International Political Theory

**Series Editor**

Gary Browning
Oxford Brookes University
UK

**Aims of the Series**

*The Palgrave Political Theory Series* provides students and scholars with cutting-edge scholarship that explores the ways in which we theorise the international. Political theory has by tradition implicitly accepted the bounds of the state, and this series of intellectually rigorous and innovative monographs and edited volumes takes the discipline forward, reflecting both the burgeoning of IR as a discipline and the concurrent internationalisation of traditional political theory issues and concepts. Offering a wide-ranging examination of how International Politics is to be interpreted, the titles in the series thus bridge the IR-political theory divide. The aim of the series is to explore international issues in analytic, historical and radical ways that complement and extend common forms of conceiving international relations such as realism, liberalism and constructivism.

More information about this series at
http://www.springer.com/series/14842

Maayan Geva

# Law, Politics and Violence in Israel/ Palestine

palgrave
macmillan

Maayan Geva
Middlesex University, UK and
University of Roehampton, UK

International Political Theory
ISBN 978-3-319-34152-1 ISBN 978-3-319-34153-8 (eBook)
DOI 10.1007/978-3-319-34153-8

Library of Congress Control Number: 2016957307



Printed on acid-free paper

This Palgrave Macmillan imprint is published by Springer Nature
The registered company is Springer International Publishing AG
The registered company address is: Gewerbestrasse 11, 6330 Cham, Switzerland

*Thank you horim. Safta Mika, you are the best*
*Thank you Raia, the wonderful Helene, Inna, Shira, Ania,*
*Tamara, Alice and Michelle*

# Preface

The impetus behind this account of law and legality in war came following the events of the 2008/9 Israeli offensive in Gaza, entitled 'Operation Cast Lead', an action positioned at a puzzling junction of law and politics. Israel's military operation was at once extremely violent and characterised by an unprecedentedly extensive involvement of military lawyers and legal discourse on war. This event called up questions about law, violence and politics that in my mind had not yet been adequately considered. The book's trajectory, however, has reversed the chronology of this thought process: it opens by addressing legal-political histories in the Israeli management of the Occupied Palestinian Territories (OPT) through an investigation of the military institution's engagement with international law, and ends with an account of the offensive. Violence in Israel/Palestine is still far from ending, with the Gaza Strip and its inhabitants continuing to suffer particularly fatal assaults. Law continues to play a significant part in these events.

There were multiple occasions of increased violence in Gaza in the years that followed Operation Cast Lead. In March 2012 the Gaza Strip again saw Israeli airstrikes, and in November 2012 Israel launched an offensive titled Operation Pillar of Defense. In the summer of 2014 Israel once again carried out a full-scale attack in Gaza, entitled Operation Protective Edge. The United Nations Office for Coordination of Humanitarian Affairs in the Occupied Palestinian Territory reported that this operation caused the death of 2251 Palestinians, destroyed or severely damaged about 18,000 housing units and, at the height of the fighting, displaced 500,000 people (in the UN Independent Commission of Inquiry 2014).

Law has become a pivotal part in the design, planning and execution processes of war in the Israeli/Palestinian context. The particular type of violence seen in Gaza in 2014 cannot be understood adequately outside of a legal contextualization. In line with the trends addressed in this book, Israel continues to advance and formalise the involvement of lawyers in its military operations (The State of Israel 2014). The battle of Shuja'iya, a key target for Israeli strikes during its 2014 offensive, provides an illuminating example for the intriguing juncture of law and violence in contemporary warfare. Shuja'iya is a neighbourhood located in the northern part of Gaza, east of Gaza city and close to the pre-1967 border, or Green Line, as it is called in Israel. It is also one of the most densely populated neighbourhoods in Gaza, which as a whole is known to be among the regions with the highest population density in the world. Prior to the offensive, Israel stated that this area was an important Hamas stronghold, and a location from which hundreds of rockets were being fired at Israeli cities.

During the days preceding its massive strikes in Shuja'iya, Israeli forces broadcast warnings over radio and television, made tens of thousands of pre-recorded telephone-calls and sent text messages, all telling residents to leave and relocate to central Gaza City until further notice. These measures follow the legal obligation of armies to provide an early warning to a population residing in a territory they are planning to attack. The assault began on 19 July. The United Nations (UN) reported that initially the majority of residents did not leave their homes, but as the bombardments intensified ultimately about half of the residents relocated. Amnesty International reported that the United Nations Relief and Works Agency for Palestine Refugees in the Near East (UNRWA) facilities were overflowing (Amnesty 2014), which meant that many of those who fled had nowhere to go. Some people stayed in their homes out of choice, and some people could not have left, for various reasons.

An Israeli officer later attested: 'I was there and I can tell you, the earth moved under our feet' (Zigdon 2014). A Palestinian witness told the UN Independent Commission of Inquiry investigating this event:

> The attacks were everywhere. Everything was coming under attack, the roads and the buildings; there was no safe haven in Shuja'iya. It would have been impossible ... We walked as the missiles kept arriving. We saw bodies of people in the streets. We came across the body of ...an acquaintance of mine from our neighbourhood. We came across several other bodies of people. The corpses were of young and old persons, women, children, etc. (The UN Independent Commission of Inquiry 2014: 70).

The attack on Shuja'iya between 19 and 20 July involved intensive shelling and extensive use of explosive weapons, including artillery, mortars and rockets fired by the Israeli Air Force. The initial shelling alone led to numerous casualties and, according to UN data, the Palestinian civilian fatalities in the neighbourhood amounted to 55 people, including 19 children and 14 women (The UN Independent Commission of Inquiry 2014: 76). UN Secretary-General Ban Ki-moon condemned this attack, referring to it as an 'atrocious action' (OCHA 2014), and Richard Falk (2014), a renowned legal scholar, called it a massacre.

There is a key legal element in Israel's military actions, and the particular employment of the measure of early warning in this case demonstrates the unexpected manner in which law has come to interact with violence. Early warning procedures in this case, rather than simply providing people with an opportunity to escape what was soon to become a battlefield, in fact take part in constituting the targets of the attack. A pivotal operational–legal assertion made subsequent to the early warnings given to the neighbourhood's residents was that, since a warning had been given, all those residents who stayed had de facto lost the protection afforded to civilians under international humanitarian law. The loss of protection is rationalised by a dual categorisation of the people who remained in the area where warning had been given: the choice to stay in the neighbourhood either identified them as being hostile operatives, or by staying the people concerned had chosen to serve as 'human shields' in service of Palestinian militants and this decision thereby transformed them from civilians into legitimate targets of attack without them necessarily taking any active part in the hostilities. This legal interpretation, even if not officially admitted, follows the same logic employed in Operation Cast Lead. In both cases, operational and legal reasoning have become intertwined in a manner which means that law serves as an element in the constitution of the battlefield and enables the exercise of violence.

This particular utilisation of law to constitute legitimate enemies as a result of the pre-emptive warning is evident in the perspectives of both legal military officers and in the experiences of soldiers taking part in this attack. For example, Pnina Sharvit-Baruch (2009), the Head of the Israeli military International Law Department (ILD) in 2003–09 stated in a similar context, in a text this book will further analyse:

> What is a military target? ... this is very flexible. A civilian object, when it is used [for military purpose], or because of its location, or even because of its potential use ... becomes a legitimate target of attack.

Major Amitai Kanarik[1] described the state of affairs by which all the people in Shuja'iya were stripped of the legal protection afforded to civilians:

> We try to create a situation whereby the area where we are fighting is sterile, so any person seen there is suspected of engaging in terrorist activity. At the same time, we make the utmost effort to remove the population, whether this means dropping flyers or shelling. Ultimately, we manage to convince even those who weren't at first persuaded, until we get to a situation where the neighbourhood becomes a ghost town, so that anyone who suddenly surfaces automatically becomes a suspected terrorist. (in Bokobza 2014)

Israeli soldiers also confirm that this was indeed the logic of the violence employed in Shuja'iya. One soldier said: 'the soldiers were briefed by their commanders to fire at every person they identified in a combat zone, since the working assumption was that every person in the field was an enemy' (Breaking the Silence 2015: 18). A second soldier similarly testified: 'The instructions are to shoot right away. Whoever you spot – be they armed or unarmed, no matter what. The instructions are very clear. Any person you run into, that you see with your eyes—shoot to kill. It's an explicit instruction' (in Bokobza 2014). And a third: 'There were no rules of engagement. If you see anyone in that area, that person is a terrorist ...They told us they have intelligence that there are practically no civilians remaining in the area, and so if someone comes towards us, that person is a terrorist' (Breaking the Silence 2014).

In the aftermath of the operation, Israel published an official report aimed at presenting the motivations for the offensive and the army's conduct in its duration. Israel's argumentation on the legality of its actions was the centrepiece of this publication. The report argued that the army had adhered strictly to legal standards, a claim that was supported by the extensive involvement of military lawyers in this operation, who were on this occasion providing advice at both regional and divisional levels.

On 29 September 2014, soon after Operation Protective Edge, Israeli Prime Minister Benjamin Netanyahu spoke at the UN General Assembly, stating:

> No other country and no other army in history have gone to greater lengths to avoid casualties among the civilian population of their enemies ...[Israel] upheld the highest moral values of any army in the world. Israel's soldiers deserve not condemnation, but admiration.

Netanyahu's claim of morality is founded on the legalisation of the Israeli army's actions. Taking into account the extreme violence employed in Gaza, these meeting points of law, politics and violence call for a thorough consideration. Who were the people protected from violence in Gaza? And who was marked as the 'enemy'? What is the influence of law in the battlefield? And how does it relate to questions of morality?

In Shuja'iya it was the particular manner in which the Israeli military-operational logic reorganised the principle of distinction between civilians and combatants, building on the measure of early warning, that shaped this attack and enabled it. Netanyahu's speech was made in an international context where much of the political battle over legitimacy, intertwined with violence on the ground, is formed in legal arguments and concepts. This book offers, through a contextualised investigation of military legal practice, an historical perspective into the dynamics, occurrences and institutions taking part in the constitution of these settings in Israel/Palestine, the legal-political state of affairs that made these events possible.

## Note

1. Major Kanarik heads the Military Doctrine Section at the headquarters of the Chief Infantry and Paratroopers' Officer's Department.

## References

Amnesty (2014). Israel/Gaza: Attacks on medical facilities and civilians add to war crime allegations, available at: https://www.amnesty.org/en/latest/news/2014/07/israelgaza-attacks-medical-facilities-and-civilians-add-war-crime-allegations/[accessed 10.1.2016].

Bokobza, A. (2014). 'Collecting on the Frontline.' BaYabasha, Ground Forces Journal **29**: 62.

Breaking the Silence (2014). Just blasting things away, soldier testimony, available at: http://www.breakingthesilence.org.il/testimonies/database/802169 [accessed 10.1.2016].

Breaking the Silence (2015). 'This is how we fought in Gaza', available at: http://www.breakingthesilence.org.il/pdf/ProtectiveEdge.pdf [accessed 10.1.2016].

Falk, R. (2014). Massacre in Gaza: Can international law provide justice for Palestinians? 22.7.2014, available at: http://www.aljazeera.com/indepth/opinion/2014/07/massacre-gaza-201472283548249 89.html [accessed 10.1.2016]. Al Jazeera (online)

OCHA (2014). Gaza Emergency Situation Report of 22 July 2014. At: http://www.ochaopt.org/documents/ocha_opt_sitrep_22_07_2014.pdf [accessed 10.1.2016]

Sharvit Baruch, P. (2009). Conference Paper. Hamas, the Gaza War and Accountability under International Law. Jerusalem, available at: http://media-line.co.il/Events/Jcpa/Law-Conference/Heb.aspx [accessed 28.4.15].

The State of Israel (2014). The 2014 Gaza Conflict: Factual and Legal Aspects, May 2015, the State of Israel, pp. 140–141, accessible at: http://mfa.gov.il/ProtectiveEdge/Documents/2014GazaConflictFullReport.pdf [accessed 10.1.2016].

The UN Independent Commission of Inquiry (2014). Report of the detailed findings of the Commission of Inquiry on the 2014 Gaza Conflict, accessible at: http://www.ohchr.org/EN/HRBodies/HRC/CoIGazaConflict/Pages/ReportCoIGaza.aspx - report [accessed 10.1.2016].

Zigdon, Y. (2014). Shuja'iyas earth was moving; September 2014, No. 57, 18–19, unofficial translation available at: http://www.beithatothan.org.il/magazin/30_10_2014/book.html - p=19 [accessed 10.1.2016]. Tamid Tothan, Association of artillery veteran's magazine.

# Contents

CHAPTER 1

# Introduction: Israel's Management of the Occupied Palestinian Territories (OPT) and International Humanitarian Law

## 1.1 Recent Developments in Law and Politics, the Israeli Occupation, and the Military Legal System

Since around the mid-1990s the role of law and the question of legality have been gaining prominence in Western militaries and their involvement in situations of warfare (Dunlap 2001a, b; Lohr and Gallotta 2003; Kennedy 2006; Dunlap 2009). Brigadier General Charles Dunlap pointedly observes, 'savvy American commanders seldom go to war without their attorneys' (Dunlap 2001a, p. 6). The Israeli military has seen a similar shift. Perspectives are divided about the meaning and significance of the Israeli engagement with international law. Persistent voices are arguing that law merely serves as lip service, a tool in the hands of political powers. These voices range across the political spectrum, from Alan Dershowitz, a prominent legal scholar and right-wing supporter of Israel, who referred to international law in a 2013 conference as 'a construct in the mind of a bunch of left wing academics' (Dershowitz 2013), to critics from the left arguing that Israel has been politicising law in a manner emptying it of its original intents and substantive values (Ben-Naftali and Michaeli 2003; Ben-Naftali and Shany 2004; Ben-Naftali et al. 2005; Falk 2009a; Ben-Naftali 2011). Others simply argue that the increased involvement of lawyers in Israel's military affairs reinforces the argument that it adheres to law (Weiner and Bell 2009; Cohen 2010). In this vein the US Joint Chiefs Chairman Martin Dempsey reported in 2014 that a team of



M. Geva, *Law, Politics and Violence in Israel/Palestine*,
DOI 10.1007/978-3-319-34153-8_1

officers and commissioners was sent to learn the Israeli military legal methods (Bernstein 2014). Finally, and as one might expect, the Israeli army's legal practitioners stress the legality of this institution's operations, which is assumed to be reinforced by the growing involvement of lawyers in the army's activities (Ronen 2009; Mendelblit 2009).

Recent Israeli military attacks and the involvement of lawyers in these attacks have raised questions about law's role in these events. The 2008/9 offensive in Gaza, then Israel's most destructive attack in the occupied Palestinian territories (OPT) since its 1967 seizure, and an offensive that involved legal practitioners more extensively than ever before, is a key occasion within this discussion. The 2008/9 offensive, dubbed by Israeli authorities Operation Cast Lead, was launched on 27 December 2008 and lasted three weeks. The exact number of lives lost in Gaza is still disputed. Human rights organisations estimate that the number of fatalities was close to 1380, among them at least 760 civilians. Thousands more were wounded (Amnesty 2009; PCHR 2010; B'Tselem 2011). The attack also resulted in the vast destruction of buildings and extensive damage to the Gaza Strip's infrastructure. In comparison with past strikes in Gaza, the ratio of casualties between Palestinian civilians in comparison to one Israeli soldier had increased drastically, from six at the time of the first Intifada (1987–91), nine in the second Intifada (2000–roughly 2005), 33 after Israel's 2005 'disengagement' from the Strip, and 86 during Operation Cast Lead (Levy 2010).

The legal responses to the offensive in Gaza included no fewer than three UN committees and investigation bodies, an abundance of academic analysis and human rights non-governmental organisations (NGOs)' writing (for example, Cohen 2009; Gearty 2009; Goldstone et al. 2009; Human Rights Watch 2009; Sharp 2009; Weiner and Bell 2009; Shandi 2010; Wells-Greco 2010; Kot 2011). Some accounts were particularly interested in the reconciliation of this operation's extended reliance on international legal practice on the one hand and its extreme violence on the other (Blau and Feldman 2009; Weizman 2009, 2011). Notably, while the involvement of lawyers reached a peak in this operation, their close engagement with operational decision-making was no novelty for the military establishment. By 2009, the processes pushing forward the incorporation of legal practice in battle had been in motion for nearly a decade (Cohen 2011). Moreover, in more general historical terms, law has been a key element in Israeli socio-political settings, grounding the legitimacy of the Zionist project.

The Military Advocate General Corps (MAG Corps) is the military establishment's legal system. As described in its mission statement (MAG Corps), its goals and responsibilities include law enforcement in the armed forces; supervising the disciplinary procedures in the military; providing legal defence to soldiers standing trial in a military court; providing legal advice to units and command authorities throughout the military; and providing legal advice on international and operational legal issues. In institutional terms, the MAG Corps is subject to the authority of the civil Attorney General and the Ministry of Justice rather than to the army's chain of command. The military legal system retains considerable influence and power in relation to the civil legal authorities. Notably, the Ministry of Justice does not have a branch or department focused on supervising the army's legal decisions. Instead, this role is divided between several bodies, none of which maintains a specific specialty in this area (Roytman 2013). The diffusion of authority within the civil authorities means that, by and large, despite the formal hierarchy, the Israeli civil legal system distances itself structurally from supervising the MAG Corps and the army's conduct (Benvenisti 2011; Shany et al. 2011).

However the military legal system's unprecedented close engagement with operational decision-making in the attack in Gaza, this action by and large has not prompted a substantive discussion on the position of law and lawyers in war. Moreover, the military legal system is one of Israel's key institutions responsible for the application of international law in the OPT, but despite of this institution's position and the great interest in the legal aspects of Israel's occupation, accounts of its work are scarce. This scarcity is surprising, even when taking into account the obstacles of military secrecy and limited access to data. Questions about the role of lawyers in military and government warfare-related policies were, for example, the centre of debate in the USA following the discovery of the Torture Memos, in which lawyers approved violent interrogation methods as part of the Bush administration's War on Terror (Rhode 2000; Bilder and Vagts 2004; Weisberg 2004; Clark 2005; Sands 2008). By and large, there was no noteworthy parallel debate in Israel. Rather, in response to questions about Operation Cast Lead's legality, military legal practitioners defended their work and stated, for example, that the deaths of civilians, even if there are many, is no proof of a violation of law (Blau and Feldman 2009; Mendelblit 2009). In view of law's increased involvement in war and the counter-intuitive statements made by its military-legal practitioners in Israel, rejecting a connection between the deaths of civilians and the legality of actions, study and analysis of law's contemporary relationship with war are all the more necessary.

International law entered the work of the Israeli military not least as a result of the 1967 War, a landmark event which began the Israeli occupation of the West Bank and Gaza. Within the MAG Corps, the main body dealing with this law is a unit founded in 1968, soon after the occupation. On its establishment this body was called the International Law Division, but some 20 years later it improved its status and was reorganised as the International Law Department (ILD), a body that included several divisions.

Law provides the vocabulary for many arguments and actions in and about Israel and the OPT. These legal activities are varied, ranging from the army's own legal practice and its critique, the Boycott Divestment and Sanctions (BDS) movement, through human-rights-based appeals (or threats of appeals) to the High Court of Justice as well as various international legal forums, state-initiated legal 'counter-terrorism' measures, and the codification of legal restriction on Israeli NGOs opposing the occupation and its various policies. International law has played a key part in the Israeli occupation, consistently since its very beginning, gaining it the title of 'the most legalized occupation in world history' (Kretzmer 2002; Ben-Naftali 2011).

The role of law in this context, however, has not been constant. A chief turning point in Israel's legal practice emerged in 2000. At this time the Israeli military complex fundamentally altered its premise of action by shifting its handling of the OPT from the legal framework of 'law enforcement' to that of International Humanitarian Law. This legal change was prompted by the second Intifada, the Palestinian uprising, and in both practical and conceptual terms it has led to a novel array of legal policies and debates. From the perspective of the military's legal system, the turn to international humanitarian law significantly widened legal practitioners' leeway to act under law. This change had been controversial and was made possible by the more legally permissive atmosphere of the War on Terror. This legal framework provided the toolkit the military used in its 2008/9 offensive in Gaza. The International Law Department Commanding Officer, Daniel Reisner,[1] describes this legal change, the opposition it faced and places its acceptance in an international political context:

> When we started to define the confrontation with the Palestinians as an armed confrontation, it was a dramatic switch, and we started to defend that

> position before the Supreme Court. In April 2001 I met the American envoy George Mitchell and explained that above a certain level, fighting terrorism is armed combat and not law enforcement. His committee [which examined the circumstances of the hostilities commencing in 2000] rejected that approach. Its report called on the Israeli government to abandon the armed confrontation definition and revert to the concept of law enforcement. It took four months and four planes [the September 11th attacks] to change the opinion of the United States, and had it not been for those four planes I am not sure we would have been able to develop the thesis of the war against terrorism on the present scale. (Reisner, in Feldman and Blau 2009)

International Humanitarian Law, the laws of war, is made up of treaty, customary and case law. Treaty law relies on states signing and ratifying treaties, and customary law is the general 'custom' and is considered obligatory regardless of a particular state's voluntary acceptance of it. The collection of cases decided in courts adds to these laws. The legal body of treaties is constructed in a lengthy and politically complex process and does not readily undergo revision. The complexity of this process is a chief argument that states evoke when they interpret law in ways that are not entirely in line with the existing treaties. The broad phrasing of international humanitarian law's provisions, and the fact that some time has passed since its codification, along with the significance attributed to the means and methods of warfare having changed, also add to the legal arguments made. The result is that the ways most states practise law and the acceptability of their practice gradually becomes a part of law itself.

Law's reliance on practice contributes to it being a site of contest, a space in which states make law by way of war. Eyal Weizman (2009) argues to this effect 'it is the border between the allowed and the forbidden that is the most intense legal battlefield. International law can be thought of not as a static body of rules but rather as an endless series of conflicts over this border'. Thus the edges of what is legal are in constant movement. ILD Commanding Officer Reisner goes even further in this vein, inadvertently resonating Walter Benjamin's (1978) insight on state violence as constitutive of law, and explicitly states Israeli military practice is an enterprise making law through its violation:

> After we bombed the reactor in Iraq, the Security Council condemned Israel and claimed the attack was a violation of international law. The atmosphere was that Israel had committed a crime. Today everyone says it was preventive self-defense. International law progresses through violations.

> We invented the targeted assassination thesis and we had to push it. At first there were protrusions that made it hard to insert easily into the legal moulds. Eight years later it is in the center of the bounds of legitimacy. (Reisner, in Feldman and Blau 2009)

Several pivotal questions about law and war rise from these depictions of international law and its position in Israel and the OPT. What is the nature of law's contemporary relationship with conflict and violence? Are we witnessing a new phase in law's and lawyers' positions in war? What power and position do lawyers have, and what role do they play, vis-à-vis military operations? What is the nature of current legal practice? Is law merely a political instrument? This book investigates international law by examining the Israeli military's engagement with this law in relation to the OPT. This investigation explores law grounded in trends and shifts in Israeli military legal practice at focal points of the Israeli–Palestinian relationship. It examines military legal practice historically and then focuses on the contemporary state of affairs.

This section of the chapter has introduced the centrality of international law to Israel and the OPT, and briefly described the Israeli military's contemporary engagement with international law and the chief institution responsible for the application of law in the army, the MAG Corps. It then listed the key questions this book addresses. Section 1.2 presents existing research on the engagement of different Israeli institutions with international law in the OPT. These institutions include the MAG Corps, the High Court of Justice and human rights NGOs. It presents these studies and considers their limitations. In Section 1.3 International Humanitarian Law is discussed, including the principles of this law, the effects it has over violence, and its recent shifts. It then considers the Israeli application of this law in the OPT. Section 1.4 addresses discussions on law's relationship with politics. This debate engages with different standpoints about the separateness of law and politics—i.e. whether these concepts are separable from one another in practice or in theory—and then considers the implications of these standpoints to morality. Section 1.5 introduces Bourdieu's sociology of the field as an analytical and methodological basis for an innovative account of international law. It presents the novel perspectives this framework opens up for the study of Israel's engagement with international law in the OPT, and shows how it goes beyond existing scholarship of this topic. Section 1.6 provides an outline of the book's different chapters.

## 1.2 Questions of International Law in Israel's Handling of the OPT

A large amount of writing and research has been dedicated to analysing the Israeli practice of international law in the OPT. The extent of existing scholarship correlates with the centrality of law in this regime. This section will introduce key existing studies of the most important Israeli legal institutions influencing state practice in the OPT, namely the MAG Corps, the High Court of Justice and human rights NGOs. It will also consider the theoretical and practical limitations of these accounts and the gaps in this literature.

Notably, this account of law is focused on Israeli institutions and does not include Palestinian bodies. This analytical situation is in line with a political setting that affords little power to Palestinians. Indeed, Palestinians are subject to these systems rather than playing an active part in this power-driven constellation of law and politics.

The MAG Corps, the military's legal system, is a key institution in the operation of the Israeli occupation. In the face of considerable scholarly interest in Israel and the OPT in a legal context, the Israeli military legal system has been surprisingly under-studied. Existing research had been carried out mainly by retired officers of this system. These include accounts focused on the MAG Corps' early days (Shamgar 1971; Shefi 1983; Inbar 2002; Shamgar 2003; Inbar 2005), its work during the first Intifada (Yahav and Amit-Kohn 1993; Straschnov 1994), the second Intifada (Finkelstein 2002), and the 2006 conflict in Lebanon (Sharvit-Baruch and Neuman 2011). The professional background of these writers gives credence to their claims to insider knowledge and access to information that is otherwise confidential. However, these accounts provide descriptions of military legal practice rather than suggesting any critique. Indeed, the authors' background means that they are unlikely to pose inherent or structural criticism in relation to the military's legal policies. Several writers external to this system have produced studies about the MAG Corps. These accounts are not particularly illuminating, but their description will follow since there are no alternative studies of this institution. These accounts include Amichai Cohen's (2005) study of Israel's management of international law in the OPT. Cohen, a legal scholar, argues that law in this context is made in a struggle between the army and its political allies, on one hand, and the judiciary, politicians, NGOs and the media on the other. My own analysis rejects this evaluation of force and alliances and suggests, instead, that an analysis focused on different legal institutions better captures law and its power. In a different study Amichai Cohen and Stuart Cohen (2011) argue that the ILD has gained substantial influence over army operations as a result of Israeli institutional acknowledgment of law's 'moral imperatives' and 'intrinsic value', claims that remain unsubstantiated. Keren Cohen (2009) also contributed to this scholarship in research dedicated to the ILD's involvement in military operations since 2000, enquiring if this new form of legal practice is desirable. This study, however, makes the problematic assumption that the extended involvement of lawyers in warfare increases the fulfilment of law. And so the existing scholarship leaves a substantial gap in the literature about the military legal system in terms of the character of legal practice and its influence on military operations.

Among accounts of Israeli legal handling of the OPT, the High Court of Justice has received considerable attention (Harpaz and Shany 2010). Two studies historically examine the cumulative impact of court petitioning over the OPT. The first of these accounts was Moshe Negbi's (1981) research, and the second was David Kretzmer's (2002). These accounts reached very different conclusions, the former asserting that the court has been an effective arena for Palestinians to raise claims and advance interests, and the latter questioning any such positive contribution. Moreover, Kretzmer goes further, beyond negating the court's positive contribution, and argues that by exercising a limited measure of liberal justice the court might have legitimised the occupation both internationally and nationally, and in this way contributed to its continuance. The 21 years that passed between the writing of these two accounts inevitably impacts their analysis in view of the occupation's temporality and consequent character. But even beyond this distance in time the difference between these perspectives is related to the nature of expectations from the court, and ultimately from law as such. In this sense, unlike Negbi, Kretzmer steps outside of the boundaries of legal argumentation and critically questions the implications of law on the occupation in the non-legal terms of legitimacy. Other studies address the court's tendencies to defer to the military commander (Davidov and Reichman 2010), and the shifts in the weight the court assigns to the interests of the Palestinian population in comparison to the military and settlers' security considerations (Gross 2007; Harpaz and Shany 2010).

Human rights organisations operating in the OPT have also attracted scholarly attention. These accounts focus on the emergence of the Israeli human rights movement and the connections between this emergence and the political situation in the OPT (Gordon and Berkovitch 2007), these organisations' limited success in gaining public support (Meydani and Mizrahi 2006), the reasons for varying measures of success among organisations (Gordon 2008), the relationship between funding and organisational strategy and policy (Berkovitch and Gordon 2008), and the organisations' choices of areas of focus, namely the general avoidance of claims regarding Palestinians being made refugees by the 1948 establishment of Israel, the Palestinian Nakba, 'the catastrophe' (Orr and Golan 2014). Eyal Weizman (2010a, b) added to this literature through an investigation into changes in human rights NGOs in relation to modifications in the military's legal system. Weizman's accounts detect in these organisations a shift towards the language and logic of international humanitarian law, a change that undermines a human rights agenda. This argument makes a distinctive contribution to the study of the Israeli human rights movement. Even beyond its central argument it is unique in comparison with previous accounts in that it analytically positions human rights organisations in relation to the military. In this sense Weizman contributes to a broader analysis of the institutions and powers in play in the Israeli context shaping the practice of international law in the OPT.

Beyond literature addressing specific institutions, the bulk of writing about Israel's legal actions and policies relating to the OPT addresses particular cases and situations rather than posing broader, more ambitious questions about the relationship between law and the violence of the occupation. Structural queries about law in the context of the OPT, such as questions about the relationship forged between this law and violence, or with morality, are largely left out of the discussion. Orna Ben-Naftali (2011) suggests that the legal scholarly tendency to focus on specific instances is a result of the legal profession's impact over its epistemology. The impact, Ben-Naftli contends, directs writing to focus on a case rather than constructing a systemic approach or considering law's medium or long-term effects. These tendencies in research about Israel should be placed in a broader context. Costas Douzinas and Adam Gearey (2005) argue to this effect that the study of law as a social phenomenon has lost its prominence in contemporary scholarship. While great philosophers, from Plato to Hobbes, Kant, Hegel and Marx turned to law in order to analyse the organisation of society, contemporary legal scholarship has adopted a technical, etymological approach to law. In this way, the disciplinary boundaries defining legal scholarship by and large confine accounts about Israel and the OPT to perspectives centred on measuring cases and 'realities' in comparison with the legal code and refraining from asking broader questions about law. This account's methodological and conceptual positioning does not aim to reject or affirm arguments about particular violations of, or adherence to, the legal code but rather suggests a fundamentally alternative perspective on law.

Notwithstanding the tendency to examine specific cases rather than the general state of affairs, several accounts do formulate a broader picture of law and its impact over the OPT (for example, Falk 2000; Ben-Naftali and Shany 2004; Ben-Naftali et al. 2005; Gross 2007; Ben-Naftali 2011; Cohen and Cohen 2011). To demonstrate, Ben-Naftali et al. (2005) examine the legality of the occupation as a whole, a question surprisingly under-studied, while other studies investigate the overall status of human rights in the OPT (Ben-Naftali and Shany 2004; Gross 2007). However, these analyses are still largely shaped by legal scholarship's self-imposed limitations, leading them to direct their attention to a dichotomised legal/illegal point of view. For example, Ben-Naftali (2011) argues that law has been implicated in 'legalising' the illegal occupation of Gaza and the West Bank, and has created a reversal between the legal rule and its exception. In this sense, even in this highly critical account, where Ben-Naftali identifies law as a factor enabling state power veiled as justice, legalising the illegal, the writer refrains from articulating a fundamental critique of law and instead argues that law has been 'infected' by taking part in shaping the occupation (Ben-Naftali 2011, p. 131). If law may be infected it then follows that it may also be pure, i.e. detached from political interest. The analytical flaw lies with the fact that this supposed division between law and its political 'infection' was never questioned. This book's theoretical point of departure rejects a predetermined separation between law and politics. Instead, it examines the involvement and implications of law in the OPT in a manner forgoing the assumption that law may be practised in a correct manner and the implicit assumption that follows, that when put into practice correctly, law is a fundamentally positive force.

## 1.3 International Humanitarian Law's Principles, Its Recent Developments and Application in Israeli Military Practice

The key principles of International Humanitarian Law, the law governing war and occupation, were codified in the 1907 Hague Convention and regulations, the 1949 Geneva Conventions and their 1977 additional

Protocols. Rather than addressing matters regarding the infliction of war and conflict (*jus ad bellum*), international humanitarian law regulates state conduct in times of war (*jus in bello*). In the context of an occupation this legal framework is to apply whenever a territory comes under the effective control of hostile foreign armed forces. The Hague Regulations and the Fourth Geneva Convention instruct that these forces are to take measures to restore and ensure, as far as possible, public order and safety, and to satisfy basic living standards for the population under occupation. These standards cover hygiene and arrangements relating to public health, education, and the provision of food and medical care. These obligations mean that the occupying power takes on considerable control. At the same time, this law provides some bills of rights protecting the occupied population. An additional fundamental principle of this law is that occupation does not constitute sovereignty. The 1907 Hague Regulations instruct, 'The occupying State shall be regarded only as administrator and usufructuary of public buildings, real estate, forests, and agricultural estates belonging to the hostile State, and situated in the occupied country' (The 1907 Hague Regulations Convention IV, Art. 55). The occupying forces' own laws would not apply in this territory. Rather, the applicable law is the same law that governed prior to the occupation, subject to changes made by military orders. In the Israeli context, the conventions and clauses to apply to the OPT created an occasion for negotiation. Not long after the occupation, officials had declared that the territories seized were in fact 'liberated' and 'administrated' rather than occupied, and that it then followed that the Fourth Geneva Convention, which stipulates otherwise, does not apply (Kretzmer 2002; Sfard 2004). Immediately after the occupation took place, the military's legal system began to produce military orders to govern the OPT, a collection now including thousands of orders (MAG 2015).

The position and role of the Israeli military's International Legal Department is grounded in the Geneva Conventions. The first additional protocol to this convention instructs signatory parties to promote compliance to the legal code by the appointment of legal advisers. The relevant article states:

> The High Contracting Parties at all times, and the Parties to the conflict in time of armed conflict, shall ensure that legal advisers are available, when necessary, to advise military commanders at the appropriate level on the application of the Conventions and this Protocol and on the appropriate instruction to be given to the armed forces on this subject. (Protocol I Additional to the Geneva Conventions, Art. 82, 1977)

Notably, these legal instructions are general and do not include specific requirements for the timing, location or context in which legal advice is to be provided. Many militaries, among them British, USA, French, Australian, Russian and German, have codified obligatory involvement of legal advisers into their practice. The German military's regulations, for example, instruct that every division must include a legal adviser. In the USA, every division and brigade includes several legal officers (Neuman 2007). The Israeli army has yet to make public any such regulations. At present, the MAG Corps' system of legal consultancy is made up of three departments: The Legislation and Legal Advice Department (*Mahleket Yeauts ve'Hakika*), Legal Adviser in Judea and Samaria (*Yoamash Ayosh*) and the ILD. The ILD is responsible for consultancy relating to international law (Mendelblit 2011). As noted earlier, within the military's structure the MAG Corps is separate from operational branches. Instead, the MAG, the head of the military legal system, is subject to the authority of the civil Attorney General. This means that, on the one hand, legal officers are not hierarchically subordinate to decision-making commanders and, on the other, they do not have a capacity to command, i.e. their legal opinions are not formally binding.

One of the primary debates on international humanitarian law revolves around the implications of the very existence of an established legal framework for war. In this, the basic question is whether this law, by definition, legitimises war and counters efforts to abolish it. Jean Pictet, one of international humanitarian law's most renowned scholars, presents a pragmatic argument, that wars occur and it is therefore necessary to have law governing hostilities: 'as long as governments maintain vast armies, even for defensive purposes, and thereby demonstrate that they do not believe war to be impossible, people attenuating the evils of war cannot shirk the duty of encouraging the adoption of safeguards while there is still time' (Pictet 1985, p. 82). Hersch Lauterpacht (1952), perhaps the most prominent international jurist of his time, argued for the centrality of the 'humane' in international humanitarian law. Grounded in an account of the goals that the creators of this law had in mind, Lauterpacht argues that the prevention or mitigation of anguish and saving lives are the chief aims of this law. Some contemporary accounts join in this discussion in support of law's humanity based on a different line of argument and identify in international humanitarian law a gradual humanisation under the influence of human rights law (Teitel 2002, 2011; Meron 2006; Iverson 2014). Ruti Teitel argues in this vein that 'the new paradigm weds traditional humanitarianism with the law of human rights, causing a shift away from states as the dominant subjects of international law to include "persons" and "peoples"' (Teitel 2002, p. 363).

Other legal scholars argue differently and stress that international humanitarian law's provisions direct action that accepts violence as its point of departure (*jus in bello*). Seen in this way, and unlike Pictet's and Lauterpacht's accounts, the analytical emphasis changes and identifies a significant gap between, on one hand, law as a preventive measure and on the other as a regulating force. Emphasising law's regulative effect, Michael Walzer (1977), a prominent contributor to discussions on the concept of 'just war', detects in international humanitarian law a circularity by which legal codes necessarily yield positive results for the questions they supposedly attempt to determine. Walzer discusses 'military necessity' in this light:

> In fact, it is not about necessity at all; it is a way of speaking in code, or a hyperbolical way of speaking, about probability and risk. Even if one grants the right of states and armies and individual soldiers to reduce their risks, a particular course of action will be *necessary* to that end only if no other course improved the odds of battle at all. But there will always be a range of tactical strategic options that conceivably could improve the odds. (Walzer 1977, p. 144; emphasis in original)

Chris Jochnick and Roger Normand (1994) contribute to this critical perspective of law and argue that one of international humanitarian law chief influences is that it legitimises war based on the misleading assumption that a war managed in law, i.e. a legal war, is more humane and moral than an illegal one. Recent decades have seen significant changes in the practice of international humanitarian law, and these shifts necessitate a reconsideration of these different perspectives about law's influence.

The 11 September 2001 attacks, and the American War on Terror that followed, had a great influence on international humanitarian law in general (Burke 2007), and on the Israeli ILD's practice in particular (Reisner, in Feldman and Blau 2009). In legal-military terminology, the War on Terror is linked directly to the definition of conflicts as 'asymmetric warfare' (Sassoli 2011). The Israeli military legal system makes frequent discursive use of 'asymmetry' in reference to the OPT (The State of Israel 2010a, b). In general terms the description of conflicts as asymmetric relates to those battles fought between belligerents significantly differing from one another in status, power and tactics, most commonly states and non-state armed groups (Baarda 2009). Within legal circles, asymmetry also frequently relates to an argument on compliance with international law, by which states abide by international humanitarian law while non-state armed groups do not (Cohen 2010). This term commonly provides argumentation in support of a revision of law through its practice of allowing states more leeway in relation to, for example, the identification of combatants and of military targets, based on the argument that the existing law is incompatible with contemporary wars (Baarda 2009; Bowyer 2009; Cook and Conversino 2009). international humanitarian law's shift in relation to the War on Terror is the backdrop of this account of law.

## 1.4 The Laws of War and Politics

The relationship between law and politics has long occupied scholars, theorists and philosophers, and international law presents a particular case for this relationship. First and foremost, the absence of a sovereign in international law changes the premise of this discussion. Anne Orford suggests that for this precise reason international law makes 'an extremely productive site for the exploration of modern responses to the pervasive uneasiness about authority and its legitimacy' (Orford 2004, p. 443). The controversies about international law and politics have been the centre of various accounts, from Lauterpacht's *The Function of Law in the International Community* (1933), through Louis Henkin's *How Nations Behave: Law and Foreign Policy* (1968) to the seminal scholarship of Martti Koskenniemi (1990, 1999, 2011). These perspectives differ substantially in terms of their understandings of law's role and its relationship with politics.

A key division in scholarship about the relationship between international law and politics is between those considering law to be by its very nature subject to political will and inseparable from politics, and those suggesting, to the contrary, that this separation is possible. The category of scholarship identifying an inseparable connection between international law and politics accommodates a wide array of research and writing from those considering law to be an instrument of political power (Kirchheimer 1961; Teubner 1997; Schmitt, in Koskenniemi 2009) through post-colonial scholars, detecting in the very creation of international law politics aimed at governing and supressing peoples through a 'civilizing project' (Berman 2004a, b; Anghie 2006; Megret 2006), to critical analysis of law's relationship with politics, exploring the possibility that law may be intensifying politically motivated violence (Kennedy 2006; Diamond 2010; Weizman 2011). The category of writing and perspective arguing that law is either separate from politics, or that it could or should be separate from it, also accommodates conflicting standpoints. These perspectives range from the scientific conceptualisation of law as a closed system (Kelsen, in Koskenniemi 2009), through concerns that law is unwarrantedly restricting state action (Buzan 2002; Lohr and Gallotta 2003) and to a struggle coupling legal theory and practice in a battle against politics and for a universal application of international law, indeed the heart of the international liberal project (Teitel 2002, 2011).

The imagery of law cleansed of politics plays a key part in liberal perceptions of the state. Koskenniemi (2011) investigates liberal positions on the politics—international law encounter and detects a common perception by which the fight for international rule is a combat against politics. In this picture, politics is understood as a tool furthering subjective desire and interest, and this desire is depicted as the very opposite of law. The assumption in this perspective is that while perhaps realistically some measure of politics is inevitable, it should be constrained by non-political rules. If only prejudices were to be eliminated or excluded, jurists could then construct a just world. Koskenniemi both challenges the assumption that law and politics are separable from one another, and that these concepts are fundamentally distinct.

This discussion about law's origins and relationship with politics echoes a parallel divide relating to the concept of morality. The naturalist and positivist traditions demonstrate this tension, with the former locating law's origin outside the will of humankind, in 'nature', 'divine law' or morality (Feinberg and Coleman 2003) and the latter locating it in human discretion, i.e. morality is a part of law in so far as it had been incorporated into it by political authority. Notwithstanding the contemporary dominance of positivism, legal argumentation commonly relies on a combination of both the positivist and naturalist schools of thought (Rubin 1997). These 'combinations' often manifest contradictions and also have direct bearing over legal practice. Positivism's dominance does not fit the imagined liberal legal-political separation neatly, because positivism is at odds with liberal perspectives, implying that law intrinsically encompasses a promise of justice (Kahn 2006). Human rights discourse also frequently demonstrates the endurance of naturalist assumptions. It does so by arguing for rights arising from one's humanity as such, a condition that is at the same time both moral and natural (Taylor 1996).

Much of the scholarship discussing law and morality in relation to current wars is dedicated to the 'asymmetry' of this warfare. Formal definitions aside, in this literature the term asymmetry often signals dissatisfaction with what is seen as unreasonable expectations that states have to meet when conducting war. This scholarship mainly argues for law's reformulation in the vein of improving states' legal position in comparison with their non-state rivals (Bowyer 2009; Frank 2009; Toiskallio 2009). In the Israeli context, Asa Kasher and Amos Yadlin (2005), the former being a retired senior military officer and the latter an academic publicly dubbed 'the Israeli Defence Forces philosopher', build on arguments about asymmetry and morality to construct a taxonomy of people, measuring the value of different lives. This essay will be debated more elaborately in Chapter 4 of this book. Gabriella Blum (2010), a legal scholar and former member of the ILD, suggests that some current situations of conflict call for a moral rejection of legal code. A 'lesser-evil' solution to these war-related dilemmas, Blum argues, may involve a violation of law. The question which inevitably follows is who will decide what is moral and what is evil (Diamond 2010). Notably, Blum's opinion is in the minority among her peers at the military legal institution and in its surrounding academic circles. These practitioners more commonly object to an explicit abandonment of law and oppose a codification of new legal tools. Rather, they prefer to maintain the current legal status quo, allowing, from their perspective, sufficient interpretive freedom (Mendelblit 2012). Notwithstanding the specific implications of these arguments and their depiction of morality, in conceptual terms Kasher and Yadlin's account is distinct from Blum's. While the former essay assumes as a point of departure a connection between law and morality, one that necessitates a remaking of law, Blum in fact abandons law in her quest for wartime morality.

Since the 1990s, researchers have identified a novel formation of the relationship between international law and politics by which this law has been gaining greater power over politics. David Kennedy's (2006) account of law and politics in war is a pivotal contribution to scholarship addressing this relationship. In Kennedy's perspective these relations have undergone a compound process intertwining law and politics, by which law has gained power by equipping politics with a new vocabulary and sets of meanings:

> For more than a century, law—and particularly international law ...has sought in any possible way to become a practical vocabulary for politics.

> The revolt was successful. Law has become more than the sum of its rules; it has become a vocabulary for judgment, for action, for communication. Most importantly, law has become a mark of legitimacy—and legitimacy has become the currency of power. (Kennedy 2006, p. 45)

Kennedy emphasises that it is important to consider the identity of those achieving this 'victory' in order to grasp the complex legal socio-historical drivers of this change. These forces include various institutions such as state legal authorities, inter alia military legal systems, but also international organisations such as the UN and the International Committee of the Red Cross (ICRC), legal scholars, human rights lawyers and NGOs. In this sense, law's contemporary power over politics and war is the result of a 'successful' battle fought by seemingly unlikely allies.

Kennedy's compelling articulation of this convoluted dynamic suggests that any attempt at providing a neat conceptual distinction between law and politics is impossible. Law's novel entanglement with politics has meant that politics gained some of law's power in the form of legitimacy, as a result of law's assumed moral grounding. Law, for its part, has been reallocated to political forums, a process inevitably changing its considerations, emphases and results. This depiction of a conceptual and practical entanglement of law and politics means that an examination of these topics requires a dynamic outlook that is not attached to predetermined definitions of either law or politics. Israel makes a particularly interesting site for an examination of law's contemporary relations with politics in war. Israel is, on the one hand, characterised by a momentous liberal ethos and dubbed by some 'the only democracy in the Middle East', while on the other, it manages an ongoing occupation. The recent processes of legalisation in the Israeli army and Israel's destructive military operations push questions about the implications of these changes to the extreme.

## 1.5 The Sociology of 'The Field' Applied to the Israeli Military Legal System

In theoretical and methodological terms, this book builds on Pierre Bourdieu's sociology of the field to construct an analysis of law as a social phenomenon and to engage with the existing scholarship of international law. While an analytical apparatus drawing on Bourdieu's ideas is developed in Chapter 2, the basic rationale proposed is to explore Israel's *practice* of international law in the OPT, in the past as well as the present, as a power-entrenched social dynamic. In line with the sociological concepts of the field analysis, this argument builds on the interplay of two fundamental elements: one is the legal field's 'inner logic', comprised of components such as legal conventions, legal procedures and the values and meanings ascribed to law; and the second is the power relations between the field's various institutions, including in this case the MAG Corps, the High Court of Justice, human rights organisations and the Ministry of Justice. This is a conceptual and practice-oriented re-examination of law exploring its past and contemporary formulations in a particular context.

In epistemological terms this project follows the core of Bourdieu's reflexive sociology, in which sociology's primary purpose is to radically re-examine the themes it investigates, and reject their predetermined definition: 'The first and most pressing scientific priority …would be to take as one's object the social work of construction of the pre-constructed object.' (Bourdieu and Wacquant 1992, p. 229). In this way, the purpose of a sociological account of law's manifestations is to unravel its supposedly neutral understanding and trace its processes of formation. The concept of the field enables an examination of 'the relationship between systems of thought, social institutions and different forms of material and symbolic power' (Johnson 1993, p. 1), as all these take part in the making of law. Based on this approach, the book's historicising of legal practice, institution and code not only relativises these as products of specific social settings, but also takes the concepts out of their implied positioning as necessary by relating to the social conditions of their genesis (Bourdieu 1996).

This book's conceptualisation of law enables an innovative consideration of politics vis-à-vis its relations with law. It considers both law and politics to be products of a dynamic social process. In this perspective, these concepts are constructs of a practice, an activity that, at the same time, is founded in existing conditions and contributes to the ongoing formation of these settings. Thus the book rejects the very possibility of 'pure' or 'correct' law and politics that were in the past, or could potentially in the future, be detached from a power-entrenched social context. Instead, it aims to engage with contextual understandings of international law and politics as products of concrete events, practice and a division of power between institutions. This outlook challenges the discussions presented about law's intrinsic relationship with politics or its relations with morality in terms of origin or 'truth'. Any of these assumptions about law remain useful analytically to the extent that they comprise the field's logic and are manifested in its practice. Methodologically, this translates into an investigation based on various source materials that uncover logics of action, institutional set-ups and distributions of power. Besides historical and institutional analysis, these include various materials, primarily interviews and documents produced by the Israeli military legal system. Grounded in these materials, the book debates and analyses shifts and trends in the legal field and its impact on Israel's conduct in the OPT as a means of discussing international law and politics in occupation and war.

Conceptually building on the sociology of the field means that this account of law is fundamentally different from the bulk of existing legal scholarship hitherto devoted to debating Israel's policies and actions vis-à-vis international law. To recall, as Costas Douzinas and Adam Gearey (2005) compellingly argue, contemporary legal scholarship has adopted a technical, etymological approach to law and now focuses on measuring cases and 'realities' against the legal code rather than asking more fundamental or ambitious questions about law. The framework of the field aims to facilitate a move away from assertions about adherence to or violation of law. Instead, in order to understand law we are to detect the power relations among legal institutions and the field's logic—its internal set of rules and meanings. To demonstrate, this perspective indicates that accounts about Israel's actions of 2008/9 in Gaza that sought primarily to identify Israel's level of compliance with law (for example, Amnesty 2009; Cohen 2009a, b; Gearty 2009; Human Rights Watch 2009; Jerusalem Center 2009; Weiner and Bell 2009; Falk 2009a; Wells-Greco 2010) make up a limited examination of law's role in those events. Questions aiming to detect whether law has been followed in this operation fail to address the dynamic shifts of legal practice, its current power and form in relation to politics, and the very logic it builds on. The political scientist Philip Liste challenges in this vein legal accounts devoted to the detection of legal 'truths': 'What is important is not who is right or whose interpretation of the constitutional text is more accurate. The "legal regime of truth" is a discursive category and it is, thus, subject to change' (Liste 2008, p. 43). This book's discussion of law provides a contextual account of the social institutions, conditions and processes of change making up legal 'truths' in Israel's legal management of the OPT.

A consideration of law in the framework of the field leads to an analysis of Israeli legal institutions and practices set in context. This means that an examination of the MAG Corps necessitates an in-depth interrogation of this system's relative power in relation to other key institutions in the field such as the court, the Ministry of Justice and human rights NGOs.

The diversity of institutions, perspectives and actions in the field all make up its form. Mikael Madsen, a sociologist interested in law, articulates the centrality of diverse opinions to a field-based analysis:

> The multiple points of entrance to the field ...serve to challenge the officialised discourses of the actors. The objective is basically to break up the 'officialised story' into its many overlapping and even opposing texts and identify its many co-writers. Coming back to the *field*, these conflicting narratives ultimately reflect its many stakes, as well as they highlight the central conflicts of its historical progression. (Madsen 2006, p. 38; emphasis in original)

And so the multiplicity of discourses and motivations all construct the field. The dynamic division of power directs the extent of validity of different perspectives as all these points of view together shape what law is and how it is put to work in a given context.

Building on this understanding of law, specific discussions about International law are transformed analytically. To demonstrate, controversy over the perception of law as either a preventive or regulative force is no longer a discussion about the ideas law's creators had in mind or about which is a more 'correct', truer legal interpretation. Instead, this book suggests a historical, contextual account of law based on Israeli military legal practice. In this vein, when inquiring whether law has regulated or if it has prohibited violence, this question necessitates an interrogation of legal practice, made up of legal interpretations, lawyers' perspectives and these practitioners' extent of power over military conduct. Conclusions about this question feed into the overall conceptualisation of law. Drawing critically on Bourdieu's sociology of the field, the book contextualises military legal practice in temporal and spatial terms, encompassing at the same time historical change in the army, the law and the wider social relations in the field, primarily made up of several key institutions. The temporal aspect leads to an examination of the major shifts the military legal system's international legal practice has undergone since the 1967 occupation of the West Bank and Gaza, through landmark moments, and up to the 2008/9 offensive in Gaza. The bleak events of the 2008/9 Israeli offensive in Gaza provide an opportunity to examine the contemporary phase in the relationship of international law, politics and war as an occasion at the same time reflecting law's state and forging it.

Analytical attention is focused in particular on the military legal system's practice of international law as the key locus of political-legal practices within the field. The military Division that became the International Law Department, specialising in international law, changed significantly over time in terms of its role and impact regarding Israeli handling of the OPT. Rather than simply evaluating the 'impact' of this institution over policy, this account explores the making of law and 'the legal' through the contextualised practice of these lawyers. Based on this site in its past and present, existing accounts and assumptions about law are challenged. Such military—legal shifts have not been examined thoroughly in existing scholarship. This contextual consideration of the military legal system's practice in the OPT makes a contribution to both scholarship dedicated to this understudied institution as well as to the general discussions on Israel's engagement with law, and international humanitarian law's contemporary state in broader terms, that go far beyond this locality.

## 1.6 Chapter Summaries

The next chapter provides an explanation for Bourdieu's sociology of the field and positions the Israeli military system and additional legal institutions within this scheme. It then explains the translation of its theoretical assumptions and assertions into methods of research. Chapter 3 puts the field into practice by constructing a dynamic map of the Israeli legal field. It describes the emergence of a legal field revolving around the OPT in a gradual process that began soon after 1967. The chapter develops a map of the field through analysis of historical turning points, changes in particular legal institutions and discursive articulation of difference between organisations and their practitioners. Chapter 4 takes a closer look at Israel's military legal practitioners as influential agents affecting the field's logic, its differentiation from politics and its overall power. It then considers military lawyers' influence with reference to recent forms of conflict and legal practice in Israel. Chapter 5 builds on the analytical map of the field and the investigation of military legal officers' positions to interrogate the 2008/9 offensive in Gaza. It examines legal practice relating to specific policies and actions in this operation in the context of the field's present logic, its power and boundaries vis-à-vis politics. Chapter 6, in conclusion, reflects on the key transformations military legal practice and the field have undergone over time, and based on this analysis considers the contemporary state of law.

## Note

1. See Appendix I for a full list of ILD Commanding Officers.

## Bibliography

Amnesty (2009). Israel/Gaza: Operation 'Cast Lead': 22 days of death and destruction, available at: http://www.amnesty.org/en/library/asset/MDE15/015/2009/en/8f299083-9a74-4853-860f-0563725e633a/mde150152009en.pdf, [accessed 28.4.15].

Anghie, A. (2006). "The evolution of international law: Colonial and postcolonial realities." Third World Quarterly **27**(5): 739–753.

B'Tselem (2011). "Fatalities during operation "Cast Lead", available at: http://www.btselem.org/english/statistics/casualties.asp?sD=27&sM=12&sY=2008&eD=18&eM=01&eY=2009&filterby=event&oferet_stat=during, [accessed: 28.4.15]."

Baarda, v., T. (2009). The Moral Dimensions of Asymmetrical Warfare: Counter-terrorism, Democratic Values and Military Ethics - an introduction The Moral Dimension of Asymmetrical Warfare: Counter-terrorism, Democratic Values and Military Ethics. T. A. v. Baarda and D. E. M. Verweij. Leiden, Boston, MARTINUS NIJHOFF: 1–28.

Ben-Naftali, O. (2011). PathoLAWgical Occupation: Normalizing the Exceptional Case of the Occupied Palestinian Territory and Other Legal Pathologies. International Humanitarian Law and International Human Rights Law: Pas de Deux. O. Ben-Naftali. Oxford, Oxford University Press: 129–200.

Ben-Naftali, O., et al. (2005). "Illegal Occupation: The Framing of the Occupied Palestinian Territory." Berkley Journal of International Law **23**.

Ben-Naftali, O. and K. R. Michaeli (2003). "We Must Not Make a Scarecrow of the Law: A Legal Analysis of the Israeli Policy of Targeted Killings." Cornell International Law Journal **36**(2).

Ben-Naftali, O. and Y. Shany (2004). "Living in Denial: The Application of Human Rights in the Occupied Territories; Ben-Naftali, Orna; Shany, Yuval." Israel Law Review **37**.

Benjamin, W. (1978). Critique of Violence, New York: Schocken Books.

Benvenisti, E. (2011). Submission to the Public Commission to Examine the Maritime Incident of 31 May 2010, available at: http://turkel-committee.com/files/wordocs/5210benbenishti.pdf, [accessed 28.4.15].

Berkovitch, N. and N. Gordon (2008). "The Political Economy of Transnational Regimes: The Case of Human Rights." International Studies Quarterly **52**(4): 881–904.

Berman, N. (2004a). 'The Appeals of the Orient': Colonized Desire and the War of the Riff. Gender and Human Rights. K. Knop. Oxford, Oxford University Press.

Berman, N. (2004b). "Privileging Combat? Contemporary Conflict and the Legal Construction of War." Columbia Journal of Transnational Law **43**(1).

Bernstein, D. (2014). Joint Chiefs Chairman Dempsey undermines Obama administration criticism of Israeli actions in Gaza, available at: http://www.washingtonpost.com/news/volokh-conspiracy/wp/2014/11/10/joint-chiefs-chairman-dempsey-undermines-obama-administration-criticism-of-israeli-actions-in-gaza/, [accessed 28.4.15]. The Washington Post 10.11.2014.

Bilder, R. B. and D. F. Vagts (2004). "Speaking Law to Power: Lawyers and Torture." American journal of international law **98** (4): 689–695.

Blau, U. and Y. Feldman (2009). How IDF legal experts legitimized strikes involving Gaza civilians. HAARETZ 23/01/09.

Blum, G. (2010). "The Laws of War and the Lesser Evil." Yale Journal of International Law **35**(1): 1–69.

Bourdieu, P. (1996). The rules of art: genesis and structure of the literary field. California, Stanford University Press.

Bourdieu, P. and L. J. D. Wacquant (1992). An Invitation to Reflexive Sociology. Chicago, University of Chicago Press.

Bowyer, D. (2009). The Moral Dimension of Asymmetrical Warfare: Accountability, Culpability and Military Effectiveness. The Moral Dimension of Asymmetrical Warfare: Counter-terrorism, Democratic Values and Military Ethics. T. A. v. Baarda and D. E. M. Verweij. Leiden, Boston, MARTINUS NIJHOFF: 137–167.

Burke, A. (2007). Beyond Security, Ethics and Violence: War against the other. New York, Routledge.

Buzan, B. (2002). Who May We Bomb? Worlds in Collision. K. Booth and T. Dunne. New York, PALGRAVE MACMILLAN: 85–94.

Clark, K. (2005). "Ethical Issues Raised by the OLC Torture Memorandum." Journal of National Security Law **1**: 455–472.

Cohen, A. (2005). "Administering the Territories: An Inquiry into the Application of International Humanitarian Law by the IDF in the Occupied Territories " Israel Law Review **38**(3): 24–79.

Cohen, A. (2009). "The Principle of Proportionality in the Context of Operation Cast Lead: Institutional Perspectives " Rutgers Law Record **35**.

Cohen, A. (2010). Proportionality in Modern Asymmetrical Wars. Jerusalem: Jerusalem Center for Public Affairs, Jerusalem Center for Public Affairs.

Cohen, A. (2011). "Legal Operational Advice in the Israeli Defense Forces: the International Law Department and the Changing Nature of International Humanitarian Law." Connecticut Journal of International Law **26**(2).

Cohen, A. and S. A. Cohen (2011). "Israel and International Humanitarian Law: Between the Neo-Realism of State Security and the 'Soft Power' of Legal Acceptability." Israel Studies **16**(2): 1–23.

Cohen, K. (2009). Is operational legal advice in the IDF desirable? (Seminar presentation). Faculty of Law Tel Aviv.

Cook, M. L. and M. Conversino (2009). Asymmetrical Air War: Ethical Implications. The Moral Dimension of Asymmetrical Warfare: Counter-terrorism, Democratic Values and Military Ethics. T. A. v. Baarda and D. E. M. Verweij. Leiden, Boston, MARTINUS NIJHOFF: 47–60.

Davidov, G. and A. Reichman (2010). "Prolonged Armed Conflict and Diminished Deference to the Military: Lessons from Israel." Law & Social Inquiry **35**(4): 919–956.

Dershowitz, A. (2013). Legality and Legitimacy: An Evening with Prof. Alan Dershowitz,availableat:http://www.inss.org.il/index.aspx?id=4480&eventid=6093 [accessed 28.4.15]. The Institute for National Security Studies. Tel Aviv University.

Diamond, E. (2010). "Before the Abyss: Reshaping International Humanitarian Law to Suit the Ends of Power." Israel Law Review **43**(2).

Douzinas, C. and A. Gearey (2005). Critical Jurisprudence: The Political Philosophy of Justice. Oxford and Portland, Oregon, Hart Publishing

Dunlap, C. J. (2001a). Law and Military Interventions: Preserving Humanitarian Values in 21st Conflicts, available at: http://people.duke.edu/~pfeaver/dunlap.pdf [accessed 28.4.15]. Humanitarian Challenges in Military Intervention Carr Center for Human Rights Policy, Kennedy School of Government, Harvard University.

Dunlap, C. J. (2001b). "The Revolution in Military Legal Affairs: Air Force Legal Professionals in 21st Century Conflicts." Air Force Law Review **51**.

Dunlap, C. J. (2009). "Lawfare: A Decisive Element of 21st-Century Conflicts?" JFQ: Joint Force Quarterly(54): 34–39.

Falk, R. (2000). "International Law and the al-Aqsa Intifada." Middle East Report(217): 16–18.

Falk, R. (2009a) Israel's war crimes, Transnational Institute, available at: http://www.tni.org/article/israel%E2%80%99s-war-crimes [accessed 28.4.15].

Feinberg, J. and J. Coleman (2003). Philosophy of Law Belmont, London, Thomson/Wadsworth

Feldman, Y. and U. Blau (2009). Consent and advise. HAARETZ 29.1.2009. accessible at: http://www.haaretz.com/consent-and-advise-1.269127[accessed 19.4.15]

Finkelstein, M. (2002). "Law in a Time of War." IDF Law Review **16**(1).

Frank, T. (2009). Reframing Asymmetrical Warfare: Beyond the Just War Idea. The Moral Dimension of Asymmetrical Warfare: Counter-terrorism, Democratic Values and Military Ethics. T. A. v. Baarda and D. E. M. Verweij. Leiden, Boston, MARTINUS NIJHOFF.

Gearty, C. (2009) Israel, Gaza and international law, Open Democracy, available at: http://www.opendemocracy.net/article/israel-gaza-and-international-law [accessed 28.4.15]

Goldstone, R., et al. (2009). Report of the United Nations Fact Finding Mission on the Gaza Conflict, available at: http://daccess-dds-ny.un.org/doc/UNDOC/GEN/G09/158/66/PDF/G0915866.pdf?OpenElement [accessed 10.1.2016].

Gordon, N. (2008). "Human Rights, Social Space and Power: Why do some NGOs Exert More Influence than Others?" The International Journal of Human Rights **12**(1): 23–39.

Gordon, N. and N. Berkovitch (2007). "Human Rights Discourse in Domestic Settings: How Does it Emerge?" Political Studies **55**(1): 243–266.

Gross, A. M. (2007). "Human proportions: Are human rights the emperor's new clothes of the international law of occupation?" The European Journal of International Law **18**(1).

Harpaz, G. and Y. Shany (2010). "Israeli Supreme Court and the Incremental Expansion of the Scope of Discretion under Belligerent Occupation Law." Israel Law Review **43**.

Henkin, L. (1968). How nations behave: law and foreign policy. Michigan, The Council on Foreign Relations, F. A. Praeger.

Human Rights Watch, N. (2009). Precisely Wrong: Gaza Civilians Killed by Israeli Drone-Launched Missiles, New York, available at: http://www.hrw.org/sites/default/files/reports/iopt0609web_0.pdf [accessed 28.4.15].

Inbar, Z. (2002). "The MAG Corps and the Held Territories " Law and Military: the IDF legal system's publication **16**(1).

Inbar, Z. (2005). Scales and Sword: The basis of military law in Israel Israel Defense Forces Publishing, MAG Corps.

Iverson, J. (2014). "Revolution or Reform: Has Humanitarianism Established a New Legal Order? Should It?." Leiden Journal of International Law **27**: 269–281.

Jerusalem Center, f. P. A. (2009). Hamas, the Gaza war and accountability under international law, available at: http://media-line.co.il/Events/Jcpa/Law-Conference/Heb.aspx [accessed 28.4.15]. Jerusalem, Jerusalem Center for Public Affairs Conference.

Jochnick, C. and R. Normand (1994). "Legitimation of Violence: A Critical History of the Laws of War." Harvard International Law Journal **35**(1): 49–96.

Johnson, R. (1993). Editor's Introduction: Pierre Bourdieu on Art, Literature and Culture The Field of Cultural Production: Essays on Art and Literature. R. Johnson. New York, Columbia University Press.

Kahn, P. W. (2006). "Judicial Ethos and the Autonomy of Law, Yale Law School, Faculty Scholarship Series. Paper 322. available at: http://digitalcommons.law.yale.edu/fss_papers/322 [accessed 28.4.15]."

Kasher, A. and A. Yadlin (2005). "Military Ethics of Fighting Terror: An Israeli Perspective." Journal of Military Ethics **4**(1): 3–32.

Kennedy, D. (2006). Of War and Law. Princeton, Princeton University Press.

Kirchheimer, O. (1961). Political Justice: The Use of Legal Procedure for Political Ends. Princeton, New Jersey, Princeton University Press.
Koskenniemi, M. (1990). "The Politics of International Law." European Journal of International Law **1**: 4–32.
Koskenniemi, M. (1999). Between Commitment and Cynicism: Outline for a theory of International Law as Practice. Collection of Essays by Legal Advisers of States, Legal Advisers of International Organizations and Practitioners in the field of International Law. U. Office of Legal Affairs. New York, United Nationas Publications.
Koskenniemi, M. (2009). "The Function of Law in the International Community: 75 Years After." British Year Book of International Law **79**.
Koskenniemi, M. (2011). The Politics of International Law. Oxford and Portland, Hart Publishing
Kot, J.-P. (2011). "Israeli Civilians versus Palestinian Combatants? Reading the Goldstone Report in Light of the Israeli Conception of the Principle of Distinction." Leiden Journal of International Law **24**(4): 961–988.
Kretzmer, D. (2002). The Occupation of Justice: The Supreme Court of Israel and the Occupied Territories. New York, State University of New York Press.
Lauterpacht, H. (1933). The Function of Law in the International Community. Oxford, Clarendon Press.
Lauterpacht, H. (1952). "The Problem of the Revision of the Law of War." British Yearbook of International Law **29**: 360.
Levy, Y. (2010). "The Tradeoff between Force and Casualties: Israel's Wars in Gaza, 1987–2009." Conflict Management and Peace Science September **27**(4).
Liste, P. (2008). "Articulating the Nexus of Politics and Law: War in Iraq and the Practice within Two Legal Systems." International Political Sociology **2**: 38–55.
Lohr, M. F. and S. Gallotta (2003). "Legal Support in War: The Role of Military Lawyers." Chicago Journal of International Law **4**(2): 465–478.
Madsen, M. R. (2006). "Transnational Fields: Elements of a Reflexive Sociology of the Internationalisation of Law." Retfaerd **3**(114): 23–41.
MAG (2015). Law in Judea and Samaria, accesible at: http://www.law.idf.il/209-he/Patzar.aspx?PageNum=14 [accessed 19.4.15]. MAG.
MAG Corps "Mission Statement." http://www.law.idf.il/320-en/Patzar.aspx.
Megret, F. (2006). From 'Savages' to 'Unlawful Combatants': A Postcolonial Look at International Humanitarian Law's 'Other'. International Law And Its 'Others'. A. Orford. Cambridge Cambridge University Press.
Mendelblit, A. (2009a). Consultancy Under Fire. HAARETZ 29.1.2009.
Mendelblit, A. (2011). Second response to the Turkel Comission regarding mechanisms of check and investigation concerning complaints and claims about vio-

lations of the laws of war Public Commission to Examine the Maritime Incident of 31 May 2010 (Turkel Comission).

Mendelblit, A. (2012). "Lawfare - the IDF's legal front." Military and Strategy **4**(1).

Meron, T. (2006). The Humanization of International Law. Leiden; Boston, Martinus Nijhoff Publishers.

Meydani, A. and S. Mizrahi (2006). "The Politics and Strategies of Defending Human Rights: The Israeli Case." Israel Law Review **39**(1).

Negbi, M. (1981). Justice Under Occupation: The Israeli Supreme Court versus the Military Administration Jerusalem, Cana.

Neuman, N. (2007). "Legal Consultancy in Battle." Systems (Ma'arachot) **411**: 36–41.

Orford, A. (2004). "The Destiny of International Law." Leiden Journal of International Law **17**(3): 441–476.

Orr, Z. and D. Golan (2014). "Human rights NGOs in Israel: collective memory and denial." The International Journal of Human Rights **18**(1): 68–93.

PCHR (2010). Genuinely Unwilling: An Update, available at: http://www.pchrgaza.org/files/2010/Genuinely Unwilling - An Update.pdf [accessed 28.4.15].

Pictet, J. (1985). Development and principles of international humanitarian law. Dordrecht; Lancaster, Nijhoff.

Rhode, D. (2000). In the Interests of Justice: Reforming the Legal Profession. Oxford; New York, Oxford University Press.

Ronen, M. (2009). Legalised Lead (Oferet Hakuka). Yedioth Aharonot 19.1.09.

Roytman, Y. (2013). "Inner legal supervision in time of combat " The Gates of Trial (Sha'arei Mishpat) **6**.

Rubin, P., A. (1997). Ethics and authority in international law. Cambridge, Cambridge University Press.

Sands, P. (2008). Torture Team: deception, cruelty and the compromise of law. London, Allen Lane.

Sassoli, M. (2011). The Role of Human Rights and International Humanitarian Law in New Types of Armed Conflicts. International Humanitarian Law and International Human Rights Law: Pas de Deux. O. Ben-Naftali. Oxford, Oxford University Press.

Sfard, M. (2004). "International Litigation in Domestic Courts." The Trial (HaMishpat) **9**.

Shamgar, M. (1971). "The Observance of International Law in the Administered Territories " Israel Yearbook on Human Rights **1**: 262.

Shamgar, M. (2003). Shamgar Book. Tel Aviv, The Israel Bar Publishing House

Shandi, Y. (2010). "Israel's Claim of the "Legitimate Right of Self- Defence" regarding the Gaza Strip in Light of International Law A Palestinian Lawyer's Position." Journal of East Asia & International Law **3**(2): 387–406.

Shany, Y., et al. (2011). Response on behalf of the researchers of the Israel Democracy Institute's Terrorism and Democracy project to claims or suspicions in regard to violation of the Laws of War. I. D. I. s. T. a. D. project.

Sharp, H. (2009). Gaza conflict: Who is a civilian? BBC News 5.1.09, available at: http://news.bbc.co.uk/1/hi/world/middle_east/7811386.stm[accessed 28.4.15].

Sharvit-Baruch, P. and N. Neuman (2011). "Warning civilians prior to attack under international law: theory and practice." Israel Yearbook on Human Rights **41**: 137–195.

Shefi, D. (1983). "The Status of the Legal Adviser to the Armed Forces: His Functions and Powers." Military Law Review(100): 119–134

Straschnov, A. (1994). Justice Under Fire. Tel Aviv, Yedioth Aharonoth Books.

Taylor, C. (1996). "A World Consensus on Human Rights?" Dissent **Summer**: 21–25.

Teitel, R., G. (2002). "Humanity's Law: Rule of Law for the New Global Politics." Cornell International Law Journal **35**(2): 355–387.

Teitel, R., G. (2011). Humanity's Law. Oxford, Oxford University Press.

Teubner, G. (1997). Law in the Collision of Discourses Law, Society and Economy. R. Rawlings. Oxford, Clarendon Press.

The State of Israel (2010a). "Gaza Operation Investigations: a Second Update, available at: http://www.mfa.gov.il/MFA_Graphics/MFA Gallery/Documents/GazaUpdateJuly2010.pdf [accessed 28.4.15]."

The State of Israel (2010b). "Gaza Operation Investigations: an Update, available at: http://mfa.gov.il/MFA_Graphics/MFA Gallery/Documents/Gaza OperationInvestigationsUpdate.pdf [accessed 29.4.15]."

Toiskallio, J. (2009). Ethics in the Core of Officer Education. The Moral Dimension of Asymmetrical Warfare: Counter-terrorism, Democratic Values and Military Ethics. T. A. v. Baarda and D. E. M. Verweij. Leiden, Boston, MARTINUS NIJHOFF: 263–278.

Walzer, M. (1977). Just and Unjust Wars: a moral argument with historical illustrations. New York, Basic Books.

Weiner, J. R. and A. Bell (2009). "The Gaza War of 2009: Applying International Humanitarian Law to Israel and Hamas." San Diego International Law Journal **5**(11): 5–42.

Weisberg, R. H. (2004). Loose Professionalism or Why Lawyers Take the Lead on Torture. Torture: A Collection. L. Sanford. Oxford, Oxford University Press.

Weizman, E. (2009). "Lawfare in Gaza: legislative attack, Open Democracy, available at: http://www.opendemocracy.net/article/legislative-attack [accessed 29.4.15]."

Weizman, E. (2010a). "Forensic Architecture: Only the criminal can solve the crime." Radical Philosophy **164**.

Weizman, E. (2010b). Only the Criminal Can Solve the Crime. ArteEast Public Lecture The New School, New York, The Sheila C. Johnson Design Center
Weizman, E. (2011). The Least of All Possible Evils: Humanitarian Violence from Arendt to Gaza. London, Verso Books.
Wells-Greco, M. (2010). "Operation Cast Lead: Jus in bello proportionality." Netherlands International Law Review 57(3): 397–422.
Yahav, D. and U. Amit-Kohn (1993). Israel, the "intifada" and the rule of law. Jerusalem, Israel Ministry of Defense Publications.

CHAPTER 2

# Conceptual Framework and Research Methods for the Israeli Legal Field in the OPT

## 2.1 Introduction

The previous chapter introduced this book's key aims and mapped related areas of study, namely international law in Israel's dealings with the occupied Palestinian territories (OPT), the laws of war, and the relationship between international law and politics. This chapter addresses law as a social phenomenon and lays out its methodological approach and tools of inquiry, set within a conceptual framework.

As discussed in Chapter 1, Israel's complex legal management of the OPT has been studied widely. These studies include general overviews of Israel's conduct (Falk 2000; Ben-Naftali et al. 2005; Ben-Naftali 2011; Cohen and Cohen 2011), with some accounts examining the applicability and status of human rights in this territory (Ben-Naftali and Shany 2004; Gross 2007) and the work of human rights organisations (Meydani and Mizrahi 2006; Berkovitch and Gordon 2008; Gordon 2008; Weizman 2010a, b), the High Court of Justice (Negbi 1981; Kretzmer 2002; Harpaz and Shany 2010), and the military legal system (Shamgar 1971; Yahav and Amit-Kohn 1993; Inbar 2002; Cohen 2005; Inbar 2005; Cohen 2011; Roytman 2013). This account also deals with international law in the work of the MAG Corps, the High Court of Justice and human rights organisations. This chapter will show how this book's theoretical-conceptual positioning leads it in directions different from the studies reviewed. A key aspect of this book, which is by and large lacking in these



M. Geva, *Law, Politics and Violence in Israel/Palestine*,
DOI 10.1007/978-3-319-34153-8_2

existing accounts, as described in the previous chapter, is a contextual positioning of military practice in relation to historical and institutional processes of change.

The key outcomes of this contextualised account are, first, novel perspectives on Israeli legal practice in the OPT, and second, an insight into the social dynamic process forming law and legality. A fundamental aspect of this analysis is a grounded consideration of the ever-present conundrum in examinations of international law—its relationship with politics. From this perspective, our account builds on and engages with studies of international law in political perspective in the specific case of Israel (Weizman 2009, 2011), but also in general terms (Koskenniemi 1990, 1999, 2011; Kennedy 2006; Rasulov 2006).

In methodological terms, this investigation of law builds primarily on Bourdieu's sociology of the field as a means of unpacking international law's past and present in the Israeli/Palestinian locality, its process of constitution and its constituted character. This framework captures the simultaneous changes in legal norms, sets of actors and their extent of influence, and ultimately the overall making of 'law' and 'legality'. Accounts that neglect any of these elements fail to address crucial aspects of this social phenomenon. This chapter will show and discuss how this perspective enables compound analysis of the legal enterprise at hand. This theoretical avenue enables a multi-layered perspective on this area of social production that is firmly grounded in legal work, histories, actors, institutions and power, and formulates a broad analysis articulating the social meanings, processes and influences making law.

The chapter lays out the conceptual foundations and methodological paths devised for this account. It consists of three parts, compiling as a whole an approach weaving together conceptual and practical layers of analysis. The first part is a preliminary discussion of Bourdieu's field analysis and consideration of the field framework in the context of law. It includes sections dedicated to key aspects in Bourdieu's field theory—agency and structure, stability and change. The second part positions Israeli institutions and actors in the field's framework and includes an introduction to key institutions and agents. This is the basis for the relational analysis of these bodies, which will unfold in the chapters that follow. The third part explains this book's use of lawyers as a conceptual doorway into law—its logic, power and the dynamic constitution of its borders.

## 2.2 The Field

Bourdieu's field is a 'radical contextualisation' (Johnson 1993, p. 9), a web made of people and institutions continually acting and reacting to one another. It is a construct grounded in an epistemologically charged set of analytical concepts and commitment to an empirical investigation (Grenfell and Lebaron 2014). In Bourdieu's terms, this analytical structure is:

> A network, or a configuration, of objective relations between positions. These positions are objectively defined, in their existence and in the determinations they impose upon their occupants, agents or institutions, by their present and potential situation (situs) in the structure of the distribution of species of power (or capital) whose possession commands access to the specific profits that are at stake in the field, as well as by their objective relation to other positions (domination, subordination, homology, etc.). (Bourdieu and Wacquant 1992, p. 52)

Thus, Bourdieu's premise is a deeply contextual account and one particularly invested in a multi-level consideration of position and power.

The field, weaving together Bourdieu's notions of capital, habitus and practice has provided fertile ground for sociological accounts of diverse areas and themes, from arts (Johnson 1993) and sports (Clément 1995) to international politics (Pouliot 2008; Bigo 2011; Adler-Nissen 2012) and law (Madsen and Dezalay 2002; Parikh and Garth 2005; Lenoir 2006; Madsen 2006, 2011; Dezalay and Madsen 2012). These accounts are all built on the fundamental power-immersed assumption by which 'a field is a social configuration structured along three primary dimensions: relations of power, objects of struggle, and taken-for-granted rules' (Bourdieu, in Pouliot 2008, p. 274). Thus all investigations reject objective apprehensions of any state of affairs and instead look at the context in which specific meanings are made—the goals set, means of evaluating success, authority and the logic making sense of actions and actors.

Power relations between agents and institutions are embedded in a doxa. The doxa comprises 'all that is accepted as obvious, in particular the classifying schemes which determine what deserves attention and what does not' (Pouliot 2008, p. 275). The power of a doxa is reflected in the fact that all agents in the field, powerful and powerless, those who gain from the doxa and those who do not, abide by its rules. This common ground implies a key Bourdieusian assumption, that all the agents in a particular field share the interest of maintaining the field's distinctiveness from other fields, as the field is the source of their power. The identification of the doxa as a taken-for-granted set of rules rather than simply fact also implies that inequalities among agents within a particular field are a product of the specific character and shape of capital at stake, which are themselves historically constructed (Bourdieu 1990). These idiosyncratic capitals and struggles define fields' autonomy or separation from one another.

Each field's institutions and agents operate in relation to capital, the extent of the power they each possess. Agents' capital is relative, and correspond with their field's particular configuration. In this sense, the measure of an agent's capital cannot be understood in isolation from the context of the field (Bourdieu and Wacquant 1992, p. 101). This also implies that power is not an inherent quality, but a relative state of affairs. Notably, taking this into account, the term 'objective' does not imply that the field and the relations it encompasses are fixed or immune to change. Rather, and as will be further discussed, the field is sustained continuously and thus inherently includes a measure of instability. Its objectivity is the extent of the persistence of social power relations, which infers, alongside constant movement, a degree of stability. In methodological terms, this implies contextual analysis, i.e. one considering an institution's position in the field and its relationship with other agents and organisations. In this, an agency's origins, the measure and extent of power it has and its variations throughout time, are all to be conceptualised and analysed in consideration of the context of other bodies operating in the same field.

Bourdieu identified three types of capital—economic capital, directly convertible to money; social capital, comprised of 'personal' connections; and cultural capital, which may manifest in educational qualifications, prestige, authority and reputation (Bourdieu 1986, p. 242). The specific character of the capital structuring the field is in itself an object of struggle. This book's discussion of law and power in the legal field builds largely on capital that correlates with Bourdieu's 'cultural capital'.

The field is at the same time both dynamic and stable. It is in constant movement, but the movement is taking place in an already-structured context. The field's structure and contents are made up continuously by its agents and institutions; agents and institutions' activities form and take place in the structured context of the field. In Bourdieu's words, the field is a system of:

> durable, transposable dispositions, structured structures predisposed to function as structuring structures, that is, as principles which generate and organize practices and representations that can be objectively adapted to their outcomes without presupposing a conscious aiming at ends or express mastery of the operations necessary in order to attain them. (Bourdieu 1990, p. 53)

These two elements are the core of the field analysis—first, it is continuously constituted and sustains power relations driven by its configuration of authority. This structured dynamism is simultaneously the conceptualisation of stability and change, repetition and diversion. Second, structure directs the ongoing maintenance of the field. Agents maintain existing power relations without necessarily calculating the aim of each specific action. In this sense, the field often operates in a manner that is to some degree independent of intent. Thus the interplay of field does not go hand in hand with a simple intention-derived interpretation of action.

Structure in Bourdieu's work is a methodological construct created by a researcher rather than a social 'truth'. Structures are primarily methodological devices that have a pragmatic value in social scientific research. Structural methods do not stem from the underlying nature of the world and social relations. This position makes the field agnostic in terms of ontology (Lizardo 2010).

### 2.2.1 *Agency in the Field: Dissolving the Subjectivist—Objectivist Polarity*

Bourdieu's theory engages with a key sociological question about the relationship between people and social context. His conceptualisation of agency builds on a break with essentialist structuralism. This departure was in part a result of what he identified as this theory's set of dichotomies, first in this subjectivism versus objectivism. Other dichotomies that follow are individual versus society and freedom versus necessity. Subjectivism in this sense relates to individuals' perspectives, and objectivism refers to social order detached from personal experience. Negating these oppositions, Bourdieu positions the objectivist and subjectivist moments in dialectical terms (Bourdieu 1989, p. 15). In this sense, an agency in the field is located in a position encompassing clashes between, and combinations of, supposedly polar elements, and brings together the necessary and the free. Post-structuralist accounts question this positioning and the very assumption of subjectivity that pre-dates society and culture (for example, Butler 1999), but this direction of inquiry is beyond the scope of this book.

Bourdieu's habitus is a conceptual tool providing a crystallised moment of the agency and structure relations. This is a term relating to a subject situated in social systems and webs of power, weaving together practice and social conditions: 'one has to return to practice, the site of the dialectic of the *opus operatum* and the *modus operandi*; of the objectified products and the incorporated products of historical practice; of structures and *habitus*' (Bourdieu 1990, p. 52). Thus, habitus is at the same time action and reaction, product and producer of social conditions, history in the making. It is a synthesis of the past into the present enacted by agents and social context. In these terms, habitus allows observation of the mutually constitutive dynamics between agency and structure. Moments of change, such as the significant modifications in legal interpretations that this book examines, are useful opportunities to observe and investigate the relationship between structure and agency, because these are occasions in which agents push boundaries and reshape the field and their position in it.

The conceptual positioning of an agent in a social context is a facet of the continuous making of social relations. It is a recurring moment in which disposition leads, at most, to the inclination to regenerate existing social power structures and consequently the agent's position within them. The element of intent or strategic calculation is not entirely excluded, but rather is located within a structured context which implies that intent is inseparable from social settings. The contextualisation of intent means that it cannot be seen as a result of objective calculation, but as an action embedded within a given structure.

### 2.2.2 *Structure and Change*

Building on the consideration of habitus as a site encompassing dynamism and stability, this section now approaches the simultaneous endurance and instability of the social. This discussion, aimed at accounting for both continuity and change, is one of the field's most pertinent conceptual endeavours. Stability is made by the field's structure—power division and doxa laying out the settings for the operation of agents and habitus. At the same time, as the field is in constant movement, made and remade continually, it is, to some extent, unstable. In this sense, a perspective detecting the dynamism of social relations has the potential to destabilise an existing state of affairs (Bourdieu 1990, p. 141). This is a viewpoint of social relations negating both a naïve perception of the possibility of social change and a depiction of a fixed structure unable to account for shifts in the division of power. Translated into research ventures, the goal is to construct analytical tools that allow a heuristic stabilisation of social dynamism that still captures movement adequately.

This perspective implies an additional formative premise—power relations constructing the field are inseparable from 'reality':

> The object of social science is a reality that encompasses all the individual and collective struggles aimed at conserving or transforming reality, in particular those that seek to impose the legitimate definition of reality, whose specifically symbolic efficacy can help to conserve or subvert the established order, that is to say, reality. (Bourdieu 1990, p. 141)

The stability of power relations is interwoven with perceptions of 'reality'. 'Reality' cannot be understood in isolation from the field's power relations. In terms of research this leads to a commitment to a methodological construct sensitive to the formative implications of power.

While this book uses the field as its conceptual grounding, it is also necessary to acknowledge the limits and oversights of this arrangement. First, an obvious shortcoming of field analysis lies in its very bordering of the field. In this, its weakness is the flipside of its strength—this relational perspective relies on a distinction between a field and its surroundings, but this is also an act a priori excluding alternative factors, processes and agents. This same bordering leads to a series of related problems, that this construct cannot account for social process, change or for a situation that is not positioned in a distinct field, or one that is located in or made up of a myriad of influences that cannot be traced to a unified field. Along the lines of this same argument, individuals may also be located in a variety of fields rather than just one (Atkinson 2012). In this sense, the positioning of agents in a single particular field cannot fully account for their perspectives and action. Translated into the terms of this book, an obvious question is the very positioning of military legal work in the legal field. Alternative accounts may suggest that military legal practice is best captured as a fundamentally political or military enterprise. To this effect I explain my analytical decisions by relating to the field and its structure as methodological constructs rather than objects existing 'out there'. In this sense, the field is a tool rather than a truth. I find that this is a framework allowing insight into law but also taking into account questions about politics and about the army.

As I have mentioned already, my own analysis is indebted to Bourdieu's sociology, but goes beyond his theory in its efforts to unpack the Israeli legal field. The particular terms and character of this departure will be discussed in the next chapter, alongside the analysis of the Israeli legal field.

## 2.3 Applying Bourdieu's Field Analysis to Law

Bourdieu applied his sociology of the field to the legal sphere in his essay 'The Force of Law: Toward a Sociology of the Juridical Field' (1987). Bourdieu is interested in the 'social practices of law', i.e. the operations of the field as manifested in its practice. In this perspective, the field is made by two interconnected elements—first, by legal 'inner logic',[1] which 'constantly constrains the range of possible actions' and 'limit[s] the range of specifically juridical solutions' (Bourdieu 1987, p. 816); and second, by power relations between this field's agents and institutions. By and large, Bourdieu's theoretical engagement with law has not been significantly acknowledged or developed[2] (Dezalay and Madsen 2012).

While scholars of law may pose questions relating to power, Bourdieu's approach nevertheless remains distinctive. One of the facets of this distinctiveness is that power is detected everywhere, 'inside' and 'outside' of law. Legal agents and institutions have different degrees of capital, and these unequal relationships structure the field. Dynamics between these bodies take place in a space made of the field's particular logic. Power dynamics not only shape relationships between parties, but are also intertwined with the contents of legal work and law. In this sense, law is made by these interplays of power: 'The juridical field is the site of a competition for monopoly of the right to determine the law' (Bourdieu 1987, p. 818). From the outside, the field's power as a whole also impacts the practice of law.

In comparison with alternative accounts of law, Bourdieu's analysis breaks free from two familiar avenues of legal scholarship—formalism and realism. Formalism relies on the interpretation of legal rules and codes, legal proceedings and judgments and the degree of their fulfilment, i.e. analysis bound within law. Realism commonly attributes law and legal practice to politics, in an analysis essentially external to law. The formalist—realist division resonates with the theoretical division between Hans Kelsen and Carl Schmitt, the former identifying law's validity within the legal doctrine itself and the latter in political authority external to law

(Koskenniemi 2009). Bourdieu points out that both of these antagonistic views equally ignore the social-dynamic *practice* of law. The field informs an analysis that is neither solely internal nor external to law. It incorporates both the theoretical territories of legal rule, code and document, as well as the power relations in action within the legal arena.

Bourdieu's analysis builds on a consideration of power relations in the legal field, embedded in law's 'logic'. Thus both legal codes and the division of capital among actors are substantive analytical factors. The dynamics of power-embedded relationships between agents and institutions constantly make and remake the field's logic. The 'field' is characterised by a specific logic that is determined by two factors. First, there are the specific power relations of all its participants—judges, practitioners and academics—which give it its structure. These power relations order the competitive struggles or conflicts over competence. The second factor is the 'internal logic of juridical functioning which constantly constrains the range of possible actions' for its participants, and 'limit the range of specifically juridical solutions' (Bourdieu 1987, p. 816). These situated dynamics are the essence of the field analysis—structure as a contextual construct, and at the same time both cause and effect of power relations.

Law's logic is also a pivotal factor directing meaning and action in the field. Participation in or entry to the field largely implies the acceptance of its logic, thus it already shapes much of the content of any action within its territory. This is an obvious argument, but also a powerful one—the field by definition excludes alternative types of logic and argumentation: 'Entry into the juridical field implies that tactic acceptance of the field's fundamental law, an essential tautology which requires that, within the field, conflicts can only be resolved *juridically*—that is, according to the rules and conventions of the field itself' (Bourdieu 1987, p. 831). It is obvious that bodies such as courts, for example, operate in accordance with legal logic, but those actors that actively enter the legal field at a single identifiable moment, such as newly emerging NGOs, enable a clearer consideration of this formative effect.

The field analysis, by way of investigating legal practice, aims to reconsider law as an object of study. This is the core of Bourdieu's reflexive sociology – an exploration rejecting predetermined categories or limits to its object of study. The means of investigation derive from the elements in operation within the legal field—its internal logic, relations within it and its overall power. This account paves the way for a nuanced and composite perspective on the ways law is made, the power relations involved in this making, and ultimately to its very meaning. One of the chief implications of this examination for this account is a reconsideration of law's relationship with politics. In this sense, the Bourdieusian-inspired task is to historicise and contextualise the ongoing making of law and the legal, with an agnostic view on the purity of law and its separation from or concurrence with, politics. Rather than an attempting to disentangle law conceptually from political interference, this analysis aims to detect the historical, contextual making of the legal and political in the particular Israeli case, and as a way of suggesting novel means of inquiry that could be used in other contexts.

The analytical framework of the field implies that its core, doxa, is largely stable. Nevertheless, it is affected by practice in a dynamic, continuous process. The emergence of a field, a process this book traces and examines, provides an opportunity to observe the formation of its doxa, a construction of a field from its very foundations. This situation of genesis is a particularly dynamic process of struggle that included the making of legal contents, the field's logic, the field's distinction from other fields and its power. At the same time, the situation of genesis also meant, in this case, that not many bodies were taking part in this struggle.

Bourdieusian analysis, which conceptualises 'reality' as a product of struggle, in its respective field, is unique in the case of law. Its particularity lies in its claims regarding social power. This power involves a set of socio-political processes and conditions that mean law becomes a fundamental framework for interpretations of the world. Law's impact is not only paramount but also formative: 'It would not be excessive to say that it [law] *creates* the social world, but only if we remember that it is this world which first creates the law' (Bourdieu 1987, p. 839; emphasis in original). This is a radical reversal of the common understanding of law's relationship with the world—rather than merely responding to existing situations, law establishes the understanding of events, i.e. the way things are. Paul Kahn argues along these lines: 'Law does not simply impose an order on a field of activity; rather, it is constitutive of a way in which experience is organised, through the meanings that we perceive in events' (Kahn 2000, p. 2). The shift from abstract code to the concrete example is a constitutive moment rather than being a priori contained in this code (Agamben 2008). This shift is part of the ongoing struggle over legal 'truth' in the field.

The legal field is in part characterised by the means in which it denies affiliation with any non-legal interest. This is a fundamental aspect of the field's making of its borders, and particularly vis-à-vis the distinction from politics. The common acceptability of such claims, asserting law as a non-political force, is tied intimately to the politics of the state:

> The universality of political competence as identified with respect of the law was ...conceived with the emergence of the modern State, that is with a social structure which—through its jurists, philosophers, and, later, experts—saw itself as the very opposite of a social group seeking out private interests. (Lenoir 2006, p. 16)

In this sense, the denial of non-legal interest by law's various practitioners is rooted in the liberal ideology of the state. These conceptual grounds, positioning 'the legal' as a fundamental component in the state, provide both an overarching insight relating to the field as a whole, and the context for the discussion and analysis of particular bodies within the field.

## 2.4 Lawyering in Israel

Following the general introduction to Bourdieu's sociology of the field and its application to the area of law, this section begins to position the Israeli case in the theoretical context presented. It addresses preliminary issues regarding the usage of the field in this case, as preparation for a discussion on particular actors in this field.

Legal fields differ in particular contexts, places and times. Investigating the Israeli case, Gad Barzilai (2007) found that Israel has an exceptionally high number of lawyers per capita: 204 % more than the USA, 232 % more than the UK, and 601 % more than France. Barzilai explains the astounding Israeli proportion of lawyers in reference to the country's historical socio-political context. In the 1990s, he argues, the country saw a dwindling belief in political parties that has been replaced by a growing liberal confidence in law and lawyers. Under these circumstances, lawyers have become prominent in all public bodies, from state agencies to political parties, building on a 'somewhat transnational and intergenerational myth about the virtues of their legal profession' (2007, p. 262). Despite Israeli public trust in the judiciary being in decline recently (Stern 2010), lawyers have, by and large, retained their power. According to a 2014 survey commissioned by the Israel Bar Association (BdiCode 2014), the number of lawyers per capita is steadily increasing.

The engagement of this account with the army's legal practice in the OPT means it is both similar to and distinct from the mentioned discussions on law and lawyers in Israel. On the one hand, the military legal system is a state institution, and as such it is shaped in the Israeli national setting and circumstance. The High Court of Justice's review of military conduct and its consequent involvement with military legal practice in the OPT is a key facet of this intertwined civil-military relationship. On the other hand, the Israeli administration of the OPT, gradually developing since 1967, has created a separate legal system for these territories. Moreover, the context of the army implies a particular type of legal work.

Building on the analytical arrangement of the field, this book provides a contextual account of legal military practice, grounded in multiple avenues, sources and materials. This investigation builds on several layers of analysis—a mapping of structured relations between different institutions, legal logic, the habitus of agents occupying different positions, and an assessment of the field's changing overall power. Translated into this case and the specific interest in military legal practice, this analysis positions the military legal system heuristically at its centre and investigates power in the field, state and non-state legal institutions' relationships with the military legal system and practitioners' habitus.

The Israeli legal field's 'inner logic' is comprised of varied elements—legal code, rules and judgments, and the relative positioning of different institutions, such as the court's authority to review and decide between conflicting opinions, the co-operation between military and state civil lawyers when challenged with a petition and so on. The collection of laws ordering the field has changed over time and has included some key international legal treaties, such as The Hague Regulations, the Geneva Conventions, human rights law and multiple military legal orders issued in the OPT. The position of this legal internal logic in itself deserves some attention. Bourdieu argues that law is often seen as 'the expression of universal and eternal values, transcending any individual interest' (Bourdieu 1987, p. 841). This is a fundamental point—within the liberal realm law has become a normative force that is often regarded as apolitical. While this argument regarding law's self-presentation as apolitical has merit, it is also a simplification of this state of affairs. For example, not all components of the legal inner logic have a similar status. First, the Israeli High Court of Justice decisions and the provisions of the Geneva Conventions, do not have an identical position even if they both form part of the field's inner logic. Moreover, law's own claims regarding its universal status are constantly being challenged. Challenges often manifest in the 'detection' of politics in law and legal practice, and all the more so in the case of international law. As the polar discussions regarding international law and politics demonstrate, these laws provide particularly fertile ground for controversies in relation to their extent of universality and distance from politics.

Notwithstanding challenges to law's self-depiction as universal and apolitical, the Israeli military engagement with international law certainly has a legitimising effect, one tied with law's social position. This legitimacy cannot be fully understood based on the military legal system alone. It is a product of the legal field as a whole and as such is indivisible from other legal institutions operating in this field. In this sense, legitimacy is made and sustained in a dynamic relationship with the participation and activities of all the legal actors and institutions involved. Seen in this way, NGOs and the military, for example, which are institutions regularly opposing one another's position within the field, both take part in the operation of continually affirming international law's legitimacy founded in the field's power as a single entity.

This book's engagement with the field analysis positions different actors— the military legal system, human rights NGOs, the court, the Ministry of Justice and legal academics—in relation to one another. This examination follows the premise that an investigation of law's impact on military conduct in the OPT is grounded not only in the operations of the military legal system, the direct body dealing with this work, but also in the broader context of the legal field. This contextual outlook provides the background for the following chapters' consideration of specific legal decisions as well as general trends involving different Israeli institutions.

Differences between institutions' measure of capital make up the field. The army and NGOs are placed in the most remote positions in the field in terms of legal interpretations, but there is also a vast difference between other agents such as academics and the military, or NGOs and the court. In Bourdieu's terms, these relations are seen as 'structural hostility' (Bourdieu 1987). Hostility is yet another aspect of the ongoing struggle within the field over the determination of meaning (of specific laws, the field's overall goals, or anything in between). Unequal distribution of power between institutions implies varied levels of authority assigned to claims regarding legal 'truth'. Legal interpretation of the MAG Corps, a body at present possessing considerable capital within the field, has far more power than that of a human rights organisation.

The framework of the field negates a single purposeful understanding of change. Purpose can account only partially for practitioners' actions because any such action is decided and carried out in an already-structured context and an existing habitus deeming some choices far more probable than others. In this light, the military's legal system historical gain of capital that the book discusses in detail is not simply a product of the carefully designed isolated actions of this system but rather it should be understood in the relative context of a capital-driven, structured field. This also implies a disengagement from a liberal depiction of progressive legal development. The perspective of the field does not produce a normative story of legal evolution but rather of specific processes and opportunities leading to alterations in the configuration of power resulting in changes in law.

This book's re-examination of law and legality through a contextualised—historicised account of the army's practice of international law in the OPT is in line with the field's conceptual rejection of predetermined definitions of its object of inquiry. This is reflexive sociology, or a 'double rupture', considered by some to be Bourdieu's most important theoretical contribution (Madsen 2011). It is a reconsideration of the very definition of the object of study as well as its means of inquiry. In this perspective, contextualising and historicising legal practice, institution and code at the same time relativises these as products of specific circumstances and takes the concepts out of their implied positioning as necessary and permanent by relating to the social conditions of their genesis (Bourdieu 1996).

The potential weakness of the field analysis is that regardless of its rejection of existing categories, by imposing a methodological 'field' it sets a priori limitations to its area of inquiry. In the case of the military legal system, it can be argued that its very positioning in the legal field marginalises alternative influences and contexts, primarily governmental—political and military authorities. This is the same tension that is present in the discourse of these practitioners and that of those supporting or opposing them. In other words, this is the tension articulating the boundaries of 'the legal' and its distinction from 'the political'. Notably, Bourdieu did not assume that fields are closed structures detached from external influence. Rather, he related to fields as dynamic spaces, with an open interface to other fields (Madsen and Dezalay 2002). In this light, it is important to employ the field in a nuanced manner, recognising its measure of fluidity and taking into account that it has different degrees of influence over specific bodies. With this in mind, the sociologist Mikael Madsen (2006, p. 27) suggests a portrayal of the field as a magnetic force, where bodies are variably positioned at different distances from the magnetic core. In this sense, some bodies are more affected by the field and its dynamics and others are affected to a lesser degree. Furthermore, a cautious consideration of this analytical structure enables an investigation of its limits as well as crossovers between fields and their influence over one another. And so, if employed in a nuanced manner, the field does not limit an analysis nor does it reject power and influence relating to agents external to it, but rather provides a research construct and tools allowing a focused yet flexible analysis.

## 2.5 Actors in Focus in the Israeli Legal Field: The MAG Corps, High Court of Justice and NGOs

This study's investigation of the Israeli legal field focuses primarily on the MAG Corps' International Law Division/Department,[3] the High Court of Justice and human rights NGOs. Additional actors and institutions receiving less attention are legal academics and the High Court of Justice Petitions Department, a unit at the Ministry of Justice. Choice of focus among legal institutions stems from this study's interest in military conduct in the OPT. The military legal system is thus heuristically positioned at the centre of this inquiry; this centrality does not imply that this is the field's most powerful body, but that this study is particularly interested in this organisation. Agents chosen are those which preliminary analysis showed have the most impact on this military body and those interacting most directly and intensively with it. This section sets out a preliminary map of relationships in the field. These institutions' multi-faceted relationships, dynamics and relative shifts of capital will be discussed in more detail and analysed in the chapters that follow.

The Ministry of Justice's High Court of Justice Petitions Department handles petitions against the actions of state authorities. This representation follows the division of authority by which the MAG Corps is institutionally subject to the authority of the civil justice system. In practical terms, co-operation between this department and military legal authorities is not limited to petitions (Mazuz 2013). These bodies also interact when new military ideas and policies are formed, in anticipation of potential court petitions. The position and role of the Ministry of Justice's practitioners in these discussions is complex. There is an ongoing discussion on both theoretical and practical levels about whose interests state lawyers are to represent. Responses to this query are located on a spectrum with public authorities at one end and 'public interest' at the other (Berenson 2000; Mandel 2009). In the face of this Department's formal pertinent position and role, theoretically implying a considerable capital, in reality it does not have a significant impact on the military's legal work. This department, as with the Ministry of Justice as a whole, has no particular expertise in international humanitarian law (IHL).

In this context, the legal scholar Eyal Benvenisti maintains:

> There is no independent knowledge of IHL in the Ministry of Justice. Almost the entire knowledge of IHL in the Israeli government centres on the ILD, and its opinions serve as the basis for the positions of the Israeli government in matters of the IHL. Hence, one cannot claim that the Attorney General's office actually controls the ILD. (in Cohen 2011, p. 386)

This lack of expertise means that Israeli public civil legal authorities do not exercise substantial supervision over the military's legal system (Shany et al. 2011; Benvenisti and Cohen 2013; Roytman 2013). Thus, regardless of the MAG Corps' formal subjection to the civil legal authority, in practice these civil bodies do not have substantive capital or sway over the MAG Corps.

The practice of legal academics intersects with that of the military and NGOs in various ways. One straightforward connection is on a personal level. Some academics are involved extensively in NGO work, sitting on executive boards and engaging in discussions. Others regularly organise events focused on international law and invite NGO representatives and military lawyers as speakers. Some military lawyers take up PhD studies or teaching positions at universities, and at least one prominent legal academic who did not have a military legal career serves in the ILD in a reserve capacity on occasions of extensive military operations. Overall, the position of academics is relatively marginal. They do not possess a great degree of capital within the field. Their relative position is nevertheless telling, particularly in the ways by which their marginality is maintained, on the basis of the discursive articulation of theory versus practice. Notwithstanding the academics' relatively marginal role, however, their position is in fact more complex than is often assumed. The academics' complex position will be described and discussed later in the book.

### 2.5.1 *The High Court of Justice*

The Supreme Court is the highest judicial tribunal in Israel. It comprises 14 judges, who sit in benches of three or more. The court has two key functions, a remnant of the British mandatory rule. It is both a court of appeal for decisions made in district courts and a High Court of Justice. The court's latter function is the first and last chance for petitions submitted to it. This is the primary forum dealing with issues relating to the OPT.

In the context of the field, the court and its judges occupy a significant position, one determining results of legal disputes but also an agent in the field in its own right. The court and its judges possess a certain degree of capital, and as with all other institutions it generally seeks to make the greatest impact possible over the determination of legal 'truth'. The court's characterisation as neutral (and the extent of acceptability of this claim), i.e. its portrayal as external to the power struggles of the field, is precisely its source of capital.

The High Court of Justice began to exercise its review over the operations of Israeli authorities in the OPT soon after the 1967 war and the occupation. The first petition relating to the OPT was submitted on 20 June 1967, less than two weeks after the occupation had begun (Kretzmer 2002). The court engages in judicial debate and decision-making in a highly charged political context and with tension between arguments of security on the one hand and individuals' rights on the other. In the relational terms of the field, the High Court of Justice's review of matters relating to the OPT has facilitated the constitution of a dynamic and complex web of organisational interactions and dependencies between civil and military legal bodies. This positioning and its implications are key elements in the configuration of power in the field.

Similarly to courts in other countries, the Israeli High Court of Justice is an institution provoking questions on the supposed separation between the judicial and political systems (Shamir 1994). In the face of a formal democratic separation, critics observe the inherent closeness of these institutions and the fact that courts comprise a part of the state's machinery (Griffith 1997). At the same time, the legitimacy of legal experts 'is derived from their ability to distinguish themselves from other social forces in general and from those holding state power in particular' (Shamir 1990, p. 782). Thus the court's continuous articulation of its separateness from political authority is fundamental to this institution's power. In conceptual terms, these tense grounds echo the relationship between law and politics. In terms of the field, the court and these debates are a site continually maintaining the borderline of the legal field and politics.

Research on the role of courts has sought to define these institutions' engagement with law and politics. Charles Black (1990), for example, suggests a simple and pragmatic approach designed to evaluate the court and its work. Black aims to examine a court's potential restriction of the executive, on the one hand, and its impact in terms of legitimising state politics on the other. In this approach the court's impact is intimately linked to its extent of separateness from state politics—it holds the potential to restrict state power in so far as it is distinct from it and it legitimises state politics when it is more closely affiliated with it. Approaches of this sort can, however, only scrape the surface of the politics/law intersection. The underlying assumption here is that a researcher is able to distinguish between 'true' law and law that is subordinate to politics. This assumption is based on a disregard of the dynamic making of law, and politics, and consequently of the relationship between these concepts.

In the Israeli context, some of the primary manifestations of tension between the legal and the political residing in the High Court of Justice's courtroom are the state's Jewish identity and concerns about national security on one hand, and liberal legal principles on the other (Shamir 1990; Barzilai 1997, 2000, 2004; Kretzmer 2002). These two features, of Jewishness and security, are closely intertwined—actions perceived to contrast the interests of the Jewish collective and the state's Jewish identity are considered and treated as a threat to security. These conflicts have a crucial impact in the courtroom, and judges have stated in this regard that they consider the primary role of the court is to protect the state against its enemies, enemies of security, and enemies of Jewishness (Kretzmer 2002).

The court's work with international law in relation to the OPT changed its character over time. Two fundamental principles in international law relating to occupation, providing some of the field's logic are (a) the benefit of the occupied population and (b) refraining from assuming the authority reserved for the sovereign. The second principle builds on the perception of an occupation as a temporary situation, in which the occupying power is only a guardian and does not replace the sovereign authority. The Israeli High Court of Justice allowed the military regime gradually to assume increasingly extensive powers and to make decisions, in contrast to the Palestinians' interests, while portraying the army as a 'benevolent occupier', acting for the benefit of the Palestinian population. The cumulative effect of such judgments became part of the field's logic.

In the first two decades of the occupation, the High Court of Justice allowed itself elaborate freedom in its interpretation of international law relating to the OPT, building on the existing relatively narrow legal body to design and mould the legal framework of the Israeli occupation. This situation changed alongside international legal developments, namely the

1977 writing of two new protocols to the Geneva Conventions and later again with the international tribunals debating Yugoslavia and Rwanda. In this altered situation, wheren international law was becoming an increasingly relevant framework for judgment and evaluation, national courts' decisions relating to this law were more likely to be scrutinised and criticised. This increased scrutiny, ironically, led to a trend by which, precisely while international law grew in legitimacy, protocols and provisions, the Israeli court developed a tendency to reject arguments based on it (Sfard 2004). In this trend, shifting away from international law, judges related to arguments based on international law as a challenge to national sovereignty and have been reluctant to enforce international legal standards upon the executive branch of the government (Benvenisti 1993).

The 1990s saw another trend, where the court grew closer to international law and the courtroom's reliance on international law intensified (Cohen and Cohen 2012). Chief Justice Aharon Barak articulated in a 2004 court decision the relationship between the court and international law in the context of the OPT. Barak then presented international law as a set of unavoidable obligations:

> 'Israel is not a desert island. It is a part of international setting' and 'Military conduct in battle does not occur in a legal void. There are legal norms—partly in international customary law, partly in international treaty law to which Israel is a signatory party, and partly in the fundamental rules of Israeli law—determining rules regarding the conduct of war.' (HCJ 4764/2004, pp. 385; 391)

Recent years have seen complex processes by which international law has played an increasingly important part in the High Court of Justice's practice (Shany 2012), and at the same time the interpretation of this law has become more and more flexible. The OPT has been a particularly prominent site for the High Court of Justice's dealings with this law. Guy Harpaz and Yuval Shany (2010) maintain that the High Court of Justice had become the world's most prolific civic state institution practising law in the context of a belligerent occupation. At the same time, these researchers argue, the court has been carrying out an 'incremental loosening of some of the judicial limits that the laws on belligerent occupation have placed on advancing Israeli interests in the Occupied Territories' (Harpaz and Shany 2010, p. 516). Thus the court's practice in the OPT in recent years manifests a convoluted relationship with international law.

On the one hand, the court bases its decisions increasingly on international law, and on the other it continually remoulds this law in its interpretations.

### 2.5.2 *Israeli Human Rights NGOs*

Human rights, as a legal body of covenants and conventions, emerged in the aftermath of the atrocities of the Second World War, with the Universal Declaration of Human Rights proclaimed by the UN General Assembly in 1948. Human rights organisations operate at a junction of local and global, national and international. Similarly to other areas in international law, human rights are commonly seen as an embodiment of tension between state sovereignty, on the one hand, and universal forces or values on the other (Freeman 2006). The particular socio-political space occupied by human rights organisations, at the same time local and global, is the source of both their strength and their weakness. Literature investigating NGOs commonly debates the nature and extent of the impact these organisations have over state policy and practice (Keck and Sikkink 1998; Gurowitz 1999; Forsythe 2012) or in terms of the field, the capital these organisations have. Research and opinion on states' engagement with human rights ranges from regarding these rights and their discourse as mere instruments in the hands of either global forces or external states, or to being influential agencies in their own right (Gordon and Berkovitch 2008). The influence of human rights is bound up with the internationality of this movement and globalised realities (Brysk 2005). In this sense, the debate on human rights is part of a broader discussion on the position and nature of the state in a globalised world (Evans 1997; Meyer et al. 1997; Held 1999; Krasner 1999; Meyer 2000). This ambiguous terrain between the national and international is also the space defining NGOs' capital. It derives power from its relations with an international legal discourse, but it is also at times marked as an external force, indifferent to, or even hostile towards, the interests of the state.

The issue of NGO funding reflects in these organisations' particular positioning in the tense intersection of the national and international. Israeli human rights organisations are financially dependent on donors, largely US and EU institutions and governments. The availability of funding for this work reflects a measure of capital, building on an international, liberal, rights-based discourse, but this same feature is also used to discredit NGOs. International sources of funding are seen by some as foreign interference, an argument that in the Israeli context may go so far as accusing human rights NGOs of treason (Cohen and Cohen 2011). This issue was the centre of public controversy when in 2011 Israeli parliament coalition members initiated a bill aiming to restrict foreign funds donated to human rights organisations. This bill has not been made law, but a similar one was put forward in 2013 and another in 2015.

Analytical investigations of human rights NGOs reflect critically on the impact of these organisations as being contradictory in terms of its effects as well as being a force shaping struggles rather than merely supporting them. Among accounts that regard human rights organisations as actors influencing states significantly, some argue interestingly that this movement affects states in contradictory ways— contributing simultaneously to promoting as well as pushing back the fulfilment of human rights standards (Hafner-Burton and Tsutsui 2005).Other accounts argue that human rights struggles have a formative effect on issues, people and politics. These are occasions when the logic of the field exceeds its boundaries. In this sense, the translation of grievances into legal language shapes both the problem and its potential solution. The political scientists Austin Sarat and Stuart Scheingold (2004) argue in this context that 'cause lawyers',[4] rather than merely participating in existing struggles, in fact play an active part in constructing causes and disputes. In Sarat and Scheingold's perspective, this is a discussion of what lawyers do *for* and *to* social and political movements. Lawyers' influence over struggles at the same time builds on and reinforces law's social power. Lawyers are able to impact social struggles because of the power they offer or suggest they have, and these claims and the extent of their acceptability then reinforces their power.

Israel has a vibrant human rights community, which emerged in the late 1980s and grew rapidly thereafter. The circumstances leading to the emergence of this community, presenting new actors in the Israeli legal field, are bound up with the historical—political realities of the OPT. In December 1987 the Palestinians had been living under the Israeli military regime for 20 years and had been subjected to many extremely repressive policies such as deportation, house demolitions, land confiscation and curfews. At the same time, Israel built and expanded Jewish settlements within the OPT, taking over more and more land and undermining the possibility of a future Palestinian state. The Intifada, the popular uprising resisting the occupation, started in Gaza and soon spread throughout the OPT. It included demonstrations, strikes, a boycott of Israeli goods and general unrest lasting from 1987 to 1993. In response to the uprising, the army employed harsh measures, including large-scale administrative detention, extensive house demolitions, frequent curfews and the closure of institutions such as schools and universities. The death toll of Palestinians killed by the Israeli armed forces during these events was 1,409, including 281 children and youths under the age of 17. The death toll on the Israeli side was 271 civilians and 150 members of the armed forces.[5]

The Intifada facilitated the emergence and expansion of the human rights movement. Prior to the breaking of the Intifada, only one human rights organisation operated in the country. Within the following three years, 15 new human rights organisations were established, all focusing on issues relating to the OPT. With this in mind, Neve Gordon and Nitza Berkovitch claim that the Intifada had 'led to the emergence of a rights discourse in Israel', and in this sense 'the Palestinians brought human rights to Israel' (Gordon and Berkovitch 2007, p. 251). Notably, it was the crisis of 1987 rather than the repressive policies which were part of the occupation in the 20 years prior to the Intifada that led to the emergence of this discourse and these organisations.

The human rights movement continued to grow and change in a process interwoven with changes in the legal field. By 2002 there were 26 national human rights organisations operating in Israel (Berkovitch and Gordon 2008). This organisational growth was affected by the changing attitudes within the High Court of Justice, particularly the court's increased willingness to review the military's conduct. This shift in the court drew human rights NGOs closer to the centre of the legal field. Their work was attuned to legal discourse and opportunities. NGOs activity, in turn, affected the High Court of Justice by prompting review of politically charged issues and pushing the court to continually formulate and present its positions in relation to Israeli political authorities. A discussion on the nature of this dynamic relationship will follow. Seen in this light, the court's shifting perspective and the genesis and growth of human rights NGOs were mutually influential processes, together changing the field.

Notwithstanding this book's use of Bourdieu's conceptual—methodological framework, it is neither a replication nor an uncritical adoption of his work. Moments of departure from this framework, which will be explained and discussed in Chapter 3, take place when my analysis shows that the army's ILD has been radically reforming the field in a manner that destabilises its boundary with politics. This course of action does not follow Bourdieu's basic assumption that institutions in the field share a common interest to maintain the field's integrity, a stability that supposedly secures the continuance of their power. This book also shows how, in a particular moment, the Israeli High Court of Justice transferred some of its power to the military legal system. This development also does not fit the field's theoretical assumptions. In Bourdieu's perspective, institutions struggle over power rather than handing it over to one another.

## 2.6 Lawyers' Practice Crafting Law

This chapter thus far has described the field as a methodological model devised to analyse the dynamic constellation of power, action and change in the field through its continuous practice, and has introduced the field's key actors. This section considers the military practitioners' position in this context, particularly in relation to the notions of politics, morality, violence and liberalism. This consideration lays the groundwork for three analytical layers this book suggests – the field's inner logic, the field's borders, and its overall power. In other words, this is a debate on the struggle over determinations in and of law, the continual remaking of the field's borders, and the influence the field exerts beyond these boundaries. This investigation uses lawyers as an analytical means to carry out an inquiry into 'the legal' rather than relating to this profession as an object of study in its own right. One of the key facets of this investigation of military lawyers' practice is law's boundary with, and differentiation from, politics. In this context, this study's articulation of practice in its making of logic, borders and power serves as a means of focusing on and analysing the constitution of the legal vis-à-vis the political. In this, the MAG Corps' international legal work in the politically charged OPT makes it a particularly fertile site for an inquiry into the shifting legal terrain and its relationship with the political.

Legal interpretation and the contents assigned to law are shaped in the context of the field, itself a dynamic territory. In this sense, the terrain in which legal work is practised is altered by the field's dynamism and continual marking of its borders. Lawyers play a key part in shaping this dynamism through their habitus, the maintenance and adaptation to and of the field by individuals. In socio-historical perspective, legal practitioners, far from filling prescribed roles passively, in fact make influential markers within the process defining the contents, possibilities and limits of law (see Burrage 1989; Abel 1995; Abbott et al. 2000; Weisberg 2004; Barzilai 2007, 2012; Halliday et al. 2007; Cummings 2011). The cumulative effect of daily practices constructs the entity and premise of 'the legal'. Notably, the analytical understanding of law as a construct formed in a specific context is based on a rejection of a universal truth about the nature of law, to be replaced by dynamic multiplicity (Nelken 2004). This does not imply that law does not have a meaning and power transcending the local context, but that its more general meanings are also made up of all these variations.

The junction of law and politics is addressed in social, political and philosophical debates, all drawing attention to the extent and terms of separateness between these concepts (Koskenniemi 2011). This discussion goes back to the naturalist—positivist divide, the former considering law to be autonomous and grounded in its source, the sovereign; and the latter considering law a closed system, separate from political power (Kahn 2006). International law occasions a particularly fierce battlefield for this politics—law discussion. The background to controversies is made up of the lack of a sovereign power grounding this law, its proximity to global power relations, and ongoing criticisms concerning its selective enforcement (Orford 2004). In terms of the fundamental naturalist—positivist divide, a key area of dispute is international law's separateness from politics, i.e. whether such a separation exists, and if it is even possible or desirable. If a degree of separation is established, it is then followed by questions about the measure and character of influence that law and politics have over one another.

Within this discussion, Martti Koskenniemi (1990) defines law as a vocabulary for politics. In this perspective, international law and politics share a single identity—the former being an expression of the latter. It then follows that a consideration of influence between these entities is futile. Koskenniemi's basic analysis of international law's inseparability from politics is in line with critical writings investigating this law in social and historical perspectives, with many considering colonialism as a key force moulding international law (for example, Berman 2004a, b; Anghie 2006, 2007; Megret 2006). Notably, this argumentation is not an exclusive territory of criticism from the left. Perspectives aligned with normative or analytical realism, despite carrying different political-theoretical baggage, similarly assert an inability to separate law from politics (Kahn 2006).

Following his questioning of a politics—law separation, Koskenniemi identifies a common discourse regarding the fight for international rule as a combat *against* politics. Politics in this context is understood as a tool advancing subjective desire and interest. The implicit assumption is that while some measure of politics is inevitable, it should be constrained by legal, non-political, rules. In this perspective, if political prejudices were to be excluded, jurists could achieve their goal in constructing a just world. Thus an identification of a political force or influence in a legal premise is a detection of a problem.

The assertion that politics is inseparable from law, with the former dominating the latter, i.e. 'all depends on politics', is an inadequate ending point to this discussion, as Koskenniemi (2011) himself more recently argued. In analytical terms this account suggests an alternative to an analysis drawing absolute conceptual boundaries between law and politics, instead offering a case-based investigation of the ways by which these categories are formed continually. This book thus explores the historical and contextualised, shifting articulation of law versus politics as an ongoing dynamic process. Moments of fundamental change in these categories are of particular importance. These are alterations in the inclusion/exclusion of themes and issues in/from law on the grounds of their political nature, i.e. rearticulating the border of the legal field. This does not imply an outright abandonment of an attempt to make more general claims about the law—politics nexus. Rather, grounded in a Bourdieusian perspective, this account is based on the assumption that the relations of law and politics, in either broader or narrower terms, are made up in an ongoing flow of power and influence. In this sense, specific sites producing these relations form part of an overall enterprise shaping the meanings of law and politics in the past, present and future.

A discussion of the contents of military legal work vis-à-vis politics necessitates a consideration of law's relations with violence. Robert Cover makes a contribution to this conversation by arguing that law and violence are inseparable: 'Legal interpretation takes place in a field of pain and death ... Interpretations in law also constitute justifications for violence which has already occurred or which is about to occur' (Cover 1986, p. 1601). Cover suggests that law and violence engage in a circular dynamic. In his perspective, law is intimately tied up with violence. Not only does legal interpretation occasion violence, but it also depends on it either potentially or in reality. In these terms, violence is an ever-present element in legal mechanisms and in fact it is unthinkable to visualise law without violence (Sarat 2001). Alongside these relations, law and its practitioners often maintain the implicit assumption that legal practice averts more lethal and destructive forms of violence, lurking just outside law's boundaries. Military legal practice occasions a particularly direct encounter between law and violence which resonates with Cover's depiction. Violence and law are closely linked in this institution in terms of justifications, yet law is also seen by some as a barrier to violence.

The case of Israeli military work with international law provides a particularly good opportunity for examining the law—violence matrix in action. As I show, this practice presented radical shifts between 1967 and 2009. These changes demonstrate distinctive phases in law's relationship with violence. Different phases in military practice reformulate legality vis-a-vis violence and reveal the dynamic character of this relationship. In this sense, Cover's perspective, which identifies an intimate relationship between law and violence, does not address more nuanced questions about the nature of these relations. This account pushes these questions further and asks: have the terms/extent of law's occasioning of violence changed? Has the nature of law's dependency on violence altered? What is the position of this dynamic under circumstances of increasing violence?

Morality is an additional premise interrelating with law in complex ways. The discussion about law and morality goes back to the positivist—naturalist division, the former perspective largely assuming no necessary connection between law and morality, and the latter maintaining, to the contrary, that law is fundamentally based on moral grounds (Rubin 1997; Feinberg and Coleman 2003). The law—morality intersection brings about particularly challenging questions when positioned in relation to war. Put in the context of military practice, abstract notions translate into concrete questions. Rather than a supposedly objective external appraisal of legal practice's morality, the framework of the field leads to contextualised explorations of practitioners' engagement with, and articulations of, morality. This direction of enquiry leads to questions about lawyers' standpoints on the inclusion/exclusion of moral criteria from legal work and the character of this morality, whether included or excluded. Morality, as it is shaped dynamically in practice, either by way of exclusion or inclusion, contributes to the logic of the field.

Any discussion of legality is necessarily connected to liberalism, law's ideological origin, though there are certainly varied and conflicting definitions offered for this term (Bell 2014). In many scholarly accounts law is seen as a focal component in the normative imagination of humanity as being immersed in an ongoing process of progress (Freeden 2009). The dominance of legal and liberal discourse in Israel (Barzilai 2000, 2007) makes this consideration particularly essential and productive.

Set in this liberal context, lawyers' power builds on and feeds into law's characterisation as a force ensuring impartial governance and justice, a presentation largely concealing particular historical—political struggles and processes of change. In this sense, liberalism is a key element in legal practitioners' capital and the legal field's overall power. The sociologists Yves Dezalay and Mikael Madsen (2012) argue that jurists' success in constructing a space supposedly removed from interest and power has led to a rationalisation of the state in the image of law. This configuration means that lawyers construct meaning and gain power veiled as objectivity and fairness. Notably, not all lawyers are equal in this regard. The ability to interpret law in a way that will be accepted as neutral derives from power relations within the field as well as the field's overall power. In methodological terms, this implies tracing the particular processes of lawyers' formations. Dezalay and Madsen argue in this regard:

> [T]o study processes of group formation with regard to legal professionals implies asking the question of how law and lawyers come about—that is, to study the different geneses of law in the context of varying legal-political and cultural settings ...[I]t is the jurists who, through their battles within the legal field, constitute a sort of practical metaphor of what becomes the political field. (2012, pp. 437–438)

In application to this account, historicising and contextualising military legal work means detecting the emergence and continual making of legal and political meanings in the OPT.

Liberalism's ambitious programme for law translates into an ethos. Practitioners' ethos of law is an analytical opportunity exposing implicit assumptions about law and legal tools (Kahn 2006). Building on this exposure, it serves here as means of exploration. Ethos encompasses the particularities and underlying beliefs and expectations relating to legal practice. This book examines the character and form of ethos in military international legal practice in the past and present.

To conclude, this section has set out a theoretical and methodological approach to the analysis of military lawyers' practice. This approach, building on the framework of the field, maintains that lawyers are influential agents set in a focal position, and sets out to examine military lawyers' practice in relation to politics, morality, violence and liberalism. These enquiries ground this account's examination of military practitioners' influence on multiple levels – dynamically forming law's logic, remaking the field's borderlines and utilising power outside these borders.

## 2.7 Fieldwork: Exploring Military Legal Practice Through Interviews and Documents

Fieldwork for this study has included interviews and the analysis of written materials, all focused on the Israeli legal field's engagement with international law in the OPT. This section presents and discusses the operationalisation of this book's conceptual framework. This discussion integrates explanations of methodological choices, their theoretical basis, obstacles faced in the course of fieldwork, and the ways in which this work directed and guided this account.

### *2.7.1 Theoretical Grounds for Interviews*

Interviews are a key methodological tool in the framework of the field. These interviews seek to understand respondents' perspectives and experiences. In theoretical terms, this approach follows Bourdieu's negation of the objectivist—subjectivist opposition in favour of habitus, structured individual perspective. In these terms, the interview is an experience that is simultaneously subjective and objective; it is subjective in that it conveys a personal perspective and objective in the sense that this subjectivity in itself is understood as the interplay of agency and structure.

The interview situation in and of itself calls for conceptual attention. Bourdieu's analysis is a second-order investigation, i.e. examining the contextual construction of meaning rather than pursuing truth or fact (Lizardo 2010). Seen in this light, the interview is an occasion in which power relations and meanings are formed. At the same time, an interview is an interaction, and response is provided for a specific audience. In this sense it is a mutual creation of meaning involving both interviewer and respondent, revisiting assumptions on the knowers and the known, the constructors of knowledge and the knowledge constructed (Kvale 1996). It then follows that the purpose of an interview, rather than unravelling truth residing in a respondent, is in itself a form of social action. In the words of Hammersley and Atkinson: 'accounts are not simply representations of the world; they are part of the world they describe' (Hammersley and Atkinson 2007, p. 107). Interaction is inevitably embedded in a social context, thus it is a specific site of situated meaning-making. From a Bourdieusian-inspired standpoint, the situation's positioning in a social context is not a methodological obstacle but rather in itself an occasion that calls for reflection.

In this sense, representations of law created in interviews are not external to this social phenomenon, but are part of the continual making of law.

My interviews with senior officials, mainly ex-military officers, occasioned particular questions about power relations. I found that gender was a substantial factor in the interview process, which is in line with the experiences of many other researchers (Sprague 2005). Many respondents assumed, on account of me being a woman, that I knew very little about military conduct in war. This aligns with the Israeli social context in which women are seen as outsiders regarding matters concerning the military and warfare (Sasson-Levy 2011). I did not try to assert a different position and in fact found these assumptions to be useful for my own purposes. Some of the officers shared stories with me about past interviews that resulted in negative implications for them, and they assumed that, as an outsider, I posed little threat of such potential damage. My lack of legal credentials further contributed to assumptions regarding the extent of my knowledge and understanding of the topics discussed. I found that I also benefited from these assumptions. I was probably regarded as unthreatening for these reasons too and I was then able to facilitate relatively rich and somewhat less guarded conversations.

In an assessment of my own position I am able to recognise my capital in academic and professional terms. My ability to arrange meetings and interviews was a direct result of my academic position. When contacting potential respondents I presented myself as a academic researcher. When communicating in writing I used the university's logo. Quite a few of the people I met had been interviewed by journalists and had their words presented in ways they did not appreciate. The acceptability of my academic position helped me to overcome some of their suspicions.

From my own perspective, I had anticipated confronting in interviews power relations related to Israeli gendered and militarised social structures. In this sense, I see my work as 'studying up' (Nader 1972), i.e. up the ladder of social power. One possible characteristic of such work is a position unsympathetic to research participants on the part of the researcher. In the planning process of my fieldwork one of my concerns was about how to respond to questions about my own opinions on the research themes, considering that I was critical of military legal work. However, such concerns were, in the main, unfounded. Some respondents were indeed interested in my views, but they were not the majority. When asked, I responded in a manner aiming to represent my position openly and at the same time avoiding antagonism. Since at the time the interviews were held, I was in the midst of the research process, I presented the general directions of my work rather than any concrete conclusions. This became easier as the fieldwork progressed and I became more comfortable in the position of interviewer.

My fieldwork included 14 interviews with present and past senior MAG Corps officers. Among the respondents were Meir Shamgar, head of the military legal system in 1967, and Amnon Straschnov, head of this system during the first Intifada (see Appendix II for a list of MAGs heading the military's legal system from 1967 onwards), 2 interviews with retired senior legal officials at other state branches – one at the Ministry of Justice and the other at the Ministry of Foreign Affairs, and three with human rights NGO practitioners. These were face-to-face interviews held between December 2012 and March 2013. I added to these interview materials I had collected in 2011 for the purposes of my Master's thesis, which focused on similar themes (Geva 2011). My primary interest was to interview military legal officials. I interviewed non-military state and NGO practitioners to better articulate the military legal system's positiong in the field.

As may be expected in research on sensitive issues, access to materials and people was challenging. Some attempts led to dead ends. Such were my communications with the Israel Defence Forces Spokesperson's Office. I had approached this office in November 2012 with the hope of obtaining permission to interview legal officers on active duty. My initial request was followed by ongoing email correspondence and a number of telephone calls. I was asked to fill in forms describing my study, its purposes, the questions I intend to present in interviews, my institutional affiliation and so on. I responded to all these requests, attempting to strike a balance between an open presentation of my study and one that would not deter the army spokesperson's representatives from co-operating. I do not know whether there was any chance of my request being granted approval, but I received a final negative response in January 2013. This procedure and its result revealed a recent change of policy within the army and its MAG Corps. I know this because, when writing a previous study, also focusing on the military legal system, I was not requested to fill in any forms and did obtain an approval leading to interviews with legal officers. I had later picked up informal information indicating that Noam Neuman, the serving ILD Commanding Officer, unlike his predecessor, generally avoids co-operating with researchers and journalists. This personal factor impacting on my access to interview respondents was unfortunate from my perspective, but this anecdote is also revealing in that it was not obvious that this military department would prevent interviews with its members. Time will tell whether this is a new and more restrictive trend within the military's legal system, or a personal preference of a single officer that might change again with the appointment of a replacement.

My lengthy communication process with the IDF Spokesperson's office, even before its final refusal, led me to seek alternative routes to MAG Corps officials. I managed to gain access to respondents in different ways, some via a straightforward email or telephone call, and some in less formal ways, quite typical for the Israeli context. On one such occasion I arranged an interview with a retired MAG based on personal connections, through a friend's family, which was then held at his home. When we finished the interview this respondent introduced me over the telephone to a colleague at the MAG Corps and that contact in turn led to others. Another friend's father was a senior retired official from the Ministry of Justice. He also helped me to get in touch with several respondents. Put in reflexive, Bourdieusian terms, this access is connected intrinsically to my own social capital. In this way, personal relationships linked me relatively easily to influential figures in the Israeli government and military establishment.

My study changed in its emphasis and perspective as I conducted my fieldwork. The study's centre of gravity moved towards investigating contemporary situations in a historical context rather than as an isolated state of affairs. The official military refusal of my request to interview serving officers gradually redirected my research focus. I was initially interested in examining the 2008/9 offensive in Gaza in a more elaborate manner. It was my intention, based on this case, to write about the contemporary configuration of the law/war intersection. Realising I would not be able to interview many current members of the ILD compelled me to re-evaluate my aims and rethink my interests, and I gradually developed an historical account of the army's work with international law. I remained particularly interested in contemporary legal practice, and found that a broader perspective greatly contributes to the understanding of the present. As my work progressed I came to consider this path preferable and more fertile than my initial plan.

Interviews lasted between one and three hours. Overall, the interviewees were willing to share a good range of their experiences and reflections with me. Prior to my fieldwork trip I had been debating whether I should suggest anonymous interviews. After consideration I decided to leave this choice in the hands of each respondent. My letters to prospective interviewees made this clear. I assumed the interviews, and consequently the study, would be different depending on whether quotes could be traced to their source, but decided to allow flexibility in that regard. As I began each interview I presented both options and let respondents decide if the interview would be on or off the record. Most chose to be interviewed on the record. In one case an interview became particularly interesting towards its end and the respondent changed his mind just as we parted and chose to be quoted anonymously.

During the fieldwork I had with me written interview questions, which I adapted to each respondent based on their professional background, the time they had served in the army and any other relevant information I had available. The questions were open-ended and created semi-structured interviews. My intention was to have a conversation and to use questions for general guidance. Some interviews were easier to handle in this regard than others, with respondents becoming upset about particular questions. In some cases, when a respondent was not willing to consider a particular question I screened others that were initially meant to follow, attempting to avoid antagonism and continue the interview in the most productive way possible. When respondents brought up information that was new to me, or shared ideas that had not occurred to me previously, I followed their lead as long as it seemed interesting and potentially relevant. As my fieldwork advanced I was able to alter and develop my interview guide, though its key themes did not change.

As one might imagine, military lawyers were generally careful and calculating in their choice of words when answering interview questions. Nevertheless, they shared knowledge and insight, resulting, from my perspective, in interesting research materials. Since many of them were familiar with one another, either personally or on the basis of knowing each other's work, a number of respondents compared their own legal practice with that of their peers. When a respondent told me, for example, that his predecessor's perspective was flawed for one reason or another, I knew I was receiving valuable material. In this sense, judgments passed by these practitioners provided me with material touching on shifts in the military legal system and the directions of this movement.

For the most part, interviewees were more forthcoming when they had long been retired. The issues discussed were less charged for their part and they were less guarded about their perspectives. Some interviews left me frustrated, because I knew there was so much left unsaid. At the same time, I realised that this was an expected outcome of my choice of research topic. Conditions of secrecy led to there being very little work being done on this area and this was a key factor in my decision to study these matters. All in all, despite their limits, the interviews produced a rich set of materials enabling a thorough analysis of the military's work with international law. Interview materials confirmed and substantiated other data, to be presented shortly, as well as providing perspectives that could not have been found elsewhere.

### 2.7.2 *Theoretical and Practical Approach to Documents*

The production and consumption of written materials are central features of contemporary organisations (Atkinson and Coffey 2011). Positioned in the framework of the field, my intention in engaging with documents is not to seek a truth, which may or may not affirm the standpoints presented in interviews, but to use materials to further investigate these perspectives. In epistemological terms, documents are situated practice, at the same time both product and producers of a bureaucratic, legal and political state of affairs.

Access to materials relating to the army's operations in general and its legal system in particular is highly restricted. Thus publicly-available documentation of the MAG Corps' work in the OPT is scarce. Under these circumstances, I aimed to trace all possible sources of materials to access as much documentation as possible.[6] I was most interested in finding documents produced by the military legal system's international unit and relating to the OPT. I was given some materials by respondents; some documents were publicly available, such as MAG Corps publications—annual reports, or publications concerning specific events. I also collected writings and presentation notes of the MAG Corps officers, including research materials, memoirs, films, recorded lectures, public talks, radio broadcasts, testimonies officers gave to public commissions, and High Court of Justice materials. I read, watched and listened to all these materials with the aim of learning about officers' perspectives regarding their ongoing practice, moments of change, and their reflections about law's goals, the relationship between the military legal system and other legal bodies and so on.

One of the collections I visited was the Israel Defence Forces Archive. This is an institution combining a general approach of secrecy with complicated bureaucratic procedure. According to Israeli law, military documents become available to the public 50 years after they had been deposited in the archive. However, even those materials that are supposedly meant to be accessible are organised in a way which makes them practically inaccessible. Perhaps these hurdles are a result of an intentional policy or perhaps it was simply never in anyone's interest to make these materials more easily accessible, but in any case the end result is known. Despite these hurdles I was able to obtain from this archive several relevant documents. These were memoranda written by the legal system's officers and providing commanding officers with guidance based on international law. Most of these documents were produced in the early days of the occupation.

I also looked for materials representing military legal practice more distantly. These included media materials such as journals published by the Israeli army and directed mainly at a military readership (*Ba'Mahane*, *Ma'arahot*). I also went over all the issues of Israel's three leading newspapers—*Ma'ariv*, *Yedioth Ahronoth* and *Haaretz*—published between the middle of December 2008 and January 2009, the time of Operation Cast Lead in Gaza. I was specifically interested in interviews with military legal officials and these officers' statements rather than their media representations. I also studied human rights NGOs' publications and UN reports to supplement the core body of materials.

The documents I collected are diverse and range over a long period of time, from the MAG Corps' annual reports in the years that followed the occupation (MAG 1968, 1969), the military legal system's written guidance for commanders (Shamgar 1967a, b; MAG 1972) to different media publications on the military's work with international law (Kapra and Negbi 1997; Harel 2003; Grinberg 2006; Fogelman 2010; Levy 2012), booklets published by the ILD describing legal practice revolving around the offensive in Gaza (The State of Israel 2009) and the Winograd Report (2008), the publication of a government-appointed commission, among other issues debating appropriate relations between legal work and military operational decision-making. These documents and others, containing legal work, positions and perspectives, constitute a collection serving as a basis for an analysis of law in this case. This collection is far from exhaustive, because, as described, many military documents are inaccessible, but it nevertheless allows for a thorough and nuanced account of this study's major interests—law's logic and power, and its transformations and dynamic relations with politics throughout Israel's dealings with the OPT.

## 2.8 Conclusion

This chapter presented the study's methodological and analytical framework. It opened with a discussion of its basic theoretical grounding, Bourdieu's sociology of the field. The field is a network of institutions, positions and relations arranged and rearranged continually by their relative power and the field's logic. The chapter focused on pertinent aspects of this theory, namely the relationship between agency and structure, and social stability versus change. It then continued with a consideration of the application of the field framework to law, an under-developed area of study, an analysis combining legal logic (norms, conventions, judgments, different perspectives on law and so on) and power relations. These materials and relationships make up the field in interplay between the field's logic and the division of power between its different actors. The chapter continued by examining legal practice in Israel and the institutions forming this legal field, assessing their power and relative positions. It then turned to a discussion about law's conceptual grounding, specifically in relation to politics, but also morality, violence and liberalism. These are all elements the study investigates later as notions made in legal practice. Finally, the chapter described and reflected on fieldwork conducted for the purposes of this study and its theoretical grounding. Building on this methodological and theoretical basis, the book continues with a chapter analysing the Israeli legal field, its logic, main actors and key transformations.

## Notes

1. The term 'logic' does not imply a coherent or rational system of meaning, but a set of codes and rules structuring the field, constructing possibilities and limitations.
2. Dezalay and Madsen suggest that this is a result of, first and foremost, socio-legal researchers' lack of willingness to engage thoroughly with the conceptual and methodological implications of Bourdieu's reflexive sociology. An additional factor, they argue, is Bourdieu's focus on the European continental legal context, which is unappealing for researchers interested in the USA.
3. This unit was established as a division, and developed into a department in the 1990s. Blau and Feldman (2009). How IDF legal experts legitimized strikes involving Gaza civilians. *HAARETZ* 23 January 2009.
4. David Luban defines 'cause lawyering' as the activity of practitioners 'using legal skills to pursue ends and ideals that transcend client service—be those ideals social, cultural, political, economic or, indeed, legal' in Scheingold,

S. A. and A. Sarat (2004). *Something To Believe In: Politics, Professionalism and Cause Lawyering*. California, Stanford Law and Politics.

5. Source for data: B'Tselem – The Israeli Information Center for Human Rights in the Occupied Territories, accessible at: http://www.btselem.org/statistics/first_intifada_tables [accessed 19 April 2015].
6. See Appendix IV for a full list of sources and archives reviewed.

## Bibliography

Abbott, K. W., et al. (2000). "The Concept of Legalization." International Organization **54**(3): 401–419.

Abel, R. L. (1995). Politics By Other Means: Law and the Struggle Against Apartheid, 1980–1994. New York, Routledge.

Adler-Nissen, R. (2012). Bourdieu in International Relations: Rethinking Key Concepts in IR. London, Taylor & Francis.

Agamben, G. (2008). State of Exception. Chicago, University of Chicago Press.

Anghie, A. (2006). "The evolution of international law: Colonial and postcolonial realities." Third World Quarterly **27**(5): 739–753.

Anghie, A. (2007). Imperialism, Sovereignty and the Making of International Law. Cambridge, Cambridge University Press.

Atkinson, P. and A. Coffey (2011). Analysing Documentary Realities Qualitative Research: Issues of Theory, Method and Practice. D. Silverman. Los Angeles, SAGE: 77–92.

Atkinson, W. (2012). "Where Now for Bourdieu-inspired Sociology?" Sociology **46**(1): 167–173.

Barzilai, G. (1997). "Between the rule of law and the laws of the ruler: The Supreme Court in Israeli legal culture." International social science journal **49**(2): 193.

Barzilai, G. (2000). "Fantasies of Liberalism and Liberal Jurisprudence: State Law, Politics, and the Israeli Arab-Palestinian Community." Isr. L. Rev. **34**: 425–452.

Barzilai, G. (2004). How Far Do Justices Go: The Limits of Judicial Decisions Critical Issues in Israeli Society A. Dowty. Westport, Connecticut; London Praeger: 55–68.

Barzilai, G. (2007). The Ambivalent Language of Lawyers in Israel: Liberal Politics, Economic Liberalism, Silence and Dissent. Fighting for Political Freedom: Comparative Studies of the Legal Complex and Political Liberalism T. C. Halliday, L. Karpik and M. M. Feeley. Oxford, Hart Publishing.

Barzilai, G. (2012). "The ambivalence of Litigation: A Criticism of Power, Jadal 13, available at: http://mada-research.org/en/files/2012/05/Jadal13/Eng/Gadi-barzilai.pdf, [accessed 28.4.15]."

BdiCode (2014). Publication: Lawyers 2014, Information Group, available at: http://www.bdicode.co.il/Page_HEB/836/%D7%A2%D7%95%D7%A8%D7%9B%D7%99 %D7%93%D7%99%D7%9F 2014, [accessed 28.4.15].

Bell, D. (2014). "What is Liberalism?" Political Theory **42**(6): 682–715.

Ben-Naftali, O. (2011). PathoLAWgical Occupation: Normalizing the Exceptional Case of the Occupied Palestinian Territory and Other Legal Pathologies. International Humanitarian Law and International Human Rights Law: Pas de Deux. O. Ben-Naftali. Oxford, Oxford University Press: 129–200.

Ben-Naftali, O., et al. (2005). "Illegal Occupation: The Framing of the Occupied Palestinian Territory." Berkley Journal of International Law **23**.

Ben-Naftali, O. and Y. Shany (2004). "Living in Denial: The Application of Human Rights in the Occupied Territories; Ben-Naftali, Orna; Shany, Yuval." Israel Law Review **37**.

Benvenisti, E. (1993). "Judicial Misgivings Regarding the Application of International Law: An Analysis of Attitudes of National Courts." European Journal of International Law **4**.

Benvenisti, E. and A. Cohen (2013) War is Governance: Explaining the Logic of the Laws of War from a Principal-Agent Perspective, available at: http://ssrn.com/abstract=2199016, accessed 28.4.15.

Berenson, S. K. (2000). "Public Lawyers, Private Values: Can, Should, and Will Government Lawyers Serve the Public Interest." Boston College Law Review **41**(4).

Berkovitch, N. and N. Gordon (2008). "The Political Economy of Transnational Regimes: The Case of Human Rights." International Studies Quarterly **52**(4): 881–904.

Berman, N. (2004a). 'The Appeals of the Orient': Colonized Desire and the War of the Riff. Gender and Human Rights. K. Knop. Oxford, Oxford University Press.

Berman, N. (2004b). "Privileging Combat? Contemporary Conflict and the Legal Construction of War." Columbia Journal of Transnational Law **43**(1).

Bigo, D. (2011). "Pierre Bourdieu and International Relations: Power of Practices, Practices of Power." International Political Sociology **5**(3): 225–258.

Black, C. (1990). The people and the court: judicial review in a democray. New York, Macmillian.

Blau, U. and Y. Feldman (2009). How IDF legal experts legitimized strikes involving Gaza civilians. HAARETZ 23/01/09.

Bourdieu, P. (1986). The forms of capital Handbook of theory and research for the sociology of education. J. Richardson. New York, Greenwood: 241–258.

Bourdieu, P. (1987). "The Force of Law: Toward a Sociology of the Juridical Field." Hastings Law Journal 805 **805**(38).

Bourdieu, P. (1989). "Social Space and Symbolic Power." Sociological Theory 7(1): 14–25.

Bourdieu, P. (1990). The logic of practice. California, Standford University Press.
Bourdieu, P. (1996). The rules of art: genesis and structure of the literary field. California, Stanford University Press.
Bourdieu, P. and L. J. D. Wacquant (1992). An Invitation to Reflexive Sociology. Chicago, University of Chicago Press.
Brysk, A. (2005). Human Rights and Private Wrongs: Constructing Global Civil Society. London, Routledge.
Burrage, M. (1989). Revolution as a Starting Point for the Comparative Analysis of the French, American, and English Legal Professions. Lawyers in Society: Comparative Theories R. L. Abel and P. Lewis. Berkeley, Los Angeles, London, University of California Press. **3**.
Butler, J. (1999). Gender Trouble: Tenth Anniversary Edition. London, Routledge
Clément, J.-p. (1995). "Contributions of the Sociology of Pierre Bourdieu to the Sociology of Sport." Sociology of Sport Journal **12**(2): 147–157.
Cohen, A. (2005). "Administering the Territories: An Inquiry into the Application of International Humanitarian Law by the IDF in the Occupied Territories " Israel Law Review **38**(3): 24–79.
Cohen, A. (2011). "Legal Operational Advice in the Israeli Defense Forces: the International Law Department and the Changing Nature of International Humanitarian Law." Connecticut Journal of International Law **26**(2).
Cohen, A. and S. Cohen (2012). Israel's National Security Law: Political Dynamics and Historical Development. London, Routledge.
Cohen, A. and S. A. Cohen (2011). "Israel and International Humanitarian Law: Between the Neo-Realism of State Security and the 'Soft Power' of Legal Acceptability." Israel Studies **16**(2): 1–23.
Cover, R. M. (1986). "Violence and the Word." The Yale Law Journal **95**(8): 1601–1629.
Cummings, S. L. (2011). Introduction: What Good are Lawyers? The Paradox of Professionalism: Lawyers and the Possibility of Justice. S. L. Cummings. Cambridge Cambridge University Press.
Dezalay, Y. and M. R. Madsen (2012). "The Force of Law and Lawyers: Pierre Bourdieu and the Reflexive Sociology of Law." Annual Review of Law and Social Science **8**(1): 433–452.
Evans, P. (1997). "The Eclipse of the State? Reflections on Stateness in an Era of Globalization." World Politics **50**(1): 62–87.
Falk, R. (2000). "International Law and the al-Aqsa Intifada." Middle East Report(217): 16–18.
Feinberg, J. and J. Coleman (2003). Philosophy of Law Belmont, London, Thomson/Wadsworth
Fogelman, S. (2010). Shock and awe. HAARETZ 31.12.2010.
Forsythe, D. P. (2012). Human Rights in International Relations. Cambridge, Cambridge University Press.

Freeden, M. (2009). Liberal Languages: Ideological Imaginations and Twentieth-Century Progressive Thought, Princeton University Press.

Freeman, M. (2006). Human Rights: An interdisciplinary approach Cambridge Polity.

Geva, M. (2011). Dynamics of Law, Organisation and Morality in Contemporary Warfare: The right to life in the case of the Israeli military International Law Department. Human Rights Practice, School of Global Studies, University of Gothenburg. **MA**.

Gordon, N. (2008). "Human Rights, Social Space and Power: Why do some NGOs Exert More Influence than Others?" The International Journal of Human Rights **12**(1): 23–39.

Gordon, N. and N. Berkovitch (2007). "Human Rights Discourse in Domestic Settings: How Does it Emerge?" Political Studies **55**(1): 243–266.

Grenfell, M. and F. Lebaron, Eds. (2014). Bourdieu and Data Analysis Methodological Principles and Practice: Conclusion. Oxford, Oxford University Press.

Griffith, J. A. G. (1997). The Politics of the Judiciary London, Fontana Press.

Grinberg, H. (2006). The Assassinations HCJ Case: Relief at the MAG Corps, Ynet 14.12.06, available at: http://www.ynet.co.il/articles/0,7340,L-3340211,00.html [accessed 28.4.15]

Gross, A. M. (2007). "Human proportions: Are human rights the emperor's new clothes of the international law of occupation?" The European Journal of International Law **18**(1).

Gurowitz, A. (1999). "Mobilizing International Norms: Domestic Actors, Immigrants, and the Japanese State." World Politics **51**(3): 413–445.

Hafner-Burton, E. M. and K. Tsutsui (2005). "Human Rights in a Globalizing World: The Paradox of Empty Promises." American Journal of Sociology **110**(5): 1373–1411.

Halliday, T. C., et al. (2007). The Legal Complex in Struggles for Political Liberalism Fighting for Political Freedom: Comparative Studies of the Legal Complex and Political Liberalism. T. C. Halliday, L. Karpik and M. Feeley. Oxford, Hart.

Hammersley, M. and P. Atkinson (2007). Ethnography: Principles in Practice. New York, Routledge.

Harel, A. (2003). MAG: We will not approve war crimes, but it is not possible to investigate 2,000 death incidents. HAARETZ.

Harpaz, G. and Y. Shany (2010). "Israeli Supreme Court and the Incremental Expansion of the Scope of Discretion under Belligerent Occupation Law." Israel Law Review **43**.

HCJ (4764/2004). Physicians for Human Rights vs. Commander of IDF forces in Gaza.

Held, D. (1999). Global Transformations: Politics, Economics and Culture. California, Stanford University Press.
Inbar, Z. (2002). "The MAG Corps and the Held Territories " Law and Military: the IDF legal system's publication **16**(1).
Inbar, Z. (2005). Scales and Sword: The basis of military law in Israel Israel Defense Forces Publishing, MAG Corps.
Johnson, R. (1993). Editor's Introduction: Pierre Bourdieu on Art, Literature and Culture The Field of Cultural Production: Essays on Art and Literature. R. Johnson. New York, Columbia University Press.
Kahn, P. W. (2000). "Speaking Law to Power: Popular Sovereignty, Human Rights and the New International Order." Chicago Journal of International Law **1**(1).
Kahn, P. W. (2006). "Judicial Ethos and the Autonomy of Law, Yale Law School, Faculty Scholarship Series. Paper 322. available at: http://digitalcommons.law.yale.edu/fss_papers/322 [accessed 28.4.15]."
Kapra, M. and M. Negbi (1997). The Legal Battlefield Ma'ariv 26.12.97.
Keck, M. E. and K. Sikkink (1998). Activists Beyond Borders: Advocacy Networks in International Politics. New York, Cornell University Press.
Kennedy, D. (2006). Of War and Law. Princeton, Princeton University Press.
Koskenniemi, M. (1990). "The Politics of International Law." European Journal of International Law **1**: 4–32.
Koskenniemi, M. (1999). Between Commitment and Cynicism: Outline for a theory of International Law as Practice. Collection of Essays by Legal Advisers of States, Legal Advisers of International Organizations and Practitioners in the field of International Law. U. Office of Legal Affairs. New York, United Nationas Publications.
Koskenniemi, M. (2009). "The Function of Law in the International Community: 75 Years After." British Year Book of International Law **79**.
Koskenniemi, M. (2011). The Politics of International Law. Oxford and Portland, Hart Publishing
Krasner, S. D. (1999). Sovereignty: Organized Hypocrisy. New Jersey, Princeton University Press.
Kretzmer, D. (2002). The Occupation of Justice: The Supreme Court of Israel and the Occupied Territories. New York, State University of New York Press.
Kvale, S. (1996). InterViews: An Introduction to Qualitative Research Interviewing. Los Angeles, SAGE Publications.
Lenoir, R. (2006). "Pierre Bourdieu and the Law: An intellectual and Personal Encounter " Retfaerd **3**(114): 7–22.
Levy, A. (2012). True Face (*Panim Amitiyot*), 2.11.2012. available at: http://panim.nana10.co.il/Article/?ArticleID=939325 [accessed 28.4.15] Channel 10

Lizardo, O. (2010). "Beyond the Antinomies of Structure: Levi-Strauss, Giddens, Bourdieu, and Sewell." Theory and Society: Renewal and Critique in Social Theory **39**(6).

Madsen, M. R. (2006). "Transnational Fields: Elements of a Reflexive Sociology of the Internationalisation of Law." Retfaerd **3**(114): 23–41.

Madsen, M. R. (2011). "Reflexivity and the Construction of the International Object: The Case of Human Rights." International Political Sociology **5**(3): 259–275.

Madsen, M. R. and Y. Dezalay (2002). The Power of the Legal Field: Pierre Bourdieu and the Law, 189–204. An introduction to Law and Social Theory. R. Banakar and M. Travers. Oxford - Portland Oregon, HART.

MAG (1968). 1967/8 MAG Annual Report MAG. Israel.

MAG (1969). 1968/9 MAG Annual Report MAG. Israel.

MAG (1972). Commanders' Document, number 10, self-guidance in the laws of war MAG.

Mandel, O. (2009). "On Lawyering in the High Court of Justice's Petitions Department." Ma'asei Mishpat **2**.

Mazuz, M. (2013). Interview with Maayan Geva, 6.2.13.

Megret, F. (2006). From 'Savages' to 'Unlawful Combatants': A Postcolonial Look at International Humanitarian Law's 'Other'. International Law And Its 'Others'. A. Orford. Cambridge Cambridge University Press.

Meydani, A. and S. Mizrahi (2006). "The Politics and Strategies of Defending Human Rights: The Israeli Case." Israel Law Review **39**(1).

Meyer, J. W. (2000). "Globalization: Sources and Effects on National States and Societies." International Sociology **15**(2): 233–248.

Meyer, J. W., et al. (1997). "World Society and the Nation-State." American Journal of Sociology **103**(1): 144–181.

Nader, L. (1972). Up the Anthropologist: Perspectives Gained From Studying Up. Reinventing Anthropology. D. H. Hymes. New York, Pantheon Books: 284–311.

Negbi, M. (1981). Justice Under Occupation: The Israeli Supreme Court versus the Military Administration Jerusalem, Cana.

Nelken, D. (2004). "Using the Concept of Legal Culture." Australian Journal of Legal Philosophy **29** 1–28.

Orford, A. (2004). "The Destiny of International Law." Leiden Journal of International Law **17**(3): 441–476.

Parikh, S. and B. Garth (2005). "Philip Corboy and the construction of the Plaintiffs' personal injury bar." LAW AND SOCIAL INQUIRY **30**(2): 269–304.

Pouliot, V. (2008). "The Logic of Practicality: A Theory of Practice of Security Communities." International Organization **62**(02): 257–288.

Rasulov, A. (2006). "From Apology to Utopia: the Structure of the International Legal Argument by Martti Koskenniemi: Review." Law and Politics Book Review **16** 583–591.

Roytman, Y. (2013). "Inner legal supervision in time of combat " The Gates of Trial (Sha'arei Mishpat) **6**.

Rubin, P., A. (1997). Ethics and authority in international law. Cambridge, Cambridge University Press.

Sarat, A. (2001). Law, Violence, and the Possibility of Justice. New Jersey, Princeton University Press.

Sasson-Levy, O. (2011). "From the Military as a Gendered Organization to Militarized Inequality Regimes: Research on Gender and the Military in Israel." Israel Studies Review **26**(2): 73–98.

Scheingold S. A. and A. Sarat (2004). Something To Believe In: Politics, Professionalism and Cause Lawyering. California, Stanford Law and Politics.

Sfard, M. (2004). "International Litigation in Domestic Courts." The Trial (HaMishpat) **9**.

Shamgar, M. (1967a). Reaction to the finding of weapon, 14.6.2967. MAG.

Shamgar, M. (1967b). Ribon's article in Ha'aretz, 22.10.1967. MAG**:** 1.

Shamgar, M. (1971). "The Observance of International Law in the Administered Territories " Israel Yearbook on Human Rights **1**: 262.

Shamir, R. (1990). ""Landmark Cases" and the Reproduction of Legitimacy: The Case of Israel's High Court of Justice." Law & Society Review **24**(3): 781–805.

Shamir, R. (1994). "Ha'Politika shel Ha'Svirut [The Politics of Reasonableness.]." Teoria u'Bikoret(5): 7–22.

Shany, Y. (2012). Should the Implementation of International Rules by Domestic Courts be Bolstered? Realizing Utopia: The Future of International Law. A. Cassese. Oxford, Oxford University Press.

Shany, Y., et al. (2011). Response on behalf of the researchers of the Israel Democracy Institute's Terrorism and Democracy project to claims or suspicions in regard to violation of the Laws of War. I. D. I. s. T. a. D. project.

Sprague, J. (2005). Qualitative Shifts: Feminist Strategies in Field Research and Interviewing Feminist Methodologies for Critical Researchers. Walnut Creek; Lanham; New York; Toronto; Oxford, Altamira Press.

Stern, Y. Z. (2010). Decade in Review: A Rocky Road for Israeli Courts, The Israel Democracy Institute, available at: http://en.idi.org.il/analysis/articles/decade-in-review-a-rocky-road-for-israeli-courts [accessed 28.4.15].

The State of Israel (2009). The operation in Gaza 27 December 2008 – 18 January 2009: Factual and legal aspects, available at: http://mfa.gov.il/MFA_Graphics/MFA Gallery/Documents/GazaOperation w Links.pdf [accessed 29.4.15].

Weisberg, R. H. (2004). Loose Professionalism or Why Lawyers Take the Lead on Torture. Torture: A Collection. L. Sanford. Oxford, Oxford University Press.

Weizman, E. (2009). "Lawfare in Gaza: legislative attack, Open Democracy, available at: http://www.opendemocracy.net/article/legislative-attack [accessed 29.4.15]."

Weizman, E. (2010a). "Forensic Architecture: Only the criminal can solve the crime." Radical Philosophy **164**.

Weizman, E. (2010b). Only the Criminal Can Solve the Crime. ArteEast Public Lecture The New School, New York, The Sheila C. Johnson Design Center

Weizman, E. (2011). The Least of All Possible Evils: Humanitarian Violence from Arendt to Gaza. London, Verso Books.

Winograd (2008). Winograd Commission Report - The commission of inquiry into the events of military engagement in Lebanon 2006.

Yahav, D. and U. Amit-Kohn (1993). Israel, the "intifada" and the rule of law. Jerusalem, Israel Ministry of Defense Publications.

CHAPTER 3

# A Map of the Israeli Legal Field Operating in the OPT: Structuring Law, Structuring Power

## 3.1 Introduction

This chapter advances the discussion of law and the Occupied Palestinian Territories (OPT), guided by this study's methodological framework. This analysis incorporates a mapping of continually restructured relations between positions competing for authority and power. In light of this, the chapter describes and debates processes of change and turning points, participants and relations in the Israeli legal field, paying particular attention to relatively recent developments and contemporary configurations of power. As I shall show, the Israeli legal field has distinctive phases, each positioning military legal practice in a different role.

The chapter begins with the genesis of the legal field at hand, tracing pivotal decisions and processes of change contributing to its early form. It continues by drawing a dynamic historical map of the field, an account based on shifts in power, discursive articulations, and relations between agents and institutions. This discussion builds on several avenues and cases – the High Court of Justice's assertion of power and remaking of legal logic through the term 'justiciability', i.e. this institution's distinction between legal and political areas, an exploration of NGOs and their power, the discursive making of 'theory' and 'practice' in the field, court debates taking place in the 2000s revolving around the army's change of approach towards the framework of international humanitarian law, and the policy of targeted killing. This discussion's particular focus on relatively recent changes in the field follows this account's interest in the contemporary legal state



M. Geva, *Law, Politics and Violence in Israel/Palestine*,
DOI 10.1007/978-3-319-34153-8_3

of affairs. Having drawn this map of power, the chapter positions the MAG Corps and its ILD in this context, in an act of 'radical contextualisation' (Johnson 1993). This contextualisation defies a division between internal and external understandings of law, allowing a conceptual—practical reconsideration of powers in play through the practice of law. In this sense, it is an attempt to avoid predetermined definitions of legal institutions and law in analysing military legal work and marking carefully the elements and dynamics constituting law.

## 3.2 The Emergence of an Israeli Legal Field Centred on the OPT

This section traces and analyses the genesis of the Israeli legal field centred on the OPT. Tracing this field's emergence and its subsequent transformations follows Bourdieu's pursuit of identifying and examining the formation of a social object rather than accepting its current shape as being neutral or inevitable. This endeavour is the core of Bourdieu's sociology: 'The first and most pressing scientific priority … would be *to take as one's object the social work of construction of the pre-constructed object*' (Bourdieu and Wacquant 1992, p. 229; emphasis in original).

The Israeli army's legal system, the MAG Corps, emerged from the existing structures of the 'Haganah', a Jewish paramilitary organisation operating between 1920 and 1948, alongside the British Mandate of Palestine (Inbar 2005). The military legal system is formally subordinate to the civil justice system. More specifically, the MAG is subjected to the authority of the civil Ministry of Justice rather than to the army's chain of command. The MAG Corps' officers are not hierarchically subject to military commanders but to the Attorney General. The military legal system's engagement with international law largely began in 1967, following the Six-Day War ending in Israel seizing the Gaza Strip, the Sinai Peninsula, the West Bank and the Golan Heights. The MAG Corps had in fact made preparations prior to 1967 for a situation in which it would administer an occupied territory through the application of international law. As early as 1963 the military legal system assembled a set of materials of basic legal orders and documents in readiness for a potential occupation (Inbar 2002, pp. 149–153). These boxes were sealed in 1963 and brought into use four years later. In that same year legal advisers were stationed, for the first time, in military units (Shamgar 2002).

In legal terms, this was a period of transformation—the 1967 occupation led to chaos, which was followed by the institution of a novel legal system in the OPT. Within the West Bank, as Jordanian rule ceased to operate, prisoners escaped from jails. Some used this opportunity to commit crimes in the absence of a police or justice system. Gaza, which prior to 1967 was controlled, though not annexed, by Egypt, was declared by the Israelis to be a closed military zone (Kretzmer 2002). Gaza was considered by the Israeli authorities to be a particularly problematic territory, densely populated and hostile. In 1967, 60 % of its inhabitants were refugees from the 1948 war (Azoulay and Ophir 2012). In 1968, MAG Meir Shamgar established the military's International Law Division, the body that later changed its title and became the International Law Department. This division was made responsible for co-ordinating all legal work in the occupied territories. In its early days it included just three legal practitioners. Shamgar was appointed Attorney General later that same year and played a pivotal role in shaping the newly emerging civil and military legal systems handling the OPT in his capacity as both MAG and Attorney General.

Legal practice is explained at the same time by the positions and power relations that structure the field and its internal logic. The year 1967 was the point in time at which the field was beginning to emerge. Subsequent to the act of occupation, Israeli authorities made two important decisions shaping this field's logic and structure, and laying out the grounds for the operation of the military international law team. The first decision was about legal obligations—the acceptance of the Hague Regulations, establishing law for conduct in war on land, considered customary law, and the rejection of the Fourth Geneva Convention, law dealing with the protection of civilians during war or under an occupation. The second fundamental decision was to allow the Israeli Supreme Court's review of issues concerning the OPT.

The first decision, a selective acceptance of the international law of belligerent occupation, was the result of various pressures and the consideration of potential future consequences (Kretzmer 2002). The military orders that the MAG Corps had prepared in 1963, and that had been disseminated in the OPT in June 1967, did include the Fourth Geneva Convention. A military order issued in August 1967, however, replaced the order devised four years earlier and excluded the Fourth Geneva Convention from the body of law governing the Israeli occupation. Discussions concerning the application of the Geneva Convention had apparently not entirely ended by that point, or perhaps they had ended but the decision was intended to remain somewhat vague. Despite the undeniable content of the August military order, Meir Shamgar, in an archived memorandum dated October 1967, instructs an unknown receiver to remain ambiguous about this issue, and recalls a related discussion with the Ministry of Foreign Affairs:

> I hereby repeat the Ministry of Foreign Affairs' request to refrain from unnecessarily emphasizing the question of whether or not the 1949 Geneva Convention applies to the territories we hold. The grounds for this request were explained in the past, and the circumstances have not changed. (my translation, Shamgar 1967a)

Four years after the start of the occupation, Shamgar (1971), at that time the Attorney General, declared that while Israel did not acknowledge a formal and abiding application of the Geneva Convention over the OPT, Israeli authorities would nevertheless adhere ***voluntarily*** to the convention's humanitarian provisions. However, he did not declare which of this law's provisions Israel considered to be humanitarian. This same position has since been affirmed repeatedly by Israeli officials and authorities.

Building on this legal premise, the international law team, in cooperation with additional MAG Corps units specialising in other bodies of law, gradually and consistently developed a collection of military orders governing the Palestinian population, and detailing how military conduct in the OPT should operate. This legal enterprise, which began in the abstract in 1963 and in reality in 1967, still continues and at present encompasses thousands of military orders, with topics ranging from education to fiscal matters, and to the confiscation of land. These legal activities constitute an operation establishing and constructing the field and its inner logic. Every military order is an addition to the law applied in the OPT and becomes an element legal institutions in the field are obliged to take into account. The significance of these orders varies—some are negligible and others extremely influential, but all feed into the field's inner logic. This military law-making takes place in a structured context, directed by this institution's relative position and capital.

The second key legal decision made by political and legal authorities regarding the OPT was the opening of the Israeli Supreme Court's doors, in its capacity as the High Court of Justice, to appeals by Palestinians. This meant that state authorities had decided that the court was to review appeals of non-citizens, relating to issues regarding territories external to Israel's borders.[1] International law does not oblige a state to allow an occupied population access to its courts. In its work in this regard, the Israeli court accepted and relied on legal standards derived from multiple sources, among them the principles of customary public international law, the law in place prior to the occupation (i.e. Jordanian law), and the general codes of judicial review derived from Israeli administrative law. Notably, even though the court had in principle taken up the review of matters relating to the OPT, in the first decades of the occupation many petitions were rejected on the grounds of their identification as political. Notwithstanding these conditions, the court's engagement with petitions regarding the OPT had a formative impact on the field. First, the court itself then became part of the field; and second, its review has had a significant influence over the inclusion and relative power of institutions in the field, namely the Ministry of Justice in the capacity of its responsibility for the representation of the military's position on the occasion of petitions and, later, the human rights community.

In the years since 1967, the Israeli—OPT centred legal field has been shaped continually by the power relations among its participants—various state bodies and practitioners, academics, NGOs and others. The relative positions of these bodies and their unequal capital feed into the competitive struggles over power and legal competence. The following sections discuss the transformations the field has undergone, cutting through different analytical axes, and all contributing to the map of the field.

## 3.3 Justiciability and the High Court of Justice's Jurisdiction: Formations and Transformations of the Field's Power, Inner Logic and Boundaries

This section describes and examines the changes the High Court of Justice has undergone in recent decades, paying specific attention to its power and the extent of its influence over military affairs in the OPT. It conceptualises this change and considers the High Court of Justice's dynamic capital within the field and beyond it, as well as its influential participation in the making of the field's inner logic and boundaries. The consideration of the High Court of Justice is pivotal to this study, first because it is a significant body in the field, and second because it played a central part in the crucial process beginning in 2000 and leading to the military legal system's gaining prominence and substantial capital.

In recent decades the Israeli Supreme Court has undergone significant changes in terms of its position and involvement in society and politics. A key facet of this change has been labelled 'judicial activism'. This activism entailed the court's willingness to ease the insistence on the rules of standing, i.e. the demonstration of sufficient connection to the action challenged to support a party's participation in the case, thus allowing the review of government actions in cases that did not have a direct impact on the rights or liberties of the petitioning individuals. This trend, which meant that the court became increasingly involved in many more social-political issues than previously, had significant implications for its review of matters relating to the OPT (Kretzmer 2002). This shift is largely connected to the work of Justice Aharon Barak, who played a leading role in the High Court of Justice from the 1980s until his retirement in 2006.

A fundamental aspect of the court's process of change, led first and foremost by Justice Barak, was a remaking of the court's 'jurisdiction', a change manifested in the term justiciability. Justiciability is an articulation of the areas of life and conduct the court considers possible and appropriate to subject to its review (Bendor 1997). Until the 1970s, the High Court of Justice exercised a rather narrow understanding of judicial review, and refrained from reviewing cases considered 'too political' (Barzilai 1997, p. 195), an assumption including, for example, many aspects of political parties and politicians' conduct, as well as matters relating to security. Barak's approach towards the court's jurisdiction changed this state of affairs radically. His work in this respect has even been referred to as a 'revolution of justiciability' (Barak-Erez 2009). Barak (in Barak-Erez 2008) made a distinction between normative and institutional justiciability, the former relating to whether law contains a provision/standard that could potentially be applied to the specific matter in question, and the latter to the desirability of the court's involvement in terms of institutional balance and division of power between the state branches. Barak argued that normative justiciability, in principle, is practically non-existent, and that institutional justiciability should be in most cases either reduced or avoided entirely.

Justice Barak had an ambitious vision of law and the role of legal practitioners. In 1977, prior to his appointment to the Supreme Court, he stated:

> As legal practitioners, we are not limited by interpretation and implementation of existing law. We are at the forefront of the ambition for more desirable

> law, better [law] ...We are the architects of social change. We have the skills to construct a better legal system that is fairer. We don't perceive our role as limited to legal technicality; we consider our role to include legal statesmanship. (in Shamir 1994, p. 10; my translation)

This approach reflects a fundamental change in the High Court of Justice's claim of capital, prompted by its practitioners. Distancing himself from his predecessors, who had generally argued for legal authority on the basis of their expertise in law, Barak's perspective is in fact a novel take on law's social position. Law in his terms sets out to reform society, and to partake actively in governance rather than merely to determine the results of cases brought to court (Shamir 1994). This perspective prompted and indicated change in the legal field's logic and power, which thereby expanded to include many more matters and areas than ever before.

The court's process of change is situated historically in the context of strong liberal shifts in the Israeli society that gave the legal field as a whole considerable power. In the 1980s' political arena the two major parties had not gained sufficient electoral support to allow either to formulate a stable coalition. Amid instability, corruption and social rifts, the court was regarded as the country's most reliable civil institution (Barzilai 1997). The following decades were characterised by the High Court of Justice's unparalleled prominence. The court then took up almost all of the controversial affairs in the country (Barzilai 2004). Thus the extent of the Supreme Court's power and influence had changed significantly, from having a marginal impact on state policy in 1948 to an extent of power that by the late 1980s had been compared to its US counterpart (Edelman 1994).

One of the key facets of the court's shift in justiciability and the intertwined reformulation of the legal field's logic was its substantially increased involvement in military and security-related action and policy. This meant that petitions on matters that would previously have been rejected on the grounds of justiciability were then reviewed. Justice Barak argued forcefully:

> In the past the security character of administrative discretion discouraged judicial review ... Over the years it has become clear that when it comes to judicial review there is nothing special about security considerations ... Just as judges are qualified and bound to examine the reasonableness of professional discretion in every sphere, they are qualified and bound to examine the reasonableness of discretion relating to security. (HCJ 680/1988)

Among others, cases reviewed in court included petitions relating to the construction and route of the Separation Wall, a barrier located in the West Bank and designed to protect Israelis at the expense of Palestinians' land and freedom of movement, and the legality of the Israeli military's use of Palestinian 'human shields', i.e. the deliberate placement of civilians in or around military targets with then intention of deterring the enemy from attacking these targets. Overall, this was a direct challenge to state authorities posed by the court, operating in areas formerly defined as political, and hence outside its jurisdiction. Cohen and Cohen (2012) go so far as to argue that since the 1990s the High Court of Justice has undertaken a process of legalising Israel's national security framework, considering itself the only non-military institution capable of influencing these policies.

Shifts in the court's perception of justiciability had significant consequences for the capital of other legal bodies, their positions and relationships. A key result of the court's move towards an increased inclusion of security matters in its jurisdiction was a change in the power and position of the military legal system. The court's review of military practices challenged by Palestinians meant that the MAG Corps was obliged to defend these practices in court. Even beyond concrete court petitions, this alteration meant that the army was pushed to take into account the court's potential intervention (Cohen and Cohen 2011, p. 12). From the perspective of the MAG Corps, and specifically its international law team, the potential need to argue in court in defence of military practices necessitated a reformulation of legal positions and roles. As will be described and analysed in more detail in Chapter 4, this new situation occasioned frequent clashes between the military's legal system and its operational rank. In this regard, the character of discussion between legal practitioners on the one hand, and political and military decision-makers on the other, had changed. The court's changing practice, brought about by the reformulation of its justiciability, altered the position, power and terms of involvement of the military's legal system in this institution's operations.

As one might expect, the court's reformulation of the legal terrain and its assertion of increased capital was met with a struggle on the part of multiple political powers. The chief accusation directed at the court in this regard was that it had become politicised (Barzilai 1997). Justice Barak's counter argument was a denial in the form of a discursive distinction between law and politics, arguing on behalf of the court's judges that 'the northern star, guiding us, is the law. Our loyalty to law is the response to any argument of politicisation' (HCJ 1635/1990). This argument, predictably, did not convince many groups and institutions objecting the court's novel assertions and new claims of power. This occasion of change in the law—politics nexus was interpreted in a number of different ways. Ronen Shamir (1994), for example, argues that the court has acted as an expansionist legal power. This expansion, in his account, meant an endeavour to transform any social-political dispute or struggle into a rational and impartial legal procedure. The result, for Shamir, was a new type of politics presented as the repression of politics. Gad Barzilai (2004) argues that the myth of judicial separation and its supremacy vis-à-vis political power allowed judges to deny their own institutional interests and the political meanings of their decisions. For Barzilai, these claims allowed the court to acquire a great deal of political power. This state of affairs, however, Barzilai argues, in which the court's power relies on its discursive distinction from politics, has a double effect. On the one hand it enables the court to gain power, but on the other its declared 'political neutrality' means that it is unable to challenge the state systematically, precisely because such a challenge is likely to be perceived as political. Our study is also interested in this process of the court's rearticulation of law, and consequentially, politics, and does not aim to define pure law or identify the 'true' political nature of a discourse labelling itself as legal. Instead of pursuing legal 'truth', this book traces the processes, means and implications of the dynamic constitution of law.

Shifts in the Israeli court are intertwined with international trends. In the era of the 'War on Terror', many courts in liberal democracies seek to reaffirm liberal values by reviewing matters relating to security (Benvenisti and Downs 2009). This trend has some ironic implications. Much of the Israeli High Court of Justice's recent practice relies on international law to safeguard national practice and institution from external, i.e. international, influence, a goal at odds with this law's global mission (Benvenisti 2008). Alongside these trends in courts, the international legal arena has seen major changes, among these the coming into force of the Rome Statute in 2002, constituting the permanent International Criminal Court. In addition, several states have been exercising the doctrine of universal jurisdiction (Roth 2001), compelling national courts to adjudicate international crimes.

The exact matters that the Israeli High Court of Justice reviewed as a result of its shift in justiciability were those that were either potentially or actually subjected to the review of international courts or national courts in other countries, operating on the premise of universal jurisdiction.

Chief Justice Barak himself had made this point, arguing that avoiding the court's review on the grounds of non-justiciability would act as a double-edged sword, because any matters rendered non-justiciable in the court in Jerusalem would become precisely the material subject to the review of the International Criminal Court (Barak, in Lahav 2002). This argument follows international law's premise by which national courts were to be the primary sites of legal debate. Only if adequate legal process does not take place in these institutions would international legal bodies be able to take up the issue at hand. To exemplify the influence international legal mechanisms have over the Israeli court, the High Court of Justice made its decision on the Separation Wall in the area of Beit Surik just as the International Court of Justice was finalising its general advisory opinion on the wall. This was, of course, no coincidence, and is connected to the Israeli court's calculation that reaching its own decision, especially one seriously taking into account, rhetorically or otherwise, considerations of Palestinians' human rights, would lessen the blow of the International Court of Justice's opinion (Barak-Erez 2008).

The court's assertion of wider grounds of justiciability, while changing the legal terrain and leading to the review of many security-related matters, did not bring about a legal revolution in the OPT through its judgments. First, the court has not been consistent in its approach towards claims of the justiciability of security matters (Bendor 2007), and second, and most important, despite significant discursive changes it de facto refrained from interfering in the vast majority of politically charged disputes brought to it for review (Barak-Erez 2002, 2009). Despite its self-positioning as a defender of both human and civil rights in Israel and the OPT, in its legal practice the court positioned these rights as subordinate to, and in conflict with, security (Sharfman 1993). Notwithstanding the limited direct influence of the court's decisions, as I shall show below, the implications of the changes initiated by the court were significant, but many of these took place outside the courtroom.

The court in its decisions in fact approved of almost all state-military practices in the context of the OPT. Notwithstanding these approvals, the court employed two other channels to impact on state conduct in the OPT. The first is the strengthening of procedural rights, such as the right of appeal, or the opportunity to argue in court prior to the execution of extreme measures such as deportation or house demolition. Second, by its mere involvement, the court pushed state agencies to shape their actions while taking into account its potential review. Kretzmer (2002) argues that the court had some constraining impact in the OPT, but the results of this impact were neither uniform nor coherent. Cohen and Cohen (2012, p. 205), for example, argue in this context that one of the cumulative effects of the court's review of security matters has been that it provided politicians with a pretext to refrain from the legislative construction of a framework for Israel's security policy, claiming that any grievances regarding security policies could be handled through court petitions.

Critics argue that beyond merely allowing existing policies to continue, by its very participation in the dynamic of reviewing petitions from the OPT the court lends its credibility to strengthen a set of oppressive practices. According to this depiction, the court has been playing an active key role in the operations of the occupation. Barzilai (1997) claims in this regard that 'By and large, the court operated as a legitimising agent granting Israel the formal tools to legalize its ideological and political control over the territories. The court supplied the Israeli political and legal culture with the collective illusion that the "rule of law" prevailed in the territories' (Barzilai 1997, p. 202). Following a similar line of argumentation, Shamir (1990) argues that the rare cases in which Palestinian petitioners have succeeded in court were not followed by similar results in comparable cases. At the same time, none of these cases have had significant effects on the Israeli authorities' later policies. Exceptional successful cases, Shamir argues, serve as symbols of justice rather than providing evidence of 'balanced' legal practice. Both of these discussions—of a legal illusion and legal symbolism—rely discursively on an imagery of legal truth versus a legal façade. These accounts are inevitably part of the ongoing struggle over law and its logic.

The perspective of the field further challenges the conclusiveness of Barzilai and Shamir's observations on the court's decisions by directing attention to the court's influence on and engagement with its surrounding field. This is not to say that the court's practice complies in a better or worse way with law, or that it has or hasn't reinforced state policy, but that this dynamic has multiple dimensions that evade these analyses. To demonstrate, as mentioned, while the success rate of appeals raised by Palestinians, commonly facilitated by NGOs, is indeed low, the court has taken measures as encouraging compromises, applying pressure to restrain state practice and instructing procedural restraints over military actions (Dotan 1999; Kretzmer 2002). Government lawyers, concerned about the possibility of losing a case in court, are likely to forgo risky cases and encourage alternative courses of action (Kretzmer 2002, pp. 190–191).

While these measures do not constitute 'victory' in legal terms, they have had significant implications for state and non-state legal bodies and practice. Even if not making many direct and forceful decisions in the context of the OPT, the court and its remaking of justiciability have in fact played a major role in a reformulation of the legal field, leading to significant consequences for the OPT. This impact is intertwined with the activities, power and relations of bodies such as NGOs, academics, civil state legal mechanisms, and most important, the military legal system. A description and debate of these processes of change will follow later in this chapter, in the sections dedicated to human rights NGOs and the military legal system.

The 'appropriate' boundaries of legal review are in constant motion, never entirely coherent and ever a source of controversy. In 2002 the Israeli Bar Association held a conference focused on the theme of 'Law under Fire'. MAG Menachem Finkelstein on this occasion criticised the High Court of Justice's willingness, headed by Justice Barak, to review the policy of targeted killing, i.e. including the subject within the boundaries of justiciable matters. Barak, in this same conference, presented a two-pronged approach and stated that the time had come to clarify the High Court of Justice's adequate extent of involvement in questions relating to security:

> The time has come to set aside clichés of 'all is justiciable' and focus, as practical legal professionals, on questioning where to place the limit ... Is this good or bad for public officials in Israel, civilians and soldiers, for the court to say what is and isn't allowed according to international law? And is it wise for the court to enter into this territory? (in Gorali 2002; my translation)

Barak's standpoint is a discursive retreat from his previous position, which rhetorically rejected any limits to justiciability. This retreat should be viewed in light of the changing relationship between this institution and the army, and in particular the court's influence on the MAG Corps' position in the army. This complex process will soon be addressed in more detail.

In recent years, Israel has seen a gradual and substantive decline in the court's public status (Stern 2010). This process will have an impact on the court's future approach to justiciability, and lessen the extent of its involvement in matters relating to the OPT. The relational context of the field means that change in the court's position is structurally tied up with the position and power of all other related bodies. Consequentially, the field as a whole will undoubtedly change, presenting new challenges and opportunities for legal institutions.

## 3.4 Human Rights NGOs' Stake in the Field

This section considers human rights NGOs' relational position and capital in the context of the court's political—legal movements. The circumstances of a court enabling the review of issues that had previously been out of bounds has allowed NGOs to litigate on many matters relating to the OPT. The practice of human rights NGOs in Israel has always been controversial and has led to some resentment. In 1994, Yitzhak Rabin, then Prime Minister and Minister of Defence, said in a televised speech on the recently signed Oslo Accords that the Palestinian Authority will do a better job at overcoming Hamas in comparison to the Israeli authorities, as it will do so 'without the High Court of Justice and without B'Tselem [a prominent human rights organisation]'. This statement grouped human rights NGOs with the court, implying that all these legal institutions obstruct effective political authority. Rabin's statement has since become a phrase in common use. It is employed by those wishing to criticise the human rights movement and the court's challenges to the state, as well as by those criticising political authorities' desire to dismiss the legal supervision of the executive branch. The account that follows debates NGOs' practice—their capital, relational positions and contributions to the articulation of law and politics.

The circumstances of the Israeli human rights movement's emergence, the outbreak of the Intifada and changes relating to the High Court of Justice to review matters relating to security (Gordon and Berkovitch 2007), meant that soon after this movement's establishment it became a highly active participant in the legal field. Assessing the extent of these organisations' capital is a difficult task. Cohen and Cohen, for example, claim that NGOs have been exerting an unwarranted degree of influence over Israel's security policies through 'unconventional' means:

> [T]hose campaigns do not take the form of attempts to exert conventional political pressure—an approach which, considering the unpopularity of Israeli NGOs, would, if adopted, doubtless have been doomed to failure. Rather, working in conjunction with their overseas colleagues, Israeli human rights activists have sought to influence Israel's national security policies by

> presenting petitions to the ISC [Israeli Supreme Court] based on principles of international law. This has proved to be an especially effective method. (Cohen and Cohen 2011, p. 14)

Both this estimation of NGOs' power, as well as the normative assumptions about appropriate and inappropriate means of influence, are questionable. It is unclear how the writers assess the NGOs' impact and their 'correct' measure of influence. In addition, their critique relies on the vague and problematic notions of 'conventional' and 'unconventional' political pressure. This section aims to estimate and analyse organisations' capital, position and impact on the court and the army more cautiously.

The community of human rights organisations is in itself diverse in terms of influence. Organisations employing similar strategies yield different measures of success. Neve Gordon (2008) points out that key factors in this variation are closeness to sites of power—government, administrative and judicial institutions as well as corporations—affect organisations' extent of economic, cultural and social capital. In Gordon's account, the particular degree of organisations' capital is also connected to the specific possibilities and limits of the human rights discourse, agenda and struggle. Organisations richer in capital are those making less radical arguments and petitioning issues relatively closer to mainstream trends. In this sense there is a circular logic in play – those organisations closer to the establishment have more power, but this same position means that they are structurally less likely to fundamentally challenge state practices.

The relationships between NGOs and state and military authorities have changed significantly since the emergence of these organisations in the early 1990. While a measure of hostility certainly prevails throughout these relationships, it has altered in form and extent. Changes within the army, which will soon be presented, marked a new phase in these organisations' practice, both in terms of their relationship with this institution and in terms of their own capital and habitus.

The comparison between military and NGO legal practitioners has attracted some scholarly attention. David Luban, analysing the discursive differences between these groups, contends that they maintain two distinct visions of law that have no point of contact. This divide is manifested discursively in these practitioners' different terms relating to the same law. The law that NGO lawyers refer to as International Humanitarian Law (IHL); is known as the Laws of Armed Conflict (LOAC) to government and military lawyers. According to Luban, this discursive divide reflects a fundamental difference in interpretive approaches:

> Where legal restrictions operate in the margins of military necessity under the LOAC vision, IHL strains to relegate war to the margins of peacetime rights. As a result, its mode of legal interpretation is maximalist in just those places—the restraints and obligations of warriors—where LOAC is minimalist, and minimalist in the places where LOAC is maximalist; in discretion and deference to the military ... [T]hey reach different conclusions because they assign military necessity and human dignity a different logical priority. (2013, p. 329)

Thus these are fundamentally different perspectives on law, one placing at its centre the protection of individuals and the other the army's warfare conduct. These perspectives identify different goals and priorities in law.

In Bourdieusian terms, this is a manifestation of 'structural hostility' (1987) within the field. In this sense, hostility is yet another expression of the ongoing struggle over the determination of law's logic building on lawyers' particular habitus, guiding their beliefs and efforts in different directions. In this context, these positions seem to be opposites, and while indeed they do stem from distinct motivations and rely on different arguments, the framework of the field ties their operations together. These institutions are competing with one another to make the greatest possible impact on law. NGOs and the army make continuous efforts to mark their own practice as *legal*, i.e. as being representative of the field's 'true' logic, and distinct from the political sphere (Weizman 2010a). Clashes between NGOs and the army are a key arena for the battle over the field's boundary with politics. Common manifestations of this battle are mutual accusations of the abuse of law in the service of politics, a central part of the conversation between these institutions. Neither is more correct than the other—this is not a question of truth, but rather of the very making of these areas and their separation. NGOs, having far less capital than the military legal system, have proportionally less sway in these struggles. The result is that the discourse of NGOs is, for the most part, kept outside the legal, i.e. in the framework of politics, while the military's discourse, based on this institution's paramount capital, is largely made legal.

NGOs and the military legal establishment sustain a web of connections and dependencies tying them together. These lawyers meet in courts, exchange legal opinions and debate in academic and political forums. To demonstrate the complexity of these relations, it is important to consider that the work of NGOs serves military lawyers by providing an argument for furthering the incorporation of legal advisers to military operations. ILD Commanding Officer Noam Neuman (2007) demonstrates this line of argumentation in an article, stating that the presence of legal advisers would make it easier for the army to respond efficiently to claims of illegal conduct made by NGOs, and could then prevent the submission of petitions to court. Moreover, Neuman argues that even if NGOs and military practitioners commonly disagree on legal interpretations, the army's participation in this discourse lessens the blow of the NGOs' contentions. Thus, in this sense, NGOs impact on legal forces within the army, pushing to further promote the integrative reform of legal work in battle.

And so Israeli NGOs have been active participants in the legal field since their emergence in the early 1990s. While these organisations are usually seen simply as the opposite of the military legal system, placed in the framework of the field their practice is relative, founded on common ground with the army and it has a complex impact on military legal practice. As Neuman's (2007) arguments demonstrate, while NGOs do impact the army, this influence is not necessarily warranted from the perspective of these organisations. The terms of this impact will be debated below in sections dedicated to key court cases unfolding in the 2000s. In these cases, NGOs' efforts to influence the field's logic entered into complex institutional dynamics and have led to crucial and unexpected results.

Following the discussions of NGOs and the High Court of Justice, the next section analyses dynamics and shifts in the field based on three avenues—first, the articulation of theory and practice; second, court debates revolving around the term Armed Conflict Short of War; and third, the court case centred on targeted killing. All these debates are part of the dynamic mapping and analysis of the field, its structure, inner logic, power relations and the habitus of its participants.

## 3.5 Theory versus Practice: A Discursive Articulation of Difference Structuring the Relations Between Academics, NGOs and the Military

Theory and practice are two fundamental notions structuring the field discursively. The theory—practice distinction implies a clear-cut division between those practitioners immersed in thought removed from the realities of conflict and those located 'on the ground', making decisions 'that really count'. These articulations of difference form part of the habitus of agents, an internalisation of structural settings. The discursive creation of 'practical practice' and its separateness from 'theoretical practice' in the field plays a key part in maintaining the army's capital. This section explores the conventions underlying these concepts and the inconsistencies they conceal.

The distinction between theoretical and practical legal practice is key to understanding power and hierarchy in the field. It was present in the work of the High Court of Justice in the 1970s (Sfard 2004), and is most prominent in the discourse of the military legal system's representatives claiming to 'practice' rather than 'theorise'. It is not surprising that military practitioners are the most vocal advocates of this division, taking into account that this state of affairs grants them power. Former MAG Mendelblit demonstrates this discourse vividly by presenting military practice in contrast to 'theory': 'Legal consultancy on operational decisions is not theoretical and not academic. It results in practical crucial decisions commanders make. It doesn't have room for vague and undecided style, sometimes a characteristic of academic thought and writing' (Mendelblit 2009; my translation). This separation is also the message often conveyed in the MAG Corps' public communication with NGOs. Since the beginning of the second Intifada, in 2000, and regardless of the topic debated, letters produced by the MAG Corps to respond to any NGO report commonly begin with a similar presentation of the setting for the military legal system's decision-making—the harsh realities of the 2000s, including hostility and terrorist attacks (see, for example, Shnayderman 2005; Diamond 2007; Feuerstein 2007). The repetitive narrative sends a clear message—NGOs' legal standpoints, unlike the army's, do not take 'reality' into account. In this picture, military practical work is related closely to 'the ground'. It has direct consequences, and is clear and decisive. In contrast, NGOs' practice is abstract and does not seriously consider the harsh reality. Of course, there are vast differences between military legal practice and NGO or academic practice, but, as I now show, an opposition or a clear-cut division between these areas is an inaccurate and contradictory description of these relations. Notwithstanding its contradictions, this polar division plays a major part in continuously establishing the MAG Corps' capital.

Ironically, when dealing with decision-makers within the military establishment, i.e. outside the field, legal officers often present themselves to be theorists, removed from 'the ground' and 'reality'. As I shall discuss later in this chapter, in the context of legal practitioners' increasing involvement in the battlefield, they attempt continually to assert their practical grounding in the face of resistance, and their being represented as being detached from 'the ground'.

The theory—practice debate requires the introduction of additional actors to this discussion, academics. Academics and academic institutions maintain multi-faceted relations with the army, the court and the NGOs. Israeli academia is in itself diverse, with some legal and social science academics and departments fostering different positions in relation to military-legal practice. Yoram Dinstein, for example, is a prominent legal scholar and also one who is affiliated most closely with the military establishment. Asa Kasher, another prominent academic trained in philosophy and linguistics, is known as 'the IDF's philosopher' (Matar 2006). Established academics, such as Yuval Shany, Eyal Weizman and David Kretzmer, play an active part in NGO human rights work, sitting on boards and participating in formulating these organisations' strategic planning.

A contradictory aspect of the theory—practice division can be traced on a personal level. Many ILD and MAG Corps officers acquire advanced degrees, and some even teach in university legal departments.[2] Pnina Sharvit-Baruch, a former ILD Commanding Officer, involuntarily provided an example of the complex relationship between academia and the MAG Corps in this context. Sharvit-Baruch, who served in the army during Operation Cast Lead, retired from active duty later in 2009 and later took up a teaching position with Tel Aviv University's Law Faculty. Her appointment caused controversy, resulting in petitions, demonstrations and newspaper articles arguing both for and against (HAARETZ editorial 2009; Ilani 2009), even occasioning a supportive response from the Prime Minister himself, Ehud Olmert (Ravid 2009). Despite the controversy, Sharvit-Baruch began her teaching career as planned. She currently teaches and works as a researcher at the Institute for National Security Studies, an institution affiliated with the same university. The former MAG Avichai Mendelblit was also a researcher at this institution until his appointment as Cabinet Secretary in 2013. The Institute for National Security Studies employs a number of retired chief officers, among these legal ones, in the capacity of security experts. The involvement of retired MAG Corps officers in teaching and research implies a trickle of 'practice' into 'theory'. Moreover, the Israeli army's systematic reliance on reservists means that even after retirement from regular duty, these academics are still a part of the military structure and are likely to be called to report for duty at the army's discretion.

An additional contradictory aspect in the supposed theory—practice division is present in High Court of Justice proceedings involving the army and NGOs. While military practitioners depict themselves as being entirely different from academic theorists, these officers base many of their court arguments on academic writing. Had academic practice been entirely disconnected from military practice, it would make no sense for the army to base its court arguments on academic literature.

Another challenge to the separation between theory and practice is the multiple meeting points between 'theorists' and 'practitioners', in both personal and discursive terms. Academics, NGOs and military lawyers participate in the same conferences, publish in the same journals and teach in the same departments. To demonstrate, the ILD, in its legal documents published post-Operation Cast Lead (The State of Israel 2009, 2010a, b), made frequent reference to both academic writing and to arguments made by NGOs. Of course, it does so in a strategic manner, but had there been a clear separation between 'theory' and 'practice' such references would have been entirely irrelevant. Another example of such meetings is forums arranged by the Israel Democracy Institute. This is not a human rights organisation per se, but an NGO operating on a similar premise, which holds regular meetings bringing together academics and military legal officers. This NGO's capacity to arrange these forums reflects its capital, which manifests in close ties with both military and state institutions. Most of the contents of these discussions are made public, but some are confidential. Presumably the purpose of confidentiality is to allow military personnel to communicate more freely than they would have otherwise been able. On the part of the Israel Democracy Institute this secrecy is ironic, considering this institution's declared commitment to the promotion of democratic transparency. The agreed confidentiality of these meetings certainly reflects this organisation's trusting relationship with state authorities, and a measure of capital by which state officials share sensitive information and knowledge exclusively with the institution's research staff. While the multiplicity of encounters does not provide 'hard proof' for mutual influence, the proximity and continual discussion between so-called opposites calls into question their supposed antagonism.

To conclude, the discursive separation between theory and practice, positioning academics and NGO practitioners as the opposites of military lawyers is a central element structuring the field. This characterisation serves, first and foremost, the interests of the army's lawyers. As I have shown above, this polar representation cannot account for many issues, from personal overlaps when legal officers become academics and occasionally return to their military capacity, to the army's reliance on academic writing in court argumentation and discussion groups where academics, NGO practitioners and military legal officers exchange opinions. Seen against the oppositional depiction of practice versus theory, these multiple sites of entanglement create a more nuanced presentation of the field, where all institutions and actors engage in a process of mutual influence, with the terms of this mutuality mediated by the different institutions' relative capital.

## 3.6 'Armed Conflict Short of War': The Remaking of Legal Logic and Transformative Shift in the Field's Constellation of Power

In the year 2000 the Israeli state legal system initiated a transformative change, defining the framework for its treatment of the second Intifada, the Palestinian uprising, as 'Armed Conflict Short of War'. Reference to the OPT with the term Armed Conflict Short of War was initially presented in a document provided by Israeli officials to the US Mitchell Committee.[3] This committee rejected the Israeli position and advised that Israel should continue administering the OPT governed by the logic of law enforcement, as it had done up to that point. The later 11 September attacks changed the US perspective, however, and had a substantial impact on the Israeli legal field. As ILD Commanding Officer Daniel Reisner (in Blau and Feldman 2009) attests, these attacks enabled the ILD to 'develop' its legal interpretations in a much more flexible manner.

The authorities' stand was soon challenged in court in several petitions, occasioning interaction between the army, NGOs, academics and judges. The second Intifada began in September 2000 and lasted roughly to 2005. The trigger for the uprising was the visit of Ariel Sharon, then opposition leader, to the compound of the al-Aqsa Mosque. This visit was seen as a political statement made to reflect Israel's (and specifically the opposition party's) intention to keep East Jerusalem under Israeli rule (Mitchell 2001). Root causes of the uprising were the occupation and its abusive policies, fuelled by the disillusionment of the 1994 Oslo Accords process and the recent failure of the 2000 Camp David Summit. The uprising began on the day following Sharon's visit, with violent demonstrations in the Old City of Jerusalem that were met with a harsh response on the part of the Israeli armed forces. The uprising soon spread throughout the West Bank and Gaza. To demonstrate the gravity of Israel's actions, during October alone, the first month of the Intifada, Israeli armed forces fired over a million bullets (Eldar 2004). Over the following years, the Intifada continued with demonstrations, strikes and violent action in the form of attacks on Israeli armed forces and civilians, including lethal bomb attacks in Israeli cities. The Palestinian death toll in clashes with the armed forces between September 2000 and December 2005 was 3294 (1531 in the West Bank and 1763 in Gaza). The Israeli death toll for this period was 309 armed forces personnel and 665 civilians.[4]

The military legal system's shift to the framework of Armed Conflict Short of War was a decisive turn facilitating an array of novel practices. One of the crucial implications of the shift to a legal frame nearing war is that killing civilians then became permissible, no longer the exception as in the context of law enforcement. The magnitude of this shift was exemplified by a statement of MAG Mendelblit on Palestinian casualties:

> Supposedly, our critics have a winning argument: 2,000 casualties, zero convictions. But there is no automatic investigation for every case of casualty. Of course we will not approve of war crimes, but it is not possible to carry out 2,000 investigations for 2,000 cases of death, when many of the cases are related to combat activity. (Mendelblit, in Harel 2003; my translation)

This situation, wherein instances of death are not investigated automatically, is a direct result of the legal shift in question. Mendelblit's observation, that the number of fatalities is no indication of 2000 war crimes, is demonstrative of the field's new-found logic. The key element here is the changed perspective on civilian deaths, which under the new framework is a generally acceptable even if it is an unwanted result of military activity. This is a moment of legal transition from death as an exception, to death as a structural result of a policy.

As I shall show shortly, this statement had become accepted systematically by the field's participants, constituting a crucial change in the field's logic. The acceptance of this logic does not imply that all NGOs and academics will agree on the 'necessity' of any, or all, cases of death, but that the field's new logic, facilitated by processes of change had transformed radically the perspectives and possibilities of all the institutions and agents in the field. This legal situation, in which civilian deaths are an acceptable and legally permissible state of affairs reveals a new phase in the military-law composition.

The dynamics between legal bodies in this case were a mutually constructive process involving predominantly High Court of Justice judges and state lawyers. While one might imagine state legal representatives had considered the meanings and implications of the shift to an Armed Conflict Short of War when initially introducing it and then translating it into military policy and action, this was not the case. Shai Nitzan (in Meridor and Fass 2006), then Deputy State Attorney for Special Affairs, had said in this regard that state legal authorities had only a vague idea of what the shift might entail when they decided to introduce this term to the Israeli system. In fact, Nitzan attests that, from his perspective, state legal representatives articulated and developed this concept through the court proceedings and with the backing of High Court of Justice judges, which Nizan refers to as 'hinted encouragement'. ILD Commanding Officer Daniel Reisner, who played a central role in the formation of this legal shift, describes the interaction between the High Court of Justice and the ILD as a legally constitutive operation. To this effect, Reisner said that the High Court of Justice judges, in this case and in others, knowingly demanded that the state legal system, and particularly the ILD, provide it with legal opinions on matters that had not yet been decided. The court's purpose in this, in his perspective, was to push the MAG Corps to develop novel legal interpretations, which the court could then review (Reisner, in Meridor and Fass 2006, p. 206). And so rather than reviewing an existing situation or assessing the legal validity of arguments presented, the court used its own capital to facilitate the instigation of new legal elements as part of the field's logic. The intentions of state lawyers and judges are important, but these provide only a part of this picture of change. The change was made possible because of structural conditions, namely the increasing prominence of international law, facilitated by the court, academics and NGOs on the one hand, and the MAG Corps and the High Court of Justice's capital on the other.

The court discussions revolving around Armed Conflict Short of War demonstrate the interplay of influence that diverges from formal legal procedure. It is common to consider the operation of the court as one adjudicating between two conflicting sides, in this case NGOs and state representatives. In this picture, the court is a body reviewing state operations from a distance. The case at hand, however, was one in which the court in fact took part in generating the military legal position. The NGOs' positions were entangled in dynamics by which the court was a priori interested in reaching new legal interpretations through interaction with state representatives. This is not to say that arguments raised by NGOs played absolutely no part in the court's decision, but that the state of affairs in which these NGOs entered cannot be accounted for in formal legal procedure, and that some cases play to the hands of state institutions. It also follows that the potential processes of change and implications of an NGO petition cannot be predicted, even beyond a victory or a loss. Thus, in this case, submitting a petition to the High Court of Justice implied initiating a complex process of interplay between the court and the state's civil and military legal systems, and possibly a precarious move as seen from the NGOs' perspective.

The acceptance of a legal framework that nears war reduced the army's legal requirements and hence also reduced the court's potential involvement in its activities. Put in more general terms, the court's decision to accept the army's suggestion for a novel legal framework shifted capital in the field, on the one hand lessening the power of the High Court of Justice and on the other adding to that of the MAG Corps. This situation, as I shall show, gave rise to the military legal system. In theoretical terms, this analysis challenges Bourdieu's assumptions about interests in the field. In Bourdieu's analysis, each institution attempts to advance its own capital, but this situation is reversed. This is not, however, a major deviation from the overall scheme of the field, because it is reasonable to assume that the court's judges acted as they did in order to expand the field's influence over military action through the army's legal system.

The debate on the application of the Armed Conflict Short of War continues. In 2010, in response to claims that the situation in the West Bank no longer fits this framework, MAG Mendelblit stated that the Armed Conflict Short of War framework and that of policing reside on a spectrum rather than being mutually exclusive (Mendelblit 2010, p. 28). In this context, Mendelblit argued, the specific events with which soldiers are faced (for example, a demonstration or an arrest in the West Bank), and the particular atmosphere in the area at the time, determines which legal framework applies. This flexibility leaves considerable power in the hands of military legal practitioners. The MAG Corps retains the power to decide how any situation should be defined, and in this decision it sets the legal rules for the army's activities.

## 3.7 Targeted Killing and the Structural Transference of Capital to the ILD

'Targeted killing' is the military term for the practice of killing individuals suspected of involvement in terrorism. Human rights organisations refer to this same practice as assassinations. According to the Strasberg-Cohen Report (2011), the publication of a government-appointed commission, this practice has become part of the Israeli army's arsenal of actions largely since its 2002 Operation Defensive Shield. This operation, in the middle of the second Intifada, was at the time Israel's most extensive military operation in the OPT since 1967. Targeted killing was then institutionally established as a merited and efficient practice among military and government authorities. Between September 2000 and until Operation Cast Lead, 232 people were targeted and killed by the Israeli army in such operations, among them 150 in Gaza and 82 in the West Bank. Casualties of these operations, including both those targeted and people around them at the time, amounted to 277.[5]

ILD Commanding Officer at that time, Daniel Reisner, is the named legal 'architect' of targeted killing (Blau and Feldman 2009). At the time he was asked about the legality of this practice and in response formulated a set of requirements. These requirements included five parameters: targets must be actual terrorists or commanders rather than political or religious leaders operating the organisation's support structure; the operation is permissible only if there is no viable opportunity of arrest; any attack is subject to the principle of proportionality; the army can only use this practice in areas where Israel does not have security responsibilities (this criterion builds on the delegation of limited control to the Palestinian Authority); and operations require ministerial-level approval (Craig 2009). MAG Menachem Finkelstein, Reisner's superior, soon afterwards signed off a similar set of criteria (Strasberg-Cohen 2011).

The High Court of Justice's consideration of this practice touched on fundamental issues relating to the field's logic. It involved questions about this practice's justiciability, the appropriate legal framework to be applied to the OPT, and the specific interpretations of this framework. A petition against this practice was filed in 2001 but was quickly rejected on the grounds of non-justiciability. State representatives argued on this occasion that the court should not interfere with the state's choice of its means of combat. The judges concurred: 'In this judgment it was held that "the choice of the method of combat that the respondents employ in order to prevent murderous terrorist attacks before they are committed is not one of the subjects in which this court will see fit to intervene"' (HCJ 769/2 2006, p. 469). The Public Committee against Torture, a human rights NGO, filed a second petition in January 2002. On this occasion, the judges rejected the state's argument of non-justiciability and the case was reviewed. The debates and proceedings of this petition began in January 2002 and did not end until December 2006.

A preliminary key question was about the generally appropriate legal framework for evaluating military conduct in the OPT (Ben-Naftali and Michaeli 2003). The state's position was that the laws of war provide the most suitable legal frame. The petitioners opposed this position and continued by arguing that even if the laws of war were to apply, targeted killing violates the principle of distinction between civilians and combatants. This final argument was to refute the state's conclusive and fatal determination of the status of the people targeted as combatants.

Finally making its decision in 2006, the court concurred with the state regarding the general acceptance of the laws of war as the appropriate frame to govern Israeli conduct in the OPT rather than law enforcement. Gabriella Blum, a former ILD officer, and the legal scholar Philip Heymann relate to this decision as 'a middle ground between a more aggressive law enforcement paradigm and a tamer wartime paradigm' (2010, p. 159). In fact, by this time the court had accepted the framework of international humanitarian law in several other decisions. The court also decided that targeted killing as such was neither legal nor illegal. This judgment was based on the First Protocol to the Geneva Convention exception to the protection granted to civilians, appearing in clause 51(3): 'Civilians shall enjoy the protection afforded by this section, unless and for such time as they take a direct part in hostilities.' Grounded in this principle, the judgment established three criteria: it is only permissible to target a person taking part in hostilities; this participation must be *direct*; and protection is lost only in *such time* as this participation is taking place. In addition to these criteria, the operation is subject to the measure of proportionality. The court's decision was received as a success from the MAG Corps' perspective (Grinberg 2006) and a failure from the standpoint of the petitioning NGOs (Feldman 2006).

The ramifications of these judicial debates proved to be far broader than this particular case. The court's decision pushed towards a rearrangement of power in the field, shifting capital to the army's legal system. The transference of capital manifested in the following way: the court's formulation of legal criteria determining the permissibility of targeted killing attacks meant that it was no longer a party to discussions about these operations, and political and military decision-makers were then compelled to seek legal advice from the ILD's practitioners prior to carrying out such actions. The court decision affected the ILD profoundly, promoting its involvement in military operations considerably (Cohen 2011). Thus legal interaction revolving around this case, beginning with an NGO court petition, invoked a complex movement in the field and led to a change in the form of an increase in the MAG Corps and ILD's power and involvement in operational decision-making.

The continuing discursive division between theory and practice played a part in this court petition. During discussions the petitioners filed an expert opinion authored by Antonio Cassese, a renowned scholar and the first president of the International Criminal Tribunal for the former Yugoslavia. Cassese argued that targeted killing is illegal under the laws of war, unless military action is directed at a person concretely engaged in combat at the time of the attack. State representatives rejected Cassese's argument through a discursive articulation of the theory—practice divide. Pnina Sharvit-Baruch, Commanding Officer of the ILD at the time, referred to Cassese as an 'odd person' and described his perspective as theoretical, i.e. irrelevant: 'I've met him, I talked to him; he's an agreeable man, but I think his perspective is not so grounded and slightly detached from reality' (Yoaz 2005). Justice Barak, the chief author of the court decision, was inclined to relate to Cassese's opinion in a more careful manner. Amichai Cohen and Stuart Cohen (2011) argue that Barak's writing reveals a deliberate attempt to refer to Cassese's arguments. Barak included such reference precisely because his final decision did not accept Cassese's stand. In this sense, then, while Sharvit-Baruch expressed an outright rejection of 'theory', Barak chose a middle way, discursively positioning himself, and by implication the court, in the middle ground between theory and practice.

The court's decision had direct implications for Israel in the context of the enforcement of international law. One of Israel's most controversial targeted operations was its July 2002 killing of Salah Shahadeh. On this occasion, an Israeli Air Force plane dropped a one-ton bomb on Shahadeh's home, which was located in a densely populated residential neighbourhood in Gaza City. Shahadeh was killed along with 14 other people, among them eight children, and many more were injured. Shahadeh's home was destroyed, as well as nine other houses in the vicinity. An additional nine houses were partially destroyed, and 20 others moderately damaged. In 2006, after the court had made the decision in which it instructed the army to consider the measure of proportionality in its targeted killing operations, NGOs demanded an independent investigation of Shahadeh's killing. Barak supported the NGOs' demand and in 2008 the Strasberg-Cohen Commission was formed to examine this case. Based on these occurrences, a Spanish court decided against reviewing the case on the grounds of universal jurisdiction (Rosenzweig and Shany 2009).

The court's consideration of both the Armed Conflict Short of War framework and targeted killing, and the implications of its rulings, demonstrate the usefulness of analysis integrating legal logic and interplay of power among institutions and agents. These events are best captured through an analysis of legal conventions and the division of capital in the field, both prior to and following the legal decision described. These cases were turning points in terms of the military system's establishment of power both inside and outside of the army. Having set up a map of organisations and change, the next section contextualises the book's key focus, the International Law Department.

## 3.8 The International Law Department in the Field

Over the years of its operation, from 1968 to present day, the army's international law team has undergone significant changes in terms of its capital, institutional positioning and the nature of its practice. On its establishment in 1968, the International Law Division had only three team members. In the 1990s it was still staffed by just a handful of members, but by 2011 it included around 25 lawyers plus support staff. In times of intense conflict, such as Operation Cast Lead, the ILD adds to its personnel reservists, complementing the work of its regular officers. The ILD's reserve unit includes approximately 30 lawyers. In relative terms, the ILD's overall growth makes it one of the fastest-growing units in the Israeli army (Cohen 2011, p. 376).

The MAG Corps had begun to provide advice based on international law as early as 1967, in the first days of the occupation. MAG Meir Shamgar, in a memo directed at the Chief of Staff and dated 14 June 1967, only four days after the occupation began, demonstrates such guidance:

> In a meeting with the Central Regional Commander, the commander of Brigade 5 commented that he blows up houses in which he finds ammunition.

> I maintain that this type of reaction is to be avoided: firstly, it is in contrast to the 1949 Geneva Convention, and even regardless of this, the reaction seems to me undesirable in all political and practical senses. (Shamgar 1967a, my translation)

The international division's team soon entered the scheme of the MAG Corps' institutionalised outputs. In annual reports publicised in the years subsequent to the occupation, the MAG Corps reported to have provided legal advice to military commanders based on international law (MAG 1968, 1969).

On 3 July 1968, Yaakov Shapira, the Minister of Justice, made a statement, at the same time stressing the authority given to the army and its legal system governing the OPT and taking pride in this legal work:

> The Ministry of Justice's work is relatively easy as far as it concerns the areas of land …which were freed by the IDF. The actual governance there is carried out by the military forces and the legal questions which are related to it are handed over to the IDF's legal system, headed by the MAG. The army's legal mechanism handles this task in a manner which can set an example for far more experienced militaries, in countries which have traditions of strict adherence to the principles of public international law. (in Inbar 2002, p. 150; my translation)

A key element in this statement is the civil state system's handing over of legal responsibilities and power to the army. As this statement demonstrates, the army's legal system has been a central body in the field governing the OPT since the field's emergence. Other factors have changed immensely over time, among them the field's inner logic, the MAG Corps' power beyond the borders of the legal field, and the very definition of these borders.

On the establishment of the International Law Division in 1968 this unit had only a marginal impact beyond the legal field, i.e. over military conduct. One of the founding members of the team describes the situation: 'We started from zero. The army was not willing to be given advice and to let legal considerations to be a part of its decision making process' (Officer E 2012). The officer's reflection on this team's marginal influence is better understood in the context of general perspectives on international law within the army at this time. In a 1961 memo, the MAG Corps itself related apologetically to international law: 'Admittedly, the instructions of international law are enforced partly by morality and international courtesy and partly by international agreement ... International law cannot be considered "law" in the standard meaning of this term' (MAG 1961). In 1968 the MAG Corps' International Law Division was positioned at the centre of an emerging field, but this field's overall power was not substantial and consequentially the division's power over military conduct was negligible. This situation would later change dramatically.

The 1987 breaking of the popular uprising, the Intifada, occasioned novel legal questions at a time when the MAG Corps did not have much power over military conduct. Newly formed human rights organisations raised numerous complaints and petitioned against various military practices. MAG at the time, Amnon Straschnov (2013), described this situation in an interview: 'Decision-makers didn't tend to consult with us unless they absolutely had to'. To recall, in 1989 the international law team was still a small unit, including only five lawyers (Craig 2009).

In its work described thus far, the MAG Corps' international law team largely carried out its activities in a position distant from military operations in terms of time and space. Practitioners largely wrote legal advice in preparation for action, as part of preliminary discussions, or in the aftermath account of occurrences. Until and throughout the 1990s legal practitioners took part only sporadically in devising legal advice to decision-makers when military operations were taking place (Cohen 2011). Court deliberations in the 2000s, ending with the adoption of international humanitarian law as a framework governing the OPT rather than law enforcement measures, were a turning point for the ILD in this respect. This change facilitated a significant increase in the MAG Corps and ILD's involvement in military practice (Mendelblit 2007; Cohen 2011) and in its extent of influence over the army. In 2003, MAG Finkelstein said: 'During this last year we have become involved and engaged in different aspects of war in a way that is unprecedented in the IDF's history. The participation of the MAG Corps' officers in decision making processes dealing with operational issues, the integration of legal perspectives to the army's orders, on-the-spot legal consultation with forces in the field—all these are daily actions in the IDF's reality of combat' (in Roytman 2013, p. 320). The ILD's commanding officer in the early 2000s, Daniel Reisner, vividly describes the moment of change in legal officers' involvement in operational decision-making: 'In the first discussions on targeted killings there was a very strange feeling. Officers didn't understand why lawyers were in the room. I would go myself—I was senior enough, so no one could tell me to leave, but it was a bit like an enema—you had to do it with plenty of Vaseline. You had to make them feel that we were not there to replace them' (in Blau and Feldman 2009). Legal officers were indeed 'not there' to replace commanders, but rather to transform military practice. Alongside this trend deepening the involvement of legal professionals in military operation, the MAG was at that point made a permanent member of the army's central decision-making forum (Finkelstein, in Meridor and Fass 2006).

Processes of change within the army were part of broader alterations in the position and power of international law in state authorities. This was a shift intertwined with legal changes in international arenas. Meni Mazuz, Attorney General 2004–2010, describes parallel shifts in government in an interview given for the purposes of this study:

> It used to be the case that we, the legal practitioners, would have to be proactive in order to get involved …Here, both military and political decision makers wanted this assurance. This didn't happen out of the blue …it's about personal criminal responsibility—the Rome Statute, the International Criminal Court. People in the political and military system gradually realised that there is a personal price to pay, on top of the political one, for decisions violating international law. I think this made them more careful and eager to get on-site legal backing. (Mazuz 2013)

An ILD member described his work at this same time in an interview: 'the presence of the legal practitioner became crucial. When it was time to make a decision, people would ask "where's the legal adviser?" …In the past there was far more supply than demand; the situation has reversed' (Keidar 2012). Both the ILD officer and Mazuz describe a radical change. Rather than legal practitioners pushing military and political decision-makers to consult them and take international law into account, decision-makers were at that point seeking lawyers. These altered dynamics indicate a dramatic change in the power the military legal system had gained, and exercised beyond the field's borders.

The 2006 conflict in Lebanon was an additional landmark in the process remaking the position and power of the military legal system. Legal advisers were becoming involved in military forums more extensively than ever before. They took part in preliminary discussions, participated in the composition of a target list and consulted battle-time decision-making. Lawyers were stationed in headquarters forums and in Northern Command, providing on-site legal advice. Attorney General Meni Mazuz, in his testimony to the Winograd Commission, which was appointed to investigate this conflict in Lebanon, had testified that this was the most legalistic conflict Israel has ever led:

> Today, we've essentially reached a situation that was [first] seen in the Lebanon war; in every centre of military decision making, in every command, in the Air Force, in the Navy, in the General Staff, in the forum for approving targets, in the forum for approving flights—almost in every forum, or even without the 'almost', there were representatives from the military legal department, and issues were raised by decision makers making echelons, and answers were given on the spot, and this is beyond the opinions and 'annuals' disseminated throughout the year. This is a process that peaked during the Lebanon War. (Mazuz 2007, p. 5)

In the aftermath of the conflict in Lebanon, the military legal system institutionalised its novel on-site involvement in military affairs. MAG Mendelblit, also in a testimony given to the Winograd Commission, argued for formalising the MAG Corps' novel practices (2007, p. 12), and the army indeed shifted in this direction. The ILD then initiated a project titled 'Operational Advice Project', aiming to provide advice based on international humanitarian law both before and during military operations. This project was a result of different factors pushing in the same direction—it had been planned by the MAG Corps, but also reflected the demands of commanders on the ground (Winograd 2008, p. 487). Both forces from within the field, namely the military-legal institution and from outside it, military and non-military state authorities, were promoting a reshaping of the measure and extent of the military legal system's power over military practice.

Thus the ILD's new position and power in the military establishment were formed in the context of the field. In this sense, the shift taking place was facilitated by the intent of agents and structurally-made opportunities. This legal unit's altered position in turn affected its surrounding institutions. Subsequent to the conflict in Lebanon, ILD officer Noam Neuman authored an article seeking to 'negate concerns regarding the involvement the legal advisor in decision-making processes during combat' (2007, p. 36). Neuman, in his article, positions the increasing military legal practice in relation to other institutions in the field:

> Legal consultancy for the IDF on combat with Palestinian terrorism has contributed greatly to the handling of petitions submitted to the High

> Court of Justice in this regard. For example, because of the involvement of legal advisers in the decision-making process and their familiarity with situations on the ground it has been possible, in many cases, to submit a quick and detailed response to the court … as a result the High Court of Justice accepted the state's position on the legality of operations in the vast majority of cases. (Neuman 2007, p. 39, my translation)

Neuman's line of argument again demonstrates the interconnected nature of the field: change in the position and power of the military legal system are tied in with the actions of and shifts in other legal bodies. From this perspective, NGO petitioning and the court's review both played a part in the process leading to military legal practitioners being seen as necessary.

The process reforming the power of legal military authorities had not gone unnoticed. The government-appointment Winograd Commission, for example, criticised the MAG Corps severely, and in particular the ILD's work on the Lebanon conflict. One of the commission's panel members had expressed concern about this at the time of MAG Mendelblit's testimony: 'the question that troubles me … your involvement in setting goals, targets—you take part in decision making. In fact, I think you've become [part of the] decision-making rank rather than legal rank' (Mendelblit 2007, pp. 16–17). In its concluding report, the Commission expressed disapproval of legal practitioners' involvement in on-site decision-making. It explained its disapproval in two ways: first, in that the increased involvement of legal advisers might shift responsibility away from decision-makers to these advisers; and second, in that legal advice may tamper with military goals. The Commission concluded that the MAG Corps should only participate in the preparation and aftermath accounts of military operations and not in their duration (Winograd 2008, p. 487). The Commission's position was an attempt to assert greater institutional distance and distinction between military operations and legal practice facilitated by spatial and temporal separation. In broader perspective, the commission called into question the MAG Corps' acquired power and its new position in relation to the legal/political intersection. Taking into account the considerable forces driving changes in the MAG Corps position, which, as I have shown, are far greater than this military body alone, the Commission is seemingly fighting a losing battle.

Criticisms of military legal practice's contemporary formation rightly detect a substantial alteration in this legal engagement. As the Winograd Commission members detected, new trends in legal work cannot be captured by an immediacy of legal involvement. In this sense, the altered position of legal practitioners is not simply 'more of the same'. Meni Mazuz, in an interview, argues in this context that a significant implication of this process is an increase in legal practitioners' responsibility. This change in the extent of responsibility, in his opinion, occurs regardless of formal conditions by which legal work merely constitutes consultancy:

> There is no doubt on this matter—on-the-spot involvement increases legal practitioners' share of responsibility as compared to 'sterile' advice, devised in advance. There is always responsibility ... but there is no doubt that if he [the military adviser] takes part in on-site decision making, then he is seen as [an actual player] in the decision-making forum, not just an advisor. (Mazuz 2013)

Mazuz's observation on the changed extent of responsibility is, however, only the tip of the iceberg. In substantive terms, this shift in responsibility of personnel indicates a fundamental change in the ways decisions are made, in the parameters and criteria taken into account, and ultimately in the way that warfare is conducted, as well as the very making of both law and politics.

## 3.9 Conclusion

This chapter developed a historical dynamic map of the field, placing in its centre the MAG Corps and its international law team. The dynamism and continual development of the institutions and of the field are essential element in this inquiry, seeking to negate the current state of affairs as a taken-for-granted point of departure. Rather, this map of the field's structure in the making lays out the relative contextual histories of key institutions in the field, considering the power relations and legal logic being created. This account is built on various axes and trajectories—the historical decisions leading to the emergence of the field, allowing the review of the High Court of Justice over the OPT, and the inclusion and exclusion of legal conventions; the High Court of Justice's articulation of its power on the grounds of justiciability; the genesis and practice of human rights NGOs; discursive articulations of difference in the field and the dynamics leading to the 2000s transference of power to the army's ILD. All these avenues reflect the dynamic and intertwined character of the field, in which the action and policy of different institutions affect one another.

As this historical account demonstrated, the army's international law team has altered significantly over time, from being a small and marginal team at its 1968 establishment to becoming a highly influential body since the early 2000s. Turning points in this process of change were the 1987 first Intifada, the 2000s' new approach towards international humanitarian law, and the 2006 conflict in Lebanon. Alterations were multi-faceted, comprising an increase of capital in the field accompanied by amplified power over military conduct and fundamental changes in legal practice—from a distant position, separate from the battlefield, to on-the-spot practice, in which the lawyer's presence is a requirement. This process is intertwined in dynamics of the legal field, and should be seen, in part, as a response to a demand of legal bodies to promote the adherence to law in combat.

This mapping of the field sets the scene for the next chapter's discussion of military legal practitioners, positioning military lawyers as its central focus and analysing these practitioners' shifting habitus and structural positioning as a means of tapping into the dynamic creation of the field.

## Notes

1. The notions of citizenship and borders can and should be questioned in the light of Israel's enduring control over the OPT, but I use these terms here in a narrower manner.
2. In fact, I managed to gain access to several officers who became research respondents through mutual academic contacts at Israeli law faculties.
3. Also known as the 'Sharm El-Sheikh Fact-Finding Committee', an American commission chaired by former US Senator George Mitchell, seeking to inquire into the failure of the 2000 Camp David Summit and Israeli—Palestinian violent occurrences of the Second Intifada.
4. Source of data: B'Tselem – The Israeli Information Center for Human Rights in the Occupied Territories, accessible at: http://www.btselem.org/statistics/fatalities/before-cast-lead/by-date-of-event [accessed 19 April 2015].
5. Source for statistics: B'Tselem: Data on participation in the hostilities and targeted killing, accessible at: http://www.btselem.org/statistics/fatalities/before-cast-lead/by-date-of-event [accessed 19 April 2015].

## Bibliography

Azoulay, A. and A. Ophir (2012). Abandoning Gaza. Agamben and Colonialism. M. Svirsky and S. Bignall. Edinburgh Edinburgh University Press.

Barak Erez, D. (2002). "Judicial Review of Politics: The Israeli Case." Journal of Law and Society **29**(4): 611–631.

Barak-Erez, D. (2008). "The Justiciablity Revolution: An Evaluation " The Attorney (Hapraklit) **50**: 3–27.

Barak-Erez, D. (2009). "Broadening the Scope of Judicial Review in Israel: Between Activism and Restraint." Indian Journal of Constitutional Law **8**(3): 118–136.

Barzilai, G. (1997). "Between the rule of law and the laws of the ruler: The Supreme Court in Israeli legal culture." International social science journal **49**(2): 193.

Barzilai, G. (2004). How Far Do Justices Go: The Limits of Judicial Decisions Critical Issues in Israeli Society A. Dowty. Westport, Connecticut; London Praeger: 55–68.

Ben-Naftali, O. and K. R. Michaeli (2003). "We Must Not Make a Scarecrow of the Law: A Legal Analysis of the Israeli Policy of Targeted Killings." Cornell International Law Journal **36**(2).

Bendor, A. L. (1997). "Are There Any Limits to Justiciability - The Jurisprudential and Constitutional Controversy in Light of the Israeli and American Experience." Indiana International & Comparative Law Review 7(2).

Bendor, A. L. (2007). "Justiciability of the Israeli Fight Against Terrorism." George Washington International Law Review **39**(1149-1164).

Benvenisti, E. (2008). "Reclaiming Democracy: The Strategic Uses of Foreign and International Law by National Courts." The American Journal of International Law **102**(2): 241–274.

Benvenisti, E. and W. G. Downs (2009). "National Courts, Domestic Democracy, and the Evolution of International Law." The European Journal of International Law **20**(1): 59–72.

Blau, U. and Y. Feldman (2009). How IDF legal experts legitimized strikes involving Gaza civilians. HAARETZ 23/01/09.

Blum, G. (2010). "The Laws of War and the Lesser Evil." Yale Journal of International Law **35**(1): 1–69.

Bourdieu, P. (1987). "The Force of Law: Toward a Sociology of the Juridical Field." Hastings Law Journal 805 **805**(38).

Bourdieu, P. and L. J. D. Wacquant (1992). An Invitation to Reflexive Sociology. Chicago, University of Chicago Press.

Cohen, A. (2011). "Legal Operational Advice in the Israeli Defense Forces: the International Law Department and the Changing Nature of International Humanitarian Law." Connecticut Journal of International Law **26**(2).

Cohen, A. and S. Cohen (2012). Israel's National Security Law: Political Dynamics and Historical Development. London, Routledge.
Cohen, A. and S. A. Cohen (2011). "Israel and International Humanitarian Law: Between the Neo-Realism of State Security and the 'Soft Power' of Legal Acceptability." Israel Studies **16**(2): 1–23.
Craig, A. (2009). "Lebanon 2006 and the Front of Legitimacy." Israel Affairs **15**(4): 427–444.
Diamond, E. (2007). Crossing the Line: Violation of the Rights of Palestinians in Israel without a Permit, available at: http://www.btselem.org/sites/default/files2/publication/200703_crossing_the_line_eng.pdf [accessed 28.4.15], B'Tselem - The Israeli Information Center for Human Rights in the Occupied Territories.
Dotan, Y. (1999). "Judicial Rhetoric, Government Lawyers, and Human Rights: The Case of the Israeli High Court of Justice during the Intifada." Law & Society Review **33**(2): 319–363.
Edelman, M. (1994). Courts, Politics, and Culture in Israel. Charlottesville, University Press of Virginia.
Eldar, A. (2004). His True Face HAARETZ 11.6.04.
Feldman, A. (2006). Croaking swan song: It is hard to pluck from Aharon Barak's rulings an independent statement that stands courageously on its own legs. HAARETZ 28.12.06.
Feuerstein, O. (2007). Ghost Town Host Town: Israel's Separation Policy and Forced Eviction of Palestinians from the Center of Hebron, B'Tselem - The Israeli Information Center for Human Rights in the Occupied Territories, The Association for Civil Rights in Israel, available at: http://www.btselem.org/sites/default/files2/publication/200705_hebron_eng.pdf [accessed 28.4.15].
Gorali, M. (2002). Justice Barak Wishes to Warn. HAARETZ 7.5.2002.
Gordon, N. (2008). "Human Rights, Social Space and Power: Why do some NGOs Exert More Influence than Others?" The International Journal of Human Rights **12**(1): 23–39.
Gordon, N. and N. Berkovitch (2007). "Human Rights Discourse in Domestic Settings: How Does it Emerge?" Political Studies **55**(1): 243–266.
Grinberg, H. (2006). The Assassinations HCJ Case: Relief at the MAG Corps, Ynet 14.12.06, available at: http://www.ynet.co.il/articles/0,7340,L-3340211,00.html [accessed 28.4.15]
HAARETZ editorial (2009). Inappropriate appointment, HAARETZ 29.1.2009. available at: http://www.haaretz.com/print-edition/opinion/inappropriate-appointment-1.269094 [accessed 28.4.15].
Harel, A. (2003). MAG: We will not approve war crimes, but it is not possible to investigate 2,000 death incidents. HAARETZ.
HCJ (680/1988). "Schnitzer vs. Chief Military Censor."

HCJ (769/2002). Public Committee against Torture in Israel vs. Government of Israel.
HCJ (1635/1990). " PD 45 (1) Zarzevsky vs. The Prime Minister."
Ilani, O. (2009). Lecturers say IDF officer who justified Gaza strikes should not teach law. HAARETZ 26.1.2009.
Inbar, Z. (2002). "The MAG Corps and the Held Territories " Law and Military: the IDF legal system's publication **16**(1).
Inbar, Z. (2005). Scales and Sword: The basis of military law in Israel Israel Defense Forces Publishing, MAG Corps.
Johnson, R. (1993). Editor's Introduction: Pierre Bourdieu on Art, Literature and Culture The Field of Cultural Production: Essays on Art and Literature. R. Johnson. New York, Columbia University Press.
Keidar, R. (2012). Interview with Maayan Geva on 17.12.2012.
Kretzmer, D. (2002). The Occupation of Justice: The Supreme Court of Israel and the Occupied Territories. New York, State University of New York Press.
Lahav, D. (2002). Background paper for a discussion of the International Criminal Court. Jerusalem, The Knesset Research and Information Center
Luban, J. D. (2013). "Military Necessity and the Cultures of Military Law." Leiden Journal of International Law **26**(2): 315–349.
MAG (1961). Military Authorities in an Occupied Territory
MAG (1968). 1967/8 MAG Annual Report MAG. Israel.
MAG (1969). 1968/9 MAG Annual Report MAG. Israel.
Matar, A. (2006). "How is Asa Kasher Possible?." Mi'taam **6**.
Mazuz, M. (2007). The testimony of the Attorney General, Meni Mazuz, to the Winograd Commission, available at: http://www.vaadatwino.gov.il/statements.html - null [accessed 28.4.15]
Mazuz, M. (2013). Interview with Maayan Geva, 6.2.13.
Mendelblit, A. (2007). The testimony of the MAG, Avihai Mendelblit to the Winograd Commission, available at: http://www.vaadatwino.gov.il/statements.html - null [accessed 28.4.15]
Mendelblit, A. (2009a). Consultancy Under Fire. HAARETZ 29.1.2009.
Mendelblit, A. (2010a). The testimony of the MAG, Avihai Mendelblit, in front of the Public Commission to Examine the Maritime Incident of 31 May 2010, Turkel Commission, Part 2.
Meridor, D. and H. Fass (2006). The Battle of the 21st Century: Democracy Fighting Terror. Jerusalem, The Israel Democracy Institute Press.
Mitchell, G. (2001). Sharm El-Sheikh Fact-Finding Committee Report, available at: http://eeas.europa.eu/mepp/docs/mitchell_report_2001_en.pdf[accessed 29.4.15].
Neuman, N. (2007). "Legal Consultancy in Battle." Systems (Ma'arachot) **411**: 36–41.
Officer E, E. (2012). Interview with Maayan Geva, 28.11.12.

Ravid, B. (2009). IDF colonel to teach TAU law course, despite critics' bid to stop her: PM calls professors who opposed appointment of IDF Colonel to TAU law school 'arrogant hypocrites.'. HAARETZ 24.6.2013.
Rosenzweig, I. and Y. Shany (2009) Update on Universal Jurisdiction: Spanish Court of Appeals Decides to Close the Inquiry into the Targeted Killing of Salah Shehadeh, available at: http://en.idi.org.il/analysis/terrorism-and-democracy/issue-no-8/update-on-universal-jurisdiction-spanish-court-of-appeals-decides-to-close-the-inquiry-into-the-targeted-killing-of-salah-shehadeh/[accssed 28.4.15].
Roth, K. (2001). The Case for Universal Jurisdiction, Council on Foreign Relations, available at: https://www.foreignaffairs.com/articles/2001-09-01/case-universal-jurisdiction [accessed 28.4.15].
Roytman, Y. (2013). "Inner legal supervision in time of combat " The Gates of Trial (Sha'arei Mishpat) **6**.
Sfard, M. (2004). "International Litigation in Domestic Courts." The Trial (HaMishpat) **9**.
Shamgar, M. (1967a). Ribon's article in Ha'aretz, 22.10.1967. MAG: 1.
Shamgar, M. (1967b). Reaction to the finding of weapon, 14.6.2967. MAG.
Shamgar, M. (1971). "The Observance of International Law in the Administered Territories " Israel Yearbook on Human Rights **1**: 262.
Shamgar, M. (2002). "Conversation with Cheif Justice (retired), Meir Shamgar " IDF Law Review **16**(3).
Shamir, R. (1990). ""Landmark Cases" and the Reproduction of Legitimacy: The Case of Israel's High Court of Justice." Law & Society Review **24**(3): 781–805.
Shamir, R. (1994). "Ha'Politika shel Ha'Svirut [The Politics of Reasonableness.]." Teoria u'Bikoret(5): 7–22.
Sharfman, D. (1993). Living Without a Constitution, Civil Rights in Israel. New York, M.E Sharpe.
Shnayderman, R. (2005). Take No Prisoners: The Fatal Shooting of Palestinians by Israeli Security Forces during "Arrest Operations", available at: http://www.btselem.org/sites/default/files2/publication/200505_take_no_prisoners_eng.pdf [accessd 28.4.15].
Stern, Y. Z. (2010). Decade in Review: A Rocky Road for Israeli Courts, The Israel Democracy Institute, available at: http://en.idi.org.il/analysis/articles/decade-in-review-a-rocky-road-for-israeli-courts [accessed 28.4.15].
Strasberg-Cohen, C. (2011). Report by the special Commission investigating targeted killing - Saleh Shh'ade, available at: http://mfa.gov.il/MFA/AboutIsrael/State/Law/Pages/Salah_Shehadeh-Special_Investigatory_Commission_27-Feb-2011.aspx [accessed 28.4.15].
Straschnov, A. (2013). Interview with Maayan Geva 31.12.12.
The State of Israel (2009). The operation in Gaza 27 December 2008 – 18 January 2009: Factual and legal aspects, available at: http://mfa.gov.il/MFA_

Graphics/MFA Gallery/Documents/GazaOperation w Links.pdf [accessed 29.4.15].
The State of Israel (2010a). "Gaza Operation Investigations: a Second Update, available at: http://www.mfa.gov.il/MFA_Graphics/MFA Gallery/Documents/GazaUpdateJuly2010.pdf [accessed 28.4.15]."
The State of Israel (2010b). "Gaza Operation Investigations: an Update, available at: http://mfa.gov.il/MFA_Graphics/MFA Gallery/Documents/GazaOperation InvestigationsUpdate.pdf [accessed 29.4.15]."
Weizman, E. (2010a). "Forensic Architecture: Only the criminal can solve the crime." Radical Philosophy **164**.
Winograd (2008). Winograd Commission Report - The commission of inquiry into the events of military engagement in Lebanon 2006.
Yoaz, Y. (2005). There is no need for shame: targeted killing is legal HAARETZ 8.3.2005.

CHAPTER 4

# Military Lawyers Making Law: The Contextual Transformations of the MAG Corps' Legal Practice and the Constitution of Law

## 4.1 Introduction

So far we have seen that military legal practice is set in a field and shaped by this field's logic and a variety of institutions and forces, rather than being an isolated operation. The preceding chapters have investigated this field and set up a map of its institutions, and their relative power and relationships, as these changed over time. This analysis has not yet addressed the MAG Corps' practice in detail, the changes this practice has undergone over time, and the relative impact it exerts both over the field and beyond its boundaries. This chapter investigates military legal practice by examining closely the character of, and changes in, the profession of military lawyer set within the map of the field outlined in the previous chapter. This discussion positions military legal practitioners as the central focus of its attention, interrogating their practice through interview materials and documents. The interrogation of this site provides analytical and practical means for tapping into the legal field and the making of its logic and power. This enquiry highlights a crucial facet of the historical shifts the Israeli legal field has undergone.

Set within this framework, the chapter is divided into two sections. The first sets out a triple-layered analysis of military legal practice in its making of (a) legal logic; (b) the field's boundaries with politics and military agenda; and (c) the power of the legal field. This discussion builds on various aspects of transformation that military legal practice underwent between 1967 and 2000, with reference to the goals of legal practice,



M. Geva, *Law, Politics and Violence in Israel/Palestine*,
DOI 10.1007/978-3-319-34153-8_4

law's potential impact over military conduct, perspectives on law vis-à-vis violence and morality, and lawyers' institutional positioning. The second section of the chapter analyses recent trends in law in the context of these discussions, i.e. the making of legal logic, the field's boundary and power, in the specific context of the army's post-2000 interpretation, reliance and use of international humanitarian law.

Existing research on state lawyers has identified distinctive characteristics for civil and military practitioners. The civil and military institutions are founded on different grounds in social, organisational and ideological terms, and each is characterised by particular interests and goals. A fundamental area investigated in research on these themes is the supposed meeting point, or clash, between obligations and demands stemming from law, and those originating from the army and the state (Rhode 2000; Shamgar 2003; Bilder and Vagts 2004; Weisberg 2004; Clark 2005). The key question these writings address is where these lawyers' loyalty lies. Perhaps contrary to common assumptions, these studies do not argue that military lawyers are necessarily more loyal to the military institution rather than to law, or that they are more easily swayed by a military agenda in comparison with civil lawyers—some have actually argued the contrary case (Sands 2008).

Describing a conflict between national ideology and law, the American legal scholar David Luban phrases the question: 'How can a military officer separate the duty of a patriot from that of an advocate?' (2010, p. 2004). But this very question, as with any other account that assumes a clash between civil and military institutions or between a military or legal agenda, is lacking analytically. The problem is that this perspective presupposes it is possible to practise law detached from power relations and politics, and to detect, analytically and practically, a departure from law in favour of a political or military agenda. This position is grounded implicitly in the assumption that law, somewhere, somehow, exists in a 'pure' form. It then follows that such perspectives may assume that, for example, the state's civic mechanisms uphold truer legal standards than a military legal system or vice versa, and that there is an inherent clash between 'true' law and military interest. This is a static, ahistorical perception of law that cannot account for law's continual change and transformation. In this field-based, contextual, power-sensitive account of law, practitioners' own perspectives on political, organisational or other tensions are important analytically, not because of the extent of their interference with a legal truth, but because these are articulations of military lawyers' positions and expressions of their practice. Such analytical positioning follows this account's understanding of law as a dynamic, contextual and structurally-shaped creation of power relations and the field's inner logic. A military agenda, which Luban identifies as a non-legal disruption or as a challenge inherent in military legal practice, plays a part in the making of the field to the extent that it is incorporated into legal practice and the field's logic. This means that there is some correlation between the significance of military goals in a legal context and the MAG Corps' relative power in the field. The military legal system's particular measure of capital feeds into law's logic, which then becomes, in one way or another, part of the practice of all the field's institutions and agents. This interplay of logic and power is in fact the production process of law rather than a diversion from it.

## 4.2 Military Lawyers' Contribution to the Field's Logic, Boundaries and Power

This section examines how international military legal practice contributed to socio-historical changes in law between 1967 and 2000. Shifts are conceptualised by a three-tier analysis, comprising the making of logic, the field's boundary, and its power. This investigation is founded on multiple avenues and materials—fundamental changes in the body of legal conventions applied to the OPT; legal interpretations formed; practitioners' habitus, i.e. the manifestations of structure in views and perspectives; organisational alterations; and lawyers' positions about morality and violence, as elements making up part of the field's logic. This analysis identifies transformative moments leading to distinctive phases in the history of Israeli military legal practice in the context of the OPT. These turning points are the international division's 1968 establishment and the 1987 Intifada. Set in the context of the field, an analysis of incremental shifts in the work of the MAG Corps and its international legal team provides, based on interviews and documents, an opportunity to examine lawyers' practice, sustaining and recreating law.

On 10 June 1967, as Israel seized control of the West Bank and Gaza, officers of the MAG Corps opened sealed boxes containing basic documents of international law, which, as noted in Chapter 3, the military legal system had prepared in advance for a potential occasion of an occupation (Kretzmer 2002; Shamgar 2013). This setup follows international law's principles, by which this law is to govern the situation of an occupation. That moment marked the beginning of a new legal era. Military order number one, waiting in these boxes and printed in both Hebrew and Arabic, asserted the authority of the Israeli army as the sovereign power in the newly occupied territories. Military orders, those the MAG Corps had prepared in advance and the many more to follow, constituted and formed the character of Israel's control over the OPT. This new situation of occupation required the army's legal system to provide expertise in international law. A division specialising in international law was established the following year to serve this purpose.

As noted earlier, on its establishment in 1968, the International Law Division had only three officers and its impact over military conduct, i.e. power beyond the legal field, was marginal. Israel had only recently begun to engage systematically with international law, and as a result, the newly founded military International Law Division was an institution positioned in an emerging field that included only a few other bodies and had very little power. An additional key institution in the field was the High Court of Justice, which dealt with petitions concerning the OPT. There were no organisations systematically and structurally opposing the army's legal system and this meant that struggle over legal logic in this field was limited.

The legal toolkit informing the International Law Division's practice and its contribution to the field's logic was based on the Israeli authorities' decisions regarding the application of legal conventions. These decisions asserted the application of the Hague Regulations, but not the Fourth Geneva Convention; however, it did declare a voluntarily application of the 'humanitarian' clauses of the latter (Kretzmer 2002). Notably, Israeli authorities did not disclose which of the Geneva Convention's clauses they considered 'humanitarian' (Sfard 2004). Regardless of Israel's policies, in the early years of the occupation international humanitarian law included relatively few conventions and tools made to protect civilians in war and under occupation. International legal tools were written later, and these changes were to affect the Israeli legal field. The existing legal conventions in 1968 were the basis for the military officers' practice, who then built on this framework to formulate multiple legal orders made to govern the OPT. Israeli military legal practice, in its writing of orders based on international law, is an operation making law unconstrained by the substantive and formal procedures set in a civil context. Unlike law-making in the civil Israeli context, wherein a bill is brought to parliament votes, the military legal system simply codifies law. This means that the MAG Corps exercises great power in the OPT, power that cannot be compared to a civil legal system. The difference between the Israeli civil system and the military legal system applied to the OPT reflects the distinctive relationships of the Israeli public and its state's authorities, on the one hand, and the Palestinian people and its occupying power on the other.

The general legal framework defining the MAG Corps' premise of action, i.e. which conventions and provisions will be included and which excluded from the legal body governing Palestinians and military conduct in the OPT, were to continue and change over time, and have a great effect on both the army and the Palestinian governed population. Despite the controversial choice of inclusion and exclusion of specific legal provisions, in the early days of international law, division lawyers considered their work to be an ardent application of a legal code and one that also carried significant normative weight. This contradiction between the strategic selection of legal tools and a self-perception of earnest and moral legal practice was a result of the authorities' political—legal calculation on the one hand and legal practitioners' legal habitus, which entailed a solid grounding in a liberal ethos, on the other. Presenting an earnest belief in law, a senior member of the team said in an interview given for the purposes of this study: 'The idea was to work by the book ... We applied the law as is, without tricks. I didn't try to be smart with the convention ... Morality guided our work all the time' (Officer E 2012). This officer's perspective sees the legal governing of the occupation as a straightforward operation and one detached from power relations, namely political power ('tricks' in this context, hinting at politics). Legal work in this regard is seen as almost a technical task, an application of a ready-made system of rules to the specific situation of the OPT. This officer also made explicit reference to morality, in this account legal practice is founded on a moral basis.

Shamgar, MAG at the time, adds in an interview his own perspective, also one heavily embedded in normative terms: 'My ambition was to educate people to possess knowledge of international law. My dream was then, and I still believe it will come true, at least partially, that we will run an exemplary military regime adhering to all the rules required by international law' (Shamgar 2013). Shamgar's statement demonstrates a grand ethos of law and is of particular importance in the light of his own formative impact over both the military and civil legal systems dealing with the OPT. His vision of a law-abiding occupation is a declaration of belief in international law and its capacity to construct appropriate and just authority. Zvi Hadar (1972), MAG in 1978–73 contributed his perspective on law's ties with morality and published an article debating the legal obligation of soldiers to disobey their commanders on the occasion of illegal orders.

Thus in the early days of the occupation, in the face of the chaotic legal realities of a changing regime, the MAG Corps officers referred to their collection of legal documents in order to reinstate order and sense. The officers' outlooks reflected a solid belief in the fairness and impartial nature of international law, one that they considered largely untouched by politics. Practitioners at this time assumed an intrinsic connection between law, justice and morality. Law in this context is a positive force that exceeds the sum of its parts. Practitioners' habitus manifested in these terms sees lawyers as facilitators of an honest and fair operation. Notwithstanding their beliefs and conviction, the military's international legal practitioners had a negligible impact on military activities at this time, were positioned in the backrooms, and were not obvious partners in decision-making processes. Dov Shefi, the first Commanding Officer of the International Law Division, substantiated this point by writing in an article: 'The exact nature of the cooperation between the legal adviser and the combatant forces is still not clear ... the legal adviser can assist in solving problems arising in the field even from his or her position in the rear' (Shefi 1983, p. 130).

And so lawyers' perspective and practice in the early days of the occupation and the International Law Division reflect a particular phase in law. The Division was at once a credible institution in the emerging legal field and a marginal body in terms of its power in the military institution. This situation reflects law's position in the OPT in more general terms—the military legal system was the key legal institution overseeing the army's conduct in these territories, but it did not have much impact over the army's actions and operations. The MAG Corps officers had an epic perspective of their role and the position of law in relation to the OPT. This perspective regarded law as being a positive force advancing justice. This advancement of justice was seen as a straightforward administration of existing rules rather than a flexible operation, making lawyers vessels rather than entrepreneurs. The Division's limited power beyond the boundaries of the legal field means that it did not challenge political authorities or the status quo regarding the separation of authority between the legal and political fields.

The 1987 popular uprising, the Intifada, radically changed the MAG Corps and its International Law Division's practice. This was a novel phase in the occupation, when largely unarmed mass demonstrations and resistance were met with harsh military measures. The army, in consultation with its MAG and the International Law Division, developed various policies to deal with the uprising. Among these measures were large-scale administrative detentions, house demolitions, curfews, the closure of Palestinian institutions, and a reformulation of the rules governing military violence. The High Court of Justice was then flooded with hundreds of petitions, many submitted by the recently-established NGOs (Kretzmer 2002). The MAG Corps seniors testify that the Intifada was the most legalistic military confrontation the Israeli army had carried out up to that point (Yahav and Amit-Kohn 1993; Straschnov 1994).

From the perspective of MAG Corps officers, the Intifada marked a shift into a new phase of legal practice. Faced with unprecedented violent situations in the OPT, the army's legal practitioners felt that the existing law was inadequate, and that legal innovation was needed in order to handle these situations. At this point, legal work became at once a creative operation and its practitioners were unequivocally and explicitly reforming the field's logic. The International Law Division's Commanding Officer at the time, David Yahav, said in an interview given for the purposes of this study:

> There were no precedents to the things we did with international law. We couldn't open a book and see what's the solution ... Everything was very new. International law addresses peace and addresses war. It doesn't address a situation of a popular uprising that is partly violent and partly not so violent ... there were no legal sources for that, and we had to create them. (Yahav 2013; my translation)

Amnon Straschnov, MAG 1986–91 described this situation in similar terms:

> While the law of peace and war was written mainly in Geneva and the Hague based on the lessons of the battlefields of Europe, the laws of popular uprising were created and institutionalised in Tel Aviv and Jerusalem, based on the riots and disturbance of public order in Nablus, Gaza and Jenin. (Straschnov 1994, p. 10; my translation)

The comparison between the international forums of Geneva and the Hague on the one hand and the Israeli military legal system on the other, encapsulates the MAG Corps' spirit in its handling of law at this time, engaging with it in a constitutive manner and with a considerable measure of chutzpah. Despite international legal practice in the Israeli army having changed immensely from the late 1980s to the present day, the quality of innovation has been a persistent facet of these lawyers' practice and habitus ever since.

The spirit of innovation indicated the military legal system's contribution to the remaking of the field's inner logic through flexible legal interpretations and the creation of orders reinventing the OPT's governance. One example of the legal changes introduced related to the army's rules of engagement, i.e. instructions for and restrictions on opening fire. In the course of the Intifada, military commanders and legal practitioners held intense ongoing negotiations regarding these instructions, leading to their continuous modification (Straschnov 1994). Aspects negotiated between lawyers and military decision-makers included the permitted distance between a soldier shooting and the person to be shot in the case of confrontations between Israeli soldiers and Palestinians, permitted kinds of ammunition, and the consideration of new types of weaponry.

Among the military means introduced at this time were rubber bullets. These are steel bullets covered in rubber, which the army began to use in August 1988 (Talmor 1990) and had become something of a symbol of Israel's handling of the Intifada. In this symbolic discussion, these bullets supposedly exemplified 'soft' violence. The army's Chief of Staff stated that rubber bullets are not lethal when fired from a distance exceeding 70 metres, and that orders prohibited the firing of them at close range (Ginosar 1988). Despite these declared safeguards, however, the bullets proved to be lethal. In January 1989 the IDF Spokesperson admitted that 47 Palestinians had been killed as a result of rubber-bullet shooting, and by March 1990 the number had risen to 128 (IDF 1990). From the MAG Corps officers' perspective the negotiations around the introduction and use of rubber bullets were part of the legal system's efforts to curtail the use of force, and prevent injuries and fatalities among Palestinians (Straschnov 1994).

Another manifestation of innovative, logic-producing practice was the treatment of children who threw stones at soldiers. The age of legal liability in the OPT under the military regime was 12, thus younger children could not be held liable for their actions. In these circumstances, the MAG Corps devised a military order in May 1988 instructing parents of children younger than 12 who had been accused of throwing stones to place a monetary deposit with the military authorities. The deposit was to be repaid in a year's time, provided the child had not been charged with throwing stones subsequent to the initial incident. NGOs challenged this policy in a court petition but the High Court of Justice found it legal (HCJ 591/1988). This policy de facto rearranged the position of children in relation to the legal system. This novelty made children part of the military legal order, as age no longer marked an exception in terms of liability. All were then potentially subject to the army's punitive system.

The MAG Corps' efforts to assert power and make a significant impact on the army's operation led to conflicts with the political authorities. Legal practitioners testify that their work at this time involved a continuous and challenging attempt to restrain the demands of political and military decision-makers. Confrontations between political decision-makers and legal practitioners are manifestations of the struggle over the legal field's boundary with politics. Straschnov (1994) made these confrontations the key narrative of his memoir published after the Intifada and titled 'Justice under Fire'. Ilan Shiff, the MAG who followed Straschnov, dryly described this struggle in an interview given for the purposes of this study: 'The MAG Corps has always seen itself as the watchdog of the rule of law, and this led to uneasy arguments' (Shiff 2013). The restriction of violence and the grounding of this restriction in morality was a central theme in practitioners' perspectives. These practitioners' perspectives reflect a perception of law as a means of limiting and restraining violence stemming from military and political powers.

Some of these legal—political disagreements revolved around the issue of beating. This became a key struggle between political decision-makers and the military legal system in the Intifada—how to evaluate and handle beatings by soldiers of Palestinians involved in the uprising. Around the beginning of the Intifada, Yizhak Rabin, then Minister of Defense, was famously quoted as instructing military commanders to 'break arms and legs' as a means of repressing the uprising (*New York Times* 1990). David Yahav, the ILD's Commanding Officer at the time attests: 'There was that phase of "Break their arms and legs'" and I told him [Amnon Straschnov, the MAG] that if there was no direct guidance from the Chief of Staff [to stop the beatings], then I would quit ... I felt that the situation was very frail' (Yahav 2013). In his memoir, MAG Straschnov (1994) writes of circulating a memo aimed at stopping beatings that was received with harsh criticism from military and political officials alike.

The battle over lawyers' jurisdiction and law's boundaries occurred alongside a struggle between the High Court of Justice and the civil political authorities over the areas the court was to review and the measure of influence the court was to have. To recall, in the 1980s, the two major parties, Ha'Avoda and Ha'Likud, did not have sufficient electoral support to form a stable coalition and the High Court of Justice then filled up the space of authority (Barzilai 1997). Gad Barzilai (2004) argues that, in the absence of political stability, the High Court of Justice was regarded as the country's most reliable civil institution and it gained unparalleled prominence, taking on the consideration of almost all controversial affairs in the country. The court's shift in justiciability, described in the previous chapter, meant a reformulation of the field's power and its boundaries. The MAG Corps' practice in the Intifada was feeding into and had affected the court's transformation. The MAG Corps' authority was supported by the potential or the actual review of the army's policies in court. In this context, military and political decision-makers had to take into account the court's power and involvement when engaging with the MAG Corps. At the same time, the military legal system's own decisions produced material that the court had to take into account. The army's sound position in Israeli politics, intertwined with the structural prioritisation of Israeli interests over those of Palestinians, meant that the court was inclined to support the MAG Corps' decisions. The clash between politics and law during the Intifada was a key element in the habitus of the MAG Corps' practitioners. This clash gave visibility to lawyers' perspectives on law and their own practice because, faced with harsh military violence, these practitioners articulated the military legal system's role and position in relation to politicians and military operational decision-makers.

Thus beyond the cases of rubber bullets, children's legal status and beatings, the Intifada was both an intense and innovative period in the work of the military legal system, and one that occasioned the MAG Corps' intense formulation of legal logic as well as the system's and law's relations with politics. Innovation entailed a multitude of new instructions and rules remaking legal logic and practice. It was also an effort on the part of the legal system to exert as much power as possible over military conduct. These efforts were met with resistance by the political authorities. In light of this, ongoing disputes between legal practitioners on the one hand and military and political decision-makers on the other indicate a struggle over the location and extent of the legal jurisdiction and its power over military operations. From the perspective of legal practitioners, this struggle, at its core, was about upholding a degree of justice and defending individuals from the power of the military and political authorities.

The trend increasing the involvement of legal officers in military conduct that we have seen emerging in the Intifada was a factor that encouraged the formation and growth of human rights NGOs. Another significant factor involved in this trend was the High Court of Justice's increased review of issues concerning Palestinians. This legal dialogue was made possible by the High Court of Justice's shift in justiciability and willingness to review security-related matters. The interaction between the army and NGOs facilitated by the court's review was a self-perpetuating process, by which these bodies' actions feed into one another, pushing towards an increase in the other's activity. NGOs' petitions meant that the MAG Corps was required to present its position in court. NGOs' reports and position papers required it to respond publicly to claims about the army's conduct. In turn, the military legal system's activity triggered more activity on part of the NGOs in the form of public responses to the army's actions, publications and further litigation.

The second Intifada, which began in 2000, again led to the military legal system's resculpting of legal logic, a reconstitution of law vis-à-vis politics, and a major increase in this institution's power. As already discussed, until 2000, the operations of the Israeli army in the OPT were handled within the framework of 'law enforcement', aiming to restore public order, resting on a logic governing police activity rather than a more militarised form of governance. As discussed in the previous chapter, this legal transformation was also directed by the actions of, and relationships between, institutions in the field, namely the High Court of Justice and NGOs. It was the petitioning of NGOs that occasioned discussions about a fundamental change in the legal framework applied in the OPT that led to the High Court of Justice's decision to shape this framework, in co-operation with the MAG Corps. The introduction of the 'Armed Conflict Short of War' framework indicated a radical change, in that the army had begun to use international humanitarian law in an entirely different manner to conduct its operations in the OPT. To analyse the character of changes in law in terms of its logic, power and articulation, interwoven with the shift to the framework of Armed Conflict Short of War, the next section will introduce International Humanitarian Law. This introduction builds on an investigation of two pillars of international humanitarian law: the principle of distinction and the principle of proportionality.

## 4.3 International Humanitarian Law and Its Practice in the Israeli Army: The Contemporary Constitution of Law's Logic, Power and Boundaries

The 1907 Hague Regulations, the four 1949 Geneva Conventions and their 1977 additional protocols make up the primary legal body governing war and belligerent occupation. This section describes and debates the provisions of these conventions in regulating the wartime status of civilians and the scale of proportion in military attacks.

The distinction between civilians and combatants is one of the pillars of international humanitarian law, wherein combatants are a legitimate target of hostilities, and civilians are to be protected from violence: 'The civilian population and individual civilians shall enjoy general protection against dangers arising from military operations; the civilian population as such, as well as individual civilians, shall not be the object of attack' (Protocol I Additional to the Geneva Conventions, Art. 51, 1977).

This distinction inevitably leads to questions about the identity and identification of those classified in each category. Researchers and military lawyers alike argue that contemporary warfare presents particular challenges to this distinction (for example, Best 1984; Hoffman 2000; Kanstroom 2003; Sassoli 2003; Dinstein 2004; Schmitt 2009; Gade 2010). In response to these challenges, the International Committee of the Red Cross, the institution named under international humanitarian law as its controlling authority, published in 2008 a document titled 'Interpretive Guidance on the Notion of Direct Participation in Hostilities under International Humanitarian Law' (ICRC 2008). This text aims to clarify the circumstances by which a civilian is deemed to have participated directly in hostilities and consequently loses his/her protection. Notwithstanding the novelties of contemporary warfare, controversy about the notion of the civilian is hardly a new discussion. Hugo Slim (2003), in his study of this term, shows that while commentators debate contemporary challenges to the definition of 'the civilian' as though it were a novel discussion, this has actually been a contested concept in varied historical, social, theological and political contexts. Slim traces this thread from the Bible to European medieval knights, imperial authorities, and to the 'new wars' of the 1990s. Presenting the contestation of the civilian—combatant division from an Israeli perspective, Amos Yadlin and Asa Kasher, the former being a retired senior military officer and latter an academic publicly dubbed the 'Israeli Defence Forces philosopher' and the author of the 'IDF Code of Conduct', published an article outlining a 'legal doctrine for war' (2005). This doctrine is supposedly an ethical revision of international humanitarian law, adapting international law to the context of terrorism and asymmetrical warfare. The inherent immorality of terrorism, the writers argue, necessitates a reformulation of the legal code. One of the core elements of Kasher and Yadlin's document is a new definition of 'the enemy', one deconstructing the distinction between civilians and combatants. The document lays out a taxonomy of groups of people by which the lives of Israeli soldiers are to be prioritised over those of Palestinian civilians:

> According to the ordinary conception underlying the distinction between combatants and non-combatants, the former have a lighter package of state duties than the latter. Consequently, the duty to minimize casualties among combatants during combat is last on the list of priorities or next to last, if terrorists are excluded from the category of non-combatants. We reject such conceptions, because we consider them to be immoral. A combatant is a citizen in uniform. In Israel, quite often he is a conscript or on reserve duty. His blood is as red and thick as that of citizens who are not in uniform. His life is as precious as the life of anyone else. (Kasher and Yadlin 2005, p. 17)

This legal deconstruction of the distinction between civilians and combatants has not been adopted formally by the Israeli army, nor was it reviewed by the court, but examinations of military operations indicate that in practice it has been, by and large, accepted. These tendencies are not an Israeli particularity—research focused on Israel's armed conflicts (Levy 2010; Kot 2011) and studies of US and UK wars (Shaw 2005) has similarly shown that all these militaries have in fact been operating in line with similar assumptions relating to the hierarchy of lives in war.

International humanitarian law builds on its distinction between civilians and combatants to prohibit attacks that do not discriminate between these two categories of persons. In Article 51 of the additional Protocol I of 1977, the prohibition of indiscriminate attacks creates an equation of proportion. An attack is illegal if its expected incidental damage to civilians is *excessive* in relation to predicted military gain:

> Indiscriminate attacks are prohibited; Among others, the following types of attacks are to be considered as indiscriminate ...an attack which may be expected to cause incidental loss of civilian life, injury to civilians, damage to civilian objects, or a combination thereof, which would be excessive in relation to the concrete and direct military advantage anticipated.

Critical researchers of international humanitarian law debate the evasive nature of this code and the problems that accompany an evaluation of such proportions (Walzer 1977; Berman 2004; Weizman 2009). In this way, an important area of concern and dispute relates to the weighing up of components and of what constitutes 'excessive' in terms of loss of lives, injury and destruction. An additional concern highlighted is that a scale of proportion is, by its very nature, limitless in that it can potentially defend attack of any magnitude, as long as the military advantage anticipated is comparably major (Kennedy 2006).

Beyond difficulties relating to assessing proportionate attacks, the idea of the wartime calculation of proportionate violence itself deserves analytical attention. Conceptualising the roots of the notion of proportion, Eyal Weizman (2011) locates this calculation on the conjunction of morality and economy, or justice and accounting. Weizman traces this pattern in Abraham's negotiation with God over the fate of Sodom, the city of sinners. In response to God's wish to destroy the city, Abraham pleads for it and suggests a numeric evaluation. He asks God if the city should be destroyed if it has a hundred just men or if it has only ten. God engages in this negotiation and accepts Abraham's plea. For Weizman, this is similar to the legal calculation of advantage and collateral damage, bringing justice to the economy of destruction.

David Kennedy (2006) also points out that the international humanitarian law equation of 'proportionality' or limitation of civilian death becomes, through an interpretive legal process, a contradictory consideration that in fact undermines the civilian—combatant distinction. The legal limit is that no more civilians should be killed than is 'necessary' in order to advance the military agenda. But the calculation of 'proportion' as such relativises civilians compared to combatants, and in this sense undermines the fundamental distinction between the two categories. This means that in international humanitarian law's codes, civilians and combatants are in fact measured against one another. Thus there is an inherent tension between proportionality and the distinction between civilians and combatants.

The military legal system's adoption of international humanitarian law facilitated significant alterations in the practice of law in the OPT. The field's logic was revised, leading to major changes in policies regulating the army's conduct. Among these were the rules of engagement, and the investigation and potential indictment of soldiers. This was also a decisive moment that reshuffled relations in the field, and the relative division of capital structuring the field and its logic. The settings of international humanitarian law lead to fewer and less restrictive obligations on the part of the army. Consequently, this alteration diminished the possibility of subjecting military actions and practices to the court's review (Finkelstein 2002), instead increasing the MAG Corps' capital since its practice became less likely to be scrutinised in court.

The turn to international humanitarian law was a key factor in the intensification process of legal work in the Israeli army. This intensification, which meant amplified legal practice applied to the army's operations, was a profoundly innovative task. The practice included the construction of multiple policies and regulations for the Israeli army in the OPT. Practitioners' innovation in law was a significant facet in this change, prompting a radical change of legal logic and a reform of the limits and terms of law's involvement in military operations. A senior MAG officer serving at this time said in an interview:

> We were the first to recognise, within the IDF, that what we have, to all intents and purposes, is a war, an armed conflict. This was incredible innovation ... the perception up until that point was that an armed conflict can only occur between two armies, and not between an army and a terrorist organisation. This decision resulted in a shift in the paradigm of armed conflict. One difference is that civilians may be killed. It had operational implications regarding consultancy, and concrete matters such as targeted killing. This was the root of the intensification of legal consultancy, which reached much deeper than ever before. (Officer D 2013)

This officer's proactive spirit is telling—this is not a case of legal officers responding to pressure or to specific questions. Rather, it is a case of profoundly innovative legal practice. This innovation was a driving force for fundamental change in the governance of the OPT. Targeted killing operations, discussed in Chapter 3 of this study, provide an example of lawyers' novel involvement in military operations. Concrete decisions about warfare targeting have now become a legal issue, and lawyers have become essential partners in the planning processes of warfare.

Within the work of the MAG Corps, the shift to the framework of humanitarian law has had multi-faceted implications. This shift was, first, a reformulation of the body of law that provides the field's logic, i.e. the 'materials' structuring its struggles, directing the means available for the institutions involved in such wrangles and these struggles' possible outcomes. Moreover, the integration of international humanitarian law into the Israeli army's operations was a process of repositioning legal practice within the army, bringing lawyers into decision-making forums and closer to the battlefield. This repositioning was not simply a formality, but a substantive remaking of law as such in a military context. It was a reshaping of the boundaries of the legal field—a process shifting law's authority into areas and questions previously located in operational and political arenas, and outside the reach of legal practitioners. This change was interwoven with an increase in the capital of the MAG Corps and its ILD within the legal field, as the court's approval of this legal framework transferred power to the military system. This increase in capital in the field was then translated into a rise in the influence the MAG Corps and the ILD had over non-legal military forums, i.e. an increase in power these bodies exercised outside the boundaries of the legal field.

Earlier modes of military legal practice wherein legal officers were largely physically distant from the battlefields and were not part of the on-the-spot wartime decision-making both reflected and formed a particular separation between the legal, on the one hand, and the political and operational on the other. Later, the increased proximity of legal practitioners to the physical battlefield reformulated both of these categories and their terms of differentiation. The intensification of legal work within the army is inseparable from multi-faceted changes in law and legal practice—the changing contents of law when law no longer limits violence but instead takes part in its planning and execution; a redrawing of the boundaries of 'the legal' through its practice, as law is no longer separate from operational—political discussions; an increase in the military legal system's capital within the field in light of the court's distancing from military affairs; and the army legal system's power over military operations. In this sense, shifts in the position of military legal practitioners, including spatial and temporal modifications, reflect and create novel articulations of law. Unlike earlier phases of military legal practice, this configuration of law and politics no longer constitutes a fundamental clash between these areas.

As the power of military legal practitioners changed and grew, a new type of discussion emerged, one concerned with lawyers exercising an excessive degree of power over decision-making processes and an anxiety about a 'confusion' about the location of responsibility and authority. The government-appointed Winograd Commission argued to the effect that military lawyers should provide advice prior to operations and review the results of attacks in their aftermath, but refrain from taking part in on-the-spot decision-making during operations (Winograd 2008, p. 488). Critical perspectives on this recommendation described it as a discarding of the lawyers when decisions are actually being made (Blau and Feldman 2009; Cohen 2011). Gabriella Blum (2009), an ILD past practitioner and legal scholar at present, approaches this situation from the perspective of the lawyer and argues that governments are choosing to be overly dependent on legal advice as a substitute for political decision-making. Blum makes these arguments in a particular political context, namely the criticism directed at US government attorneys in the wake of controversial legal guidance revolving around the US 'War on Terror'. Both the Winograd Report and Blum's standpoints are at odds with the Israeli legal field's novel boundaries with military—political authority and the MAG Corps' increased power.

Law's contemporary form presents more blurred separations between 'the legal' and 'the political' in comparison with its past phases. This movement also implies a key distancing from elements that were at one point essential to its logic. Two of these elements that have changed significantly are morality and violence. Law in its current phase reflects and feeds into lawyers' changed articulation of the relationships between both law and morality, and law and violence. Unlike their predecessors, the ILD's post-2000 practitioners no longer consider morality to be an inherent part of the job. Unlike legal practitioners in the early days of the occupation, they do not regard law as a just force, fairly governing the OPT or even aiming to govern it fairly. On this point, an officer said in an interview: 'We are not moral advisers ... We are legal advisers, and our advice is legal ... everyone has a moral perspective: every commander, every soldier and us too' (Officer B 2011). Another officer said to this effect in an interview: 'We are not responsible for morality. Morality is not relevant for the work of this team ... The question of whether or not the IDF is a moral army is of no concern to us' (in Geva 2011, p. 35). MAG Mendelblit similarly refused to make use of the cliché common in the national context referring to the Israeli army as the 'world's most moral army'. He said, instead: 'I determine that the IDF acts lawfully. I don't consider myself to be an expert in morality' (in Harel 2009).

Legal practice and law's weaker ties with morality as reflected in the Israeli army ironically, but unsurprisingly, coincide with the supposed structural transference of moral battlefield responsibility to law. David Kennedy argues convincingly in this context:

> We no longer need to decide for ourselves whether war is civilized, whether killing this civilian is a good idea, whether attacking the town is ethically defensible. The law of armed conflict will do that for us—while lending itself to strategic deployment. (Kennedy 2006, p. 141)

In this sense, the inclusion of legal criteria determining an acceptable measure of destruction and death means that legal practice takes up the space of a moral debate, regardless of lawyers' own perspective on their practice and its relationship with moral questions. The involvement of lawyers in decision-making forums and the moral weight assigned to law in these situations means that, de facto, much of the moral weight had shifted to lawyers precisely when legal practice itself had moved away from moral considerations, instead deferring to law that has no moral aspirations. This means that in these decision-making debates a moral account is assumed to occur elsewhere and, in fact, does not take place.

The growing closeness between legal practice and operational decision-making implies a significant alteration in law's relationship with violence. Practitioners no longer consider the limitation of violence to be a fundamental part of their role as lawyers, in stark contrast to the perspectives of legal officers serving in the first Intifada. An ILD officer serving in the 2000s describes his professional goal in these circumstances in the following words: 'Our purpose is not to place restrictions on the army, but to provide it with the tools for victory, in a way that is legal' (Blau and Feldman 2009). This perspective is fundamentally different from that of officers serving in parallel positions in earlier times, when lawyers related to their work in terms of promoting a legal and just vision, restraining violence. The new legal practice provides tools, directs and shapes violence. This novel situation was the background for legal practice carried out by the army in its 2008/9 offensive in Gaza. The next chapter will explore this military operation as a means of investigating the contemporary legal state of affairs.

## 4.4 Conclusion

This chapter addressed military legal practice and practitioners' habitus and perspective as these altered historically, as a means of understanding the making of law in this context. The chapter's analysis was grounded in three dynamic dimensions—the field's logic, its power, and its boundaries. This investigation identified three distinctive phases in the MAG Corps' practice. The first began in the early days of the occupation, the second emerged in 1987, in the face of the first Intifada, and the third, and current, phase began in 2000. A major difference between these phases is the collection of legal conventions the military legal system applies to the OPT. An additional key factor is the spirit of legal practice, which shifted in the late 1980s from a formalist standpoint to an innovative perspective on law. This feature continues to characterise law's present practice. Other central changes are the MAG Corps' capital in the field and its power beyond the field's boundaries. The International Law Division was in its early days an important institution in the field, but the field as a whole did not have much power and this Division did not have a significant impact on the army's conduct. This balance changed in the face of the first Intifada, when the MAG Corps claimed greater power, facilitated by the High Court of Justice. The third phase again rearranged this situation, making the renamed International Law Department an important institution that forms part of the army's strategic discussions and concrete operational planning.

Alongside these changes, law's logic altered fundamentally in relation to both morality and violence. In its transitions, law has abandoned its status as a supposed facilitator of justice and morality. It has also moved away from past efforts to limit violence and restrict military operations. This change manifests in the terms of differentiation between legal advice and operational decision-making. Whereas in the past legal officers retained a spatial, institutional and conceptual distance from operations, today these separations are more blurred. This is not to say that law has been compromised, but that this is law's contemporary character.

Law's particular phases engaged with politics differently. These differences relate to law's own characteristics in terms of power, roles and the challenges it presents to political authorities. A fundamental change in this context took place in the transition between law's second and third phases. Whereas the first Intifada brought about multiple clashes between legal officers on the one hand, and military and operational decision-makers on the other, law's current phase does not entail a fierce struggle between these powers. This is an indication of law's current form, which no longer presents fundamentally different roles and ambitions in comparison to political authorities. The next chapter focuses on the 2008/9 offensive in Gaza to examine closely law's contemporary phase based on its practice. It interrogates legal practice relating to military policies and specific attacks in order to articulate law's current phase.

## Bibliography

Barzilai, G. (1997). "Between the rule of law and the laws of the ruler: The Supreme Court in Israeli legal culture." International social science journal **49**(2): 193.

Barzilai, G. (2004). How Far Do Justices Go: The Limits of Judicial Decisions Critical Issues in Israeli Society A. Dowty. Westport, Connecticut; London Praeger: 55–68.

Berman, N. (2004). "Privileging Combat? Contemporary Conflict and the Legal Construction of War." Columbia Journal of Transnational Law **43**(1).

Best, J. (1984). "Civilians in Contemporary Wars: A Problem in Ethics, Law, and Fact." 35 Air University Review: 29–40.

Bilder, R. B. and D. F. Vagts (2004). "Speaking Law to Power: Lawyers and Torture." American journal of international law **98** (4): 689–695.

Blau, U. and Y. Feldman (2009). How IDF legal experts legitimized strikes involving Gaza civilians. HAARETZ 23/01/09.

Blum, G. (2009). "The Role of the Client: The President's Role in Government Lawyering " Boston College International & Comparative Law Review **32**: 275–287.

Clark, K. (2005). "Ethical Issues Raised by the OLC Torture Memorandum." Journal of National Security Law **1**: 455–472.

Cohen, A. (2011). "Legal Operational Advice in the Israeli Defense Forces: the International Law Department and the Changing Nature of International Humanitarian Law." Connecticut Journal of International Law **26**(2).

Dinstein, Y. (2004). The conduct of Hostilities under the law of international armed conflict. Cambridge, Cambridge University Press.

Finkelstein, M. (2002). "Law in a Time of War." IDF Law Review **16**(1).

Gade, E. K. (2010). "Defining the Non-Combatant: How do we Determine Who is Worthy of Protection in Violent Conflict?" Journal of Military Ethics **9**(3): 219–242.

Geva, M. (2011). Dynamics of Law, Organisation and Morality in Contemporary Warfare: The right to life in the case of the Israeli military International Law Department. Human Rights Practice, School of Global Studies, University of Gothenburg. **MA**.

Ginosar, S. (1988). Editorial. Davar 5.10.1988.

Hadar, Z. (1972). "Illegal Command." Systems (Ma'arachot) **225**.

Harel, A. (2009). MAG, Brigadier General Mendelblit, speaks about Cast Lead, Chico Tamir and B'Tselem, HAARETZ 18.9.09, available at: http://www.haaretz.co.il/misc/1.1281465 [accessed 28.4.15]

HCJ (591/1988). "Taha vs. Minister of Defense."

Hoffman, M. (2000). "Emerging combatants, war crimes and the future of international humanitarian law." Crime Law and Social Change **34**(1): 99–110.

ICRC (2008). Interpretive Guidance on the Notion of Direct Participation in Hostilities under International Humanitarian Law.
IDF (1990). Press Release 4.3.1990. I. O. IDF Spokesperson.
Kanstroom, D. (2003). "Unlawful Combatants" in the United States: Drawing the Fine Line Between Law and War, Human Rights Magazine, available at: http://www.americanbar.org/publications/human_rights_magazine_home/irr_hr_winter03_unlawful.html [accessed 28.4.15].
Kasher, A. and A. Yadlin (2005). "Military Ethics of Fighting Terror: An Israeli Perspective." Journal of Military Ethics **4**(1): 3–32.
Kennedy, D. (2006). Of War and Law. Princeton, Princeton University Press.
Kot, J.-P. (2011). "Israeli Civilians versus Palestinian Combatants? Reading the Goldstone Report in Light of the Israeli Conception of the Principle of Distinction." Leiden Journal of International Law **24**(4): 961–988.
Kretzmer, D. (2002). The Occupation of Justice: The Supreme Court of Israel and the Occupied Territories. New York, State University of New York Press.
Levy, Y. (2010). "The Tradeoff between Force and Casualties: Israel's Wars in Gaza, 1987–2009." Conflict Management and Peace Science September **27**(4).
Luban, J. D. (2010). "Lawfare and Legal Ethics in Guantánamo." Stanford Law Review **60**: 1981–2026.
New York Times (1990). Israel Declines to Study Rabin Tie to Beatings. 12.7.1990.
Officer B, B. (2011). Interview with Maayan Geva, 20.2.11.
Officer D, D. (2013). Interview with Maayan Geva, 16.1.13.
Officer E, E. (2012). Interview with Maayan Geva, 28.11.12.
Rhode, D. (2000). In the Interests of Justice: Reforming the Legal Profession. Oxford; New York, Oxford University Press.
Sands, P. (2008). Torture Team: deception, cruelty and the compromise of law. London, Allen Lane.
Sassoli, M. (2003). "Unlawful Combatants": The Law and Whether It Needs To Be Revised, including remarks by Daniel Reisner. Ninety-Seventh Annual Meeting Of The American Society Of International Law.
Schmitt, M. N. (2009). "Human Shields in International Humanitarian Law." Columbia Journal of Transnational Law **47**.
Sfard, M. (2004). "International Litigation in Domestic Courts." The Trial (HaMishpat) **9**.
Shamgar, M. (2003). Shamgar Book. Tel Aviv, The Israel Bar Publishing House
Shamgar, M. (2013). Interview with Maayan Geva, 25.2.13.
Shaw, M. (2005). The new western way of war: risk-transfer war and its crisis in Iraq. Cambridge, Polity.
Shefi, D. (1983). "The Status of the Legal Adviser to the Armed Forces: His Functions and Powers." Military Law Review(100): 119–134

Shiff, I. (2013). Interview with Maayan Geva, 30.1.13.
Slim, H. (2003). "Why Protect Civilians? Innocence, Immunity and Enmity in War." International Affairs **79**(3): 481–501.
Straschnov, A. (1994). Justice Under Fire. Tel Aviv, Yedioth Aharonoth Books.
Talmor, R. (1990). The Use of Firearms by the Security Forces in the Occupied Territories, B'Tselem - The Israeli Informaiton Center for Uhman Rights in the Occupied Territories.
Walzer, M. (1977). Just and Unjust Wars: a moral argument with historical illustrations. New York, Basic Books.
Weisberg, R. H. (2004). Loose Professionalism or Why Lawyers Take the Lead on Torture. Torture: A Collection. L. Sanford. Oxford, Oxford University Press.
Weizman, E. (2009). "Lawfare in Gaza: legislative attack, Open Democracy, available at: http://www.opendemocracy.net/article/legislative-attack [accessed 29.4.15]."
Weizman, E. (2011). The Least of All Possible Evils: Humanitarian Violence from Arendt to Gaza. London, Verso Books.
Winograd (2008). Winograd Commission Report - The commission of inquiry into the events of military engagement in Lebanon 2006.
Yahav, D. (2013). Interview with Maayan Geva, 5.3.13.
Yahav, D. and U. Amit-Kohn (1993). Israel, the "intifada" and the rule of law. Jerusalem, Israel Ministry of Defense Publications.

CHAPTER 5

# The International Law Department at War in Gaza

## 5.1 Introduction

Chapter 3 in this book interrogated the Israeli legal field involved in the OPT as a historical—contextual product of power relations steeped in the field's inner logic. Its fourth chapter continued this analysis by examining military legal practice as both a product and a production site for the field's logic and its division of capital. Grounded in these settings, it identified distinctive phases in military legal practice and logic, each characterised by different elements, among them a particular extent of capital and specific understandings of law vis-à-vis violence and morality. These different legal phases were the basis for this study's analysis of fundamental changes in law, manifested in the field's logic, the power it exerts beyond its boundaries, and the very location of these boundaries. These changes in law ultimately challenge and rearrange law's relationship with politics. This chapter now builds on these discussions to develop an analysis of law's contemporary phase, based on an interrogation of the Israeli 2008/9 offensive in Gaza.

The chapter opens with a brief overview of the existing literature on the offensive, highlighting its limitations and oversights. It continues with a historical—political introduction to the offensive, describing the conditions and processes leading to this event. The chapter positions the military operation in the context of the field and its different institutions. It continues by analysing the ILD's legal practice in Operation Cast Lead, considering this team's engagement with international humanitarian



M. Geva, *Law, Politics and Violence in Israel/Palestine*,
DOI 10.1007/978-3-319-34153-8_5

law's fundamental distinction between civilians and combatants, and the measure of proportionality. The discussions of specific policies and actions serve as an entry point to a broader debate on the contemporary character of law in war in Israel/Palestine.

The 2008/9 offensive in Gaza has been debated widely in academia, the media, civil society and other forums, with analysis focusing largely on the legal aspects of the operation (for example, Amnesty 2009; Human Rights Watch 2009; Jerusalem Center 2009; B'Tselem 2009a; Falk 2009a; Macintyre 2010). The UN alone launched three different investigations into this event.[1] Some of these accounts were written and received in the face of revelations about the military legal system's extended involvement in this operation. The MAG Corps' practitioners, it has been revealed, participated in this offensive more extensively than in any past operation (Blau and Feldman 2009). While the military legal system's extent of involvement in this operation continued an existing trend rather than being an exception, this was nevertheless an issue attracting discussion by those interested in international law in the context of Israel and the OPT. Many of the existing accounts of the Gaza offensive examined this attack, building exclusively on legal rules and codes. These accounts, directed by their own tools of inquiry, conclude by asserting either that Israeli forces abided by or had violated international law (for example, Sharp 2009; Weiner and Bell 2009; Shandi 2010; Wells-Greco 2010; Zimmermann 2011).

Justus Reid Weiner and Avi Bell, for example, present a legal analysis stating that Israel had abided by international humanitarian law in its actions in Gaza. The authors support this thesis by referring to the extensive involvement of military lawyers in the operation:

> All reported Israeli strikes in the December 2008—January 2009 round of fighting have been aimed at legitimate targets and none has caused excessive collateral damage. Legal advisors attached to Israeli military units review proposed military actions. They apply an extremely restrictive standard of both distinction and proportionality, in accordance with intrusive Israeli Supreme Court rulings that have imposed far stricter legal standards on the Israeli military than those found in international law. (Weiner and Bell 2009, p. 22)

Some of the accounts of the offensive, specifically those arguing that Israel acted in violation of law, push aside law altogether by claiming that it did not have a substantial role in the offensive, but rather paid lip service poorly concealing a political agenda (Gearty 2009; Falk 2009b). Conor Gearty, for example, argues along these lines that international law had a negligible impact on Israel's conduct: 'It would be wrong to say that none of this international activity has had any effect at all ... But in the absence of any kind of enforcement mechanism, the legal effect of all this international noise has been for all practical purposes zero' (Gearty 2009). Richard Falk (2009b) similarly contends:

> The timing of the attacks seemed prompted by a series of considerations: most of all, the interest of political contenders, the Defense Minister Ehud Barak and the Foreign Minister Tzipi Livni, in demonstrating their toughness prior to national elections scheduled for February ... Such Israeli shows of force have been a feature of past Israeli election campaigns ... That such a human catastrophe can happen with minimal outside interference also shows the weakness of international law.

Existing research offers limited perspectives on this offensive as a legal phenomenon, because the majority of accounts are constrained analytically by their means of inquiry that can lead only to a conclusion by which arguing that these events fall either inside or outside of law. In conceptual—disciplinary terms, the dominance of this dichotomised discourse is a result of, first, the prominent position of legal experts, itself interwoven with the power of the legal field, and second, the withdrawal of the humanities and social sciences from engagement with law, a trend discussed in this book's introduction. The dominance of legal scholars translates into there being few researchers positioned in other disciplines engaging with law. A key implication of this state of affairs is that, by and large, existing accounts of law in this context do not offer an analysis that reaches beyond the legality and illegality divide, a perspective examining law as either a force governing political decision-making or a tool being subjected to political use.

Guided by the analytical setting laid out in the previous chapters—the contextual map of the field and the investigation of military legal practice—this chapter engages with the occurrences in Gaza while reaching beyond the perspectives described thus far. It moves beyond an attempt to determine the compatibility of this operation to a static legal code, or to claim that law is altogether irrelevant and does not play a significant part in dictating military and state action. This chapter's enquiry positions military legal practice in the context of the field as a site made up of power and inner logic, and argues that this particular practice is a key operation contributing to the make-up of the field. Building on the identification of a distinctive phase of military legal practice beginning in 2000, this chapter examines the offensive in Gaza as a manifestation of this phase. This examination endeavours to articulate law's contemporary form and, by interrogating law, to analyse its relationship with politics and the implications of these legal—political formations for conflict and war.

## 5.2 Historical—Political Background to Operation Cast Lead

Israel has been subjecting Gaza to a variety of repressive policies since its 1967 occupation. As debated previously, Israel's control of the Strip has historically been more restrictive in comparison with the West Bank, and policies have become particularly severe since the second Intifada. A key aspect in this was the Gaza Strip's connections with the West Bank, localities closely related in politics, history and demographics. Since the breaking of the second Intifada, Israeli policy and practice have restricted Palestinians' freedom of movement severely to and from the Strip, leading to a de facto separation between Gaza and the West Bank.

In 2005, Israel carried out its unilateral Disengagement Plan, withdrawing settlers and ground military posts from Gaza, with the declared purpose of ending its relations with the Strip. Nevertheless, Israel has retained considerable control over Gaza's borders, including passage to the West Bank and the Strip's airspace and territorial waters. Even after the 2005 ground withdrawal, Israel continues to exercise considerable control over important aspects of everyday life in Gaza. Restrictions on the import and export of goods to and from the Strip have led to extreme poverty. In more general terms, the disengagement constituted Gaza as a no-man's-land, placing it outside the scope of Israeli sovereignty, and yet in many respects it was still subject to considerable Israeli control. Within legal discourse, this situation was translated into a dichotomised question—whether Gaza was still under Israeli occupation—a question that fails to address adequately the complex situation at hand (Shany 2008), while either a positive or negative answer make little difference to Gazans.

In June 2007, Hamas overtook the Strip and, with Egypt's co-operation, Israel tightened its own control over the Gazan crossings, rarely allowing Palestinians to enter or leave Gaza or to import or export goods. Several months later, and with the continued firing of Qassam rockets at Israel, the Israeli security cabinet declared Gaza a 'hostile entity'. Israel's actions were also prompted by Hamas taking captive in 2006 an Israeli soldier, Gilad Shalit, whom the organisation held captive for five years. The declaration of Gaza as a hostile entity was followed by punitive measures, including a reduction in electricity and fuel supplies. Israel's policies led to shortages in basic food items and medicine, and a sharp rise in prices. Under these circumstances, the majority of factories and many businesses closed, leading to a drastic increase in unemployment. According to UNRWA (2009), in the second half of 2008 more than 125,000 Gazans were unemployed, comprising about 40% of the Strip's workforce.

Analysing Israel's conduct, Ariella Azoulay and Adi Ophir (2012), researchers highly critical of these policies, argue that at this period, after the Oslo Accords process weakened and finally stopped, Israel sought simultaneously to control Gaza and abandon it, leaving it to its own devices. This endeavour employed two extreme elements—a tightened grip on the one hand and minimising responsibility on the other (Li 2006). Israel's restrictive policies led to extreme hardship among Gazans, but it was notable that the extent of this hardship was managed continually. In this sense, scarcity was itself a policy rather than a by-product of policy. Israel's management of scarcity was demonstrated by the disclosure of a confidential governmental document, titled 'Food Consumption in the Gaza Strip—Red Lines' (Ministry of Defense 2008). This document is indicative of the thinking behind the extent and nature of control that Israel exercises over Gaza under siege. This is a document produced by the Ministry of Defense in co-operation with the Ministry of Health, aiming to 'identify the point of intervention for prevention of malnutrition in the Gaza Strip'. It includes detailed charts of minimal caloric intake for the Strip's population taking into consideration gender and age, and then translates these figures into quantities of goods to be allowed into Gaza. On the exposure of this document, officials were quick to state that this policy was a suggestion that was never actually exercised, but the Israeli human rights NGO Gisha (Gisha 2012) compared the number of trucks appearing in this document to those actually admitted into the Strip, and concluded that the numbers were in fact very similar. In the year that followed Hamas's takeover of the Strip (July 2007–June 2008) the number of trucks allowed into Gaza with goods was even lower.

Operation Cast Lead was a massive attack launched on 27 December 2008 ad lasting three weeks. While a military offensive had been expected around that time, the precise timing of its launch was nevertheless surprising for many in both Gaza and Israel. Its surprising timing was understood in retrospect as a key strategic element (Fogelman 2010). Commentators argue that the element of surprise, combined with extensive casualties and destruction, was an application of the American practice termed 'shock and awe' that US forces employed during the March 2003 invasion of Iraq (Harel 2008). Shock and awe is an out-of-proportion surprise attack intended to cause panic and eradicate the will to resist. The exact number of lives lost in Gaza as a result of the attack remains disputed and is not expected to be agreed upon. Human rights organisations estimate that the number of fatalities was close to 1380, with among them at least 760 civilians (Amnesty 2009; PCHR 2010; B'Tselem 2011).

Discussions about the targets of this attack continue—the vast destruction of buildings (11,000 housing units) compared with the numbers of fatalities has led some commentators to argue that the Israeli army aimed to maximise destruction and at the same time minimise harm to civilians. In this context, Azoulay and Ophir quote a military official stating, 'We did not wish to kill Palestinians, we wanted to hit them in their pockets' (in Azoulay and Ophir 2012, p. 195). If this is the case and Israeli forces had indeed intended to minimise casualties, then either these intentions were translated into action in an ineffective way, or perhaps the goal the army set considered 1400 fatalities an acceptable result.

This military operation, raising controversy because of its grave consequences, was followed by multiple calls for investigations. Soon after it had ended, Israeli NGOs, academics and journalists called for an Israeli independent investigation of the occurrences. The army's legal authorities objected, arguing that international law does not oblige such an action (Libman 2009). The army's opinion was accepted and there was no national forum investigating the attack. There were, however, as mentioned earlier, three UN-appointed committees that examined the offensive. The best known of these investigations was the Goldstone Fact-Finding Mission, headed by Richard Goldstone, a South African judge who served as the prosecutor of the United Nations International Criminal Tribunal for the former Yugoslavia and for Rwanda. The members of the mission were Christine Chinkin, a London School of Economics (LSE) professor who was a member of a previous UN fact-finding mission; Hina Jilani, former Special Representative of the Secretary-General on Human Rights Defenders; and Desmond Travers, a former officer in the Irish Armed Forces and member of the Board of Directors of the Institute for International Criminal Investigations.

This mission concluded in its report that Israel had violated international law severely in its actions,[2] and had in fact, in this offensive, made Gaza its target rather than having any specific aims: 'While the Israeli Government has sought to portray its operations as essentially a response to rockets attacks in the exercise of its right to self-defence, the Mission considers the plan to have been directed, at least in part, at a different target: the people of Gaza as a whole' (Goldstone et al. 2009, p. 523).

## 5.3 Law and Operation Cast Lead: The ILD's Exercise of Capital and Power, In and Outside the Field

Operation Cast Lead was in 2008 Israel's most destructive attack on the Strip since its 1967 occupation. At the same time, as previously discussed, it was an attack involving the army's legal mechanism more extensively than ever before. The ILD was the prominent body making legal judgments during the operation and in the preparations leading up to it (Blau and Feldman 2009). The ILD's extended involvement in the operation indicates an increase in the power it exercises beyond the boundaries of the legal field. The combination of the operation's horrendous consequences and the involvement of the army's ILD raises questions about the character of legal practice, the logic driving it, and the ILD's relative position in the field at this time.

These contextual questions arise from the assumption that notwithstanding the ILD's power, this body's influence cannot be understood in isolation. It is bound up intrinsically with the legal practice, capital and dynamics within the field as a whole. This means that an investigation of military legal work necessitates a consideration of the field at the time of the attack. This section debates relationships and dynamics in the field, building on, first, three court petitions related to the offensive, filed to the High Court of Justice by NGOs; and, second, a general analysis of the relations between the court, NGOs and the army at that time.

Notably, the army and other state authorities affected the field's state of affairs during the attack by restricting the freedom of movement to and from the Strip. These restrictions meant that much of the information about the offensive was kept secret at the time it was carried out. The army, as expected, kept its own discussions confidential, and the Israeli authorities banned journalists from the Strip (Bronner 2009), making the flow of information difficult and scarce. In the context of the legal field, this meant that legal institutions and practitioners other than military and governmental bodies had very limited access to information and consequently reduced possibilities for action.

NGOs submitted two court petitions during the offensive and another in its aftermath, initiating interaction between themselves, military and non-military state lawyers, and the High Court of Justice (HCJ 201/09; 248/09). The first of these petitions, filed by Physicians for Human Rights, centred on state—military handling of the wounded and medical personnel. The petition described the army shooting medical teams as well as preventing the evacuation of the wounded, preventing the emergency services from obtaining medical supplies and the removal of bodies to be taken for burial. The second petition, filed by the NGO Gisha, centred on the shortage of electricity, a situation caused by the army's prevention of the transfer of industrial diesel oil into Gaza. This prevention had led to the shutdown of the Strip's power station and damaged seven of the 12 electricity lines that transferred electricity from Israel. The shortage prevented the effective functioning of hospitals and clinics, and of the operation of water supply and sewage systems.

The court rejected both petitions (HCJ 201/09; 248/09). In its decision it asserted, on the one hand, the justiciability of these cases, i.e. their inclusion in its jurisdiction, but on the other placed the legal responsibility and power relating to these situations with the army. Chief Justice Beinisch concluded, 'Cases in which the court examines the legality of military operations while they are happening are not uncommon occurrences … It is the role of the court, even in times of combat, to determine whether … the obligation to act in accordance with legal guidelines is upheld—both in the context of Israeli law and international humanitarian law.' And later, 'It was made clear to [the court] that the IDF and the high-level command authorities acting on its behalf are aware of and prepared to carry out their humanitarian obligations' (HCJ 201/09; 248/09, pp. 105–106). The judges' practice first presented the court's principle position in the field and its potential power over matters relating to the OPT, and then affirmed the contemporary configuration of power relations within the field. From this perspective, the court asserts theoretical power over the army but de facto distances itself from the actual execution of such a review, and instead locates/positions power, legal awareness and criteria within the army. Hence, in its decision, the court follows the trend gaining prominence since the year 2000, by which the legal field's power over military conduct is channelled to the MAG Corps.

An additional petition was filed in May 2011, centring on the army's use of white phosphorus, a spontaneously flammable chemical (HCJ 4146/2011). Use of this substance in populated areas is prohibited by the Third Protocol to the Convention on Certain Conventional Weapons. Israeli officials claimed in court that the army only used this chemical in ways that were not in conflict with law. This petition occasioned a process somewhat different from the previous two. While the High Court of Justice rejected this petition as it did in the two other cases, it reached this decision after state representatives announced that the army would reduce its use of this chemical substance significantly. In this case, it would have been more difficult for the court to simply reject the petition in light of international law's explicit prohibition of specific uses of this substance. The hypothetical possibility of a court decision prohibiting the substance caused the army to declare a change in its policy. The end result of this petition was that the army stated it will reduce its use of the chemical in question, but at the same time, the court did not explicitly prohibit its usage. In this sense, even though the petition led to change, it is difficult to assess its precise nature. It is unclear whether court proceedings ended de facto in favour of the petitioners by resulting in this military statement, or whether the court's reluctance to provide a prohibition in fact implicitly approved use of this substance or others similar to it in the future.

From the perspective of the army, this legal process ended in a change in its weaponry and means of battle. From the NGOs' perspective, the legal result is ambiguous. On the one hand the petition had an effect on the army's conduct, but the precise character of this impact is not entirely clear. In more general terms, this ambiguity reflects the considerations organisations take on board when deciding whether to file a petition—from their perspective, the court's reluctance to prohibit a particular policy after reviewing it may be less desirable than there being no court position at all. In this sense, a petition submitted and the court's review puts an end to the existence of its hypothetical decision against a military policy, which may have been a deterrent for both state authorities and the army.

The petitioning and the High Court of Justice's decisions around the offensive did not alter the relations in the field, but rather provided an affirmation of a state of affairs already in existence, by which the army's legal system possesses a considerable amount of capital and the court does not exercise much direct power over the MAG Corps. This does not indicate that the High Court of Justice is entirely removed from involvement, as the petition concerning white phosphorus demonstrates. As this case exemplifies, the court's capital affects the field even when it does not produce a concrete judgment prohibiting or supporting a policy. In more general terms, there is a status quo in the field by which the court supports the MAG Corps' handling of military legal affairs in the vast majority of cases, but at the same time the army takes into account the court's imagined or potential positions. In this vein, David Kretzmer (2002) identifies a mismatch between the court's decisions in practice, which have hardly restricted the army in the OPT, and the state and military lawyers' apprehension of the court's potential involvement, which seemingly anticipates a more restrictive review. I consider the court's capital as being made up of both its actions as well as its authority, which includes assumptions about it and its capabilities that may or may not be based on fact. In this sense, assumptions relating to its authority are an element in its capital that is as 'real' and significant as its statements and judgments.

Following from the study's mapping of capital shifts in the field, the ILD's practice in Gaza should be placed in its historical context. The MAG Corps and the ILD's practice are best understood in the context of the dynamic processes taking place in the field in the decade preceding this offensive. This practice was made possible by the processes described in this narrative—first in these is the introduction of international humanitarian law as an adequate legal framework for the evaluation of military conduct in the OPT. After the High Court of Justice's acceptance of this framework in general terms, its application in Gaza after the 2005 withdrawal was an obvious implication. The court's decision, as described, was followed by the ILD's institutional repositioning in the army, a transference of capital from the High Court of Justice to the army's legal system, and the ILD's assertion of power over military decision-making.

The flow of power in the field is an interdependent continual dynamic. The MAG Corps sustains its power outside the field by relying on the capital of the High Court of Justice, and even that of NGOs and academics. In this constellation of power, the legal process of petitioning to court, regardless of its result contributes to the validation of the military legal system's capital. Demonstrating this interdependency, in its publications relating to the Gaza offensive the ILD refers to NGO petitions, the court's activities and even academic writing as proof of its own appropriate application of legal procedure and, by implication, the necessity of its involvement in military decision-making. For example, a text produced by the ILD argued that:

> The Israeli Supreme Court has demonstrated that it can and will intercede in actual hostilities between the IDF and Palestinian terrorist organisations—including the Gaza Operation. In January 2009, while IDF forces were still fighting Hamas in Gaza, the Court reviewed two petitions by human rights groups challenging the IDF's efforts to satisfy humanitarian obligations to Palestinian civilians ...Israel's Supreme Court has earned international respect for its jurisprudence and its independence in enforcing international law. Its rulings balancing security and individual rights are highly regarded by jurists and academic scholars of international law, and have been cited favourably by foreign courts, including the Supreme Court of Canada, the House of Lords in the United Kingdom, and the European Court of Justice. (The State of Israel 2010a, pp. 10–11)

In this text, the court's practice is depicted as creating a balance between security and individual rights, and then serves the ILD as an element contributing to its own credibility. The ILD's assertions in this text also employ the capital of NGOs and academics to strengthen its own position. NGO petitioning seen from this perspective is thought to provide proof of a fair legal system. Academics studying the court are used discursively to validate this institution's authority. By building on NGOs and academics' capital, the ILD pushes aside the practice—theory discursive dichotomy that in another context it uses to label these practitioners' perspectives as irrelevant.

The relation of the MAG Corps to NGOs is a key facet in the field's contemporary structure. By the time of the offensive, the discursive interaction between these institutions had already incorporated the deadly terminology and logic of international humanitarian law. Change in human rights NGOs' discourse was part of the field's shift in the direction of international humanitarian law during the 2000s, as discussed previously. NGOs were compelled to follow other legal bodies in order to communicate in the language that is often in conflict with human rights law, and the implications of this 'adjustment' were substantial. A key result of this shift is a growing similarity between the discourse of these organisations and the army—institutions operating, in Bourdieusian terms, from positions structurally hostile to one another. NGO statements made during the offensive evaluated specific attacks based on the international humanitarian law criteria of the distinction between civilians and combatants and proportionality (ACRI et al. 2009; B'Tselem 2009a). MAG Avichai Mendelblit illustrated this growing proximity in the aftermath of Operation Cast Lead by expressing on several occasions his appreciation of the work of human rights NGOs (Mendelblit 2010). In one such example he pointed out explicitly the commonality between the MAG Corps and NGOs practice: 'B'Tselem [a prominent human rights organisation] endeavours to get to the bottom of events, as do we' (Harel 2009a, my translation). NGOs and the army are the institutions furthest from one another within the field, but at the same time the distance between them has diminished. This similarity of opposites is an indication of the altered character of the field as a whole, its move towards international humanitarian law and its growing acceptance of the logic of war.

NGOs' engagement with international humanitarian law meant that they adapted their means of argumentation and research to match those of the army. To recall, international humanitarian law is a legal body that calculates permitted destruction and killing rather than promoting an end to hostilities or providing a blanket prohibition on killing, as do human rights provisions. The participation of human rights NGOs in this discourse completes the entire field's movement in this direction and will inevitably also remake the goals and habitus of these organisations, which are bound to change as their means of practice alter. In an article titled 'Only the criminal can solve the crime', Eyal Weizman (2010) examines the profound implications that the discursive turn to international humanitarian law has had over NGOs. The key effect Weizman detects is a growing similarity between NGOs and the military. Weizman demonstrates this argument based on a story of a former defence professional turned NGO practitioner. This career path, he argues, is indicative of NGOs' current state. Since these organisations now set out to conduct military-like interrogations to confront state arguments about the application of international humanitarian law, the optimal human rights researcher is, in fact, the perpetrator of attacks.

## 5.4 The ILD's Practice in Operation Cast Lead: Contemporary Legal Logic, Capital and Power in Play

This section debates the ILD's legal practice in Operation Cast Lead, paying particular attention to key legal decisions made regarding the classification of civilians and combatants, and the proportionality of attacks. The section considers the ILD practitioners' contribution to the field's logic, their institutional position and influence as a manifestation of capital in the field and power exercised beyond its boundaries.

Operation Cast Lead thus far has occasioned the ILD's involvement in battle in its maximalist form. Lawyers became more involved than ever before in the military command structure. The ILD stationed its lawyers in divisional commands, and these practitioners then took part in operational decision-making. Many plans and operational decisions were to go ahead only on being approved by either the appointed ILD lawyer on the ground or the ILD's central command. ILD practitioners were then made regular participants in 'operations meetings', the forums making major decisions about planned attacks (Cohen 2011, p. 375).

In an op-ed publicised shortly after the operation had ended, MAG Mendelblit described the MAG Corps' work during this offensive, emphasising its extended involvement:

> During Operation Cast Lead, the IDF's legal practitioners, led by myself and the International Law Department, accompanied combat from decision-making hubs at the General Headquarters, Southern Command, and the division. The decision to accompany combat activity legally should not be taken for granted. It reflects commanders' recognition of the importance of the law in the operational decision-making process, and the IDF's perspective by which warfare is carried out within law rather than outside of its boundaries. It reflects our professional apprehension that commanders are in need of available and skilled legal advisers who will point out the boundaries of the forbidden, and indeed the permissible. (Mendelblit 2009; my translation)

In this text, as in others, Mendelblit discusses the acceptance of law within the army, and the army's aim to conduct itself within the boundaries of law. This dichotomised discourse of 'in' or 'out' excludes the dynamic ways in which legal judgments and law's logic are constituted. Moreover, by directing its attention to the changes commanders have undergone in relation to law, it pushes aside the vast changes that legal practice and law have undergone to arrive to their current position. The following sections explore the dynamic formation of law through its military practice in Gaza.

### 5.4.1 *The ILD and the Civilian: Legal Classifications Ordering the Battlefield*

As discussed in the preceding chapter, many researchers have shown that the legal category of 'civilian' and its related principle of distinction are controversial matters in contemporary warfare (for example, Best 1984; Hoffman 2000; Kanstroom 2003; Sassoli 2003; Dinstein 2004; Schmitt 2009; Gade 2010). In fact, these current controversies echo the political-historical tensions pre-dating contemporary conflicts (Nabulsi 2001; Slim 2003). David Kennedy (2006) suggests that such controversies are bound up with a clash between two trends: the one increasing continuity between war and peace, and the other a rhetorical assertion of their distinctiveness. The particular discussion regarding civilian and combatant in the case of Israel and the OPT manifests such a contradictory interplay of continuity and distinctiveness—on the one hand relating to ambiguous forms of participation in combat, and on the other asserting clear-cut classifications leading to decisions about life and death. This section investigates legal practice relating to civilians as reflected in decisions and discussions about police forces in Gaza. This investigation begins with a specific military action and then broadens its scope to consider police forces and the civilian/combatant categorisation in more general terms.

The attack that opened Operation Cast Lead on Saturday, 27 December 2008 was an air force strike on the Arafat City Police Station in Gaza City. This incident was later titled 'the police line-up', as the officers were lined up for a ceremony when they were hit. The first missile launched caused the instant death of 48 people, and five more were injured, two of whom subsequently died. A few seconds later, either one or two more missiles were fired at a second nearby yard, causing the additional deaths of 28 officers. The total number of fatalities from the whole attack was even higher, amounting to a total of 89. Videos from the scene taken with mobile phones show the brutal results of the airstrike—bodies and body parts lying on the floor, some still arranged in the line-up formation, medical personnel helpless, shouting in disbelief and horror.

Legal debates in the aftermath of this event focused on the distinction between civilians and combatants, and whether the people targeted were combatants, i.e. legitimate targets of attack. The official Israeli statements relating to this case, formed by the ILD, have been debated in multiple arenas – journalistic, academic and governmental (Moshe 2009; Fogelman 2010).

One argument raised by the ILD regarding the combatant/civilian classification of Gaza's police force was that Gazan police personnel were legitimate targets of attack because if attacked they would potentially fight back (Blau and Feldman 2009). This legal argumentation is indicative of military legal practice's proactive character, intrinsically connected to the practitioners' spirit of innovation. The action of the Israeli military transforms police officers from civilians to combatants via hypothetical participation in combat. In this sense, the launching of missiles is at once an operational and legal action in that it is not only a physical assault but is also the constitution of a legal status that permits killing.

From this perspective, the combatant identity, or departure from the civilian category, does not lie with the police officers as such, but rather in the operation of the Israeli forces, grounded in law. Legal practice in this case constructs an order in war. It does not merely point out a situation already in existence but rather forms a systemic logic by constructing enemy targets. Law, as it was practised in this case, established categories that order violence. In conceptual terms, it is indifferent to the consequences of its classifications. Thus the classification process as such does not aspire to create a moral judgement and does not intend to protect people. The creation of targets and their ordering into categories allowing or prohibiting attack neither intensifies nor restrains military violence per se; rather, it rearranges it.

Another aspect of the attack debated was its proportionality. This equation inevitably depends on the classification of individuals as either legitimate targets of attack or not. The ILD argued in this respect that some of the police officers in the line-up at the Arafat City Police Station were involved in Hamas military activity (Fogelman 2010). A publication sponsored by the Israeli government accuses only some of the policemen of involvement in terrorist activity, leaving 34 of them with no link to any such actions (Goldstone et al. 2009). If this is the case, then in legal terms while some of the policemen might have been considered combatants, and thus a legitimate target for attack, the action still needs to adhere to the test of proportionality. A more elaborate consideration of the ILD's practice of proportionate attacks will soon follow.

The ILD negated any differentiation between police and military forces in the context of Gaza's Hamas regime, i.e. arguing that all police personnel are to be considered as combatants (State of Israel 2010a, b). The ILD's arguments are based in part, on the High Court of Justice's decision regarding targeted killing. As discussed in Chapter 3 above, this decision set out a dual criterion—both substantive and temporal—by which a civilian taking part in hostilities loses protection. In substantive terms, the participation must be direct; in temporal terms, protection is lost only at *such time* as this participation is active. The court's decision leaves in the hands of military lawyers the power to determine the precise interpretation of these substantive and temporal elements deciding the civilian/combatant division.

The ILD's decision to consider Gazan police as a military force on the grounds of these elements reshaped the battlefield. An ILD member described this transformative moment laconically in a media interview: 'This is a very large group of people who were supposedly, at that moment, civilians, and the following day turned into legitimate military targets' (Blau and Feldman 2009). A spokesperson for the Israeli army described in an additional interview the layout of the novel legal—operational order: 'Our definition is that anyone who is involved with terrorism within Hamas is a valid target. This ranges from the strictly military institutions and includes the political institutions that provide the logistical funding and human resources for the terrorist arm' (Bowen 2009). This interpretation is at odds with the ILD's position on targeted killing as presented in court. The classification of police stations and personnel as legitimate targets of attack had extreme implications. Out of a 100 targets attacked by Israeli artillery during the first day of the military operation, twenty-four were police stations. By the time the operation's artillery attacks were stopped, all 60 Gazan police stations had been struck (Fogelman 2010). In line with this decision, in the ILD's official publications, Gazan police are referred to repeatedly as 'police', with the word placed within inverted commas (The State of Israel 2009, 2010a, b). In this discourse, Gaza has only 'police' and no genuine police as such, a rhetorical signalling of its classification as a combatant entity, a terrorist force in disguise.

ILD Commanding Officer during the offensive in Gaza, Pnina Sharvit-Baruch, provides an account of the ILD's innovative practice of the principle of distinction and the legal constitution of the battlefield:

> The principle of distinction is, by definition, flexible. It requires that you make a distinction between a military target that is legitimate for attack, and a civilian object that is illegal for you to set as a target. Now, what is a military target? … this is very flexible. A civilian object, when it is used [for military purposes], or because of its location, or even because of its potential use … becomes a legitimate target of attack. (Sharvit-Baruch 2009; my translation)

Sharvit-Baruch's statement provides an additional demonstration of the ILD's practice, wherein potentiality suffices for the classification of objects (and subjects) permissible targets of attack. The criterion builds on the intent and positioning of the Israeli army in order to classify individuals as combatants rather than relating necessarily to the characteristics of the subjects as such. This argument again exemplifies how legal practice forms a military target rather than identifies an already-existing one. This constitutive effect of the classification of warfare targets coincides with military violence and cannot be understood in isolation from it. At the same time, law's prominence in current policy-making hubs indicates that military violence cannot be understood separately from law. Put together, we see a particular relationship between law and violence where military activities have become dual—both operational and legal.

Another participant in this debate, the NGO B'Tselem—the Israeli Information Center for Human Rights in the Occupied Territories—chose a midway classification for Gazan police personnel. While the organisation states on its website that the police line-up attack should be investigated with regard to its adherence to the principle of distinction (B'Tselem 2009b), the list of fatalities publicised on the organisation's website places the names of police casualties on a list separate from both civilians and combatants.[3] This division follows the 2008 ICRC publication debating 'direct participation', i.e. the situations in which civilians lose protection from hostilities (ICRC 2008). This statement is an expression of the field's current logic. The NGO's discourse is based on the premise of international humanitarian law and, as a result, is not fundamentally different from that of the army.

Military legal categorisation interlinks with contemporary means and methods of warfare. Legal practice reshaping the battlefield based on the classification of civilians and combatants is linked to Western warfare patterns, minimalising risk for soldiers. A sweeping categorisation, such as the classification of the police as a military force, is compatible with weapons operated from afar. Legal—military decisions in this regard are in line with Amos Yadlin and Asa Kasher's taxonomy of lives based on a revision of international humanitarian law (2005). As described, these authors suggest a classification of soldiers and civilians versus terrorists and enemy civilians, leading to different 'weights' in terms of state responsibility for protection. The decision to open the offensive with a massive airstrike, posing little risk to Israeli soldiers but causing great loss of life among Palestinians, clearly reflects state—military priorities in this regard, assigning more weight to Israeli soldiers than to Palestinian civilians. While the MAG Corps and ILD do not subscribe officially to Yadlin and Kasher's 'doctrine', several sources account for its adoption in practice. Officers testified that it has been made part of the army's 'guidelines' (Kot 2011,

p. 963). Other officers stated that military conduct in Gaza followed this typology (Harel 2009b), and the historical study of the death toll among Israeli soldiers and Palestinian civilians indicates a decisive trend prioritising the former over the latter (Levy 2010). Furthermore, a MAG Corps official stated explicitly in an interview given at the time of the operation that the army indeed considers the lives of its soldiers to be more valuable than those of Palestinian civilians (Ronen 2009). The reasoning the officer provides for this assertion is identical to that of Kasher and Yadlin (2005)—that the Israeli army's reliance on conscription deems a clear-cut distinction between Israeli civilians and combatants to be irrelevant. This categorisation and subsequent prioritisation of lives is yet another facet of legal—operational military action demonstrating violence and law intertwined.

### 5.4.2 *The ILD and Proportionate Attacks: Law Guiding the Extent of Destruction*

This section investigates the ILD's practice of the international humanitarian law principle of proportionate attacks in the context of broader discussions about this legal provision. Elements investigated in this regard are the evasive nature of this provision and its subjective character (for example, Walzer 1977; Berman 2004a, b; Weizman 2010a) and the inherent tension between the distinction of civilians and combatants, and the evaluation of proportionate attacks. This tension, as Kennedy (2006) argues, is omnipresent in legal discussions and follows the fact that militaries weigh the value of combatant targets with anticipated civilian deaths.

On 1 January 2009 the Israeli air forces bombed the home of Hamas senior Nizar Rayan in Jabalya refugee camp. The blast killed Rayan and 15 of his family members—four women and 11 children (Harel and Stern 2009). In an official statement, the Israeli military spokesperson said that: 'The house served as a large munitions warehouse and a war room. Under the house was an escape tunnel for terrorist members of Hamas's military wing' (IDF 2009). Both Israeli and Palestinian sources confirmed that Rayan had been warned of the coming attack (Katz 2009; *The Telegraph* editorial 2009). This particular military action led to controversies in the field about the proportionality of this attack, the classification of people as either civilians or combatants, and the implications of early warning procedures.

Following this incident, the NGO B'Tselem released a statement arguing that this was a grave breach of international humanitarian law (B'Tselem 2009a). The NGO maintained that while Nizar Rayan, being a senior Hamas military official, was likely to be a legitimate target for attack, his family members were not. Under the circumstances of the ongoing military campaign, the organisation argued, it is not clear how this attack was expected to secure a military advantage that was proportionate to the loss of civilian lives.

In the aftermath of the operation, ILD members revealed that the legal decision-making in this case was in part based on the exclusion of Rayan's family members from the 'civilian' category (Blau and Feldman 2009). An ILD officer argued that in the context of this case and others similar to it, where a warning of an intended attack had been given, people who chose to remain lost their civilian protection and became legitimate military targets. Following this logic, the women and children of the Rayan family were not part of the evaluation of a proportionate attack, i.e. not regarded as 'collateral damage', because they were no longer seen as being entitled to protection. This legal interpretation builds on the High Court of Justice's decision regarding targeted killing (HCJ 769/2002), distinguishing between voluntary and involuntary human shields. The former, the judges asserted, are to be considered a legitimate military target. The court's decision, however, does not clarify what constitutes 'voluntarism' and how it should be identified. The ILD built on this assertion to construct its own legal practice classifying the Rayan family and others in similar situations to be unprotected from military assault. The legal interpretation in this case shows how the ILD's practice, in its innovative spirit, pushes the boundaries of legal logic to exclude people from the protection of law.

This legal practice which determined that the Rayan family had lost its civilian protection, illuminates an additional facet of law's contemporary relationship with violence. Similar to the decision made about Gaza's police, the civilian/combatant distinction, the preliminary condition for the evaluation of proportion is, in the case of the Rayan family a product of the military action rather than any characteristic of the individuals involved. Unlike Nizar Rayan, who might have fitted into the combatant category regardless of a particular Israeli military operation, his family members were not in a similar position. This legal practice echoes Sharvit-Baruch's analysis – a person or location may be classified as a legitimate target for attack on the basis of what it becomes in light of the aggressor's action. The implications of this perspective, as the Rayan attack exemplifies, are radical—family members, the youngest a baby, are not classified as civilians to be protected from hostilities.

Now examining the issue of proportionate attacks in general terms, a quantitative question is key. A journalist posed this precise question to MAG Mendelblit. How many civilians would the Israeli army be willing to kill in order to hit a targeted person? The MAG's response was hesitant: 'I can't … very, very low numbers … I can't go into that … but the numbers … the number is close to zero' (Levy 2012; my translation). Perhaps this is simply a wholly disingenuous account, but to the extent that it is truthful it is revealing of the ILD's practice of the civilian/combatant classification. If the actual permissible number of civilians killed is indeed very low, then taking into account the death toll in Gaza it is possible to deduce that the ILD employed a highly flexible classification of both civilian and combatant, deeming many individuals ineligible for civilian protection. Another conclusion is that while the equation of proportion is indeed subjective, the ILD's legal practice goes much further in negotiating law, transforming the measuring tools, and the elements measured.

Sweeping classifications of combatants are bound up with early warning, another legal requirement. Early warning is a key international humanitarian law component relating to the obligation to protect civilians from hostilities. ILD officers describe making great efforts in this regard:

> [T]he amount, scope, and specificity of warnings issued to civilians have dramatically increased in the conflicts fought since the beginning of this century. Probably the most elaborate and systematic warnings were issued by Israel in its conflict in Lebanon in 2006 and especially in its operation in the Gaza Strip in 2009. (Sharvit-Baruch and Neuman 2011, pp. 359–360)

The Israeli army had delivered early warnings in large areas of Gaza in the form of leaflets, radio broadcasts and even text messages. An additional and highly controversial method of warning was dubbed by the army 'roof knocking'; this is the use of relatively low-explosive 'teaser' bombs or missiles aimed at houses designated for destruction. From this, the inhabitants of the house are to understand this is a warning message, communicating that the facility will soon be shelled. This legally induced missile again exemplifies the character of the ILD's legal practice—legal procedure translated into weaponry; law and violence interwoven.

A significant ramification of early warning procedures is the subsequent status of those locations and the people warned. While international law does not direct that this is a final measure after which civilians are no longer protected from hostilities, this was, in practice, the result in Gaza. Notably, this same argument was made in the case of the Rayan family. In more general terms, officers indicate that Palestinians who had remained in such houses or locations after the warnings were in fact stripped of their civilian protection. One of these officers describes the directions given on the ground and the status of those who stayed: 'any movement must entail gunfire. No one's supposed to be there ... if you see any signs of movement at all you shoot. This is essentially the rules of engagement' (in Macintyre 2010). Thus, the ILD's practice of early warning shaped battlefield proportionality even before, or without deciding on a legally permissible number of, civilian casualties because it assigned sweeping classifications serving as a basis for the calculation of proportion.

The ILD's practice of early warning embodies a transformation of a legal code potentially protecting some people from hostilities, to a code covering an entirely different activity. Early warning in this case formed a battlefield and established military activity that is at once operational and legal. It provides either a practical or a hypothetical chance to escape, and marks all those who stay as legitimate targets of attack. Again, the transition from a person protected to one who is not is a result of legal practice rather than that person's characteristic or active involvement in combat. Legally induced notifications, including all the means employed— leaflets, radio broadcasts, text messages and 'roof knocking' weaponry as means of 'communication'—shaped the battlefield and created 'enemies'.

Returning to the question of proportion, this is a central international humanitarian law parameter, and one that is particularly flexible and subject to ambiguity. In this light, the ILD's determination of permissible, proportionate attack provides a lucid opportunity to examine the character of legal practice. Several ILD members describe the operationalisation of the proportion criterion:

> There is no legal answer to the question what is proportionate. It's not that I can say: this is proportionate, that is not. You have to take into account considerations A, B, C and D, look at this and that, and then consider the whole question. (Officer A 2010)

> There are many difficult decisions ... times when I can't say if the decisions are proportionate or not. I can ask questions: Did you think of that? Do you have information about X? ... Do you know of sensitive objects nearby the place of attack? (Officer B 2011)
>
> Proportionality is a complex logic with many variables—but how do you compare these? There is no choice but to ask the question, compare and calculate. Proportionality does not tell us what to include in the calculation, what is the equation and what is the exchange rate. Should a man of combatant age be counted as a civilian? If so, does he count for more or for less? How do you count women in relation to men? How do you count the death of children? Does one dead child equal one dead grownup, or does he equal five grownups? As a lawyer I need numbers to work with. I need thresholds in order to instruct the soldiers, any number could become a useful benchmark. But when the ground of the law is shaking I am also unstable. (Resiner in Weizman 2011, p. 13)

Legal practitioners' accounts of proportionality in war are revealing about the subjectivity of this rule and the fluidity of its metaphorical 'balance'. Indeed, the very task of measuring and comparing lives, on the one hand, with military goals on the other, cannot lead to any straightforward criterion. Notably, the open-ended character of this legal code does not imply that its practice is similarly abstract. Considering the coincidence of the Israeli shift to international humanitarian law with the incorporation of legal practitioners into the battlefield and the intensification of their work, the implication is that legal practitioners are now required to practise law in a manner more concrete than ever before. Thus these concrete requirements arose precisely when legal logic became open-ended.

To recap, David Kennedy (2006) suggests that the equation of proportion undermines the premise of distinction because it necessitates a comparison or conversion rate between the lives of civilians against combatant targets. The ILD's practice in fact reflects and creates many more entanglements between these legal provisions. In the ILD's practice, the army's violence actually has the capacity to constitute the identification of combatants and in this way establish the terms for measuring battlefield proportion.

Alternative discussions of wartime proportionality and civilian—combatant distinctions suggest a reversal in perspective: looking for the attack's aim in its 'collateral' rather than its stated target (Weizman 2011; Cronin 2013). In this perspective, the collateral, the attack's 'excessive' violence and pain, is used as a political tool and is at the heart of the offensive rather than being located on its margins. Translated into patters of war, this interpretation nears the military practice titled 'shock and awe'. In October 2008, two months prior to the offensive in Gaza, the IDF's Northern Command Commanding Officer, Major General Gadi Eisenkott, described in an interview the strategy he called 'Dahiya Doctrine', based on the army's operation in Lebanon: 'What happened in the Dahiya Quarter of Beirut in 2006 will happen in every village from which shots are fired in the direction of Israel… We shall use disproportionate force against it and cause immense damage and destruction. From our perspective these are not civilian villages but military bases. This is not a recommendation, this is a plan and it has already been approved" (Eisenkott, in Fishman and Ringel-Hoffman 2008; my translation).

Eisenkott's account may be seen as an outright rejection of legal principles. His use of the term 'disproportionate' is particularly telling in this regard. At the same time, the ILD's practice of the principles of distinction and proportion may still go hand in hand with this statement. If potential threats are considered to be combatant targets, if people remaining after a warning had been given lose their civilian status, then entire villages may be seen as the legally-made 'enemy'. Returning to the discussion suggesting the consideration of collateral as the central focus of analysis (Weizman 2011), a preliminary step in this light is to understand what is the target, and what is the destruction that accompanies it. Eisenkott's statement and some of Israel's actions in Gaza make it impossible to distinguish between the two.

## 5.5 Conclusion: New Law and New War in Gaza

This chapter was an account of military legal practice in Operation Cast Lead as a case reflecting the contemporary configuration of law and war. Historical consideration of the relative capital in the field shows that the MAG Corps and ILD's intense involvement in this operation was the result of a dynamic process of change taking place in the field since the early 2000s. As a result of the field's shifts, at the time of the operation the ILD had both considerable capital in the field and power outside the field's boundaries, guiding military actions.

This operation did not bring about major changes in the relational context of the field. Rather, it evoked dynamics grounded in an already established state of affairs. The High Court of Justice, for the most part, claimed its discursive justiciability over military affairs, but in practice negated direct participation in reviewing the army's actions, instead reaffirming its transference of capital to the army's legal system. Human rights NGOs were engaged discursively in the legal language of international humanitarian law, a logic dictating from the outset much of the response to the legal questions posed. In this perspective, the practice of the NGOs reflected their present positions in the field, which has moved closer to that of the army.

The ILD's innovative practice operates at the edges of law and continually pushes and expands the ends of its logic. ILD Commanding Officer Reisner vividly describes this practice:

> We've defended policy that is on the edge—neighbour routine, demolishing houses, deportation, targeted killing. We've defended all the magic solutions for fighting terrorism …If the army says 'here's a magic solution, is it within the possible?' then I will say 'I'm willing to try and defend it, but I may be unsuccessful.' In white I'll allow, in black I'll forbid, but in grey I'll take part in the dilemma. I don't stop in grey. (in Blau and Feldman 2009)

The ILD's exploration of grey zones, the practitioners' novel crafting of law, altered both law and military practice. The ILD's innovative practice and the making of legal logic is enabled by the permissive grounds of international humanitarian law and this department's established capital in the field and power over military practice.

The ILD's practice during the offensive in Gaza of both the legal principles of distinction and proportionality demonstrated a new relationship between law and violence. Legal practice on this occasion was activity constituting the battlefield. Rather than identifying civilian or military objects/subjects already in existence, legal practice played an active part in their creation. The ILD's interpretation of the civilian category demonstrated this type of practice—the army's own strategy can lead to a person's exclusion from the category of those people protected from hostilities. This may be a result of his/her location, the army's intentions, or their remaining in a space that had already been warned of a coming attack. Legal policies regarding classifications order the battlefield, they draw the line between legitimate and illegitimate military targets, participate in measuring military gain versus loss of civilian lives, translation of the legal obligation of early warning into weaponry, and as a whole weave together law and war.

The following and final chapter of this book will tie together the analysis of the offensive in Gaza with broader historical—socio-political processes of change. In this way, it will construct a contextualised account of law, politics and war grounded in changes in legal logic, its power and the legal field's shifting boundary.

## Notes

1. The first of these was a Board of Inquiry appointed by UN Secretary-General Ban Ki-moon, examining incidents relating to UN facilities in the Strip. The second was the Goldstone Fact-Finding Mission appointed by the UN Human Rights Council. Unlike the situation with the first Board of Inquiry, Israel refused to co-operate with the UN Mission. The Goldstone Report recommended a follow-up body to scrutinise local investigations of alleged violations of IHL. This recommendation led to the establishment of a third UN body, the Tomuschat Committee.
2. Richard Goldstone published a letter in 2011 'reconsidering' the mission's conclusions by which Israel violated international law. Notably, rather than providing new evidence, Goldstone based his new assertion on Israel's investigations of specific actions and its declaration regarding a willingness to comply with the legal code. Goldstone, R. (2011). Reconsidering the Goldstone Report on Israel and war crimes. *The Washington Post*, 1.4.11, accessible at: http://www.washingtonpost.com/opinions/reconsidering-the-goldstone-report-on-israel-and-war-crimes/2011/04/01/AFg111JC_story.html [accessed 19 April 2015].
   The co-authors of the report quickly released a joint statement objecting to Goldstone's recanting of the report's assertions, arguing that there was no new evidence that might have disqualified the report's original conclusions. Jilani, H. et al. (2011). Goldstone report: Statement issued by members of UN mission on Gaza war, 14 April 2011, *Guardian*.
3. http://www.btselem.org/statistics/fatalities/during-cast-lead/by-date-of-event.

## Bibliography

ACRI, et al. (2009). Background Document: Violations of Human Rights in Gaza and Israel As the Fighting Rages, available at: http://www.acri.org.il/pdf/Gaza140109.pdf, [accessed 28.4.15].

Amnesty (2009). Israel/Gaza: Operation 'Cast Lead': 22 days of death and destruction, available at: http://www.amnesty.org/en/library/asset/MDE15/015/2009/en/8f299083-9a74-4853-860f-0563725e633a/mde150152009en.pdf, [accessed 28.4.15].

Azoulay, A. and A. Ophir (2012). Abandoning Gaza. Agamben and Colonialism. M. Svirsky and S. Bignall. Edinburgh Edinburgh University Press.
B'Tselem (2009a). "4 Jan. '09: The killing of Nizar Rayan and 15 members of his family, available at: http://www.btselem.org/gaza_strip/20090104_killing_of_nizar_rian_and_13_family member, [accessed: 28.4.15]."
B'Tselem (2009b). Israeli human rights organizations: Clear and present danger to the lives of tens of thousands of civilians, available at: http://www.btselem.org/press_releases/20090114, [accessed: 28.4.15].
B'Tselem (2011). "Fatalities during operation "Cast Lead", available at: http://www.btselem.org/english/statistics/casualties.asp?sD=27&sM=12&sY=2008&eD=18&eM=01&eY=2009&filterby=event&oferet_stat=during, [accessed: 28.4.15]."
Berman, N. (2004a). 'The Appeals of the Orient': Colonized Desire and the War of the Riff. Gender and Human Rights. K. Knop. Oxford, Oxford University Press.
Berman, N. (2004b). "Privileging Combat? Contemporary Conflict and the Legal Construction of War." Columbia Journal of Transnational Law **43**(1).
Best, J. (1984). "Civilians in Contemporary Wars: A Problem in Ethics, Law, and Fact." 35 Air University Review: 29–40.
Blau, U. and Y. Feldman (2009). How IDF legal experts legitimized strikes involving Gaza civilians. HAARETZ 23/01/09.
Bowen, J. (2009). BBC NEWS 9.2.2009, available at: http://news.bbc.co.uk/1/hi/world/middle_east/7878711.stm, accessed 28.4.15.
Bronner, E. (2009). Israel Puts Media Clamp on Gaza. The New York Times 6.1.2009, accessible at: http://www.nytimes.com/2009/01/07/world/middleeast/07media.html?_r=0 [accessed 19.4.15].
Cohen, A. (2011). "Legal Operational Advice in the Israeli Defense Forces: the International Law Department and the Changing Nature of International Humanitarian Law." Connecticut Journal of International Law **26**(2).
Cronin, B. (2013). "Reckless endangerment warfare: Civilian casualties and the collateral damage exception in international humanitarian law." Journal of Peace Research **50**(2): 175–187.
Dinstein, Y. (2004). The conduct of Hostilities under the law of international armed conflict. Cambridge, Cambridge University Press.
Falk, R. (2009a) Israel's war crimes, Transnational Institute, available at: http://www.tni.org/article/israel%E2%80%99s-war-crimes [accessed 28.4.15].
Falk, R. (2009b) Understanding the Gaza Catastrophe, The World Post, available at: http://www.huffingtonpost.com/richard-falk/understanding-the-gaza-ca_b_154777.html, [accessed 28.4.15].
Fishman, A. and A. Ringel-Hoffman (2008). Israel warns Hizbullah war would invite destruction. Yedioth Aharonot 3.10.2008.
Fogelman, S. (2010). Shock and awe. HAARETZ 31.12.2010.

Gade, E. K. (2010). "Defining the Non-Combatant: How do we Determine Who is Worthy of Protection in Violent Conflict?" Journal of Military Ethics **9**(3): 219–242.

Gearty, C. (2009) Israel, Gaza and international law, Open Democracy, available at: http://www.opendemocracy.net/article/israel-gaza-and-international-law [accessed 28.4.15]

Gisha (2012). ""Red Lines" presentation: New details about the old policy, while the current policy remains shrouded in secrecy, Gisha - Legal Center for Freedom of Movement, available at: http://www.gisha.org/item.asp?lang_id=en&p_id=1699 [accessed 28.4.15]."

Goldstone, R., et al. (2009). Report of the United Nations Fact Finding Mission on the Gaza Conflict, available at: http://daccess-dds-ny.un.org/doc/UNDOC/GEN/G09/158/66/PDF/G0915866.pdf?OpenElement [accessed 10.1.2016].

Harel, A. (2008). ANALYSIS/IAF strike on Gaza is Israel's version of 'shock and awe'. HAARETZ 27.12.2008.

Harel, A. (2009a). MAG, Brigadier General Mendelblit, speaks about Cast Lead, Chico Tamir and B'Tselem, HAARETZ 18.9.09, available at: http://www.haaretz.co.il/misc/1.1281465 [accessed 28.4.15]

Harel, A. (2009b). The philosopher who gave the IDF moral justification in Gaza. HAARETZ 6.2.2009.

Harel, A. and Y. Stern (2009). IDF targets senior Hamas figures. HAARETZ 2.1.2009.

HCJ (201/09; 248/09). Physicians for Human Rights vs. the Prime Minister.

HCJ (769/2002). Public Committee against Torture in Israel vs. Government of Israel.

HCJ (4146/2011). "Hess and 116 petitioners vs Chief of General Staff of the Israel Defense Forces."

Hoffman, M. (2000). "Emerging combatants, war crimes and the future of international humanitarian law." Crime Law and Social Change **34**(1): 99–110.

Human Rights Watch, N. (2009). Precisely Wrong: Gaza Civilians Killed by Israeli Drone-Launched Missiles, New York, available at: http://www.hrw.org/sites/default/files/reports/iopt0609web_0.pdf [accessed 28.4.15].

ICRC (2008). Interpretive Guidance on the Notion of Direct Participation in Hostilities under International Humanitarian Law.

Jerusalem Center, f. P. A. (2009). Hamas, the Gaza war and accountability under international law, available at: http://media-line.co.il/Events/Jcpa/Law-Conference/Heb.aspx [accessed 28.4.15]. Jerusalem, Jerusalem Center for Public Affairs Conference.

Kanstroom, D. (2003). "Unlawful Combatants" in the United States: Drawing the Fine Line Between Law and War, Human Rights Magazine, available at: http://www.americanbar.org/publications/human_rights_magazine_home/irr_hr_winter03_unlawful.html [accessed 28.4.15].

Kasher, A. and A. Yadlin (2005). "Military Ethics of Fighting Terror: An Israeli Perspective." Journal of Military Ethics **4**(1): 3–32.

Katz, Y. (2009). IDF kills top Hamas terrorist Rayyan. The Jerusalem Post 2.1.2009.

Kennedy, D. (2006). Of War and Law. Princeton, Princeton University Press.

Kot, J.-P. (2011). "Israeli Civilians versus Palestinian Combatants? Reading the Goldstone Report in Light of the Israeli Conception of the Principle of Distinction." Leiden Journal of International Law **24**(4): 961–988.

Kretzmer, D. (2002). The Occupation of Justice: The Supreme Court of Israel and the Occupied Territories. New York, State University of New York Press.

Levy, A. (2012). True Face (*Panim Amitiyot*), 2.11.2012. available at: http://panim.nana10.co.il/Article/?ArticleID=939325 [accessed 28.4.15] Channel 10

Levy, Y. (2010). "The Tradeoff between Force and Casualties: Israel's Wars in Gaza, 1987–2009." Conflict Management and Peace Science September **27**(4).

Li, D. (2006). "The Gaza Strip as Laboratory: Notes in the Wake of Disengagement." Journal of Palestine Studies **35**(2): 38–55.

Libman, L. (2009). The investigation of alleged violations of the Laws of War during operation "Cast Lead". ILD**:** 10.

Macintyre, D. (2010). Israeli commander: 'We rewrote the rules of war for Gaza'. The Independent 3.2.2010.

Mendelblit, A. (2009a). Consultancy Under Fire. HAARETZ 29.1.2009.

Mendelblit, A. (2010a). The testimony of the MAG, Avihai Mendelblit, in front of the Public Commission to Examine the Maritime Incident of 31 May 2010, Turkel Commission, Part 2.

Ministry of Defense (2008). Food Consumption in the Gaza Strip – Red Lines, unofficially translated version available at: http://www.gisha.org/UserFiles/File/publications/redlines/red-lines-presentation-eng.pdf, [accessed 28.4.15].

Moshe, R. (2009). Constituted Lead [Oferet Hakuka]. Yedioth Aharonot 19.1.09.

Nabulsi, K. (2001). Evolving Conceptions of Civilians and Belligerents: One Hundred Years after the Hague Peace Conferences. Civilians in War. S. Chesterman. Boulder, International Peace Academy**:** 9–24.

Officer A, A. (2010). Interview with Maayan Geva, 21.12.10.

Officer B, B. (2011). Interview with Maayan Geva, 20.2.11.

PCHR (2010). Genuinely Unwilling: An Update, available at: http://www.pchrgaza.org/files/2010/Genuinely Unwilling - An Update.pdf [accessed 28.4.15].

Ronen, M. (2009). Legalised Lead (Oferet Hakuka). Yedioth Aharonot 19.1.09.

Sassoli, M. (2003). "Unlawful Combatants": The Law and Whether It Needs To Be Revised, including remarks by Daniel Reisner. Ninety-Seventh Annual Meeting Of The American Society Of International Law.

Schmitt, M. N. (2009). "Human Shields in International Humanitarian Law." Columbia Journal of Transnational Law **47**.

Shandi, Y. (2010). "Israel's Claim of the "Legitimate Right of Self- Defence" regarding the Gaza Strip in Light of International Law A Palestinian Lawyer's Position." Journal of East Asia & International Law **3**(2): 387–406.

Shany, Y. (2008). "Binary Law Meets Complex Reality: The Occupation of Gaza Debate." Israel Law Review **41**.

Sharp, H. (2009). Gaza conflict: Who is a civilian? BBC News 5.1.09, available at: http://news.bbc.co.uk/1/hi/world/middle_east/7811386.stm [accessed 28.4.15].

Sharvit-Baruch, P. (2009). Conference Paper. Hamas, the Gaza war and accountability under international law. Jerusalem.

Sharvit-Baruch, P. and N. Neuman (2011). "Warning civilians prior to attack under international law: theory and practice." Israel Yearbook on Human Rights **41**: 137–195.

Slim, H. (2003). "Why Protect Civilians? Innocence, Immunity and Enmity in War." International Affairs **79**(3): 481–501.

The State of Israel (2009). The operation in Gaza 27 December 2008 – 18 January 2009: Factual and legal aspects, available at: http://mfa.gov.il/MFA_Graphics/MFA Gallery/Documents/GazaOperation w Links.pdf [accessed 29.4.15].

The State of Israel (2010a). "Gaza Operation Investigations: an Update, available at: http://mfa.gov.il/MFA_Graphics/MFA Gallery/Documents/GazaOperation InvestigationsUpdate.pdf [accessed 29.4.15]."

The State of Israel (2010b). "Gaza Operation Investigations: a Second Update, available at: http://www.mfa.gov.il/MFA_Graphics/MFA Gallery/Documents/GazaUpdateJuly2010.pdf [accessed 28.4.15]."

The Telegraph editorial (2009). Militant Hamas leader Nizar Rayan killed in air strike 9.1.09. The Telegraph, available at: http://www.telegraph.co.uk/news/worldnews/middleeast/israel/4060236/Militant-Hamas-leader-killed-in-air-strike.html [accessed 28.4.15]

UNRWA (2009). The Gaza Labour Market in 2008, available at: http://www.unrwa.org/userfiles/2010011974016.pdf [accessed 28.4.15].

Walzer, M. (1977). Just and Unjust Wars: a moral argument with historical illustrations. New York, Basic Books.

Weiner, J. R. and A. Bell (2009). "The Gaza War of 2009: Applying International Humanitarian Law to Israel and Hamas." San Diego International Law Journal **5**(11): 5–42.

Weizman, E. (2010). "Forensic Architecture: Only the criminal can solve the crime." Radical Philosophy **164**.

Weizman, E. (2011). The Least of All Possible Evils: Humanitarian Violence from Arendt to Gaza. London, Verso Books.

Wells-Greco, M. (2010). "Operation Cast Lead: Jus in bello proportionality." Netherlands International Law Review **57**(3): 397–422.

Zimmermann, A. (2011). Abiding by and enforcing international humanitarian law in asymmetric warfare: the case of 'Operation Cast Lead'. Institute for International Law and Justice: International Legal Theory Colloquium. New York.

CHAPTER 6

# Conclusion: Lawfare: Law's Contemporary State

## Introduction

This study has mapped out the Israeli legal field involved in the OPT based on the interplay of two fundamental interlinked elements: the logic of the field and the power relations within. Chapter 3 described and analysed the shifts of power in the field and related transformations of its logic. Practices of the military legal system, the High Court of Justice, human rights NGOs, the Ministry of Justice and academics were examined in this context and evaluated in relational terms. Positioning the military legal system in the relational setting of the field underscored the considerable capital gained by this institution. Moreover, the analysis showed that this shift of capital has altered the field's logic, driving it to incorporate international humanitarian law into all pertinent institutions.

Chapter 4, focusing on the military legal system, showed that this institution's legal practitioners have been key agents in making and remaking the field's logic, boundaries and power. It also noted distinct phases in the MAG Corps' practice, maintaining and generating different law. These phases of practice have particular implications for violence and morality, in addition to reshaping the relation of law to politics. Chapter 5 analysed military legal practice in Operation Cast Lead as a manifestation of the law's current phase.

The key questions this study initially set out to tackle were: what is the nature of law's contemporary relationship with conflict and violence? Are we witnessing a new phase in law and lawyers' position in war? What



M. Geva, *Law, Politics and Violence in Israel/Palestine*,
DOI 10.1007/978-3-319-34153-8_6

power and position do lawyers have, and what role do they play, vis-à-vis military operations? What is the nature of current legal practice? And is law merely a political instrument? The field's theoretical-methodological framework required engagement with an additional set of more fundamental questions as a preliminary step. Before enquiring into law's impact on the military handling of the OPT, it was first necessary to reconsider presumptions about law, its goals and intents, and to ask: what *is* law in this particular context, and how has it arrived at its current position? To what extent does the military legal system affect other legal institutions, and how is it affected in return? How has legal practice changed since the beginning of the occupation? Based on these analyses, it was then possible to examine the historical and contemporary character of law's relationship with politics. The response to these questions is a contextualised/historicised account of law.

This concluding chapter ties together the different parts of the study by constructing an analysis of the ILD's engagement with the field's logic, boundaries and power, as a means of articulating law's current phase and its relationship with politics. This analysis builds on the multiple processes of change discussed in the study, including conventions that serve as the basic rules for the field's activities, the reallocation of capital, and legal practitioners' habitus, positioning and power, to make way for a conceptual articulation of the law at present.

This part of the chapter presents the questions and scholarship with which the study set out to engage, and considers the ways that the field's methodological and theoretical frameworks affected this engagement. The chapter's second part describes the term lawfare and its common use as a preparation for this book's novel use of this concept as a means of articulating law's contemporary phase. The following sections analyse lawfare's implications for morality and violence. The chapter then considers the High Court of Justice and the NGOs' position in view of law's new phase. A final section considers the ILD's aspirations to affect law beyond Israel and the OPT, and the future of law.

This book contributes to scholarship regarding Israel's actions and policies in view of international law in the OPT. As described in the introductory chapter, while international law is, and has been, a key feature of Israel's occupation of the West Bank and Gaza, and even though this feature has been the centre of many scholarly accounts, the literature still has considerable gaps. This stems from the tendency of many studies to engage with law in terms that are either internal or external to it. Accounts internal to law generally assess the extent to which Israeli actions and policies are compatible with legal conventions and standards, or diverge from them. Studies external to the law commonly assume that law in this context is merely a political tool, thus rendering it analytically irrelevant. This account, building on Bourdieu's sociology of the field, set out to avoid such presumptions and their analytical implications. Instead, law was analysed as an entity constructed in continual interaction between formal legal instruments, including legal conventions, but also power relations and the ongoing articulation of the relationship between law and politics.

In conceptual and theoretical terms, this examination of the Israeli legal management of the OPT responds to more general accounts addressing the relationship between law and politics. This account's position negates assumptions about law's 'origins' and intended goals (for example, Meron 2000; Teitel 2002; Berman 2004; Anghie 2006). It also rejects perspectives that disqualify law as a substantial factor by understanding it as a political instrument (Kirchheimer 1961; Teubner 1997; Megret 2006). Instead, this book suggests a nuanced consideration of the law—politics relationship as manifested in practice in a specific context.

While the military legal system remained at the centre of this study, theoretical and methodological choices led to contextualisation of this practice in relation to other legal institutions. Bourdieu's framework of the field led to the consideration of various aspects of legal practice taking place in a range of organisations. These facets of law include the participation of different institutions in the process of creating law and its logic, the division of capital among them, their relationships, the habitus of their practitioners, and the influence of bodies on the field's boundaries and power. All these elements provide insight into how the current structure and configuration of power is sustained, and how it is challenged.

## Lawfare and Different Perceptions of Law in Military Conflicts

In recent years, the term 'lawfare' has been appearing increasingly in academic and media discussions. Charles Dunlap is commonly named as the person who popularised it. Dunlap uses this term to describe legal argumentation and legal action as weaponry employed by the weaker side of a conflict with the intention of distorting law:

> Lawfare describes a method of warfare where law is used as a means of realising a military objective … There are many dimensions to lawfare, but the one increasingly embraced by U.S. opponents is a cynical manipulation of the rule of law and the humanitarian values it represents. Rather than seeking battlefield victories, per se, challengers try to destroy the will to fight by undermining the public support that is indispensable when democracies like the U.S. conduct military interventions. (Dunlap 2001, p. 4)

Legal scholar Laurie Blank (2010) applies this term in a similar manner to Israel and Gaza, assessing the Goldstone Report in this vein: 'misapplication of IHL in the Goldstone Report exacerbates the manipulation of IHL by insurgents and terrorists, who use the law, and Western militaries' adherence to the law, as a tool of war in today's conflicts' (Blank 2010, p. 281). This depiction has two noteworthy implications vis-a-vis the law's current state: first, that the Goldstone Fact Finding Mission's legal assertions equate to terrorism, and second, that the Israeli army's actions, precisely because they are governed by law, allow the lawfare attack to come about.

Academic opponents of these arguments claim that the supposed similarity between legal action and terrorism undermines the rule of law (Sadat and Geng 2011), and that this term is used simply to disqualify critical legal positions (Schabas 2011). David Luban (2010) goes further, reversing the argument about the manipulation of law against its creators. Luban contends that those accusing others of exerting lawfare 'are themselves engaged in lawfare' (Luban 2010, p. 3). In this sense, Luban rhetorically disarms the lawfare argument and implies it is no more than a discursively aggressive way to contradict a legal opinion.

To recap this book's introduction, similar discussions relating to legal activity as a form of war take place in political policy-making forums. The US Department of Defense argued to that effect that, 'our strength as a nation state will continue to be challenged by those who employ a strategy of the weak using international fora, judicial processes, and terrorism' (US Department of Defense 2005). Echoing the same discourse in the Israeli context, Prime Minister Benjamin Netanyahu, speaking in a special parliamentary session, listed as the three key threats Israel faces: Iran's nuclear capacity; missiles fired at Israeli territories; and the 'Goldstone threat' (Netanyahu 2009).

I propose a different use of the term lawfare. I use the term to depict law's contemporary condition vis-à-vis military affairs. This depiction constructs a three-layered analysis of law, building on the ILD's influence on the field's logic, the shifting of the field's boundaries, and the power exercised beyond those boundaries. In his accounts of international humanitarian law and conflict in Israel and the OPT, Eyal Weizman (2009, 2011) suggests building on this concept as a gateway to considering the new relationship between law and war, but does not develop this particular analysis much further. I follow up on this suggestion and articulate the term in the course of my analysis.

The term lawfare suggests an alternative to the usual depiction of state military legal practice, where it is often assumed that practitioners negotiate some kind of balance between law and the state's political interests (Rhode 2000; Shamgar 2003; Bilder and Vagts 2004; Clark 2005). The ILD's contemporary phase of legal practice challenges this depiction. Rather than balancing law and the military/state political agenda, as two separate and fixed elements, I argue that practitioners in fact create an entirely new legal—military manner of war.

## Lawfare: The ILD in Warfare and the Remaking of Law

The Israeli trend of making military lawyers standard participants in decision-making forums, and bringing them closer to battlefields (Neuman 2007; Weizman 2009; Cohen 2011) is in line with modifications in Western militaries (Dunlap 2001a, b; Lohr and Gallotta 2003; Kennedy 2006). One facet of this change is quantitative. The ILD grew significantly between 1968 and 2009, at a rate making it the army's fastest-growing body (Cohen 2011, p. 376).

Alongside this quantitative change, the team underwent qualitative transformations. Lawyers' current proximity to decision-making hubs is a key facet of law's new logic. In the past, legal discussions were separate from operational debates. Legal advisers would formulate guidelines and advice far from the battlefield, and were not invited to join discussions leading to political—operational decisions. The separation in time and space allowed for two distinct forms of discussion to take place. In contrast with the image of law's 'truer' practice at a safe distance from military affairs (Mazuz 2007, 2013), its contemporary positioning is entangled with operational—political combat decisions. In terms of the field, this new situation is a remaking of law's logic and boundaries. Operational discussions, once off-limits for legal practitioners, now fall under the jurisdiction of the field.

The active, on-site participation of lawyers in warfare decision-making has made them more amenable to considerations relating to operational agendas. In other words, the place at the table occupied by lawyers in decision-making forums is closely related to their presenting a rationale for reduction of possible conflict between law and military affairs. An ILD officer said as much in the context of the offensive in Gaza: 'Our goal was not to fetter the army, but to give it the tools to win in a lawful manner' (in Blau and Feldman 2009). Similarly, MAG Mendelblit stated: 'We need to help the army win at the end of the day, and we can't forget that … *But* winning within law, and it is possible, if you don't tie things down too much' (Mendelblit 2010, p. 65). In an interview, an ILD officer reiterated this position: 'The only reason why they [military lawyers] can sit beside commanding officers and be listened to, and have their say taken into account, is that they are a part of the system' (in Geva 2011, p. 30). This proximity of intentions signals that relations between law and military operational practice have become entwined in a circular dynamic. Lawyers can only influence military action because they are part of 'the system' and do not 'tie things down too much' – yet being part of this system also directs their actions and their practice of law.

### 6.1.1 *Lawfare and Morality*

A historical review of the MAG Corps and the habitus of its ILD practitioners over the decades that followed the occupation reveals significant changes in the understanding of the legal project vis-à-vis morality. Current practitioners' habitus in this regard is very different from that of their predecessors. In the occupation's early days, practitioners viewed law as a force promoting justice and morality by setting limits to the army's agenda. This approach was spearheaded by Meir Shamgar, who was the MAG in 1967, and a great believer in law's moral and normative capacity. Military lawyers serving during the first Intifada, in the late 1980s, sustained similar perspectives on law. In a characteristic account, a senior ILD officer serving at that time says: 'Our job was to protect human rights … there are universal norms and values. We had a key role to play in that' (Yahav 2013). MAG at that time, Amnon Straschnov, made a similar statement: 'If there was a restraining factor guarding human rights in the Intifada it was the MAG Corps' (Straschnov 2013). These officers considered the defence of individual rights and countering the military agenda as a key aspect of their work. The habitus and perspectives on law of legal officers serving today are radically different.

The departure of law from a position protective of individuals goes hand in hand with it moving away from the notion of morality. In an interview conducted after the operation in Gaza, MAG Mendelblit, in response to a question regarding the extent of the Israeli army's morality, was notably reluctant to describe it as the world's most moral army (Harel 2009), a common cliché among local military and political leaders. That is not to say that he disagrees with this statement, but that the question is irrelevant because as a legal practitioner he does not consider himself to be in a position to make an 'expert' claim about the army's morality. ILD officers similarly said in interviews: 'We are not moral advisers ... We are legal advisers, and our advice is legal ... everyone has a moral perspective: every commander, every soldier and us too' (Officer B 2011). Another officer said to this effect: 'We are not responsible for morality. Morality is not relevant for the work of this team ...The question of whether or not the IDF is a moral army is of no concern to us' (in Geva 2011, p. 35).

### *6.1.2 Lawfare Innovation in Violence Pushing the Limits of Law*

Innovation is also a chief facet of contemporary military legal practice. It implies both a continual remaking of the field's legal logic and a constant pushing of the borders of this logic. Eyal Weizman refers to this innovation as the making of 'elastic law' (Weizman 2011). In the case of Israeli military practice, the second Intifada and the new incorporation of international humanitarian law into the field's logic was a turning point in this regard. The shift of capital to the army's legal system, lawyers' recently acquired seat at the decision-making table and to their being equipped with the international humanitarian law tool box were all forces that allowed for tremendous legal innovation. The effects of change in legal logic and law's new positioning has meant, in fact, a reshaping of the field's boundaries, trespassing on operational areas at one time considered to be exclusively political.

The ILD's innovative practice, backed by this institution's newly acquired considerable capital, was translated into new warfare policies. The classification of Gaza's police forces is an illuminating example of this influence. The ILD's decision to classify police as a combatant entity, and hence a legally permissible target, guided military violence. This was a constitutive action, as a legal officer described it: 'This is a very large group of people who were supposedly, at that moment, civilians, and the following day turned into legitimate military targets' (Blau and Feldman 2009). The rationale for this legal decision is the key analytical point. The legal definition of an enemy plays a major part in warfare choices. The legally induced classification of combatant forces is not limited to people actually and already engaged in combat. This means that from the ILD's perspective the possibly difficult question about what constitutes actual participation in battle is not necessarily even put on the table. The legal argumentation relied on a hypothetical scenario, the anticipated actions of the Israeli army itself and the Gazan police forces' expected response to these actions. In this sense, the action of the Israeli army intertwined with legal practice constituted this enemy group. Notably, this decision was not an exception in terms of its rationale. To recall, as Pnina Sharvit-Baruch, the ILD's Commanding Officer during Operation Cast Lead, clearly stated in a conference presentation: 'Now, what is a military target? …this is very flexible. A civilian object, when it is used [for military purpose], or because of its location, or even because of its potential use …becomes a legitimate target of attack' (Sharvit-Baruch 2009a, b).

The ILD's interpretation of the principle of proportionality similarly reveals innovative constitutive practice. Legally-induced early warning procedures provide people with either a practical or a hypothetical chance to escape, marking all those who stay put as legitimate targets for attack, much like the practice guiding the division between combatants and civilians on grounds of their being potential military threats. In some cases the transition from being a civilian, a person protected from hostilities, to one who is not, is a result of the legal practice of early warning rather than this person's actual involvement in combat.

In this legal—operational constellation of action, law does more than establish supposedly acceptable violence: it actually participates in deciding the components of the battlefield. In separating between civilians and combatants, it does not necessarily seek to identify any action or characteristic of its target. The reasoning for the distinction may originate from the intentions and actions of the army itself, actions that are in part a result of legal practice. In this sense, law participates in the making of targets—enemies—the objects and subjects of military assault. It not only provides the tools to assess, for example, whether an attack is proportionate, but also takes part in constituting the subjects measured with those tools.

As discussed in the introductory chapter, scholars present conflicting opinions about the fundamental impact of international humanitarian law on war: whether it helps to lessen the suffering that would have otherwise transpired, or if it enables and legitimises war. Jean Pictet (1985), one of international humanitarian law's most renowned scholars, represents the former position. Pictet argued that wars occur and it is therefore a moral imperative for law to govern these hostilities. Michael Walzer (1977, p. 144), demonstrates a different perspective, arguing that law only creates the pretence of regulation. This book's conceptualisation of legal practice as an activity that shapes war and guides new forms of warfare means that discussions of international humanitarian law that consider law's impact solely in terms of legitimacy or prevention do not address its full effect.

The ILD's contemporary practice of the laws of war does not inherently aspire to restrict violence. Unlike earlier phases of military legal practice, this type of law is not the likely opponent of military and political decision-makers. Law's de facto construction of novel military battles camouflages it within military surroundings, making it an active facet of contemporary warfare. This legal—military phase is therefore starkly different from law's earlier forms. The legal officers in the early days of the occupation, as well as those serving at the time of the first Intifada, were focused on restricting the army's operations. In the past, confrontations between political decision-makers and legal practitioners were a key element in the habitus of officers, who regarded themselves as the protectors of civil rights. These perspectives no longer represent the military legal system and its relationship with violence. A senior MAG Corps officer explicitly demonstrated this change in relation to Operation Cast Lead in an interview conducted for this study: 'They [commanders] thought it is not allowed to attack mosques, but I, the legal practitioner, tell them that it is allowed. You can attack, no problem' (Officer D 2013). In another interview, a senior MAG Corps officer, who played a major part in the same military operation, responded with difficulty to my asking whether law restricted violence and protected civilians in this case. It was an honest moment on his part, and his pauses reflected difficulty in composing his sentence and setting the thought free: 'Do we prevent harm to civilians? … I don't know … maybe … I'm not sure … I'm not sure it [law] lessens harm … The opposite is sometimes true' (Officer D 2013). Immediately after this moment, he said that he would like this interview to be used anonymously.

## The Current Positions of the High Court of Justice and Human Rights NGOs

As shown in the Chapter 3, the High Court of Justice's decisions since the year 2000 have been central in rearranging the division of capital in the field and transferring power to the MAG Corps. In this process, the court has actually diminished its own influence in favour of the military legal system. This was a pivotal step: in transferring capital to the army, the court placed the authority to decide about crucial issues in the MAG Corps' hands. This shift then led to a process of change in the army's legal system, lessening the legal power of forums removed from battlefields and positioning it instead in discussions interwoven with warfare. In this way, the court played a complex part in remaking the field's logic.

This transferral of capital from the High Court of Justice to the army's legal system, and the general unequal division of capital between legal institutions, do not change the field's joint premise. Law, when understood as the product of the field, is by its nature a joint operation, including all the field's agents and organisations. This intertwined dynamic and law's contemporary character leads NGOs to question their part in the current state of affairs. Michael Sfard, a prominent human rights lawyer, wrote an article posing questions along these lines. One was: 'Am I nothing but a collaborator to this huge mechanism, which needs me to occasionally soften the sharp edges of the military domination and hence enable the occupation to operate?' (Sfard 2005, p. 167). The question implied is: what if NGOs were to dissolve, leaving the state legal system to its own devices? David Kretzmer's account of the High Court of Justice presents the same question in relation to the court – what if it wouldn't review cases concerned with the OPT? Both these questions lead us to the edge of the field. This is a speculative direction of inquiry, but what is certain is that as long as these institutions play a part in the field, even if they occupy a position of structural hostility in relation to the MAG Corps, as NGOs do, they still contribute to the field's power.

The convoluted dynamic of the field also means that the very character of institutions participating in the field is shaped by this relational context. NGOs have been affected greatly by the army's legal shifts. Following the army's novel entry into the realm of international humanitarian law, NGOs used this language in court petitions and in their interactions with the army, but also in their own publications and media materials. This led to NGOs discursively shifting closer to militaries. Eyal Weizman analysed this process in the article he titled 'Only the criminal can solve the crime' (Weizman 2010b), critically examining the implications of the human rights movement's engagement with the evaluation of military conduct, and highlighting a growing similarity between these institutions.

## Local Practice, International Impact

The ILD's lawfare, the current remaking of law and pushing of boundaries—between the legal and the illegal, between the legal and the political—takes place in the meeting point between national and international forums. The ILD's practice aspires to transcend the Israeli-Palestinian locality. Lawyers' innovation seeks international recognition and impact. Senior ILD officers describe legal practice in such terms:

> If you're right, law shifts to your direction. Now, it takes time and practice, but when you understand that this is the way that international law works, you understand how hard it is to say 'illegal' and 'legal' in grey zones. (in Geva 2011, p. 32)
>
> If you do something long enough, the world will accept it. International law as a whole is built on the premise that an act deemed illegal today may become legal if a sufficient number of states are doing it. If this were the case in private law, then the speed limit would be 115 kilometres per hour and income tax would be 4 %. So there is no connection between the question 'Will it pass?' and the legality of an action (in Blau and Feldman 2009)

> The way in which international law evolves ... is the way of practice. This means that the actions of states, the ways in which they act, including the ways in which they explain what they do, creates law ...When states are confronted with new kinds of threats ...like terrorist organisations, in combat they act and employ principles and rules with adaptations that are required by the new situations. Through these adaptations they are, in fact, creating new law. (Pnina Sharvit-Baruch at the Jerusalem Center for Public Affairs Conference 2009)

Statements made by US officials, such as the Chairman of the Joint Chiefs of Staff, Martin Dempsey's announcement of a mission sent to Israel to study the ILD's successful practice, provides a confirmation of such an acceptance (Bernstein 2014).

The current form of law in war in the context of Israel and the OPT is alarming to all those entrusting law with the mitigation of violence and the protection of lives. The perspective of the field can offer the sole comfort of contextualisation and provide a reminder of different possibilities of legal practice and law. The laws of war are not oblivious to violence, nor do they exclude moral considerations per se. The situation we witness today is not inevitable or set in stone. The present-day state of law and the configuration of relations between law and politics are dynamic and never a given constellation of power. While lawfare is grounded in, and maintained by, structures of power, the field's constant movement means that the future of law is undetermined.

## Bibliography


Anghie, A. (2006). "The evolution of international law: Colonial and postcolonial realities." Third World Quarterly **27**(5): 739–753.

Berman, N. (2004). 'The Appeals of the Orient': Colonized Desire and the War of the Riff. Gender and Human Rights. K. Knop. Oxford, Oxford University Press.

Bernstein, D. (2014). Joint Chiefs Chairman Dempsey undermines Obama administration criticism of Israeli actions in Gaza, available at: http://www.washingtonpost.com/news/volokh-conspiracy/wp/2014/11/10/joint-chiefs-chairman-dempsey-undermines-obama-administration-criticism-of-israeli-actions-in-gaza/, [accessed 28.4.15]. The Washington Post 10.11.2014.

Bilder, R. B. and D. F. Vagts (2004). "Speaking Law to Power: Lawyers and Torture." American journal of international law **98** (4): 689–695.

Blank, L. R. (2010). "Finding Facts but Missing the Law: The Goldstone Report, Gaza and Lawfare." Case Western Reserve Journal of International Law **43**(1): 279–306.

Blau, U. and Y. Feldman (2009). How IDF legal experts legitimized strikes involving Gaza civilians. HAARETZ 23/01/09.

Clark, K. (2005). "Ethical Issues Raised by the OLC Torture Memorandum." Journal of National Security Law **1**: 455–472.

Cohen, A. (2011). "Legal Operational Advice in the Israeli Defense Forces: the International Law Department and the Changing Nature of International Humanitarian Law." Connecticut Journal of International Law **26**(2).

Dunlap, C. J. (2001). Law and Military Interventions: Preserving Humanitarian Values in 21st Conflicts, available at: http://people.duke.edu/~pfeaver/dunlap.pdf [accessed 28.4.15]. Humanitarian Challenges in Military Intervention Carr Center for Human Rights Policy, Kennedy School of Government, Harvard University.

Geva, M. (2011). Dynamics of Law, Organisation and Morality in Contemporary Warfare: The right to life in the case of the Israeli military International Law

Department. Human Rights Practice, School of Global Studies, University of Gothenburg. **MA**.

Harel, A. (2009). MAG, Brigadier General Mendelblit, speaks about Cast Lead, Chico Tamir and B'Tselem, HAARETZ 18.9.09, available at: http://www.haaretz.co.il/misc/1.1281465 [accessed 28.4.15]

Kennedy, D. (2006). Of War and Law. Princeton, Princeton University Press.

Kirchheimer, O. (1961). Political Justice: The Use of Legal Procedure for Political Ends. Princeton, New Jersey, Princeton University Press.

Lohr, M. F. and S. Gallotta (2003). "Legal Support in War: The Role of Military Lawyers." Chicago Journal of International Law **4**(2): 465–478.

Luban, J. D. (2010). "Lawfare and Legal Ethics in Guantánamo." Stanford Law Review **60**: 1981–2026.

Mazuz, M. (2007). The testimony of the Attorney General, Meni Mazuz, to the Winograd Commission, available at: http://www.vaadatwino.gov.il/statements.html - null [accessed 28.4.15]

Mazuz, M. (2013). Interview with Maayan Geva, 6.2.13.

Megret, F. (2006). From 'Savages' to 'Unlawful Combatants': A Postcolonial Look at International Humanitarian Law's 'Other'. International Law And Its 'Others'. A. Orford. Cambridge Cambridge University Press.

Mendelblit, A. (2010a). The testimony of the MAG, Avihai Mendelblit, in front of the Public Commission to Examine the Maritime Incident of 31 May 2010, Turkel Commission, Part 2.

Meron, T. (2000). "The Humanization of Humanitarian Law." The American Journal of International Law **94**(2): 239–278.

Netanyahu, B. (2009). "Speech at a special Knesset session, http://mfa.gov.il/MFA/PressRoom/2009/Pages/PM-Netanyahu-addresses- Knesset-Special-Session-23-Dec-2009.aspx."

Neuman, N. (2007). "Legal Consultancy in Battle." Systems (Ma'arachot) **411**: 36–41.

Officer B, B. (2011). Interview with Maayan Geva, 20.2.11.

Officer D, D. (2013). Interview with Maayan Geva, 16.1.13.

Pictet, J. (1985). Development and principles of international humanitarian law. Dordrecht; Lancaster, Nijhoff.

Rhode, D. (2000). In the Interests of Justice: Reforming the Legal Profession. Oxford; New York, Oxford University Press.

Sadat, L. N. and J. Geng (2011). On Legal Subterfuge and the so called "Lawfare" debate, Case Western Reserve University School of Law. **43:** 153–161.

Schabas, W. (2011). "Gaza, Goldstonem and Lawfare." Case Western Reserve Journal of International Law **43**(1): 307–312.

Sfard, M. (2005). "Book Review: The Human Rights Lawyer's Existential Dilemma: The Occupation of Justice, the Supreme Court of Israel and the Occupied Territories." Israel Law Review **38**.

Shamgar, M. (2003). Shamgar Book. Tel Aviv, The Israel Bar Publishing House

Sharvit Baruch, P. (2009). Conference Paper. Hamas, the Gaza war and accountability under international law. Jerusalem, available at: http://media-line.co.il/Events/Jcpa/Law-Conference/Heb.aspx [accessed 28.4.15].

Straschnov, A. (2013). Interview with Maayan Geva 31.12.12.

Teitel, R., G. (2002). "Humanity's Law: Rule of Law for the New Global Politics." Cornell International Law Journal **35**(2): 355–387.

Teubner, G. (1997). Law in the Collision of Discourses Law, Society and Economy. R. Rawlings. Oxford, Clarendon Press.

U.S. Department of Defense (2005). "The National Defense Strategy of the United States of America 5, http://www.defense.gov/news/Mar2005/d20050318nds2.pdf..

Walzer, M. (1977). Just and Unjust Wars: a moral argument with historical illustrations. New York, Basic Books.

Weizman, E. (2009). "Lawfare in Gaza: legislative attack, Open Democracy, available at: http://www.opendemocracy.net/article/legislative-attack [accessed 29.4.15]."

Weizman, E. (2010b). Only the Criminal Can Solve the Crime. ArteEast Public Lecture The New School, New York, The Sheila C. Johnson Design Center

Weizman, E. (2011). The Least of All Possible Evils: Humanitarian Violence from Arendt to Gaza. London, Verso Books.

Yahav, D. (2013). Interview with Maayan Geva, 5.3.13.

# Appendices

## Appendix I: International Law Division/Department Commanding Officers

| *Name* | *Period of service* |
|---|---|
| Dov Sheffi | 1968–1973 |
| Zvi Efrat | 1973–1978 |
| Yoel Zinger | 1978–1989 |
| David Yahav | 1989–1991; 1994–1995 |
| Ahaz Ben Ari | 1991–1994 |
| Daniel Reisner | 1995–2003 |
| Pnina Sharvit Baruch | 2003–2009 |
| Liron Libman | 2009–2011 |
| Noam Neuman | 2011– |

*Source*: MAG Corps' Spokesperson's Office


M. Geva, *Law, Politics and Violence in Israel/Palestine*,
DOI 10.1007/978-3-319-34153-8

# Appendix II: Military Advocate Generals Serving After 1967

| *Name* | *Period of service* |
|---|---|
| Meir Shamgar | 1961–1968 |
| Zvi Hadar | 1968–1973 |
| Zvi Inbar | 1973–1979 |
| Dov Sheffi | 1979–1984 |
| Ben Zion Farhi | 1984–1986 |
| Amnon Straschnov | 1986–1991 |
| Ilan Shiff | 1991–1995 |
| Uri Shoam | 1995–2000 |
| Menachem Finkelstein | 2000–2004 |
| Avihai Mendelblit | 2004–2011 |
| Dani Efroni | 2011–2015 |
| Sharon Afek | 2015– |

# Index




M. Geva, *Law, Politics and Violence in Israel/Palestine*,
DOI 10.1007/978-3-319-34153-8

The manufacturer's authorised representative in the EU is Springer Nature Customer Service Centre GmbH, Europaplatz 3, 69115 Heidelberg, Germany. If you have any concerns regarding our products, please contact ProductSafety@springernature.com

Printed and bound by CPI Group (UK) Ltd, Croydon, CR0 4YY
23/09/2026
02221520-0001

# The Origins of Economic Regions in France, 1918–1940

Terence Cudbird

# The Origins of Economic Regions in France, 1918–1940

palgrave
macmillan

Terence Cudbird
University of Oxford
Oxford, UK

ISBN 978-3-032-04421-1    ISBN 978-3-032-04422-8 (eBook)
https://doi.org/10.1007/978-3-032-04422-8



This Palgrave Macmillan imprint is published by the registered company Springer Nature Switzerland AG.
The registered company address is: Gewerbestrasse 11, 6330 Cham, Switzerland

# Acknowledgements

I am grateful for the support I have received from my D Phil supervisors, Dr. David Hopkin of Hertford College, Oxford and Dr. Adrian Gregory, Pembroke College, Oxford. I also acknowledge the advice I received from Professor John Horne of Trinity College, Dublin; Professor Julian Wright of Northumbria University; and Clotilde Druelle-Korn of the Université de Limoges, France. I thank many archivists and librarians who assisted my research in France, particularly Frédérique Galin and her colleagues at the Bibliothèque du Patrimoine, Clermont-Ferrand, Laurent Barbier, and her colleagues at the Bibliothèque Stanislas, Nancy, Anais Avossa at MUCEM, Marseille; and Anne Alonzo and her colleagues at the Archives de Saint Gobain, Blois. I am also grateful to Nicholas Davidson at St. Edmund Hall, who listened to my ideas and set me off on an application to the history faculty, to David Priestland and to Wes Williams, my college advisor, for always listening sympathetically to accounts of my progress. I also benefited from discussions with a wide circle of academic colleagues including Dr. Cesare Vagge who contributed to my thinking about the links between regionalism and corporatism

As a mature researcher I also need to acknowledge some older debts of gratitude—to my tutors at Peterhouse and also to the late Patrick Bury of Corpus Christi, Cambridge, whose special subject on Napoleon III first awakened my interest in modern French history; to the late Professor Douglas Johnson of University College London who supervised me during a failed attempt to complete a PhD on French attitudes to England in the mid-nineteenth century and finally, to Robin Reeve, Norman Isaacs and their colleagues at KCS Wimbledon who laid the foundations for my lifelong interest in history and in France.

My work is also the fruit of reflection during three years spent tramping around France and writing about my experiences in two books—*Walking the Hexagon* and *Walking the Retreat, 1914*. During this time, I met many people and made French friends who have encouraged me on the path I have taken. I would like to record particular thanks to the Bussac family for their hospitality during my research and for drawing my attention to some important books, to Jacques Prouff who was my companion on many expeditions and his wife Sylvie, and to Annette and the late Alain Desaulty, himself a writer on modern French history as well as a distinguished surgeon.

Lastly, I must thank my wife for her support and having to put up with the lows as well as the highs of this project.

# Contents

# About the Author

**Terence Cudbird** is an associate member of the History Faculty in Oxford. He took a B.A. in History at Cambridge and, after a career in business, gained a D Phil in History from Oxford for a thesis entitled *The Impact of the Great War on French Regionalism 1900–1924* (2020). He has also published two books on France: *Walking the Hexagon, an Escape Around France on Foot* (2012) and *Walking the Retreat, the March to the Marne 1914 Revisited* (2014), as well as an article "The Clémentel moment: the reform of 1918 and the beginnings of regional economic planning in France" (*French History*, volume 37, no. 2, June 2023).

# List of Figures

CHAPTER 1

# Introduction

The relationship between Paris and the diverse regions of France has been one of the main factors in French history. It has affected not only politics and the development of state institutions but also economics and social and cultural issues. The subject of this book, the activities of the economic regions between 1918 and 1940, is part of this much broader and longer story.

The tension between Paris and the provinces existed under the *Ancien Régime*. For the monarchy, control was important, particularly to ensure the security of the kingdom. Rebellious provinces were a constant preoccupation. Control of the administration was exercised through the *intendants*, but a certain diversity of regional institutions was tolerated. Provinces maintained an identity. Provincial estates existed in some such as the Languedoc. While French was the official language of the French monarchy, provincial languages and dialects flourished particularly among rural populations.

For our purposes the story begins with the French Revolution. The threat to the future of the republic from internal revolts set up a suspicion of provincial particularism which lasted for 200 years. Moreover, the Revolution also saw the abolition of many corporate institutions which stood between the state and individuals. The French republic was based on the assumption that the general interest could be protected by creating a direct relationship between the state and each citizen. Intermediate



T. Cudbird, *The Origins of Economic Regions in France, 1918-1940*,
https://doi.org/10.1007/978-3-032-04422-8_1

corporate bodies were seen as inimical to that general interest. This political and philosophical inheritance overshadowed every attempt subsequently to grapple with the problem of governing a country of extraordinary regional diversity. Pierre Rosanvallon has described the dominant Jacobin political discourse which continued to be a feature of French political thought. This discourse on the virtue of generality was directly opposed to the recognition of different interests including regional interests.

However, Rosanvallon has also shown that a gap developed between the theory and actual practice as the state dealt with the development of society in the nineteenth century. The chambers of commerce, which were clearly non-state corporations, were allowed to continue throughout the nineteenth century as channels of communication between business and central government. In practice large numbers of non-governmental associations were tolerated from the later nineteenth century. These included charitable associations, literary societies, mutual aid bodies, industrial societies, cooperative organizations and of course political parties. A legal framework for business corporations was codified, organs of local government acquired legal powers and in 1884 labour unions were given legal status. A new law in 1901 gave all associations that the government deemed to be of public utility legal recognition. Various sorts of associations and intermediary bodies became political agents of the state and supported its activities in a number of functional areas such a health and social welfare.[1] Rosanvallon described these developments as creating the network state, although he says nothing about regionalism as a phenomenon and does not mention the development of economic regions after 1918.[2] The Third Republic was characterized by an institutional pluralism which meant that power was more diffuse than the Jacobin model might suggest and that it was distributed horizontally and vertically through a variety of political, economic and geographic mediating structures.[3] In the thinking of social Catholics and sociologists like Durkheim, these intermediary bodies were sometimes described as corporations, a generic category to remedy the atomization of society.

[1] P. Rosanvallon, The Demands of Liberty: Civil Society in France Since the Revolution, trans. A. Goldhammer (Harvard, 2007), 149–230.

[2] Rosanvallon, Demands of Liberty, 231–253.

[3] J. Wright and H.S. Jones (eds), Pluralism and the Idea of the Republic in France (Basingstoke, 2012), 1–22.

This toleration of non-governmental organizations did not extend to giving regions representation. Many politicians in the dominant Radical party after 1870 believed that any regionalist programme, including the devolution of power to the regions through the creation of regional assemblies, was a threat to the Third Republic. It implied a return to a traditional society, based on the old provinces of the *Ancien Régime* and under the influence of the Catholic church. It might encourage separatism in areas with a distinctive culture and language which were not French, like Brittany. This view may have softened a little in the years immediately before the First World War, but it still influenced public debate. Many Radicals thought that traditionalists would use regional reform to restore the power of the Catholic church. The policy of *laicité*, particularly in education, which dated back to the laws inspired by Jules Ferry between 1880 and 1882, was of overriding importance for Radicals.[4] Their suspicion of regionalism was no doubt also influenced by the widespread revival of interest in regional cultures throughout France in the later nineteenth century which commenced with Mistral's Félibrige association to promote Provencal language and literature in the 1850s. Some of those who supported regional cultures argued that love of a region was not incompatible with national patriotism. Indeed two of the flag bearers of French nationalism in this period, Charles Maurras founder of the Action Française, and Maurice Barrès, believed local roots were very important. Maurras was attached to Mistral's movement and Barrès to Lorraine. However the conservative position of these two opinion leaders was seen by Radicals as anti-Republican. While cultural associations in Brittany were mostly not interested in politics in the nineteenth century, this was not the case with the Union Régionaliste Bretonne founded by the Marquis de l'Estourbeillon in 1898.

The history of regionalism in France is closely connected with two other debates on decentralization and deconcentration which also grew during the nineteenth century. These two terms covering policies for the development of government institutions have different meanings although they are connected. Decentralization refers to the idea of devolving power from the central government in Paris to local institutions, giving them greater responsibility for certain matters rather than having to refer everything to the centre. It was thought that this would mean quicker and less costly government action which would speed up economic and social

[4] S. Berstein, Histoire du Parti Radical, la recherche de l'âge d'or (Paris, 1980), 323–324.

development and save money. This debate had a long history. In the early nineteenth century, some royalists, particularly the Legitimists, favoured a decentralized government. They looked for a return to the *Ancien Régime*'s provincial liberties and corporate privileges. Their decentralist sentiment stemmed from a belief in organic, local institutions like *parlements*, guilds, and provincial estates. They were strong in certain areas with strong regionalist sentiments like Brittany and the Vendée. Joseph de Maistre and Louis de Bonald emphasized the importance of local traditions. Decentralization was a feature of the Nancy programme, which appeared in 1865 during the Second Empire, and was also supported by a number of prominent writers like De Tocqueville, who feared the loss of civil liberties in a centralized state, and Fréderic Bastiat, a classic economic liberal who believed in free markets. A different reason for supporting decentralization was offered by Proudhon who believed in the dissolution of centralized state power in favour of autonomous associations. This federalist tradition was influential among those who supported regional institutions in the twentieth century.

Belief in decentralization underpinned the granting of greater powers to local municipalities in the early years of the Third Republic. It was a constant feature of discussions in regionalist groups, for example, in the FRF, throughout the years up to the First World War, as my thesis on regionalism shows.[5] Of course, decentralization covered changes to many other government institutions apart from regions, for example, municipalities and departments. It also called into question the control which the prefects, the agents of central government in the departments, exercised over actions by local bodies through the *tutelle* (administrative supervision). They could reverse local authorities' actions without going to the courts.

Deconcentration referred to the idea of delegating some powers from central government organs to local agents of the central administration, but not to independent local government institutions with a separate legal personality. It was thus simply a reorganization of powers within the administrative hierarchy of the state. It might lead to greater efficiency and faster decisions without central government losing its control of policy. It was an attempt by those in the Jacobin tradition to answer calls for greater efficiency, but it did not satisfy the aspirations of regionalists and others

[5] T. Cudbird, The Impact of the Great War on French Regionalism 1900–1924 (Oxford DPhil, 2020), 34–35, 110, 168.

who wanted local citizens to have the power to shape their own environment.

The pressures of the First World War on the French state and the growing strength of the regionalist movement influenced Étienne Clémentel, Minister of Commerce, to introduce the first economic regions in 1918, assisted by the geographer Henri Hauser, a disciple of Vidal de la Blache, the founder of the French school of Geography whose *Tableau de la Géographie de la France* was published in 1903. These regions were based on groupings of chambers of commerce and incorporated regional committees created during the war to mobilize resources for the war effort. Clémentel was a regionalist in the sense that he was interested in his native Auvergne's culture. He also had connections with regionalist circles and believed in moving some powers closer to local people to make government more effective. However, the formative experience behind his reform was his period as Minister of Commerce for four years during the First World War. This convinced him that French industry needed to make itself more competitive, once the war was over, to compete with Germany and other large economies. He set about forming a number of representative bodies to involve business leaders in a programme of modernization of industrial practices and of the infrastructure which supported a modern economy. The new economic regions were one manifestation of this policy of creating intermediate bodies in a campaign of modernization.[6] These were bodies representative of particular economic interests but in no sense could they claim the democratic mantle of national representative bodies like the Chamber of Deputies. They were no threat to the Republican state.

This interest in intermediate bodies to help the state manage the economy did not stop in 1918. It continued and developed in the inter-war period. Examples of new bodies which were created include the *chambres d'agriculture* and the Conseil National Économique. In my article in *French History* I assessed the contextualization of Clémentel's reform within the changing political culture of French republicanism by associating it with the term 'corporatist'.[7] His policy involved what Wright and Jones have described as modern political scientists' definition of corporat-

[6] Terence Cudbird, 'The Clémentel moment: the reform of 1918 and the beginnings of regional economic planning in France,' *French History*, volume 37 number 2, June 2023, pp. 126–141.

[7] Terence Cudbird, 'the Clémentel moment', 128.

ism, namely "the institutionalized representation of functional interest groups within the political system." These groups were clearly in part dependent on the state.[8] According to Michel Letté, it is appropriate to frame Clémentel's policies in the inter-war context of the construction of systems for directing the economy under the leadership of the state.[9] Adrian Rossiter in his 1986 Oxford DPhil thesis frames Clémentel's regional reform within the 'corporatist politics' of the inter-war period, which sought to modernize the state by encouraging the formal representation of economic interest groups. Corporations representing such groups would introduce fresh technocratic expertise in planning the economy. In his speech to the inaugural meeting of the Eastern region in 1918, Clémentel said he wanted to see new interest groups join together with the regional groupings of chambers of commerce in regional assemblies. His aim in this regard was never carried out, but his focus on expanding the number of representative corporate bodies is clear. This approach Rossiter characterizes as "corporative pluralism."[10]

This book takes Rosanvallon's analysis as a starting point but extends it into a discussion of the development of regional government, starting with the economic regions of the inter-war period. Many historians have discussed regionalism, but no one has dealt with the activity of the economic regions and other economic bodies throughout France between the First World War and the enactment of Mitterrand's major regional reform of 1982. This book is based on much original research on the activities of the economic regions and assesses what they achieved. Its main focus is infrastructure development such as new railways and canals, electricity generation and technical education. Involving regional bodies in economic modernization marked a pivotal moment in the history of regionalism.

Hitherto the strand of regionalism which wanted to preserve regional cultures and even some of a past way of life tended to be dominant. Regionalism before the First World War drew its strength from attachment to regional languages and customs in the countryside and among a limited

[8] J. Wright and H.S. Jones (eds), Pluralism and the idea of the Republic in France (Basingstoke, 2012), 11–12.

[9] M. Letté, 'Le pré-planificateur: le rapport général sur l'industrie française, sa situation, son avenir en 1919', in Étienne Clémentel: politique et action publique sous la Troisième République, ed. M-C. Kessler and G. Rousseau (Brussels, 2018), 323.

[10] A. Rossiter, 'Experiments with Corporatist Politics in Republican France 1916–1939', (Oxford DPhil, 1986), 1–10, 83.

number of the educated middle class in regional centres. Maurras was a staunch monarchist and Catholic, and Barrès's patriotism was strongly rooted in the soil of Lorraine. A good example of this traditionalist regionalism is to be found in the writings of Henri Pourrat, the Catholic writer in the Auvergne who admired Barrès and the Action Française and the values of a rural life. He distrusted the towns and foresaw the pollution which would be caused by an industrial civilization to which he was opposed. Another interesting example of this traditionalist tendency in pre-war regionalism was Louis Marin, whose nationalism ran alongside a very traditional view of social relations. He believed every region like Lorraine had its own character and that an upbringing in a village had a profound effect on individuals. His interest in Lorraine was in the countryside, not the new Lorraine of industry and large towns.[11] He was greatly influenced by Catholic family values and supported the movement led by Jules Méline for a return to the land.[12] This emphasis on the values of the land is evident in his collection of Lorraine folk tales.[13] These views went back to his time as president of the *Fédération régionaliste française* before 1914. He was very involved in the development of anthropology in France between the wars, but his thinking was narrow and old-fashioned.[14] After 1918 regionalism was gradually re-oriented to harnessing the energies of the regions to modernize regional economies. This book deals with this decisive shift.

In considering Clémentel's reform and its outcome, there are three key considerations. How far did an interest in a region's culture and pride in its identity motivate the business leaders in their practical programmes? Secondly, how far were they implementing the concept of economic regionalism developed in the pre-1918 period? Thirdly, how far did they extend the influence of the state in economic life? Various secondary sources discussed next all throw some light on these questions.

[11] L. Marin, Regards sur la Lorraine: réflexions sur des notions fondamentales, particularités du caractère lorrain (Paris, 1966), pp. 15–18, 25–26, 54–57, 121–131.

[12] Méline's post war statement of this programme was published in 1919, J. Méline, Le Salut par la terre et le programme économique de l'avenir (Paris, 1919).

[13] L. Marin, Contes traditionnels en Lorraine. Institutions de transfert des valeurs morales et spirituelles (Paris, 1944).

[14] H. Lebovics, 'Le Conservatisme en anthropologie et la fin de la Troisième République', Gradhiva, Revue d'Histoire et d'Archives de l'Anthropologie, no. 4 (été 1988), pp. 3–17, particularly pp. 13–14. H. Lebovics, True France, the Wars over Cultural Identity 1900–1945 (Cornell and London, 1992), pp. 16–50.

Regarding the role of Clémentel, Alain Chatriot has explained how he set up the regions and what further attempts were made to modify them. He does not deal with the practical performance of the regions which is the main subject of my book.[15] Clotilde Druelle-Korn also covers the influences on Clémentel's thinking and draws attention to the philosophy of solidarism developed by Léon Bourgeois, a philosophy based on the identification of mutual interests which could be pursued by people joining together for the common good. However she agrees that the practical experience of the Great War had the greatest influence on his subsequent reforms. She says the results of the chamber groupings are still to be assessed but that they gave a decisive push to transport and electrification in the regions[16]

A practical approach to economic policy making is very much at the centre of Julian Wright's study of pre-First World War regionalism, *The Regionalist Movement in France 1890–1914: Jean Charles-Brun and French Political Thought* (Oxford, 2003). He identifies the praxis which was characteristic of Charles-Brun's thinking. This praxis was fundamental to the concept of economic regionalism, the devolution of some powers to regional bodies to lead a revival of regional economic development. He also shows that regionalism was a broad church and that therefore this new economic regionalism was closely linked to the rediscovery of the culture of France's regions. He shows how Charles-Brun was successful in raising regionalism as an issue up the political agenda before 1914 and this momentum continued into the war years. Clémentel was clearly influenced by the ideas being discussed in regionalist circles.

The strength of the regionalist movement in pre-First World War France was much wider than the Fédération Régionaliste Française run by Charles-Brun, even though the latter had some influential members in political and academic circles. It was a revival of interest in regional culture

[15] Marie-Christine Kessler et Guy Rousseau (dir.), Étienne Clémentel, Politique et action publique sous la Troisième République (Peter Lang Brussels, 2018). Alain Chatriot's essay here is 'Les régions Clémentel: débats et expériences' (pp. 327–341).See also 'Les régions économiques d'une guerre à l'autre: aménagement du territoire, discours, projets et pratiques,' in P. Caro, O. Dard, J-C. Daumas (dirn.), La politique d'aménagement du territoire: racines, logiques et résultats (Rennes, 2002).

[16] Druelle-Korn, C., 'Un Laboratoire réformateur, le Département du Commerce en France' (Thèse de doctorat, Institut d'Études Politiques, Paris, 2004). Druelle-Korn, C., 'De la pensée à l'action économique: Étienne Clémentel (1864–1936) un ministre visionnaire', Histoire@Politique, Politique, culture, société, n° 16, (janvier–avril 2012), 40–54.

and history led by middle-class writers and intellectuals, often grouped together in provincial literary societies throughout the French provinces. It started in Provence led by Mistral and spread in several other regions, for example, to the Cantal in the Auvergne, as described by J-F Chanet.[17] Without this renewed pride in regional identity, it is unlikely the idea of economic regions would have gathered strength. Clémentel was a typical product of this movement with his personal interest in the history of his native Auvergne. Writers with an interest in the character of their regions like Henri Pourrat in the Auvergne were increasingly influential.[18] Fundamental to this movement was the desire to teach children about their regional heritage in the schools.[19]

R. F Kuisel's work helps us understand how Clémentel's initiatives formed part of a greater involvement of the French state in the economy during this period.[20]

The French Third Republic largely adhered to liberal economic principles, with the state playing a limited role in economic management. It intervened selectively in areas such as railways, postal services and armaments. This laid early foundations for the later acceptance of a more active economic role. The First World War forced the state to take a much more active role—mobilizing resources, managing industries and coordinating production, especially in armaments. Wartime agencies, such as war supply boards, foreshadowed later planning bodies. This was a critical juncture that legitimized state coordination of the economy. The war brought industrialists and the state into closer collaboration, helping to ease prior antagonisms and demonstrating the utility of state intervention. After the war, there was a strong ideological reversion to free-market orthodoxy. Some planning proposals emerged (e.g., from technocrats and industrial engineers), but they lacked political support. The Depression of the thirties intensified critiques of liberalism and exposed structural weaknesses in the French economy (e.g., over-fragmentation, low productivity). The crisis gave more visibility to technocratic elites who advocated planning,

[17] J-F. Chanet, Les Félibres cantaliens : aux sources du régionalisme auvergnat 1879-1914 (Clermont-Ferrand, 2000).

[18] A-M. Thiesse, Écrire la France; le movement littéraire régionaliste de langue française entre la belle époque et la libération (Paris, 1991).

[19] A-M. Thiesse, Ils apprenaient la France: l'exaltation des régions dans le discours patriotique (Paris, 1997). J-F. Chanet, L'École républicaine et les petites patries (Paris, 1996).

[20] Kuisel, R.F., Capitalism and the State in Modern France: Renovation and Economic Management in the Twentieth Century (Cambridge, 1981). 66–69, 90–92, 96, 114–127.

rationalization and modernization—though still marginal in political influence. Kuisel shows how the Popular Front government of Léon Blum promoted social reforms but was hesitant to embrace full economic planning. While the pre-1940 period does not yet institutionalize economic planning, Kuisel identifies the growing intellectual and administrative groundwork for postwar *dirigisme.* Up to 1940, the French state's economic role was reactive rather than strategic—responding to crises rather than shaping long-term development.

The weakness of the economic regionalism which emerged through Clémentel's reform was that it depended on the central government to bring it into being and it met opposition from the outset. Traditional Republicans distrusted it. It was dependent on the cooperation of sometimes fractious chambers of commerce. As a result of opposition, the regions had no legal personality and relied on persuasion only to carry initiatives forward. This led some historians like Flory and Pitte to describe the regions as failures.[21] I argue that this is to take a very narrow view of their achievements. The political scientist R. K. Gooch's *Regionalism in France,* first published in New York in 1931, suggested that regionalism could develop gradually based on existing structures without the need for government legislation to introduce new regional structures. Thinkers like Lagardelle in Toulouse suggested professional bodies could get together to pursue common objectives without official sanction. When Gooch used the term "spontaneous regionalism," he meant regionalism which grew up from the grassroots. This book aims to build on Gooch's idea and discover how spontaneous regionalism actually worked in the economic sphere. Gooch also recognized the importance of the new strand of economic regionalism.[22]

I have found the books by Romain Pasquier very suggestive—*La capacité politique des régions: une comparaison France-Espagne* (Rennes, 2004), and *Le Pouvoir régional* (Paris, 2012). He identifies what he calls political capacity as critically important in explaining a region's success in the post-1945 period. I have concluded that it was also fundamental in the pre-1940 period. By "capacité politique," he means a way of acting which the leaders inherit in their regions from beliefs and practices going back

[21] T. Flory, Le Mouvement Régionaliste Français (Paris, 1966), 94–96. J.R. Pitte , Philippe Lamour, père de l'aménagement du territoire en France 1903-1992 (Paris, 2002), 24 (fn. p. 297), 32.

[22] R.K. Gooch, Regionalism in France (New York, 1931), 104–124.

many years. He stresses a region's ability to act autonomously and to influence national decisions. Political capacity involves institutional resources, strategic vision, leadership, coalition building and administrative know-how to carry out a regional programme. It also involves the capacity to construct and project a territorial identity, which helps legitimize the region's role and political claims. We will find so many of these characteristics in the successful pre-1940 region of Lorraine.[23]

We have seen that up to 1918 there was an important regionalist movement based on pride in a region. A new institutional framework was set up in that year to help develop each region's economy. What we need to understand is what the new economic regions did in practice over the next 20 years. What influenced their effectiveness? How did they relate to the state? These are issues that I aim to resolve. Some regional studies have been published which point the way forward.

First of all I have made extensive use of my doctoral thesis: "The Impact of the Great War on French Regionalism 1900–1924: A study of the Auvergne and Lorraine," completed in 2020. In this thesis I made extensive use of primary sources to illuminate not only the impact of the war on regionalism but also the results the economic regions actually achieved in the immediate post-war period. I studied in particular the papers of Camiile Cavallier, the head of the Pont-à-Mousson company and vice-chairman of the Nancy Chamber of Commerce and those of Jean Charles-Brun and the FRF. I also used the records of the principal chambers of commerce and the economic journals published by the regions. The minutes of the regions meetings have not survived in extenso.

Veitl has provided a book on the Alpine region post-1918, Druelle-Korn an essay on the Limousin in the same period and Eck likewise on the Nord.[24] Veitl describes how influential economic leaders and geographers created a vision of a region based on hydro-electric power. The study does not, however, show in detail what was achieved. Druelle-Korn and Eck

[23] R. Pasquier, La Capacité Politique des Régions: une comparaison France, Espagne (Rennes, 2004), 26–29, 206–207.

[24] P. Veitl, L'Invention d'une région : les Alpes françaises (Grenoble, 2013). C. Druelle-Korn, 'La modernisation inachevée de l'aménagement du territoire, le cas de la VIIe Région (Limousin, Poitou, Charentes)', in A. Aglan, M. Margairaz, P. Verheyde (eds), De la croissance à la crise (1925-1935): Le moment Tannery, une tentative avortée de modernisation conservatrice et libérale à l'heure de la mondialisation (Paris, 2014), 155–172. J. F Eck, 'Une expérience de modernisation économique: la première région économique,' in A. Aglan et al., De la Croissance à la crise (1925-1935), 139–154

show that the results achieved in the Limousin and the Nord were limited. In the Limousin some improvements resulted, for instance, the plan to generate hydro-electricity from the Dordogne river. In the Nord there was rivalry between different commercial interests which seemed to prevent a concerted drive for regional development. Giandou's book on the setting up of the Compagnie Nationale du Rhône to facilitate the passage of shipping, the irrigation of agriculture and the generation of electricity has much to say about the effectiveness of leadership in the regions based on Lyon, Grenoble and Marseille. In this case the project was driven through to an effective result.

I have not conducted my own research in the areas covered by these historians. What all these studies show is that performance varied from region to region. Lorraine and the Auvergne were more active than any of the others with the exception of those in the Rhône valley. These studies suggested that it was important to survey a wide number of regions to get a fair picture of progress in regional development in France as a whole.[25] This I have attempted to do by covering the Toulouse and Bordeaux regions and also Normandy and Brittany. I have also assessed the work of the institutions set up in the regions to represent agriculture and tourism. These have not been covered at all by other historians.

In looking at these new regions I have also used regional press extensively and particularly regional periodicals which focus on economic affairs. I have discovered a number of such journals which articulated the main economic issues which the regions faced and sought to encourage wider support for change. I have also used the printed records of chambers of commerce in the main regional centres. It is important to understand that the presidents of the regions were often president, or at least a member, of the chamber of commerce of the regional centre. In that sense the main chamber of commerce also 'ran' the region and an examination of its deliberations is important. Fortunately the proceedings of the regions have survived in whole or for some years in the case of these new regions and I have used them extensively. For agriculture I have examined the journals of the main regional federations of agricultural syndicates. For tourism I have looked at the proceedings of regional federations published in various journals and also at the *Bullletn de l'Union des Fédérations des Syndicats d'Initiative*. I have looked at some works published by key

[25] A. Giandou, Compagnie Nationale du Rhône 1933-1998, histoire d'un partenaire régional de l'état (Grenoble, 1999).

figures regionally. In assessing the achievements of the regions, I have looked outside the membership of the regional committees themselves to a wider group of economic leaders in each region—politicians, business leaders, journalists, engineers.

I have used secondary sources as well. For the post-1945 period, I have consulted the plentiful secondary sources written by historians but also by political scientists and economists, who are concerned to elucidate how regional institutions work in France today. I have also looked at the writings of some of the main actors who turned the Socialist party toward a policy of decentralization and regionalization, such as Michel Rocard, eventually a Socialist Prime Minister, and Robert Lafont, a leading Socialist thinker, as well as Mitterrand himself. This was a historic shift from the pre-war socialist distrust of all things regionalist.

In the second chapter I begin by analysing the influences which brought about Clémentel's reform at the end of the First World War and exactly how it took place. I then show how subsequent attempts to give the economic regions the legal powers they lacked ended in failure. All this provides the essential context for what the economic regions actually achieved. In the next two chapters, I demonstrate what was achieved in Lorraine and the Auvergne. This provides an essential benchmark for what follows. I show that the economic development agenda included railway and canal transport, power generation, technical education, capital provision, tourism, post-war reconstruction and natalism and I deal with each of these issues in turn. It is significant that these were the two regions where Clémentel thought he had the best chance of success and which he visited personally. In the next two chapters, I revisit the two regions in turn and analyse the success factors in each. First of all, I deal with the strength of regional feeling and regional solidarity. Then I show how the chambers of commerce operated, the nature of their leadership, its effectiveness and their networks of influence. In Chap. 7, I carry out a similar analysis on the region centred around Toulouse, showing how despite the evident feeling of regional identity, the attitude of the regional leadership was very different. I describe the difference in approach between the regional chairman who was against interventions in regional development and the regional secretary who had a much more activist approach. I then use regional records to see how far the achievements of Lorraine, the Auvergne and Toulouse were reflected in Bordeaux and Normandy. I have also included some material on Brittany because it corroborates what has been covered elsewhere. None of these regions were as active as the Rhône, Lorraine and the Auvergne, with the possible exception of Bordeaux and Toulouse's management of airports and the maritime port in the case of Bordeaux. Bordeaux's role in the latter has parallels in Normandy. Chapter 8 covers the achievements of the special regional bodies representing agriculture and tourism, which were not on the whole the subject of deliberations in the economic regions. In the case of tourism, we see the setting up of bodies by the industry in order to promote tourism effectively to customers. They received limited government funds, but the real initiative lay with industry representatives. Tourism is one of the best examples of economic regionalism in action. In the case of agriculture, the agricultural unions and the *chambres d'agriculture* became very effective lobbying organizations. Chapter 9 discusses the legacy of the activities of the pre-1940 regions for the bodies set up under Vichy and particularly during the period 1945–1982. The end point of this book is the regional reform enacted by the Socialist government in 1982. This established permanent regions, broadly with the powers they have today. Chapter 10 draws together some conclusions for the pre-1940 economic regions and their place in the history of regionalism in modern France.

## Bibliography


Berstein, S. (1980). *Histoire du Parti Radical, la recherche de l'âge d'or.*

Chanet, J.-F. (1996). *L'École républicaine et les petites patries.*

Chanet J.-F. (2000). *Les Félibres cantaliens : aux sources du régionalisme auvergnat 1879-1914.*

Chatriot, A. (2002). Les régions économiques d'une guerre à l'autre: aménagement du territoire, discours, projets et pratiques. In P. Caro, O. Dard, & J.-C. Daumas (Eds.), *La politique d'aménagement du territoire: racines, logiques et résultats.*

Cudbird, T. (2020). *The impact of the Great War on French regionalism 1900–1924.* Oxford DPhil.

Cudbird, T. (2023). The Clémentel moment: The reform of 1918 and the beginnings of regional economic planning in France. *French History, 37*(2), 126–141.

Druelle-Korn, C. (2004). *Un Laboratoire réformateur, le Département du Commerce en France.* Thèse de doctorat, Institut d'Études Politiques.

Druelle-Korn, C. (2012, janvier–avril). De la pensée à l'action économique: Étienne Clémentel (1864–1936) un ministre visionnaire. *Histoire@Politique, Politique, culture, société.*

Druelle-Korn, C. (2014). La modernisation inachevée de l'aménagement du territoire, le cas de la VIIe Région (Limousin, Poitou, Charentes). In A. Aglan,

M. Margairaz, & P. Verheyde (Eds.), *De la croissance à la crise (1925-1935): Le moment Tannery, une tentative avortée de modernisation conservatrice et libérale à l'heure de la mondialisation* (pp. 155–172).
Eck, J. F. Une expérience de modernisation économique: la première région économique. In *A. Aglan et al. De la Croissance à la crise (1925-1935)* (pp. 139–154).
Flory, T. (1966). *Le Mouvement Régionaliste Français.*
Giandou, A. (1999). *Compagnie Nationale du Rhône 1933-1998, histoire d'un partenaire régional de l'état.*
Gooch, R. K. (1931). *Regionalism in France.*
Kessler, M.-C., & Rousseau, G. (Eds.). (2018). *Étienne Clémentel, Politique et action publique sous la Troisième République.* Peter Lang.
Kuisel, R. F. (1981). *Capitalism and the state in modern France: Renovation and economic management in the twentieth century.* CUP.
Lebovics, H. (1988). Le Conservatisme en anthropologie et la fin de la Troisième République. *Gradhiva, Revue d'Histoire et d'Archives de l'Anthropologie, 4.*
Lebovics, H. (1992). *True France, the wars over cultural identity 1900–1945.* Cornell and London.
Marin, L. (1944). *Contes traditionnels en Lorraine. Institutions de transfert des valeurs morales et spirituelles.*
Marin, L. (1966). *Regards sur la Lorraine: réflexions sur des notions fondamentales, particularités du caractère lorrain.*
Méline, J. (1919). *Le Salut par la terre et le programme économique de l'avenir.*
Pasquier, R. La capacité politique des régions: une comparaison France-Espagne (Rennes, 2004), and *Le Pouvoir régional* (Paris, 2012).
Pitte, J. R. (2002). *Philippe Lamour, père de l'aménagement du territoire en France 1903-1992.*
Rosanvallon, P. (2007). *The demands of liberty: Civil society in France since the revolution* (A. Goldhammer, Trans.).
Rossiter, A. (1986). *Experiments with corporatist politics in Republican France 1916–1939.* Oxford DPhil.
Thiesse, A.-M. (1991). *Écrire la France; le movement littéraire régionaliste de langue française entre la belle époque et la libération.*
Thiesse, A.-M. (1997). *Ils apprenaient la France: l'exaltation des régions dans le discours patriotique.*
Veitl, P. (2013). *L'Invention d'une région : les Alpes françaises.*
Vidal de la Blache, P. (1910, nov–déc). Régions de France. *Revue de Paris*, 821–849.
Wright, J., & Jones, H. S. (Eds.). (2012). *Pluralism and the idea of the Republic in France.*

CHAPTER 2

# Clémentel's Regional Reform of 1918

As we have seen, the inspiration for Clémentel's reform of 1918 was in part derived from the regionalist movement which grew in strength prior to 1914. While regional institutions were frowned on for much of the nineteenth century, there was an extraordinary growth of interest in regional history, cultures and languages. This interest grew among the educated middle class. Chanet's study of the Félibrige in the Cantal revealed that the founders of the movement there were mostly intellectuals.[1] The learned societies became very active in this field often supported by men with a role in government. More local cultural associations were founded and practical municipal government was more highly esteemed. As an example the Félibrige, Frédéric Mistral's movement to revive the language and literature of Occitania, flourished and received support from prominent politicians. There was a regionalist school of novelists, described by Anne-Marie Thiesse,[2] regional artists and new regional styles of architecture. Teachers were encouraged to teach children about their regional

[1] J-F. Chanet, Les Félibres cantaliens : aux sources du régionalisme auvergnat 1879-1914 (Clermont-Ferrand, 2000).

[2] A-M. Thiesse, Écrire la France; le movement littéraire régionaliste de langue française entre la belle époque et la libération (Paris, 1991).



T. Cudbird, *The Origins of Economic Regions in France, 1918–1940*, https://doi.org/10.1007/978-3-032-04422-8_2

heritage in schools in the belief that love of the *petite patrie* of the region supported love of the *grande patrie* of France.[3]

Sympathy for the introduction of regional assemblies tended to be strongest among those of the traditionalist and Catholic right who were attracted to the thinking of its leading figures like Charles Maurras, Maurice Barrès and the Marquis de L'Estourbeillon, founder of the URB (Union régionaliste bretonne). Several of them were connected with the Action Française founded in 1899, of whom Maurras was an early supporter. An example is the Catholic writer in the Auvergne, Henri Pourrat. Such thinking emphasized the gradual evolution of institutions and the importance of patriarchal and collective values derived from working on the land. Barrès's concept of *la terre et les morts* appealed to many of these traditionalists. It tied in well with the idea of *la petite patrie.* Both emphasized that a feeling of belonging derived from identification with the history of the land and the local community. Barrès himself felt close to his native Lorraine. He wrote about the importance of local roots in his novel *Les Déracinés.* This conservative strand of regionalism continued to be influential after the First World War. Separatist movements existed in Alsace and Brittany during the inter-war period. Regionalist conservatives found a home in the Vichy regime.

The founding of the Fédération Régionaliste Française in 1900 by Jean Charles-Brun was a significant milestone in the awakening of regionalism, because it brought together such a diverse range of sympathizers in one lobby group, which encouraged a pragmatic approach to regional issues. Those who wanted to champion the setting up of elected regional assemblies did so because the departments were felt to be too small to deal with many contemporary challenges. A new strand in regionalist thinking based on the work of Vidal de la Blache, author of *Tableau de la Géographie de la France* (1903), and his followers in the French school of geography challenged the traditionalist position early in the twentieth century. Vidal argued before the war that any concept of regional government based on the *Ancien Régime* provinces was out of date. Industrialization had created some large regional centres throughout France, whose power of attraction spread far beyond departmental or even old provincial boundaries. The call for decentralization throughout the regionalist movement, including in Lorraine, was given focus by Vidal de la Blache and his

[3] A-M. Thiesse, Ils apprenaient la France: l'exaltation des régions dans le discours patriotique (Paris, 1997). J-F. Chanet, L'École républicaine et les petites patries (Paris, 1996).

followers with their analysis of the key role played by the large towns as hubs for economic development.[4]

In August 1917 Étienne Clémentel, Minister of Commerce, announced his project to divide France into economic regions (Fig. 2.1). This is often seen as the first attempt to create a regional structure for government in modern French history. It was not a radical reform but a cautious measure and built on the existing chambers of commerce of which there were 149 throughout France. Clémentel did not start with a clean sheet of paper and determine a brand-new structure. Rather he used a provision in the 1898 law on chambers of commerce which allowed individual chambers to cooperate with each other in the pursuit of some agreed common objective. Clémentel proposed a scheme for chambers to work together in regional groupings which his ministry defined. It was clear, however, that a chamber could refuse or perhaps suggest an alternative grouping. After the scheme was published, Clémentel personally visited the groupings in Lorraine, the Auvergne and Bordeaux to seek their agreement and to discuss any proposed changes. His officials visited all the other regions. There were 18 to start with. The scheme was discussed by the Chamber of Deputies in the autumn of 1918 and the decree was promulgated in April 1919. Clémentel did not need to propose primary legislation; he could rely on his existing powers.[5] In 1918 the *Comités consultatifs d'Action économique*, originally set up in 1915 in each military region, were incorporated into the structure of regional groupings of chambers of commerce.

The fact that he chose to use a decree is significant. He knew there was likely to be opposition within the governing Radical party to a measure of regional reform involving primary legislation. As we have seen, many Radical politicians after 1870 believed that the regionalist programme was a threat to the Third Republic. However, Clémentel also knew he would face opposition from regionalists who wanted a comprehensive regional reform. They were likely to be disappointed with a measure they might see as half-hearted. Since the founding of the *Fédération Régionaliste Française* (FRF) in 1900, there had been an active campaign to devolve powers to new regional assemblies, and in the years before the war this was showing some signs of success. Aristide Briand, 11 times président du conseil, formed a new government in 1910 and issued a programme which

[4] P. Vidal de la Blache, 'Régions de France', Revue de Paris, (nov–déc 1910), 821–849.

[5] Ministère du Commerce et de L'Industrie, Direction des affaires commerciales et industrielles, Organisation des Régions économiques (Paris, 5 avril 1919).

included a number of regionalist ideas. He was not the only prominent republican politician to be attracted to regional reform. Clemenceau had flirted with it before the wine growers' crisis of 1907. Paul-Boncour, Deschanel and Clémentel were supportive. Paul-Boncour was a Radical before the First World War and later an influential Socialist and at one time président du conseil. Deschanel was a noted orator as president of the Chamber of Deputies. Even Poincaré showed interest and there was the possibility of linking administrative reform to a change in the voting system. During the 1910 elections, administrative reform appeared in the election addresses of over 400 deputies (Figs. 2.1 and 2.2).[6]

**Fig. 2.1** Portait of Étienne Clémentel, courtesy of the Bibliothèque Nationale de France

[6] J. Wright, The Regionalist Movement in France 1890–1914: Jean Charles-Brun and French Political Thought (Oxford, 2003), 164–198.

With the outbreak of war, there seemed little hope of reform. No FRF congress was held in 1914 and its paper *L'Action régionaliste* ceased publication until 1920. However, regionalist agitation did not slacken once war was declared; rather it intensified. This was largely due to a deputy for the Charente, Jean Hennessy, scion of the famous Cognac family. A conservative anti-Dreyfusard at the start of his political career, close to Deroulède and the *Ligue des Patriotes*, he moved toward a progressive republican position as his thinking developed. He formed a *Ligue de représentation professionnelle et d'action régionaliste* to agitate for his objective of creating assemblies which would represent the professional interests in each region, as well as having members elected by direct suffrage. These corporatist ideas were heavily influenced by contemporary social Catholic thought. Alfred de Mun, the prominent social Catholic thinker, was his father-in-law.[7] He worked alongside the FRF and its secretary Charles-Brun, but in reality he was the driving force.

Supporters of the FRF claimed that the war showed the need for urgent reform of the way France was governed. They said that the excessive centralization of France's bureaucracy stifled local initiative. Too much had to be referred to Paris for a decision. France had to make the best use of all its resources to win the war and rebuild the country after victory. To do this, the central government had to engage the energies of the leaders of industry, commerce, the administration and the universities in the various regions. The best way of achieving this goal was to create regional assemblies representing local interests which had access to finance and some power to initiate projects to meet local needs, such as transport infrastructure.

A friend wrote to Charles-Brun on 21 May 1916 that he was due to give a lecture in Paris on 4 June on the lessons of the war:

> *I am giving a lecture on Sunday 4th June in the Ch*âteaubriand Hall also known as L'Étoile on the lessons of the war. I will not hide from you that the most important of these lessons concerns regionalism and Hennessy's project, i.e. our project.[8]

[7] Dubasque, Hennessy, 80–81 for the influence of social Catholicism on Hennessy and 79–140 for Hennessy's political action during the war.

[8] MUCEM, Charles-Brun 2 AP 2, Correspondance domaine privé Courrier I 1892–1946, dossier 1911–1918, letter to J. Charles-Brun from unknown correspondent, 21 mai 1916.

The *Courrier parlementaire* on 8 June 1918 drew attention to the regionalist argument that the war had destroyed the narrow bounds of France's old administrative organizations—departments, districts (*arrondissements*) and cantons.[9] In September of that year, the editor of *La Nouvelle Revue* wrote thus:

> The frightful storm which has battered the world for four years and the terrible situation of France before the victory compels us at once not to neglect anything which might revive the prosperity of the fatherland, organize society in a way most likely to raise the ruins again and repair the disaster, develop all the means of production which are still intact, and enhance all our resources. The heresy of old and superannuated administrative structures must give way to rational concepts suitable for modern requirements. Life is about perpetual renewal, which is never fixed. Why impose on society an unchanging administrative regime when everything around it and depending on it is being transformed incessantly?[10]

After the initial shock of the war, the FRF re-started its regular meetings in Paris in February 1915 on the third Thursday of each month.[11] In the first half of 1917, a series of meetings was organized in Paris on sentimental regionalism; decentralization; economic regionalism and regionalism among intellectuals and the universities.[12] The full annual congresses re-commenced in Paris from 29 May to 2 June 1917 with consideration of the definition of regions and regional assemblies. The FRF decided to examine regionalism in all its many facets and what lessons the war had brought to light.[13] The congress passed resolutions in favour of the creation of morally and administratively independent regions based on the *pays* of France; supporting a more active national publicity campaign; inviting members of the Chamber of Deputies to start work on new laws; supporting electrification of the country; revising the law of 1912 in order

[9] MUCEM, Charles-Brun 2 AP 26, folder of press cuttings gathered by J. Charles-Brun, 'le Régionalisme, sa doctrine et ses partisans, ce qu'en pense M. André Berthelot et M. Jean Hennessy'.

[10] MUCEM, Charles-Brun 2 AP 36, folder of press cuttings gathered by J. Charles-Brun, La Nouvelle Revue, t xxvii (Sept 1918), 101–102.

[11] MUCEM, Charles-Brun 2 AP 35, La Semaine auvergnate 8 avril 1915.

[12] MUCEM, Charles-Brun 2 AP 35, Le Limousin de Paris 24 décembre 1916, 25 février 1917, 11 mars 1917.

[13] MUCEM, Charles-Brun 2 AP 2, letter from Jean Hennessy to Charles-Brun 30 avril 1917; 2 AP 35, press cutting Le Journal 29 mai 1917.

to make ports even more autonomous; transferring teachers from the authority of the prefect to the local rector of the academy and, lastly demanding that these teachers educate their pupils in all the features of their region. Some 60 organizations took part including Hennessy's *Ligue de représentation professionnelle et d'action régionaliste.*[14]

In 1918 *Journées régionales* were held in Paris instead of a full congress.[15] There were sessions on the regions transformed by the war, on the delimitation of regions, on the economic traditions of France and on projects for regional reform coming from the Chamber of Deputies or government, led by Jean Hennessy. The congress closed with a public session led by Édouard Herriot, a senator and mayor of Lyon.[16] From all these war time discussions, it is clear that a tension was developing between those who saw regional structures responding to the needs of the modern economy and those who believed they should be based on traditional historic communities.

Jean Hennessy had submitted a draft law in 1913 which called for the election of regional assemblies with a mixed suffrage. There would be elected representatives of different professional groups—farmers and farm workers, merchants and their employees, industrialists and workers, the liberal professions and civil servants—but also some members chosen by those who did not have such an affiliation. It was referred to the Chamber of Deputies' commission for general administration and no further action was taken.[17] However, Hennessy did not give up. He became secretary of the Commission of General Administration in 1914. He presented his 1913 project for a second time in 1915 and again without success. So in July of that year he brought forward a fresh proposal for consultative economic committees in each military district. He believed the purpose of these committees should be to inform the state about local resources in order to facilitate the supply of food and other essential commodities. In October the Chamber of Deputies accepted this idea and so the government was forced to bring in its own proposal. The new committees would examine transport, imports and exports, and the productive capacity of

[14] MUCEM, Charles-Brun 2 AP 32, Le Monde latin (juillet–août 1917), 8.

[15] MUCEM, Fonds FRF 6 AP 8, Organisation of congresses 1918.

[16] MUCEM, Fonds FRF 6 AP 8, printed programmes for meetings; letters L. Marin to J. Charles-Brun 27 mars 1918, 3 avril 1918; Daniel Vincent to L. Marin 8 avril 1918; E. Herriot to J. Charles-Brun 9 avril 1918, 8 mai 1918. MUCEM, Charles-Brun, 2 AP 26 La Rennaissance 11 mai 1918

[17] Dubasque, Hennessy, 79–140.

industries in the respective regions. However, these committees were subordinate to the Minister of War and had few funds to carry out their work. Hennessy continued to battle for his ideas. In 1917 he was defeated in elections to be President of the Commission on General Administration. The Minister of the Interior started his own enquiry on the subject of regional reform, but, unlike Hennessy, he was not disposed to abolish the department as being too small to encompass the economic life of a region. Another proposal for regional assemblies elected by the *conseils-généraux* of the departments was defeated in 1918.

This was the background to Clémentel's proposal to group together the chambers of commerce in different regions. He faced opposition from two main directions, both inside the Chamber of Deputies and also from the chamber of commerce of Paris.[18] In the Chamber, he faced a number of objections of which the most important was from Victor Peytral, a Radical deputy for the Hautes-Alpes. On 18 October 1918, he suggested that Clémentel's reform concerned the responsibilities of the Minister of the Interior who ought to be involved. Departments were being moved between regions without being consulted, and the role of the departmental *conseils-généraux* was being ignored. Clémentel replied that he was not addressing the question of administrative reform but merely dealing with problems created by the large number of chambers of commerce. If they were grouped in regions, it would be easier for his department to consult with them on matters of national importance like increasing productivity.[19] The Paris chamber of commerce also opposed the changes on the grounds that they could only be put into effect by primary legislation and a wider regional reform. They may have been concerned about the threat to their traditional pre-eminence among all the chambers of commerce in France. Clémentel successfully argued that his measure was watertight from a legal point of view.[20]

It might be thought that Clémentel was being a little disingenuous in the reasons he gave for his reform on 18 October 1918. A number of historical studies in recent years have uncovered several reasons why

[18] A. Chatriot, 'Les Régions Clémentel: débats et expériences', in Kessler, Rousseau, Clémentel, 327–341.

[19] Journal officiel de la République française, débats parlementaires, Assemblée Nationale, 18 octobre 1918, 2735–2740.

[20] A. Chatriot, 'Régions Clémentel', 333.

Clémentel brought forward his 'regional' proposal.[21] The historical context and the pressures of the war on the French economy are very important. During the war, Clémentel took hitherto unprecedented powers over the shipping and consumption of vital raw materials in cooperation with his British allies. These included the formation of purchasing consortiums for different goods which had the power to direct where imports would be used and to set prices.[22] For these consortia to work effectively, Clémentel's ministry needed a clear idea of the productive potential of industries in different parts of France. It quickly became apparent that French industry had to raise its game, both to win the war and to compete effectively in the post-war world. The combined chambers of commerce had set up an *Association nationale d'expansion économique (ANEE)* to plan for future economic growth. Clémentel asked this body to carry out a survey of the whole of French industry, and it was with this task that he asked Henri Hauser, Professor of Geography at Dijon, to assist.

Hauser had already observed the ruthless focus of the German government before the war on supporting national industry at home and abroad. A dossier compiled by the Ministry of Commerce contains two reports on the grouping of chambers of commerce in Germany. The second report with Hauser's name at the bottom has a covering note dated 20 November 1917 saying the report shows how urgent it is now to create economic regions in France.[23] Hauser foresaw a continued retreat from free trade principles after the war and believed that France must be ready to compete with Germany once victory was achieved. Clémentel shared Hauser's concerns. He wanted to turn his Ministry of Commerce into a virtual ministry

[21] Kessler, M-C., Rousseau, G. (eds), *Étienne Clémentel: politique et action publique sous la Troisième République* (Bruxelles, 2018). Druelle, C., 'Le Ministère du Commerce et de l'Industrie pendant la Première Guerre Mondiale: Étienne Clémentel ou la volonté de moderniser la France' (Mémoire pour le Diplôme d'Études Approfondies, Institut d'Études Politiques, Paris, 1993). Druelle-Korn, Laboratoire réformateur, particularly 126–150. S-A. Marin, G-H. Soutou (eds), Henri Hauser 1866–1946 humaniste-historien-républicain (Paris, Sorbonne, 2006), 147–183. Druelle-Korn, 'De la pensée à l'action économique'. H. Hauser, Le Problème du régionalisme (Paris, 1924). G. Rousseau, Étienne Clémentel 1864–1936 (Conseil-Général du Puy-de-Dôme, Archives départementales, Clermont-Ferrand, 1998). Veitl, Invention d'une région, 55–92, 179–208.

[22] For Clémentel's industrial policy in the war, see J.F. Godfrey, Capitalism at War, Industrial Policy and Bureaucracy in France 1914–1918 (Leamington Spa, 1987), 82–105; R.F. Kuisel, Capitalism and the State in Modern France: Renovation and Economic Management in the Twentieth Century (Cambridge, 1981), 44–48.

[23] AN F 12 8037, dossier groupement des chambres de commerce en Allemagne.

of the national economy which would make plans for French industry to improve productivity and have a governing role in encouraging appropriate measures by firms in different sectors. He could not achieve his objectives without a more effective mechanism for consulting the professionals in different industrial sectors, hence the reform which he introduced. The grouping of the chambers of commerce was not his only step in this direction. He also encouraged the formation of national associations for different professional groups such as the first national association of employers.

Some modern historians have suggested that Clémentel was a regionalist from the beginning of his political career.[24] Like other Third Republic Radical politicians, he had deep roots in his native department, the Puy-de-Dôme, where he was brought up and educated. He became a notary in Riom before being elected to represent his home region in the Chamber of Deputies in 1900. During his formative years, he came under the influence of Emmanuel des Essarts, Professor of Literature, at the University of Clermont-Ferrand. Together they wrote a drama about Desaix, the general from the Auvergne who grasped victory from defeat for Napoleon at Marengo and died as a result. At the end of his life, Clémentel wrote another work about an Auvergnat leader, Vercingétorix, who resisted the Romans and became a republican hero. Clémentel knew other Auvergnat writers such as Henri Pourrat. He maintained his connection with the Auvergne throughout his career as a local deputy and later senator, as well as president of the conseil-général of the Puy-de-Dôme and mayor of Riom, where he had a property in a nearby village.

In 1903 Clémentel was appointed *rapporteur* of the budget of the Ministry of the Interior, and he made a speech supporting the idea of decentralizing the French government.[25] In 1905 he contributed a piece on the same theme to a work edited by Paul-Boncour and Charles Maurras.[26] In the same year, he was appointed Minister of Colonies, and

[24] G. Rousseau, 'Les Racines d'une pensée idéaliste', in Kessler, Rousseau, Clémentel, 50; G. Rousseau, 'Étienne Clémentel et l'Auvergne', in Kessler, Rousseau, Clémentel, 109–127; A. Chatriot, 'Régions Clémentel', 330. Druelle, 'Ministère Commerce Industrie', 5.

[25] C. Bellon, 'Étienne Clémentel et l'organisation administrative de la France (1903). Rapport parlementaire sur le budget du Ministère de l'Intérieur', Parlement[s], revue d'histoire politique, no. 20 (2013/2), 127–131.

[26] E. Clémentel, 'Organisons la démocratie', in J. Paul-Boncour, C. Maurras (eds), Un Débat nouveau sur la République et la décentralisation, opinions de E. Buré, G. Clemenceau, E. Clémentel, J. Dessaint, E. Fournière, J. Reinach, L.-Xavier de Ricard, P. Strauss, le "Temps", A. Varenne (Toulouse, 1905), 148–161.

he encouraged the transfer of some power to native and colonial populations. For example, in Madagascar, he followed a policy, started by the military governor Galliéni, of transferring responsibility to the native officials and giving them a provincial budget.[27] The native populations would be associates of the French in the development of their country.[28] *L'Action régionaliste* noted this with approval. Clémentel told a delegation from the FRF, "I am going to do some decentralization in the colonies."[29] Research in the archives of the FRF and in *L'Action régionaliste* has not revealed any other references to Clémentel until 1922 when, as a senator, he spoke at an FRF congress. However, we do know that Hauser, his spokesman, attended a number of FRF meetings during the war. Given the lengthy exposition of the benefits of economic regionalism in the official documents on the reform, as well as in the works of Henri Hauser who masterminded it, it is reasonable to say it had a 'regionalist' inspiration. However, it was regionalism of a different kind from the strand espoused by Charles Maurras, by the Marquis de L'Estourbeillon in Brittany or even by Henri Pourrat. It was a regionalism which preserved the regional identities of the past but also embraced the developments of the modern world.

The archives of Charles-Brun contain a number of unpublished speeches which describe the growth of large towns in France and how they had made the narrow boundaries of a department irrelevant from an economic point of view.[30] Such towns were important centres for commercial transactions covering industry, commerce and agriculture over a wide region. They were also hubs for communication by road, rail and water (either canals or maritime transport in the case of ports like Marseille or Bordeaux). They were centres for the development of technical expertise, particularly after the setting up of regional universities in 1896. The power of attraction of a city like Lyon spread way beyond the confines of the department of the Rhône. However, this concept did not originate with the FRF. It was developed by the French school of geography and in particular by its leader Paul Vidal de la Blache. His seminal work *Tableau géographique de la France* (1903) contains very few references to this phenomenon. It

[27] G. Ferragu, 'Le Ministère des Colonies', in Kessler, Rousseau, Clémentel, 282–284.

[28] Y. Paillard, 'Domination coloniale et récupération des traditions autochtones: le cas de Madagascar de 1896 à 1914', Revue d'histoire moderne et contemporaine, tome 38 no. 1 (janvier–mars 1991), 73–104; see particularly 92–93.

[29] L'Action régionaliste (janvier 1906), 351.

[30] MUCEM, Charles-Brun 2 AP 13, speech in Montpellier 1915, 89, 91–92; speech to Congrès de la Propriété bâtie 1915, 390.

deals with older divisions between geographic areas based on geology and physical features. However, by 1914 he had started to emphasize the role of *grandes villes* in the contemporary economy.[31] His last work before he died was *La France de l'Est* (1917), written in part to justify France's claim to Alsace-Lorraine, but describing the links between eastern France and the lost provinces.[32] The professor of Geography at Nancy University, Lucien Brocard, described the influence of the great Lorraine industries spreading far outside Lorraine itself.[33] These ideas were taken up by Henri Hauser when he set out his ideas in 1918 to advise Clémentel on the setting up of the groupings of chambers of commerce.[34]

Philosophically Clémentel was not an economic liberal who believed the state should have no role in the national economy. Nor was he a socialist in the Marxist sense, who argued for state ownership of the means of production. He was heavily influenced by the thinking of Léon Bourgeois, which is sometimes described as solidarist. Bourgeois emphasized the virtues of social solidarity, of the need for individuals to associate together to achieve social goals, and of an organized liberalism with oversight by the French state. He saw men developing through their mutual interdependence. The state and society were simply expressions of the free association of men for their own benefit.[35] The following passage from Bourgeois's book could stand as a description of how contemporaries saw economic development:

> The free development of human faculties and activities, in a word of the human being, cannot be obtained, for each person, except through interaction with the faculties and activities of contemporaries, and only achieves its current level of development thanks to the faculties and activities of men of the past.[36]

We can find numerous references to the need for organization in Clémentel's writings.[37]

[31] P. Vidal de la Blache, 'Régions de France', Revue de Paris (nov–déc. 1910), 821–849.

[32] P. Vidal de la Blache, La France de l'Est (Paris, 1917).

[33] L. Brocard, 'Le Développement économique de la Lorraine française', Séance de la Société d'économie sociale (Paris, 14 avril 1913), 733.

[34] H. Hauser, Les Régions économiques; préface de M. Clémentel, (Paris, 1918).

[35] L. Bourgeois, Solidarité (Paris, 1896), 50–51, 87, 90–91.

[36] Bourgeois, Solidarité, 137.

[37] C. Druelle-Korn, 'La Construction d'une action économique', in Kessler, Rousseau, Clémentel, 60, 66.

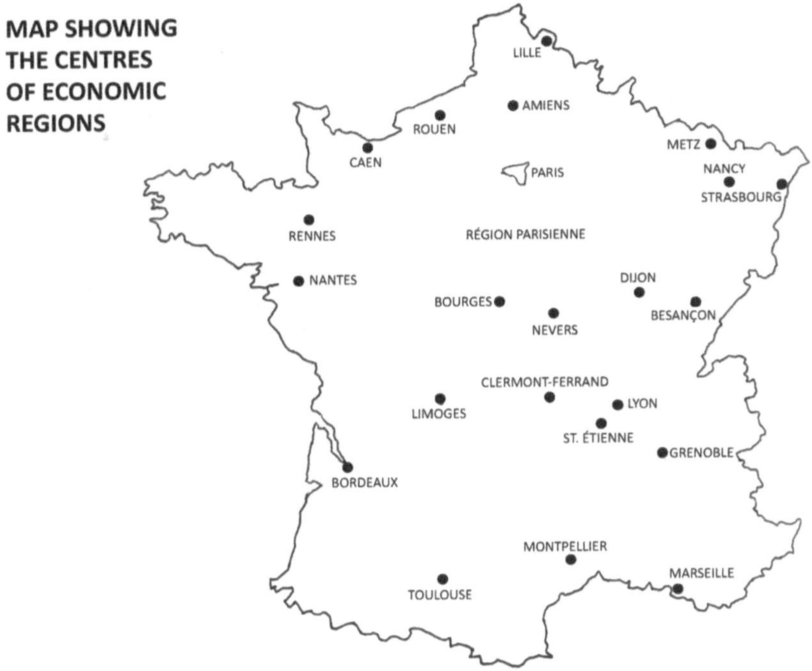


**Fig. 2.2** Map showing the centres of the economic regions

Clémentel's reform was also one measure among many he encouraged to create corporate bodies between the state and private interests to participate in the management of the national economy.[38] Clémentel believed that the engagement of these intermediary bodies in a common enterprise of economic modernization would make France stronger in a competitive post-war world. One of the defining characteristics of the economic regionalism of the post-war period is the activity pursued within an institutional framework at regional level. In this sense, it was regionalist but also pluralist and made widespread use of intermediary corporate bodies (Fig. 2.2).

There were practical problems in setting up the new regions, particularly in defining the boundaries. Lorraine and the Auvergne can serve as

[38] T. Cudbird, 'The Clémentel moment: the reform of 1918 and the beginnings of regional economic planning in France,' French History, vol. 37 no. 2, June 2023, pp. 126–141.

examples. We can also see in more detail what Clémentel thought the regions' objectives should be. The first region in which he sought support for his reform was Lorraine. He met with representatives of the regional chambers of commerce in Paris on 19 March 1918.[39] The ministerial document setting out the minister's plans proposed that the region based on Nancy should cover the departments of Ardennes, Marne, Aube, Meuse, Haute-Marne, Meurthe-et-Moselle, Vosges, the Territoire de Belfort and Haute-Saône (partie) and the chambers in Charleville, Sedan, Châlons-sur-Marne, Reims, Troyes, Bar-Le-Duc, Saint-Dizier, Nancy, Épinal, Saint-Dié, Belfort and Lure. The document noted that Nancy was very conscious of its regional role. The Nancy chamber of commerce envisaged the region spreading over a wide area. The pre-war secretary Laffitte had conceived a plan for this region, spreading as far as Burgundy and the Franche-Comté, and it had been taken up in the formation of the *Office des Transports de l'Est*. The ministerial document noted that the *Union économique de* l'Est, a journal published by the Nancy chamber, had a similar view. The document and Hauser's subsequent article in *L'Union économique de l'Est* highlighted the role of regional banks based in Nancy and also the cooperation of academics and industrialists in creating technical institutes. It noted the regional spread of the metallurgical and other industries.[40] The document proposed a smaller region than some Lorrainers desired.[41] In his address to the assembled chambers of commerce of the East, Clémentel referred to Nancy's valiant struggle to keep life going in the face of the enemy as a reason for selecting it as the first region. He emphasized that cooperation between different firms and industries, working with the authorities, was the key to victory and to economic prosperity after the war. France had to raise the pace of its economic development significantly.[42] Hauser, in his comments, explained that this measure of devolution would make coordination between the different government

[39] Union économique de l'Est, 2e année (1 avril 1918) 79. Hauser, Problème du régionalisme, 85.

[40] Hauser, Problème du régionalisme, 84. Union économique de l'Est, 2e année (1 août 1918), 187–190.

[41] Ministère du Commerce, de l'Industrie, des Postes et des Télégraphes, Projet de division de la France en régions économiques (Paris, 1917), 19–20.

[42] 'La France économique et la Région économique de l'Est', Union économique de l'Est, 2e année, numéro special, (1 août 1918), 185–187.

and private agencies quicker as constant reference to Paris would be avoided.[43]

In the article in *L'Union économique de l'Est*, Henri Hauser elaborated on the reasons for the minister's proposals. He had approached Lorraine first because it was here that the idea of an economic region had been born. Hauser referred to Nancy's role as a regional hub, exactly as conceived by Vidal de la Blache. To define the region, it was necessary to run along the lines of influence spreading out from Nancy. He conceded that the attachment of Belfort, while based on the metallurgical interests there and in the Meurthe-et-Moselle, might change in future. Indeed, Belfort had disappeared from the Lorraine region when the official ministerial decree was promulgated in 1919.[44] Of course Nancy seemed to be the natural capital for Lorraine in 1918 as the war ended. Ever since 1870, when Metz and its hinterland were annexed by Germany, Nancy was the economic and cultural centre of French Lorraine. Yet once Metz was re-integrated into France, it had a claim to be an economic centre on a par with Nancy because of its proximity to the iron industry. It also had a cultural heritage as a French city dating back to 1552. This conflict would continue in the post-war years.

*L'Union économique de l'Est*, in its special number, set out a programme for the new regional organization. It was a very long list—social questions such as increasing the birth rate, professional and technical education, agriculture, reconstruction of industry, commercial development with an emphasis on new markets and export, finance including a Nancy stock exchange and credits for reconstruction, railways, roads and canals, laying telephone lines, the list was endless. Certainly, the Eastern region did not lack ambition.[45]

The second region which Clémentel visited was his native Auvergne on 29 April 1918. He chaired a meeting of the Clermont-Ferrand chamber of commerce to which representatives of the other chambers in the proposed region had been invited. It was important to Clémentel that the Auvergne region was the second founded in France.[46] The other chambers involved were Moulins-Lapalisse, Montluçon-Gannat, Aurillac, Mende, Le Puy,

[43] Union économique de l'Est, 2e année (1 août 1918), 187–190.

[44] Ministère du Commerce et de L'Industrie, Direction des affaires commerciales et industrielles, Organisation des Régions économiques (Paris, 5 avril 1919), 15–16, 59.

[45] Union économique de l'Est, 2e année (1 août 1918), 219–221.

[46] La Région du Centre, no. 1(mars–avril 1921), 3–4 quoted in Rousseau, 'Étienne Clémentel et l'Auvergne', 117.

Thiers, Ambert and Riom. Clémentel's senior advisers from the Ministry of Commerce also attended along with the prefects of Puy-de-Dôme, Allier, Haute-Loire, Cantal and Lozère. Clémentel said that the government had made every effort to foster the industries needed to support the war and it needed to continue this action to win the peace as well. He talked of cooperation between the government and industrialists to make better use of raw materials and to buy less of these from abroad. He said that after the war, more cooperation was needed between the different factors of production. The new regions would not alter existing administrative structures but would facilitate projects on a regional basis like regional entrepôts, electricity generating plants and regional banks for export. The regions could commission new communication channels such as canals, roads and railways by sharing the expense; also telephone and telegraph networks. All the chambers represented agreed to join the new region with two exceptions. Mende in the Lozère preferred to join with Montpellier and Le Puy, while saying it would not join, suggested the creation of a new chamber in the west of the Haute-Loire at Brioude. This would join the Clermont-Ferrand region.[47] The ministerial plan of 1917 had envisaged this solution for the Haute-Loire with the arrondissements of Le Puy and Yssingeaux being attached to Lyon. The plan also agreed that Mende oscillated between Clermont and Montpellier. It had also said that the attachment of Moulins and Montluçon to Clermont was questionable, but its preference was to maintain this because of the need to proceed with the canalization of the Allier river which ran between the two areas.[48] It is clear from these and other regions that Clémentel took a fairly pragmatic attitude in these discussions on regional boundaries. In the case of the division of the Haute-Loire, the ancient identity of the Velay, centred on Le Puy and dating back to the *Ancien Régime*, had reasserted itself. Brioude had always been anti-clerical and republican, whereas the Velay was Catholic, with the pilgrimage centre at Le Puy, and aligned to the right in politics. The definition of the regions was not an easy matter. It had bedevilled the various proposals for regional reform from before the war. These new regions soon entered the public debate on economic development. An article in *Le Moniteur du Puy-de-Dôme* on 21 June 1918

[47] Travaux Clermont-Ferrand, 1918, (séance 29 avril 1918), 29–33.
[48] Projet Régions économiques, 21–22.

on the future of Clermont referred to the new region when justifying the growth of Clermont-Ferrand as a transport hub for the whole region.[49]

Clémentel's regional reform grew directly out of the wartime conditions which he faced. However, it would be a mistake to portray the war as marking a radical departure in French regionalism. As we have seen, the reform was a cautious measure. The new economic regionalism based on the powers of attraction of major cities pre-dated the war. Next we will examine how far Clémentel's regional institutions were changed in the inter-war period.

## Development of the Economic Regions 1918–1938

As we have seen, there was considerable momentum behind the creation of economic regions in 1918. The benefits of economic regionalism had been proved by the *comités consultatifs d'action économique* during the war. There was every expectation that they would start to produce useful results. However, first we have to confront the judgement that these regions were ultimately failures because they had no legal basis. They simply provided a mechanism for chambers of commerce to work together if they so wished.

The momentum behind economic regionalism started to dissipate during the 1920s, and no further changes were made to their status until 1938. Clémentel himself no longer had direct influence on policy making. He lost his seat in the Blue Horizon election of 1919 and joined the Senate until 1935. He did serve for a brief spell as Finance Minister (1924-25) (Fig. 2.3) and was later frustrated in his attempt to form a ministry with himself at the head. He was president of the conseil-général of Puy-de-Dôme and died in 1936.

The government decided in November 1922 to submit a draft law which made the groups of chambers of commerce into public bodies, which would mean they could make contractual commitments. Supported by a report by Mario Roustan, senator for the Hérault, the draft law was given a first reading in the Senate in May 1923. It now included an amendment which raised the question of whether a chamber of commerce should have to adhere to one grouping. However, this proposal never came before the Chamber of Deputies. It was withdrawn in December 1924 and again

[49] Le Moniteur du Puy-de-Dôme (21 juin 1918), 3 col a–b.

**Fig. 2.3** Photo of Clémentel greeting Winston Churchill at the Gare du Nord, courtesy of the Bibliothèque Nationale de France

in February 1925.[50] There was a debate among the chambers of commerce, who defended their administrative and financial independence. They were independent legal entities.[51] Dupuy, a member of the Toulouse chamber, strongly opposed Roustan's proposal. A number of chambers elsewhere like Lyon and Grenoble supported it provided that the entire freedom of individual chambers to refuse support for a project could be maintained. The chambers of commerce who formed the economic regions could not agree whether they should federate with one region only. Neither could they agree to be bound to the cost of projects supported by a majority of chambers in their region. In founding regions, the Ministry of Commerce had wanted to move chambers of commerce away

[50] La Région Économique de Toulouse et des Pyrénées (Bulletin officiel du Groupement des Chambres de Commerce) abbreviation RETP, mai-juin 1928, 57–59.

[51] A. Chatriot, 'Les régions économiques d'une guerre à l'autre; aménagement du territoire, discours, projets et pratiques,' in (dirn.) P. Caro, O. Dard et J-C Daumas, La politique d'aménagement du territoire: racines, logiques et résultats, (Rennes, 2002), 60–61.

from their natural individualism but seemed to have failed.[52] In 1923 the Toulouse region wanted a modest increase in its 1924 budget from 43,000 francs to 60,000 francs, which would increase Toulouse's contribution from 16,000 francs to 19,600. Dupuy argued vigorously against contributing to the increased budget. He said that the law of 1898 allowed chambers of commerce to act together in pursuit of some important project if they wanted, so the expense of a permanent region was unnecessary. He suspected that the state was trying to force the regions to finance items which it should fund centrally. He believed that the regions might eventually reduce the individual chambers' fiercely guarded independence. In the end, the Toulouse chamber approved the budget increase. It also approved Roustan's proposal provided individual chambers kept their freedom of action.[53]

The Toulouse chamber also passed the budget for 1925 provided there was a thorough debate at once on future plans for the region. They asked that Lagardelle, the regional secretary, deliver an activity report to the chamber on a quarterly basis.[54] A further discussion on regional projects concluded that the region was sometimes too small to finance projects and inter-regional cooperation was needed.[55] The debate exposed the individualism of the chambers in this part of France, and elsewhere, which acted as a brake on regional development. The position of the region as a whole in 1928 was to back the proposal to grant regions a legal personality, provided chambers were not forced to contribute to a project and could continue to participate in more than one region.[56] This was still their position when the regions were granted full legal powers by the government in 1938.[57] The total budget for the whole region only increased from 60,000 francs to 85,000 by 1932.[58]

Clémentel made a further call for a new law on the economic regions at the *journée des regions économiques* organized by the Fédération Régionaliste Française on 27 May 1926. The *Action Régionaliste* for January 1927 noted that the proposed new law on the regions was not

[52] Bulletin de la Chambre de Commerce de Toulouse, procès-verbaux des séances de 1923, séance 14.3.1923, 75.

[53] Bulletin de la Chambre de Commerce de Toulouse, 12 mai 1923, 145.

[54] Bulletin CCT, 11 juin 1924, 157; 25 juin 1924, 161, 163, 165.

[55] Bulletin CCT, procès-verbaux des séances de 1925, séance du 25 février 1925, 46.

[56] 'Réunion du comité régional 30 janvier,' RETP, mai-juin 1928 nos. 5–6, 57–59.

[57] 'Réunion du comité régional 22 juin 1938,' Ibid., juin-juillet 1938, 77–78.

[58] 'Réunion du comité régional 23 fevrier 1931,' RETP, no. 4 avril 1931, 41.

clear how far a majority of chambers in a region could engage others' resources for a major project which could take many years to complete.[59] The Lyon chamber was against one chamber being forced to contribute to a project. Jean Coignet, senator for the Rhône and until 1922 president of the Lyon chamber of commerce, and Roustan were authorized by the government to try and find a solution.[60] Clémentel was involved in the discussions. There was also continued concern about forcing chambers to adhere to only one region. The Toulouse region protested against this in July–October 1927. Bordeaux, Dijon and Limoges supported this point of view and were also unhappy with majority voting on financial projects. A new text was defended by Clémentel in the Senate in 1928, again without results.[61]

We can see here the weakness of Clémentel's original reform, when he was forced to base the economic regions on existing chambers of commerce. They could be self-interested bodies, and some observers were sceptical of their ever being suitable vehicles for reform. Bertrand de Jouvenel wrote an article on the reform of the state in the journal *Notre Temps* on 1 May 1928:

> Most often the most active young men don't bother to get involved in the region. The chambers are full of sententious old men, to whom we owe agendas betraying a lamentable economic orthodoxy that newspaper editors, lacking copy, place on the fourth page in very small type under the not very tempting headline: Wise Advice! However, let's leave on one side these children of Bastiat (free trade economist of the nineteenth century).[62]

De Jouvenel, a philosopher and economist who took posts in several leading universities, was one of the Young Turks of the Radical Party. He argued in *L'Économie dirigée* (Paris, 1928) for a planned economy rather than liberal capitalism.

So by the end of the 1920s there was no change in the legal status of the economic regions. Discussion about the future of economic regionalism after the war took place as a wider debate started on the structure of the state and its relationship with the national economy. This discussion focussed on the apparent failure of the French state to deal with the

[59] Action Régionaliste, xxviie année, janvier 1927, 3.
[60] RETP, mai-juin 1928, 57.
[61] Chatriot, 'D'une guerre à l'autre,' 60–61.
[62] B. de Jouvenel, in Notre Temps 1 mai 1928, 78–79.

economic crises which confronted it—first, the currency crises of the 1920s and then the Great Depression of the 1930s. There was criticism of the weakness of the government relative to the Chamber of Deputies which culminated in proposals by Gaston Doumergue for the reform of the state in 1934. Doumergue had been president of France 1924 to 1931 and led a unity government in 1934 in the face of social unrest. Some held the view that the executive needed to be strengthened; for example, André Tardieu who led a ministry from 1929 to 1930. He set out his ideas in a book published in 1934. He said France was a body without a head and there was no authority in the state. He wanted to give the executive the right to dissolve the Chamber of Deputies without the Senate's consent, and also to remove the right of deputies to propose expenditure for the benefit of particular individuals or organizations. He also wanted votes for women and consultative referenda.[63]

The debate was framed by the question of how to deal with a capitalist system which seemed at times on the brink of total collapse—with mass unemployment, wild fluctuations in prices and currency failures. A number of influential thinkers argued that the laisser-faire approach of classical liberalism had failed. They believed that the government did not have the economic expertise to come up with solutions. They tended to favour a corporatist solution, in which representative bodies of capital and labour for different sectors would come together to regulate production and prices and to resolve disputes between capital and labour. This belief in a concerted approach to planning the economy is to be found in journals like Philippe Lamour's *Plans*.[64] *Plans* was founded by Philippe Lamour and Jeanne Walter and published from 1931 to 1933 and aimed to express modern ideas on technical progress and artistic expression. Radicals and Radical Socialists supported consultative bodies for economic policy, as did the Socialists and Redressement Français. Redressement Français, founded by Ernest Mercier in 1925, was an association of businessmen and intellectuals who wanted to restore the authority of the French state which had been weakened by government mistakes. Naturally, the Socialists wanted to include worker representatives.[65] Mercier was an influ-

[63] A. Tardieu, La Réforme de l'État (Paris, 1934), 128, 130–131.

[64] P. G. Nord, France's New Deal, From the Thirties to the Postwar Era (Princeton, 2010), 22, 25; J.R.Pitte , Philippe Lamour, père de l'aménagement du territoire en France 1903-1992 (Paris, 2002), 59–71.

[65] A. Israel, La Réforme de l'État devant les partis (Paris, 1934), 26, 32, 58–59.

ential industrialist in government circles, a leader in the power generation industry and director of the Compagnie Française des Pétroles. Tardieu also wanted worker and professional representation in policy making.[66] *L'Homme Nouveau* (1934-1937) a short-lived journal associated with Marcel Déat supported similar ideas. Déat was a Socialist who, in the 1930s was excluded from the party because of his authoritarian ideas. He was attracted to fascism and eventually became a Vichy government minister. However, the Radical party would not adopt a fully corporatist approach despite pressure from its young Turks in 1934.[67]

There was no incompatibility between 'corporatism' and the idea that the needs of the regions should be represented by some specifically regional bodies. Indeed, as my recent article on Clémentel's regional reform argued, the governance of the Third Republic was characterized by a pluralism of corporate bodies between the state and the private individual. Clémentel himself encouraged the formation of such bodies to cope with the challenges of the war and its immediate aftermath. His regional reform needs to be seen in this context.[68] The thinkers who debated the apparent failures of the French state from the late twenties onwards were building on Clémentel's ideas.

As we shall see in the chapter covering Toulouse, some thinkers within the regions themselves supported the formation of regional professional organizations. The Fédération Régionaliste Française continued to press the case for economic regionalism. A diverse range of thinkers in different journals supported regionalist ideas. De Jouvenel, for example, wanted to replace the Senate with delegates from the departmental *conseils-généraux*.[69] He said elsewhere that these *conseils* should be used to inform deputies who knew nothing about economic life outside Paris.[70] Lucien Romier, a journalist who was heavily involved with *Redressement Français* and later with the Vichy regime, wrote in his *Explication de Notre temps* that economic regionalism had been successful because it was based on a

[66] G. Mer, 'L'appel de M. Tardieu à l'État moderne,' État moderne, 1 janvier 1930, 488–493.

[67] S. Berstein, Histoire du Parti Radical vol. II Crise du radicalisme 1926-1939, (Paris, 1982), 101–125 and 312–331.

[68] T. Cudbird, 'The Clémentel moment: the reform of 1918 and the beginnings of regional economic planning in France,' French History, vol. 37 no. 2, June 2023, pp. 126–141.

[69] De Jouvenel, L'Économie dirigée (Paris, 1928), 188–189.

[70] Notre Temps, 1 mai 1928, 78–79.

solidarity of interests and supported the nation.[71] At the first national congress of *Redressement Français* in 1927, one speaker said that:

> We want to entrust to regional assemblies, chosen from professional bodies or by co-option, the task of running economic and social government services.

Redressement Français was an association formed under the leadership of the industrialist Ernest Mercier to agitate for economic modernization.

Decentralization would make for a more effective administration and regionalism was essential in this regard.[72] After 1945, Phillipe Lamour was a driving force in regional development. An article published in December 1931 in his journal *Plans* saw regions becoming more important in Europe and the state abandoning the economy to representatives of economic interests like chambers of commerce and workers' and industrialists' unions.[73] Lamour wanted to create regional 'estates' with administrative autonomy. He saw regions which had an economic unity as a building block of the state.[74] *Ordre Nouveau* was another influential monthly review founded by historian Robert Aron whose founding principles published on 1 May 1933 included the following:

> The fertile contact of the human personality with its peer group and its homeland can only be obtained by federalist decentralization, in which the professional corporation rejoins its natural region.

*L'Ordre Nouveau* was against the overweening power of the state and in favour of regional economic planning.[75]

The debate about regionalism and corporatism affected another discourse during the 1920s on whether the economic regions should make formal or informal links with other regional bodies, particularly the new *chambres d'agriculture*. There was no progress on this idea towards a new

[71] L. Romier, Explication de Notre temps (Paris, 1925), 184.

[72] Bulletin mensuel du Redressement français, 1 mai 1927 2eme année no. 11, 20.

[73] R. Dupuis, 'Le problème de l'Europe et la question de l'état,' Plans, décembre 1931, 15–16.

[74] Pitte, Philippe Lamour, Père de l'Aménagement du territoire, 33, 45, 66.

[75] L'Ordre Nouveau 1 mai 1933 9, 18; 15 janvier 1934 8, 19–21; R. Dupuis and A. Marc, 'Retour à la coutume,' 15 janvier 1934 1–3.

vision for regionalism, but the discussion illustrates the prevailing intellectual climate and the difficult issues involved.

Clémentel's original wish had been for regional assemblies grouping all the active forces in a region, but he had to confine himself to chambers of commerce because of lack of support in the Chamber of Deputies.[76] A number of thinkers suggested that the departmental *chambres d'agriculture* founded in 1924 should be grouped together with the economic regions. For example, Jacques Bardoux, who was later to lead the parliamentary commission set up by Doumergue on the reform of the state, gave a speech to a Redressement Français meeting at the end of 1930 in which he talked of the necessity of grouping representatives of chambers of commerce, chambers of agriculture and workers and agricultural federations.[77] Bardoux became a senator and after the Second World War deputy for the Puy-de-Dôme. The person who more than anyone else espoused this cause in the 1920s was Hubert Lagardelle, Secretary-General of the ninth region based in Toulouse. Lagardelle was one of the few in his position who really thought through what the region was for. He started life as a revolutionary syndicalist, before retreating to Toulouse and devoting himself until 1927 to regional development. Later he joined *le Faisceau*, was a contributor to Lamour's review *Plans* and was attracted by fascism, particularly the Italian model. He eventually became Minister of Labour under Vichy. He started a short-lived journal in 1920–21 *La Région de Toulouse et des Pyrénées*, published a book on the South-West region and contributed regularly on economic development to *Sud-Ouest Économique*.[78]

Lagardelle wrote down some of his ideas about how the economic regions should ideally function in these publications. In *Sud-Ouest une région française*, he talked about the need to organize all the professional groups in the region, who had had some experience of participating in regional affairs during the war in the *comité consultative d'action économique*. For Lagardelle this wartime experience was formative. Clémentel had said in the Chamber of Deputies on 12 October 1918 that he wanted more regional bodies involved than just chambers of

[76] 'Journée régions économiques, Fédération Régionaliste Française, 27 mai 1926,' in Région du Centre juillet 1926, 243–244.

[77] Bulletin mensuel du Redressement français, 1 janvier 1931, assembly of provincial supporters 22-23 décembre 1930, 8.

[78] H. Lagardelle, Sud-Ouest, une région française (Paris, 1929).

commerce. Ever since Lagardelle regarded the current structure as 'régionalisme économique mutilé.' Clémentel's original vision for the regions was not being fulfilled. Lagardelle said that a number of bodies had recently suggested joining the *chambres d'agriculture* with the economic regions, including the General Assembly of Chambers of Commerce and the General Assembly of Chambres d'Agriculture. He was in favour of this change as the two bodies had many interests in common such as improved transport and electrification of the countryside. He was secretary of the *chambre d'agriculture* for the Haute-Garonne. He wrote that his chamber wanted to create a regional *chambre d'agriculture* and then work with the economic region.[79] Lagardelle also set up a South-West region branch of the Confédération nationale des Associations Agricoles. Agricultural customers ought to be represented in the new *Office régional d'Énergie électrique* created in 1931 at the initiative of the economic region.[80] Agriculturalists also had an interest in rural railway lines, a matter discussed by the regional *Office des Transports.*[81].The chamber of commerce of Toulouse was suspicious of change because it did not want its authority diluted. In 1929 the Toulouse region said it supported working with the *chambres d'agriculture* on areas of common interest.[82] This idea received the backing of Joseph Faure, senator for the Corrèze and involved in the work of the agricultural unions. It was then taken up by the Minister of Commerce who asked the chambers of commerce for their opinion. This was a step towards integrated regionalism, true to its founder's vision.[83] However, Lagardelle wanted to go further. If the government would not change the status of the economic regions, he thought they should make what changes they could themselves—what he called spontaneous regionalism.[84] What he was advocating was a sort of DIY regionalism by direct action, not surprising perhaps for a revolutionary syndicalist.[85] He believed

[79] RETP, décembre 1928, no. 12, 125–126.

[80] H. Lagardelle, 'Producteurs et consommateurs d'électricité dans le Sud-Ouest,' Sud-Ouest Économique, décembre 1931, 1480.

[81] H. Lagardelle, 'Petits Pays et Transports dans le Sud-Ouest,' Sud-Ouest Économique, 25 janvier 1927, 120–121.

[82] RETP, octobre 1929, 124–125.

[83] H. Lagardelle, 'Régions Économiques et Chambres d'Agriculture,' Sud-Ouest Économique, octobre 1930, 1037–1038.

[84] H. Lagardelle, Sud-Ouest une région française (Paris, 1929), 152–153, 155–156.

[85] H. Lagardelle, 'Le movement régionaliste,' La Revue de Toulouse et des Pyrénées, mars 1921, 56–57; Sud-Ouest Économique, 5 août 1928, 1037–1038.

his cause would be helped by new regional structures being created for various branches of the national administration, for example, in universities, the judiciary and the military. Lagardelle believed the regional universities had an important role to play. An article in *La Région de Toulouse et des Pyrénées* in August 1921 explained how the University of Toulouse helped define the region and gave it technical expertise.[86] He wanted the regions to have real management responsibilities, rather than being purely consultative bodies.[87]

Lagardelle believed that a technocratic elite should be involved in running the regional economy. He believed in "la profession organisée dans la region organisée" to combat the individualism unleashed by the revolution. To this end he set up the *Union interprofessionnelle régionale des pays Languedoc-Gascogne-Pyrénées* to discuss and exercise pressure on key regional issues.[88] To recover from the disruption of the war, the intellectual leaders of the regions needed to be involved in reconstruction he believed. The regional assembly of professions would coordinate all regional forces for change.[89] In *Sud-Ouest Économique* Lagardelle commented on a recent congress of the *Assemblée régionale professionnelle* saying that they had to act because the state was failing economically. The region was, he said, the natural framework for economic activity.[90] At the opening meeting, one member sounded the trumpet for regionalism:

> Do you recognise that Paris, the brain of France, monopolises to an exaggerated degree the vital forces of the nation? Unite to usher in an era of decentralization and of regionalism.[91]

[86] La Revue de Toulouse et des Pyrénées, août-septembre 1921, 4–9.

[87] H. Lagardelle, 'Sud-Ouest une région française,' Sud-Ouest Économique, 10eme année, no. 190, septembre 1929, 1162–1163. The article contains an extract from HL's book.

[88] H. Lagardelle, 'Un essai de région professionnelle à Toulouse,' Sud-Ouest Économique, 7eme année, no. 135, 23-31 juillet 1926, 921–923.

[89] H. Lagardelle, 'Nécessité d'une organisation permanente,' Bulletin de l'Assemblée régionale professionnelle, 1924 no. 1, 56–57.

[90] Hubert Lagardelle, 'Les manifestations économiques de Toulouse,' Sud-Ouest Économique, 7ème année, no. 131, 23-31 mai 1926, 647–649 and H. Lagardelle, 'Un essai de région professionnelle à Toulouse,' Sud-Ouest Économique, 7ème année, no. 135, 23-31 juillet 1926, 921–923.

[91] M. Doat, industriel, Président du Syndicat général de commerce et de l'industrie, 'Le commerce et l'industrie dans la région,' Réunion Constitutive 22 décembre 1923, Bulletin de l'Assemblée régionale professionnelle, 1924 no. 1, 12.

In a summary of his book on the South-West which appeared in *Sud-Ouest Économique*, Lagardelle trumpeted the virtues of association between interested parties as the basis of social organization and economic progress in the new age.[92] The chaos created by economic liberalism must be brought to an end and associations should support the government in the task of reconstruction.[93] All the region needed to progress was self-confidence in its own destiny.[94] The Toulouse region, he added, needed a wide organization to give it that self-confidence. The departments were not big enough on their own.[95]

Lagardelle was not alone. *Chambres d'agriculture* around the country started to ask for representation in the regions, for example, in the Offices des Transports whose work was clearly of interest to them. After all, the *chambre d'agriculture* in the Sarthe said, we represent half the population.[96] Despite Lagardelle's advocacy, the chambers of commerce in his region remained opposed to immediate fusion with the *chambres d'agriculture*. Boubenès, president of the ninth region, preferred to keep industry and agriculture separate because otherwise meetings would be unwieldy and too long.[97] He was in favour of industry and agriculture working together but not being formally linked.[98] This was also the position of the Bordeaux and Nancy based regions.[99] In the Bordeaux region, there was no merger but friendly cooperation between groupings of *chambres d'agriculture* and the economic region.[100] In Brittany, chambers of

[92] H. Lagardelle, 'Sud-Ouest, une région française,' Sud-Ouest Économique, novembre 1928, 1162–1163.

[93] H. Lagardelle, 'Nécessité d'une organisation permanente,' Bulletin de l'Assemblée régionale professionnelle, 1924 no. 1, 56–57.

[94] H. Lagardelle, 'Aspects économiques de la région Toulousaine,' Sud-Ouest Économique, 10e année no. 184, mars 1929, 213–237.

[95] H. Lagardelle, Sud-Ouest, 158–167; C. Bouneau, Hubert Lagardelle, un bourgeois révolutionnaire et son époque 1874-1958 (Talence, 2000), 231, 235.

[96] Revue Économique de L'Ouest, 1 avril 1928, 53–55.

[97] Sud-Ouest Économique, mars 1929, 347.

[98] 'La deuxième foire de Toulouse, discours de M. le président Boubènes,' RETP, octobre 1929, no. 10, 124.

[99] Région économique de l'Est, assemblée générale du 9 mars 1927, Union Économique de l'Est (UEE), 11e année, no. 7, 1 avril 1927, 80 and Région économique de l'Est, assemblée annuelle du comité économique régional, UEE, 13e année, no. 7, 1 avril 1929, 83–84. Bulletin officiel de la Région économique de Bordeaux et du Sud-Ouest (REBSO), no. 24, septembre-octobre 1927, 102.

[100] Région économique de Bordeaux et du Sud-Ouest Bulletin Officiel, juillet-août 1928, 38–39; novembre-décembre 1928, 58.

commerce and *chambres d'agriculture* met together by 1937.[101] Friendly cooperation between economic regions and *chambres d'agriculture* became the norm but not formal fusion. This only happened after the major regional reform in 1938.[102]

Another alteration in the economic regions which Lagardelle supported was for there to be more cooperation across regional boundaries. An inter-regional commission on rural electrification was set up in 1926 covering the Bordeaux, Toulouse and Languedoc regions in an arc from Bordeaux to Marseille.[103] This committee also got involved in assessing hydro-electricity projects.[104] Lagardelle argued for such inter-regional cooperation in Sud-Ouest Économique.[105] He believed in a Grand Midi region covering the whole of the south of the country.[106]

In all these proposals, Lagardelle was moving towards a corporatist philosophy, which was hostile to the centralizing state.[107] For Lagardelle, syndicalism and regionalism were two approaches which sought to interpose new social groups between the individual and the state. He wanted to see the country governed by skilled elites, a new spirit of association and an end to parliamentarism and dead bureaucracy.[108]

Another factor in the debate about economic regions was that during the 1920s other channels were found to carry out development projects covering a wider area than one department. We do see during this period a mushrooming of bodies with an interest in regional economies. We have already noted the *chambres d'agriculture*. The laws of 1919 and 1924 also facilitated *chambres régionales d'agriculture* and *Offices régionaux agricoles*, the latter being staffed with experts who undertook technical improvement programmes.[109] There was also substantial growth in the number of regional tourism federations, a subject which will be covered in a later chapter. Albert Sarraut was Minister of the Interior from 1926 to 1928. In

[101] Bulletin Trimestriel de la VIe région économique (Rennes), avril 1937, 32–33.

[102] C. Bouneau, Lagardelle, 235.

[103] RETP, juin 1927, 84–85.

[104] RETP, avril 1928, 44.

[105] Hubert Lagardelle, 'L'interrégionalisme,' Sud-Ouest Économique, 7ème année, no. 122, 8-15 janvier 1926, 9–10.

[106] C. Bouneau, Lagardelle, 236–237.

[107] C. Bouneau, Lagardelle, pp.238–239.

[108] Hubert Lagardelle, 'Sud-Ouest une région française,'Sud-Ouest Économique, 10ème année, no. 190, 1929, 1162–1163.

[109] Chatriot, 'D'une guerre à l'autre,' 61.

1926 he introduced some reforms by decree in which the *conseils de préfecture* were replaced by *conseils de préfecture interdépartementaux*. Departments could also form inter-departmental commissions to undertake particular tasks. Lastly they could form more permanent associations or syndicates, which had a legal personality and a budget, so they could undertake projects to improve infrastructure such as rural electrification.[110] There are frequent references in the regional records which exist to inter-departmental commissions. For example, the record for Basse-Normandie based in Caen refers on 1 November 1928 to the use of such a commission to examine the feasibility of a canal from Rouen to the coast. This creation of inter-departmental commissions makes it clear that the Ministry of the Interior wanted to keep control of projects within its own structures and not allow them to be carried out by economic regions consisting of independent chambers of commerce.

There is, however, another perspective on the situation of the economic regions at this time. In December 1925, the Secretary-General of the Auvergne economic region, Charles Mathiot, attended one of a number of regular meetings for such secretaries-general at the Ministry of Commerce. Among the topics was mobilization in time of war. He presented his views which he had previously shared with his own regional committee. He believed that control of stocks, raw materials and skilled labour for factories was vital. He also believed that the last war had taught that this was best done on a regional basis despite the difficulty of some departments being attached to more than one region. After all, the current military regions were fairly closely aligned with the economic regions.[111] Contact between the Ministry of War and the regions on this subject had started soon after 1919. After 1925, discussions were pursued with the regions, for example, in 1927 and 1928 in Basse-Normandie.[112] At a meeting of secretaries-general of the economic regions with the Ministry of War and Ministry of Commerce on 25 February 1928, it was clear that the government saw regions playing a key role in mobilizing the economy in time of war. First of all, they could gather information on

[110] Lagardelle, Sud-Ouest, 158; Chatriot, 'D'une guerre à l'autre,' 61, 64. Hubert Lagardelle, 'Le régionalisme à Toulouse,'Sud-Ouest Économique, 7ème année, no. 145, 16-31 décembre 1926, 1597–1599. This article discussed the Assemblée Régionale Professionnelle meeting on 6 November 1926, held jointly with Redressement Français.

[111] C. Mathiot, La Mobilisation Économique (Clermont-Ferrand, 1926), 25–62.

[112] Comité régionale, séance du 22 mars 1928, IVe region économique, groupement de basse normandie (Caen), 22 mars 1928, 11–14.

productive capacity in each region.[113] The government wanted the regions to make decisions on the distribution of important materials in wartime.[114] It seems that in practice the state still saw the regions as useful vehicles.

Mathiot also made some points which have a wider significance for the debate on the role of the economic regions in the inter-war period. He wrote that a number of ad hoc reforms had been carried out to deal with the inadequacies of the existing departmental structure. Each separate reform was carried out by a government department without considering how it might relate to other government regional services. Foreigners might say that France was being very conservative in its approach and had shied away from a comprehensive regional reform.[115] Despite this it is clear that he thought the regions could show greater initiative than many realized. They had a spirit of independence, enjoyed direct relationships with central government and had gone as far as asking for concessions to undertake major public works, as his region had done. The leaders of the regions were mostly leading businessmen and some were deputies. They could not accept enjoying a purely consultative role. As a result, they had created new bodies of their choice, presided over by experts, such as the Offices des Transports, Offices d'Énergie Électrique and Chambres de Métiers (chambers of trades). This activity represented the will of France to work and be productive.[116] We shall examine later how far leadership attitudes affected performance in undertaking regional development projects in different regions.

In the 1930s, demands for the reform of the state became stronger with the onset of the Great Depression and the governmental crisis of 1934. In that year, Doumergue appointed Jacques Bardoux to lead a committee of experts to work on proposals for reform. As they emerged, these proposals involved strengthening central government at the expense of the legislature. They sparked much public debate as well as in the Chamber of Deputies but were defeated by the Socialists and Radical-Socialists who were suspicious of an increase in executive power.[117] Blum set out his ideas for the reform of the state in his *Lettres sur la réforme gouvernementale* published in 1918. He suggested various changes to make the

[113] IVe region économique, groupement de basse normandie (Caen), janvier-mars 1928, 11–14.

[114] RETP, juin 1927, 86; also 26 mai 1933, 83.

[115] Mathiot, Mobilisation, 47–49.

[116] Mathiot, Mobilisation, 12–14.

[117] M. Tandonnet, André Tardieu l'incompromis, (Paris 2019), 188–191.

government more effective, but he was opposed to tinkering with the constitution. He had too much respect for parliamentary sovereignty which derived from the will of the people. However, he had nothing to say about decentralization or regional organizations.[118] Socialists were often suspicious of regionalist ideas. They saw regionalists as opposed to lay education, which was particularly important to Socialists.

However, regionalism was an issue in debates on reform of the state.[119] Bardoux's committee put forward additional proposals for regional reform which were not debated in the Chamber of Deputies. These included provision for regional prefects with executive power in 26 new regions and also conseils régionaux, with members elected from conseils-généraux of departments, from professional representative bodies such as chambers of commerce, or some coopted for their expertise. The *tutelle* of this regional administration would be modified, so that the government could only challenge its actions in the courts, rather than through the prefects, except on budgetary matters. The regional councils could impose some additional taxation and would deal with transport, education, health, social security and commercial development.[120]

The Doumergue proposals and the debate on reform of the state also led to discussion on the role of the Conseil National Économique (CNE). This body caused concern among some of the economic regions. At a meeting in March 1933, the Eastern region opposed proposals for a revised CNE as superfluous. In its proposed new form, it would duplicate existing bodies representing business and labour. The region favoured the existing body but with increased representation for the economic regions. It opposed any suggestion of an 'économie dirigée.'[121] The region expressed concern again on 12 October 1934 that the government was ignoring chambers of commerce and going straight to the CNE.[122]

[118] L.Blum, Oeuvres, vol. III.i 1914-1928 includes la Réforme gouvernementale (Paris, 1954). S. Berstein, Léon Blum, (Paris, 2006), 147–153 for a discussion of La Réforme gouvernementale.

[119] Chatriot, 'D'une guerre à l'autre,' 61.

[120] J. Bardoux, La France de Demain, son gouvernement, ses assemblées, sa justice; textes du comité technique pour la réforme de l'état, (Paris, 1936), 43–49, 179–181, 189–191, 194–195. Chatriot, 'D'une guerre à l'autre,' 61.

[121] '24 chambres de commerce et chambres consultatives, 1 chambre d'agriculture, assemblée générale annuelle du 7 mars 1933,' Union Économique de L'Est, 17e année, no. 7, 1 avril 1933, 78.

[122] Bulletin de la Chambre de Commerce de Nancy, séance 6 novembre 1934, 313–314.

Alexandre Dreux, president of the Nancy Chamber and the Eastern region and leading iron master from Longwy, wrote to Garnier, the president of the assembly of presidents of chambers of commerce in Paris, complaining about the enlargement of the role of the CNE to the detriment of chambers of commerce. He opposed the idea of creating a large consultative committee answering to the Président du Conseil, which would give its views on many questions: draft laws, decrees on economic matters. Delegates from chambers of commerce and agriculture would be better qualified. He cited two recent economic matters on which the chambers of commerce had been bypassed. Ministers were more inclined to neglect chambers of commerce and consult other professional groups. Dreux said they must try and reverse this trend. Garnier replied suggesting there could be a motion passed at a forthcoming assembly of chambers of commerce on 8 November when the role of the CNE would also be discussed.

Again in 1935 Nancy asked the Minister of Commerce to keep the economic regions at the centre of advice he received. The Toulouse region supported this view.[123] All these protests seem to have fallen on deaf ears. In 1936 the government proceeded to create a new structure for the CNE, which gave it an enhanced role. It would be asked to comment on proposed government measures but also to suggest measures of its own. The Président du Conseil would be in the chair. It would be divided into 20 professional sections, each one consisting of an equal number of *patrons* and workers. The CNE would also include representatives from chambers of commerce and agriculture and a range of other economic bodies. The Nancy chamber expressed its concerns that chambers of commerce, economic regions and the national assemblies of these in Paris were being excluded from consultation by the government. It was worried about the CNE developing as a corporatist organization to manage the economy.[124] To add another layer of consultation, a government initiative also instituted new local committees for commerce and industry to encourage beneficial cooperation. These started work by the end of 1936.[125]

[123] RETP, juillet 1935, séance 20 mai 1935, 89–90.

[124] Bulletin C de C Nancy avril-juin 1936, séance du 7 avril 1936, 34e année, no. 129, 138–140, 146–152; see séance du 6 novembre 1934, Ibid., 1934, 32e année, no. 125, 313–314. Chatriot, 'D'une guerre à l'autre,' 62–64.

[125] Procès-verbal de la réunion du comité régional du 26 octobre 1936, REBSO, no. 64, 15 novembre 1936, 406–408 for the new national committee and 408 for the regional committee; see also Bulletin C de C Nancy, octobre-décembre 1936, 34e année, no. 131, séance

Meanwhile in Toulouse some of the corporatist ideas which Lagardelle had espoused in the twenties started to gain traction. A report from the chamber of commerce in Toulouse in March 1936 favoured a corporate organization of the economy in order to organize production, to get firms to cooperate and to regulate relationships between capital and labour. This discussion was felt to be necessary because of the Great Depression. *Laisser-faire* had led to disaster. The government felt it had to interfere in the economy but did not always do this well because it did not possess the expertise. It needed advice. The economic regional meeting felt the proposal at this stage was too vague. It would disrupt the whole way the economy was managed. Further discussion took place in June and November 1936 and February 1937 with no clear resolution. There was particular concern about the Popular Front policy on collective conventions on agriculture, which it was feared would transfer power to the government and lead to virtual nationalization.[126] The Toulouse region presented further ideas for a change to a more corporatist system of management later in 1937. The president of the Toulouse chamber said industry was in chaos; demand and supply were out of balance; strong firms were exploiting their position to send weaker ones to the wall. Corporate bodies were needed to regulate prices, production and labour rates. The government, it was argued, should hand over the management of the economy to professional bodies.[127] This interest in a corporatist formula was echoed in the Brittany region in 1937. Here there was a particular interest in the Italian model.[128]

Despite an intellectual climate across a broad range of commentators not at all hostile to regionalism, the development needs of regions were not perceived as important. Fostering regional development was not seen before 1940 as answering the nation's economic needs. One illustration of this state of mind is that Tardieu made the re-equipping of France his

du 6 octobre 1936, 282, séance du 8 décembre 1936, 363–364, and Union Économique de l'Est, 15 décembre 1936, 270–271.

[126] RETP, juin 1936, séance 23 mars 1936, 77–81; septembre-octobre 1936, séance 8 juin 1936, 115–123; janvier 1937, séance 9 novembre 1936, 11–20; séance 22 fevrier 1937, 43–47.

[127] RETP, août-septembre 1937, 98–100.

[128] Charles Bodin, doyen honoraire de la faculté de Droit de Rennes, Le problème du corporatisme en France, Bulletin Trimestriel de la VIe région économique (Rennes), 1e année, no. 4, octobre, 115–129.

central economic policy but said nothing about regional development.[129] The damaging effect of regional imbalances on the national economy was not realized as it was after 1945. Regional geographers did not describe them as Gravier did in 1947 in his *Paris et le désert français*, with the exception of Albert Demangeon who asked the question in the conclusion of his 1933 book on the Paris region:

> Is there not a risk that one day this large head will become too heavy for the equilibrium of the country?

However, he does not try to answer it.[130] Demangeon was a Professor of Social Geography at the Sorbonne and the leading human geographer of the 1930s.

Regional development needs and possibilities were described in a number of regional economic journals, some of them founded by administrators or businessmen closely associated with their economic region. However, these regional development discourses did not seem to percolate through to debates at a national level in Paris. Examples include *Sud-Ouest Économique*, published in Bordeaux but covering a wide area in the South-West including Toulouse (Fig. 2.4). It dealt with infrastructure developments including ports, canals, railways and the industrial development unleashed by electrification through the network developed by the railway Compagnie du Midi.[131] It also covered agriculture extensively. The two economic regions covering Normandy had similar publications—*La Revue Économique de l'Ouest* and *L'Ouest Économique*, which included articles on an organization called *Ouest Expansion* (Fig. 2.5). This covered an area west of a line passing through Dieppe-Paris-Orléans-Limoges-Agen-Tarbes and promoted investment in infrastructure. Sometimes such journals were published with the cooperation of the economic region but tried to cover commercial developments and to bang the drum for their region. Examples include *Région du Centre* covering the Massif Central and *Union Économique de l'Est* which promoted developments in Lorraine and Alsace (Figs. 2.6, 2.7). Apart from the manufacturing and extractive

[129] F. Monnet, Refaire La République, André Tardieu, une dérive réactionnaire 1876-1945 (Paris, 1993), 140–145.

[130] A. Demangeon, Paris, la ville et sa banlieue, (Paris, 1933), 61.

[131] Sud-Ouest Économique, 9ème année no. 171, 29 fevrier 1928. A special number on hydro-electricity, the electrification of the Chemins de Fer du Midi and the economic growth of the region.

**Fig. 2.4** Cover of Sud-Ouest Économique (8–15 January 1926), courtesy of the Bibliothèque Nationale de France

industries covered in these journals, some included tourism, particularly the *Région du Centre* which devoted a lot of space to the subject.

The *Exposition internationale des arts et des techniques dans la vie moderne* in Paris in 1937 shows how there were conflicting views about the potential of the regions. It included an important centre showcasing regional cultures. The intention of the organizing committee in Paris was to demonstrate their diversity with artisan products, gastronomy and the arts. It was intended that the 27 pavilions in the regional centre in the exhibition should exemplify regional architectural styles, rather than modernism per se. The committee believed that such an exhibition would

Deuxième Année - N° 34 30 Novembre 1928 Le Numéro : 1 fr. 50

# L'OUEST ECONOMIQUE

REVUE BI-MENSUELLE

Téléphone : 50.29 RÉDACTION & ADMINISTRATION : 7, Rue André-Caplet — LE HAVRE Téléphone 50.29

## L'Enseignement Professionnel à Rouen

**Fig. 2.5** Masthead of L'Ouest Économique (30 November 1928), courtesy of the Bibliothèque Nationale de France

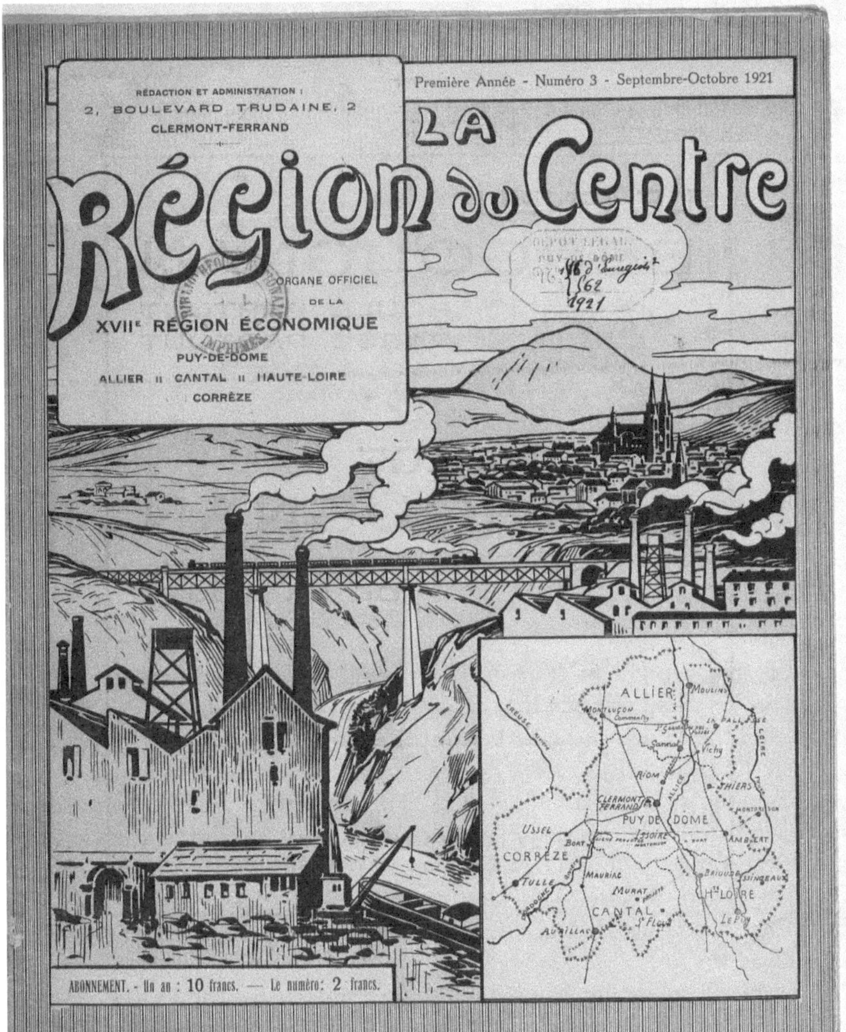


**Fig. 2.6** Cover of La Région du Centre (March–April 1921), courtesy of the Bibliothèque Nationale de France

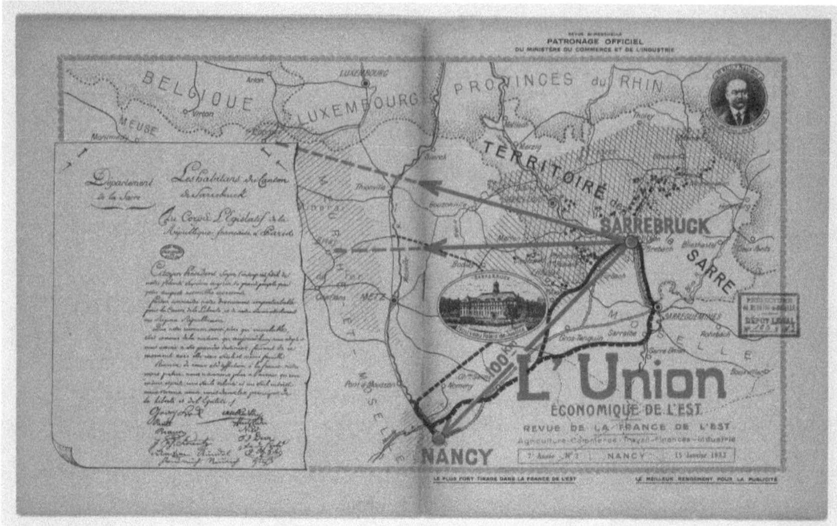


**Fig. 2.7** Cover of Union Économique de l'Est (15 January 1923), courtesy of the Bibliothèque Nationale de France

facilitate the growth of tourism in France's regions. It was after all the character of these regions that visitors came to experience. Jean-Charles Brun, still the leader of the FRF, saw the exhibition as a major opportunity to push the regionalist cause. The diversity of the regions would strengthen the Republic rather than weaken it. This argument had not moved on since the turn of the century. The development of interest in ethnography saw the creation a museum of French folklore under the inspiration of Georges-Henri Rivière. The new museum was housed in the Palais de Chaillot in Paris which had been constructed in anticipation of the 1937 exhibition.[132]

Shanny Peer, in her book on the exhibition, highlights the tension between the central committee in Paris which had a very clear view about what it wanted and the committees in the regions tasked with producing suitable exhibits. The central committee felt they had to compromise on the sort of exhibits they wanted in order to elicit the support and funds

[132] G-H. Rivière, Un Musée-laboratoire; le musée des arts et traditions populaires, (Paris, 1947), 147–149, 154.

needed from the regional organizations. Shanny Peer says that, as a result, the regional centre in the exhibition became more industrial and commercial in character. In April 1936, the regional commission in Paris sent a letter to local business leaders to persuade them to support their plans. These leaders provided the presidents of the 27 regional organizing committees who were influential. Eight of these presidents were presidents of their local chamber of commerce and three were presidents of an economic region. There were three industrialists and three senators or deputies. Of the rest, a number were artists and architects, but some were administrators or lawyers.[133] The chair of the organizing committee, Edmond Labbé, claimed in his concluding report that a balance had been struck between building on the past and reflecting progress. He said that the departmental committees did not want to confine regionalism in a cult of the past. The *centre régional* was not just a picturesque exhibition but designed to show the revival of the French regions. It showed France at work, not under direction of Paris.[134]

However, if we examine the official publications for each region which list the exhibits, we do not find commercial or industrial exhibits so prominent as we might expect. Indeed, the majority of exhibits seem to fit in the Parisian organizing committee's concept. In Alsace, there was some mention of textiles. The Languedoc featured aviation and metallurgy. In Lorraine the chambers of commerce mounted some exhibits as did the coal industry and three out of the many iron forges including Pont-à-Moussson. Mining, quarrying and chemicals were also represented. In Flandres-Artois, textiles were represented by the carpet industry, but there was no mention of the coal field. In the Auvergne, industry was better represented with exhibits from Michelin and Bergougnan in the rubber industry, as well as exhibits from construction, the electrical industry, lighting and heating and hydro-electricity. There were exhibits from the Allier iron industry. In the Lyonnais exhibition, the silk industry was naturally prominent, and in Guyenne and Gascony the port and shipyards of Bordeaux.[135]

[133] S. Peer, France on Display, Peasants, Provincials and Folklore in the 1937 Paris World's Fair, (Albany, 1998), 71 and 85.

[134] E. Labbé, Exposition Internationale des Arts et Techniques dans la vie moderne 1937, Rapport Général, Tome 1 (Paris, Ministère du Commerce et de l'Industrie, 1938), 224–226, 233.

[135] Exposition internationale des arts et techniques dans la vie moderne, 2e édition tome I, Liste des Exposants, BNF Gallica. Exposition Internationale. Arts and Crafts in Modern Life. Official Guide (Paris, 1937, English Edition), 104, 109, 111–112.

Despite the concern among certain chambers of commerce about their diminishing influence, it appears the government was listening. In 1937 the government proposed to give a legal status to the Assembly of Presidents of Chambers of Commerce as a public body.[136] Then in 1938, in a series of decrees dating from April, through June to September, the Popular Front government gave the economic regions a legal status. Chambers were still allowed to affiliate with more than one region but had to agree their compulsory financial contribution with each region before they joined and the decision had to be ratified by the Minister of Commerce. The number of regions was increased. Édouard Daladier, Président du Conseil 1938-1940, said that that they needed a clearer legal status in view of their responsibilities, particularly relating to economic mobilization in time of war. Also the Ministry of Commerce was finding it difficult to sort out differences because of this lack of clarity.[137] The regions got proper secretariats and a modest increase in their budgets. The Radical Party congress in 1938 claimed credit for this as a reform they had carried out, ironic as the party had frustrated attempts at reform for 20 years.[138] An influential voice in this reform may have been Paul Bastid, Minister of Commerce from 1936 to 1937. He was certainly in favour of regionalism as a philosophy and was also deputy for the Cantal and president of the *conseil-général* there. He made a visit to the Auvergne economic region, recorded in *Région du Centre*, in February 1937. He said he was following in the spirit of Clémentel who had died the previous year. He applauded regional achievements like the hydro-electricity dams on the Dordogne, said the region had made the best use of some shaky legal texts and implied he would look at the basis on which the regions operated.[139]

So the regions now enjoyed full legal status as public bodies. As such they could legally organize and finance projects as one body, rather than having to engineer progress through individual chambers of commerce and other organizations. Unfortunately, they could not make much further progress before war broke out a year later.

[136] RETP, juin-juillet 1937, séance 18 mai 1937, 79–85.

[137] Chatriot, 'D'une guerre à l'autre,' 63–64.

[138] 35e Congrès du Parti Républicain Radical et Radical-Socialiste 26-30 Octobre 1938, Marseille. (Paris, the Executive Committee, 1938), 20–21.

[139] Région du Centre, février 1927, 45–47.

## Bibliography


(1938). *35e Congrès du Parti Republicain Radical et Radical-Socialiste 26-30 Octobre 1938, Marseille.* The Executive Committee.

*Action régionaliste* 1906, 1926, 1927.

AN F 12 8037, dossier groupement des chambres de commerce en Allemagne.

Bardoux, J. (1936). *La France de Demain, son gouvernement, ses assemblées, sa justice; textes du comité technique pour la réforme de l'état.*

Bellon, C. (2013). Étienne Clémentel et l'organisation administrative de la France (1903). Rapport parlementaire sur le budget du Ministère de l'Intérieur. *Parlement[s], revue d'histoire politique, 20*(2), 127–131.

Berstein, S. (1982). *Histoire du Parti Radical vol. II Crise du radicalisme 1926-1939.*

Berstein, S. (2006). *Léon Blum.*

Blum, L. (1954). *Oeuvres* (Vol. III.i).

Bouneau, C. (2000). *Hubert Lagardelle, un bourgeois révolutionnaire et son époque 1874-1958.*

Bourgeois, L. (1896). *Solidarité.*

Brocard, L. (1913, avril 14). Le Développement économique de la Lorraine française. In *Séance de la Société d'économie sociale* (p. 733).

*Bulletin de l'Assemblée régionale professionnelle (Toulouse),* 1924, 1926.

*Bulletin de la Chambre de Commerce de Nancy,* 1934, 1936.

*Bulletin de la Chambre de Commerce de Toulouse,* 1923, 1924.

*Bulletin mensuel du Redressement français,* 1927, 1931.

*Bulletin Trimestriel de la VIe région économique* (Rennes), 1937.

Chatriot, A. Les Régions Clémentel: débats et expériences. In Kessler, Rousseau (Ed.), *Clémentel* (327–341).

Chatriot, A. (2002). Les régions économiques d'une guerre à l'autre; aménagement du territoire, discours, projets et pratiques. In P. Caro, O. Dard, & J.-C. Daumas (Eds.), *La politique d'aménagement du territoire: racines, logiques et résultats.*

Clémentel, E. (1905) Organisons la démocratie. In J. Paul-Boncour & C. Maurras (Eds.), *Un Débat nouveau sur la République et la décentralisation.* opinions de E. Buré, G. Clemenceau, E .Clémentel, J. Dessaint, E.Fournière, J. Reinach, L. Xavier de Ricard, P. Strauss, le "Temps", & A. Varenne, 148–161.

Cudbird, T. (2023). The Clémentel moment: The reform of 1918 and the beginnings of regional economic planning in France. *French History, 37*(2), 126–141.

Demangeon, A. (1933). *Paris, la ville et sa banlieue.*

Druelle-Korn, C. La Construction d'une action économique. In Kessler, Rousseau (Ed.), *Clémentel,* 59–76.

Druelle-Korn. *De la pensée à l'action économique.*

Druelle-Korn. *Laboratoire réformateur,* particularly 126–150.

Druelle, C. (1993). *Le Ministère du Commerce et de l'Industrie pendant la Première Guerre Mondiale: Étienne Clémentel ou la volonté de moderniser la France.* Mémoire pour le Diplôme d'Études Approfondies, Institut d'Études Politiques.
Dubasque, F. (2008). *Jean Hennessy 1874–1944, argent et réseaux au service d'une nouvelle république.*
Dupuis, R. Le problème de l'Europe et la question de l'état. *Plans*, 15–16.
*Exposition internationale des arts et techniques dans la vie moderne* (Vol. I, 2nd éd., Liste des Exposants).
(1937). *Exposition Internationale. Arts and Crafts in Modern Life. Official Guide* (English edition).
Ferragu, G. Le Ministère des Colonies. In Kessler, Rousseau (Ed.), *Clémentel* (282–284).
Godfrey, J. F. (1987). *Capitalism at war, industrial policy and bureaucracy in France 1914–1918.*
Hauser, H. (1918). *Les Régions économiques*; préface de M. Clémentel.
Hauser, H. (1924). *Le Problème du régionalisme.*
Israel, A. (1934). *La Réforme de l'État devant les partis.*
*IVe region économique, groupement de basse normandie (Caen)* 1928.
(1918, octobre 18). *Journal officiel de la République française*, débats parlementaires, Assemblée Nationale, 2735–2740.
Jouvenel, B. de. (1928). *L'Économie dirigée.*
Kessler, M.-C., & Rousseau, G. (Eds.). (2018). *Étienne Clémentel: politique et action publique sous la Troisième République.*
Kuisel, R. F. (1981). *Capitalism and the state in modern France: Renovation and economic management in the twentieth century.*
Labbé, E. (1938). *Exposition Internationale des Arts et Techniques dans la vie moderne 1937, Rapport Général* (Vol. 1). Ministère du Commerce et de l'Industrie.
Lagardelle, H. (1929). *Sud-Ouest, une région française.*
Marin, S.-A., & Soutou, G.-H. (Eds.). (2006). *Henri Hauser 1866–1946 humaniste-historien-républicain.* Sorbonne.
Mathiot, C. (1926). *La Mobilisation Économique.*
Mer, G. (1930, janvier 1). L'appel de M. Tardieu à l'État moderne. *État moderne*, 488–493.
Ministère du Commerce, de l'Industrie, des Postes et des Télégraphes. (1917). *Projet de division de la France en régions économiques.*
Ministère du Commerce et de L'Industrie, Direction des affaires commerciales et industrielles. (1919, avril 5). *Organisation des Régions économiques.*
*Moniteur du Puy-de-Dôme* 1918.
Monnet, F. (1993). *Refaire La République, André Tardieu, une dérive réactionnaire 1876-1945.*
MUCEM, Charles-Brun 2 AP 13, speech in Montpellier 1915, 89, 91–2; speech to Congrès de la Propriété bâtie 1915, 390.

MUCEM, Charles-Brun 2 AP 2, Correspondance domaine privé Courrier I 1892–1946, dossier 1911–1918, letter to J. Charles-Brun from unknown correspondent, 21 mai 1916.
MUCEM, Charles-Brun 2 AP 2, letter from Jean Hennessy to Charles-Brun 30 avril 1917; 2 AP 35, press cutting Le Journal 29 mai 1917.
MUCEM, Charles-Brun 2 AP 26, folder of press cuttings gathered by J. Charles-Brun, 'le Régionalisme, sa doctrine et ses partisans, ce qu'en pense M. André Berthelot et M. Jean Hennessy'.
MUCEM, Charles-Brun 2 AP 32, *Le Monde latin* (juillet–août 1917), 8.
MUCEM, Charles-Brun 2 AP 35, *La Semaine auvergnate* 8 avril 1915.
MUCEM, Charles-Brun 2 AP 35, *Le Limousin de Paris* 24 décembre 1916, 25 février 1917, 11 mars 1917.
MUCEM, Charles-Brun 2 AP 36, folder of press cuttings gathered by J. Charles-Brun. (1918, September). *La Nouvelle Revue, xxvii*, 101–102.
MUCEM, Charles-Brun, 2 AP 26 *La Rennaissance* 11 mai 1918.
MUCEM, Fonds FRF 6 AP 8, Organisation of congresses 1918.
MUCEM, Fonds FRF 6 AP 8, printed programmes for meetings; letters L. Marin to J. Charles-Brun 27 mars 1918, 3 avril 1918; Daniel Vincent to L. Marin 8 avril 1918; E. Herriot to J. Charles-Brun 9 avril 1918, 8 mai 1918.
Nord, P. G. (2010). *France's new deal, from the thirties to the postwar era.*
*Notre Temps* 1928.
*Ordre Nouveau* 1933, 1934.
Paillard, Y. (1991). Domination coloniale et récupération des traditions autochtones: le cas de Madagascar de 1896 à 1914. *Revue d'histoire moderne et contemporaine, 38*(1), 73–104.
Peer, S. (1998). *France on display, peasants, provincials and folklore in the 1937 Paris World's Fair.*
Pitte, J. R. (2002). *Philippe Lamour, père de l'aménagement du territoire en France 1903-1992.*
Région du Centre 1921, 1926,
Région économique de Bordeaux et du Sud-Ouest Bulletin Officiel, 1928, 1936.
*Région Économique de Toulouse et des Pyrénées* (Bulletin officiel du Groupement des Chambres de Commerce) *abbreviation RETP* 1921, 1927, 1928, 1929, 1931, 1933, 1935, 1936, 1937, 1938,
*Revue Économique de L'Ouest* 1926, 1928.
Rivière, G.-H. (1947). *Un Musée-laboratoire; le musée des arts et traditions populaires.*
Romier, L. (1925). *Explication de Notre temps.*
Rousseau, G. Étienne Clémentel et l'Auvergne. In Kessler, Rousseau (Ed.), *Clémentel* (109–127).
Rousseau, G. Les Racines d'une pensée idéaliste. In Kessler, Rousseau (Ed.), *Clémentel.*

Rousseau, G. (1998). *Étienne Clémentel 1864–1936*. Conseil-Général du Puy-de-Dôme, Archives départementales.

*Sud-Ouest Économique*, 1923, 1927, 1928, 1929, 1930, 1931.

Tandonnet, M. (2019). *André Tardieu l'incompromis.*

Tardieu, A. (1934). *La Réforme de l'État.*

*Travaux de la chambre de commerce de Clermont-Ferrand*, 1918.

Union économique de l'Est 1918, 1927, 1929, 1936.

Veitl, P. *Invention d'une région.*

Vidal de la Blache, P. (1910, November–Décember). Régions de France. *Revue de Paris*, 821–849.

Vidal de la Blache, P. (1917). *La France de l'Est.*

Wright, J. (2003). *The regionalist movement in France 1890–1914: Jean Charles-Brun and French political thought.*

CHAPTER 3

# Achievements of Economic Regionalism in Lorraine

## Economic Regionalism in Lorraine After the War

This chapter will examine the achievements of the economic region and the Nancy chamber of commerce in the fields of transport, technical education, regional banking, a regional stock exchange, reconstruction after the war and most importantly the exploitation of the Rhine to generate hydro-electricity, improve navigation and irrigate agriculture. It is important to show how a regional economic programme arose from consideration of the very difficult economic circumstances which Lorraine and indeed France faced after the war. As the war drew to a close, members of the regional elite started to develop a programme to rebuild Lorraine's economy. Apart from the physical process of reconstruction, their deliberations focused on issues like the labour shortage and re-population, revamping the transport infrastructure, and technical education to train a new generation in the skills needed for industry and commerce to make good the losses of the war. They were concerned about energy supply, particularly making good the shortage of coal for the iron and steel industry. They also considered improving agricultural productivity to make up for the loss of labour on farms, and new ways of channelling capital to industry. Camille Cavallier, vice-president of the Nancy chamber of commerce and head of the iron foundry at Pont-à-Mousson, set out a reconstruction programme incorporating some of these themes.



T. Cudbird, *The Origins of Economic Regions in France, 1918–1940*,
https://doi.org/10.1007/978-3-032-04422-8_3

The programme of economic reconstruction was given direction by the creation of the new regional groupings of chambers of commerce brought about by Clémentel, the Minister of Commerce. We will focus on how the regional elite developed their programme for regional development through the agency of the Nancy chamber of commerce which, as we shall see in Chap. 5, was in practice the driving force in Lorraine in the new regional structure, rather than the regional grouping.

Before doing this, it is essential to set the context for this discussion. We need to identify those parts of their programme which had a specifically regional context. It is these which can be legitimately described as manifestations of economic regionalism. The Nancy chamber was asked to review a wide range of laws and administrative actions, but many of these had no specific regional context. Economic regionalism did not consist in discussing issues affecting the whole of France but which might have more resonance in one region for specific reasons. It involved identifying specifically regional issues, like transport networks, where regional action or lobbying (as opposed to local or national) might produce results and which could be channelled through regional organizations with relevant powers or at least the influence to get their views carried out by others.

Lorraine's industries faced a huge task of reconstruction after the armistice. Most iron ore mines and iron and steel plants were either occupied by German forces or severely damaged by shelling. Many of those in occupied territories were deliberately damaged. Other industries like the textile plants in the Vosges were also affected. The department of the Meuse was particularly badly hit. A lot of agricultural land was laid waste and farms needed rebuilding. However, the disruption meant that many materials needed for reconstruction were in short supply. Particularly important was the shortage of coking coal needed for the iron and steel industry and power generation. Lorraine had traditionally depended on supplies from the adjacent Saar coalfield, now administered by France, from Belgium/ Luxembourg and from the Ruhr. These were disrupted in the war and its aftermath. Destruction of the railway network, or interruptions due to military use, made transporting heavy materials difficult. Railway companies needed to raise freight rates to compensate for rising costs and lack of traffic, but this only made the situation more difficult for industrial customers. Lorraine, in common with other areas of France, was short of labour, and particularly skilled workers, because of loss of life and injuries caused by the conflict. The Lorraine metallurgical industries were particularly badly hit, because before 1914, they had become dependent on foreign labour, particularly from Italy. These workers went home in 1914, and it took some time to recruit them again after the war.

The *Union économique de l'Est*, a journal set up to push an agenda of regional reconstruction under the patronage of the chambers of commerce of the region, had foreseen some of these problems in a series of articles which appeared in 1917 on the future of the metallurgical industries inspired by Camille Cavallier.[1] The home market was underdeveloped.[2] France needed to increase the birth rate to provide more workers and a larger home market. Improvements in efficiency were needed to economize on the use of labour by using the latest methods (Taylorism) and also by investing in better machines. Recruitment abroad was not the whole solution. There was also a need for capital to be provided quickly after the war to pay for re-equipment, particularly of the Briey iron field, when it was returned to France.[3] Cavallier believed that the leaders of French metallurgy in Lorraine and elsewhere should be pushing for a measure of tariff protection, training facilities for factory supervisors, measures to combat tuberculosis, alcoholism and syphilis and to provide better housing for workers. There should be more investment in hydro-electric power. In general, governments should place more emphasis on economic policy, a marked departure from the *laisser-faire* approach before the war.[4] This programme outlined by Cavallier was picked up and expanded by other writers in *L'Union économique de l'Est*. Lorraine industry and consumers had to become less dependent on German products after the war.[5] Lorraine industries had to export more.

By the beginning of 1920, France was facing a full blown balance of payments crisis and a consequent collapse in the value of the franc which made necessary imports more expensive. Exports could not grow to cover the cost of much needed imports until productive potential was fully restored. The situation was alleviated for a time by a collapse in international raw material prices but then aggravated by Germany's failure to adhere to the clauses of the Treaty of Versailles which required the prompt payment of reparations and the timely delivery of coking coal. In 1923

[1] Bulletin de la Chambre de Commerce Nancy, vol. 15 1917, (séance10 février 1917), 19.

[2] Union économique de l'Est, 1e année (1 août 1917), 8–10, (15 octobre 1917), 10–13.

[3] Union économique de l'Est, 1e année (1 novembre 1917), 6–9.

[4] Union économique de l'Est, 1e année (15 novembre 1917), 6–9.

[5] 'L'Office des industries nouvelles, contribution à la préparation de l'après-guerre', Union économique de l'Est, 1e année (1 juin 1917), 7–8.

France sent troops into the Ruhr, beyond the area it was already occupying in the Rhineland.[6]

In February 1920, the Minister of Commerce wrote to all chambers of commerce asking for their views on how to tackle the trade gap, particularly on how exports could be increased.[7] Iron master Alexandre Dreux, as president of the Nancy chamber of commerce, fired off a reply straight away, as soon as he had a limited number of answers to inquiries made of various firms. He said it was very difficult to increase exports significantly until something like normal productive capacity could be restored. At the time of writing, factories in operation were only using a third of their potential. In his opinion, the government had been wrong to allow free importation after the war and now non-essential imports should be restricted.[8] The chamber discussed the situation at length, a report was requested from the commission on customs and international trade, and this was presented by Marcel Paul and iron master Charles Fould in June.[9] Marcel Paul was Cavallier's son-in-law who helped run Pont-à-Mousson as well as being a member of the Nancy chamber. The conclusions of the Paul and Fould report were that coal supplies must be restored. As François de Wendel had pointed out on 9 March, the metal industries needed 600,000 tons a month and were only receiving 240,000 in a good month.[10] The supply of labour had to increase and the transport situation improve. The law of 1919 which created the eight-hour working day should be repealed. Concessions on freight rates were needed for the metal industries.[11] Addressing energy, labour and transport shortages—these were the three pillars of the economic programme of the regional elite in Nancy, as their continued discussion in the Nancy chamber, in documents in the Cavallier papers at Saint Gobain and in the pages of the publications sponsored by the chamber and the *Société industrielle de l'Est* shows.[12]

[6] J-C. Asselain, Histoire économique du XXe siècle, vol. 1 la montée de l'état 1914–1939 (2 vols, Paris 1995), 95–113.

[7] Chambre de Commerce Nancy, vol. 18 1920, (séance 10 février 1920), 51–53.

[8] Chambre de Commerce Nancy, vol. 18 1920, (séance 15 février 1920), 54–60.

[9] Chambre de Commerce Nancy, vol. 18 1920, (séance 9 mars 1920), 43–48; (séance 13 avril 1920), 80–83; (séance 11 mai 1920), 99; (séance 8 juin 1920), 115–118; rapport de MM. Ch. Fould et M. Paul, (séance 8 juin 1920), 159–198.

[10] Chambre de Commerce Nancy, vol. 18 1920, (séance 9 mars 1920), 44.

[11] Ibid., (séance 12 octobre 1920), 231.

[12] R. Hartmann, 'Contribution à l'étude des combustibles solides', Bulletin de la Société industrielle de l'Est, no. 144 (janvier 1919), 7; R. Hartmann, 'L'Utilisation des combustibles dans les foyers industriels', Bulletin de la Société industrielle de l'Est, no. 145 (février 1919),

This programme was driven forward by the leaders of the chamber, in particular by Alexandre Dreux. He was in the habit of giving a summary of the chamber's programme of work at the beginning of each year. These summaries pick out many of the points which were important for the regionalist programme. For example, in 1923, he identified seven questions—abolition of the eight hour working law, fiscal reform, reducing transport tariffs, improving transport infrastructure, modernization of the telecommunications network, improving workers' housing and reforming the training of apprentices.[13] In 1924 he looked back at those issues on which a clear stance had been adopted through chamber resolutions—a new canal for the North-East, new railway connecting lines, new telephone lines, pressure for further reductions in transport tariffs, support for founding a chamber for trades in the region, the launch of the new stock exchange in Nancy and the creation of the company to study the canalization of the Rhine and associated hydro-electric power stations. Looking forward he could see more work to do on housing improvements, transport tariffs and infrastructure and of course on the Rhine studies.[14] We can see in these summaries the emergence of the regional themes: transport improvement, technical training, power generation, capital provision.

Dreux received powerful support from Camille Cavallier. He believed the government must be made to take more notice of what he called 'the productive class.'[15] He had a very clear view of the important role industrial leaders could play in rebuilding France at a critical time, and he saw a strong partnership with Dreux in fulfilling this mission.[16] A year later he set out in a note the key themes for their work. Some of these are national issues, but some mirror the regional issues we have already identified; wrapping up the war and settling Franco-German differences, dealing with France's financial problems including a reduction in government

3; L. Bailly, 'Le Problème français du charbon, conférence à la Société industrielle de l'Est 20 septembre 1920', Bulletin de la Société industrielle de l'Est, no. 159 (oct–déc 1920), 12–46; M. Travers, 'La Crise des carburants et les remèdes proposés, la situation particulière de la France', Bulletin de la Société industrielle de l'Est, no. 173 (avril–juin 1924), 31–68. SGA 7247, dossier février–mars, note by Daum, president of commission on electric energy, on meeting of 10 février 1920; note by Marcel Paul 2 mars 1920 on a recent meeting of the commission for transport concerning new railway lines.

[13] Chambre de Commerce Nancy, vol. 21 1923, (séance 9 janvier 1923), 2–4.

[14] Chambre de Commerce Nancy, vol. 22 1924, (séance 8 janvier 1924), 12–17.

[15] Chambre de Commerce Nancy, vol. 20 1922, (séance 10 janvier 1922), 12.

[16] SGA 7248, dossier correspondance 1917–1924, letter from Cavallier to Dreux 27 janvier 1922.

expenditure, installing an energetic government which dealt with disruptive elements like communists, repealing the eight hour working law, reducing railway tariffs, tackling issues relating to natalism, for example, setting up schools for household management and cracking down on crime and drunkenness, and lastly restricting unnecessary imports.[17] Improving the railways was a key regional theme. Natalism, which addressed both the supply of labour and the demand for goods, was a programme which, as we shall see later, the Nancy chamber made all its own.

Cavallier developed some of his ideas during the war. After his retirement from the chamber, he published a number of pamphlets. In *L'Avenir de la France,* he set out many of the elements of the regionalist programme—further development of technical education, development of hydro-electric power to match Germany, restoring the race (natalism) and making up France's deficit of coal and other combustibles.[18] In *Notes économiques,* he returned to the challenge faced by his industry of rising input prices which made selling prices too high. Labour rates had multiplied by four times since the beginning of the war and coal prices three and a half times.[19] On the question of coal at least the temporary acquisition of the Saar might help as he wrote in *La Sarre par un Franco-Sarrois.* However, the Saar would need investment, particularly in transport links to France.[20] In *La Crise économique,* he also focused on the ballooning national debt caused by reconstruction and on the need for economies. He then went on to attack the railway companies for their rising tariffs and suggested they economize even more.[21] In *La France de demain,* he set out the big challenges facing the country, including of course the lack of coal and the need to raise the population.[22] In this paper, he set out Pont-à-Mousson's future mission, to improve the health of the nation by making the pipes which would carry fresh water to the towns of France. Repopulation became something of an obsession for Cavallier in his final

[17] SGA 7247, dossier 1923, note by Cavallier dated 12 février 1923.

[18] SGA, DOC PAM 22.13, C. Cavallier, 'L'Avenir de la France, réformes nécessaires, avant propos de Maurice Herbette', 8, 19, 31.

[19] SGA, DOC PAM 21.50, 'Notes économiques d'un métallurgiste'.

[20] SGA, DOC PAM 22.21, 'La Sarre par un Franco-Sarrois', June 1923.

[21] SGA DOC PAM 21.52, 'La Crise économique: transports par chemins de fer', 1 février 1924'. SGA DOC PAM 21.65, 'Séance du 24 février 1922 Office des Transports'.

[22] SGA, DOC PAM 21.51, 'C. Cavallier, La France de demain: paix et prospérité par le travail, la natalité, l'hygiène', août 1923.

years. We see this in the collection of his writings, *La Sagesse du chef,* and also in another pamphlet, *La France victorieuse.*[23]

So the regional issues which emerged from the economic debate outlined above were transport, power supply, technical education to combat the shortage of skilled labour, and financial institutions affecting the supply of capital. We will now examine each of these in turn, followed by consideration of the development of regional organizations to speed up reconstruction and also natalist policies.

## Transport—Railways and Canals

Transport matters—roads, canals and railways—were often top of mind for prominent members of the chamber, including Camille Cavallier. An internal company memo dated 28 March 1919 from Cavallier to his assistant Dubois reminded him to forward a list of matters to raise with the Minister for the Liberated Regions, Albert Lebrun, the next day. The hand written list at the bottom includes roads, doubling of railway lines, canalization of the Moselle, a north-east canal, suburban and industrial tramways, improvement of railway traffic and modification of tariffs.[24]

In 1917 the Nancy chamber of commerce had taken the initiative in setting up an *Office des Transports* to bring the combined weight of 21 chambers in the eastern region to bear on operational issues for roads, canals and railways and on future development. They modelled their project on a similar office in the South-East.[25] The policy of the Nancy chamber, and indeed of its neighbouring organization in Metz, was to lobby hard for extensions to the railway and canal networks to facilitate the transport of goods, particularly heavy materials like iron, steel and coal. New railway lines were usually financed with state support and operated by the regional railway companies. The government agreed a new convention with the railway companies in 1921.[26] For the railway network, the

[23] Sagesse du chef, lettres et notes inédites de Camille Cavallier (Paris, 1937). C. Cavallier, La France victorieuse (Nancy, 7 septembre 1923).

[24] SGA 7319, dossier correspondance avec Albert Lebrun, 'Note de service 28 mars 1919'.

[25] Chambre de Commerce Nancy, vol. 15 1917, (séance 5 mai 1917), 61; (séance 7 juillet 1917), 72.

[26] SGA 7247, dossier octobre 1920, 'Commission des Transports, séance 12 octobre 1920, le régime des chemins de fer'. F. Caron (ed), Les Grandes Compagnies de chemin de fer en France 1823–1937, Archives économiques du Crédit Lyonnais (Geneva, 2005), 327–335, 342–352, 376–377.

big regional issues were the integration of Alsace-Lorraine's railways into the French structure and improving links across the old frontier, and secondly improving communications from Nancy to the iron and steel manufacturing areas to the north, to the Moselle department and the Saar beyond it. The Lorraine elite were also aware of the benefits of electrification of the network.[27]

Canals played a major part in the transport of heavy goods in France. Major developments in the network continued into the twentieth century. New canals were also financed by the state, although municipalities, *conseils-généraux* and the new regional groupings of chambers of commerce could become shareholders, and even individual industrial firms sometimes participated in projects. As Lorraine industry faced renewed competition with Germany after the war, the deficiencies of the water transport network in France, compared with Germany, were a pressing concern. Lorraine needed access to raw materials, markets and energy more than ever. Accordingly, the *Revue industrielle de l'Est* published two articles entitled U*n péril national, l'encerclement par l'eau*, referring to the German network based on navigable rivers like the Rhine linked to the North Sea.[28]

The priorities for canals were to improve links from Lorraine to the Rhine, and also via Luxembourg into Belgium. Lorraine was quite close to the Rhine. If the Moselle could be canalized for heavier barges, then the route out to the Low Countries and their ports and also to the Ruhr's coalfield was fairly straightforward. Such plans would improve supplies of coal from Germany and Belgium and also help exports via Antwerp and Rotterdam. The temporary acquisition of the Saar coal mines also raised the issue of canal links there. At the same time, the Nancy chamber wanted to see the construction of a Nord-Est canal—in effect, a series of new canals, linking with existing canals, to join the Lorraine iron basin to the Pas-de-Calais coalfield and the port of Dunkerque.

There was a strategic choice to be made here for the landlocked Lorraine industries on the German frontier. Which projects were more urgent—those facilitating links to the north and east, or those linking with the rest of France ? And of course there was an issue of cost. The links to the East were generally less costly to improve, for example, the canalization of the

[27] SGA 7247, dossier juin 1920, 'Analyse de la brochure de M. R. Paul, Directeur des Chemins de Fer du Midi, L'Électrification des chemins de fer français'.

[28] Revue industrielle de l'Est (24 mars 1918), 343, 345; (31 mars 1918), 359, 361.

Moselle river for heavy barges. Linking existing canals to make a continuous Nord-Est canal was complicated. There were also political considerations here in the context of France's fraught relations with Germany: post-war disputes on issues like the Treaty of Versailles. Should France develop canal links to the Saar when eventually its inhabitants might choose to rejoin Germany in the plebiscite agreed for 1935? Should France be financing canals which would make it easier for competitive German industries to penetrate the French market? Given the general suspicion of Germany after the war, it is not surprising that such questions were asked. Clémentel and his advisers thought German competition would become formidable again once the conflict was over.

## Railways

The first debate on railways concerned the future of the network in the former Alsace-Lorraine. This had been managed as part of the German system until November 1918. Now the question arose of what its long-term future in France should be. How should it be integrated into the French network? Should it be given to the *Compagnie des Chemins de Fer de l'Est* to manage or possibly be put into a separate company owned by the state?[29] There were technical issues to be resolved in operating the two networks. Timetables and tariffs needed to be coordinated. The two networks were designed to run with stops at the frontier and sometimes connections across the old frontier were not logical. German railways ran on a different side of multiple tracks. Signalling was different. Personnel with German nationality would have to be replaced in line with government policy on the recovered territories.

From the start the Nancy chamber felt the right course was to pass the Alsace-Lorraine network over to the *Compagnie de l'Est* at once. They passed a resolution to this effect in January 1919 as indeed did the council of the *Office des Transports de l'Est*. At the same time Imbeaux, the chief engineer of *Ponts-et-Chaussées*, presented two new routes to run through the Vosges mountains which were being actively considered.[30] The

[29] Union économique de l'Est, 3e année (1 février 1919), 33–35.

[30] Chambre de Commerce Nancy, vol. 17 1919, (séance 25 janvier 1919), 124. SGA 7248, 'Avant projet de voeu de l'Office des Transports de l'Est 8 janvier 1919'. Union économique de l'Est, 3e année (1 février 1919), 33–35; (15 février 1919), 50–51.

chamber preferred the most direct route through Saint-Maurice-Wesserling.[31] The chamber naturally enough favoured one unified tariff for goods transported on railways throughout France.[32] The matter took a long time to resolve. In 1921 the Nancy chamber passed a new resolution which laid out in some detail the economic, defence and political reasons to have one national network. From a regional point of view, the network in the east would run much more smoothly, and this would be economically beneficial.[33] The Metz chamber also wanted better co-ordination of trains between the east of France and the former Alsace-Lorraine, with fewer stops at the frontier.[34] In November 1922, the Nancy chamber noted with satisfaction that a draft law had been submitted to the Chamber of Deputies covering the attachment of the Alsace-Lorraine network to the *Compagnie de l'Est*. Unsurprisingly the chamber in Strasbourg was opposed to this loss of independence.[35] So it appears that constant lobbying by the Nancy chamber supported by Metz had helped push the government into action beneficial to the functioning of the Eastern region.

The need for the further development of railways in the regions was highlighted in the *Union économique de l'Est* in an article emphasizing the importance of different regions being able to connect with each other directly without going through Paris. Otherwise, the article asked, what was the point of talking about regionalism and of setting up regional economic groupings?[36]

Starting in 1919 the Nancy chamber wanted to shorten the railway journey to the Saar, to facilitate trade with a territory where France was administering the mines.[37] In March 1920 Marcel Paul attended the transport commission of the Nancy chamber and recorded a discussion on various ways to improve the railway links between Sarrebruck and Nancy–Pont-à-Mousson. Naturally his company would have a particular

[31] Chambre de Commerce Nancy, vol. 19 1921, (séance 8 novembre 1921), 240. Union économique de l'Est, 5e année (15 octobre 1921), 217–218.

[32] Chambre de Commerce Nancy, vol. 18 1920 (séance 9 novembre 1920), 262.

[33] SGA 7248, memo attached to note of 4 juillet 1921 from Dubois, Pont-à-Mousson to Cavallier. Chambre de Commerce Nancy, vol. 19 1921, (séance 8 juillet 1921), 184–186.

[34] Communications de la Chambre de Commerce de Metz, 1e année, no. 2 mars 1922, (séance 25 février 1922), 6.

[35] Chambre de Commerce Nancy, vol. 20 1922, (séance 7 novembre 1922), 230; (séance 6 décembre 1922), 263–264.

[36] 'Lignes transversales, horaires nouveaux', Union économique de l'Est, 3e année (15 avril 1919), 103.

[37] Chambre de Commerce Nancy, vol. 17 1919, (séance 9 décembre 1919), 256–258.

interest in this.[38] However, the Nancy chamber ran into a number of obstacles. Firstly, the whole matter was referred to an inter-departmental commission of the Moselle and the Meurthe-et-Moselle.[39] Secondly the military wanted to develop a new route further to the east passing through Château Salins. The chamber preferred a more westerly routing because it could serve the new coal mining concessions in the Moselle more effectively. It would also go straight past Pont-à-Mousson. They fired off letters to the Minister of War, the Minister of Public Works and the Minister of Commerce.[40] No doubt they were disappointed to learn in June that year that their wish for a more westerly route could not be implemented first, because the military wanted to do work on the eastern route straight away.[41] However, by May the following year, the military had changed its mind and was backing the route preferred by the chamber.[42] Cavallier's papers contain a letter from General Ragueneau of the General Staff, and a member of the *Conseil supérieur des Chemins de Fer*, to the Nancy chamber and dated 20 March 1923, saying that the westerly route via Dieulouard and Remilly was preferable from a strategic point of view.[43] Cavallier made some very caustic remarks about the military attitude to building railways:

> Here is another example of the stupidity of soldiers and of the military spirit in particular, concerning the question of knowing which railways should be built and which should be rejected. It is not the first example I have seen of lines which should be rejected but a little later on are requested again. It all depends on one's point of view. It is extraordinary how much money is wasted in France, and the French people pass for being the most intelligent. Only its intelligence is spent on words.[44]

[38] SGA 7247, dossier février–mars 1920, 'Note de Marcel Paul pour Cavallier 2 mars 1920'.

[39] Chambre de Commerce Nancy, vol. 19 1921, (séance 8 mars 1921), 80.

[40] Chambre de Commerce Nancy, vol. 19 1921, (séance 12 avril 1921), 107–110.

[41] Chambre de Commerce Nancy, vol. 19 1921, (séance 7 juin 1921), 173.

[42] SGA 7248, dossier correspondance 1917–1924, 'Compte-rendu de la Commission des Communications de 31 mai 1922 par Marcel Paul'.

[43] SGA 7249, dossier renseignements divers, letter from Ragueneau to Nancy chamber of commerce 20 mars 1923.

[44] SGA 7248, dossier correspondance 1917–1924, 'Note de service de Cavallier pour Marcel Paul 5 juin 1922'.

In 1923 the route supported by the Nancy chamber was opposed by their colleagues in Metz who wanted a different route.[45] However, Imbeaux reported to the Nancy chamber in June 1923 that the Dieulouard–Remilly line had now been definitively selected.[46]

This line was one of several projects on which the Nancy chamber was asked to comment. This particular story shows that the economic leaders of the region in the Nancy chamber fought their corner vigorously for what was in the economic interests of Lorraine as they conceived them. In their considerations, the interests of the iron masters played a major part. The new line went near to their plants.

## Canals

The strategic choices to be made on canals sparked a lively debate among members of the regional elite with an economic interest in the outcome. These issues were discussed in two articles in the *Union économique de l'Est*, the first by Imbeaux on 1 January 1919 and the second in an editorial, probably written by chamber of commerce secretary Fayolle, in June.[47] Imbeaux alerted Camille Cavallier to the opportunities for his company from canal development in northern Lorraine in a letter of April 1919. He said that the Committee of Navigable Waterways for the North and East reporting to the *Conseil supérieur des Travaux publics* had adopted a report he had prepared calling for the canalization of the French Moselle and also to create two new canals in the North East serving some of the iron and steel basin. These should be financed by the industrial interests they would serve, including Cavallier's company.[48] Meanwhile Fayolle warned the representatives of the *Ligue maritime française* meeting in Nancy in May 1919 that canalization of the entire Moselle might meet with German opposition.[49]

[45] Communications Metz, 2e année, no. 3 mars 1923, (séance 24 mars 1923), 3; nos. 4–5 avril–mai 1923, (séance 27 avril 1923), 2–4.

[46] Chambre de Commerce Nancy, vol. 21 1923, (séance 8 juin 1923), 100.

[47] Union économique de l'Est, 3e année (15 janvier 1919), 26–29 and (15 juin 1919), 148–151.

[48] SGA 7393, dossier voies navigables, letter from Imbeaux to Cavallier 2 avril 1919.

[49] SGA 7248, dossier correspondance 1917-1924, 'Réception des représentants de la Ligue maritime française, Chambre de Commerce de Nancy, 19 mai 1919; exposé fait par M. Fayolle sur la question des transports, notamment métallurgiques, dans l'Est et la canalisation de la Moselle'.

Alexandre Dreux set out many of these issues in a speech to the Congrès de Navigation intérieure at Strasbourg on 2 September 1919.[50] Chief Engineer Imbeaux had already set out plans to link the basins of the Moselle and the Saar with the French canal network and eventually with the Rhine. However, Dreux pointed out that the only effective route was through the *Canal de la Marne au Rhin* which would not be able to cope with increased traffic. Dreux said that Imbeaux's plans did not include an extended Canal du Nord-Est which would provide the links between all the Lorraine industrial basins, the Ardennes and the *Nord* and Dunkerque, and also Luxembourg. This Nord-Est canal project, linking together existing canals with some new sections, was part of Freycinet's plan for the canal network drawn up in 1881 and had been ranked as a top priority by the government since, but the funds to complete it were never available. (Freycinet was an engineer who became Minister of Public Works and eventually Président du Conseil.) Current plans also did nothing to help the industrial basin of Longwy, where Dreux's own plants were situated, and also the Briey iron field occupied by Germany in the war and severely damaged. Dreux went on to say that that German factories in the Moselle had not yet been brought back under French control and the firms in the Saar were of course German owned. The Saar firms already had special privileges of access to the French market. In 15 years, the Saar might choose to stay German. The congress passed a series of resolutions to develop the locks on the *Canal de la Marne au Rhin* and the *Canal des Houillères de la Sarre* and to install electric traction, to canalize the Moselle between Metz and Thionville so the Moselle could receive Rhine barges and to make a start on the Nord-Est canal with canal works in the Lorraine basin.

All these projects were to be the subject of extensive lobbying by the Nancy chamber over the next few years. Cavallier was a little cynical about whether anything would come of all this activity. He wrote to Fayolle on 8 September 1919 that he doubted whether anything much would be done:

[50] Chambre de Commerce Nancy, vol. 17 1919, (séance 4 novembre 1919), 201–216 with a full text of the speech at Annex I 217–232.

> As soon as anyone wants to construct a section of canal in France, all the departments get their deputies to campaign for their own canal, so that the cost of all the canals requested cannot be entertained.[51]

It seems that by May 1920, the government had decided on a programme, but the representatives of the metallurgical industries felt that it put too much emphasis on linking the Saar to Paris. Dreux and Cavallier believed the priorities should be firstly, joining the Lorraine metallurgical basin to the French canal network, with a possible link to Luxembourg, and only secondly, the canalization of the Saar which would link with the Moselle and the Rhine.[52] By March 1921 hostility to the central government scheme had increased in Lorraine, because its whole thrust seemed to be to direct traffic to Paris and Rouen and not to Dunkerque. The Lorraine iron masters wanted to make a start on joining Lorraine to the Pas-de-Calais coalfield.[53]

In 1922 the Metz chamber of commerce got behind the project to canalize the Moselle. The chamber wanted to form a consortium consisting of the department of the Moselle, towns and interested industrialists. They proposed to borrow money and advance 77 million francs to the state administration to carry out the works. Bankers were said to be supportive. The Minister of Public Works met with a delegation including leading iron master Humbert de Wendel, the president of the Metz chamber, on 22 July. The Minister indicated he was willing to put the necessary legislation in place to allow the consortium to go ahead. By October the *conseil-général* of the Moselle, the cities of Metz and Thionville and the *Association minière d'Alsace et de Lorraine* had given their formal backing to the project.[54] In October Dreux believed the government would go ahead but leave out the links to Briey and Longwy (Dreux's home

[51] SGA 7420, dossier divers, Cavallier letter to Fayolle, 8 septembre 1919.

[52] Chambre de Commerce Nancy, vol. 18 1920, (séance 11 mai 1920), 100–101 and Annexe II 107–110; Union économique de l'Est, 4e année (15 juin 1920), 145–146.

[53] SGA 7247, dossier 1921, papers on canal of Moselle 11 mars 1921. SGA 7249, dossier Transports, 'Analyse de Dubois, Chambre de Commerce, Canal du Nord-Est 14 mars 1921'. Chambre de Commerce Nancy, vol. 19 1921, (séance 8 juillet 1921), pp. 194–195. SGA 7249, dossier transports, 'Rapport de M. Alexandre Dreux au Congrès national de la Navigation intérieure à Rouen, 4–8 juillet, Canal du Nord-Est', copy dated 30 septembre 1921'.

[54] Communications Metz, 1e année, no. 3 avril 1922, (séance 1 avril 1922), 2; nos. 5–6 juin–juillet 1922, (séance 27 mai 1922), 2–3; no. 9 octobre 1922, (séance 2 septembre 1922), 2, (séance 7 octobre 1922), 3.

territory). He fired off a letter of protest, and in November received an assurance that the two areas would be catered for.[55]

Dreux had not given up on the *Nord-Est* canal. In his review in January 1924, he said that this canal "would happily complete the economic infrastructure of our region."[56] The next national congress on internal navigation considered the matter yet again. Dreux could not obtain backing there for the whole concept,[57] but in October he got Lebrun to help him obtain the support of the *Conseil-général* of Meurthe-et-Moselle for the *Nord-Est* canal as he had originally conceived it.[58] The Metz chamber also supported it but said that the canalization of the Moselle was the top priority.[59]

Although the history of lobbying for the *Nord-Est* canal over the six years after the war was inconclusive, the debate in the Nancy and Metz chambers of commerce had achieved much. The government now supported in principle extensive improvements to the canal network into France and potentially outwards to the Rhine. Furthermore, to expedite the canalization of the Moselle, various parties in the Moselle had come together to provide financial backing. The chambers had a clear view of where their regional interests lay and took what steps they could to turn their vision into reality. This was exactly the kind of activity being carried out by chambers of commerce which Clémentel had envisaged, albeit the main impetus came from individual chambers rather than the grouping as such.

## Energy

The leaders of the chamber of commerce in Nancy discussed not only water transport but also the provision of new sources of energy. These two concerns came together in consideration of a project to exploit the resources of the Rhine. The *Union économique de l'Est* outlined the

[55] Chambre de Commerce Nancy, vol. 20 1922, (séance 10 octobre 1922), 205–210; (7 novembre 1922), 238–239.

[56] Chambre de Commerce Nancy, vol. 22 1924, (séance 8 janvier 1924), 13.

[57] Chambre de Commerce Nancy, vol. 22 1924, (séance 8 juillet 1924), 169.

[58] Chambre de Commerce Nancy, vol. 22 1924, (séance 7 octobre 1924), 190–193. SGA 7249, dossier questions diverses, L'Est républicain reported the conseil-général's resolution in detail on 2 octobre 1924, cutting passed by Dubois to Cavallier.

[59] Communications Metz, 3e année, nos. 11 and 12 novembre–décembre 1924, (séance 29 novembre 1924), 2–4.

importance of the Rhine to commerce in a long article in July 1922.[60] The regional grouping of chambers of commerce formed a *Société des Études pour la Navigation du Rhin* which focused on navigation improvements and also the possibility of hydro-electric power generation from the fall in the Rhine when a lateral canal was constructed. This project needs to be considered in detail because it represents just the sort of initiative which Clémentel envisaged when he created the regional groupings of chambers of commerce.

The context of the Rhine project was grave concern about France's acute shortage of coal after the war and high prices. This was the subject of many articles in the press controlled by the Nancy chamber and the *Société industrielle de l'Est* and also of discussions within the chamber itself. The *Union économique de l'Est* covered the subject in articles on 1 April, 1 July and 1 August 1920. Camille Cavallier rated the writer L. Bailly as highly expert even if he did not agree with all of his views.[61] Bailly called for more intensive exploitation of what reserves France had and legal reforms to make it easier for prospectors to search for new coal mines.[62] He gave a lecture entitled *Le Problème français du charbon* at the *Société industrielle de l'Est* on 20 September 1920, subsequently published in the society's bulletin, which also carried other articles on the issue.[63] Cavallier, like other industrial leaders, was well aware of the problem. His papers contain a note dated 3 November 1920 which said that France only received 75% of the fuel which it needed and over half of this came from abroad. There is also in the Cavallier papers the draft of a pamphlet, *La Question des combustibles en France*, which talked about the necessity of increasing French coal production, economizing on the use of energy in the manufacturing process and finding new sources of coal and new fuels altogether.[64] Industrialists like Cavallier were investing in new production in the Saar. Marcel Paul made these points in his report to the Nancy chamber on 7 December 1920 adding that of course Germany must

[60] Union économique de l'Est, 6e année (1 juillet 1922), 151–158.

[61] SGA 7247, dossier août–septembre 1920, letter Cavallier to Fayolle 23 août 1920.

[62] Union économique de l'Est, 4e année (1 avril 1920), 89; (1 juillet 1920), 157–158 and (1 août 1920), 198—9.

[63] Bulletin de la Société industrielle de l'Est, no. 159 (octobre–décembre 1920), 12–46.

[64] SGA 7247, dossier novembre 1920, 'Note pour M. Cavallier, Approvisionnement de la France en charbon, résumé d'un extrait du Bulletin de la Société d'Études et d'Informations 3 novembre 1920' and 'La Question des combustibles en France'.

deliver the quantities of coal which it had undertaken to do.[65] In 1921 the Nancy chamber organized a series of five lectures on the use of fuel and also an exhibition run by the *Office économique de l'Est* which it had set up.[66]

This obsession continued over the next few years. In an account written four years later, Dreux said that more recent events had shown up France's continued dependence on foreign coal, for example, during the French occupation of the Ruhr in 1923.[67] In January 1924 the *Union économique de l'Est* published an article directed, it said, at the regional elite, which argued that much of the power of countries depended on access to coal, and in the future oil. France was poorly provided. It produced only 40 million tons of coal a year, as against consumption of 60 million. Germany and the UK each produced 300 million and the USA 600 million.[68]

Expanding hydro-electric capacity was widely seen as the answer to over-dependence on foreign coal. Such capacity doubled during the war encouraged by the state because power was important for national defence.[69] Philippe Veitl explained the reason for the development of hydro-electricity in his work on the creation of the Alpine economic region.[70] We shall also come across this belief in hydro-electricity in the chapter on the Auvergne. Dreux, in the introduction to Libault's book on the Rhine project, referred to the Dordogne hydro-electricity project being undertaken by the regions of the centre of France, as similar in scope.[71]

The key legislation which governed the grant of concessions for hydro-electric plants was the law of 16 October 1919. Under this law the state could take over the rights of holders of land alongside rivers which were

[65] Chambre de Commerce Nancy, vol. 18 1920, (séance 7 décembre 1920), 290–300.

[66] Chambre de Commerce Nancy, vol. 19 1921, (séance 12 avril 1921), 112; (séance 10 mai 1921), 132–133; (séance 7 juin 1921), 168; (séance 8 juillet 1921), 180. SGA 7248, dossier correspondance 1917–1924, letters from Fayolle to Cavallier 3 mai 1921 and 2 août 1921'. See also SGA 7249 dossier exposition des combustibles.

[67] A. Libault, Le Rhin et le Grand Canal d'Alsace, préfaces d'A. Dreux, Président de la Région économique de l'Est et D. Mieg, Président de la Société industrielle de Mulhouse (Paris, 1924), ix–x. Libault was secretary of the technical and information committees of the Société des Études pour la Navigation du Rhin.

[68] Union économique de l'Est, 8e année (1 janvier 1924), 2–3.

[69] M. Lévy-Leboyer, H. Morsel (eds), Histoire générale de L'Électricité en France, T.II 1919–1946 L'Interconnexion et le Marché (Paris, 1994), 632.

[70] Philippe Veitl, L'Invention d'une région: les Alpes françaises (Grenoble, 2013)

[71] Libault, Le Rhin, ix.

not navigable (the state already had such rights for navigable rivers) and grant concessions for their exploitation for hydro-electricity. New concessionaires would have to make 25% of the energy generated available at an advantageous rate to the department where the plant was situated. As a result, concessionaires could obtain financial assistance from the state for construction costs and the state could even take up shares in the venture. The concessionaire had to pay 5c per KW to the state for ten years and the concessions would last for 75 years. From this and subsequent legislation on rural electrification and the provision of high tension lines followed a general acceptance that the state should have a role in the electrification of France in the general interest.[72] This tendency was reinforced by the arguments of influential Radical-Socialists and Socialists in government.[73]

In the 1920s the position of hydro-electric plants relative to thermal power stations worsened because of inflation in the construction costs of the former. Hydro-electric plants were relatively much costlier to build and dependence on loans from banks made them financially riskier. On the other hand, they absorbed less labour and avoided dependence on uncertain and costly coal supplies.[74] Hydro-electricity accounted for 45% of French power generation capacity in 1923.[75]

In 1919 Dreux proposed a scheme to share current generated by hydro-electric plants on the Rhine which was conceived as a way to help areas far from sources of coal supply. Such a sharing scheme was seen as an excellent way of demonstrating the usefulness of the new economic region of the East.[76] The *Union électrique du Nord-Est* would include not only the power generation companies but also chambers of commerce and consumer representatives. The initial report to the Nancy chamber was made by Desforges, a banker from the *Société nancéienne de Crédit industriel et de Dépôts.*[77] The new vehicle could draw eventually on hydro-electricity generated by the Rhine, but meanwhile it could look at new sources of energy, for example, gas generated by blast furnaces. This sharing arrangement could cover a wide area including the Ardennes, the Meuse, the

[72] Histoire générale de L'Électricité, 43–46, 54–56

[73] Ibid., 356.

[74] Histoire générale de L'Électricité, 56, 59, 61,

[75] Ibid., 733.

[76] Chambre de Commerce Nancy, vol. 17 1919, (séance 4 novembre 1919), 211–212.

[77] Chambre de Commerce Nancy, vol. 19 1921, (séance 10 février 1921), 21–23, 28–34; (séance 9 décembre 1921), 256. 'L'Énergie électrique dans l'Est', Union économique de l'Est, 3e année (15 décembre 1919), 278–279.

Vosges and the Marne. Imbeaux pointed out that wide participation was needed to get government backing.[78] It was from regional networks developed in the 1920s and 1930s that the French national grid was eventually created.[79]

The Eastern region started the Rhine exploitation project with a study visit in July 1920. The group of representatives of chambers of commerce looked at hydro-electric power plants on the Swiss Rhine and then met with a group of Alsatians considering a bid for a concession on the French Rhine at Kembs. The meeting took place at the industrial centre of Mulhouse and included Daniel Mieg, president of the newly formed *Société des Forces motrices du Haut-Rhin*. It was agreed that any new French consortium would cooperate with the *Forces motrices* and consider taking further concessions downstream from Kembs. Imbeaux, the waterways engineer and member of the Nancy chamber of commerce, conducted the visit and was retained as a consultant.[80] The economic region envisaged taking a majority holding in any new venture but this was later to cause some dispute.[81]

From the start Alexandre Dreux, the president of the Nancy chamber, spearheaded this project. He thought that energy producers could not always look to the state for help, particularly in view of the pressures on the public purse after the war. Users of energy had to take the lead and work with the state to get suitable projects off the ground.[82] This was exactly what Clémentel had envisaged his new economic regions doing. To get the backing of interested parties including politicians, the region took steps to make sure their ideas were well publicized. The Nancy chamber's journal *Union économique de l'Est* published two articles setting out the scope of the project and the expected benefits from a canal parallel to the Rhine on the French side which would improve navigation, control flooding and irrigation, and most important offer the opportunity to

[78] SGA 7247, dossier janvier 1920, 'Énergie électrique de l'Est, réunion de la commission spéciale 31 janvier 1920'.

[79] C. Bouneau, 'La Contribution de l'électrification à la genèse de l'aménagement du territoire en France durant la première moitié du XXe siècle', in P. Caro, O. Dard, J-C. Daumas (eds), La Politique d'aménagement du territoire: racines, logiques et résultats (Rennes, 2002), 31–52.

[80] Chambre de Commerce Nancy, vol. 18 1920, (séance 8 juin 1920), 137, (séance 6 juillet 1920), 201.

[81] Union économique de l'Est, 4e année (15 avril 1920), 101.

[82] Libault, Le Rhin, ix–x.

install turbines at each dam to profit from the fall of the water.[83] The Nancy chamber noted that the Treaty of Versailles specifically gave France the exclusive right to exploit the Rhine which now ran along its frontier. However, they knew that the Germans and some Swiss interests would be opposed to the scheme.[84]

A key meeting took place with the Minister of Public Works on 18 May 1921. All the chambers of commerce in the Eastern region were represented plus the chambers of Bas-Rhin, Haut-Rhin, Belfort, Dijon and Gray-Vesoul and also the *Forces motrices*. The principle of setting up the *Société des Études du Rhin* was agreed subject to the approval of the Minister of Commerce. A key obstacle was overcome when legal experts in Paris ruled that chambers of commerce could take shares in such an enterprise by virtue of the law of 16 October 1919 concerning hydraulic energy. Other public bodies could also lend financial support.[85] Of course not all regional interests agreed on how the project should be executed. There was opposition to the proposed structure of the company from the Alsatian chambers and particularly Strasbourg. Strasbourg wanted to increase the proposed shareholding of the Bas-Rhin and Haut-Rhin and to include not only the *Forces motrices* but also the Port of Strasbourg as shareholders. Some concessions were eventually agreed to Strasbourg's point of view.[86]

Twenty-four bodies were involved as shareholders when the first assembly of the new company took place in Nancy in May 1922. All the major players had positions of influence. Dreux was the president, and the vice-presidents were Herrenschmidt from the Strasbourg chamber, Mieg from *Forces motrices*, and Perrigot, the president of the Épinal chamber. Humbert de Wendel from Metz was a member of the board of directors. It was agreed with the Minister of Public Works that the company would

[83] Union économique de l'Est, 4e année (15 juillet and 1 août 1920), 181–183 and 193–195. This account was published later the same year as a separate brochure Rhin français, projets d'aménagement du fleuve, force motrice, navigation (Union économique de l'Est, Nancy).

[84] Chambre de Commerce Nancy, vol. 18 1920, (séance 15 octobre 1920), 236–237.

[85] Chambre de Commerce Nancy, vol. 19 1921, (séance 12 avril 1921), 115; (séance 10 mai 1921), 146; (séance 7 juin 1921), 169–171; (séance 8 juillet 1921), 188–191.

[86] SGA 7249, dossier Société régionale des Études du Rhin, 'Société des Études du Rhin: Réunion 29 novembre 1921 Procès-Verbal; projets de statuts de la société, analyse et critique, 5 décembre 1921'. SGA 7359, dossier Le Rhône et Le Rhin, letter from Président de la Chambre de Commerce de Strasbourg to Alexandre Dreux 7 octobre 1921, analyse 10 octobre 1921, note de service Pont-à-Mousson 11 octobre 1921'.

eventually spawn a separate vehicle to build and manage the canal and hydro-electric plants.[87] Later that year an offshoot company to manage French navigation on the Rhine was created. Again a number of industrial interests took shares (members of the *Comité des forges*, including Pont-à-Mousson, the railway companies and the *Comité des armateurs* or ship owners) as well as the city, chamber of commerce and port of Strasbourg.[88]

The crucial next steps were to obtain the concessions for the new hydro-electric plants. Most important the company had to build the case for investment by estimating demand and talking about the price of the electricity generated to potential consumers. Dreux ensured he was in control of this crucial process by creating an economic committee of the *Société d'Études* and basing it in Nancy.[89] In March 1924, the draft project for the Grand Canal d'Alsace in all its ramifications was agreed.[90] In a discussion at the Nancy chamber in November, Paul Hellé, *Compagnie lorraine d'Électricité*, argued that this energy project was not so good for Lorraine because the price per Kwh at 20 centimes (of which transmission accounted for 5-6c) was not competitive with coal unless the price of the latter increased substantially. When the project started, its backers were motivated by the thought that the force of the Rhine was equivalent to half the annual coal production of the Saar basin.[91] However, it now seemed that the goal of reducing dependence on foreign coal might be more difficult to achieve. Also two billion francs were needed to complete the project. There were limits to the guarantees the state could give.[92]

The project was delayed by German and Swiss opposition, but in December 1927, *Énergie électrique du Rhin* was incorporated to construct

[87] Union économique de l'Est, 6e année (15 avril 1922), 92; (15 mai), 121–122; (1 juin), 134.

[88] SGA 7331, dossier navigation sur le Rhin, 'Note de service du service des participations de Pont-à-Mousson pour M. Cavallier 5 novembre 1922'. SGA 7359, dossier Le Rhône et Le Rhin, letter from Tannery, Société des Minerais lorrains to Cavallier, 30 novembre 1923. SGA 7331, dossier navigation sur Le Rhin, letter from Tannery to Cavallier listing the shareholdings, 3 juin 1924.

[89] SGA 7359, dossier Le Rhône et le Rhin, 'Réunion du conseil, société d'études, 20 avril 1923'.

[90] Chambre de Commerce Nancy, vol. 22 1924, (séance 11 mars 1924), 73.

[91] Rhin français, projets d'aménagement du fleuve, force motrice, navigation (Union économique de l'Est, Nancy, 1920), 1.

[92] Chambre de Commerce Nancy, vol. 22 1924, (séance 11 novembre 1924), 237–239.

**Fig. 3.1** View of the dam at Kembs on the Rhine 1932, courtesy of the Bibliothèque Nationale de France

the station at Kembs.[93] Work on the *Grand Canal d'Alsace* or *canal latéral* eventually started in 1928. The first hydro-electric generating station at Kembs opened in 1932 (Fig. 3.1). The other three such stations on the canal had to wait until after 1945. This story shows that a large number of public and private interests over the Eastern region and beyond could come together with the state's support to get a major infrastructure project off the ground. It demonstrates that private and public interests in the region were willing to back such a project financially. It also shows that adjustments had to be made between different regional perspectives. Although Strasbourg played a significant role, the project was driven by an iron master from Nancy, the core of the Lorraine region. Lastly it was a complex project which demonstrated the ambition of the regional elite in economic affairs. It was seen as a way of helping the East of the country,

[93] Histoire générale de L'Électricité, 642.

which had suffered so grievously in the recent conflict.[94] It is one of the best demonstrations of economic regionalism in the inter-war period.

## Technical Education

During its discussions on how to combat the shortage of coal, the Nancy chamber suggested that the newly formed *Institut minier* could play a significant role by fostering research into new energy sources.[95] The Nancy chamber and prominent members like Cavallier believed that one of the greatest challenges facing Lorraine's industries after the war was the shortage of skilled manpower. This was an issue on which they knew they could take effective action. Before 1914 they had been instrumental in setting up a number of technical institutes attached to the University of Nancy. The year 1919 was to see the founding of yet another, the mining institute, and also the development of more general management education.

The university made the decision to set up the Metallurgical and Mining Institute on 28 May 1919, and it opened in the autumn of that year.[96] Students would be able to graduate as engineers from the University of Nancy. French metallurgical firms had taken over sequestered German assets in Lorraine, and France was involved in exploiting the mines of the Saar. As a result of these developments, the industry was 400 engineers short. This was a gap which the Faculty of Science was keen to fill with a practical training which would put Nancy above Strasbourg or Metz. The *École des Mines* in Paris and the similar school in St.-Étienne had said they could not meet this skills gap.[97] The desire to compete effectively with Germany after the war was a motivating force. The new institute would be a hybrid institution—partly a university faculty and partly a *grande école* over which the *Corps des Mines*, a state institution, would have influence. Later it would change its name from *Institut métallurgique et minier* to *École supérieure de Métallurgie et des Mines.*

From the start, the institution depended on financial support from the relevant industries which were heavily involved in running it. Dreux took the lead in obtaining industry backing. Four bodies—the *Comité des Forges*

[94] Rhin français, 12.

[95] Chambre de Commerce Nancy, vol. 19 1921, (séance 8 février 1921), 26–27.

[96] This account is drawn from F. Birck, *L'École des Mines (ENSMN) 1919-2012 ; entre université, grand corps d'État et industrie* (Nancy, 2013), 85–113.

[97] F.Birck, A.Grelon, (eds), *Des Ingénieurs pour la Lorraine XIXe–XXe siècles* (Nancy, 2007), 173.

*de France*, the *Comité central des Houillères de France(coal mines)*, the *Comité des Forges et Mines de fer de Meurthe-et-Moselle* and the *Société industrielle de l'Est*—provided start-up funding of 300,000 francs. The Nancy chamber provided 10,000 francs over five years and the *Office économique* 45,000. In total the institute needed 300,000 francs to open and 258,000 francs per annum to cover running costs. The *Comité des Forges de France* said it would cover any annual costs not met by agreed subsidies.[98] In time annual subsidies amounted to 100,000 francs which just about covered staff costs. Paul Petit, the Dean of the Faculty of Science, was appointed as director. He had seen the difficulties of running an institution inadequately supported by industry, the *École de Brasserie (brewing)*, and was anxious to tie industry into this new venture. The industry would have a say in the running of the school, the course content and the appointment of staff. A majority of the board of directors would be nominated by trade associations, the Nancy chamber of commerce, the *Office économique de l'Est* and the *Société industrielle de l'Est*. Dreux was on the council as were Cavallier, Antonin Daum, the glass maker, and François de Wendel, the president of the *Comité des Forges*.[99]

It was clear from their correspondence that both Cavallier and Dreux wanted to be in the driving seat.[100] The committee of patronage included leading industrialists and members of chambers of commerce from throughout eastern France and not just the Eastern region as such.[101] Cavallier tried to suggest other industrialists who had been left out.[102] He was also in constant correspondence with the school about the course content.[103] He wanted the school to open a service to look at common technical problems experienced by the metallurgical and mining industries.[104] By 1922 there were 282 candidates applying for places of which only 65 came from the Eastern region.

[98] Chambre de Commerce Nancy, vol. 17 1919, (séance 4 novembre 1919), 215.

[99] Chambre de Commerce Nancy, vol. 17 1919, (séance 6 mai 1919), 164–165.

[100] SGA 7248, dossier correspondance 1917–1924, letters from Dreux to Cavallier 3 octobre 1919 and Cavallier to Dreux 11 octobre 1919.

[101] SGA 7313, dossier Institut métallurgique et minier de Nancy 1920–26, 'Comité d'actions chargé de préparer l'organisation et le fonctionnement de l'Institut métallurgique et minier 6 mai 1919.'

[102] Ibid., Cavallier letter to Fayolle 25 mai 1919.

[103] Ibid., Cavallier letters to Petit, director of the institute, 10 février 1922, 20 février 1922.

[104] Chambre de Commerce Nancy, vol. 17 1919, (séance 6 mai 1919), 164–165.

**Fig. 3.2** École Supérieure de Commerce, Nancy, by permission of the website www.image-est.fr

The Nancy chamber took a considerable interest in two other technical education projects after the war. The first was the *Institut commercial* set up with help from the chamber of commerce and the *Société industrielle de l'Est*. Before the war, it had been financially self-sufficient but needed help after the war. Bourcart, the Professor of Commercial Law in the *Faculté de Droit* and a *membre correspondant* of the Nancy chamber, was the director.[105] The purpose of the institute was to provide an advanced commercial education either to graduates of the *École supérieure de Commerce* (Fig. 3.2) or to graduates in other fields. To reduce costs, the *institut* decided to reduce its course to one year. The chamber of commerce committed 15,000 francs over three years to be paid via the *Office économique de l'Est*, and the city of Nancy, and the *Sociétés industrielles de l'Est et de Mulhouse*,

[105] Chambre de Commerce Nancy, vol. 17 1919, (séance 25 janvier 1919), 131. Union économique de l'Est, 3e année (1 avril 1919), 89.

smaller amounts.[106] By 1922 the situation of the *institut* seemed to have stabilized; the academic results and finances were reported as excellent.[107]

The other more complex project was the establishment of a chamber for trades (chambre de métiers) in Nancy to organize apprenticeship training in a more systematic way. While large firms already had training programmes, many small- and medium-sized firms did not. The chamber started to consider apprenticeships for a number of reasons. There was government legislation on the subject, but this did not deal with the problem in a comprehensive fashion. In 1920 the government initiated a survey to find out about current practice. There was a departmental committee for technical education which wanted action. There were national congresses to discuss the issue, and Nancy was aware that a number of towns had taken matters into their own hands and founded a chamber for trades without waiting for a framework of government legislation. An article appeared in a local paper pointing out that chambers had been formed already in Strasbourg, Limoges, Angers and other towns.[108]

The chamber of commerce's commission on teaching and apprenticeships reported in July 1920 in favour of setting up a chamber for trades in Nancy. Only four training schools currently existed in Nancy—the *École d'Apprentissage du Bâtiment*, the *École professionnelle de l'Est*, the *École primaire supérieure* and the *École des Beaux-arts*. A wider coverage of all trades was essential.[109] There was a division of views in the Nancy chamber between those who wanted centrally organized instruction in a school in Nancy and those, like Dreux, who wanted training to be carried out on the job, supplemented occasionally by a local course.[110] It was considered that the chamber for trades should be independent of the chambers of commerce, but the latter should appoint some members of the board of directors. The chamber for trades should clearly organize apprenticeships in firms, govern conditions of work and examinations.[111] The Nancy

[106] Chambre de Commerce Nancy, vol. 17 1919, (séance 15 mars 1919), 152–154; (séance 6 mai 1919), 164–165; vol. 18 1920, (séance 6 juillet 1920), Annexe IV Institut commercial, 222–225.

[107] Chambre de Commerce Nancy, vol. 20 1922, (séance 11 juillet 1922), 178.

[108] SGA 7247, dossier mai 1920, 'Note sur l'apprentissage, 6 mai 1920.'

[109] Chambre de Commerce Nancy, vol. 18 1920, (séance 11 mai 1920), 101–102; (séance 6 juillet 1920), 202–204 and Annexe III 215–219.

[110] SGA 7247, dossier mai 1920, 'Note sur l'apprentissage, 6 mai 1920.'

[111] Chambre de Commerce Nancy, vol. 19 1921, (séance 8 novembre 1921), 244–246, Annexe II chambre de métiers 259–263.

chamber got involved in discussions with other chambers in Paris and also with the Nancy city council.[112] By November 1922 a number of industrialists and professionals had lost patience with the legislative delays and so the chamber of commerce voted to instruct its commission to produce a report on how a chamber for trades should be set up. Nancy did not like to be behind in a new social or economic development. The commission's report contains this telling remark, "our region, which has always been a leader on major social issues."[113]

In March 1923 it was a committee set up by the department of Meurthe-et-Moselle which produced a report on how the new chamber for trades would be set up.[114] The plans included courses in most towns, advanced courses, competitions and exhibitions, exams, prizes, bursaries, regulations and an office to manage the process and to facilitate placements. The board of directors would consist of one third each elected representatives of the *patronat* and the workers and one third from bodies like the chamber of commerce and the *Société industrielle de l'Est*. The whole philosophy would be to spread best practice from the bigger firms to the smaller. A conference of all interested parties in Nancy was held on 12 May when the statutes were agreed.[115] The story of the chamber for trades' foundation is a good example of local initiative, involving a variety of local interests, producing a result in the economic field when central government had failed to act.

So we have found evidence of an authentic economic regionalism among the industrial and commercial leaders of Lorraine in the chamber of commerce of Nancy. They tackled problems of transport infrastructure, power generation and technical education on a regional basis. The regional elite also took pride in the role of local banks in financing industry, providing support not forthcoming from Parisian banks. Representatives of the *Société nancéienne de Crédit industriel et de Dépôts* and the *Banque Renauld* were members of the chamber. We now turn to examine the support the chamber gave to improving the provision of capital to local firms, by

[112] Chambre de Commerce Nancy, vol. 20 1922, (séance 6 mars 1922), 45; (séance 11 avril 1922), 95–96.

[113] Chambre de Commerce Nancy, vol. 20 1922, (séance 7 novembre 1922), 237, 240–243.

[114] For the role of the comité départemental see SGA 7249, dossier chambre de métiers février–mars 1923.

[115] Chambre de Commerce Nancy, vol. 21 1923, (séance 9 mars 1923), 50–54; (séance 12 juin 1923), 119–120.

encouraging the founding of *banques populaires* but most directly by organizing the opening of a stock exchange in Nancy, a project which had been discussed before the war.

## Regional Stock Exchange

Almost as soon as the war was over, members of the chamber of commerce in Nancy were thinking about reviving the project to create a stock exchange for the city. A note in Cavallier's papers dated 25 January 1919 reflects on the enormous task of raising capital to re-equip after the war and also the developing regional role of Nancy's banks:

> The war has spread the horizon of Nancy, the regional capital, further throughout the region and particularly to the East. It has precipitated the development of regionalism, at least in economics, and, in enlarging the field of action of our local banks, to whom the situation now offers new tasks; the war forces us to have recourse to new and more numerous ways of doing business, to new collaborations, to a more powerful and extensive set of banking tools, without which regional needs cannot be satisfied.[116]

The chamber of commerce took up the issue formally on the same day and set up a commission to look into it. The discussion highlighted the likely doubling of the market capitalization of firms in the east resulting from the return of Alsace-Lorraine. Cooperation between the chamber, the municipality and local businessmen was urgent. A stock exchange would be:

> An organisation called to render great services to the region, to the numerous companies who have a registered office or other establishments there or in Nancy itself.

The commission appointed, apart from the *bureau*, included six other members including Gustave Simon, the mayor of Nancy, Matray from the local branch of the *Banque de France*, chamber of commerce vice-president Alfred Krug and Bourcart, the Professor of Commercial Law.[117] Cavallier wrote to Fayolle from Paris, having seen some personal contacts in the Ministry of Finance, to urge going for a full-scale stock exchange with six

[116] SGA 7234, dossier bourse des valeurs, note on bourse des valeurs 25 janvier 1919.
[117] Chambre de Commerce Nancy, vol. 17 1919, (séance 25 janvier 1919), 127–128.

*agents de change* and a tribunal, even though this meant a lengthier approvals process. It was vital to persuade local banks to back the scheme as some had opposed it before the war.[118] Gustave Simon said that the municipality would support anything which increased the prestige of the city. He remarked:

> But it appears that there is a place for a stock exchange in the Eastern region, and that such an exchange can be of great service in stimulating regional activity. The chamber of commerce of Nancy, which has already taken many favourable initiatives for the region, must undertake this one.[119]

Reconstruction would create a big demand for financial credit which might persuade some firms to raise new capital, although share valuations were low which could deter some owners. The Paris shares market did not favour shares in smaller Lorraine companies which suffered alongside major groups.[120] Nancy could feel Strasbourg breathing down its neck. Dreux wrote to Fayolle that the chamber of commerce there was moving forward which removed some of the objections in Nancy.[121]

At the beginning of 1920, the municipality of Nancy got actively involved in the project and set up a commission to push the matter to a conclusion, working with the chamber of commerce and leading personalities such as François de Wendel and also the directors of banks in Nancy including national banks such as the *Société Générale* and *Crédit Lyonnais*. The municipal group favoured a smaller stock exchange—only four *agents de change* without a tribunal.[122] The chamber of commerce was prepared to provide premises on conditions to be discussed.[123] In November the chamber supported the plan for four agents only, while noting that the

[118] SGA 7234, dossier bourse des valeurs, Cavallier letter to Fayolle 11 février 1919, Cavallier letter to Bertrand-Oser 16 novembre 1919.

[119] SGA 7247, dossier 1918–1919, 'Compte-rendu de la commission 25 février 1919, bourse des valeurs'.

[120] SGA 7234, dossier bourse des valeurs, report by commission on bourse des valeurs 14 mars 1919, Pont-à-Mousson note de service to Cavallier 1 avril 1919.

[121] Ibid., Dreux letter to Fayolle 15 novembre 1919.

[122] Chambre de Commerce Nancy, vol. 18 1920, (séance 9 mars 1920), 50 and Annexe VII 75. SGA 7234, dossier bourse des valeurs, 'Création d'une bourse des valeurs à Nancy, personnalités pressenties en vue de la constitution d'une commission extra-municipale', (attachment to letter from the Maire de Nancy to Cavallier as member of the commission of the chambre de commerce on the bourse des valeurs, 9 avril 1920).

[123] Chambre de Commerce Nancy, vol. 18 1920, (séance 8 juin 1920), 134.

exchanges in Lyon, Marseille, Bordeaux, Toulouse, Nantes and Lille were larger (six agents and a tribunal).[124] The note presented by Fayolle to the stock exchange commission and included in the official record as an annex draws attention to the activity of Nancy's banks as an example of financial decentralization and urges that it be encouraged further by the creation of an exchange:

> In our time, when the principle of decentralization is in favour, Nancy has a just claim to be one of the provincial centres which has witnessed the most fortunate and well ordered activity.
>
> The local and regional banks there have been among the first to set an example of financial decentralization. They have had very great success. It seems to some credit houses in this place and in the region that they would develop more if there was a stock exchange in Nancy.
>
> The choice of Nancy as the seat of this exchange will be among the most fortunate, by reason of the considerable activity of its banking organisations and of its geographical situation 353 kilometres from Paris, 418 from Lyon and 358 from Lille, towns which each have a stock exchange.[125]

At this stage the major obstacles had been overcome. In 1921 the procedure to give official approval to the new *agents de change* was completed and the exchange could start business.[126] We can see here how the Nancy chamber's involvement in the creation of a stock exchange was tied to a positive view of how financial institutions in Nancy could transform the region's prospects. They specifically referred to regionalism as an economic phenomenon.

It was entirely consistent with this approach that the chamber should give its support to a *banque populaire* when asked by the prefecture and the Ministry of Commerce. These mutual institutions were designed to provide credit for small- and medium-sized commercial and industrial firms. A new law which gave them a much clearer legal status was passed by the Chamber of Deputies in 1917. *Banques populaires* could get help in

[124] Chambre de Commerce Nancy, vol. 18 1920, (séance 9 novembre 1920), 257–258 and Annexe I 267–272.

[125] Chambre de Commerce Nancy, vol. vol. 18 1920, (séance 9 novembre 1920), 272. SGA 7247, dossier octobre 1920, 'Note sur la bourse des valeurs de Nancy, 26 octobre 1920, réunion de la commission de la bourse des valeurs le 30 octobre 1920', (attachment to letter from Vilgrain to Cavallier announcing meeting, 27 octobre 1920).

[126] Chambre de Commerce Nancy, vol. 19 1921, (séance 8 mars 1921), 80–81 and (séance 12 avril 1921), 104–105.

raising capital in the form of a government loan.[127] The *Banque populaire de l'Est* opened in Nancy in December 1919. The Nancy chamber was asked by the government whether it would recommend that the bank be given approval for a government loan. The chamber signified that it was favourable in 1920.[128] The new bank in Nancy was not the only one to open soon after the law was passed. There were also *banques populaires* in Épinal and Bar-Le-Duc.[129]

## Reconstruction

To demonstrate the success of economic regionalism in Lorraine, we will now turn to consider post-war reconstruction, a massive task which absorbed the energies of Lorraine's leaders for several years. We can see its impact on Camille Cavallier as he sought to rebuild his business. His main plant had been damaged, installations in the Briey basin had been occupied and damaged also, supply lines of raw materials had been disrupted, and access to markets at home and abroad had to be restored. Equally, rebuilding towns and villages and making farms productive again was a huge task. The chamber of commerce was not in the driving seat on most of the issues, but they were of great concern to members. So here we will explore how reconstruction was organized in a regional context. In particular we will examine the creation and operation of reconstruction cooperatives, a movement in which Lorraine took the lead among the former front line regions.

At the end of the war, the French government passed a law on *dommages de guerre* (17 April 1919). In it they accepted responsibility for the costs of reconstruction, on the basis of course that they would recuperate the cost from Germany. A process was set up whereby those who had suffered damage could make a claim for reimbursement. It was of great concern to the Nancy chamber that these claims were settled as quickly as possible. Already on 25 January 1919 the chamber was complaining about the delay in passing the law on war damage. Cavallier proposed a resolution saying it was a matter of utmost urgency.[130] The chamber itself had suffered in the war because some of its subscribing businesses were in

[127] Chambre de Commerce Nancy, vol. 17 1919, (séance 10 juin 1919), 181.
[128] Chambre de Commerce Nancy, vol. 18 1920, (séance 11 mai 1920), 163.
[129] R. Bour, Histoire de la banque populaire de Lorraine (Metz, 1989), 29, 47, 81, 117.
[130] Chambre de Commerce Nancy, vol. 17 1919, (séance 25 janvier 1919), 125–127.

occupied territories or the war zone.[131] Naturally the chamber wanted the government to make sure Germany paid the reparations.[132] Cavallier believed that private firms in Germany, who had profited from the deliberate destruction of French industry, which he himself had witnessed when he visited his installation in Briey in December 1918, should pay for the damage through a tax.[133]

Soon the industrialists whose businesses had been damaged experienced the problem which affected all those who had suffered damage. The French government could not keep up the flow of payments because of Germany's failure to adhere to the reparations schedule and its own financial problems. In July 1921 the Nancy chamber noted that the Office for Industrial Reconstruction had suspended payments. Firms in different industries were combining to seek loans guaranteed by their war damage titles or their provisional certificates so they could undertake the work needed. These loans would be guaranteed by the state. An example quoted was the sugar industry. Cities such as Verdun and Reims also looked for loans. Accordingly, the Nancy chamber passed a resolution asking the government to authorise a loan of 800 million francs to the metallurgical industries, which no doubt pleased the many iron masters who were members.[134]

As reconstruction progressed, the chamber saw itself as the defender of the rights of those who had suffered war damage against any government attempt to whittle them down.[135] In this they were supported by Lorraine politicians like Louis Marin, founder of the leading conservative grouping the Fédération Républicaine and Minister for the Liberated Regions in 1924. For example, in 1924 the chamber along with others in the North and East protested against government attempts to claw back certain supplementary payments made to industrialists to cover the replacement costs of damaged stocks.[136] The chamber also complained constantly about the

[131] Chambre de Commerce Nancy, vol. 17 1919, (séance 10 juin 1919), 185.

[132] Chambre de Commerce Nancy, vol. 18 1920, (séance 8 juin 1920), 134–135.

[133] SGA 7385, visit note by Cavallier on Briey-Longwy 11 décembre 1918. SGA 7248, dossier correspondance 1917–1924, 'Note de service de Cavallier 6 février 1919'.

[134] Chambre de Commerce Nancy, vol. 19 1921, (séance 8 juillet 1921), 182–184.

[135] Chambre de Commerce Nancy, vol. 21 1923, (séance 12 juin 1923), 117–118.

[136] SGA 7247, 'Réunion des représentants autorisés des chambres de commerce des dix départements dévastés par la guerre et d'Alsace-Lorraine à Lille 3 décembre 1924'; 'Réunion avec Édouard Herriot et 36 chambres de commerce 8 décembre 1924 au Ministère des Affaires Étrangères'.

administration of the Ministry for the Liberated Regions and particularly the high salaries of contractors paid directly by them, which were depriving firms and farms of labour.[137]

The Nancy chamber did not in fact spend a lot of time debating reconstruction, compared with other subjects. Businesses organized their own works, either individually or through their trade associations. They protested through various channels including the chamber when difficulties occurred. Reconstruction was not just an issue for Lorraine but affected much of the North and East and indeed the economy of France as a whole. It also caused controversy in relations with Germany and France's former allies. Firms like Pont-à-Mousson were no doubt big enough to fend for themselves. Pont-à-Mousson re-lit the first of its furnaces in April 1919 and had the others operational by June 1920.[138] Cavallier had a direct relationship with Albert Lebrun, Lorraine politician and Minister for the Liberated Regions until November 1919. For small enterprises and particularly for farmers and rural communities, it was a different matter. On their own they would struggle with the organization of reconstruction and the government paperwork. Here we should examine the emergence in 1919 of reconstruction cooperatives, a remarkable example of regional initiative and solidarity, which took root first in Lorraine and then spread to other devastated areas. As Desforges, from the *Société nancéienne* and the chamber of commerce, said in a speech in 1922:

> It is in Meurthe-et-Moselle that private initiative has given the liveliest impetus to the development of reconstruction cooperatives, without which small proprietors would have been impotent.[139]

They were very effective in helping Lorraine's economy and society recover after the war.

*Le Bon Grain*, the organ of the union of Lorraine farmers' unions, also acted as publicist for the work of the cooperative movement. As early as May 1919 it was making the case for cooperatives, saying it would be

[137] SGA 7247, dossier février–mars 1920, 'Chambre de commerce réunion 9 mars 1920'; Dreux letter to Isaac, Minister of Commerce, 15 février 1920, 4; Cavallier letter to Dreux, 27 février 1920; Dreux inquiry to members to obtain evidence of complaints, 25 février 1920.

[138] SGA Série A fasc. 31 A, DOC PAM 21.24, 'Fête de la reconstitution aux usines de Pont-à-Mousson 18 juillet 1920', 6.

[139] Speech to the Association des Anciens Élèves de l'École libre des Sciences politiques, Union économique de L'Est, 6e année (1 mai 1922), 108–110.

much easier for farmers to re-build using centralized expertise, for example, building entrepreneurs, architects and accountants.[140] How did their extraordinarily rapid growth in Meurthe-et-Moselle come about? By April 1919 there were 40 such organizations, by May, 60 and at the start of 1920, 180. A lot was due to one man, the Abbé Thouvenin, who visited his home village of St. Généviève in January 1919 and was convinced that cooperatives were the way forward. The Abbé had had some experience with schemes for housing workers in the north of the department before the war. The cooperatives which were eventually adopted in Meurthe-et-Moselle were similar to those that allowed the reconstruction of flooded areas on the Marne in 1911.[141] Early in 1918, Thouvenin joined forces with the Abbé Fiel, eventual secretary of the union of cooperatives, Dupan of the *Génie rural* and Mirman the prefect and, encouraged by Albert Lebrun, founded the first cooperative at Norroy-lès-Pont-à-Mousson in February 1919.[142] Lorraine politician Lebrun was Minister for the Liberated Regions from 1917 to 1919 and later the last president of the Third Republic. Louis Marin also supported the movement and addressed meetings. With the backing of the bishop of Nancy, the prefect and the relevant officials, Thouvenin went on a tour of the department to encourage support for his ideas.

His second innovation was to realize that individual cooperatives, which were quite small and often represented just one village, needed support. They needed help with choosing suitable architects and builders, and also advice on how to cope with the mass of government legislation and regulations. They had to learn how to work closely with the public authorities.[143] Thouvenin and De Warren, the local deputy, told them they needed to understand the difficulties they would have operating on their own and the benefits of having access to advice.[144] Thouvenin set up a union of cooperatives in June 1919, of which there were initially 54 members, again with the active encouragement of his bishop. He was the first president. One hundred and fifty people came to the first meeting including

[140] Le Bon Grain, 13e année nos. 3 and 4 (15 mai and 1 juin 1919).

[141] P. Fiel, 'La Reconstruction des régions dévastées en Lorraine,' Le Pays lorrain, 27e année, nouvelle série quatrième volume (1935), 6.

[142] R. Préaud, P. Fiel, Les Coopératives de reconstruction du département de Meurthe-et-Moselle (Nancy, 1922), 5. Préaud was chef de service du contrôle des coopératives de Meurthe-et-Moselle.

[143] Préaud, Fiel, 'Les Coopératives', 7.

[144] Le Bon Grain, 13e année no. 2 (avril 1919), 32–35.

representatives of the prefecture, four priests from the diocese, architects and builders, and of course the administrators of the cooperatives.[145] The meeting discussed in great detail what cooperatives needed to do. The church offered to pay the cooperatives' registration costs and help came in from other well-wishers like deputy de Warren. The union guided the cooperatives in creating their dossiers and 11,000 copies of Thouvenin's *Guide des Sinistrés* (those who had suffered damage) were distributed.[146] The church subsidized courses on creating dossiers.[147] In addition, cooperatives could turn to a journal, *La Reconstruction lorraine*, for authoritative advice.[148]

In its July 1919 issue, *La Reconstruction* announced the opening by the *Société industrielle de l'Est* of an *Office de Dommages de Guerre* to offer help to those who had suffered war damage. It was supported in this by the *Société d'Assistance aux Réfugiés et Sinistrés de Meurthe-et-Moselle* (*president iron master Maurice de Wendel*), the *Société centrale d'Agriculture* and the *Comité lorrain de Reconstitution des Régions éprouvées.*[149] In fact, the minutes of the *Société d'Assistance* show that this body had been discussing this project since December 1918. They envisaged the office not only giving out information but also actively contacting mayors of affected communes to help them. The March 1919 minutes suggested the mayors should nominate people to come to the office for training in how to gather the information on damage needed to make claims and they should then go back to work in their communes.[150]

By the end of 1919, encouraging progress was being made in a number of communes such as Ancerviller, discussed at length by Abbé Fiel at a

[145] 'Union lorraine des Coopératives de Reconstruction assemblée générale, 9 juin 1919', Le Bon Grain, 13e année no. 8 (15 juillet 1919), 127–140.

[146] Préaud, Fiel, 'Les Coopératives', 9–10.

[147] Ibid., 11.

[148] This account draws on two articles by H.D. Clout, 'War and recovery in the countryside of north-eastern France: the example of Meurthe-et-Moselle,' Journal of Historical Geography, 23, 2 (1997), 164–186 and 'The Revival of Rural Lorraine after the Great War,' Geografiska Annaler, series B, Human Geography, vol. 75, no. 2 (1993), 73–91.

[149] La Reconstruction lorraine (15 juillet 1919), 294.

[150] SGA 7448, dossier Société d'Assistance aux Réfugiés, Évacués, Sinistrés de Meurthe-et-Moselle: compte-rendu de réunions, divers (1918–1920), minutes of the meetings of the committee of the Société d'Assistance aux Réfugiés et Sinistrés de Meurthe-et-Moselle, décembre 1918, mars 1919, avril 1919. See also SGA 7229, dossier Assistance aux réfugiés, évacués (1920).

further meeting of the union on 15 November.[151] However, considerable problems still remained. For example, there were not enough skilled volunteer administrators and architects, and some materials were difficult to obtain. Also the statutes of the cooperatives were legally defective in certain respects.[152] Groups of two to three cooperatives were advised to combine to hire an accountant.[153] A law of 15 August 1920 set standards for cooperatives and required them to register. Architects and builders had to be approved by the prefecture and financial accounts audited. Cooperatives already set up in Meurthe-et-Moselle had to apply for registration and they were duly approved.[154] Thouvenin and the union of cooperatives guided individual cooperatives through the new legislation. The union itself had to change its legal status.[155] We have already seen that industrial sectors were considering loans secured by entitlement to compensation and backed by the state to ease cash flow. In 1921 the *Société nancéienne* and the *Banque Renauld* offered to lend the union of cooperatives two and a half times its deposits if the state suspended payments.[156]

Delegations came from elsewhere in northern France to study how the cooperatives in Meurthe-et-Moselle worked. The Minister of Liberated Regions recommended the prefect of the Nord to follow the methods adopted in Meurthe-et-Moselle.[157] By early 1922 there were 205 cooperatives in 228 communes. These now included specially formed cooperatives to deal with the reconstruction of churches, *mairies* and schools. In 1921 the church launched a 15 million franc loan to pay for the reconstruction of the Nancy diocese's 107 damaged churches and it was successful.[158] Abbé Thouvenin received recognition from central government when he was asked to join the *Comité supérieur de la Reconstruction* and was made a Chevalier of the Légion d'Honneur.[159] The church's example of taking out a loan was followed by others fairly quickly. The *Conseil-général de*

[151] 'Assemblée générale de l'union des coopératives 19 novembre 1919', Le Bon Grain, 13e année nos. 17 and 18 (1 et 15 décembre 1919), 284–287. Ancerviller finished reconstruction quickly by Autumn 1921, see Clout, 'Rural Lorraine', 82.

[152] Le Bon Grain, 13e année nos. 17 and 18 (1 et 15 décembre 1919), 282–283.

[153] Préaud, Fiel, 'Les Coopératives', 10.

[154] Ibid., p. 12.

[155] Le Bon Grain, 15e année no. 3 (1 février 1921), 38–39.

[156] Préaud, Fiel, 'Les Coopératives', 25.

[157] Fiel, 'La Reconstruction', 8.

[158] Ibid., 12–13.

[159] Préaud, Fiel, 'Les Coopératives', 13.

*Meurthe-et-Moselle* raised two loans for 190 million francs. Isolated war damage victims were grouped together by Brun of the *Société industrielle de l'Est* and 11 million was raised. Similar loans were floated in the Meuse and the Vosges.[160]

The reconstruction cooperatives are yet another example of regional leaders in Lorraine coming together to solve important problems affecting the region's future. So we have widespread evidence of a strong current of economic regionalism in Meurthe-et-Moselle and in Lorraine more widely. The regional elite was willing to act on its own initiative to try and achieve defined economic objectives, whether it could legally undertake projects directly or had to lobby the public authorities to do so. There is no doubt that regional institutions like the chambers of commerce and others thought they were acting in the interests of their region, which they occasionally referred to as Lorraine.

## Natalism

The economic and potential military challenge presented by Germany after the war was the basis of the natalist movement. This covered the whole of France, but the issues central to its platform chimed in well with the central concerns of the Lorraine elite after the war. Lorrainers played a very prominent role within the movement. There were further tensions here between different discourses on the role of the region after the war. Traditional Catholic teaching on the family and the role of women ran alongside social Catholic ideas on improving the living conditions of workers, suspicion of Germany and economic modernization.

The starting point for this movement was France's much inferior population growth compared with Germany and other European countries. This phenomenon was thought to be partly due to high infant mortality,[161] but mainly the result of a lower birth rate. The issue was of concern to Lorraine's leaders for a number of reasons—fewer children meant fewer sons to defend France and Lorraine. However, lower population growth also had economic effects—fewer trained workers in factories and a smaller home market of consumers. The effect of slower growth was particularly keenly felt in agriculture, because even before the war the countryside was being drained of labour seeking higher wages in the towns. This meant

[160] Fiel, 'La Reconstruction', 13.

[161] Union économique de l'Est, 4e année (1 avril 1920), 87–88.

some farms became impossible to manage and drove a series of dramatic changes in agricultural practice. These changes were also of great concern to the Auvergne and support for natalism was not lacking there either. Lorraine held the first of a series of annual national congresses on natalism in Nancy in September 1919. Clermont-Ferrand followed in 1925.

One of the driving forces behind the Lorraine natalist movement was Krug of the Nancy chamber of commerce, who also wrote a report on the mechanization of agriculture. Krug had published a report on *La Natalité française* in 1916 proposing a congress. He believed that the middle classes were setting a bad example because they simply wanted to avoid having children. They had to be educated out of this attitude in Krug's opinion. He also focused on abortion which should be legislated out of existence. He discussed better child care in the home and the need for crèches in the workplace for working mothers. He also believed alcoholism, venereal disease and tuberculosis were weakening the race and procreation. Venereal disease was a common pre-occupation among the regional elite—witness articles which appeared in the *Bulletin of the Société industrielle de l'Est* after the war.[162] This pre-occupation was also shared by Camille Cavallier.[163] Another major issue was the housing crisis—not enough affordable homes for workers. Charles Guyot of the Académie Stanislas tackled this issue by drawing attention to the existence of poor housing even in a fine town like Nancy. The city council was taking action, but there was a lot more to do.[164] Working incomes were often insufficient to bring up families and Krug thought firms should be encouraged to give financial help to large families.[165]

Krug published a further report on population in 1918. Here he expanded on the type of re-education he felt was necessary. Young women had to be taught to take pride in motherhood. Young people had to be instilled with the discipline to be good patriotic fathers and mothers. All

[162] Dr. Macé, Professeur d'Hygiène à la Faculté de Médicine de Nancy, 'La Lutte contre la syphilis dans le basin de Briey', Bulletin de la Société industrielle de l'Est, no. 157 (avril 1920), 46–54; 'La Lutte contre le péril vénérien', no. 169 (avril–juin 1923), 19–30.

[163] SGA 7248, dossier correspondance 1917–1924, Cavallier letter to Fayolle 22 décembre 1921.

[164] C. Guyot, 'Un Problème urbain, logements insalubres et habitations à bon marché', Mémoires de l'Académie Stanislas, CLXXIe année, 6e série, t. xviii 1920–1921 (Nancy, 1921), 1–4.

[165] A. Krug, La Natalité française (Nancy, 1916, supplement to the Bulletin de la Société industrielle de l'Est), 5.

European nations suffered from the diseases he had highlighted in his previous report. The crucial difference in France was the lack of a desire for children. This was a moral issue. The bourgeoisie had set a bad example, being too concerned about splitting their inheritance at death.[166]

Many of these ideas were discussed and adopted at the first national natalist congress organized by the Nancy chamber in Nancy, 25 – 28 September 1919. This attracted 350 attendees from all professions and from all over France. A further 500 registered as supporters. Support for natalism spread far wider than the traditional Catholic faithful. Clémentel was invited but unfortunately could not attend. The president was Auguste Isaac from Lyon, who later became Minister of Commerce himself. The congress was closed by a keynote speech by Paul Deschanel, president of the Chamber of Deputies. The opening speech was made by Alexandre Dreux who posed the question—will our race decline? Germany, he said, was not resigned to her defeat. We must, he said, combat the egotism of families restraining births and make sure that all the sacrifices of the war years had not been in vain.[167]

Six commissions were set up covering teaching, religion, health and childcare, legislation, action by business owners and propaganda. It fell to Marcel Paul, Cavallier's son-in-law, to report back to the plenary session on the commissions' work. An important recommendation was that business owners should join with the state to support employees with a supplementary income if they had families. There were some more radical suggestions for state intervention including creating a family vote, with fathers exercising the suffrage on behalf of children. The Chamber of Deputies voted for this in principle in 1924. A member of the *Conseil supérieur de la Natalité* claimed that there had been a change of tone in Paris on population and family issues since the war. Poincaré was behind a policy which sought to increase population and made family interests a priority.[168] However, like Krug, the commissions recognized that legislative interventions would not solve the problem. It was a matter of religious and moral education and the congress called for the state to work

[166] A. Krug, Pour La Repopulation (Nancy, 1918), 3–6, 12–13.

[167] Congrès national de la Natalité 1919, premier congrès de la natalité tenu à Nancy du 25 au 28 septembre 1919, compte-rendu part I (Nancy, 1919), 7–13. See also SGA 7420, dossier Congrès de la Natalité.

[168] F. Hoverat, 'Allons-nous avoir une politique familiale?' Union économique de l'Est, 8e année (15 janvier 1924), 24.

with the church on this.[169] The language of the recommendations suggested a moral crusade:

> We want the public authorities to carry out their task of exercising control and pursuing (wrong doers). We demand that enterprises involving lust and corruption, pornography. abortion and neo-malthusian propaganda be severely punished.[170]

Paul said that they needed:

> Vigorous efforts to purify hearts, to strengthen wills against bad temptations, to enlighten intelligence and cleanse consciences[171]

and also to combat:

> This terrible plague of undisciplined habits and depopulation.[172]

These views were widely shared among the elite of Lorraine connected to the Nancy chamber, who were also well networked into natalist circles in Paris. Foremost among the Lorraine natalists was Camille Cavallier. He wrote to Krug in 1918 saying that he supported the latter's work on natalism and the high cost of living.[173] Later he was to publish his own brochures dealing with *natalité*, like *La France victorieuse*, which he sent to Krug with the comment:

> Where I deal with this agonising question of the birth rate which preoccupies us all,[174]

and also *La France de Demain*, written in 1923. Here he made a direct connection between health, personal hygiene, clean water and the need for pipes for new water mains in most towns. This became Pont-à-Mousson's key business in the years ahead. This was a case of a correct

[169] Congrès Natalité, 35, 37–39.
[170] Congrès Natalité, 33.
[171] Congrès Natalité, 38.
[172] Ibid., 39.
[173] SGA 7342, dossier Pupilles, Cavallier letter to Krug 29 avril 1918.
[174] SGA 7247, dossier 1923, Cavallier letter to Krug on natalité and La France victorieuse, 5 octobre 1923.

moral attitude reaping financial rewards. Like Krug he saw the problem as moral and psychological, dealing with the effects of the war, as much as economic, combatting the pressure on living standards after 1918, which the state could attack directly through measures on taxes and healthcare.[175] He believed towns had a role to play in providing better housing for working families, for example, by reserving plots for building for large families.[176] He was heavily involved in discussions on family benefits being paid by employers in Lorraine and he favoured setting up a regional fund for all employers.[177] He also pressed his fellow iron masters to support the Nancy chamber's own Wards scheme, which gave grants from the chamber to selected families with five or more children. Solvay agreed to give 20,000 francs in October 1918.[178] The Wards scheme was helping over 150 families by the early twenties.[179] It drew support from a wide circle of subscribers, not just a few big firms.[180]

There was more than a hint in all this of bourgeois men striking moral and patriotic attitudes at the expense of the working poor and also women. Cavallier wrote to Fayolle, the permanent secretary of the Nancy Chamber in 1918 saying he was against women having the vote or having any say in important meetings. He wrote:

> The woman is in essence a being with impulsive feelings and logic does not live in her brain.[181]

Cavallier also advocated at one point that a partner in a marriage which had not produced four children within ten years should be entitled to an automatic divorce.[182] Such a suggestion would have been abhorrent to

[175] SGA 7331, dossier Natalité, 'Note de service, études sur les moyens de combattre la dépopulation (7pp.), pour Cavallier fin avril 1923'.

[176] SGA 7247, dossier 1923, notes for Union économique de l'Est on answers to their questionnaire on future of France 17 janvier 1923.

[177] SGA 6754, Congrès Natalité, Nancy, 'Cavallier note de service 4 avril 1919'.

[178] SGA 7342, dossier Pupilles (Wards), Cavallier letter to E. Ferry at Rupt 10 février 1918. For the Wards scheme see also Chambre de Commerce Nancy, vol.17 1919, (séance 30 août 1919), 198–204, 207–208, 210–216; vol. 22 1924, (séance 11 mars 1924), 74.

[179] SGA 7342, dossier Pupilles, 'Note de service, Dubois à Cavallier 1 décembre 1920'.

[180] SGA 7420, dossier Pupilles, 'Pupilles de la Chambre de Commerce de Nancy, souscriptions 1917'; 2–6; 'Pupilles, souscriptions uniques et annuelles 1918', 7pp.; 'Oeuvre des Pupilles de la Chambre de Commerce de Nancy 4 février 1918', 2.

[181] SGA 7342, dossier Pupilles, Cavallier letter to Fayolle 16 février 1918.

[182] SGA 6754, Congrès Natalité, Nancy, Cavallier letter to Morin 17 avril 1917.

faithful Catholics. Divorce was more usually blamed for the low birth rate, a connection made by Michon, a contributor to the deliberations of the Académie Stanislas. In supporting the sanctity of marriage he referred to:

> The crisis of the birth rate, which today puts the existence of France in peril.[183]

Cavallier's views were shared by others in his circle of industrial contacts such as Henri Cavallier at the Foug foundry which belonged to Pont-à-Mousson. In a letter in 1919 Henri echoed the argument that the *haute bourgeoisie* did not set a good example. They did not want to divide inheritances and wives wanted to appear alongside their husbands and enjoy themselves. For those lower down the middle-class social scale, like *fonctionnaires*, life was tough and the cost of living had gone up considerably since 1918. Like Camille Cavallier and Krug, he expected the state and *patrons* to step in and help families in need.[184] Earlier Henri Cavallier had pledged 25,000 francs for a fund for large families and Morin replied approvingly, noting:

> As a good pupil of M. Camille Cavallier, I consider that the question of the birth rate comes before all else.[185]

Members of the Lorraine elite had good contacts with the four key national bodies which had an influence on policy on natalism, apart from the Chamber of Deputies itself. Firstly, the *Association nationale d'Expansion économique* set up a special commission on *natalité*. Cavallier claimed to have initiated this.[186] François Villain was a member.[187] Cavallier was in regular touch on the issue with Paul Bureau, the secretary of the commission.[188] Secondly, there was the national campaigning group for

[183] M.L. Michon, 'La Natalité et le divorce', Mémoires de l'Académie Stanislas, 1920–1921, 13.

[184] SGA 7398, dossier ANEE commission Natalité, H. Cavallier letter to Morin 26 avril 1919.

[185] SGA 7398, dossier ANEE commission Natalité, H. Cavallier letter to Morin 19 avril 1919; Morin to H. Cavallier 24 avril 1919.

[186] SGA 7331, dossier Natalité, internal Pont-à-Mousson note by Camille Cavallier 4 avril 1919.

[187] SGA 6754, Congrès Natalité, Nancy, F. Villain letter to Cavallier 4 février 1918.

[188] Ibid., internal note of Pont-à-Mousson on a visit by Paul Bureau to Roubaix to study family benefits there 11 avril 1919; minutes of commission de la natalité, ANEE, 17 mars 1918, 13 janvier 1919.

natalism (*Alliance nationale pour l'Accroissement de la Population française*) run by Dr. Bertillon. André Michelin was on the council and Cavallier was in contact with him on the issue. Michelin invited Cavallier to attend a lecture in Paris by Dr. Bertillon.[189] Thirdly, the Minister of Health set up a *Conseil supérieur de la Natalité* and nominated Louis Vilgrain, president of the Nancy chamber until 1919, as a member.[190] Lastly there was an organization called *Pour la Vie* in which the leading light was Paul Bureau. Cavallier was in regular contact with him.

In the natalist movement in Lorraine, there were overlapping concerns about future economic development, competition with Germany and moral and social regeneration. The demands of economic development and the need to maintain social cohesion also existed in the rural world. The campaign against the depopulation of the countryside and the shortage of farmers, common to both Lorraine and the Auvergne, also took on the character of a moral crusade. An editorial in *Le Bon Grain* described the young deserting the land for a terrible life in the towns. This criticism of urban life and its attractions was certainly echoed in the Auvergne by writers like Pourrat.[191] H. Cote, the president of the *Syndicat départemental d'Agriculture et Viticulture*, railed against the deceptive attractions of the large towns. Being a peasant farmer should be seen as a noble calling.[192] From the Vosges, champion of agriculture Jules Méline hoped that, after the war, people would turn their back on the luxuries of the towns.[193] Charles Guyot wrote about the industrialisation of agriculture and the decline of the rural population. He said it would mean fewer good recruits for the army as peasants made better soldiers. There was a collapse of morale among rural populations, particularly as most of their natural leaders among the bourgeoisie were absentee land owners. The answer lay in better schooling for country dwellers, reductions in taxes, changes to the

[189] SGA 6754, Congrès Natalité, Nancy, A. Michelin letter to Cavallier 3 septembre 1918.

[190] Chambre de Commerce Nancy, vol.18 1920, (séance 10 février 1920), 18. SGA 7331, dossier Natalité, Note de service for Cavallier and Marcel Paul 30 janvier 1920.

[191] 'Les Déserteurs de la terre', Le Bon Grain, 13e année, no. 12 (15 septembre 1919), 191–192.

[192] Revue du Syndicat départemental agricole du Puy-de-Dôme, 34e année, no. 3 (mars 1921), 12–13.

[193] J. Méline, Le Salut par la terre et le programme économique de l'avenir (Paris, 1919), 83.

inheritance laws to avoid splitting up farms and *remembrement* (schemes to join up scattered plots of land in a single holding).[194]

## Conclusion

The records of the region published in the *Union Économique de L'Est* from 1925 onwards show that the policy guidelines laid down immediately after the war were followed for the remainder of the inter-war period. The region and the major chambers of commerce continued to focus on railways, power and canals and introduced airways into the transport mix. They achieved much in all these fields. Lorraine continued to be a coherent region with a dynamic approach to regional development, despite the economic adversities of the inter-war period. Nancy and Metz fulfilled important roles as major regional centres. Fayolle, the regional secretary, wrote in 1929 that economic regionalism was really invented in Lorraine. We will see later that it was in this region that the concept was strongest.[195]

## Bibliography

Asselain, J.-C. (1995). *Histoire économique du XXe siècle, vol. 1 la montée de l'état 1914–1939* (2 Vols).

Birck, F., & Grelon, A. (Eds.). (2007). *Des Ingénieurs pour la Lorraine XIXe–XXe siècles.*

Birck, F. (2013). *L'École des Mines (ENSMN) 1919-2012 ; entre université, grand corps d'État et industrie.*

Bouneau, C. (2002). La Contribution de l'électrification à la genèse de l'aménagement du territoire en France durant la première moitié du XXe siècle. In P. Caro, O. Dard, & J.-C. Daumas (Eds.), *La Politique d'aménagement du territoire: racines, logiques et résultats* (pp. 31–52).

Bour, R. (1989). *Histoire de la banque populaire de Lorraine* (pp. 29, 47, 81, 117).

*Bulletin de la Chambre de Commerce Nancy* 1917, 1919, 1920, 1921, 1922, 1923, 1924.

*Bulletin de la Société industrielle de l'Est*, 1919, 1920, 1923, 1924.

Caron, F. (Ed.). (2005). *Les Grandes Compagnies de chemin de fer en France 1823–1937, Archives économiques du Crédit Lyonnais.*

[194] C. Guyot, 'À propos d'un livre récent, le passé et l'avenir de la Lorraine, agriculture et industrie', Extrait des Mémoires de l'Académie Stanislas 1918–1919 (Nancy, 1919), 27–46. Guyot was Secrétaire perpétuel de l'Académie Stanislas.

[195] B. Fayolle, "La region économique de lEst, historique," Union Économique de l'Est 1 mars 1929, 55.

Cavallier, C. (1923, septembre 7). *La France victorieuse.*

Cavallier, C. (1937). *Sagesse du chef, lettres et notes inédites de Camille Cavallier.*

Clout, H. D. (1993). The revival of rural Lorraine after the Great War. *Geografiska Annaler, series B, Human Geography, 75*(2), 73–91.

Clout, H. D. (1997). War and recovery in the countryside of north-eastern France: The example of Meurthe-et-Moselle. *Journal of Historical Geography, 23*(2), 164–186.

*Communications de la Chambre de Commerce de Metz* 1922, 1923, 1924.

(1919). *Congrès national de la Natalité 1919, premier congrès de la natalité tenu à Nancy du 25 au 28 septembre 1919, compte-rendu part I* (pp. 7–13).

SGA 6754, Congrès Natalité, Nancy, Cavallier letter to Morin 17 avril 1917.

Guyot, C. (1919). À propos d'un livre récent, le passé et l'avenir de la Lorraine, agriculture et industrie. In *Extrait des Mémoires de l'Académie Stanislas 1918–1919* (pp. 27–46).

Guyot, C. (1921). Un Problème urbain, logements insalubres et habitations à bon marché. *Mémoires de l'Académie Stanislas*, CLXXIe année, 6e série, t. xviii 1920–1921, 1–4.

Krug, A. (1916). *La Natalité française* (supplement to the Bulletin de la Société industrielle de l'Est).

Krug, A. (1918). *Pour La Repopulation.*

*La Reconstruction lorraine* 1919.

*Le Bon Grain*, 1919, 1921.

*Le Pays lorrain*, 1935.

Lévy-Leboyer, M., & Morsel, H.(Eds.). (1994). *Histoire générale de L'Électricité en France, T.II 1919–1946 L'Interconnexion et le Marché.*

Libault, A. (1924). *Le Rhin et le Grand Canal d'Alsace*, préfaces d'A. Dreux, Président de la Région économique de l'Est et D. Mieg, Président de la Société industrielle de Mulhouse.

Méline, J. (1919). *Le Salut par la terre et le programme économique de l'avenir.*

Michon, M. L. (1920–1921). La Natalité et le divorce. *Mémoires de l'Académie Stanislas*, 13.

Préaud, R., & Fiel, P. (1922). *Les Coopératives de reconstruction du département de Meurthe-et-Moselle.*

*Revue du Syndicat départemental agricole du Puy-de-Dôme*, 1921.

*Revue industrielle de l'Est* 1918.

*Rhin français, projets d'aménagement du fleuve, force motrice, navigation* (*Union économique de l'Est.*

SGA 6754, Congrès Natalité, Nancy, 'Cavallier note de service 4 avril 1919'.

SGA 6754, Congrès Natalité, Nancy, A. Michelin letter to Cavallier 3 septembre 1918.

SGA 6754, Congrès Natalité, Nancy, F. Villain letter to Cavallier 4 février 1918. Internal note of Pont-à-Mousson on a visit by Paul Bureau to Roubaix to study family benefits there 11 avril 1919; minutes of commission de la natalité, ANEE, 17 mars 1918, 13 janvier 1919.

SGA 7229, dossier Assistance aux réfugiés, évacués (1920).

SGA 7234, dossier bourse des valeurs, 'Création d'une bourse des valeurs à Nancy, personnalités pressenties en vue de la constitution d'une commission extra-municipale', (attachment to letter from the Maire de Nancy to Cavallier as member of the commission of the chambre de commerce on the bourse des valeurs, 9 avril 1920).

SGA 7234, dossier bourse des valeurs, Cavallier letter to Fayolle 11 février 1919, Cavallier letter to Bertrand-Oser 16 novembre 1919.

SGA 7234, dossier bourse des valeurs, note on bourse des valeurs 25 janvier 1919.

SGA 7234, dossier bourse des valeurs, report by commission on bourse des valeurs 14 mars 1919, Pont-à-Mousson note de service to Cavallier 1 avril 1919. Dreux letter to Fayolle 15 novembre 1919.

SGA 7247, 'Réunion des représentants autorisés des chambres de commerce des dix départements dévastés par la guerre et d'Alsace-Lorraine à Lille 3 décembre 1924'; 'Réunion avec Édouard Herriot et 36 chambres de commerce 8 décembre 1924 au Ministère des Affaires Étrangères'.

SGA 7247, dossier 1918–1919, 'Compte-rendu de la commission 25 février 1919, bourse des valeurs'.

SGA 7247, dossier 1921, papers on canal of Moselle 11 mars 1921.

SGA 7247, dossier 1923, Cavallier letter to Krug on natalité and *La France victorieuse*, 5 octobre 1923.

SGA 7247, dossier 1923, note by Cavallier dated 12 février 1923.

SGA 7247, dossier 1923, notes for *Union économique de l'Est* on answers to their questionnaire on future of France 17 janvier 1923.

SGA 7247, dossier août–septembre 1920, letter Cavallier to Fayolle 23 août 1920.

SGA 7247, dossier février–mars 1920, 'Chambre de commerce réunion 9 mars 1920'; Dreux letter to Isaac, Minister of Commerce, 15 février 1920, 4; Cavallier letter to Dreux, 27 février 1920; Dreux inquiry to members to obtain evidence of complaints, 25 février 1920.

SGA 7247, dossier février–mars 1920, 'Note de Marcel Paul pour Cavallier 2 mars 1920'.

SGA 7247, dossier février–mars, note by Daum, president of commission on electric energy, on meeting of 10 février 1920; note by Marcel Paul 2 mars 1920 on a recent meeting of commission for transport concerning new railway lines.

SGA 7247, dossier janvier 1920, 'Énergie électrique de l'Est, réunion de la commission spéciale 31 janvier 1920'.

SGA 7247, dossier juin 1920, 'Analyse de la brochure de M. R. Paul, Directeur des Chemins de Fer du Midi, L'Électrification des chemins de fer français'.

SGA 7247, dossier mai 1920, 'Note sur l'apprentissage, 6 mai 1920'.

SGA 7247, dossier novembre 1920, 'Note pour M. Cavallier, Approvisionnement de la France en charbon, résumé d'un extrait du Bulletin de la Société d'Études et d'Informations 3 novembre 1920' and 'La Question des combustibles en France'.
SGA 7247, dossier octobre 1920, 'Commission des Transports, séance 12 octobre 1920, le régime des chemins de fer'.
SGA 7247, dossier octobre 1920, 'Note sur la bourse des valeurs de Nancy, 26 octobre 1920, réunion de la commission de la bourse des valeurs le 30 octobre 1920', (attachment to letter from Vilgrain to Cavallier announcing meeting, 27 octobre 1920).
SGA 7248, 'Avant projet de voeu de l'Office des Transports de l'Est 8 janvier 1919'.
SGA 7248, dossier correspondance 1917-1924, 'Réception des représentants de la Ligue maritime française, Chambre de Commerce de Nancy, 19 mai 1919; exposé fait par M. Fayolle sur la question des transports, notamment métallurgiques, dans l'Est et la canalisation de la Moselle'.
SGA 7248, dossier correspondance 1917–1924, 'Compte-rendu de la Commission des Communications de 31 mai 1922 par Marcel Paul'.
SGA 7248, dossier correspondance 1917–1924, 'Note de service de Cavallier pour Marcel Paul 5 juin 1922'.
SGA 7248, dossier correspondance 1917–1924, Cavallier letter to Fayolle 22 décembre 1921.
SGA 7248, dossier correspondance 1917–1924, letter from Cavallier to Dreux 27 janvier 1922.
SGA 7248, dossier correspondance 1917–1924, letters from Dreux to Cavallier 3 octobre 1919 and Cavallier to Dreux 11 octobre 1919.
SGA 7248, dossier correspondance 1917–1924, letters from Fayolle to Cavallier 3 mai 1921 and 2 août 1921'.
SGA 7248, memo attached to note of 4 juillet 1921 from Dubois, Pont-à-Mousson to Cavallier.
SGA 7249 dossier exposition des combustibles.
SGA 7249, dossier chambre de métiers février–mars 1923.
SGA 7249, dossier questions diverses, *L'Est républicain* reported the conseil-général's resolution in detail on 2 octobre 1924, cutting passed by Dubois to Cavallier.
SGA 7249, dossier renseignements divers, letter from Ragueneau to Nancy chamber of commerce 20 mars 1923.
SGA 7249, dossier Société régionale des Études du Rhin, 'Société des Études du Rhin: Réunion 29 novembre 1921 Procès-Verbal; projets de statuts de la société, analyse et critique, 5 décembre 1921'.
SGA 7249, dossier Transports, 'Analyse de Dubois, Chambre de Commerce, Canal du Nord-Est 14 mars 1921'.

SGA 7249, dossier transports, 'Rapport de M. Alexandre Dreux au Congrès national de la Navigation intérieure à Rouen, 4–8 juillet, Canal du Nord-Est', copy dated 30 septembre 1921'.

SGA 7313, dossier Institut métallurgique et minier de Nancy 1920–26, 'Comité d'actions chargé de préparer l'organisation et le fonctionnement de l'Institut métallurgique et minier 6 mai 1919'. Cavallier letter to Fayolle 25 mai 1919. Cavallier letters to Petit, director of the institute, 10 février 1922, 20 février 1922.

SGA 7319, dossier correspondance avec Albert Lebrun, 'Note de service 28 mars 1919'.

SGA 7331, dossier Natalité, 'Note de service, études sur les moyens de combattre la dépopulation (7pp.), pour Cavallier fin avril 1923'.

SGA 7331, dossier Natalité, internal Pont-à-Mousson note by Camille Cavallier 4 avril 1919.

SGA 7331, dossier Natalité, Note de service for Cavallier and Marcel Paul 30 janvier 1920.

SGA 7331, dossier navigation sur le Rhin, 'Note de service du service des participations de Pont-à-Mousson pour M. Cavallier 5 novembre 1922'.

SGA 7331, dossier navigation sur Le Rhin, letter from Tannery to Cavallier listing the shareholdings, 3 juin 1924.

SGA 7342, dossier Pupilles, 'Note de service, Dubois à Cavallier 1 décembre 1920'.

SGA 7342, dossier Pupilles, Cavallier letter to E. Ferry at Rupt 10 février 1918.

SGA 7342, dossier Pupilles, Cavallier letter to Fayolle 16 février 1918.

SGA 7342, dossier Pupilles, Cavallier letter to Krug 29 avril 1918.

SGA 7359, dossier Le Rhône et le Rhin, 'Réunion du conseil, société d'études, 20 avril 1923'.

SGA 7359, dossier Le Rhône et Le Rhin, letter from Président de la Chambre de Commerce de Strasbourg to Alexandre Dreux 7 octobre 1921, analyse 10 octobre 1921, note de service Pont-à-Mousson 11 octobre 1921'.

SGA 7359, dossier Le Rhône et Le Rhin, letter from Tannery, Société des Minerais lorrains to Cavallier, 30 novembre 1923.

SGA 7385, visit note by Cavallier on Briey-Longwy 11 décembre 1918. SGA 7248, dossier correspondance 1917–1924, 'Note de service de Cavallier 6 février 1919'.

SGA 7393, dossier voies navigables, letter from Imbeaux to Cavallier 2 avril 1919.

SGA 7398, dossier ANEE commission Natalité, H. Cavallier letter to Morin 26 avril 1919.

SGA 7398, dossier ANEE commission Natalité, H. Cavallier letter to Morin 19 avril 1919; Morin to H. Cavallier 24 avril 1919.

SGA 7420, dossier Congrès de la Natalité.

SGA 7420, dossier divers, Cavallier letter to Fayolle, 8 septembre 1919.

SGA 7420, dossier Pupilles, 'Pupilles de la Chambre de Commerce de Nancy, souscriptions 1917'; 2–6; 'Pupilles, souscriptions uniques et annuelles 1918', 7pp.; 'Oeuvre des Pupilles de la Chambre de Commerce de Nancy 4 février 1918', 2.

SGA 7448, dossier Société d'Assistance aux Réfugiés, Évacués, Sinistrés de Meurthe-et-Moselle: compte-rendu de réunions, divers (1918–1920), minutes of the meetings of the committee of the *Société d'Assistance aux Réfugiés et Sinistrés de Meurthe-et-Moselle*, décembre 1918, mars 1919, avril 1919.

SGA DOC PAM 21.52, 'La Crise économique: transports par chemins de fer', 1 février 1924'.

SGA DOC PAM 21.65, 'Séance du 24 février 1922 Office des Transports'.

SGA Série A fasc. 31 A, DOC PAM 21.24, 'Fête de la reconstitution aux usines de Pont-à-Mousson 18 juillet 1920', 6.

SGA, DOC PAM 21.50, 'Notes économiques d'un métallurgiste'.

SGA, DOC PAM 21.51, 'C. Cavallier, La France de demain: paix et prospérité par le travail, la natalité, l'hygiène', août 1923.

SGA, DOC PAM 22.13, C. Cavallier, 'L'Avenir de la France, réformes nécessaires, avant propos de Maurice Herbette', 8, 19, 31.

SGA, DOC PAM 22.21, 'La Sarre par un Franco-Sarrois', June 1923.

*Union économique de l'Est*, 1917, 1919, 1920, 1921, 1922, 1924, 1929.

CHAPTER 4

# Achievements of Economic Regionalism in the Auvergne

This chapter will examine the achievements of the Auvergne region and its constituent chambers of commerce during the inter-war period. The arguments are mainly drawn from the records of the regional grouping of chambers of commerce and also of the Chamber of Commerce of Clermont-Ferrand, because it was the centre of the economic region. For the Auvergne we have a set of the published proceedings of the regional committee in the periodical *Région du Centre*, unlike for Lorraine.

Before examining individual regional economic projects, we need to understand how the elite developed an overall programme after the war. From 1917 onwards they considered the challenges the region would face once peace was achieved. There is some overlap between the issues identified in Lorraine and the Auvergne. The Auvergne supported Lorraine's lead on the economic implications of a reduced population. The Auvergne was also concerned about training a new generation in the skills needed for industry and commerce to make good the losses of the war. In the Auvergne there was great concern about the impact of war losses on the future of the region's small farms. The economic elite in the Auvergne saw the need to ramp up the development of transport infrastructure. In the Auvergne there was a particular focus on the future development of tourism.

A meeting on 22 February 1919 constituting the region was the first opportunity after the armistice to identify key regional projects. Allegret,



T. Cudbird, *The Origins of Economic Regions in France, 1918–1940*,
https://doi.org/10.1007/978-3-032-04422-8_4

an official from the Ministry of Commerce, gave a detailed review of the economic opportunities. He highlighted the importance of thermalism, mining, hydro-electricity, the mechanization of canals, good technical education, improved agricultural techniques, support for export activities and import substitution. He urged the case for a number of clearly regional projects like a regional *Office de l'Énergie électrique* and a *Musée d'Échantillons* (samples) to act as a showcase for regional manufactures. His key message was that regional economic actors must come together to get things done. In the modern economy 'unity produces strength.' The same applied to cooperation between firms in buying and selling. This was a big change from the laisser-faire economic policy of pre-war years. The new climate was to encourage corporate cooperation under the watchful eye of the state. He wanted to see the regional agent, the secretary-general of the regional committee Mathiot, spend a lot of his time knocking on doors to make progress.[1]

It is significant that Allegret gave the regional representatives a copy of the economic programme drawn up by the Eastern region.[2] While we cannot trace exactly the authorship and transmission of this programme, it is clear that the main lines of activity in the Auvergne were similar to those followed in Lorraine. This similarity is apparent in two theses written in Paris 1924–25.[3] Chadefaux's early assessment of the benefits of economic regionalism in the Auvergne is fairly positive. We can also see from Clotilde Druelle-Korn's article on the region based in Limoges that there were similarities between the programme adopted there and the thinking in Clermont-Ferrand. The Limousin region was interested in telephone and railway networks, the encouragement of foreign commerce and electricity generation using the fall of the Dordogne river.[4]

Evidence for an overall regional economic programme also comes from the *Union des Syndicats patronaux des Industriels et Commerçants du Puy-de-Dôme*, of which the president was A. Lagaye, also the secretary of the Clermont chamber of commerce and a manufacturer of *fruits confits*. In *Le*

[1] Travaux de la Chambre de Commerce de Clermont-Ferrand, 1919 (séance 22 février 1919), 42–50.

[2] Travaux Clermont-Ferrand, 1919 (séance 22 février 1919), 49.

[3] J. Diez, Le Régionalisme économique, organisation de la Région économique de l'Est (Nancy) (Thèse pour le doctorat, sciences politiques et économiques, Paris, 1925).

R. Chadefaux, La Région économique de Clermont-Ferrand (Thèse pour le doctorat, Faculté de Droit de Paris, Aurillac, 1924).

[4] Druelle-Korn, 'Modernisation inachevée', 164–168.

*Commerce* for November 1922, he outlined his ideas in an article called *Devoir Syndical.* His programme was a mixture of regional economic *dirigisme* and complete freedom for industry. He wanted the execution of large regional projects to exploit regional resources, but at the same time freedom for industry and a war on public waste in order to re-establish French credit. He favoured the organization of comprehensive technical education and the development of apprenticeships. He also wanted workers and owners to cooperate to reduce social conflict and combat communism. He favoured the natalist programme. Above all France had to put work first. It sounded like a speech by Cavallier.[5]

Over and above the individual programmes the regional elite clearly felt the need to justify the existence of their region and to beat the drum for regional progress, to inculcate a sense of regional pride. The regional committee decided to publish a regional journal to make their work more widely known, *La Région du Centre.* This was not a dry bulletin of laws and measures taken. It had striking covers with symbols of regional progress. The articles covered not only meetings of the region and project reports but also contained descriptions of the regional industries and general regional economic news. More than this the journal developed a literary section to which writers, already well-known before the war, were contributors, for example, Henri Pourrat, Amélie Murat, novelist and poet from the Auvergne; Gandilhon Gens-d'Armes, an Auvergnat poet; Desdevises du Dézert from the university; and Pourrat's friend Gachon, who wrote extensively about the Auvergne. There was a special section on tourism issues and regular reports on the Aero Club of the Auvergne. (Clermont had seen the development of the manufacture of military planes during the war.)

In the second issue of *Région du Centre,* Dr. Marcombes, the mayor of Clermont-Ferrand, wrote an editorial saying that his town was unarguably the regional capital. It was a centre for trade in the region and it had a number of cultural assets including the university.[6] The following year the journal went on to describe the historic links which bound the Auvergne together. Although mainly an agricultural region, it had significant sources of hydro-electric power and was the centre for a major rubber industry in

[5] Le Commerce, no. 72 (novembre 1922), 6.

[6] 'Clermont capitale du Centre de la France', Région du Centre, no. 2 (juin–juillet 1921), 3–4.

Clermont. (The main firms were Michelin, Bergougnan and Torilhon.) Moreover, the Auvergnats had a reputation for hard work.[7]

On 1 October 1922 the Minister of Commerce, Dior, made an official visit and met at length with the regional committee for discussions on current projects.[8] Clémentel and the prefects were also present. This extensive review served not only to check on progress on individual items but also to prove that the regionalist experiment was working well. Clémentel expressed the hope that his successor would ensure that the secretaries-general of the various regions met regularly together in Paris, and he also urged the minister to give the regions themselves the legal status they lacked in law which would enable them to make legal commitments on their own behalf.[9] The president of the Bourges region reminded the audience that they were working for the 1.5 million Frenchmen killed in the war and also for the million whose ability to work was affected by their wounds.[10] Dior referred to the overriding importance of unity, of which the Auvergne had given a good example.[11]

Advertising the achievements of the region was the objective of the major regional festival and exhibition which was staged in Clermont-Ferrand 1–8 July 1923 and which ended with the formal reception of Alexandre Millerand, president of the Republic, to celebrate the three hundredth anniversary of the birth of Pascal, the most esteemed local son.[12] Chalus, president of the Clermont-Ferrand chamber of commerce, wanted to bolster the regionalist cause. He greeted the president as:

> a convinced regionalist who wants to see tomorrow the nation regenerated by an organisation of which we will have been the precursors.

[7] F. Chambon, professeur de l'École supérieure de Commerce à Clermont-Ferrand, 'D'où est né la xviie région économique: province et région?', Région du Centre, no. 5 (janvier 1922), 5–8.

[8] Région du Centre, no. 14 (octobre 1922), 3–23.

[9] Région du Centre, no. 14 (octobre 1922), 7.

[10] Région du Centre, no. 14 (octobre 1922), 9.

[11] Ibid., 10.

[12] 'Semaine auvergnate, rapport de M. Jouve sur l'organisation d'une foire-exposition régionale'. Région du Centre, no. 20 (avril 1923), 9–10; 'La réception de M. Alexandre Millerand, Président de la République Française à la XVIIe Région économique', 'La Foire-Exposition régionale de Clermont-Ferrand', Région du Centre, no. 24 (Août 1923), 3–8, 9–11.

Chalus went on to salute 'the first regionalist of France.' In his reply, Millerand referred to the need to rebuild the economy to compete with Germany. Later in the day, the president saluted Clémentel, who was present, as the father of economic regionalism and referred to his role in launching the region locally. Millerand made it clear that he personally was a regionalist who believed in the benefits of economic regionalism, of business people getting together to defend their interests.[13]

In the following pages, we will examine major projects, several already identified in outline at the February 1919 meeting with Allegret—to create a new source of hydro-electric power on the Dordogne river; to build a lateral canal alongside the Allier river and to improve other canals, for instance, the Canal du Berri in the Bourbonnais; to create new railway links, principally East-West 'Suisse-Océan' running through Lyon and Clermont to Bordeaux; to open new technical training facilities in Clermont and create a chamber for trades; and lastly to open a *Banque populaire de la 17e Région économique*. We will deal with tourism and agriculture, which were particularly important for the Auvergne, in a later chapter.

## Railways

As in Lorraine, the future development of transport links was a major issue, particularly in an area as isolated as the Auvergne. Again as in Lorraine the chamber of commerce in Clermont-Ferrand was part of a regional *Office des Transports* set up in this case by chambers of commerce for the South-East and based in Lyon.[14] In 1918 this office enlarged its remit to take in the post, telephones and telegraph.[15] Unlike the chamber of commerce in Nancy, Clermont-Ferrand was represented in not one but two *offices des transports*, one for the Sud-Est based in Lyon and another for the Centre-Ouest based in Limoges. Representatives of the chamber attended the meetings of both. At a meeting in Lyon on 18 October 1920, the Clermont representative set out his chamber's key objectives for railways. He said that Clermont-Ferrand, as the capital of rubber, should be linked directly to Bordeaux, Lyon and hence to Marseille as soon as possible. Secondly, the express from Clermont to Paris should be as fast as

[13] Région du Centre, no. 24 (août 1923), 5 and 8.
[14] Travaux Clermont-Ferrand, 1914, (séance 7 juillet 1914), 123–137.
[15] Travaux Clermont-Ferrand, 1918, (séance 12 février 1918), 12.

that from Lyon to the capital. Thirdly, the project for a Grand Central railway must pass through Clermont. These objectives were forwarded to the Minister for Public Works as well as to the PLM (Paris-Lyon-Méditerranée) and P-O (Paris-Orléans) railway companies.[16] The Clermont chamber mobilized its parliamentary representatives behind the plan for a Grand Central via the city, which would require some new track construction in the Puy-de-Dôme.[17]

As the *Région du Centre* explained at the beginning of 1921, re-establishing the direct service from Bordeaux to Clermont via Périgueux, which had run before the war, was vital because the alternative via Limoges took far too long. The Clermont chamber was hoping for more electrification of lines to make the services more reliable. A *Grande Transversale*, passing south of Clermont but linked to it and crossing the mountains of the Forez, was a matter on which the regional committee felt strongly. Mathiot told the committee that Clémentel was behind them on this matter.[18]

In January 1921, the regional committee also considered a cause dear to the Moulins chamber, a direct line between Riom and Vichy linking eventually to the Saône-et-Loire through Paray-le-Monial. This would also improve links between Clermont and Lyon.[19] The *syndicat d'initiative* of Vichy were concerned about this because it would improve communications to their facilities. They wanted a double track for the new link, which they thought had been agreed but now seemed to have been replaced by a single track. The Vichy tourist trade approached the Auvergne region to strengthen their protest.[20] The Minister of Public Works indicated that they would get what they wanted.[21] As we have seen in Lorraine, the central government's approval for all new railway lines was vital but lobbying by regional bodies could achieve progress.

Lastly, the Clermont chamber and the region were very concerned about the poor condition of the roads in the Auvergne and were constantly lobbying the Ponts-et-Chaussées state engineers for improvements

[16] Travaux Clermont-Ferrand, 1920 (séance 17 novembre 1920), 92.

[17] Travaux Clermont-Ferrand, 1920 (séance 20 décembre 1920), 109–110.

[18] 'Comité régional 7 janvier 1921', Région du Centre, no. 1 (mars–avril 1921), 11–13., also 'Comité régional 15 mars 1923', Région du Centre, no. 20 (avril 1923), 6. Travaux Clermont-Ferrand, 1923 (séance 26 janvier 1923), 20–21.

[19] 'Comité régional 7 janvier 1921', Région du Centre, no. 1 (mars–avril 1921), 13.

[20] Région du Centre, no. 21 (mai 1923), 19–22.

[21] Travaux Clermont-Ferrand, 1923 (séance 21 avril 1923), 56.

and the government for more credits. Such improvements were particularly vital for the new tourist trade which was developing in the post-war years.[22]

As in Lorraine, development of good railway connections to the rest of France was vital if the region was to grow economically. In the Auvergne the concern was exacerbated by a feeling of geographical remoteness. As in Lorraine the economic elite in the Clermont chamber and the region had to mobilize local political leaders if they were to get the necessary approvals from the Minister of Public Works, the *Conseil supérieur des Chemins de Fer* and the local *conseils-généraux*. Their task was complicated because not everyone wanted the same improvements. Towns wanted a railway which served them, rather than the region as a whole.

## Canals

As in Lorraine improving canals was an important strategic issue. During the war the chamber in Clermont-Ferrand had revived a proposal, which dated back to before the war, for a canal alongside the Allier river which flowed through the region, a project also being taken up by the *conseil-général* of the Puy-de-Dôme. It was becoming more urgent because the 'transport crisis' on the rail system, caused by the war, showed that the region was too dependent on this mode of transport. The chamber was willing to pay a share of the cost of preliminary studies.[23] An inter-departmental commission was set up in which the chamber participated.[24] Later the chamber raised its financial contribution to 10,000 francs, a considerable sum considering its resources.[25] *Le Moniteur du Puy-de-Dôme*, the leading newspaper in the Auvergne, could see a bright future for Clermont as the industrial hub of the centre of France, if the transport links were improved. Bearing in mind the possibility of renewed international conflict in the future, production was more secure far from the north of the country. The writer of several articles on the future of Clermont in 1918 wanted to see a greater development of port facilities in Bordeaux and on the Gironde estuary and rail links from there to

[22] Travaux Clermont-Ferrand, 1923 (séance 14 novembre 1923), 88; 1924 (séance 25 juillet 1924), 143–134. Région du Centre, no. 39 (novembre 1924), 363–365.

[23] Travaux Clermont-Ferrand, 1916, (séance 23 mars 1916), 17–19, 22–23; (séance 7 juin 1916), 62.

[24] Travaux Clermont-Ferrand, 1916, (séance 5 septembre 1916), 134.

[25] Travaux Clermont-Ferrand, 1918, (séance 25 avril 1918), 26.

Clermont, thus improving the latter's links to overseas sources of supply and markets, principally the United States.[26]

Tapping into regional sources of finance was very much part of the debate. The advice of experts from Clermont-Ferrand university is also noteworthy. Studies for a *canal latéral* alongside the Allier river continued soon after the war.[27] The Clermont-Ferrand chamber of commerce contributed a further 6000 francs to the cost of studies in 1920.[28] Work on the Allier basin was not only to improve navigation. It was envisaged that the construction of reservoirs could regularize the flow, control flooding and allow the construction of hydro-electric plants. In his report to the regional committee in March 1923, Mathiot advised that various academic experts associated with the University of Clermont-Ferrand were involved, including Pourrat's friend Gachon and Arbos, Professor of Geography, who was also involved with the Dordogne hydro-electric project. The region planned for a congress in Clermont-Ferrand the following year bringing together all the experts and other interested parties.[29]

So the Allier became another major focus of attention for the new economic region. In this connection the region also adopted a project to build a new canal between Moulins and Sancoins which would feed the important Canal du Berri, a canal which served an industrial area. This could be seen as a first step in linking the Loire and the Garonne, and was consistent with railway projects to give Clermont good east-west links as well as north-south. The president of the Moulins chamber of commerce envisaged a project financed jointly by the state, the department, the town of Moulins and the chamber of commerce.[30] The Auvergne region was asked by the Moulins chamber to persuade the Clermont-Ferrand chamber of commerce and city council, the Riom chamber and the department of Puy-de-Dôme to make financial contributions.[31] The scope of canal improvements being considered by the region immediately after the war

[26] Le Moniteur du Puy-de-Dôme (2 juin 1918), 3 col a–b; (7 juin 1918), 3, col a–b; (21 juin 1918), 3 col a–b.

[27] Travaux Clermont-Ferrand, 1919 (séance 4 février 1919), 31.

[28] Travaux Clermont-Ferrand, 1920 (séance 20 décembre 1920), 112.

[29] 'Comité régional 15 mars 1923 et rapport par Mathiot sur le Congrès de l'aménagement du basin d'Allier', Région du Centre, no. 20 (avril 1923), 5–8.

[30] Région du Centre, no. 14 (octobre 1922), 21; Darfour, Président de la Chambre de Commerce de Moulins-Lapalisse, 'Élargissement du Canal du Berry, alimentation', Région du Centre, no. 16 (décembre 1922), 3–8.

[31] Travaux Clermont-Ferrand, 1923 (séance 26 janvier 1923), 10.

did not stop at the Allier. Professor Glangeaud at the University of Clermont-Ferrand also put forward the concept of a canal linking the Allier to the Dordogne, to be known as the Canal du Cantal, a fairly ambitious project through mountainous terrain.[32]

To conclude, the Auvergne region had been effective in mobilizing several interested parties behind its plans for new railways and canals. This ability was to become even more important when it tackled hydro-electricity.

## Energy

From the outset the most important project for the Auvergne region was the exploitation of the hydro-electric potential of the Dordogne. Here we can trace the development of a regional economic project exactly as Clémentel envisaged. In April 1919 the prefect of the Puy-de-Dôme opened a public enquiry about it covering the whole of the river. At this stage it was envisaged that the PO railway company would erect seven dams to power 40% of its network. Members of the Clermont chamber were concerned that such a large project would affect the hydrography of the entire region and might be prejudicial to other interests. For example, the *Société Hydro-Électrique d'Auvergne* was planning a plant on the river Rhue, an affluent of the Dordogne. The chamber decided to write to the Minister of Public Works about their concerns.[33] The project was first discussed by the Auvergne region on 19 August 1919.[34]

However, it would not be right to see the Dordogne project as the sole focus of the region's interest in hydro-electricity. Clémentel in a preface to the first edition of the new journal, *Région du Centre*, talked about the mechanical force which could be gained from the region's rivers generally, reducing dependence on foreign coal.[35] Raoul Blanchard, the geographer who according to Philippe Veitl came to Grenoble and defined the Alpine

[32] C. Mathiot, 'Étude sommaire d'un canal de la Dordogne à l'Allier', Région du Centre, no. 1 (mars-avril 1921), 39–41.

[33] Travaux Clermont-Ferrand, 1919 (séance 14 mai 1919), 68–69, (séance 28 mai 1919), 72–76.

[34] Réunion de la Région du 19 août 1919', XVIIe Région Économique, Groupement régional de Clermont-Ferrand, Compte-rendu des travaux du comité régional et du comité consultatif régional économique, séances des 29 avril 1918, 17 juin et 19 août 1919 (Clermont-Ferrand, s.d.), 45.

[35] Région du Centre, no. 1 (mars–avril 1921), 3–4.

region in terms of its hydro-electric potential, also drew attention to what could be achieved in the Massif Central. In an article written in 1922 he remarked that the Massif did not have either the height, steepness of slope, volume or regular flow of rivers in the Alps. It was therefore necessary to develop a new technique, the reservoir enclosed by a dam which would release enough power.[36] Philippe Arbos picked up the development of dams in an article for *Région du Centre* in March 1924. The war had revealed France's critical shortage of coal and so had encouraged a host of hydro-electric projects including that in the Massif Central.[37] Of the total hydro-electric potential of the Massif measured in kilowatts, the Dordogne project accounted for one third.[38]

On 7 January 1921 Mathiot outlined to the regional committee a vision of how hydro-electricity could transform not only industry and commerce in the Auvergne but also in many surrounding areas of France. The region wanted to set up an *Office régionale d'Énergie électrique* and it had the backing of the *Conseil-général du Puy-de-Dôme* for this. (Clémentel was of course the president of the latter.)[39] A number of these regional offices were set up in the inter-war years.[40] On 11 April Rambaud, the president of the Tulle chamber and the driving force behind regional hydro-electricity projects, presented a report on the hydro-electric potential of the Massif Central in general and the need for a company to exploit it. Clément Rambaud was an industrialist who in 1906 became the concessionaire for the distribution of electricity in Égletons in the Corrèze. He built power stations to supply electricity to the surrounding area. In 1919 he became a *conseiller municipal* at Meymac in the same area and mayor in 1925. He was elected a member of the chamber of commerce in Tulle in 1919 and president in 1920, continuing in office for many years.

[36] R. Blanchard, 'La Houille blanche dans le Massif Central français', Revue de géographie alpine, tome 10, n°3 (1922), 353–396. Veitl, Invention d'une région, 221–251.

[37] Blanchard, 'La Houille blanche', 380, 394. Région du Centre, no. 31 (mars 1924), 83–85.

[38] Blanchard, 'La Houille blanche', 394.

[39] 'Réunion du Comité régional 7 janvier 1921', Région du Centre, no. 1 (mars–avril 1921), 13–16.

[40] Bouneau C., 'La contribution de l'électricité à la génèse de l'aménagement du territoire en France, pendant la première moitié du xxe siècle,' in F. Caron, C. Bouneau (eds), L'UPEPO, 1922-1946 : génèse et logiques de l'interconnexion, Bulletin d'histoire de l'électricité, 1985, 6, 47.

After the war his electricity business expanded in the region.[41] He was president of an electricity supply firm Énergie industrielle (EI), which operated in the Cantal as well as the Corrèze.[42]

In his report Rambaud suggested an inter-departmental commission on the subject, covering the regions based in Bordeaux, Limoges and Clermont-Ferrand, with qualified commercial and industrial representatives.[43] Rambaud argued that public participation in projects would ensure the necessary cooperation between operators of different dams which would maximize the flow on rivers and hence the power generated. Rambaud was firmly of the view that such projects were too important to be left to the politicians. The chambers of commerce representing commercial interests had a vital role to play rather than politicians, trained in the liberal professions and often lacking the necessary technical and commercial expertise. Sixty per cent of any inter-departmental commissions appointed should consist of industrialists, and workers should be represented too. Shareholdings should be widely spread. Some of the private concessions granted by the state before the law of 1919 had not operated too well, whereas the chambers of commerce had demonstrated they could run public facilities like ports successfully. However, the state's participation along with departments would ensure the general interest was protected. Projects would have access to the corps of state engineers with the necessary expertise. The state also had to be involved because power generation was so important for France's recovery after the war. It would be a just recompense for the sacrifice of France's war heroes.[44]

At a meeting on 14 July 1921 the *Office régionale d'Énergie électrique* was formally set up. Rambaud submitted a report which envisaged this office facilitating the expansion of hydro-electricity by finding the right expertise, organizing technical studies and helping the regional committee negotiate its way through the laws and bodies with an interest, in order to obtain concessions for exploitation. An appeal had to be made to the relevant *conseils-généraux* for funds for studies.[45]

[41] 'Clément Rambaud ou la vie d'un grand Corrézien', La Montagne (19 juillet 2019); www.lamontagne.fr

[42] M. Lévy-Leboyer, H. Morsel (eds), Histoire générale de L'Électricité en France, T.II 1919–1946 L'Interconnexion et le Marché (Paris, 1994), 655, 961.

[43] 'Comité régional 11 avril 1921', Région du Centre, no. 2 (juin–juillet 1921), 17–20.

[44] 'Comité régional 11 avril 1921', Région du Centre, no. 2 (juin–juillet 1921), 21–30.

[45] Region du Centre, no. 3 (septembre–octobre 1921), 21–24.

The Dordogne project was complex, both technically and in terms of the number of interests which had to be brought on board and the financing. The prefects and the *conseils-généraux* of five departments, professional bodies, the chambers of commerce, three regions, local politicians, three ministers in Paris (Commerce, Finance and Public Works) and finally the Chamber of Deputies and the Senate, all had to be won over. There were differing views about how far the state and the departments should be involved in guaranteeing loans for construction, as they had done before to finance new railways, for example. There was a conflict between private interests, like the PO railway company, and the Auvergne region representing the various institutions of the centre of France, as to whether it was right for a quasi-public body to be managing power generation. Lastly, there was the question of distribution of electricity and the most fundamental question of all—would there be a market for the Kilowatts generated? From a fairly early stage the project was driven by the newly created regions. It became a test case for Clémentel's reform.

At the start of discussions on the project, the PO railway company wanted to take all the potential concessions on the upper Dordogne. The Auvergne region intervened and aimed to apply for a concession for the so-called 2nd section. Later it was envisaged that the region based in Limoges would take the third and fourth sections. The PO railway company would remain as concessionaire for the first section above Vernejoux. Public companies would be formed financed by a mixture of loans, with interest guaranteed by the state, and share capital. Departments and chambers of commerce as well as private interests would be involved in the financing and the project would be managed by a board of directors representing chambers of commerce and other local interests. Although there was some precedent for such a public-private vehicle, for example, on the Rhône, the project presented a number of political and administrative challenges for the French state and ultimately required a special law to be passed by the Chamber of Deputies.

To negotiate the thicket of conflicting bodies, the three regions interested in the Dordogne project set up an inter-regional commission, separate from the inter-departmental committees who had looked at it. Apart from Clermont-Ferrand, Limoges and Bordeaux, Nantes and the sub-region of Orléans were also included.[46] The Clermont-Ferrand region

[46] 'Réunion interrégionale de Paris 23 novembre 1921', Région du Centre, no. 5 (janvier 1922), 9–10.

decided that it would bid for the second section from Vernejoux to Argentat and Rambaud was authorized to approach the Minister of Public Works with their concession request.[47] Rambaud reported that the three main regions involved (Limoges, Bordeaux, Clermont-Ferrand) were broadly in agreement on this.[48] In April Mathiot could report that the Auvergne region's proposal had the Minister of Public Works and the region's parliamentary representatives on board. The region's proposal envisaged the construction of three dams at Chambon and Argentat I and II.[49] By June it appeared that the Ministers of Finance and Commerce were also behind the project. A draft law was prepared by the Minister of Public Works.[50]

A summary of the key documents published after the event emphasized the contribution which the scheme would make to the national post-war policy for industry, to increase French production and to make it more competitive on price. It would also help electrify the countryside and support the mechanization of agriculture. The region had considered not only the technical problems of construction but also potential sales and lines for distribution. Electricity consumption per household was still way behind the USA. The new plants could use the PO railway company's lines for distribution and also new networks being constructed with the direct encouragement of the government.[51]

However, it was at this stage that difficulties appeared. These centred around two issues. Firstly, opposition from private interests who wanted concessions and secondly problems over financing. Vociferous opposition from private interests that wanted concessions arose at the congress of the *Ligue fluviale* in Bordeaux in May 1922, attended by many interested in the Dordogne. At the congress Rambaud pointed out that hydro-electric energy would help France save some of the 20 million tons of coal currently imported, mainly from the UK. The reduction in the value of the franc made these imports expensive. Rambaud said the region's scheme for the second section would lead to low prices for all, rather than increasing the profits of private companies. It would also help stem rural

[47] Région du Centre, no. 6 (février 1922), 19–20.

[48] 'Comité régional 26 janvier 1922', Région du Centre, no. 8 (avril 1922), 13–17.

[49] Région du Centre, no. 8 (avril 1922), 3–4.

[50] Région du Centre, no. 10 (juin 1922), 7.

[51] XVIIe Région économique, groupement régional des chambres de commerce. Aménagement Hydro-électrique de la 2ème section du bassin de la Dordogne, notice technique et financière (Clermont-Ferrand, mai 1924), 3–6 and 15–21.

depopulation by making rural areas more attractive to live in. Indeed, the scheme was the basis of all plans to develop the regions of the centre of France. The scheme assumed the state would guarantee the payment of bank interest, an advantage not available to private firms.[52] Despite the opposition, the Minister of Public Works and other supporters, such as Clémentel, Alexander Varenne, the SFIO socialist deputy from the Puy-de-Dôme and Joseph Faure, senator for the Corrèze and a supporter of agricultural interests, held firm in their opposition to private concessions. Varenne, who at a crucial stage was the *rapporteur* for the Public Works budget in the Chamber of Deputies, contributed a piece to the *Région du Centre* in August 1922 in which he said the whole justification for the project was cheaper electricity for all customers. It should definitely not be run for private profit. It was not the only commercial activity in which the state took an active interest. He also thought it right that all interested parties should be involved in the project.[53]

However, when the Minster of Public Works' draft law was available for discussion at the regional committee on 4 December 1922, it appeared to be different in important respects from what the region thought had been agreed. It seemed to be based on a much more direct central government participation in hydro-electricity from the Auvergne to the Atlantic Ocean. However, the real sticking point was over financing. The Auvergne region scheme proposed that 90% of the cost should be covered by a loan from the Crédit Foncier guaranteed by state organizations. The state was unwilling to underwrite the Crédit Foncier loan and in the end departments and communes assumed responsibility for 90% of the capital obligations with the balance covered by chambers of commerce through shares. Regional representatives would also hold a majority of seats on the board of directors. The project could now be considered by the Chamber of Deputies itself. Mathiot believed the ministers were still supportive of the region's plan, which defended the interests of consumers against private interests.[54] He said this was important if:

> our industrialists and our businessmen no longer want to be held to ransom by producers with long teeth.[55]

[52] Région du Centre, no. 11 (juillet 1922), 7–8 and 9–15.

[53] Région du Centre, no. 12 (août 1922), 3–7.

[54] 'Comité régional 4 décembre 1922', Région du Centre, no. 16 (décembre 1922), 9–12; no. 20 (avril 1923), 3–4.

[55] Région du Centre, no. 20 (avril 1923), 4.

In October 1923 the project went onto the floor of the Chamber of Deputies in Paris. Unusually the commission of the chamber examining the project asked for the departmental guarantees to be binding before the project went any further. The Corrèze tried to extract a special tariff for electricity as the price for its agreement.[56] The horse trading on financial guarantees went on for another year. Eventually the concession of the second section to the Auvergne Region was approved by the Chamber on 30 December 1924.[57]

This was not, however, the end of the matter. The project did not go ahead in the form envisaged during the period under discussion. After further consideration a law of 6 March 1928 permitted another mixed public-private company to be formed called *Énergie électrique de la Moyenne Dordogne*, which was incorporated on 15 December 1928. Half of its capital came from eleven chambers of commerce, six chambers of agriculture, large towns such as Clermont-Ferrand, Saint-Étienne and Montluçon and six departments—Cantal, Puy-de-Dôme, Haute-Loire, Loire, Corrèze and Allier. (The 7th region around Limoges had dropped out.) The other half of the capital came from 16 electricity distribution companies. This company opted for a new site for a power station at L'Aigle (Fig. 4.1) below Marèges, where the PO railway company had now been granted a separate concession for a dam. The new mixed company was granted the concession eventually in 1934. The state provided guarantees for 60 million of the total capital obligations of 160m francs, in return for a 35% reduction in the normal tariff. (The local bodies only got a 20% reduction.) The Aigle dam was only finished after 1945. The PO dam was finished in 1937.[58] Given the risks inherent in large and costly hydro-electric projects the delay is not surprising (Fig. 4.1).

The first project to install hydro-electric dams on the Dordogne may have failed. However, the debate it unleashed is a significant demonstration of the spirit of practical economic regionalism which prevailed in the region in the years after the First World War. The prevailing climate in economic policy before the war had been to allow private industry considerable freedom and for the state only to get involved in economic activity in exceptional circumstances. Clémentel had wanted to continue some of

[56] Région du Centre, no. 26 (octobre 1923), 3–6.

[57] Région du Centre, no. 41 (janvier 1925), 7. Journal Officiel, (30 décembre 1924), 4941–4943.

[58] Histoire générale de L'Électricité, 771, 773–774.

**Fig. 4.1** The Aigle dam on the Dordogne river, courtesy of the Bibliothèque Nationale de France

the wartime controls he exercised over industry after the war, in the interests of improving French competitiveness, but was unsuccessful. In the case of the Dordogne project, however, we find a regional group of businessmen and officials trying to run an economic activity on behalf of the consumer. They also sought to bypass the local politicians in the interests of technical efficiency. It was a challenge during a period when the resources of the central government were stretched by a financial crisis. Private concessions were not as risky for the state as projects funded by a public interest guarantee.[59] That the regionalists were successful in advancing their project says something for regional solidarity and determination to bring all the interested parties on board.

The Dordogne project was not the only example of local interests coming together to bring electrification to the Auvergne. It could happen on a more modest scale. That is why the *Région du Centre* drew attention to

[59] Région du Centre, no. 39 (novembre 1924), 367–368.

a syndicate of 43 communes who combined to ensure electricity supply to the Gannat in the Allier, thus helping, it was claimed, to stem rural depopulation.[60] The journal also published an article by Pourrat's friend Lucien Gachon about electrification of another rural area, the Livradois, using hydro-electricity on a much smaller scale.[61] During the 1920s, there was political support for rural electrification. It was not always profitable for private interests, and therefore, there was encouragement for rural communes to combine to arrange distribution. The state could lend money through the Crédit agricole.[62]

## Technical Education

The chamber of commerce was also concerned about the future provision of technical education after the war. It was involved with the operation of the *Institut industriel et commercial du Centre* in Clermont-Ferrand. A proposal was made to attach this institute to the university there. The institute provided some training in industrial chemistry, but the university wanted to start a similar course itself. The future of the institute was a complicated matter involving the Ministry of Commerce which had an interest in such education, the Ministry of Public Instruction and the council of the university. The chamber got involved in lobbying in Paris to resolve the institute's future.[63] The chamber noted the national interest in improving technical education and cited the growth of such education in the University of Nancy.[64] By 1918 the matter had still not been resolved and the military had taken over occupation of the Institute's premises.[65] Soon afterwards an inspector-general from technical education in the Ministry of Commerce made a visit to consider a site for a new *École supérieure de Commerce*[66] (Fig. 4.2).

The main educational initiatives of the Auvergne region along with the chamber of commerce of Clermont-Ferrand were now to found an *École*

[60] Région du Centre, no. 37 (août-septembre 1924), 285–294.

[61] Région du Centre, no. 32 (avril 1924), 123–126.

[62] Histoire générale de L'Électricité, 55–56, 371, 373,

[63] Travaux Clermont-Ferrand, 1914, (séance 2 février 1914), 38–40; 1915, (séance 31 mars 1915), 25–31; (séance 26 octobre 1915), 55–56; 1916, (séance 9 août 1916), 74–129.

[64] Travaux Clermont-Ferrand, 1916, (séance 5 septembre 1916), 136–138.

[65] Travaux Clermont-Ferrand, 1918, (séance 12 février 1918), 10.

[66] Travaux Clermont-Ferrand, 1918, (séance 2 juillet 1918), 37; (séance 12 juillet 1918), 43–45; (séance 26 juillet 1918), 49.

**Fig. 4.2** École Supérieure de Commerce, Clermont-Ferrand Wikimedia Commons

*supérieure de Commerce* mentioned above and also a chamber for trades. The director of technical education at the Ministry of Commerce had made his visit. The problem at this stage was that there was no building in Clermont in which to house it. The Clermont chamber of commerce was looking for the town or the state to step in and then the chamber might be able to help with running expenses.[67] The problem was solved when the Ministry of War released the Caserne d'Estaing in July 1919 to the town to be used for the school.[68] The chamber of commerce appointed three members to the board of directors of the new school including Raymond Bergougnan, the rubber manufacturer. Members were also appointed from the regional committee and the municipal council of Clermont. The fitting out of the building for an estimated sum of 600,000 francs was financed by the state (250,000 francs), the city and the Auvergne

[67] Travaux Clermont-Ferrand, 1919 (séance 4 février 1919), 21.
[68] Travaux Clermont-Ferrand, 1919 (séance 24 juillet 1919), 91.

region (80,000 francs) and the balance came from a loan from the Crédit Foncier. The town also offered to help with bursaries. When the region financed a project, it meant that individual chambers of commerce had to make a commitment and the sums involved in this case caused some to hesitate. Clémentel urged them to come forward so that he could get the state contribution through the Chamber of Deputies.[69]

The school was up and running in its new home in October 1920. Michelin endowed a chair of Taylorism or what might be called industrial efficiency and standardization. Bergougnan, Chalus and other firms, including trade associations, made contributions. In the first year there were 109 pupils including 47 who had been demobilized from the army. An alumni organization was founded to help with placement of graduates and raising funds.[70] The school was an integral part of what the region was trying to achieve. As Mathiot said at the opening ceremony:

> you are officially endorsing the first organization here of official regionalism which will really make a difference in the domain of economics.

Marcombes, the mayor of Clermont, went on to say that the school was an important result of the policy of decentralization started by Clémentel, who was of course present too. The school, Marcombes said, should be considered alongside other achievements of the region like the *Office régional d'Agriculture*, the *Banque populaire* and the Musée régional d'Échantillons (samples).[71] The Clermont chamber continued to support the school every year. In 1924 it planned to donate 15,000 francs, about half the amount it gave to the region.[72]

Given the importance of tourism to the Auvergne, it is not surprising that the region wanted to set up an *École supérieure hôtelière* on the model of the *École supérieure de Commerce*. Offers of financial help had been received for such a project.[73] By May 1924 the school was an institution in its own right on the same site as the commercial school. Fifty-seven students had already been through the course. As Mathiot wrote, a large

[69] 'Réunion régionale 19 août 1919', Travaux Clermont-Ferrand, 1919 (séance 30 septembre 1919), 99–105.

[70] Région du Centre, no. 37 (août–septembre 1924), 303–304.

[71] Région du Centre, no. 3 (septembre–octobre 1921), 13–15, quote 14.

[72] Travaux Clermont-Ferrand, 1923 (séance 14 novembre 1923), 96.

[73] 'Comité régional 7 janvier 1921', Région du Centre, no. 1 (mars–avril 1921), 19–20; 'Comité régional 16 juillet 1921', Région du Centre, no. 3 (septembre–octobre 1921), 19.

number of foreign hotel workers went home before the war and not all had come back. They had to be replaced. There was also a need to develop capable managers and thus promote the growth of the industry.[74] The region and the Clermont chamber also supported other types of technical training such as professional courses run by the municipality of Clermont, the project for a cutlery school in Thiers which was a big centre for this industry, and the courses in industrial chemistry at the university which were re-started after the war.[75]

While the university did not see the rapid development of new schools of applied science as in Nancy, the institution was not asleep. Geological studies were a strong point, partly because of the mineral riches in the area. Professor Glangeaud, Professor of Geology and Mineralogy, had recently received public recognition when admitted to the Institut de France. The *Région du Centre* made the case for a new *Centre d'Études géologiques* and for the endowment of a new chair. Apart from the *Institut de Chimie*, Clermont now boasted the commercial school and a full *faculté de droit*. The university was small in relation to Nancy (in 1924, 452 students as opposed to 1908) but growing. The *Région du Centre* believed that it deserved local financial support.[76]

Just after the war members of the regional elite in Clermont-Ferrand reflected the view shared in Lorraine and indeed throughout France that there was a critical shortage of skilled labour. France needed to train more young people for skilled trades, like the Germans. Early in 1921 the region wanted to take advantage of the impetus created by national legislation and start its own chamber for trades. It encouraged local leaders and the central government to support such a proposal, with the help of the Inspector of the local Academy and the works inspector. A commission was set up to study the matter.[77]

Tourette, professor of technical education and a works inspector, visited a number of towns where chambers for trades had already been set up. In his report he said that patrons, workers and the departments should all be equally represented on the board of directors of the new regional chamber for trades proposed. They should be nominated by the economic

[74] Région du Centre, no. 33 (mai 1924), 163–165.

[75] Travaux Clermont-Ferrand, 1919 (séance 19 mars 1919), 59; 1924 (séance 8 janvier 1924), 18; (séance 5 décembre 1924), 172.

[76] Région du Centre, no. 31 (mars 1924), 87–89.

[77] Région du Centre, no. 1 (mars–avril 1921), 20; no. 2 (juin–juillet 1921), 12; no. 5 (janvier 1922), 12–16.

region, chambers of commerce, bourses du travail (workers' organisations for mutual aid), and unions representing workers and industrialists. The new chamber should concentrate on guiding young people into suitable careers, regularizing apprenticeships, setting up courses where needed and delivering certificates of qualifications. Tourette's report was agreed by the region early in 1922.[78] Mathiot set about talking to businesses about financial support for the scheme, which ideally would start at the end of the school year in July.[79]

At the first formal meeting of the board of directors on 24 June 1922 with Chalus in the chair, Mathiot was elected president of the chamber for trades. According to Tourette it was a matter of urgency to get young people into trades where there was a particular skills deficit and also to create courses where none existed.[80] The report by Leclerc, the new director, in March 1923 was encouraging. The war had accelerated the decline in skills with a further 20% reduction in trained manpower, because of death, injury or labour going abroad. The new chamber had made a good start in raising awareness of its activities and it had started making placements in a number of trades. The chambers of commerce were helping with subsidies but more were needed. In the future, the placement service needed to be improved, local offices created throughout the region and special help was needed for candidates from large families who could not afford to educate their children. Eighty per cent of the 1924 budget of 20,000 francs was provided by the department and the communes. The chamber of commerce's contributions were relatively small.[81] Apart from Vidal, the Minister for Technical Education, Clémentel was lending his support. If no longer the Minister of Commerce, his influence as senator for the Puy-de-Dôme and president of the *conseil-général* was still considerable. In 1924 a major exhibition of craft skills was held in Clermont-Ferrand.[82]

In conclusion it is clear that regional initiatives and funding were fundamental to the success of technical education. These initiatives are a clear demonstration of the importance of economic regionalism after the war.

[78] Région du Centre, no. 5 (janvier 1922), 12–16; no. 6 (février 1922), 20.
[79] 'Comité régional 26 janvier 1922', Région du Centre, no. 8 (avril 1922), 13.
[80] Région du Centre, no. 13 (septembre 1922), 10.
[81] 'Rapport sur l'exercice 1923', Région du Centre, no. 36 (juillet 1924), 243–254.
[82] Région du Centre, no. 39 (novembre 1924), 369–371.

## Banque Populaire

A new *banque populaire* of the Auvergne region was also set up in Clermont-Ferrand after the war. Lagaye produced a report for the chamber of commerce. The Minister of Commerce had asked how chambers could support the setting up of such banks in the light of the enabling law of 13 March 1917. Lagaye's report said that markets were more demanding than they had been before the war. Constant innovation in products was necessary and hence the need for credit for small- and medium-sized businesses who could not have recourse to the large commercial banks. The need to rebuild the French economy after the war had also increased the demand for capital. At this stage, the chamber of commerce indicated that it could offer some financial support and awaited the outcome of a study organized by the prefecture.[83] The bank finally opened its doors on 1 February 1921.[84] The director outlined its commercial policy in an article in *Région du Centre* in November 1922. Their function, he said, was purely to help commerce and industry, and not to get involved in other speculative banking operations. There was a central fund in Paris which received state help but the local operations were autonomous with local directors who knew the needs of local firms. There were already *banques populaires* in the region at Tulle, Montluçon and Le Puy but the Clermont bank wanted to see branches open in other regional towns.[85]

## Conclusion

We have demonstrated in this chapter that regional leaders in industry and commerce in the Auvergne, working through the chambers of commerce and the new economic region, but also with other organizations, promoted important changes in infrastructure, technical training and finance in the years following the First World War. In the case of railways and canals, it was mainly a question of pressing the government to act. In the case of the major hydro-electric project on the Dordogne river, the regional elite led the project and attempted to organize much of the financing on a regional basis. This initiative is significant because it is an

[83] Travaux Clermont-Ferrand, 1919 (séance 14 juin 1919), 81–85; (séance 24 juillet 1919), 89–90.

[84] 'Comité régional 7 janvier 1921', Région du Centre, no. 1 (mars–avril 1921), 41–42. See also Travaux Clermont-Ferrand, 1920 (séance 26 mars 1920), 43.

[85] Région du Centre, no. 15 (novembre 1922), 3–6.

early example of public authorities attempting to invest in and manage an infrastructure project rather than letting it out to private concessionaires as the state might formerly have done. In the fields of technical training, management education, and banking, the regional elite had more scope to lead and finance a project.

This is not to say there was no local initiative in these matters before the war. However, there is no doubt there was a renewed impetus for economic development in the regions after the war, to rejuvenate an economy devastated by the conflict and to make it competitive in world markets. Industrialists and businessmen in the regions sought to show central government that it did not have the economic expertise on its own to make the necessary changes. Economic necessity forced central government to allow these regional leaders to have some freedom to pursue their goals. They took full advantage while the government was dealing with pressing international problems. The economic initiatives outlined above and in the chapter on Lorraine were not a random collection of actions but part of a self-conscious and well-thought out programme.

Among regionalists before the war, there was great interest in decentralization, in freeing the regions from tight central control, in allowing responsible people in the regions to take decisions for themselves. This would lead to quicker decisions, greater efficiency and would increase support for government actions. The practical programmes of the post-war economic regionalists were fully in accordance with an important strand of regionalist thinking which stretched back before the war. Regionalism had sometimes been described as a reactionary mind-set, a hankering after a lost past. It had many manifestations. It could be backward-looking but also forward-looking, a programme for modernization and practical government.

## Bibliography

(1924, mai). *Aménagement Hydro-électrique de la 2ème section du bassin de la Dordogne, notice technique et financière.*

Blanchard, R. (1922). La Houille blanche dans le Massif Central français. *Revue de géographie alpine, 10*(3), 353–396.

Bouneau, C. (1985). La contribution de l'électricité à la génèse de l'aménagement du territoire en France, pendant la première moitié du xxe siècle. In F. Caron & C. Bouneau (Eds.), *L'UPEPO, 1922-1946 : génèse et logiques de l'interconnexion, Bulletin d'histoire de l'électricité* (Vol. 6, pp. 75–102).

Chadefaux, R. (1924). *La Région économique de Clermont-Ferrand*. Thèse pour le doctorat, Faculté de Droit de Paris.

Diez, J. (1925). *Le Régionalisme économique, organisation de la Région économique de l'Est (Nancy)*. Thèse pour le doctorat, sciences politiques et économiques.

Druelle-Korn, C. (2014). La modernisation inachevée de l'aménagement du territoire, le cas de la VII[e] Région (Limousin, Poitou, Charentes). In A. Aglan, M. Margairaz, & P. Verheyde (Eds.), *De la croissance à la crise (1925-1935): Le moment Tannery, une tentative avortée de modernisation conservatrice et libérale à l'heure de la mondialisation* (pp. 155–172).

*Journal Officiel*. (1924, décembre 30), 4941–4943.

*La Montagne*. (2019, juillet 19). *Clément Rambaud ou la vie d'un grand Corrézien*. www.lamontagne.fr

*Le Commerce*, no. 72. (1922, novembre).

*Le Moniteur du Puy-de-Dôme* 1918

Lévy-Leboyer, M., & Morsel, H. (Eds.). (1994). *Histoire générale de L'Électricité en France, T.II 1919–1946 L'Interconnexion et le Marché*.

*Région du Centre*, 1920, 1921, 1922, 1923, 1924, 1925

*Travaux de la Chambre de Commerce de Clermont-Ferrand*, 1914, 1915, 1916, 1918, 1919, 1920, 1921, 1923, 1924.

Veitl, P. (2013). *L'Invention d'une région : les Alpes françaises*.

*XVIIe* Région Économique, Groupement régional de Clermont-Ferrand, *Compte-rendu des travaux du comité régional et du comité consultatif régional économique, séances des 29 avril 1918, 17 juin et 19 août 1919* (Clermont-Ferrand, s.d.).

(1922) XVIIe Région économique, groupement régional des chambres de commerce. Aménagement hydro-électrique de la 2ème section du bassin de la Dordogne, demande de concession présentée par la Région économique du Centre (Clermont-Ferrand)

CHAPTER 5

# Economic Regionalism in Lorraine: Success Factors

Chapters 5 and 6 will attempt to identify the key factors before 1918 which contributed to making the economic regions of Lorraine and the Auvergne successful pioneers of regional economic development. This will provide a yardstick against which the other economic regions can be judged. We will concentrate on regional identity and a sense of solidarity, the power of attraction of the regional centre, the presence of a regional university since their reform in 1896 and the strength of regional leadership.

## The Regional Sense of Identity in Lorraine Before 1914

Before the First World War, the German border cut through Lorraine. The war itself further affected the feeling of regional solidarity because the front was never far distant. Before the war Nancy was a thriving regional centre and the seat of a university with several newly created technical and scientific institutes.

We start with an analysis of the ideas of those who had thought about Lorraine's identity in the pre-war years. The region and its characteristics were an important preoccupation for the elite of society whose influence was based on certain institutions. The ideas of this institutional elite in Lorraine can be divided into a number of discourses which reveal what the



T. Cudbird, *The Origins of Economic Regions in France, 1918-1940*,
https://doi.org/10.1007/978-3-032-04422-8_5

region meant to them, what was distinctive about it. There was a discourse concerned with the definition of the region of Lorraine, its boundaries, its history and culture, the character of its people and the position of the regional capital Nancy. There was also a discourse about the economy of Lorraine, pride in rapid industrialization and also in the close cooperation of its industrialists, bankers and academics to achieve economic growth. At the same time there was a consciousness that Lorraine faced particular challenges such as the improvement of transport in a land-locked region and the sourcing elsewhere of vital raw materials like coal. Encompassing these discourses was a regionalism which included discussion about how much power should be devolved to Lorraine.

Lastly there was a discourse which might be described as 'regional nationalist,' a particular variation of French nationalism brought about by the special circumstances of Lorraine. There were various shades of this "regional nationalist" discourse, from the more extreme views of men like Maurice Barrès, the writer and propagandist, to the circumspect patriotism of a politician like Poincaré. Because of the history of invasion, fear of German power was very strong in Lorraine. However, the discourse about Germany contained a number of elements which sometimes conflicted with each other. Industrialists and academics wanted to copy some German best practice as well as compete with Germany. There was hatred and fear certainly, but also admiration. There were conflicted feelings too about the German annexation of the Moselle (eastern Lorraine)—a desire to liberate the Moselle among *Lorrains français*, particularly those who had originated from occupied Alsace-Lorraine, but also an accommodation with reality among those actually living under German rule.

## Defining Lorraine

Most of France's regions in 1900 did not refer to defined geographical or administrative spaces with definite boundaries. Even the boundaries of Brittany on its peninsula were a matter of dispute. The identity of the regions was largely based on history, culture and sometimes language. Most of the distinctive features of regions related to the past, although this was not the case with Lorraine as we shall see.

Lotharingia, the ancient name for Lorraine, was the land of Lothair, the grandson of Charlemagne, and referred to the northern part of the Middle Kingdom which he was awarded by the Treaty of Verdun in 843. It had a separate existence in the Middle Ages and early modern period within the

Holy Roman Empire. There were two centres of power: the three bishoprics of Metz, Toul and Verdun and the dukedom of Lorraine based in Nancy. The bishoprics were absorbed by France in the sixteenth century and the independent dukedom in the eighteenth. Lorraine as a legal entity ceased to exist after 1789, although it was widely used in speech and literature.

The leading historian of eastern France in the early twentieth century and professor at the University of Nancy, Robert Parisot, published articles on Lorraine before the war and a major book in 1924. He founded a *Fédération historique lorraine*, which grouped a number of learned societies and also the *Société lorraine des Études locales.*[1] Addressing the *Union régionaliste lorraine,* of which he was vice-president, and the *Société des Amis de l'Université* in 1908 and later the regionalist Congress at Nancy during the exhibition of 1909, he argued that Lorraine consisted of the three departments of Meurthe-et-Moselle, Meuse and Vosges for historical, geological, geographical and economic reasons and because of the common attitudes and character of its inhabitants.[2] (The department of the Moselle had been annexed by Germany in 1871, except for the arrondissement of Briey in the west which was joined to the department of Meurthe-et-Moselle. The Moselle was returned to France in 1919.) He said that Lorraine was definitely distinct from the Franche-Comté and Champagne, but agreed that the borders were difficult to determine because the geographical, economic and historical links he had identified could work in opposite directions.

Parisot's definition of Lorraine was based essentially on the fact that it had a distinctive history. He concludes that despite a history of being split up:

> The memory of the former unity of the Moselle has not entirely disappeared; it has persisted across the ages and although weakened, it constitutes a force which the organisers of the future Lorraine region will know how to put to work.[3]

[1] P. Barral, L'Esprit lorrain, cet accent singulier du patriotisme français (Nancy, 1989), 121.

[2] R. Parisot, La Lorraine région française (Nancy, 1909), 1–15, also published in Le Pays Lorrain, 5e année (1908), 465–480.

[3] Parisot, La Lorraine région française, 8.

That the historical heritage of Lorraine was still very much a live subject for educated Lorrainers was shown by the popularity of historical pageants at the 1909 exhibition in Nancy which attracted over two million visitors.[4]

For an ethnographer like Charles Sadoul the answer to the question 'where were the frontiers of Lorraine?' was also unclear. The year 1904 saw the opening of the *Musée lorrain*. At the museum, Sadoul built up an extensive collection of the popular arts of Lorraine which he described in a book in 1920.[5] He also made an enormous personal collection of items and documents covering local folklore—popular songs, tales and beliefs. Sadoul was a very successful communicator of Lorraine's traditional culture through public meetings and the journal *Le Pays lorrain*. For Sadoul, Lorraine was partly defined by the common style of its furniture and houses and the common characteristics of its folk tales or its cooking. He had no doubt that its customs and the Francophone Lorraine *patois* were key to any definition. In practice he settled for the three departments, plus of course the occupied Moselle.[6]

If history and ethnography did not provide a totally clear answer to the question 'where is Lorraine?' it seemed best to fall back on the traditional character of the people. Robert Parisot wrote that:

> Character and aptitudes are, I would dare say not determined, but at least strongly influenced by geographical, historical and economic factors.[7]

The inhabitants were hard-working, tenacious and thrifty, even miserly, because they lived in a harsh climate and cultivated a soil which, left to itself, would not give them a living. They were warlike, reserved, defiant and cold in manner because of the constant attacks they had had to face. Like a lot of men who worked the soil, they were attached to their traditions and beliefs and not inclined to chase after new ideas. In politics they preferred sensible and moderate opinions. Their practical approach was even seen in their religious activity. For example, in the last two centuries their religious orders had been teachers and cared for the sick rather than

[4] L. Laffitte, Rapport général sur l'exposition internationale de l'Est de la France, Nancy, 1909 (Paris, 1912), 451–480, 772–818.

[5] C. Sadoul, L'Art rustique en France 1. La Lorraine, Ph. de Las Cases (ed) (Paris, 1920), 9. C. Sadoul, Le Mobilier lorrain (Ensembles et détails) (Paris, 1926), préface.

[6] D.Hopkin, 'Identity in a Divided Province : The Folklorists of Lorraine, 1860–1960', *French Historical Studies*, Vol. 23, No. 4 (Fall 2000), 655–661.

[7] Parisot, Lorraine région française, 12.

being contemplatives.[8] Lucien Brocard defined the characteristics of the Lorraine population in similar terms.[9]

The trouble with relying on the character of the Lorraine people was that such a view took little account of how Lorraine was changing. Some writers felt that the traditional Lorraine virtues were under attack, as workers left the land and large numbers of foreign immigrants arrived to work in the iron and steel industry in the early years of the twentieth century. By 1914 there were approximately 50,000 Italians living in Briey and they accounted for 60% of all steelworkers being recruited in the *Pays Haut* in the decade before the war.[10] Hottenger, in his work on the mining district of Briey, talked about the effect of rural depopulation on the sober, patient and energetic characteristics of the Lorraine peasant. This analysis and support for reforms to encourage peasants back to the land was common in many parts of France among conservatives of the period.[11] The large numbers of foreign workers recruited brought their own social problems as they were absorbed into completely new settlements in small agricultural communities. Hottenger was concerned about the effects of rapid industrialization on the morality of rootless labourers brought in from Italy.[12] Hottenger was a sociologist based in Nancy and closely allied as were some of his colleagues with the Musée Social of Ferdinand Le Play.

If defining the land according to the character of its people was not entirely satisfactory either, perhaps relying on the appearance of the Lorraine countryside might help. Revering the countryside of Lorraine seems to have been a common part of this discourse of definition. At one level regional writers like Moselly had a strong sense of where they came from. For example, Moselly's *Le Rouet d'ivoire: enfances lorraines* contains a charming description of the festival of St. Nicholas traditionally celebrated in Lorraine.[13] However, a lot of writing was not about the actual

[8] Parisot, Lorraine région française, 12–13.

[9] L. Brocard, 'Le Développement économique de la Lorraine française', Séance de la Société d'économie sociale (Paris, 14 avril 1913), 731.

[10] P-D. Galloro, A. Boubeker, Histoires et mémoires des immigrations en Lorraine (Nancy, 2013), 170.

[11] G-A. Hottenger, Le Pays de Briey (Nancy, 1911), 34–35.

[12] M. François, 'Hottenger', la France savante, (Comité des travaux historiques et scientifiques web site https://cths.fr/an/prosopographie.php, 15.12.2008). Hottenger, Briey, 110–120, 132, 204.

[13] Moselly, E., Le Rouet d'ivoire : enfances lorraines 1907, P. Goudot (ed) (Nancy, 1990), 73.

**Fig. 5.1** Portrait of Maurice Barrès, courtesy of the Bibliothèque Nationale de France

countryside at all but about some mystical recreation of it for political purposes. Writers like Barrès (Fig. 5.1) projected their own ideas onto the landscape—*la terre et les morts.* The very identity and values of Lorraine lay in the soil itself and the province's glorious past. Barrès in works like *Les Déracinés* had emphasized the importance of local roots. In this novel he developed the key idea that to be a true son of eternal France, you had to be rooted in the soil of somewhere like Lorraine.[14] He enshrined this attachment to the land in the hill of Sion-Vaudémont south of Nancy. Formerly a site, among many others, for Marian pilgrimage, it became for Barrès a place to celebrate what it meant to be truly a son of Lorraine but also French. His novel *La Colline inspirée* (1913) is very closely based on the historical events associated with the hill and he mentioned it in other

[14] M. Barrès, Les Déracinés, (Paris, 1897).

works. The first major gathering there occurred in 1873 after German troops had left French Lorraine and was a kind of expiation for past faults. The German occupation of the Moselle was sometimes described as *Po Tojo*, in Lorraine dialect '*Ce n'est pas pour toujours.*' Regular gatherings occurred up until the First World War. Barrès used to take his friends on conducted tours. He wrote in *Pages lorraines* in 1903:

> I never dreamed up there without eternal Lorraine swelling my soul that I thought was defeated.[15]

Others latched on to this mystical streak of Barrès.

So history and culture were not totally reliable guides to the sense of identity among inhabitants of Lorraine. Such definitions also looked to the past. They did not describe how Lorraine was at the turn of the twentieth century, a region of rapid industrial growth.

## The Economy of Lorraine

If the Lorrainers thought about the boundaries of their region from an economic point of view, they might come up with different answers from a historian like Parisot. Parisot described the growth of industry in Lorraine, but he did not address the wider connections of Lorraine's industries as they exploited improved communications to import raw materials and export to new markets.[16] While Brocard accepted the traditional three departments as Lorraine, as a geographer he had a much greater sense of the dynamism of modern industry, and this was the subject of a lecture on Lorraine in Paris in 1913. What he noted continually were the connections between Lorraine's industries and those of other regions:

> Thus the great Lorraine industries have engendered around them as it were waves of activity which, in reinforcing each other, have gradually spread little by little to the three Lorraine departments, to the region of the East and at last to the whole of France.[17]

[15] Quoted in P. Martin, 'la Colline inspirée : lieu d'une mémoire lorraine, nationale ou européenne', in P. Martin and F Roth (eds), Mémoire et lieux de mémoire en Lorraine (Sarreguemines, 2003), 244.

[16] Parisot, Lorraine région française, 1–15.

[17] Brocard, 'Développement économique', 733.

In his review as organizer of the 1909 exhibition, Louis Laffitte argued that the region of the East was a whole stretching from Flanders to the Franche-Comté with complementary industries. He believed this wider region could be based on the exchange of raw materials and manufactured goods.[18] This would consist of 12 departments—Ardennes, Aube, Côte-d'Or, Doubs, Jura, Marne, Haute-Marne, Meurthe-et-Moselle, Meuse, Territoire de Belfort, Vosges, Haute-Saône.[19] So the boundaries of Lorraine shifted depending on the author's knowledge and experience.

The 1909 exhibition took place in Nancy. Pride in Nancy, the regional capital, exemplified all that was new and exciting in contemporary Lorraine. Before the First World War, Nancy was the pre-eminent city in eastern France, the focus of Lorraine's identity. Metz and Strasbourg were potential rivals but had been annexed by Germany in 1870. Nancy was a transport hub for the railways and canals of the region with lines which did not have to go through Paris.[20] Its growth had been spurred by the influx of skilled refugees from Alsace-Lorraine after 1870. When the president of the session of the *Société d'Économie sociale* introduced Lucien Brocard before his lecture in 1913, he said it was perhaps Nancy which, among all the provincial cities of France, most had the attraction and the qualities of a regional capital.[21]

The 1909 exhibition gave the city the chance to show off not only its historic buildings but also new areas of urban development, new architecture and new cultural assets. Among all the industrial exhibits, it gave special prominence to the art nouveau *École de Nancy* which had made striking innovations in the decorative arts like glass making (Daum), furniture and interior design, art and sculpture (Émile Gallé and Victor Prouvé) and architecture (Emile André). André created a regional style of domestic architecture which was very influential in Nancy.[22] It was unusual to have such a flourishing artistic movement as the *École de Nancy* outside Paris, the fruit of economic growth and prosperity, reconciled to the

[18] L. Laffitte, 'Revue générale de l'exposition de Nancy 1909', Bulletin de la Société industrielle de l'Est, 27e année, no. 76 (janvier 1910), 13–17.

[19] Laffitte, 'Revue générale de l'exposition', lxvii.

[20] J. Diez, Le Régionalisme économique: Organisation de la Région économique de l'Est (Thèse de doctorat, sciences politiques et économiques, Paris, 1925), 20–21.

[21] Brocard, 'Développement économique', 728.

[22] H. Doucet, Art nouveau et régionalisme: Émile André (1871–1933), architecte et artiste (Versailles, 2004), 276–285.

modern world and using modern materials.[23] The 1909 exhibition was also important in bringing the three discourses together. Here regional historians, academics, custodians of the region's culture like Sadoul, artists and businessmen could rub shoulders and learn about each other's achievements. Many of the important institutions in Lorraine like the chamber of commerce of Nancy, the *Société industrielle de l'Est*, Nancy University, the municipal council of Nancy and the *Musée lorrain* were involved in running the event.

Lorraine's pride in its recent industrial achievements was undoubtedly an important part of its sense of identity. The exhibition of 1909 beat the drum for the economic achievements of Lorraine, the fastest growing region in France in the decade before 1914, a region which evoked admiration throughout France and beyond. The opening up of the Briey iron ore mines had some of the features of a 'gold rush,' a real boom economy. The exhibition was a showcase for all the industries of Lorraine, both new ones like iron and steel and chemicals and old established sectors such as textiles, brewing, glass making and agriculture.

Economic commentators kept coming back to the unique partnership between the university and industry as a key to success. This partnership was evident in the creation of excellent technical institutes as part of the University of Nancy in cooperation with local industrialists. Together they created schools of applied chemistry (*Institut de chimie*, 1887–90), brewing (1893), electrical and mechanical engineering (*Institut électrotechnique et de mécanique*, 1905), zoology and microbiology, and geology (*Géologie appliquée*, 1908).[24] The university enjoyed great prestige as a result in the years before the First World War. Parisot talked about this partnership between the university and industry in his lecture in 1909. He wrote:

> You will not be astonished that I recall here the role which the Faculty of Sciences of the University of Nancy has played in the development of our industry: the Faculty has provided numerous engineers and foremen for the factories and manufacturing firms of the region.[25]

[23] L. Laffitte, Rapport général, 36.

[24] Laffitte L., Rapport général sur l'exposition internationale de l'Est de la France, Nancy, 1909 (Paris, 1912), 98–104, 563–564 and 578.

[25] Parisot, Lorraine région française, 12.

It was very much the intention of the 1909 Nancy exhibition to make visible the connection between science and industry.[26] Hauser, the architect of the regional groupings of chambers of commerce in 1918, picked up this theme when he wrote for *L'Union économique de l'Est*:

> Is it not at Nancy that a fertile alliance of men of science and men of action has given birth to these university institutes, whose work has not been without use to the prosperity of your mines and forges, your caustic soda plants, your breweries, your weaving and dying plants?[27]

Brocard could not help but mention this cooperation in his 1913 lecture in Paris. He homed in on two aspects—the provision of engineers educated in the practices of regional industries and also the discovery of coal in Meurthe-et-Moselle.[28]

Of prime importance to the academic community was the desire to rival the excellence of Germany's universities in technical education. The university also gave a visible demonstration of its support for economic growth by providing commercial education. An *École supérieure de Commerce* had been created in 1896 by the chamber of commerce and the *Société industrielle de l'Est*.[29] It attracted donations from a number of industrialists and businessmen of the region.[30] A university *Institut commercial* followed in 1911 under the aegis of the *Faculté de Droit*. It received support from the chamber of commerce, the *Société industrielle de l'Est* and the *Office économique* of the chamber of commerce. They nominated half the board of directors, and the latter two bodies provided financial subsidies.[31] Between 1896 and 1914 industrialists made useful donations to a number of technical institutes, but most funds came from

[26] M-J. Choffel-Mailfert, 'La Visibilité sociale de l'alliance de la science et de l'industrie : l'exposition de l'est de la France en 1909', in F. Birck, A. Grelon (eds), Un Siècle de formation des ingénieurs électriciens, ancrage local et dynamique européenne, l'exemple de Nancy (Paris, 2006), 195–236.

[27] H. Hauser, 'La Création de la Région économique de l'Est', L'Union économique de L'Est, 2e année (15 mai 1918), 109.

[28] Brocard, 'Développement économique', 741.

[29] F. Birck, *L'École des Mines (ENSMN) 1919-2012 ; entre université, grand corps d'État et industrie* (Nancy, 2013), 59.

[30] A. Grelon, F. Birck (eds), Des Ingénieurs pour la Lorraine XIXe–XXe siècles (Nancy, 2007), 101.

[31] A. Logette, Histoire de la Faculté de Droit de Nancy 1768–1864–1914 (Nancy, 1964), 149–152.

the state.[32] Beyond organizing donations of money, businessmen were occasionally involved in other ways in the development of these institutes. The *Société industrielle de l'Est* was often the conduit through which businessmen talked to academics about these plans. The society, which was founded in 1884, had 244 members after its launch. Members of the university were invited to attend later. Its main purpose was to spread knowledge useful to business.[33]

Another element of this discourse on the economy was to highlight the support given to local industry by regional banks. Henri Hauser drew attention to this factor.[34] There were a number of home-grown banking institutions which had developed in the nineteenth century. Speaking in 1913 Lucien Brocard praised Lorraine banks as the crown on the economic region of Lorraine. He said that institutions like la Banque de Nancy, la Banque Lévy-Bettinger, la Banque Renauld and la Société nancéienne, which together had a capital of over 180 million francs, concentrated on advances to regional industries in the longer term.[35]

The Lorraine economy was characterized by the diversity of its enterprises, from steel to the decorative arts, and the complexity of their interconnections.[36] Cooperation between local industrialists was said to be another feature of the Lorraine economy. The *Société industrielle de l'Est* and the chambers of commerce were important forums for cooperation. The Nancy chamber was pre-eminent because it included the most

[32] E. Bolmont, J-R. Cussenot, 'La Faculté des sciences de Nancy: équipements, personnels et enseignements', in L. Rollet, M-J. Choffel-Mailfert (eds), Aux Origines d'un pôle scientifique; faculté des sciences et écoles d'ingénieurs à Nancy, du Second Empire aux années 1960 (Nancy, 2007), 170 bar chart 1898–1904; 285. Association amicale des anciens élèves de l'École nationale supérieure des industries chimiques (Institut chimique) (Nancy, 1920), 134–135. F. Birck, 'Des Instituts annexes de facultés aux écoles nationales supérieures ingénieurs, à propos des trois écoles nancéiennes', in A. Grelon, F. Birck (eds), Des Ingénieurs pour la Lorraine XIXe–XXe siècles (Nancy, 2007), 159–160.Birck, L'École des Mines, 55, 56–58.

[33] F. Birck, 'La Société industrielle de l'Est et la diffusion de l'information scientifique et technique, de la fin du XIXe siècle à la veille de la Première Guerre Mondiale', S. Benoit, G. Emptoz, D. Woronoff (eds), Encourager l'innovation en France et en Europe (Paris 2006), 173–198.

[34] H. Hauser, 'La Création de la Région économique de l'Est', L'Union économique de L'Est, 2e année (15 mai 1918), 109–111. See also J. Duplantier, Le Régionalisme économique et spécialement la Région économique de Bordeaux et du Sud-Ouest (Thèse de doctorat, Faculté de Droit, Bordeaux, 1929), 231–233.

[35] Brocard, 'Développement économique', 728, 737–738.

[36] Brocard, 'Développement économique', 730, 735.

important industries in the region in the department of Meurthe-et-Moselle. It set up an *Office économique* to collect and publish data about the progress of the regional economy. There were regional bodies for major industries like *Le Comité des Forges et Mines de Fer de Meurthe-et-*Moselle founded in 1906.[37] Jean Buffet, the local banker, believed this spirit of cooperation was a cause of Lorraine's industrial prosperity. He noted that, in the Nancy chamber of commerce, representatives of *la grande métallurgie* came together with less prominent industries and commerce, with intellectuals, engineers and jurists.[38] He talked about "a type of regional solidarity."

So the interconnections created a feeling of regional solidarity that the Lorraine industries belonged together and could help each other. The term solidarity was used to refer to the spirit of the 1909 exhibition.[39] No one believed that one factor caused the miracle of Lorraine's prosperity. It was due to a number of complex causes. The university, the banks, industries working together and a skilled work force all had their part of play as Albert Lebrun expressed it.[40] All these factors were well summed by Cavallier before the congress of regional bankers in 1909:

> What characterises this movement of expansion is above all its extreme and growing complexity; it is the multiplicity, the diversity of industries which grow together on Lorraine soil, it is the cohesion, the intimate collaboration, the profound solidarity of all these overlapping and indissolubly linked activities. Lorraine presents to the highest degree the spectacle of an economic unity of which the parts develop while relying on each other.[41]

We can see clearly how the region after the war would have benefited from this history of economic dynamism, with the university playing a leading role. We can also see how Nancy was the centre of this activity with a number of business and cultural institutions apart from the university.

[37] J. Moine, Les Barons du fer, les maîtres de forges en Lorraine (Nancy, 1989), 179.

[38] J. Buffet, 'Le Rôle des banques locales en Lorraine, les conditions du développement des banques locales', Chambre de Commerce Nancy, vol. 7 1909, (appendix séance 21 juillet 1909), 561.

[39] L. Laffitte, 'Discours de clôture de l'exposition', Chambre de Commerce Nancy, vol. 7 1909, (appendix séance 21 juillet 1909), 645–646.

[40] A. Lebrun, La Politique du fer au cours de la guerre, la question de Briey, conférence faite à la Société industrielle de l'Est, le 18 juin 1920 (Nancy, 1920), 22.

[41] F. Baudin, Histoire économique et sociale de la Lorraine, ii L'Essor 1870–1914 (3 vols, Nancy, 1992, 1993, 1997), 236.

If Lorraine's economy was a success story, what would be the best administrative framework to enhance the regional dynamism? Here we come to consider regionalism in a political sense. The 1909 exhibition was unashamedly regionalist in its aspirations as Louis Laffitte said in his long report published in 1912. The exhibition allowed a host of regional organizations to run congresses including the *Union régionaliste lorraine* (URL) and the *Fédération régionaliste française* (FRF) jointly. In separate sessions the URL planned to study not only decentralization of the government but also the development of the region, that is, regionalist issues. The *URL*'s secretary, Charles Berlet, entered a plea for regional reform.[42] Three original signatories of the 1865 Nancy manifesto on decentralization were present in 1909 to discuss this issue.[43]

The URL had been founded by 30 academics after a visit by Jean Charles-Brun, the secretary of the FRF, in 1902. In 1907 the URL asked the FRF's current president, Louis Marin, to talk about decentralization in Nancy. Marin said regionalism was concerned with the development of local resources and the qualities and intellectual aptitudes of the people, based on local traditions. It was all about regions realizing their full potential. It was different from what he called traditionalism, the conservation of local folklore, artistic styles, music, architecture, furniture. For Marin fostering the development of Lorraine would contribute to the development of France as a whole.[44] The URL was a more broadly based organization than the FRF. Its committee included Poincaré and Méline, 13 deputies, the Rector of Nancy University, several Lorraine mayors, the president of the Nancy chamber of commerce and the *Société industrielle de l'Est*.

## Regional Nationalism

For many Lorrainers, loyalty to the region was indistinguishable from loyalty to France. Proximity to Germany had made Lorraine the vanguard in the defence of *la patrie* against its powerful neighbour. The need to compete with Germany economically and also to be in a constant state of

[42] C.Berlet, Les Provinces au XVIII siècle et leur division en départements: essai sur la formation de l'unité française (Paris, 1913), 551–552.

[43] 'Congrès régionaliste de Nancy', Le Pays lorrain, 6e année (1909), 379–380; Laffitte, Rapport général, 808.

[44] 'Union régionaliste lorraine', Le Pays lorrain, 4e année (1907), 299.

vigilance dominated their thinking. The impact of the Thirty Year's War, the advance to Valmy in 1792, the Prusso-Austro-Russian invasion of 1814 and of course the Prussian invasion of 1870 were referred to frequently in contemporary writing and journalism.[45] *L'Est républicain* referred to the German occupation of 1870 in 17 articles between April and July 1914.[46] Most important, local school children were taught this history in primary school, as a locally produced *manuel scolaire* reveals.[47] As a frontier province Lorraine had always felt a strong identification with the army, and this feeling was still alive in 1914.

This nationalist discourse was very much in evidence at the 1909 exhibition in Nancy. Lorraine's leaders, political, economic and intellectual, wanted to show that the France of the East was growing and successful after the setback of the annexation of Alsace-Lorraine in 1871. It was this desire to compete with Germany which explained the creation of excellent technical institutes on the German model as part of the University of Nancy.

In view of the German threat it is not surprising that the desire to compete successfully with Germany coloured much thinking in Lorraine about the economy. We find it in Brocard's lecture of 1913. He asked why Lorraine's economic growth took off after the war of 1870. Several causes came together by chance to account for this leap forward, such as the discovery of the iron ore around Briey in 1880. French metallurgists were searching desperately for new sources of iron ore because Germany had taken most French mines in the Treaty of Frankfurt. Another factor was the emigration to France of industrialists from Alsace-Lorraine after 1871.[48] Louis Laffitte in 1912 explained how after 42 years of hard work and many difficulties Lorraine had rebuilt the riches and resources wrenched from France's grasp in 1870.[49]

[45] K. Varley, Under the Shadow of Defeat, the war of 1870-1 in French Memory (Basingstoke, 2008), 179–180.

[46] L'Est Républicain (6 avril 1914), 1 col a–c; (13 avril), 1 col a–c; (14 avril), 1 col a–c; (20 avril), 1 col a–b; (28 avril), 1 col c–d; (4 mai 1914), 1 col a–b; (12 mai), 1 col a–c; (18 mai), 1 col a–b; (25 mai), 1 col a–b; (1 juin 1914), 1 col a–b; (15 juin), 1 col a–b; (22 juin), 1 col a–b; (29 juin), 1 col a–b; (6 juillet 1914), 1 col a–b; (9 juillet), 1 col a–b; (20 juillet), 1 col a–b; (27 juillet), 1 col a–b.

[47] L. Bouchot, Vingt-cinq Leçons sur l'histoire de la Lorraine et du Barrois (Nancy, 1919), 66–70.

[48] Brocard, 'Développement économique', 731–732.

[49] L. Laffitte, 'L'évolution économique de la Lorraine', Annales de Géographie, t.21, no. 20 (1912), 393–417.

So the Lorrainers, like many other Frenchmen, had mixed feelings about Germany—admiration for her industrial, technical and intellectual achievements but also resentment of her occupation of Alsace and Lorraine and a fear of German economic and military power. These feelings surfaced constantly in the press. Lorraine was constantly on the *qui vive*, as one writer said, and suspicious of foreigners whose loyalty was questionable.[50] This 'regional nationalist' line was also actively encouraged by the church in Lorraine. Turinaz, the Archbishop of Nancy before and during the First World War, was known as the frontier bishop. He believed that patriotism was holy.[51]

There was one other factor peculiar to Lorraine which accounted for the suspicious discourse about Germany. In the Meurthe-et-Moselle there were 72,000 people, and in the Vosges 50,764, from Alsace-Lorraine, who had either opted for French nationality and left after the Treaty of Frankfurt, or who lived in France anyway, or who left subsequently, maybe to enrol in the French military. These *Alsacien-Lorrains* in the two Lorraine departments accounted for 23% of all those in France.[52] Emigrants from Alsace-Lorraine played a prominent role in Nancy post-1870, as described by Hélène Sicard-Lenattier in her 2002 doctoral thesis, *Les Alsaciens-Lorrains à Nancy 1870–1914, une ardente histoire*. They accounted for 30% of the population.[53] Naturally enough, more than the average Frenchman or woman, these exiles took a particular interest in how Germany was governing Alsace-Lorraine, and they did not like what they heard. The press was full of stories of petty German oppression.[54] Even the radical *L'Étoile de l'Est* ran 27 stories on this subject between April and July 1914, including news of the arrest of the writer and artist Hansi who satirized the German regime.[55]

[50] L'Éclair de l'Est (6 mai 1914).

[51] C-F. Turinaz, Discours patriotiques (Nancy and Paris, 1900), 211, 218.

[52] A. Wahl, L'Option et l'émigration des Alsaciens-Lorrains, 1871–1872 (Paris, 1974), 237. R. Gildea, Children of the Revolution (London, 2008), 295 quoting Wahl, L'Option et l'émigration, 102–34, 190–191.

[53] H. Sicard-Lenattier, Les Alsaciens-Lorrains à Nancy 1870–1914, une ardente histoire (Haroué, 2002). P. Clemendot, 'Population de Nancy (1815–1938)', Annales de Démographie Historique, 1973, 120.

[54] L'Étoile de l'Est (9 juin 1914). For the Saverne affair see Journal de la Meurthe (8 janvier 1914), 1 col b–c; (13 janvier), 1 col c; (20 janvier), 1 col c.

[55] L'Étoile de l'Est covered Hansi on (19 mai 1914), (26 juin 1914), (10, 13, 16 juillet 1914).

A prolific propagandist and printer who skilfully developed the idea of Alsace-Lorraine being French at heart was Émile Hinzelin. His belief that most of those in the occupied territories were loyal to France and could not wait to throw off the German yoke was shared by others including Maurice Barrès in his novel *Colette Baudoche* (1909), in which the heroine turns down marriage to a German school teacher to remain true to France. In fact, the picture painted by Hinzelin and Barrès was at variance with reality. The Mosellans had developed an independent identity of their own, separate from Alsace but also different from France in certain respects. This was to cause friction after 1918. The Moselle department was part of the German Empire for 48 years.[56] In practice, until the advent of war, most French speakers had accepted the reality of German rule but sought protection for their identity within the German Empire. There was support in Alsace and Lorraine for a truly separate status, similar to other German states, but *Elsass-Lothringen* (Alsace-Lorraine) remained a *Reichsland.*

However, it is true that there were elements of loyalty to France within the Moselle population. The linguistic division of the area survived and French was still spoken in the south and west. Metz, once a French-speaking city, adopted German because of the presence of the government, but French was widely spoken in the countryside. French was still used in schools in the French-speaking areas and taught as a second language in the German zones.[57] Westphalen the folklorist concentrated before 1918 on preserving the culture of French speakers in the Moselle.[58] *Le Souvenir français* was allowed to perpetuate the memory of those who had fallen in the war of 1870.

The Catholic church played a key role as a bridge between French and German Catholics. The Concordat of 1801 continued in Alsace and Lorraine which meant that the Catholic church was in effect a state church, and bishops, for example, were appointed by the government. Schools in Alsace and the Moselle were confessional schools, mostly Catholic but some Protestant. This was totally different from the lay state which resulted from the Ferry reforms of 1880–2 and the Combes reforms of 1903–5 in

[56] See F. Roth, La Lorraine annexée: étude sur la présidence de Lorraine dans l'Empire allemand, 1870–1918 (Metz, 2011).

[57] S. L. Harp, Learning to be Loyal. Primary Schooling as Nation Building in Alsace and Lorraine 1850–1940 (North Illinois University, 1998), 87–99.

[58] Hopkin, 'Identity in a Divided Province', 662–664.

France. The Archbishop of Metz, Benzler, was appointed by the German government, but he was sympathetic to the plight of French-speaking Catholics and supported their right to learn their faith, for instance, the catechism, in their own language.

## The Impact of the War on Lorraine's Sense of Identity

Lorraine's sense of identity as the advance guard of France in resisting German aggression was reinforced by the events of 1914–1918. We find in some war diaries the belief that Lorraine soldiers had the personal characteristics to take on this role. Abel Ferry, nephew of Jules Ferry, was Under-Secretary of State for Foreign Affairs at the beginning of the war and represented the Vosges. Later he played a key role in the Army Commission of the Chamber of Deputies and was killed at the front in 1918. He described the endurance of his Lorraine soldiers on 18 November 1914:

> Four fifths of our men are from the invaded lands, from the Meuse or the Nord, docile and brave. They sleep in the trench, on soaking ground. They rest badly in glacial barns without straw, with air currents blowing through; sometimes they are apathetic because of an excess of fatigue. Their resignation gives us a great lesson, a moral!![59]

There is no doubt that the shock of invasion crystalized this regional variant of French patriotism. There was intense fighting on the Lorraine front only 15 kilometres to the east of Nancy in August 1914 as the French army, after initial reverses, struggled to prevent the Germans making a decisive break through. The military casualties were high, towns and small villages were destroyed by shell fire and a flood of refugees fled west and south. John Horne and Alan Kramer in their seminal work on the German 'atrocities' concluded that they did occur in Belgium, northern France and in Lorraine.[60] Four areas were affected in Lorraine—the northern

[59] A. Ferry, Les Carnets secrets d'Abel Ferry 1914–1918 suivis de lettres et notes de guerre, A. Loez and N. Offenstadt (eds) (Paris, 2005), 355.

[60] J. Horne, A. Kramer, German Atrocities 1914, A History of Denial (Yale, 2001), 113–139, 419–431. J. Horne, A. Kramer, 'German "Atrocities" and Franco-German Opinion, 1914: The evidence of German soldiers' diaries', The Journal of Modern History, vol. 66 No. 1 (March 1994), 1–33.

steel making area of Meurthe-et-Moselle between Pont-à-Mousson and Longwy, the northern area of the Meuse department, an arc of towns to the east of Nancy, and the foothills of the Vosges. Horne and Kramer show that the German army seems to have been prey to exaggerated fears of partisans, perhaps because in close fighting in village streets, firing by retreating French troops could seem like firing by residents from buildings.

The atrocities made a huge impact on Lorraine opinion and the sense of regional identity, not only during the conflict but also for many years afterwards. They affected decisions taken after 1918 on economic and social issues as well as on defence. Despite qualifications about propaganda written after the event and the common thread of anti-German feeling across France, there was a distinctive Lorraine experience of invasion, partly because of the memories of 1870. Unlike other areas of northern France, in Lorraine the sense of outrage found a voice in a substantial city, Nancy, and its surrounding region which were not occupied.

The most publicized atrocities occurred in Noméný and Gerbéviller where 55 and 60 civilians died, respectively, and many women were raped.[61] *L'Est républicain* ran 16 stories specifically on the Lorraine atrocities in August and September 1914, *L'Étoile de l'Est* four, *L'Éclair de l'Est* six, and *L'Impartial de l'Est* twelve. *L'Est républicain* transcribed many of the French witness accounts uncritically.[62] Some of the stories, repeated in the press in Lorraine and elsewhere, were exaggerated, like reports of women and children having their hands cut off or women having their breasts removed.[63] However, for most Lorrainers in August 1914, the circumstantial evidence appeared overwhelming. The contemporary literature spawned by the atrocities is extensive: published accounts, private letters and diaries and government correspondence.

The coverage of the atrocities clearly went beyond mere reportage, and it cannot be taken at face value as an indication of shifting regional identity. In the hands of skilled writers, it became propaganda deliberately created by the press and the authorities with a number of objectives: to encourage soldiers and civilians to resist; to put France in a good light with opinion in neutral countries, particularly the United States, and to argue the case for special government help for refugees and in reconstruction.

[61] Horne, Kramer, German Atrocities, 64–66, 199 for Noméný Gerbéviller.
[62] Horne, Kramer, German Atrocities, 205.
[63] L'Impartial de l'Est (1, 3 septembre 1914).

Out of all this the cult of 'La Lorraine martyre' was born. Hinzelin coined the phrase in the title of another of his books *La Lorraine martyre.*[64]

Barrès used his pen and prestige to draw attention to Lorraine's fate in his work *La Lorraine dévastée*, part of a collection sponsored by the Franco-American committee. Having trumpeted France's superior civilization and Lotharingia as a zone of transition between the Latin and the Teutonic, he wrote a devastating attack on the atrocities including on the Bavarian General Clauss with a glass of champagne in his hand as his troops destroyed Gerbéviller.[65]

There was one area of wartime Lorraine where feelings of regional identity were very different and that was the German occupied Moselle department. Because the Moselle was very near the front and Metz was a fortress and pivot for German troop movements, the German army placed the area under martial law. Inhabitants who were suspected of French sympathies were taken into custody. Some fled to France. The French language was banned in public places, and French newspapers and journals suppressed. German papers were censored. Benzler, the Bishop of Metz, insisted on maintaining French language services in French-speaking areas. However, French assets were subject to sequestration. In general historians suggest that the harshness of German military rule made Mosellans and Alsatians much more accepting of reunification with France in 1918.[66]

## Regional Solidarity in Action in Lorraine

This regional solidarity in the face of the enemy was reinforced by the measures which the regional elite took to support the war effort and alleviate the suffering caused by the fighting through the chamber of commerce of Nancy, the *Société industrielle de l'Est* and the *Fédération des Commerçants de Nancy*.

Frequently, in making their appeals for money and other forms of support, the elite appealed not only to national patriotism but also to a sense of regional solidarity. All over France, citizens were urged by the elites to support fundraising efforts to alleviate the suffering of victims of the

[64] E. Hinzelin, La Lorraine martyre (Paris, 1915).

[65] M.Barrès, *La Lorraine dévastée* (Paris, 1919), 5, 122, 150–151.

[66] F. Roth, Robert Schumann, Du lorrain des frontières au père de l'Europe (Paris, 2008), 79–93.

conflict. There were a series of fundraising days or *journées* for national causes such as the *Journée du Poilu, Journée des Orphelins de la Guerre*, etc. In Lorraine these fundraising efforts were often presented in a way which might appeal to regional loyalties. For example, the street sellers sometimes dressed in regional costume, as in the case of the *Journée du Canon 75* in aid of the army. *L'Est républicain* recorded that the sellers put on the costumes of Alsace and Lorraine which doubled the receipts.[67]

In addition, the Lorraine elites set up special Lorraine organizations to cope with particular challenges faced by their region. First of all, they had to tackle the problems of displaced persons, those who had had to flee their homes as the German armies advanced. They created two organizations—the *Société d'Assistance aux Réfugiés, Évacués et Sinistrés de Meurthe-et-Moselle* and the *Comité d'Assistance nancéienne aux Familles réfugiées des Villages lorrains*. The former became more of a lobbying organization to represent the interests of those who had suffered losses. In due course it was concerned with the issue of compensation and help with reconstruction. The president was Maurice de Wendel, the iron master, the vice-president a judge. The secretary-general came from the iron works in Longwy. Of the nine members of the committee, four more came from iron companies, one was a judge, one, Jean Buffet, the banker from Nancy, one an industrialist unspecified, one a professor in the medical faculty and one a member of the chamber of commerce.[68] Camille Cavallier, vice-president of the chamber of commerce, had an important role in dealing with the issue of compensation for property owners who had suffered losses. He was nominated by the Minister of the Interior to sit on the national *Commission supérieure pour l'Évaulation des Dommages de Guerre*.[69]

The *Comité d'Assistance nancéienne* concerned itself with more practical help for displaced persons in the short term. For example, they set up refuges in two former barracks in Nancy, the Caserne Molitor and the Caserne Druot. Here they provided not only lodging, food and clothing, but also education, an infirmary and work placements. The chamber of commerce's concern with the plight of refugees continued right through the war. In 1917 they were active in providing clothing and shelter for those going back to villages now liberated from the German occupation.

[67] L'Est républicain (9 février 1915), 2 col c.

[68] AD M-et-M, 1 J 1288 'Bulletin de Meurthe-et-Moselle (1 décembre 1914)'.

[69] Chambre de Commerce Nancy, vol. 13 1915, (séance 10 avril 1915), 12–13.

The *Société industrielle de l'Est* was also heavily involved in programmes to alleviate the suffering caused by the war after 1914. It could of course draw on a wide range of contacts in the world of industry, commerce and academia. It concentrated in particular on the fate of Lorrainers in the army who were prisoners in Germany. It supported the retraining of soldiers injured in the war and developed schemes for finding them work.[70] It also helped many other organizations relieving those suffering from the effects of the war in a variety of ways.[71]

By 1917 the attention of the Lorraine elites was turning more seriously to the reconstruction of refugees' homes. A committee (*Comité de Reconstitution des Régions éprouvées par la Guerre, Meurthe-et-Moselle, Meuse et Vosges*) to rebuild regions damaged in the war was formed under the patronage of the Société industrielle de l'Est, and it started to publish the journal *La Reconstruction lorraine*, which became an important influence in the process.[72] The committee's focus was on the technical and financial aspects of reconstruction and also on protecting regional interests between central government and local construction projects.[73] *La Reconstruction lorraine's* overall approach was that the government could not be expected to do everything. It could only give general direction and therefore private organizations would have to step in.[74] As the war progressed reconstruction became the dominant issue for the Lorraine elite. The formation of appropriate local organizations was key as we have already seen. Lorraine was signalling that it wanted to be master of its own destiny and not have solutions imposed from Paris.

So far we have seen that by 1918 Lorraine had a strong sense of identity and solidarity which meant the initiatives taken by the post-war economic region were generally supported. Nancy was clearly equipped to take a leadership role in the region, particularly because it had a distinguished university. We turn now to the question of regional leadership.

[70] La Société industrielle de l'Est pendant la guerre 1914–1918 (Paris, 1919), 4.

[71] Société industrielle pendant la guerre, 30.

[72] L'Est républicain (2 août 1917), 2 col a.

[73] Bulletin de la Société industrielle de l'Est, no. 129 (1917), 14–18. La Reconstruction lorraine (15 juillet 1917), 4–5, (15 août 1917), 1–2, (15 septembre 1917), 1, (15 octobre 1917), 1, (15 août 1918), 1.

[74] La Reconstruction lorraine (15 juillet 1917), 1–3.

## The Nancy Chamber of Commerce and Other Regional Institutions

To assess the leadership role adopted by the Nancy chamber of commerce, we have to understand what sort of institution it was. The chambers of commerce in France were partly a public service and partly independent corporations to further their members' interests. The French sometimes referred to them as *corps intermédiaires*.[75] They operated according to laws passed by the Chamber of Deputies, the most recent of which for our purposes dated from 1898 and 1908. Their role was mainly consultative and they had three main purposes. Firstly, they were asked by government for their views on economic matters and they could of their own initiative send opinions to relevant ministries or authorities. Secondly, they represented their area in official councils and other organizations. Thirdly, they could run services like providing information for business, journals, instruction in relevant subjects and operating trading enterprises like *bourses de commerce* (commodity trading) and *magasins généraux* (general stores). They could become concessionaires for public works like ports or navigable waterways, and with the Minister of Commerce's agreement take out loans.[76] They were legally constituted bodies who could sign contracts and own property, unlike the new economic regions. The officers of each chamber (president, vice-presidents, secretary, treasurer) and the members were chosen in organized elections by designated businesses who paid the *patente*, or business tax. The number of businesses so designated was 8,000 in Meurthe-et-Moselle out of a total of 27,000 *patentés*.[77] Local committees decided the split of members to be chosen between manufacturing industry and commerce. The number of businesses voting in the biennial elections for a third of all members was normally 10% or less, although it could reach 20% among industrialists as it did in Nancy in

[75] C. Druelle-Korn, Introduction, in C. Druelle-Korn (ed), Les Corps intermédiaires entre l'état et le marché (Limoges, 2011), 7–27.

[76] C. Thouvenel, 'Étude sur la Chambre de Commerce de Nancy d'après les procès-verbaux des séances de 1871 à 1914' (Thèse D.E.S., Université de Nancy, Juin 1967), 16. C.Druelle-Korn, 'La Modernisation inachevée de l'aménagement du territoire, le cas de la VIIe région, (Limousin, Poitou, Charentes), in A. Aglan, M. Margairaz, et P. Verheyde (eds), De la croissance à la crise (1925-1935) Le moment Tannery; Une tentative avortée de modernisation conservatrice et libérale à l'heure de la mondialisation (Paris, 2014), 157.

[77] M. Paul-Cavallier et B. Fayolle, Trente ans d'action économique 1905–1935, la Chambre de Commerce de Nancy (Nancy, 1936), 11.

the first round elections in December 1919.[78] Chambers of commerce drew revenue from an addition to the *patente* tax, a regular amount which could be increased after consultation with the Minister of Commerce.[79] The elected members could also co-opt a number of additional members, *membres correspondants*, who had relevant expertise in industry, commerce, banking or the academic world. The maximum number was fixed by law. At the beginning of 1919, there were 17 *membres titulaires* in the Nancy chamber and 23 *membres correspondants.*

In the case of the Nancy chamber, the members were drawn exclusively from the wealthy industrial, commercial and professional bourgeoisie. They represented a limited number of mainly larger firms. Their influence rested on the quality of their membership and the way they used their powers to represent the economic interests of their region and to effect change. It is clear that the members of the Nancy chamber realized this from a discussion in January 1919. Vilgrain, the president, said that it was now up to businessmen to win the peace by rebuilding France. Chambers of commerce had limited powers so their greatest service was to make themselves heard because they represented important interests. Cavallier called for more representatives of economic interests to get involved in politics, and Dreux, the future president, said they could represent their legitimate interests through the press.[80] Dreux also stressed that the members must attend regularly and produce high-quality work in the various commissions if their opinions were to be given consideration.[81]

We will start by examining the membership of the Nancy chamber in the post-war period and how far they were committed to the chamber by looking at their attendance. We will also consider the commissions of the chamber where much of the important work was done. These commissions were subcommittees on various topics and were chosen by the full chamber. We will cover certain permanent organizations set up by the chamber to promote its aims. Lastly we will consider the membership of an important organization with overlapping membership and aims, the *Société industrielle de l'Est,* which operated out of the same building as the chamber of commerce.

[78] SGA 7247, dossier janvier 1920, election results déc 1919–jan 1920; the printed record gives turnout and the number of registered electors and firms.

[79] Thouvenel, 'Chambre de Commerce', 11–19.

[80] Chambre de Commerce Nancy, vol. 17 1919, (séance 25 janvier 1919), 122–123.

[81] Chambre de Commerce Nancy, vol. 17 1919, (séance 6 mai 1919), 159.

The main officers of the chamber were a tightly knit group who provided continuity of leadership over a considerable period. In 1919 there was a change in this group of officers known as the *bureau*. Louis Vilgrain, president of the Grands Moulins of Nancy, long time president and a member since 1895, became a *président d'honneur* and was replaced by *maître de forges* Alexandre Dreux, who remained president throughout the post-war years under consideration here. As head of the *Aciéries de Longwy,* he had stayed behind enemy lines throughout the war near his works. Camille Cavallier, another *maître de forges* and head of *Pont-à-Mousson,* was first vice-president. Bertrand-Oser was secrétaire-membre. He was an industrialist who had held interests in brewing (Grands Brasseries de Maxéville) and chemical products (Meyer, Bertrand-Oser et fils). Antonin Daum from the glass-making enterprise was treasurer.

At the end of 1921 Cavallier retired because of ill health, although he was still influential as a *président honoraire* and took an active interest in the chamber's affairs. Alfred Krug became a vice-president. At that time, he was also a member of the board of directors of the *École nationale des Eaux et Forêts* in Nancy. Albert Tourtel, owner of a well-known brewery in Nancy, joined the *bureau* as treasurer, replacing Daum who became secrétaire-membre. Bertrand-Oser also became a vice-president. All of these officers had been members for at least ten years, some longer. At the end of 1923, there was yet another re-shuffle of roles in the *bureau*. Krug left and Marcel Paul became treasurer. Daum became a vice-president and Tourtel secrétaire-membre. Paul had been co-opted at the end of 1920 and elected as a *membre titulaire* the following year. He was the son-in-law of Camille Cavallier and a director of Pont-à-Mousson. He served the chamber until 1944, becoming president in 1936 in succession to Alexandre Dreux.[82] During all these changes, Benjamin Fayolle provided continuity as the paid secretary of the chamber. He had been an employee of Pont-à-Mousson and was a constant point of contact between Cavallier and the chamber after Cavallier resigned, as their voluminous correspondence in the Cavallier archives at Saint Gobain reveals.[83]

In any consideration of the Nancy chamber, one question which immediately arises is how important were the *maîtres de forges*? There were more

[82] Details of membership and attendance at meetings have been extracted from the Chambre de Commerce Nancy, 17e année 1919 to 22e année, 1924.

[83] SGA 7248, dossier correspondance 1917–1924, Cavallier letter to Vilgrain 10 février 1919.

representatives of this industrial sector than any other, but their number was not preponderant. In 1919 there were three other elected *maîtres de forges* apart from those on the *bureau:* Fernand de Saintignon from *Longwy Bas*, Ernest Nahan from *Micheville* (in which Pont-à-Mousson had a shareholding) and Paul Labbé from *Gorcy*. In 1919 engineer François Villain was a *membre correspondant*. They were joined at the beginning of 1920 by Théodore Laurent from *Homécourt* and François de Wendel, from the family who were the most powerful of iron masters. He was also a member of the Chamber of Deputies. At the same time Paul Nicou from *Micheville* (replacing Nahan) and Charles Fould from *Aciéries Pompey* joined as *membres correspondants*, followed *at the start of 1922* by Auguste Dondelinger of *Société métallurgique Senelle-Aubeuge, Longwy and* Édouard Dreux, son of Alexandre, also from *Aciéries de Longwy*. (Édouard Dreux died suddenly in 1923.) Jean Raty, another iron master from *Saulnes*, joined as a co-opted member in 1924. It is also significant that when the Moselle chamber of commerce was relaunched in 1922, Humbert de Wendel became president.[84] Correspondence in the Cavallier archive suggests strongly that the *maîtres de forges* wanted at least to maintain their position among the chamber's membership. A letter from Dreux to Cavallier on 14 January 1921 says that if he persists in his plan to resign, then they are minded to replace him with his son-in-law Marcel Paul.[85] However, he does agree that it would be excessive for one firm to have two representatives.[86] Another note dated 2 December 1921 from Nicou of *Micheville* to Cavallier makes it clear that, now Nahan of the same business has resigned, he is putting his name forward to take over.[87] Cavallier wrote to Fayolle on 27 September 1923 saying that were Dreux ever to resign, then he must be replaced by another metallurgist.[88] Moine concludes in his chapter on the chambers of commerce in *Les Barons de fer* that the Nancy chamber did present a convenient way for the *maîtres de forges* to defend their interests while putting their demands forward along

[84] Communications de la Chambre de commerce de Metz, 1e année, No. 2 mars 1922, (séance 4 février 1922), 2.

[85] SGA 7248, dossier correspondance 1917–1924, Dreux letter to Cavallier 14 janvier 1921.

[86] Ibid., letter Cavallier to Fayolle 20 janvier 1919.

[87] SGA 7248, dossier correspondance 1917–1924, letter Nicou to Cavallier 2 décembre 1921.

[88] SGA 7247, dossier 1923, Cavallier letter to Fayolle 27 septembre 1923.

with other industrialists. We will see later how they pressed issues of particular concern to them.[89]

The number of iron masters may have been growing but other sectors were represented. Among industrialists there were representatives from *Cristalleries Baccarat*, the Belgian chemical firm *Solvay* based near Nancy and the *Société des Filatures de l'Est*, the textile industry being an important employer in the region. The regional banks were represented by the *Société nancéienne de Crédit industriel et de Dépôts* and the *Banque Renauld*. The energy generating sector had members and also the *Chemins de Fer de l'Est*. The university was consistently represented by its Professors of Commercial Law and for a time by Brocard, the Professor of Geography. Imbeaux of *Ponts-et-Chaussées* was a constant presence. Agriculture was not within the remit of the chamber, although it was discussed from time to time. Louis Michel, one of Lorraine's leading agriculturalists and a senator, became a *membre correspondant* in 1920. In view of the massive programme of reconstruction, the building trade was important. Gustave Simon, formerly Mayor of Nancy during the war and a leading builder and industrialist, joined the chamber as a co-opted member and was later elected directly.

The practical level of support from members by attending chamber meetings was quite high. *Bureau* members were present for almost all meetings, except when called away by other duties, as Dreux and Cavallier were from time to time. Turnout among elected members was usually well over 50%. The same applied among co-opted members, although it dropped below this more frequently. Some co-opted members hardly showed up at all and were eventually replaced. The time commitment for fully engaged businessmen was considerable. We can see this when examining the correspondence of Cavallier and his associates. Cavallier frequently had to ask someone else to step in and Dreux as president appealed in the same way to Cavallier. Being a member not only involved attending between nine and eleven meetings a year. There were nine commissions in 1919, but this figure almost doubled as more subjects became of concern to members during the phase of reconstruction of the economy. In 1920 these commissions covered legislation, roads, railways and canals, transport and tariffs, finances, L'Office économique, customs and international economic relations, teaching and apprenticeships, agriculture, general economic organization and re-population policy. In addition, there were

[89] J. Moine, Les Barons du fer; les maîtres de forges en Lorraine (Nancy, 1989), 211.

temporary commissions on the peace treaty, reconstruction, the stock exchange, the Eastern region, the Office des Transports de l'Est and the Énergie électrique de l'Est.[90]

The bulletins of the chamber also list around 12 national consultative bodies each year in which various leading members of the chamber were involved and through which they could exercise their influence. They covered areas such as railways, interior navigation nationally and for the north-east, postal and telephone services, war damage, the *Chemin de Fer de l'Est*, the *Mines de la Sarre*, natalism, international chambers of commerce, colonies, public assistance and arts and manufactures. Most of the burden of attending these was shared between the president and the vice-presidents. Dreux, for example, was nominated to the board of directors of the *Mines de la Sarre*, now under French control.[91] He also sat on the *Conseil supérieur des Chemins de Fer* in Paris, which made important recommendations on policy to the minister.[92] There was also a *Conseil supérieur du Commerce et de l'Industrie* with representatives from chambers of commerce.[93]

Dreux was also expected to attend regular meetings of the presidents of all the chambers of commerce in France in Paris. This was a very important forum through which an individual chamber like Nancy could gain support for its initiatives. The secretary Fayolle attended similar meetings for secretaries-general.[94]

To add to its network of influence, the chamber had set up two additional organizations—the *Office économique de l'Est* to provide timely information to businessmen and the *Office des Transports* which drew together all the chambers of the wider region of eastern France and discussed with the railway companies (and canal operators) everything from rolling stock, tariffs and timetables to new lines. (The various *Offices des Transports* had a national committee on which Dreux also sat.)[95]

The Nancy chamber also spread its ideas through publications. During the war it had set up the *Union économique de l'Est*. In 1920 Krug was asked to review the future of this publication and change the remuneration of its director, Fayolle, also the secretary of the Nancy chamber. In a

[90] Chambre de Commerce Nancy, vol. 18 1920, xi–xiv.
[91] Chambre de Commerce Nancy, vol. 17 1919, (séance 9 décembre 1919), 254.
[92] Chambre de Commerce Nancy, vol. 21 1923, (séance 9 mars 1923), 54.
[93] Union économique de l'Est, 8e année (1er juillet 1924), 254.
[94] SGA 7249, dossier renseignements divers, note dated octobre 1922.
[95] Chambre de Commerce Nancy, vol. 21 1923, (séance 9 mars 1923), 54.

note attached to a letter to Dreux on 19 February 1920, Krug said that the journal had been set up in the war to defend the economic interests of the region and to prepare for the return to normal working, by well documented and objective studies.[96] At the same time Fayolle also set up *le Petit Officiel du commerce français*, a weekly designed to inform businessmen about all relevant administrative acts.[97] Propaganda through such publications continued to be a pre-occupation of the chamber, and particularly of Camille Cavallier. Pont-à-Mousson already had a shareholding in the main Nancy paper *L'Est républicain*.[98] Cavallier was involved in several projects for new journals covering economic affairs after the war. They either failed to get off the ground or lasted a limited period. In 1918 he subscribed to a new publication called *la Démocratie nouvelle* to which the Michelin brothers also gave money. It lasted until 1925. As we shall see Cavallier was very concerned about two issues in particular—the repopulation of France after the war and the provision of reliable supplies of coal. He thought that the press could play a role in espousing these causes.[99]

The regional elite used another influential industrial institution in Nancy, the *Société industrielle de l'Est,* to spread its influence. Here we find a similar type of membership to the chamber of commerce, perhaps with a greater emphasis on relevant professions such as engineers, chemists, lawyers and professors, than on firms. After all, the function of this society was to spread relevant knowledge to industry rather than to represent its interests. Of 19 members of the *bureau* between 1883 and 1920, six were members of the chamber of commerce including Louis Vilgrain and François Villain. The membership of the society's various councils also included a number of members of the chamber of commerce including Antonin Daum, Krug, Hammer of the *Compagnie générale électrique* and Imbeaux, Cavallier, Édouard Dreux and Fould.[100]

[96] SGA 7247, dossier 1920/février-mars, letter from A. Krug to A. Dreux 19 février 1920 and 'projet de règlement concernant les publications crées pendant la guerre, rapport de M. A. Krug, secrétaire-membre, Président de la Commission de l'Office économique'.

[97] Ibid., 'Note de service 1 juillet 1920'.

[98] SGA 7289, papiers divers, dossier L'Est républicain, 'Notes de service du service des participations (M. Fremiot) à Monsieur Cavallier, 21 mars 1925, 27 mars 1926'.

[99] Moine, Barons du fer, 271–275.

[100] L. Rollet, Liste des membres des conseils de la Société industrielle de l'Est (1883–1920) (Laboratoire d'Histoire des Sciences et de Philosophie, Archives Henri Poincaré, Histoire des Institutions scientifiques et éducatives de Nancy (HISE), Université de Lorraine, http://hise-nancy.ahp-numerique.fr/items/show/13).

The *Région économique*, the grouping of 12 chambers of commerce of the East set up on Clémentel's initiative, was run from the Nancy chamber's offices under Dreux's chairmanship. The question arises as to how much importance the Eastern region's discussions had as opposed to those within individual chambers. Unfortunately, no official record of the region's deliberations seems to have survived.[101] There are brief summaries in the journal *Union économique de l'Est* published by the Nancy chamber. The region did not appear to be the driving force of change in the region. Rather it was a forum where action between different chambers could be coordinated when this was advantageous. It was responsible for setting up the *Société régionale des Études du Rhin* to see how the river could be better used for transport and power generation. A series of articles by Benjamin Fayolle, secretary of the Nancy chamber, written in 1926 described some of the activities of the region—the *Office des Transports*, the *Office économique de l'Est*, which we have already noted, and the setting up of a regional exhibit at a major industrial fair in Paris.[102] It seems that the general assembly of the region only met annually and that action between meetings was initiated by the *bureau* of two representatives from each adhering chamber.[103] Marcel Paul, writing some years later, claimed that the real initiatives came from the Nancy chamber.[104]

Why, one might ask, did these no doubt very busy men running important firms and organizations give themselves so much work. Attending the meetings of all these bodies put a heavy load on the chamber of commerce's officers, principally on Alexandre Dreux. Apart from the national committees noted above, he chaired the meetings of the *Région économique, the Office des Transports,* and the *Société des Études du Rhin*. On 9 and 10 March 1923, Dreux spent two days in Nancy chairing all his meetings.[105] It seems reasonable to assume that these businessmen felt the effort

[101] (Note made November 2020) - Any archives in the Nancy chamber of commerce building were transferred to the Archives départementales some years ago. Before the pandemic the Archives départementales were closed for over a year because of a move so I was unable to consult them in person on this subject. However, the electronic catalogue sent to me very recently does not suggest they possess any records likely to change the account of the eastern region given here.

[102] Union économique de l'Est, 10e année (15 avril 1926), p. 95.

[103] Union économique de l'Est, 5e année (15 octobre 1921), p. 54. SGA 7247, 'Note de service pour Cavallier 24 juin 1920'.

[104] M.Paul-Cavallier et B.Fayolle, Trente ans d'action économique 1905–1935, la Chambre de Commerce de Nancy (Nancy, 1936), 22.

[105] Chambre de Commerce Nancy, vol. 21 1923, (séance 10 avril 1923), p. 62.

essential, because they could implement some beneficial changes regionally and also influence central government on other matters. They ran a powerful lobbying organization with connections regionally and into central government and various quangos. It also had a publicity machine.

## Conclusion

In summary we have isolated a number of factors which account for the subsequent success of the Lorraine region after 1918—a strong sense of identity and regional solidarity; a growing economy pre-1914 allied to an agreed need for reconstruction after the war; a pre-eminent regional centre in Nancy; strong leadership with a sense of mission and a powerful network through which they could exercise influence; robust links between regional institutions, industry and commerce and lastly the strength of Nancy University and its technical institutes. In many ways Lorraine was a model for what Clémentel hoped the other regions would become. The activity level and commitment to development of the region's economic leaders in the Nancy chamber of commerce has no parallel anywhere else.

## Bibliography

AD M-et-M, 1 J 1288 'Bulletin de Meurthe-et-Moselle (1 décembre 1914)'.

*Association amicale des anciens élèves de l'École nationale supérieure des industries chimiques (Institut chimique)*. (1920).

Barral, P. (1989). *L'Esprit lorrain, cet accent singulier du patriotisme français.*

Barrès, M. (1897). *Les Déracinés.*

Barrès, M. (1919). *La Lorraine dévastée.*

Baudin, F. (1992, 1993, 1997). *Histoire économique et sociale de la Lorraine, ii L'Essor 1870–1914* (3 Vols).

Berlet, C. (1913). *Les Provinces au XVIII siècle et leur division en départements: essai sur la formation de l'unité française.*

Birck, F. (2006). La Société industrielle de l'Est et la diffusion de l'information scientifique et technique, de la fin du XIXe siècle à la veille de la Première Guerre Mondiale. In S. Benoit, G. Emptoz, & D. Woronoff (Eds.), *Encourager l'innovation en France et en Europe* (pp. 173–198).

Birck, F. (2007). Des Instituts annexes de facultés aux écoles nationales supérieures ingénieurs, à propos des trois écoles nancéiennes. In A. Grelon & F. Birck (Eds.), *Des Ingénieurs pour la Lorraine XIXe–XXe siècles.*

Birck, F. (2013). *L'École des Mines (ENSMN) 1919-2012 ; entre université, grand corps d'État et industrie.*

Bolmont, E., & Cussenot, J.-R. (2007). La Faculté des sciences de Nancy: équipements, personnels et enseignements. In L. Rollet & M.-J. Choffel-Mailfert (Eds.), *Aux Origines d'un pôle scientifique; faculté des sciences et écoles d'ingénieurs à Nancy, du Second Empire aux années 1960.*

Bouchot, L. (1919). *Vingt-cinq Leçons sur l'histoire de la Lorraine et du Barrois.*

Brocard, L. (1913). Le Développement économique de la Lorraine française. In *Séance de la Société d'économie sociale* (pp. 727–745).

(1909). *Bulletin de la Chambre de Commerce Nancy* (Vol. 7) (appendix séance 21 juillet 1909), 1915, 1919–1924.

*Bulletin de la Société industrielle de l'Est*, janvier 1910, 1917.

Choffel-Mailfert, M.-J. (2006). La Visibilité sociale de l'alliance de la science et de l'industrie : l'exposition de l'est de la France en 1909. In F. Birck & A. Grelon (Eds.), *Un Siècle de formation des ingénieurs électriciens, ancrage local et dynamique européenne, l'exemple de Nancy* (pp. 195–236).

Clemendot, P. (1973). Population de Nancy (1815–1938). *Annales de Démographie Historique.*

*Communications de la Chambre de commerce de Metz.* (1922).

Diez, J. (1925). *Le Régionalisme économique: Organisation de la Région économique de l'Est.* Thèse de doctorat, sciences politiques et économiques.

Doucet, H. (2004). *Art nouveau et régionalisme: Émile André (1871–1933), architecte et artiste.*

Druelle-Korn, C. (2011). Introduction. In C. Druelle-Korn (Ed.), *Les Corps intermédiaires entre l'état et le marché* (pp. 7–27).

Druelle-Korn, C. (2014). La modernisation inachevée de l'aménagement du territoire, le cas de la VII[e] Région (Limousin, Poitou, Charentes). In A. Aglan, M. Margairaz, & P. Verheyde (Eds.), *De la croissance à la crise (1925-1935): Le moment Tannery, une tentative avortée de modernisation conservatrice et libérale à l'heure de la mondialisation* (pp. 155–172).

Duplantier, J. (1929). *Le Régionalisme économique et spécialement la Région économique de Bordeaux et du Sud-Ouest.* Thèse de doctorat, Faculté de Droit.

Ferry, A. (2005). In A. Loez & N. Offenstadt (Eds.), *Les Carnets secrets d'Abel Ferry 1914–1918 suivis de lettres et notes de guerre.*

François, M. (2008, December 15). Hottenger. In *la France savante* (Comité des travaux historiques et scientifiques web site https://cths.fr/an/prosopographie.php)

Galloro, P.-D., & Boubeker, A. (2013). *Histoires et mémoires des immigrations en Lorraine.*

Gildea, R. (2008). *Children of the Revolution.*

Grelon, A., & Birck, F. (Eds.). (2007). *Des Ingénieurs pour la Lorraine XIXe–XXe siècles.*

Harp, S. L. (1998). *Learning to be loyal. Primary schooling as nation building in Alsace and Lorraine 1850–1940.* North Illinois University.

Hinzelin, E. (1915). *La Lorraine martyre.*
Hopkin, D. (2000). Identity in a divided province: The folklorists of Lorraine, 1860–1960. *French Historical Studies, 23*(4), 655–661.
Horne, J., & Kramer, A. (1994). German "Atrocities" and Franco-German Opinion, 1914: The evidence of German soldiers' diaries. *The Journal of Modern History, 66*(1), 1–33.
Horne, J., & Kramer, A. (2001). *German atrocities 1914, a history of denial.* Yale.
Hottenger, G.-A. (1911). *Le Pays de Briey.*
*Journal de la Meurthe.* (1914).
*L'Éclair de l'Est* 1914.
*L'Est Républicain* 1914, 1915, 1917
L'Étoile de l'Est 1914.
*L'Impartial de l'Est* 1914.
*L'Union économique de l'Est* 1918, 1921, 1924, 1926.
*La Reconstruction Lorraine*, 1917, 1918
*La Société industrielle de l'Est pendant la guerre 1914–1918.* (1919).
Laffitte, L. (1912a). L'évolution économique de la Lorraine. *Annales de Géographie, 21*(20), 393–417.
Laffitte, L. (1912b). *Rapport général sur l'exposition internationale de l'Est de la France, Nancy, 1909* (pp. 451–480, 772–818).
*Le Pays lorrain, 1907,* 1909.
Lebrun, A. (1920). *La Politique du fer au cours de la guerre, la question de Briey, conférence faite à la Société industrielle de l'Est, le 18 juin 1920.*
Logette, A. (1964). *Histoire de la Faculté de Droit de Nancy 1768–1864–1914.*
Martin, P. (2003). la Colline inspirée : lieu d'une mémoire lorraine, nationale ou européenne. In P. Martin & F. Roth (Eds.), *Mémoire et lieux de mémoire en Lorraine.*
Moine, J. (1989). *Les Barons du fer, les maîtres de forges en Lorraine.*
Moselly, E. (1907). *Rouet d'ivoire.*
Parisot, R. (1909). *La Lorraine région française.*
Paul-Cavallier, M., & Fayolle, B. (1936). *Trente ans d'action économique 1905–1935, la Chambre de Commerce de Nancy.*
Rollet, L. *Liste des membres des conseils de la Société industrielle de l'Est (1883–1920).* Laboratoire d'Histoire des Sciences et de Philosophie, Archives Henri Poincaré, Histoire des Institutions scientifiques et éducatives de Nancy (HISE), Université de Lorraine. http://hise-nancy.ahp-numerique.fr/items/show/13
Roth, F. (2008). *Robert Schumann, Du lorrain des frontières au père de l'Europe.*
Roth, F. (2011). *La Lorraine annexée: étude sur la présidence de Lorraine dans l'Empire allemand, 1870–1918.*
Sadoul, C. (1920). In P. d. L. Cases (Ed.), *L'Art rustique en France 1. La Lorraine.*
Sadoul, C. (1926). *Le Mobilier lorrain (Ensembles et détails).*
SGA 7247, 'Note de service pour Cavallier 24 juin 1920'.

SGA 7247, dossier 1920/février-mars, letter from A. Krug to A. Dreux 19 février 1920 and 'projet de règlement concernant les publications crées pendant la guerre, rapport de M. A. Krug, secrétaire-membre, Président de la Commission de l'Office économique'. 'Note de service 1 juillet 1920'.

SGA 7247, dossier 1923, Cavallier letter to Fayolle 27 septembre 1923.

SGA 7247, dossier janvier 1920, election results déc 1919–jan 1920; the printed record gives turnout and the number of registered electors and firms.

SGA 7248, dossier correspondance 1917–1924, Cavallier letter to Vilgrain 10 février 1919.

SGA 7248, dossier correspondance 1917–1924, Dreux letter to Cavallier 14 janvier 1921. Letter Cavallier to Fayolle 20 janvier 1919. Letter Nicou to Cavallier 2 décembre 1921.

SGA 7249, dossier renseignements divers, note dated octobre 1922.

SGA 7289, papiers divers, dossier *L'Est républicain*, 'Notes de service du service des participations (M. Fremiot) à Monsieur Cavallier, 21 mars 1925, 27 mars 1926'.

Sicard-Lenattier, H. (2002). *Les Alsaciens-Lorrains à Nancy 1870–1914, une ardente histoire.*

Thouvenel, C. (1967, Juin). *Étude sur la Chambre de Commerce de Nancy d'après les procès-verbaux des séances de 1871 à 1914.* Thèse D.E.S., Université de Nancy.

Turinaz, C-F. (1900). *Discours patriotiques.*

Varley, K. (2008). *Under the shadow of defeat, the war of 1870–1 in French memory.*

Wahl, A. (1974). *L'Option et l'émigration des Alsaciens-Lorrains, 1871–1872.*

CHAPTER 6

# Economic Regionalism in the Auvergne: Success Factors

We will now examine the success factors identified in Lorraine and see how far they apply in the Auvergne. We will start with the framework for thought and action which the regional sense of identity gave the elites in the Auvergne. We have seen that among regional elites, there was a very clear sense of Lorraine's identity in the years immediately before the First World War. The Duchy of Lorraine as an independent political unit had only ceased to exist 150 years before. The narrative of invasions from the east gave the Lorrainers an 'other' against which they could define themselves. Even in economic terms Lorraine's identity was strong because of the need to compete with Germany. The sense of identity in the Auvergne was not as strong as in Lorraine. This was true for a number of reasons. Firstly, there was no constant threat from a foreign 'other' to create solidarity among Auvergnats, no 'regional nationalist' discourse. Secondly, the Auvergne had even more uncertain borders than Lorraine. It stood at a crossroads between northern and southern France. Its language and culture in the Middle Ages were heavily influenced by the Languedoc to the south. However, it was one of the first regions outside the Île de France to be absorbed by the Capetian kingdom. The core consisted of the volcano country of the Puy-de-Dôme and the Cantal and the hills of the Forez to the east, surrounding the plain of the Limagne and the valley of the Allier, with Clermont-Ferrand as its centre. From Clermont it was much easier to travel north than south across the mountains or along the precipitate



T. Cudbird, *The Origins of Economic Regions in France, 1918–1940*,
https://doi.org/10.1007/978-3-032-04422-8_6

gorge of the Allier river. However, from Aurillac in the Cantal, the natural lines of communication ran south and west. Under the *Ancien Régime,* the province of the Auvergne covered the modern departments of Puy-de-Dôme and Cantal with the north-west of the Haute-Loire. The Bourbonnais to the north was a separate province, although the department of Allier in modern times was often linked to the Auvergne region. As we shall see it was included in the 17th region created in 1918. The Velay to the South-East (department of the Haute-Loire), with Le Puy at its centre, was likewise considered as having links with the Auvergne. However, it had some different cultural traditions, and Lyon and the Rhône valley were strong attractions.

Despite the huge growth in local historical studies, no crucial episode emerged which provided a regional sense of difference.[1] After its absorption into France in the Middle Ages, the Auvergne was not thought to have made a noticeable impact on the national story. This was felt to be true politically but also artistically. Georges Desdevises du Dézert was a professor in the Faculty of Literature at the University of Clermont-Ferrand. In 1914 he wrote in *La Veillée d'Auvergne* about a local art exhibition and reflected on the fact that between the end of the Middle Ages and his times, the Auvergne was a complete blank. The medieval flowering of Romanesque architecture and sculpture died not to be replaced.[2] Looking back later, Joseph Desaymard, a friend of the Auvergnat writer Henri Pourrat, and who had started writing about the Auvergne before the First World War, said that the region had not achieved much in the arts in the past because its people were too engaged in practical tasks like scratching a living from difficult terrain.[3] In the rest of France, the Auvergne was known as a relatively backward region, with wild and beautiful mountains, some quaint folklore and a reputation for meanness.

There was no discourse about economic success as in Lorraine. For a long time, the Auvergne had been known for its poverty. Agriculture was the dominant industry. Livestock was reared in the mountains and wheat and other crops grown on the plains. Most peasant farmers tried to feed their families from their own land but holdings were small compared with

[1] P. Den Boer, A. Pomerans, *History as a Profession, the Study of History in France 1818–1914* (Princeton, 2014), 18–19.

[2] G. Desdevises du Dézert, 'L'Exposition d'Arvernia à Clermont-Ferrand', *La Veillée d'Auvergne,* 6e année (15 février 1914), 33–36.

[3] J. Desaymard, *L'Art et les artistes en Auvergne* (Saint-Etienne, 1935), 3–5.

the rest of France. Most of the large estates had been broken up in the nineteenth century in the Puy-de-Dôme and the Cantal and sold to the peasant proprietors who followed traditional methods and were resistant to change. Holdings were larger in the mountains but smaller in the fertile soil of the Limagne plain.[4] The department of the Allier had larger estates and the practice of share-cropping was widespread there. There was discontent among share-croppers because of harsh conditions of work. Active agricultural unions developed there in the early twentieth century but were unknown further south in the Auvergne proper. Émile Guillaumin described his own life as a humble sharecropper in the Bourbonnais in his novel *Vie d'un simple* (1904), and it enjoyed considerable success. He engaged in union activity too.[5]

Most of the industries in the Auvergne operated on a small scale using traditional artisanal practices. These included paper-making in the Forez, ardently defended by Henri Pourrat, cutlery manufacture in Thiers and mining. The only concentrations of more modern industries were metallurgy around Commentry in the Bourbonnais and of course Clermont-Ferrand. In the regional capital an industry based on imported rubber had developed. The best-known firm was Michelin, which had 4500 employees pre-war.[6] It sucked in labour from across the department and elsewhere. Before the war only approximately 20–26% of employees had been born in the town.[7] However, there were other significant employers in the rubber industry, such as Raymond Bergougnan and Jean-Baptiste Torilhon, two considerable firms and rivals of Michelin. Raymond Bergougnan also took an active part in the social and political life of

[4] L. Gobin, *Essai sur la géographie de l'Auvergne* (Clermont-Ferrand, 1896), 213–230 and 268–94. A. Gourbeyre, *La Petite Propriété rurale dans le Puy-de-Dôme* (Thèse de doctorat, Faculté de Droit, Paris, 1900), 114–115.

[5] E. Guillaumin, *Vie d'un Simple*, (Paris, 1904). R Mathé, *Émile Guillaumin, homme de la terre et l'homme de lettres* (Paris, 1966), 475–478. N-J. Chaline, *Émile Guillaumin paysan-écrivain bourbonnais, soldat de la Grande Guerre* (Paris Sorbonne, 2014), 31–38.

[6] P. Charbonnier, *Histoire de l'Auvergne des origines à nos jours; Haute et Basse-Auvergne, Bourbonnais et Velay* (Clermont-Ferrand, 1999), 517–21.

[7] A. Moulin-Bourret, *Guerre et industrie Clermont-Ferrand 1912–1922: la victoire du pneu*, (2 vols, Faculté des Lettres et Sciences humaines de l'Université Blaise Pascal (Clermont II), publications de l'Institut d'Études du Massif Central (Centre d'Histoire des Entreprises et des Communautés), 1997), i, 119.

Clermont-Ferrand. Other industries included agricultural products such as *fruits confits*, textiles and chemical products.[8]

Another factor which inhibited regional economic development was the Auvergne's remoteness and poor communications. There was a network of railway lines by 1914. However, improvements in canal communications were desirable.[9] The Clermont-Ferrand chamber of commerce, which in most respects was not very dynamic, concentrated on transport issues.[10] A number of projects were discussed of which a lateral canal for the Allier was the most important.[11] Better transport and some modern industries had perhaps not yet made an impact on people's habits. Bréhier, professor at the Faculty of Letters in Clermont-Ferrand, remarked that transport and industry were supposed to bring modernity, but the Auvergne kept to its old customs.[12]

The economic factor most often discussed by the Auvergnat elite was rural depopulation and emigration to other parts of France and abroad. The actual population figures do not quite support the gloomy picture painted by some commentators. By 1911 the population in the Puy-de-Dôme and the Cantal had fallen between 12 and 14% from a peak in 1846. However, the population in the Allier held steady until 1911 as did that in the Haute-Loire.[13] However, the perception that numbers were declining provoked a reaction among conservative elites seen elsewhere in France. For example, Baron Lucien Reynaud addressing the *Société scientifique et agricole de la Haute-Loire* in 1911 told his audience that disaster awaited unless action was taken to halt this depopulation. He presented the town as a mirage of an easy life for the labouring poor. Who, he asked, would desert sunshine in the fields for life in a dark room? He said military service in barracks in towns corrupted young men. Like many other conservatives, he advocated an education adapted to life in the country as a farmer, improved agricultural techniques which the peasant had resisted, more

[8] Charbonnier, *Histoire de l'Auvergne*, 479–531. A-G. Manry, 'Un Siècle somnolent' in A-G. Manry (ed), *Histoire de l'Auvergne* (Toulouse, 1974), 398–416.

[9] Gobin, *Essai géographie*, 316.

[10] Moulin-Bourret, *Guerre et industrie*, 59.

[11] G. Bonnefoy, *Canal latéral de l'Allier* (Clermont-Ferrand, 1903). A. Jouve, *Création d'un canal latéral à l'Allier* (Chambres de Commerce de Clermont-Ferrand, Riom et Issoire, 1910).

[12] L. Bréhier, *L'Auvergne* (Paris, 1912), 94.

[13] Charbonnier, *Histoire de l'Auvergne*, 479.

agricultural cooperatives and an end to landlord absenteeism.[14] Similar sentiments to those of Reynaud were expressed by Mgr. Lecoeur, the Bishop of Saint-Flour, in a speech recorded in *La Veillée d'Auvergne* in April 1912.[15] The bishop denounced unnecessary emigration as leading to moral decline in the towns and urged the instruction of peasants in agriculture and the heritage of their native region.

Auvergnats left the land mainly because the small farms could not support all members of the family, and opportunities for work appeared better in the towns.[16] Some went to regional centres like Clermont-Ferrand, where 50% of the workers came from outside the town but within the Puy-de-Dôme.[17] Others went further afield and the most common destination was Paris, where there was a large Auvergnat community described by F. Raison-Jourde.[18] A smaller group examined by Duroux went as far as Madrid.[19] At first emigrants would work for a while in a large city and return home periodically. Later they stayed longer but might come back to retire. Eventually their emigration became permanent.[20] The emigrants to Paris sought help from fellow Auvergnats and tended to stick together in certain quarters. They went into particular trades such as food shops, cafés and water, coal and milk vending. They often worked hard, spending little on leisure or luxuries, saving up perhaps to invest in a property in the Auvergne.[21] Because of this way of life, they acquired a reputation for being money-grubbing ('âpre du gain'). Indeed, this stereotyping of the Auvergnat was mainly based on the Parisian experience of interacting with

[14] Baron L. Reynaud, 'L'esprit agricole et le retour à la terre', *Bulletin historique, scientifique, littéraire, artistique et agricole de la Société scientifique et agricole du Puy-en-Velay et la Haute-Loire*, 1911, fasc.3, 195–213. Gourbeyre, *Petite Propriété*, 115.

[15] 'Échos et nouvelles-Mgr Lecoeur Évêque de St. Flour 'La Dépopulation dans le Cantal'', *La Veillée d'Auvergne*, 4e année (1 avril 1912), 188–190.

[16] Manry, *Histoire de l'Auvergne*, 400.

[17] Moulin-Bourret, *Guerre et industrie*, 119.

[18] F. Raison-Jourde, *La Colonie auvergnate de Paris au XIXe siècle* (Paris, 1976). M. Boule, P. Glangeaud, G.Rouchon, A. Vernière, *Le Puy-de-Dôme et Vichy, guide du touriste, du naturaliste et de l'archéologue* (Paris, 1901), 130. M. Boule, L. Farges, *Le Cantal, Guide* (Paris, 1898), 119–125.

[19] R. Duroux, *Les Auvergnats de Castille. Rennaissance et mort d'une migration au XIXe siècle* (Clermont-Ferrand, Faculté des Lettres et Sciences-humaines, Université de Blaise-Pascal, 2018).

[20] Charbonnier, *Histoire de l'Auvergne*, 480–1.

[21] B. Solet (ed), *15 Histoires d'Auvergne* (Paris, 1981), 146.

them.[22] In both cases they acquired a love for the land of their birth, felt some nostalgia while away and gathered in social groupings to celebrate their cultural heritage.[23] The Auvergnat sense of identity was cultivated most strongly in exile from the homeland, in Paris and other centres of the very considerable Auvergnat diaspora, quite unlike Lorraine.

## The Creation of an Auvergnat Sense of Identity

We have seen how the sense of regional identity in the Auvergne was weaker than in Lorraine, because of the region's poverty and remoteness. To counter the Auvergne's reputation for economic and cultural backwardness, a group of intellectuals and the educated bourgeoisie set out to reverse perceptions. The Auvergnat sense of identity in modern times was largely their creation. They expressed their ideas in a number of journals and societies; for example, in Clermont-Ferrand, through the *Académie des Sciences, Belles-lettres et Arts*, the *Revue d'Auvergne* linked to *Société des Amis de l'Université* and the Faculty of Letters of the university itself.

Clermont-Ferrand had had a university since the law of 1896, but it was less dynamic than in Nancy. Local businessmen lent some support to management and scientific education but not on the same scale as the new institutes in the capital of Lorraine. In 1900 the university had no *faculté de droit*. Its strongest departments were geology and mineralogy.[24] In 1906 the chamber of commerce financed a course in industrial chemistry within the faculty of science.[25] In 1913 the chamber of commerce also started a management course. The department of letters made a significant contribution to local intellectual life with figures such as Georges Desdevises du Dézert, Émile Bréhier and Emmanuel des Essarts. Desdevises du Dézert was a mentor to many Auvergne enthusiasts and a close friend of Henri Pourrat. His papers contain biographical sketches of all the local intellectuals he influenced during his long life including the Cantal born poet Gandilhon Gens-d'Armes, Abbé Courchinoux, poet and

[22] D. Martin (ed), *L'Identité de l'Auvergne, mythe ou réalité historique, essai sur une histoire de l'Auvergne des origines à nos jours* (Clermont-Ferrand, Université de Blaise-Pascal, 2002), 629–649.

[23] J. Ajalbert, *En Auvergne* (Paris, 1893), 168. E. Joucla, R. Cortat, *Lectures d'Auvergne* (Aurillac, 1929), 113–114. A. Dauzat, 'Ma Petite Patrie', *La Veillée d'Auvergne*, 1e année (1 avril 1909), 192–3.

[24] *L'Université de Clermont-Ferrand* (Clermont-Ferrand, 1900), 3–5.

[25] Moulin-Bourret, *Guerre et industrie*, 59.

supporter of the Félibrige in the Cantal, Étienne Clémentel the politician, Jacques Bardoux, writer and later senator for the Puy-de-Dôme, Léon Boyer, a Cantal poet killed at Verdun, Jean Angeli, Pourrat's literary partner killed in the First World War, and Joseph Desaymard.[26] In 1903 these intellectuals founded the Musée Bargoin for art and archaeology which still stands next to the university.

The first Auvergnat regional movement, extensively researched by J-F. Chanet in his *Les Félibres cantaliens*, owed most to the Félibrige of Mistral. The Auvergne's *patois* and literature were a branch of Provençal-Occitan, and not Celtic as some liked to think. Vermenouze, who was born in Aurillac, but spent many years with his father in Spain, was writing poems in the *patois* of the Cantal in the 1870s. He announced the formation of a branch of the Félibrige in Aurillac in 1887, but it took another seven years for the society to be constituted as *L'Escolo oubergnato*. *L'Escolo's* journal was heavily supported by Auvergnats in Paris, which again demonstrates the cultural importance of the Auvergnat diaspora in the capital. *L'Escolo* covered the whole political spectrum from left to right but was mainly professional and bourgeois in character, people who used French in their everyday lives unlike the peasants of the Cantal countryside. The society in Aurillac collapsed within ten years, although the important *Revue de la Haute-Auvergne* continued. It had the same exclusive bourgeois base as a list of subscribers from 1904 shows.[27]

The story of how this movement continued also underlines how the Auvergnat sense of identity was felt most strongly outside the Auvergne itself. Auvergnats in Paris and Clermont-Ferrand took up the flame of Auvergnat culture with the foundation of *La Veillée d'Auvergne* in 1908 and the journal of that name in 1909. The first meeting was held at the Musée social in Paris on 29 November 1908 with Maurice Barrès in the chair and Charles-Brun of the FRF also present. The *Veillée* was supported by the influential newspaper *L'Auvergnat de Paris*, edited by Louis Bonnet, and the *Ligue Auvergnate* which dated back to 1886.[28] From the start *La*

[26] Patrimoine, Fonds Georges Desdevises du Dézert, 'Dossiers documentaires sur les savants, les écrivains et les artistes de l'Auvergne contemporaine réunis par Georges Desdevises du Dézert (1854–1942)', MS 1740 Gandilhon, MS 1658 Clémentel, MS 1608 Boyer, MS 1538 Angeli, MS 1453 poètes d'Auvergne, MS 1720 Louis Farges, MS 1671 Courchinoux, MS 1561 Bardoux.

[27] *Revue de la Haute-Auvergne, 7e année* (1905), 1–6.

[28] Le Musée Francisque Mandet, Riom, *Entre Chien et loup. La Veillée, naissance d'un mythe? Les Veillées en Auvergne en milieu rural et urbain, du XIXe siècle à nos jours* (Paris, 2003), 53–54.

*Veillée* was the flagship of the drive for a local culture, with articles on literature and the arts as well as news of regionalist groupings like the *Fédération régionaliste française*. It organized regular meetings and dinners in Paris and Clermont. In his launch editorial Ribier said they wanted to preserve and enhance the culture of the Auvergne and also to defend it against 'la banale et moderne uniformité.'[29] Like *L'Escolo* the supporters of *La Veillée d'Auvergne* came from the bourgeoisie or from skilled artisans and owners of small businesses with some education.

Linked to *La Veillée d'Auvergne* were a number of other Auvergnat cultural organizations with overlapping membership. *La Maintenance d'Auvergne* was formed in 1914, specifically as a branch of the Félibrige to protect the Auvergnat dialect and literature. Its majoral or leader was the Duc de la Salle de Rochemaure. Rochemaure (1856–1915) was an aristocratic friend of Henri d'Orléans who lived in a troubadour chateau in the Cantal. He was a poet in local dialect, a friend of the renowned dialect poet Vermenouze and a founder of *La Veillée d'Auvergne*. *La Maintenance d'Auvergne* attracted fifty members including Gandilhon Gens-d'Armes and a number of writers such as Marcenac, a member of the Félibrige from the Cantal; Antonin Meyniel of *La Semaine Auvergnate* (a journal for Auvergnats in Paris) friend of Rochamaure and organizer of literary soirées; Louis Delhostal, another poet in the *langue d'oc* and member of the Félibrige; Fernand Delzangles, a writer on Auvergnat songs and history; and Henri Pourrat.[30]

These Auvergnat intellectuals were constantly looking for great men from their region who exemplified the distinctiveness of the Auvergne and its way of thinking. The Duc de La Salle de Rochemaure emphasized such men's importance in his lecture on regionalism given in Clermont-Ferrand in 1909.[31] Several writers concentrated on Pascal as a great thinker who originated in the Auvergne. Rochemaure sang the praises of one of the greatest thinkers ever.[32] Jean Ajalbert suggested that Pascal's thoughts were inspired by the mountains. Pascal's famous bet was a pure example of

[29] E. de Ribier, 'À nos compatriotes', *La Veillée d'Auvergne*, 1ère année (1 janvier 1909), 4.

[30] 'La Maintenance d'Auvergne', *La Veillée d'Auvergne*, 6e année (15 février 1914), 181–3.

[31] Duc de La Salle de Rochemaure, *Régionalisme auvergnat, conférence donnée à la Faculté des Lettres de l'Académie de Clermont-Ferrand, le 23 janvier 1909* (Aurillac, 1909), 30 and 34–9.

[32] Ibid, 30.

Auvergnat pragmatism![33] Joseph Desaymard wrote about Pascal and Barrès in *La Veillée d'Auvergne*, seeking to show how one had inspired the other and how both had been influenced by the local environment. Barrès's father came from the Auvergne, although Barrès himself was not brought up there. He made several trips to the Auvergne to visit sites associated with Pascal.[34]

It seems that these Auvergnat writers were desperate to put the Auvergne on the map; to get it taken seriously by intellectual circles in Paris and elsewhere. They wanted to get rid of a sense of inferiority by talking up what the Auvergne had achieved and its great men. So these intellectuals had to find a rallying point and the most popular under the Third Republic was Vercingétorix, the leader of the Gallic tribe, the Arvernes, who opposed the Romans under Julius Caesar, triumphing at Gergovia before surrendering at Alésia and later being killed in Rome. It was the Arvernes who gave their name to the Auvergne. For the Auvergnat intellectuals of 1900, it was important to believe that the Arvernes of Roman times were not inferior in intelligence to other Gallic tribes in the rest of France. For republicans Vercingétorix was a potent symbol because he rallied his people to resist an invader. He supported contemporary ideas of freedom and liberty. For regional writers he exemplified the fiercely independent mountain people which they conceived the Auvergnats of their day to be.

We find this transposition of contemporary political ideas back to the era of Vercingétorix in several writers. The poetry of Arsène Vermenouze made a specific link between Vercingétorix and *revanche* post 1870. Vercingétorix's example would encourage the Auvergne's soldiers. In November 1887 his poem *À Vercingétorix* was read to an audience of over 1000 people at a meeting of the *Ligue auvergnate* in Paris and received a

[33] J. Ajalbert, *Auvergne* (Paris, 1932), 28 and 31. This book was a reworking of older books — *L'Auvergne* (1904), *les Veillées d'Auvergne* (1905) and *Au Coeur de l'Auvergne* (1922).

[34] J. Desaymard, 'Pascal et Barrès', *La Veillée d'Auvergne, 1e année (octobre 1909)*, 578 and 582–3. Patrimoine, MSS Joseph Desaymard JD12, Brouillons et manuscrits 1910–1914, fol. 266–76, 'Blaise Pascal et Maurice Barrès d'après un article récent'; also MSS Joseph Desaymard JD21, fasc. 63–72; Fonds Georges Desdevises du Dézert, Louis Farges MSS 1720. P. de Nolhac, *Pages Auvergnates* (Paris, 1888), 120–1. *La Veillée d'Auvergne*, 1ère année (mars 1909), 149–150. U. Rouchon, 'Les Ancêtres auvergnats de Maurice Barrès', *La Veillée d'Auvergne*, 1ère annee (juillet 1909), 321–324 and (1 août 1909), 375–383.

rapturous reception. The *Moniteur du Cantal* reported this event in patriotic terms:

> They (the stanzas) were dedicated to Vercingétorix, the great Arven, and recited with soul at a meeting of the descendants of the former Arvernii. They were received with enthusiastic bravos.[35]

Vercingétorix was the subject of many pictures during the years before 1914.[36] These sentiments were not unique to the Auvergne, however, but widely shared among patriots throughout France who were looking for a sense of redemption in defeat.[37] This celebration of Vercingétorix should be seen in the context of a national interest in the Celts of Gaul going back to the Middle Ages. Under the Third Republic there was a veritable Gallomania.[38] Claims that Vercingétorix was an Auvergnat hero were relatively muted in comparison with his portrayal as a great man of French history.[39]

There were several projects to erect statues, some abortive. A large equestrian statue of Vercingétorix was erected in the Place Jaude in the centre of Clermont-Ferrand and unveiled in a ceremony on 11 October 1903 which turned into a grand republican *fête*. The celebration was attended by Président du Conseil Combes and other members of the government. Emmanuel des Essarts' speech at the inauguration stands out because he linked the Gallic chieftain with the defence of republican liberty, the forerunner of the contemporary French nation. Des Essarts was president of the monument project committee. He was a very significant figure in the Auvergne regionalist movement, an intellectual mentor of Étienne Clémentel, later Minister of Commerce and author in 1933 of an entertainment at the Paris Opera on the subject of Vercingétorix with

[35] J. Mazières, *Arsène Vermenouze 1850–1910 et la Haute-Auvergne de son temps* (Paris, 1965), 326, 328.

[36] Exposition Musée Roger Quillot, Clermont-Ferrand (2014).

[37] M. Ozouf, *L'École de France* (Paris, 1984), 345. C. Amalvi, *De l'Art et la manière d'accommoder les héros de l'histoire de France* (Paris, 1988), 51–88.

[38] K. Pomian, 'Francs et Gaulois', in P. Nora (ed), *Les Lieux de mémoire, T. III Les France, vol.1 conflits et partages* (Paris, 1992), 40–105.

[39] A. Ehrard, 'Vercingétorix contre Gergovie? Nos ancêtres les Gaulois', (Clermont-Ferrand, June 1980), 309, https://hal-clermont-univ.archives-ouvertes.fr/hal-01410214

music by Joseph Canteloube.[40] Des Essarts was also close to Henri Pourrat.[41]

Despite the celebration of Vercingétorix, it was difficult to create an Auvergnat sense of difference out of the history of its great men. These Auvergnat intellectuals hit on a more fertile theme when they suggested that rural traditions and a simple way of life were strengths, not weaknesses, and should be preserved. Hence they revived interest in local culture and customs such as song, dances, fairy tales, local religious cults, pilgrimages and story-telling, music and sociability around the fire (*the veillées*).[42]

There was some new literature written in the local dialect, perhaps more than in Lorraine. The language was best suited to poems and also songs often accompanied by dances.[43] Among all the writers and poets admired by this movement, there was one which stood out—Arsène Vermenouze. He was a bridge between the first *félibres* in Aurillac and *La Veillée*, a *patois* poet of the first group admired by the second. He was a man of the Cantal, the true Auvergne as he saw it, and he made this *petite patrie* come to life. He evoked the pastoral life of the mountains, the cattle, stone byres and local customs like dancing the *bourrée*. He celebrated the joy of living close to one's native soil and encouraged the emigrants to return.[44]

Vermenouze was not alone among writers from the Cantal. Pierre Besson published in French in 1914 the simple story of a young man growing up in a traditional Cantal village; his days at school; his life on a working farm looking after cattle and making cheese; the *veillées* and dancing; learning his catechism with the priest. It was a rather idealized view of the Cantal in his youth with all the harsh conditions removed. Besson was born in 1873, so he was describing the Cantal of the late nineteenth

[40] M-C. Kessler, G. Rousseau, 'La trajectoire sociale d'Étienne Clémentel', in Kessler, Rousseau, *Clémentel*, 43

[41] 'Les Fêtes de Vercingétorix', *Le Moniteur du Puy-de-Dôme* (12 octobre 1903), 1 col f.

[42] Le Musée Francisque Mandet, Riom, *Entre Chien et loup. La Veillée, naissance d'un mythe? Les Veillées en Auvergne en milieu rural et urbain, du XIXe siècle à nos jours* (Paris, 2003), 25–30.

[43] Boule, Glangeaud, *Puy-de-Dôme et Vichy, 140–2.*

[44] V-E. Ardouin-Dumazet, *Voyage en France: Auvergne, Vol. II Haute-Auvergne Cantal* (Paris, 1927). 203–220. Avenin, 'Le Poète de l'Auvergne, Arsène Vermenouze', *Revue d'Auvergne*, IIe série (1911), 21–42. Mijoule, 'Arsène Vermenouze et sa poésie', *Revue de la Haute-Auvergne*, 13e année (1911), 71–83 and 140–152.

century. He became a teacher in the Cantal and then an academic inspector in the Charente when he published *Le Pâtre*.[45] Much of this writing helped create the myth of a simple life, whereas a writer like Émile Guillaumin, describing share-cropping in the Bourbonnais, did not hide the hard life and the conflicts in a village.

These Auvergnat intellectuals also believed that their sense of difference derived from the landscape of the Auvergne. There was a particular feeling for the extraordinary bleak volcanic landscape of the Auvergne mountains, effectively evoked by Jean Ajalbert when he visited the peak of Sancy and Mont-Dore.[46] Lac Pavin was another place which inspired his awe. Georges Desdevises du Dézert significantly drew attention to Audigier's love of the Auvergnat natural world, as something to be admired rather than feared. Audigier (1659–1744) was a canon of Clermont-Ferrand cathedral and wrote important annals of the Auvergne.[47]

The folklorists pointed to the distinctive songs and dances of the Auvergne as another point of difference, a factor in regional identity. Arrangements by which these have reached a wide audience are to be found in Joseph Canteloube's *Chants d'Auvergne* for soprano and orchestra, which has become an established piece in the modern concert repertoire. Canteloube came from the Ardèche but had deep roots in the Auvergne. He collected folksongs and wrote an opera with a libretto in Occitan. He also wrote the music for Clémentel's libretto on Vercingétorix.

A reviewer of Mario Versepuy's large collection of folksongs said they celebrated the naïve and tender love of its sons for the Auvergne. He created the idea that these songs spread something called the soul of the Auvergne and he hoped significantly they would be sung in schools.[48] Desaymard had said that for Chabrier, as for other Auvergnat musicians, the essence of music was rhythm as found in a dance like the *bourrée*.[49]

[45] P. Besson, *Le Pâtre du Cantal* (Paris, 1914).

[46] J.Ajalbert, *Auvergne* (Paris, 1932), 99–100.

[47] G. Desdevises du Dézert, 'Histoire d'Auvergne par le chanoine Pierre Audigier, nouvelle édition Clermont-Ferrand 1899', *Revue d'Auvergne*, 16e année, no. 1 (janvier–février 1899), 76–80.

[48] U. Rouchon, 'Le Folkore auvergnat de Marius Versepuy', *La Veillée d'Auvergne,* 1e année (novembre 1909), 527, 530, 533.

[49] J.Desaymard, *Artiste Auvergnat Emmanuel Chabrier* (Revue d'Auvergne, Clermont-Ferrand, 1908), 9.

Ajalbert explained that the sound of an Auvergnat tune, *le regret*, in the streets of Paris made him cry.[50]

The Auvergnat country dweller was thought to entertain all sorts of beliefs in the supernatural of interest to middle-class visitors.[51] Common in other areas, these beliefs took on a particular character in the Auvergne. Léon Pineau recorded beliefs in supernatural beings—wild dogs, owls inhabited by devils, sorcerers, old hags and young girls dancing in long white robes all night.[52] Boule and colleagues writing a guide book to the Puy-de-Dôme in 1901 said the country folk did not believe in fairies and supernatural wolves, but they were still afraid of sorcerers and believed in some people's abilities to effect cures. Belief in ghosts was also common.[53] Such stories were subsequently recorded for posterity by Henri Pourrat.

These descriptions of the landscape, history, folklore and art of the Auvergne were included in guidebooks, which encouraged a nascent tourism in the years before the First World War. Some were sponsored by recently formed *syndicats d'initiative* to promote tourism locally. Louis Farges, who co-authored the guidebook on the Cantal, was born in Aurillac and helped found the *escolo oubergnato* as did his colleague Marcellin Boule, born in the Cantal but later a professor in Paris. Farges created several *syndicats d'initiative* in the Cantal, as well as pursuing a career as an archivist, diplomat and politician. In 1896 Jean Masfrand, vice-president of the *Club alpin français*, drew attention to the growing number of tourists attracted by the thermal baths and the beautiful mountain scenery. They urgently needed a guide book containing not only historical and geographical information but also practical guidance on hotels and transport.[54] Major series of guides began to be published in Paris, for example, the *guides Joanne*. Their volume on the Auvergne published in 1904 was very comprehensive in terms of background as well as information on trains, coaches and accommodation.[55] The growth of thermalism at resorts like Vichy, Châtel-Guyon and Mont-Dore was encouraged by

[50] J.Ajalbert, *En Auvergne* (Paris, 1893), 278.

[51] Martin, *L'Identité de l'Auvergne*, 638.

[52] L.Pineau, 'Le Foklore de l'Auvergne', in A. Van Bever (ed), *Auvergne et Limousin Histoire, Tableaux Pittoresques, Poésies, Chansons Populaires, Contes et Légendes* (Paris, s.d.). 35.

[53] Boule, Glangeaud, *Puy-de-Dôme et Vichy*, 138–9.

[54] J. Masfrand, *Le Cantal guide du touriste, du botaniste et du géologue* (Aurillac, 1896), 247–8.

[55] P. Joanne, *Itinéraire général de la France: Auvergne et Centre* (Paris, 1904).

doctors advocating bathing in the waters as a cure for all sorts of ailments.[56] A railway was built up the Puy-de-Dôme in 1907.[57] This development of tourism alongside the Auvergnat cultural movement suggested a symbiotic relationship between the two.

Henri Pourrat became the dominant influence among these intellectuals in the years immediately before the war. More than any other writer, he invented the identity of the Auvergne in modern times, distilling the work of scholars and folklorists of previous generations. Pourrat was born in Ambert, in the hills of the Livradois east of Clermont-Ferrand, in 1887. In 1905 he had to abandon his studies at the National Agricultural Institute in Paris and return to Ambert, gravely ill with tuberculosis. For the rest of his life he was an invalid in his home in Ambert. He walked extensively in the region but rarely travelled outside it. Pourrat started to read very widely, including contemporary writers such as Maurice Barrès, whom he acknowledged as a master. He also collected folktales and traditions and met Arnold van Gennep, the founder of scientific ethnography and folklore studies in France.

The prevailing tone of the movement in the Auvergne was Catholic and conservative, close to thinkers like Charles Maurras and especially Maurice Barrès. Evidence of this affiliation is to be found in Arsène Vermenouze, a practising Catholic, Gandilhon Gens-d'Armes, and Rochemaure. Pourrat's Catholicism was fundamental to his life. A folder of spiritual jottings from a fellow Catholic, included by Pourrat among his papers, reveals very traditional Catholic beliefs, with an emphasis on purity and a preoccupation with the sexual act.[58] Pourrat was clearly interested in manifestations of popular religion, such as the belief in wells with miraculous healing powers. He was also very sympathetic to the right wing *Action Française* even at this stage of his life, as was his friend Joseph Desaymard.

Pourrat started his life-long attempt to define what being an Auvergnat meant in an article for the *Revue d'Auvergne* in 1913, *Nous qui sommes Auvergnats*.[59] Pourrat had no time for a Kantian universalism. Each province had its own way of feeling. These should be allowed to thrive and France would live better. Pourrat said that men and women should live

[56] Le Professeur Landouzy, *Le Mont-Dore, station hydrominérale et station d'altitude* (Châtelles, Vosges, 1906), 32–34. Charbonnier, *Histoire de l'Auvergne, 524–529.*

[57] Manry, *Histoire de l'Auvergne*, 412.

[58] Patrimoine, MSS Henri Pourrat HP 125, fasc. 20.

[59] Pourrat, 'Nous qui sommes Auvergnats', *Revue d'Auvergne*, xxx (1913), 73–92 and 160–187.

according to the promptings of their blood, not abstract ideas. They should follow their fathers and here he invoked Barrès' doctrine of *la terre et les morts* (the soil and the dead).[60] He reflected a lot on the impact of climate and habitat on character. The men of the mountains lived an isolated, reserved, individualistic life. They had to be practical, stubborn and tenacious just to survive. They were not avaricious but careful with money because they feared losing control of the future.[61] Some of these qualities were similar to those ascribed to the Lorraine peasant.

This analysis of Auvergnat character was widely shared by other writers.[62] Delzangles, in his popular book on Auvergnat songs, wrote that the Auvergnats had not been mixed with other racial groups because of their remoteness and therefore retained some characteristics of the ancient Gauls—physical vigour, energy, tenacity, pride, adventurousness, love of liberty and independence.[63] Bréhier, however, introduced a more nuanced picture saying the Auvergne was not just dour, mean and violent.[64] According to some there were differences between the men of the mountains and those who lived on the plain of the fertile Limagne around Clermont-Ferrand. The mountain peasants did not work as hard as the lowland peasant. They led a more independent life style.[65] There was also a widespread belief that they were a different racial physical type—short and stocky.[66]

While the regional sense of identity was weaker in the Auvergne than in Lorraine, there was a cultural concept of being an Auvergnat which

[60] Pourrat, 'Nous qui sommes Auvergnats', 73–77.

[61] Pourrat, 'Nous qui sommes Auvergnats', 81, 87, 91, 178, 181.

[62] Reynaud, 'L'Esprit agricole', 207. Gobin, *Essai géographie*, 213–230. Solet, *15 Histoires*, 146. L. Pineau, 'Le Folkore de l'Auvergne', 35–37. E. Cathala, *L'Auvergne* (Facsimile de l'édition de Paris, fin du 19e siècle; Paris, 2008), 120. P. de Nolhac, *Pages Auvergnates* (Paris, 1888), 29. Chanet, *Félibres cantaliens, 264–6*. Ajalbert, *Auvergne*, 15. Martin, *L'Identité de l'Auvergne, 629, 632, 636, 637, 639*. Rochemaure, *Régionalisme auvergnat*, 51. Joucla, Cortat, *Lectures, 113*. Boule, Glangeaud, *Puy-de-Dôme et Vichy*, 128. L. Delzon, 'La grande fête régionaliste du 4 mars, conférence de M. Louis Delzon', *La Veillée d'Auvergne*, 3e année (avril 1911), 144–5; M. Giraudet, 'La Psychologie de l'Auvergnat', *La Veillée d'Auvergne, 4e année* (mars 1912), 298–303. Patrimoine, MSS Joseph Desaymard JD12, brouillons on Pastourel.

[63] F. Delzangles, *Folklore cantalien, chants populaires d'Auvergne* (Aurillac, 1910), 60.

[64] Bréhier, *L'Auvergne,* 3, 29–30, 70, 225.

[65] H.Doniol, *La Basse-Auvergne* (Paris, 1900), 212–13. Boule, Glangeaud, *Puy-de-Dôme et Vichy,* 128–42. Cathala, *L'Auvergne,* 84.

[66] Martin, *L'Identité de l'Auvergne,* 633, 635. Bréhier, *L'Auvergne,* 69.

influenced leaders of society involved in the work of the economic region. We can see this, for example, in the articles on tourism in the periodical *Région du Centre*. While the economy was predominantly agricultural and backward, Clermont-Ferrand was developing as an industrial centre, with the three rubber firms of Michelin, Torilhon and Bergougnan being particularly important. These firms developed even faster during the First World War as they had the advantage of being far from the front. Michelin got involved in other sorts of manufacturing for the war, for example, aeroplanes. While the University in Clermont-Ferrand did not have the standing of that in Nancy, it did provide a foundation for intellectual life and later for certain sciences.

## The Impact of the War on the Auvergne's Sense of Identity

The elite in Clermont-Ferrand seemed to express their support for the war in patriotic sentiments found in other areas of France. However, how far can we talk about regional identity in war time? How far might this have influenced the regional elite to act together to combat the region's particular problems? A comprehensive search for soldiers' diaries or letters from the Auvergne, or indeed from the neighbouring Limousin, published and unpublished, did not reveal many examples where they talked about their region. They thought about 'home' quite a lot—the farm and their family, for example, but rarely specifically about the region where they lived. I found only five exceptions in the Auvergne. One from 1915 concerns two employees from the Bergougnan factory, now soldiers, who wrote to their colleagues in Clermont as follows:

> Here, while resting, we are in the land of the vine: everything recalls our dear Auvergne: Chanturgue, Mont Juset, all these smiling hillsides of vineyards, we find them here. But, Clermont and its great chimneys? They are absent; graven in our spirits and in our hearts, Clermont follows us everywhere. We live however in the hope that one day, perhaps very soon, we will see it again, bringing back with us a permanent peace for everyone.[67]

[67] AD P-de-D, Fonds du Comité de Secours des Établissements Bergougnan, F 028, 'Courrier et gazette des tranchées réalisés par deux employés de l'usine Bergougnan, de la 14e compagnie du 201e Régiment d'Infanterie', 28 juillet 1915, quoted in Puy-de-Dôme Conseil-Général, *Des Armes aux larmes 1914–1918, l'engagement patriotique du Puy-de-Dôme* (Clermont-Ferrand, Cahier des Archives, 2014).

Other diaries and some letters in the departmental archives show that some soldiers felt a strong attachment to a home space which had certain characteristics.[68]

In his epic poem *les Montgnards*, written during the war and published just afterwards, Henri Pourrat concentrated diffuse feelings of identity into the driving force behind the Auvergnat *poilus*' valiant resistance at Verdun. This was a major step in creating his own particular vision of the Auvergne. It was a vision which resonated with others in the region, who saw the peasant society of the past disappearing for good. The loss of life in the First World War was not the only cause of depopulation of the countryside, but it was sudden, obvious and traumatic. Pourrat created a greater sense of awareness of the Auvergnat peasant culture on the eve of its extinction. Auvergnat identity was born of exile and then of loss of life. In Lorraine the impact of the war was immediate in that death, destruction and refugees appeared within days of the invasion. In the case of the Auvergne the impact of the war took a little longer to be felt. It took some years of mourning for those left to realize fully what had happened.

Like many others Pourrat was deeply affected by the deaths of young men known to him personally, as well as by the extent of the carnage. The letters Henri exchanged with Joseph Desaymard are also full of sad news of friends and associates in the literary world. They record the deaths of the 18-year-old son of the Auvergnat writer Jean Ajalbert in 1915 in the Argonne and that of poet Léon Boyer in 1916, among others.[69] Pourrat's friend Desdevises lost a nephew.[70] Pourrat realized that the sons of Auvergnat peasants were being cut down in huge numbers. The latest research on deaths by region suggests that peasant areas like the Auvergne and Brittany suffered particularly severely, because it was the peasantry who ended up in the front line infantry in greater numbers.[71] France lost

[68] C. Marcoline (ed), *Un Auvergnat dans la paix et dans la guerre, chroniques auvergnates autour des journaux de la guerre 14/18 de Jean et Jacques Lacoste* (Clermont-Ferrand, s.d.), 67–69, 74, 101, 107. AD P-de-D, La Grande Collecte, 'Lettre Léger Debost, lettres Adolphe Féneyrols, carnets Eugène Martin'.

[69] H. Pourrat letter to J. Desaymard 3 janvier 1915, in C.Dalet, (ed), *Correspondance croisée Henri Pourrat–Joseph Desaymard 1913 à 1918: la Grande Guerre* (Clermont-Ferrand, 2013), 156.

[70] H. Pourrat letter to J. Desaymard 22 octobre 1918, in Dalet, *Correspondance croisée*, 289.

[71] G. Férier, 'Les Conséquences démographiques de la Grande Guerre en Auvergne', *Guerres mondiales et conflits contemporains*, 145 (Janvier 1987), 81–94.

11.3% of men aged 15 to 54 years, but 19.1% in the Cantal, Allier 14.1%, Haute-Loire 14% and 13.5% in the Puy-de-Dôme. This is on a par with the losses in Brittany—Cotes-du-Nord 20.6%, Morbihan 19.5%, Ille-et-Vilaine 15.6%, Finistère 15%.[72]

The epic poem *Les Montagnards, chronique paysanne de la Grande Guerre* received a prize from the *Académie française* in 1919. The main focus is the effect of the war on the people of the Auvergne. Of the twelve sections three deal directly with the front and the remainder mostly with the life of those left behind at home in the mountains of the Auvergne. The author is always careful to connect his two worlds; for example, when, on the march, Theil smells pine trees and thinks of home.[73] He goes to sleep with images of the Auvergne in his head—"Ah! Our homeland which does not leave us!"[74] At the end of the poem Pourrat brings the spirit of the Auvergne to the battle front, when men on leave dance a *bourrée* at Rethondes on the Aisne and there is a new light in their eyes.[75] There are many striking descriptions of the Auvergne countryside and of work on the land.[76] The three sections on the front make a very simple and direct impact. They describe the attack on Le Bois des Corbeaux at Mort-Homme at Verdun where the 92nd Infantry Regiment from the Auvergne were decimated in a German counter-attack. He evokes the endurance of the peasant soldier through all of this. It was these peasants and their endurance which saved France.[77] Because of the sacrifice made by the peasantry, Pourrat believed that the Republic had a moral debt to the *petite patrie* of the Auvergne on whose economy and society the war had had such a destructive impact.[78]

In view of the losses suffered it was almost inevitable that someone would suggest an Auvergnat monument with all the names of the fallen sons of the Auvergne inscribed on it—"to the Auvergnats who died for the freedom of the world." What better place to put it than the site of

[72] Férier, 'Les Conséquences', 93.

[73] H.Pourrat, *Les Montagnards, chronique paysanne de la Grande Guerre* (repr. Paris, 2016), 41.

[74] Ibid, 42

[75] Ibid, 108.

[76] Ibid, 49–50.

[77] Ibid, 97.

[78] P. Cornu, 'Auvergne dans la Grande Guerre. *Les Montagnards* d'Henri Pourrat et la rhétorique de la dette', *Siècles* [En ligne], 39–40 (2014), http://journals.openedition.org/siecles/2799

Vercingétorix's battle against the Romans at Gergovia, in the heart of the Auvergne with huge views. The author of the proposal was J. Reynard, a retired conservator of *Eaux et Forêts*.[79] He hoped it would encourage national and regional pilgrimages and would unite the populations of Upper and Lower Auvergne.[80]

Here too the elite showed some sense of regional solidarity in the work they undertook to support the war effort. For some emergencies they set up specifically regional organizations, for example, the *Association d'Auvergne pour les Prisonniers de Guerre*. A major conference was organized in May 1915 in the Faculty of Letters of the University of Clermont-Ferrand. It was attended by the prefect; various generals; Chalus, the president of the chamber of commerce; Desdevises du Dézert, the honorary dean of the Faculty of Letters; and Audollent, the current dean. There was an appeal for donations.[81] There was a steady flow of donations throughout the war.[82]

There was plenty of help locally for wounded soldiers. In December 1915 a *Foyer du Soldat blessé* was set up under the patronage of the prefect and other local dignitaries. Raymond Bergoungnan was the president and Audollent and Lange were involved as well as various senior officers in the local administration. The *foyer* was a house where soldiers could go for company every afternoon. Local people were encouraged to donate. Bergougnan set an example by giving 1000 francs, and Desdevises and Audollent were also in the initial subscription list.[83]

Regarding the wounded there was a particular focus on re-training them and finding them jobs as there was in Lorraine and other parts of France. Desdevises du Dézert drew attention to their plight in a typical patriotic speech to raise funds called *Les Poètes et la Guerre*. The book of poems to be sold to raise funds for practical help for the wounded included pieces by well-known Auvergnat poets we have already encountered including Gandilhon Gens-d'Armes, 'un bon Cantalien', Henri Pourrat,

[79] *Le Moniteur du Puy-de-Dôme* (22, 27 mars 1918), 3 col a, 3 col b, (1, 10, 14 juin 1918), 3 col b, 2 col c–d and 3 col b. Ehrard, 'Vercingétorix contre Gergovie?' 307–317, 481–486.

[80] Ehrard, 'Vercingétorix contre Gergovie?', 312.

[81] *Le Moniteur du Puy-de-Dôme* (11 mai 1915), 3 col b–c; *L'Avenir du Puy-de-Dôme,* (11 mai 1915), 2 col b–c.

[82] *Le Moniteur du Puy-de-Dôme* (23 décembre 1915), 3 col d; (27 janvier 1916), 3 col a, (6 novembre 1916), 4 col b–c; (11 décembre 1917), 3 col b.

[83] *Le Moniteur du Puy-de-Dôme* (8 février 1917), 3 col c.

Amélie Murat and Pierre de Nolhac.[84] Soon afterwards a local organization was formed called *Gagne-Pain des Mutilés (Bread for the Wounded)*, whose purpose was to help war wounded gain an honourable living. The committee included Audollent and several lawyers.[85] By the end of the year a school for re-training the wounded had been set up (*École professionnelle des Blessés de Guerre*), working alongside an initiative providing accommodation for wounded soldiers (A.C.M. Assistance pour les Convalescents militaires).[86] The chamber of commerce in Clermont-Ferrand gave its financial support to the school.[87]

The *oeuvre de guerre* with the most obviously Auvergnat appeal was the *Journée du Puy-de-Dôme* on 23 January 1916. This was a special fundraising effort for a previously established *oeuvre*, the *paquetage du soldat*, which sought donations for parcels to be sent to soldiers giving them a few home comforts. It was an opportunity for ordinary people to send gifts in kind rather than money and many donations were made in this way.[88] By the end of 1915 200,000 francs had been raised and an equivalent value of goods sent out.[89] On the occasion of the *Journée du Puy-de-Dôme* itself, donors were told that “giving to the Puy-de-Dôme day, is giving to all the natives of the Auvergne.”[90] Badges were sold on the streets including one depicting the arms of the Auvergne.[91] The badges sold out raising 17,000 francs on the day so there was a repeat sale on 6 February. The posters for this fundraising contained obvious references—Vercingétorix and volcano-shaped mountains.[92] Frequently such packets included warm clothing—warm hats, socks, etc (Fig. 6.1). It is worth pointing out that posters for

[84] *Le Moniteur du Puy-de-Dôme* (10 mai 1915), 3 col b–c.

[85] *Le Moniteur du Puy-de-Dôme* (24 juin 1915), 3 col b. *L'Avenir du Puy-de-Dôme* (24 juin 1915), 2 col d–e.

[86] *Le Moniteur du Puy-de-Dôme* (8 décembre 1915), 3 col d.

[87] *Travaux Clermont-Ferrand*, (séance 15 février 1917), 15.

[88] *Le Moniteur du Puy-de-Dôme* (5 février 1915), 3 col d, (11 février 1915), 3 col c, (12 février 1915), 3 col d. *L'Avenir du Puy-de-Dôme* (18 janvier 1916), 2 col d.

[89] *Le Moniteur du Puy-de-Dôme* (4 décembre 1915), 3 col d, (29 décembre 1915), 3 col c. *L'Avenir du Puy-de-Dôme* (29 décembre 1915), 3 col a–b.

[90] *Le Moniteur du Puy-de-Dôme* (20 janvier 1916), 3 col e.

[91] *Le Moniteur du Puy-de-Dôme* (22 janvier 1916), 3 col c.

[92] Patrimoine, web site Overnia, GR 12017, Affiches, Willette, A.L., *Journée du Puy-de-Dôme, Vercingétorix soldat au front, paquetage du soldat, 23 janvier 1916,* (Imprimeur Devambez, Paris, 1916). BNF, IFN-9013081, *F. Poulbot, Journée du Puy-de-Dôme, paquetage du soldat, 23 janvier 1916, “Avec ça, il ne serait pas enrhumé, papa. With that, Papa will not catch a cold.”*

**Fig. 6.1** F. Poulbot, Journée du Puy-de-Dôme, paquetage du soldat, 23 January 1916, "With that, Papa will not catch a cold." Courtesy of the Bibliothèque Nationale de France

regional fundraising days, for the Auvergne and many other regions, were produced by the well-known house of Devambez in Paris who provided appropriate designs and a finished printed product. They also produced posters for many national appeals. However, this does not invalidate the point that organizers thought their regional appeal would be more successful if an appeal was made to regional solidarity.[93]

[93] I am indebted for this insight to Pierre Purseigle of the University of Warwick, who also drew attention to similar posters used in the Languedoc in P. Purseigle, *Mobilisation, sacrifice, citoyenneté: Angleterre-France 1900–1918* (Paris, 2013), 103–109. For examples of Devambez's regional posters see R. Paillard, *Affiches 14–18* (Reims, 1986), 64, 116, 119.

There is thus some evidence that patriotism in the Auvergne in support of the war drew its strength from an identification with the region and appealed to regional loyalties in support of the French cause; the *petite patrie* supporting the *grande patrie* again.

The contrast between patriotism in Lorraine and the Auvergne is fairly clear. Regional patriotism was less fiercely expressed in the Auvergne which was far from the front. It seems to have been strongest there among the intellectual elite. Its brightest and fullest expression was to be found in a literary work, Henri Pourrat's epic poem *Les Montagnards*. Here we find a dramatic expression of the unity between the sacred soil of France defended by soldiers on the front and the soil of the *petite patrie* of their homeland. As in Lorraine regional solidarity was expressed through charitable activities during the war which appealed to an Auvergnat sense of belonging.

## The Clermont-Ferrand Chamber of Commerce

We have seen that the Auvergne had some sense of regional solidarity, an important regional centre in Clermont-Ferrand and a university of some standing. We now turn to look at the leadership of the Clermont-Ferrand chamber of commerce and the economic region. The chamber's committee and membership mainly represented smaller enterprises, with the notable exception of Raymond Bergougnan, and also included a number of officials and representatives of the local *Banque de France*.[94] The Clermont-Ferrand chamber was totally different in character from the chamber in Nancy. It was smaller with circa 25 members, as opposed to 40 in Nancy, mainly due to the latter's larger number of *membres correspondants*.[95] Average attendance was also lower, somewhere between 10 and 20. Clermont-Ferrand did not think it had much voting weight in the assembly of presidents of chambers of commerce which was organized regularly by the Paris chamber.[96]

The occupations of the Clermont members were different from those in Nancy. There were proportionately more traders as opposed to manufacturers. There were also relatively few professionals like engineers

[94] *Travaux Clermont-Ferrand*, 1914, 5–8.

[95] See *Compte-Rendu des travaux de la Chambre de Commerce de Clermont-Ferrand 1919–1920 and 1923–24* (Clermont-Ferrand published 1920–1921 and 1924–25).

[96] *Travaux Clermont-Ferrand, 1924* (séance 8 janvier 1924), 14.

or university professors. There was a coal mining engineer and also a representative of the hydro-electric company of the Auvergne. The president throughout the period in question was Maurice Chalus, the owner of a private bank in the Auvergne. Like Dreux in Lorraine, he was president of the regional grouping of chambers of commerce. He was also a member of the *Conseil supérieur du Commerce*, which met regularly in Paris.[97] He was obviously a man of means. In 1923 he made a loan to the university's chemistry institute for repairs.[98] His vice-presidents were Raymond Bergougnan of the eponymous rubber company in Clermont-Ferrand and a merchant A-A. Jouve. The secretary was A-A. Lagaye, a manufacturer of *fruits confits*. The treasurer was a distiller of liqueurs. Édouard Michelin was also a member although not on the *bureau*. Another difference from Nancy is that the prefect of the Puy-de-Dôme was an honorary president and did attend from time to time, more frequently than his opposite number in Meurthe-et-Moselle. Occasionally he sent the secretary-general of the prefecture in his place. Prefects did not have direct control over either the chambers of commerce or the new regions. Their role in the new regions was only consultative.[99]

The comparison between Bergougnan and Michelin is an interesting one. Édouard Michelin resigned in November 1923 having not attended a single meeting in the previous four years. His excuse was that he had agreed to serve during the war but had always made it clear he could not do so afterwards.[100] Generally, he held himself apart from local affairs. Raymond Bergougnan, however, was a member of the municipal council of Clermont-Ferrand, as well as being a vice-president of the chamber. He was also assiduous in actual attendance at meetings. His absences were very rare. More than this he was also vice-president of the Union of the *Syndicats patronaux of the Puy-de-Dôme* of which Lagaye was president.[101] (The union was more directly concerned than the chamber in defending the interests of business owners.[102]) Bergougnan was very close to Étienne

[97] *Travaux Clermont-Ferrand, 1924* (séance 26 juin 1924), 136.

[98] *Travaux Clermont-Ferrand, 1923* (séance 14 novembre 1923), 93.

[99] Druelle-Korn, 'Modernisation inachevée', 163.

[100] *Travaux Clermont-Ferrand, 1923* (séance 14 novembre 1923), 88–9.

[101] 'Assemblée générale des syndicats patronaux 26 décembre 1922,' *Le Commerce*, bulletin de l'Association du commerce et de l'industrie du Puy-de-Dôme, des Syndicats patronaux et de la Fédération des groups commerciaux et industriels du Centre, no. 74 (jan-février 1923), 5.

[102] A. Lagaye, 'Devoir Syndical,' *Le Commerce*, no. 73 (décembre 1922), 5–6.

Clémentel, who was on his board and was his commercial representative in Paris, at one point obtaining for Bergougnan a contract to supply tyres to the Paris bus company. Maurice Chalus's brother Joseph was also on the Bergougnan board.[103] Michelin's marketing policy was much more aggressive than say Bergougnan's.[104] Michelin had patented the pneumatic tyre, suitable for the private car which the company foresaw would eventually be produced in huge numbers. Bergougnan stayed with solid rubber tyres, more suitable for buses and trucks. In the thirties Michelin bought out the Bergougnan company.

## The Economic Region

The work of the Clermont-Ferrand chamber and its relationship to the economic region is chiefly of interest because it took place under the watchful eye of Étienne Clémentel, the most powerful Auvergnat politician of his generation. Clémentel naturally came down to his fief to initiate the proceedings of the Auvergne region, which he did on 27 April 1918. Representatives of the Clermont and other chambers of commerce in the region were present plus the prefects and some of Clémentel's aides from the Ministry of Commerce.[105] After the election in November 1919 he had more time to take an interest because he lost his seat as a deputy and therefore his position as a minister in the government. Subsequently he became president of the *Conseil-général* of the Puy-de-Dôme and a senator.

The new region was not formally constituted until 22 February 1919, two months before the ministerial decree which authorized the new groupings.[106] At this meeting the regional chambers of commerce and prefects were represented plus Allegret, an official from the Ministry of Commerce. This time Clémentel could not attend because he was heavily engaged negotiating the Treaty of Versailles. A new regional committee was chosen. Clermont-Ferrand had two votes and the other chambers

[103] Moulin-Bourret, *Guerre et industrie*, 61, 110, 114.

[104] S. Harp, *Marketing Michelin: advertising and cultural identity in twentieth century France* (John Hopkins, 2001).

[105] *XVIIe région économique, groupement régional de Clermont-Ferrand, Compte-rendu des travaux du comité régional et du comité consultatif régional économique, séances des 29 avril 1918, 17 juin et 19 août 1919* (Clermont-Ferrand, s.d.), 7.

[106] An account of this important meeting is to be found in *Travaux Clermont-Ferrand*, 1919 (séance 22 février 1919), 33–57.

one, because Clermont had far more registered businesses (*patentés*) than the other towns, which were Ambert, Riom, Montluçon, Moulins, Aurillac and Thiers. Chalus became president of the new region, the presidents of Moulins and Thiers became vice-presidents and the president of Riom treasurer. The budget for expenditure was set at 60–80,000 francs and would be met by a supplementary levy on qualifying firms.[107] A year later Clermont's contribution was set at 32,168 francs.[108]

Defining the region was not exactly straightforward. After all there was no commonly accepted definition of the region often referred to as the Auvergne. The original policy documents from the centre included the old province of the Bourbonnais, or in other words the department of the Allier, in the new Auvergne region. The main justification for this seemed to be that it was vital to improve communications between the Allier and Clermont along the line of the river basin. The chamber of commerce at Moulins accepted this and then later raised objections. It also felt an attachment to the departments of the centre of France and to Bourges. At the first normal meeting of the region on 19 August 1919, at which Clémentel was present, it was announced that Moulins had decided on 13 June to hold off joining for the moment. Mathiot, the secretary-general of the region, thought this was a totally inadmissible attitude. He said there were many common concerns which united Moulins and Clermont-Ferrand. Clermont had always been accepted as the regional capital. Clermont was the military, postal and ministry of justice chief town and had a well-established university. Moulins seemed to be playing off the Minister of the Interior against the Minister of Commerce, as Clémentel's opponents had in Paris, but Mathiot said his loyalties lay with the latter. In the end Moulins towed the line.[109] The adherence of the Allier continued to be a matter of concern to some in Clermont. The *Région du Centre* published an article in its June–July issue 1921 entitled *L'Allier doit-il être rattaché?* The conclusion was that the economic and transport links between the Allier and the Puy-de-Dôme were enough to justify the move.[110]

The question of Brioude had already been settled. Its closer links with Clermont were recognized by the chamber of commerce in Le Puy. The

[107] *Travaux Clermont-Ferrand,* 1919 (séance 22 février 1919), 55.
[108] *Travaux Clermont-Ferrand,* 1920 (séance 14 avril 1920), 46.
[109] *Travaux Clermont-Ferrand,* 1919 (séance 30 septembre 1919), 99–128.
[110] *Région du Centre,* no. 2 (juin–juillet 1921), 5–9.

solution was to create a brand-new chamber of commerce for Brioude and then attach it to the Auvergne region.[111]

Lastly there were discussions about Tulle and the department of the Corrèze. Tulle had links with three regions: with Bordeaux, Limoges and Clermont-Ferrand. At the meeting of the regional committee attended by Clémentel on 19 August 1919 Mathiot, the secretary-general, argued for the attachment of the *arrondissement* of Ussel, which was part of the Tulle chamber, to the Auvergne region. He suggested this would facilitate plans for the exploitation of hydro-electricity on the Dordogne river and also improvements to railway lines from Tulle to Clermont. Maybe it would be better if Tulle itself joined the Auvergne region, he added.[112] Clémentel's flexibility, allowing chambers to be attached to more than one region, overcame this problem and by 12 April 1921 Rambaud, the president of the chamber at Tulle had joined the deliberations of the Auvergne region's committee. He was to play a prominent part in the development of the Dordogne hydro-electric project.[113]

## Conclusions: Success Factors in the Auvergne

Like Lorraine the Auvergne had a sense of identity and regional solidarity, even if it was not so keenly felt or so widespread among the population. There were arguably areas whose attachment to the centre at Clermont-Ferrand was not strong—such as Brioude or the Bourbonnais. The Cantal was almost entirely agricultural, in contrast to the more urban Puy-de-Dôme with the industrial centre of Clermont-Ferrand. Clermont was clearly the dominant regional centre even if it was difficult for some of the population to reach. It had a university which played a part in regional life and provided advice to industry. The Clermont chamber did take a lead even if the Michelin brothers did not support it. The other chambers took an important role in pushing forward the power project on the Dordogne. Mathiot, the regional secretary, was effective and made sure the journal *Région du Centre* provided useful news to increase a regional sense of belonging in the constituent departments. It supported the regional tourist organizations which were particularly dynamic. Lastly the continued

[111] *Travaux Clermont-Ferrand*, 1919 (séance 24 juillet 1919), 91.

[112] 'Réunion de la Région du 19 août 1919', *XVIIe région économique*, 46–7.

[113] 'Réunion du Comité régional 12 avril 1921', in *Region du Centre*, no. 2 (juin–juillet 1921), 18.

presence of Clémentel in the Puy-de-Dôme as president of the *conseil-général* ensured that regional affairs were given due consideration.

## Bibliography


AD P-de-D, Fonds du Comité de Secours des Établissements Bergougnan, F 028, 'Courrier et gazette des tranchées réalisés par deux employés de l'usine Bergougnan, de la 14e compagnie du 201e Régiment d'Infanterie', 28 juillet 1915, quoted in Puy-de-Dôme Conseil-Général, *Des Armes aux larmes 1914–1918, l'engagement patriotique du Puy-de-Dôme* (Clermont-Ferrand, Cahier des Archives, 2014).

AD P-de-D, La Grande Collecte, 'Lettre Léger Debost, lettres Adolphe Féneyrols, carnets Eugène Martin'.

Ajalbert, J. (1932). *Auvergne.*

Ajalbert, J. (1893). *En Auvergne.*

Amalvi, C. (1988). *De l'Art et la manière d'accommoder les héros de l'histoire de France.*

Ardouin-Dumazet, V. E. (1927). *Voyage en France: Auvergne, Vol. II Haute-Auvergne Cantal.*

Besson, P. (1914). *Le Pâtre du Cantal.*

Bonnefoy, G. (1903) *Canal latéral de l'Allier.*

Boule, M., & Farges, L. (1898). *Le Cantal, Guide.*

Boule, M., Glangeaud, P., Rouchon, G., & Vernière, A. (1901). *Le Puy-de-Dôme et Vichy, guide du touriste, du naturaliste et de l'archéologue.*

Bréhier, L. (1912). *L'Auvergne.*

Cathala, E. (2008). *L'Auvergne* (Facsimile de l'édition de Paris, fin du 19e siècle).

Chaline, N.-J. (2014). *Émile Guillaumin paysan-écrivain bourbonnais, soldat de la Grande Guerre.*

Chanet, J.-F. (2000). *Les Félibres cantaliens : aux sources du régionalisme auvergnat 1879–1914.*

Charbonnier, P. (1999). Histoire de l'Auvergne des origines à nos jours; Haute et Basse-Auvergne, *Bourbonnais et Velay.* Clermont-Ferrand.

*Compte-Rendu des travaux de la Chambre de Commerce de Clermont-Ferrand 1919–1920 and 1923–24* (Clermont-Ferrand published 1920–1921 and 1924–25).

Cornu, P. (2014). Auvergne dans la Grande Guerre. *Les Montagnards* d'Henri Pourrat et la rhétorique de la dette. *Siècles* [En ligne], 39–40. http://journals.openedition.org/siecles/2799

Dalet, C. (Ed.). (2013). *Correspondance croisée Henri Pourrat–Joseph Desaymard 1913 à 1918: la Grande Guerre.* Clermont-Ferrand.

Delzangles, F. (1910). *Folklore cantalien, chants populaires d'Auvergne.*

Den Boer, P., & Pomerans, A. (2014). *History as a profession, the study of history in France 1818–1914*. Princeton.
Desaymard, J. (1908). *Artiste Auvergnat Emmanuel Chabrier*. Revue d'Auvergne.
Desaymard, J. (1935). *L'Art et les artistes en Auvergne*. Saint-Etienne.
Doniol, H. (1900). *La Basse-Auvergne*.
Druelle-Korn, C. (2014). La modernisation inachevée de l'aménagement du territoire, le cas de la VII[e] Région (Limousin, Poitou, Charentes). In A. Aglan, M. Margairaz, & P. Verheyde (Eds.), *De la croissance à la crise (1925–1935): Le moment Tannery, une tentative avortée de modernisation conservatrice et libérale à l'heure de la mondialisation* (pp. 155–172).
Duroux, R. (2018). *Les Auvergnats de Castille. Rennaissance et mort d'une migration au XIXe siècle*. Clermont-Ferrand, Faculté des Lettres et Sciences-humaines, Université de Blaise-Pascal.
Ehrard, A. (1980). *Vercingétorix contre Gergovie? Nos ancêtres les Gaulois*. (Clermont-Ferrand, June 1980), 309. https://hal-clermont-univ.archives-ouvertes.fr/hal-01410214
Exposition Musée Roger Quillot, Clermont-Ferrand (2014).
Férier, G. (1987). Les Conséquences démographiques de la Grande Guerre en Auvergne. *Guerres mondiales et conflits contemporains, 145*, 81–94.
Gobin, L. (1896). *Essai sur la géographie de l'Auvergne* Clermont-Ferrand.
Gourbeyre, A. (1900). *La* Petite Propriété rurale dans le Puy-de-Dôme. Thèse de doctorat, Faculté de Droit.
Guillaumin, E. (1904). *Vie d'un Simple*.
Harp, S. (2001). *Marketing Michelin: Advertising and cultural identity in twentieth century France*. John Hopkins.
Joanne, P. (1904). *Itinéraire général de la France*. Auvergne et Centre.
Joucla, E., & Cortat, R. (1929). *Lectures d'Auvergne*.
Jouve, A. (1910). *Création d'un canal latéral à l'Allier*. Chambres de Commerce de Clermont-Ferrand, Riom et Issoire.
L'Avenir du Puy-de-Dôme 1915.
*L'Université de Clermont-Ferrand* (Clermont-Ferrand, 1900).
La Salle de Rochemaure Duc de. (1909). *Régionalisme auvergnat, conférence donnée à la Faculté des Lettres de l'Académie de Clermont-Ferrand, le 23 janvier 1909*.
*La Veillée d'Auvergne* 1909, 1911, *1912*, 1914.
Landouzy Le Professeur, *Le Mont-Dore, station hydrominérale et station d'altitude* (Châtelles, Vosges, 1906).
*Le Commerce*, bulletin de l'Association du commerce et de l'industrie du Puy-de-Dôme, des Syndicats patronaux et de la Fédération des groups commerciaux et industriels du Centre, 1922, 1923.
*Le Moniteur du Puy-de-Dôme* 1903, 1915–1918.

Le Musée Francisque Mandet, Riom, *Entre Chien et* loup. La Veillée, naissance d'un mythe ? Les Veillées en Auvergne en milieu rural et urbain, du XIXe siècle à nos jours (2003).

Kessler, M.-C., & Rousseau, G. (2018). La trajectoire sociale d'Étienne Clémentel. In M.-C. Kessler, & G. Rousseau (Eds.), *Étienne Clémentel: politique et action publique sous la Troisième République.*

Manry, A.-G. (Ed.). (1974). *Histoire de l'Auvergne.*

Marcoline, C. (Ed.). (s.d.). *Un Auvergnat dans la paix et dans la guerre, chroniques auvergnates autour des journaux de la guerre 14/18 de Jean et Jacques Lacoste.*

Martin, D. (Ed.). (2002). *L'Identité de l'Auvergne, mythe ou réalité historique, essai sur une histoire de l'Auvergne des origines à nos jours.* Université de Blaise-Pascal.

Masfrand, J. (1896). *Le Cantal guide du touriste, du botaniste et du géologue (Aurillac).*

Mathé, R.. (1966). *Émile Guillaumin, homme de la terre et l'homme de lettres.*

Mazières, J. (1965). *Arsène Vermenouze 1850–1910 et la Haute-Auvergne de son temps.*

Moulin-Bourret, A. (1997). *Guerre et industrie Clermont-Ferrand 1912–1922: la victoire du pneu* (2 vols, Faculté des Lettres et Sciences humaines de l'Université Blaise Pascal (Clermont II), publications de l'Institut d'Études du Massif Central (Centre d'Histoire des Entreprises et des Communautés)).

Nolhac, P. de. (1888). *Pages Auvergnates.*

Ozouf, M. (1984). *L'École de France.*

Paillard, R. (1986). *Affiches* 14–18.

Bibliothèque du Patrimoine, Clermont-Ferrand (abbreviation Patrimoine) Fonds Georges Desdevises du Dézert, 'Dossiers documentaires sur les savants, les écrivains et les artistes de l'Auvergne contemporaine réunis par Georges Desdevises du Dézert (1854–1942)', MS 1740 Gandilhon, MS 1658 Clémentel, MS 1608 Boyer, MS 1538 Angeli, MS 1453 poètes d'Auvergne, MS 1720 Louis Farges, MS 1671 Courchinoux, MS 1561 Bardoux.

Patrimoine, MSS Henri Pourrat HP 125, fasc. 20.

Patrimoine, MSS Joseph Desaymard JD12, Brouillons et manuscrits 1910–1914, fol. 266–76, 'Blaise Pascal et Maurice Barrès d'après un article récent'; also MSS Joseph Desaymard JD21, fasc. 63–72; Fonds Georges Desdevises du Dézert, Louis Farges MSS 1720.

Patrimoine, MSS Joseph Desaymard JD12, brouillons on Pastourel.

Patrimoine, web site Overnia, GR 12017,

Pineau, L. Le Foklore de l'Auvergne. In A. Van Bever (Ed.), *Auvergne et Limousin Histoire, Tableaux Pittoresques, Poésies, Chansons Populaires, Contes et Légendes* (s.d.).

Pomian, K. (1992). Francs et Gaulois. In P. Nora (Ed.), *Les Lieux de mémoire, T. III Les France, vol.1 conflits et partages* (pp. 40–105).

Pourrat, H. (2016). *Les Montagnards, chronique paysanne de la Grande Guerre* (repr. Paris, 2016).
Purseigle, P. (2013). *Mobilisation, sacrifice, citoyenneté: Angleterre-France 1900–1918.*
Raison-Jourde, F. (1976). *La Colonie auvergnate de Paris au XIXe siècle.*
Région du Centre, 1921.
*Revue d'Auvergne*, 1899, 1911, 1913.
*Revue de la Haute-Auvergne* 1905, 1911.
Reynaud, B. L. (1911). L'esprit agricole et le retour à la terre. *Bulletin historique, scientifique, littéraire, artistique et agricole de la Société scientifique et agricole du Puy-en-Velay et la Haute-Loire, fasc.3*, 195–213.
Solet, B. (Ed.). (1981). *15 Histoires d'Auvergne.*
*Travaux de la Chambre de Commerce de Clermont-Ferrand*, 1914, 1917, 1919, 1920, 1921, 1923, 1924.
Willette, A. L., *Journée du Puy-de-Dôme, Vercingétorix soldat au front, paquetage du soldat, 23 janvier 1916,* (Imprimeur Devambez, Paris, 1916). BNF, IFN-9013081, *F. Poulbot, Journée du Puy-de-Dôme, paquetage du soldat, 23 janvier 1916,* "*Avec ça, il ne serait pas enrhumé, papa. With that, Papa will not catch a cold.*"
*XVIIe région économique, groupement régional de Clermont-Ferrand, Compte-rendu des travaux du comité régional et du comité consultatif régional économique, séances des 29 avril* 1918, 17 juin et 19 août 1919 (Clermont-Ferrand, s.d.).

CHAPTER 7

# Toulouse and Other Regions of France

We have discovered in the previous chapters the main factors which account for the successful initiation of regional development projects in Lorraine and the Auvergne. Both regions had a clearly articulated sense of regional identity based on their cultural heritage and their experiences during the First World War. Both had dominant regional centres—Nancy and Clermont-Ferrand, with important universities and new technical and scientific institutes. There was in both regions a sense of solidarity. There was also in both regions a leadership group determined to take advantage of the opportunities offered by Clémentel's reform. In Nancy the chamber of commerce was an effective organization, which was able to exploit its contacts in Paris and with other regional organizations. There was indeed some rivalry with Metz and Strasbourg, but they showed they could work together for example on the exploitation of the Rhine or the canalization of the Moselle. The influence of the Nancy chamber was dependent on the presence there of some of the leading ironmasters of Lorraine. The Lorraine iron and steel industry was of great importance to the French economy. Lorraine also had influence in Paris because of what the region had suffered during the war on the front line.

In the Auvergne the continuing political influence of Clémentel in the region ensured that regional development opportunities were not overlooked. Although he lost his seat in the Chamber of Deputies, he was elected a senator and was also president of the *conseil-général* of the



T. Cudbird, *The Origins of Economic Regions in France, 1918–1940*,
https://doi.org/10.1007/978-3-032-04422-8_7

Puy-de-Dôme. The region had an energetic and conscientious secretary in Charles Mathiot. Although there were no leaders with quite the influence of the Lorraine ironmasters, there was no shortage of business people with technical knowledge who were prepared to step up and take a leading role in developing projects. A good example is Clément Rambaud who led the charge on the development of hydro-electricity. It was the individual chambers in both regions who had to make the financial commitments involved in projects, particularly in the development of hydro-electricity. However, the two leading chambers in Clermont-Ferrand and Nancy were prepared to work through the regional committee where necessary, to use it as a way of convening support for projects they wished to pursue. In both cases the region published an important publication—the *Union Économique de L'Est* and the *Région du Centre*—which set out what they were trying to achieve. It is significant that Clémentel recognized the leading role these regions were likely to take in the development of his regional reform, when he chose to visit them personally soon after the passage of the enabling decrees.

The dynamism of these two regions poses the question, what progress was made in regional development in the other economic regions created by Clémentel? In the case of Lorraine and the Auvergne, we find a willingness among the regional leadership to execute projects themselves, making some financial commitment through the constituent chambers of commerce. Such an activist approach seems to have existed in five other regions—Limousin, Lyon, Grenoble, Marseille, Paris. We have already seen in the chapter on the Auvergne how the Limousin region was also involved in the Dordogne power project. It was unsurprisingly also concerned to improve communication links, working through the *Office des Transports for the Centre-Ouest.*[1] The Limousin region studied doubling the line from Limoges to Angoulême because of increased traffic to the coast.[2] Philippe Veitl[3] has described the movement to imagine and realize an economic region of the Alps centred on Grenoble and based on industries using hydro-electricity, *la houille blanche.*

[1] Druelle-Korn, 'La Modernisation inachevée de l'aménagement du territoire, le cas de la VIIe région, (Limousin, Poitou, Charentes), in A. Aglan, M. Margairaz, et P. Verheyde (eds), *De la croissance à la crise (1925–1935) Le moment Tannery; Une tentative avortée de modernisation conservatrice et libérale à l'heure de la mondialisation* (Paris, 2014), 164, 166.

[2] F. Prevet, *Le Régionalisme économique, conception et réalisation* (Thèse de doctorat, Faculté de Droit de Paris, 1929), 126–128.

[3] P. Veitl, *L'Invention d'une région: les Alpes françaises* (Grenoble, 2013).

One other major project where regional leaders got involved in execution was the creation of the *Compagnie Nationale du Rhône* during the period from 1921 onwards. This involved the regions based in Lyon, Grenoble and Marseille. The concept here was to create one concessionaire for the development of the Rhône, using the revenue from hydro-electricity to pay for improvements to navigation and irrigation for agriculture. The resulting vehicle was a unique *cooperative régionale d'économie mixte*, which created a precedent in French administrative law as it combined public (local authorities and the state) and private shareholders, including chambers of commerce like Lyon. Private financing was accepted because the government had insufficient funds for all the reconstruction and development urgently needed after the First World War. The Lyon chamber kick started the project with a meeting in 1899 to which interested parties were invited. The chambers in Grenoble, Marseille and Valence were also supportive. Léon Perrier was a local politician and the driving force behind the project. Like Clémentel he was a regionalist in economic matters. Perrier received invaluable support from Édouard Herriot, again a powerful figure in Lyon and later Président du Conseil in the Cartel des Gauches. An inter-departmental commission put forward recommendations and an enabling law was passed in the Chamber of Deputies in 1921. It was envisaged that the regions would have a preferential right to the current generated by the scheme. This was common for concessions granted for hydro-electricity plants under government legislation passed in 1919. After the enabling legislation, it took 12 years to get the company formed and operating in 1933. Certain local authorities were unhappy with the details. The Conseil d'État had reservations about a mixed company. The financial crisis affecting the franc in the twenties also impacted the project. It was the support of the chambers of commerce, and particularly Lyon, which kept the whole project alive. After the company was formed, work on the Génissiat power plant followed in the 1930s and also on the Herriot port in Lyon. An agricultural scheme was started in the Crau valley on the lower Rhône.[4] Meanwhile in the inter-war years, the Paris region, the 16th, initiated a project to dam the upper reaches of the Seine, thus providing drinking water, controlling floods in Paris itself which could be serious and generating some hydro-electricity.[5]

[4] A. Giandou, *La Compagnie Nationale du Rhône 1933–1998; histoire d'un partenaire régional de l'état* (Grenoble, 1999), 18–36.

[5] J. Duplantier, *Le Régionalisme économique et spécialement la région économique de Bordeaux et du Sud-Ouest* (Thèse de doctorat, Faculté de Droit de Bordeaux, 1929), 155;

In this chapter I will look at the experience of one other region in detail—the ninth region centred on Toulouse. I will then survey the effectiveness of regions in other areas of France not already discussed. The remit of the regions initially was to cover commerce and industry, not agriculture. I shall therefore return to the latter in a separate chapter and at the same time will consider tourism, which like agriculture, had its own regional organizations outside the economic regions created by Clémentel.

## Toulouse

Toulouse was an important centre for the preservation of regional culture with a university dating back to the thirteenth century. It was also conveniently situated between Bordeaux to the west and the Mediterranean littoral to the east with good communications by rail and canal. It was predominantly an agricultural area with small peasant holdings but new industries developed during the war as Toulouse was far from the battle front. Exploitation of the hydro-electric resources of the Pyrenees facilitated new enterprises in the electro-chemical and electro-metallurgical sectors. The government also decided to locate a new Office de L'Azote in Toulouse to exploit the BASF processes for manufacturing nitrate fertilizers, the rights to which had been given to France in the Treaty of Versailles. However, there was greater uncertainty here about what use should be made of the new regional structure. This internal debate revealed some of the weaknesses of Clémentel's reform. This chapter will cover all these issues in more detail.

## Cultural Heritage

The region of Toulouse was part of the Languedoc which had its own cultural traditions dating back to the time in the early Middle Ages when the province was politically independent and the Counts of Toulouse the dominant influence. The region was absorbed into the Kingdom of France after the war against the Cathar heresy, but the estates of Languedoc remained active throughout the *Ancien Régime*. Occitan language and literature were revived in the nineteenth century when Frédéric Mistral founded his Félibrige. This cultural revival was still active immediately

P. Brun, *Les Régions* Économiques (Thèse de doctorat, Sciences Politiques et Économiques, Montpellier 1928), 71–2; Prevet, 119–120.

before and after the First World War. Paul Gachon in his 1929 study of the Languedoc noted that the solidarity of this region was still very much alive through intellectual studies.[6] The Jeux Floraux celebrating Occitan poetry still took place regularly in Toulouse.[7] Clémence Issaure, the founder of the Jeux Floraux, became something of a cult in the city.[8] The *Cri de Toulouse* noted that love of the Occitan language and literature had spread far to the west of the Rhône since Mistral, which might have surprised him as he wrote in the Provençal dialect.[9] The Escola Occitana and the magazine *Lo Gai Saber* were still very active.[10] De Gélis, writing in the *Mémoires of the Academy of Sciences in Toulouse*, noted in 1921 that Occitan was still developing and adapting to modern life.[11] Anglade, who was a member of the Escola, published his history of the Troubadors in 1928.[12] Costumes, music and folkloric dancing were an important part of this cultural heritage. On 29 June 1924 an event took place in Toulouse including 400 costumes from across the Languedoc as well as popular Occitan songs.[13] In the same year an Occitan study group was founded in Paris.[14] There was also an Association Toulousaine in Paris which offered events like concerts of Languedoc music and had a publication called *Le Capitole*. There had also been regular exhibitions of Midi artists since 1910 through the Salon des Artistes Méridionaux.[15] Another publication called *L'Oeuvre Méridionale* was started in 1918 by a new association, the Fédération littéraire, artistique et économique du Midi. It celebrated expressions of Midi culture in art and music.[16] Yet another publication to cover Occitan literature was *Le Soleil de Toulouse*, a satirical journal.[17]

*La Dépêche de Toulouse*, the leading daily newspaper, published a number of Visions du Languedoc about different places within the region, which showed they thought their readers would be interested in the

[6] P. Gachon, *Languedoc* (Paris, 1921), 329.

[7] *La Dépêche de Toulouse*, 3 mai 1913, 4.

[8] *Le Cri de Toulouse*, 14 septembre 1912, 3.

[9] Ibid, 20 octobre 1929, 3.

[10] *Le Cri de Toulouse*, 20 octobre 1929, 3.

[11] M. F. De Gélis, 'La Vraie Langue d'Oc, l'ancienne et la nouvelle langue d'oc,' *Mémoires de l'Académie des sciences, inscriptions et belles-lettres de Toulouse*, 1 janvier 1921, 115–140.

[12] J. Anglade, *Les Troubadors de Toulouse* (Toulouse, 1928).

[13] *L'Express du Midi*, 29 juin 1924, 3.

[14] *La Dépêche de Toulouse*, 6 décembre 1924, 3.

[15] *Le Midi Républicain*, 66e année, dimanche le 6 juillet 1930, for artists see pp. 2–3.

[16] *L'Oeuvre Méridionale*, décembre 1918 32; avril-mai 1936, 1683.

[17] *Le Soleil de Toulouse*, 2ème année, 24 mai 1925, 4–5; 28 juin 1925, 5; 12 juillet 1925, 5.

Languedoc's history.[18] Regional identity in Toulouse was bound up with pride in the city's history and monuments.[19] In 1929 the city celebrated the 700th anniversary of the founding of the University of Toulouse.[20] Doumergue, the president of the Republic, attended the ceremonies. The university was well known, not only for the study of the liberal arts but increasingly for its scientific institutes. It was a centre of expertise for the region in the same way as the University in Nancy. The regional reform of the universities in 1896 was fundamental to the identity of the economic regions. The Toulouse faculty of sciences created in the early twentieth century an *Institut de Chimie*, an *Institut électrotechnique* (1907), an *Institut agricole* and four other agricultural research institutions. In addition, the chamber of commerce founded an *École supérieure de commerce* in 1902–3. An *École pratique de l'Industrie hôtelière* followed in 1917. An *École des Métiers* for training in craft skills was started by the *conseil-général* of the Haute-Garonne in 1922.[21]

There was also a sense of regional solidarity born of the experiences of the war. As in the Auvergne and Lorraine a number of committees were formed to help Toulousain victims of the war such as wounded soldiers, prisoners and orphans.[22] However, the weakness in the regional sense of identity in the ninth region was that cultural ties and also economic links spread far beyond its borders. Occitan language and culture pulled Toulouse towards the east, but economic links to Bordeaux. In 1926 an article appeared in *Sud-Ouest Économique*, a journal devoted to encouraging economic development across the South-West regardless of regional boundaries. It was written by Hubert Lagardelle, a leading thinker on regional issues and secretary of the ninth region. It was entitled 'Interrégionalisme, Bordeaux-Toulouse,' but it equally applied as far east as Montpellier. He pointed out the economic links which bound Toulouse to the great port of Bordeaux. He also referred to the work of the *Offices*

[18] *La Dépêche de Toulouse*, 23, 1, 30 juin 1924;1, 31 juillet 1924, 1; 25 août 1924, 1; 12 octobre 1924, 1; 22 novembre 1924, 1; 18 mai 1925, 1; 11 septembre 1925, 1.

[19] 'Chronique Toulousaine,' *Le Cri de Toulouse*, 4 décembre 1927, 251.

[20] 'Les Fêtes du VIIe centenaire de l'Université de Toulouse,' *Le Cri de Toulouse*, 9 juin 1929, 3.

[21] L. Dutil, *La Haute-Garonne et sa région*, (Toulouse, 1929), t.1., 291, 293. C. Bouneau, *Entre David et Goliath: la dynamique des réseaux régionaux: réseaux ferroviaires, réseaux électriques et régionalisation économique en France du milieu du XIXe siècles au milieu du XXe siècle* (Pessac, 2008), 372, 379, 381–2.

[22] "Les Oeuvres de Guerre,' *La Dépêche de Toulouse*, 16 octobre 1915, 4.

*des Transports*, set up to manage relationships between transport companies, principally the railways, and users. The office for the South-West covered Bordeaux, Toulouse and Montpellier. He also pointed to other regional administrative boundaries, such as the universities or the military which overlapped.[23] The journal published another article on *Le Sud-Ouest* by Maxime Leroy, president of organizations representing the South-West. He referred to the cultural heritage of Gascony and the Basque country and suggested that Toulouse economically and culturally was part of the Midi and the Languedoc but also part of Gascony. It straddled the two.[24] We can see the practical result of these divided loyalties in a discussion at the Toulouse chamber of commerce about financing the economic region. It was noted that several chambers of commerce in the ninth region also adhered to the Bordeaux region as they were allowed to do under the government decree which set up the regions.[25] In a discussion at the chamber on 12 May 1923, the president and treasurer said that neighbouring regions wanted to see the Toulouse region disappear so they could annex its chambers to their regions.[26]

On the surface the ninth region had many of the characteristics of the those based in Nancy and Clermont-Ferrand. What distinguished it from the latter was a different view among the leadership about how the regional structure should be exploited. Indeed, there was a debate about what exactly the region was for which continued throughout the post-war period. We see this most clearly when we consider their attitude to power generation and the distribution of electric current.

Boubènes, the president of the ninth region, formerly president of the Toulouse chamber of commerce and a commercial tribunal judge, spelt out clearly that his region took a different approach to developing electric power from say the Auvergne region. He thought this was a matter for private industry. The ninth region should stay out of investment in electricity plants and distribution, unless all the constituent chambers of commerce demanded it. However, the same chambers, acting through the Office régional d'Énergie électrique should regulate how power was

[23] H. Lagardelle, 'L'Interrégionalisme, Bordeaux-Toulouse', *Sud-Ouest Économique*, Janvier 1926, 8–15.

[24] M. Leroy, 'Le Sud-Ouest,' *Sud-Ouest Économique*, Janvier 1927, 115–118.

[25] *Bulletin de la Chambre de Commerce de Toulouse*, procès-verbaux des séances de 1923, séance du 14 mars 1923, 76.

[26] *Bulletin CCT 1923*, séance du 23 mai 1923, 145.

provided by private companies.[27] Lagardelle, the secretary of the region, would have agreed with him, as he spelled out to the chamber of commerce in Toulouse.[28] In 1923 he said to this chamber that Clémentel had wanted the regions to be industrial enterprises as in Clermont-Ferrand, where they set up a consortium to exploit hydro-electricity in the Massif Central. Lagardelle did not think the ninth region or the Bordeaux region could act in this way. "Its role seemed to be rather to research, to group together, to coordinate energies."[29] It could encourage private industry to invest through publicity and spell out what the opportunities were. However, it should not impinge on the domain of private firms. There should be no regional plan for the development of hydro-electricity.[30] Fortunately for the wider region, private industry was more than willing to take the lead in investment in electricity. The Pyrenees provided abundant sources of hydro-electric power and there was no shortage of investors willing to develop schemes, as the minutes of the Toulouse chamber of commerce and the regional committee show. In the crucial matter of developing adequate distribution capacity for electricity, the regional railway operator, the *Compagnie du Midi*, was willing to take a leading role. After the war it made the strategic decision to electrify all its lines throughout the south. To do this it needed a distribution infrastructure giving access to the Pyrenean hydro plants and with distribution via high voltage lines. It was fortunate to be led by engineers, technocrats with a vision for regional development, such as Maroger, president of U.P.E.P.O (Union des Producteurs d'Électricité des Pyrénées Occidentales) and Paul, CEO of the *Compagnie du Midi*. Maroger was a *polytechnicien* and engineer of the Ponts-et-Chaussées who sat on a number of industry representative bodies. J-R Paul had a similar background. They saw the opportunity to create a regional electricity network which would service their own needs and provide access to electricity for industrialists and consumers alike. To this end they set up U.P.E.P.O., a cooperative organization for the power industry. In the light of this spontaneous economic regionalism there was no need for chambers of commerce to finance power generation.[31]

[27] M.P. Boubènes, 'La Région économique de Toulouse et des Pyrénées, son rôle et son avenir,' *Sud-Ouest Économique,* dixième année no. 184, mars 1929, 348–349.

[28] Bulletin CCT, février 1929, 165.

[29] Ibid, séance du 14 mars 1923, 75.

[30] Bouneau, *Entre David et Goliath,* 369.

[31] Bouneau, *Entre David et Goliath,* -341. C. Bouneau, *Modernisation et Territoire, L'Électrification du Grand Sud-Ouest de la fin du XIXe siècle à 1946* (Bordeaux, 1997).

Alongside the rather passive leadership in the chambers of commerce and the region, Maroger and Paul were dynamic innovators. Another regional personality full of ideas was Lagardelle, the regional secretary. We have discussed his contribution to the debate on regions in chapter one. Lagardelle was not the only activist to advocate the benefits of regional action after the war. *L'Oeuvre Méridionale* based in Toulouse took up the same cause. In April 1919 Paul Dupont in an article entitled 'Le Mouvement Régionaliste' quoted the example of Provence, following Lyon's example and creating an economic forum for surrounding regions with representatives from chambers of commerce and industrial and agricultural unions. They organized study days to work on hydro-electricity in the Verdon valley, new railways and tourism.[32] This journal saw regionalism as a vital means of post-war recovery.[33]

No doubt Lagardelle was disappointed that not everyone on the regional committee and in the chamber of commerce in Toulouse shared his excitement and desire for change. In this connection the debate within the Toulouse chamber which we have already examined is very instructive. It should be noted that the Toulouse chamber approved the regional budget for 1924 mainly out of fear that if they refused and left the region, Toulouse would lose its prestige as a centre of attraction and then the region might fall apart, being absorbed by its neighbours.

The Toulouse chamber passed the budget for 1925 provided there was a thorough debate at once on future plans for the region. The chamber discussed regional activities and agreed that some were useful like its commercial information service and the compilation of statistics of production. The region published a bulletin of its proceedings. It was preparing the Commercial Exhibition in Toulouse in 1924 and the region's participation in the Exposition internationale des Arts Décoratifs et de l'Industrie moderne in Paris in 1925. It coordinated the views of the whole region on

C. Bouneau, 'La contribution de l'électricité à la génèse de l'aménagement du territoire en France, pendant la première moitié du xxe siècle,' in F. Caron, C. Bouneau (eds), *L'UPEPO, 1922–1946: génèse et logiques de l'interconnexion*, *Bulletin d'histoire de l'électricité*, 1985, 6, 75–102. C. Bouneau, 'Chemins de Fer et Développement régional en France 1852–1937: la contribution de la Compagnie du Midi,' *Histoire, économie et société*, Année 1990, 9–1, 95–112.

[32] P. Dupont, 'Le Mouvement régionaliste,' *L'Oeuvre méridionale*, 2e année, no. 7, avril 1919, 87.

[33] R. Laborie, 'La Doctrine du régionalisme,' *L'Oeuvre méridionale*, 5e année, no. 44, août 1922, 596–7.

contentious issues which might therefore carry more weight with central government. However, in view of the regional opposition to taking over the role of private industry in major projects and also the individualism of the chambers, it is not surprising that the region's achievements were more limited than in Lorraine and Clermont-Ferrand.

So what was the region for? Boubènes, the chair of the regional committee, set out its stall in an article in *Sud-Ouest Économique*, highlighting some of the features presented to the Toulouse chamber.[34] It encouraged foreign commerce for example by supporting executives getting work experience overseas. It supported improvements to the École supérieure de Commerce, such as new laboratories.[35] This school had been founded by the chamber of commerce in Toulouse in 1903. The region set up an *Office régional d'Énergie électrique* in 1931, a bit later than other regions, it had an *Office des transports* and it was likely that it would take a role in developing air services, in restoring the Canal du Midi, and in developing ports. He made similar points in an article on the Toulouse fair in *le Cri du Midi* in 1929.[36]

Perhaps the most important role the region could fulfil was to make the case for economic development and to persuade different economic and social interests to cooperate. Lorraine and the Auvergne had their journals as we have seen. In the south-west as a whole this role was fulfilled by the journal *Sud-Ouest Économique* founded in Bordeaux in 1919. Its masthead said, it was a "monthly review defending the region's interests, creating publicity and concerned with economic expansion." Again it was Lagardelle who banged the drum for the South-West's development.[37] The September 1933 issue was devoted entirely to progress in electrification and its benefits. This special issue covered electrification throughout France and contained a foreword by Albert Lebrun, the president of the Republic. It discussed the new dam at Kembs on the Rhine, the Alps, the Dordogne project and electrification of the Compagnie Paris-Orléans

[34] M.P. Boubènes, 'La Région économique de Toulouse et des Pyrénées, son rôle et son avenir,' *Sud-Ouest Economique,* dixième année no. 184, mars 1929, 345–349.

[35] *Région Économique de Toulouse et des Pyrénées* (Bulletin officiel du Groupement des Chambres de Commerce),*abbreviation RETP*, juin 1927 no. 6, 84; 'Réunion du comité régional 23 juin 1930,' juin-juillet 1930, nos. 6–7, 94, 96.

[36] P. Boubènes, 'La IXe Région économique et la Foire de Toulouse,' *Le Cri de Toulouse*, 27 octobre 1929, 4–5.

[37] H. Lagardelle, 'L'Essor Industriel de la Région du Sud-Ouest,' *Sud-Ouest Économique,* 9e année 171, février 1928, 273–276.

network as well as of the Compagnie du Midi.[38] Lagardelle set out the case for rural electrification and the need to get small peasant farmers behind it. They needed to be persuaded of the benefits of electrically operated machinery.[39] Lagardelle also used the pages of this journal to make the case for agricultural modernization, a subject which we will cover separately.

In the case of electric energy, the region and individual chambers stepped back from investment and adopted a regulatory role to protect the interests of consumers. The records of the *Office régional d'Énergie électrique* published in the regional bulletin and the sessions of the Toulouse chamber cover the subjects discussed. The Toulouse chamber reviewed every proposal for new hydro-electric installations in the Pyrenees. It tried, with expert advice, to lay down some technical standards for transmission so that the new source of power could benefit the generality of consumers. The region acted most effectively through the *Office régional*, attended by chambers of commerce and government engineers, and by producers and distributors as well.[40] The majority of members of the Office argued for reductions in tariffs. They wanted the benefit of a plentiful supply of cheap energy in the region to benefit local consumers first. To do this they supported reserving a percentage of power from a new plant for the region's use. They were opposed to a method of calculating the cost of electricity which did not reflect local circumstances. They argued for flexibility in the tariffs offered so that they matched the needs of different groups of users. In this context they were particularly concerned with the needs of domestic consumers, small businesses and farms in the countryside.[41] They believed that the new energy companies which were granted concessions under the government law of 16 October 1919 should be controlled by French directors and largely financed by French capital. They argued for low minimum consumption requirements for consumers. They fiercely defended the right of all the chambers of

[38] *Sud-Ouest Économique,* 14e année, nos. 238–9, septembre-octobre 1933.

[39] H. Lagardelle, 'L'Électrification rurale,' *Sud-Ouest Économique,* 9e année no. 171, février 1928, 294–297.

[40] 'Réunion de l'*Office régional d'Énergie électrique* (OREE) 23 juin 1930,' *RETP*, mai 1931 no. 5, 63–4.

[41] 'Réunion du comité régional 23 juin 1930,'; 'Réunion de l'OREE, 26 mai 1931,' *RETP*, août-septembre 1930, 105–110 and juin 1931, 74–75.

commerce to be consulted on new proposals. They looked for progress in the electrification of the countryside.[42]

The debate in the *Office régional d'Énergie électrique* about all these issues threw up differences of opinion, principally between Maroger, the head of U.P.E.P.O, who was an engineer, and the chamber of commerce representatives. Maroger argued that it was illogical to ask for reserves of current for local use to be increased, when they were nowhere near being used currently. What was needed, he suggested, was a more flexible tariff which satisfied the needs of different types of user. Electricity prices were higher abroad than in the region. Moreover, electricity prices had gone up less since the war than other products. The index used to calculate prices based on coal equivalents had been stabilized at the request of users, but this had retarded a natural drop in prices with the current recession.[43] Crescent, a chief engineer of the *Ponts-et-Chaussées* and director of the Service for Hydro-Electricity in the South-West, was asked to produce a lengthy report on all these issues, which was then discussed.[44] A commission of the full meeting was set up to come up with precise measures.[45] The proposals which resulted included different tariffs for lighting, domestic heating, agricultural and commercial use. Maroger said this differentiated tariff would aid consumption, as would the massive electrification of the railway network. Crescent remarked that absorption of excess current was the important issue with the onset of the recession.[46] The Office also expressed support for the development of interconnections between different regional distribution networks and more intensive propaganda to encourage usage. It ratified the proposals for a differentiated tariff. It seemed that the producers had been won over to this.[47]

So the region's representations about tariffs only really bore fruit after the advent of the recession in the 1930s when the electricity companies

[42] 'Réunion de l'OREE 26 mai 1931,' *RETP*, juin 1931, 74–75.

[43] 'Réunion de l'OREE 26 octobre 1931,' *RETP*, janvier 1932, 11–12 and février 1932, 17–24.

[44] 'Étude sur la consommation et la tarification de l'énergie électrique dans le Sud-Ouest, 31 mai 1932,' *RETP*, juin 1932, 121–160.

[45] 'Réunion de l'OREE 4 juillet 1932,' *RETP*, novembre 1932, 213.

[46] 'Réunion de l'OREE 28 novembre 1932,' *RETP*, février 1933 15, 17–19; mars 1933, 121.

[47] 'Réunion de l'OREE 26 juin 1933,' *RETP*, novembre 1933, 133–140. 'Réunion de l'OREE 14 mai 1934,' *RETP*, août –septembre 1934, 118.

had surplus energy to sell.[48] The region had negotiated with the regional producers and distributors of electricity to some effect. In 1935 the central government issued some decree laws to enforce selective reductions in tariffs nationally. These stipulated that small consumers should not be faced with requirements for minimum consumption for lighting and power. Crescent said that these decrees were motivated less by the need to reduce prices, which were not high, but more by the need to increase consumption and stimulate economic activity.[49] The debate on prices in the *Office régional d'Énergie électrique* is a good example of the body's role as a regional regulator for the industry.

Christophe Bouneau, who has studied electrification comprehensively, remarked that there were only two sectors where regional economic development projects made sense—transport and electricity. He might perhaps have added technical training.[50] Like the other regions the Toulouse region also participated in an *Office des Transports*, making the case for timetable improvements, lower tariffs, new services such as a direct train to Paris, and new lines, for example, across the Pyrenees to Spain.[51] One contentious proposal put forward by the *Compagnie du Midi* was for an auxiliary bus service to connect with railway stations. This would avoid the company having to maintain and improve lines in rural areas, where traffic was low, and at the same time provide a better service. Some in the chambers of commerce were opposed to this idea on the grounds that it might create a transport monopoly for the powerful *Compagnie du Midi*. They wanted to protect the interests of small bus operators whom they represented.[52] Lagardelle pointed out that the small bus operators were often dependent on public subsidies. The railway was willing to guarantee that no monopoly would be created and they would use small bus operators for their auxiliary services where possible. The chambers of commerce had been asked to subscribe some capital for the new service but every chamber was at liberty not to do so. Lagardelle thought that the chambers

[48] 'Réunion du comité régional du 23 juin 1930,' *RETP*, août-septembre 1930, 105–110.

[49] 'Réunion de l'OREE 2 décembre 1935,' *RETP*, novembre-décembre 1935, nos. 11–12, typed minutes without page numbers; février 1936, 25.

[50] Bouneau, *Entre David et Goliath*, 367–369.

[51] Account of the proceedings of the Office des Transports in *Bulletin CCT*, 20 juin 1928, 198. For a Toulouse-Paris service see 'Réunion de l'Office des Transports du Sud-Ouest, 8 juillet 1929,' *RETP*, août-septembre 1929, 100. Prevet, 126–8.

[52] Bouneau, *Entre David et Goliath*, 368–9.

should back the scheme. Once again he found himself in opposition to their individualism.[53]

Rail was not the only form of transport with which the South-West chambers were involved. They participated in discussions about major improvements to the Canal du Midi so that barges of much greater tonnage could use it. Other canals took much larger barges. Bordeaux supported the idea. A *Société des Études* was formed. When the Tardieu government announced plans for renewing national infrastructure at the end of 1929, the region put forward the improvement of the Canal du Midi as a priority. However, the cost was very high for the chambers and the government. The Narbonne chamber said it would be better to increase goods capacity on the railways.[54] It was decided to concentrate on more minor improvements to the canal over a period of years rather than a major project.[55]

The regional chambers also considered what support they could give to air services. The Toulouse chamber believed that the French air network would be of great importance to Toulouse and decided to join the *Comité française de Propagande aéronautique*.[56] The regional committee listened to a report which said that France was way behind Germany in developing air services.[57] They decided to support a government-backed project for a Paris-Toulouse air service. They also nominated it as a priority for the Tardieu plan for *outillage national*.[58] New air services needed an improved airport. In 1920 the Toulouse chamber budget committee had decided to provide 1000 francs towards the cost of a halt for planes at Toulouse.[59] The government later proposed to station fighter planes at Toulouse at an airport which would also be used by civil flights. However, this proposal was dependent on the Toulouse chamber making a financial contribution.[60] The cost of building the new airport was 6 million francs and the chamber

[53] H. Lagardelle, 'La région, la route, le rail,' *Sud-Ouest Économique*, 1 octobre 1928, 1306–1307.

[54] 'Réunion du comité regional 5 décembre 1927,' *RETP*, décembre 1927, 141–6; Ibid, juillet-août 1928, 83–5; 'Réunion de l'Office des Transports du Sud-Ouest 8 juillet 1929,' Ibid, août-septembre 1929, 102–103; 'Réunion du comité régional 23 juin 1930,' Ibid juin-juillet 1930, 96.

[55] 'Réunion du comité régional 26 juin 1933,' *RETP*, octobre 1933, 126.

[56] *Bulletin CCT*, décembre 1929, 200.

[57] Ibid.

[58] *RETP*, juin-juillet 1930, 96.

[59] RETP, 19 octobre 1920, 239.

[60] *Bulletin CCT*, mars-avril 1931, 149.

had to tell the mayor of Toulouse, the prefect and *conseil-général* that it did not have the resources to help.[61] In 1934 it was agreed that the chamber of commerce would in fact run the new airport with the support of the *conseil-général* and the city. It would be under the control of the Ministry of Air.[62]

In conclusion the ninth region had a degree of coherence because of the importance of the city of Toulouse. However, it was also subject to a strong commercial pull towards the port of Bordeaux to the west and it had a cultural connection with the Languedoc to the east. The region had a large agricultural sector which could have been more closely integrated into its decision making. The chambers of commerce making up the region were not in favour of supplanting private capital in developing infrastructure such as power generation and distribution. This was a classic belief of pre-war economic liberalism. Moreover, a tradition of consular independence made them suspicious of greater regional integration. The region therefore remained primarily a body to represent the views of chambers to central government in a more effective way. It also provided a commercial information service for domestic and foreign trade. In this context it helped organize exhibitions. It championed the cause of regional modernization through the press. It also acted as an effective energy regulator on behalf of consumers and in a similar way through the Office des Transports to argue for better services from the rail companies. It also pressed for improvements to the Canal du Midi. When it represented the views of the region on such matters to central government it was acting like a lobbyist. However, in the case of air services it did get more actively involved in running the airport of Toulouse through the Toulouse chamber.

Like the Alpine region based in Grenoble, the Toulouse regional committee fostered the idea of a region which could create new industries based on hydro-electric power. In the Alps the region did not invest directly in energy projects. However, they and other regional leaders created a very favourable climate for industrialists to invest and brought about a region where hydro-electricity was the key identifying factor. This new form of energy, as in Toulouse, spawned new industries like electro-chemistry and electro-metallurgy. Bankers, industrialists, geographers like Raoul Blanchard and publicists promoted the region and

[61] Ibid, janvier-février 1932, 47.
[62] Ibid, 24 octobre 1934, 255–7.

what it had to offer. An international exhibition was held in Grenoble in 1925. New media like radio was used to draw attention to the new developments.[63] The region also proposed a new railway line from Grenoble to Nice to bind the region together, but this proved to be too expensive.[64]

If we look at how other regions in France operated in the inter-war years, we will find they broadly followed a similar path to Toulouse. They were lobbyists and publicists. They set an agenda for regional development or *l'aménagement du territoire,* but they were not active executants on the whole.

## The Nord

Eck in his article on the first region of the Nord and Pas-de-Calais says there was no great regional spirit involved during the period of its formation after 1918. An Office des Transports had been set up in 1912, but Tourcoing objected to the expense and Dunkerque only agreed if Le Havre and Rouen were kept out of it. It had some impact on railway tariffs. The first region resisted the apprenticeship tax for seven years, unlike any other group of chambers of commerce in France. The industrialists of the Nord were firmly opposed to the state's involvement in economic affairs and defended consular independence. The recession of the thirties and accompanying social conflicts made them even more defensive. There was no lack of leaders or institutions, but the region lacked any vision of its future. There were divisions on free trade and protection. It is therefore not surprising that it did not achieve much. It pressed the case for new canals such as the Canal maritime des Flandres and the Canal du Nord-Est linking to Lorraine. Its secretary published plans for comprehensive re-equipment and integration of its ports, railways and waterways. It sponsored a course on regional geography. The region was slow, however, to develop interconnections between electrical distribution networks.[65]

[63] P. Veitl, *L'invention d'une region: les Alpes françaises* (Grenoble, 2013), 141–314.

[64] P.Brun, 78–9; Prevet, 126–8.

[65] Prevet, p.126; J-F. Eck, 'Chapitre VIII - Une expérience de modernisation économique: la première région économique (1925–1935)', in Alya Aglan et al., *De la Croissance à la crise (1925–1935): Le moment Tannery*, (Paris, 2014), 139–154.

## Bordeaux

The Bordeaux region adopted a more passive role like Toulouse except in the case of its port and airport. It took a similar view on giving the regions a legal personality, rejecting a motion from Montauban supporting Senator Mario Roustan's bill to make the regions public bodies. It would mean some chambers of commerce having to share in expenses they thought unnecessary. The resulting obligation to adhere to only one region would cut several places off from ports like Bordeaux and restrict their growth. However, the region was open to contact with the new *chambres d'agriculture* as Lagardelle had argued in Toulouse.[66] Later it appeared that the *chambres d'agriculture* would be formed into regional groupings and therefore the 8th region said it would cooperate with the relevant grouping.[67]

The Bordeaux region took a close interest in the port and surrounding waterways. The Bordeaux chamber ran the port and the region had three delegates on the board of directors.[68] When the Tardieu government initiated its programme to improve national infrastructure, it was natural that the Bordeaux region should put forward improvements to ports such as Bayonne, Libourne, Arcachon and St. Jean de Luz. The region also asked for backing to open the Canal du Midi and the Canal latéral de la Garonne to barges of 600 tons.[69] The region was still seeking funds from the government for dredging the canals in 1934.[70] Like Toulouse it also lobbied for railway improvements through the Office des Transports. The region wanted faster train services to Paris.[71] In the context of Tardieu's *outillage national,* a sponsored article appeared in the regional bulletin urging the government to adopt the project to radically improve the rail links across the country towards Lyon.[72] An activity report in 1931 noted that the region had failed to get government backing for Bordeaux-Geneva

[66] 'Réunion du comité régional 14 juin 1927,' *Région économique de Bordeaux et du Sud-Ouest,* bulletin officiel, septembre-octobre 1927, 98, 102.

[67] 'Réunion du comité régional 10 décembre 1928,' REBSO, novembre-décembre 1928, 58.

[68] 'Réunion du comité régional 12 avril 1926,' REBSO, mars-avril 1926, no. 15, 10.

[69] 'Réunion du comité régional 14 juin 1930,' REBSO, no. 7, août 1930, 69–74.

[70] 'Réunion du comité régional 3 avril 1934,' REBSO, octobre 1934, 205.

[71] 'Réunion du comité régional 14 juin 1924,' REBSO, juin-juillet 1924, 47.

[72] A. Bourbon, 'Amélioration de l'outillage national et les relations entre Bordeaux et Lyon,' REBSO, juin 1930, 41–43.

improvements but other more local works had been approved.[73] Evidently the railway company refused to help establish better rail connections to the east. The regional committee did not give up hope. Another article by Bourbon appeared in 1934 urging support for the link to Lyon and Geneva.[74]

The region also lobbied for the initiation of air services, both new flights and a regional airport at Mérignac near Bordeaux, where it is today (Fig. 7.1). An article appeared in the regional journal in 1926 suggesting that Bordeaux would be a key hub for air services in the south-west just as it was an important port. It could link to Morocco and South America as well as French cities and England. The writer warned that other regional cities like Marseille and Lyon were considering the issue.[75] Next the region hosted a conference on interregional air services in April 1927 with representatives from regions and chambers of commerce all around France. The conference drew up detailed plans for a company to manage these initiatives with state and the local authorities' participation. A commission was set up to progress the matter. From the start an active role was envisaged for local chambers of commerce. The role of the region was getting involved in the launch and funding publicity but not running airlines. However, in principle the state was prepared to grant the chamber of commerce of Bordeaux a concession for the airport at Mérignac. The chamber in Bordeaux sent a study group abroad. There were negotiations with the state on the financing of facilities at Mérignac because of parallel military use. The chamber did not have the resources for major construction expenditure, although it was legally allowed to make an investment in such a public utility.[76] By 1932 work was progressing on construction of the Mérignac airport which was expected to open in 1933. The chamber of commerce of Bordeaux had ensured that the state was commencing payments.[77] By 1935 the need for more regional airports was growing. It was agreed at a meeting of the region, at which the Ministry of Air was

[73] REBSO, avril 1931, 37–41. Duplantier, 165.

[74] A. Bourbon, 'Relation transversal de Bordeaux-Lyon-Génève,' REBSO, no. 51, mai 1934, 165–7.

[75] L. Valeton,' L'Avenir aéronautique de Bordeaux et de la région du Sud-Ouest,' REBSO, septembre-octobre 1926, 31.

[76] 'Réunion du comité régional 26 novembre 1927,' REBSO, janvier-février 1928, 5.

[77] 'Réunion du comité de la VIIIe région économique du 23 janvier 1933,' REBSO, no. 40, mai 1933, 50.

**Fig. 7.1** Chamber of Commerce of Bordeaux, Airport of Bordeaux-Mérignac, 1936–1937, courtesy of the Mérignac communal archives, 13 Fi 38. Acknowledgements are also due to M. Bruno Vielle

present, that a regional plan for new facilities was best drawn up by the region with technical advice. It would then be submitted to the ministry. At one point in the discussion, it was suggested this task should be carried out by departments under the direction of prefects but arguments in favour of a wider regional view won the day.[78]

The chamber of commerce in Bordeaux, like Toulouse, assumed responsibility for the École Supérieure de Commerce in the city. It used part of the proceeds of the apprenticeship tax to give financial assistance. It looked for other chambers in the region to help in a similar manner.[79] The region wanted to see an *institut supérieur commercial* set up at the University of Bordeaux in the Faculté de Droit. A project was prepared to send to the relevant ministry. If successful it was envisaged that the region would nominate a representative to the board of directors.[80] However, the region was not always united on proposals for extending technical

[78] 'Réunion du comité régional 17 juin 1935,' REBSO 15 août 1935, 304–6.
[79] REBSO, janvier-février 1929, 1–2.
[80] 'Réunion du comité régional 14 juin 1930,' REBSO, septembre 1930, 84.

education, such an important feature of economic regionalism. In 1927 the region would not support an École de Pin for the Landes because only three chambers were in favour.[81]

The *Office régional d'Énergie électrique* for the eighth region set up in 1931 adopted similar policies to those pursued in Toulouse. The discussions in the two bodies followed very similar lines. Agricultural representatives were present at the initial meeting in April 1932.[82] It was agreed that Bordeaux would use some of the publicity material created by Toulouse to encourage electricity usage.[83] The Office believed hydro-electricity should be encouraged for reasons of energy security and national defence.[84] It pronounced in favour of interconnection between high tension networks, electrification of the railways and propaganda to encourage more use domestically. It favoured a diverse tariff and continued to grant hydro-electric concessions even during the recession.[85] When the government issued its price reduction decrees in 1935, the Bordeaux Office urged the inclusion of maximum prices, mobilizing unused electricity capacity near power stations, more publicity from distributors for the reduced tariffs and better representation for *Offices régionaux d'Énergie électrique* in the Conseil Supérieur de l'Électricité.[86]

## Normandy

The economic region of Upper Normandy showed considerable interest in economic development between the wars, even if not all of it is manifest in the deliberations of the regional grouping of chambers of commerce. *L'Ouest Économique* was a bi-monthly published in Le Havre and founded in 1927. It was connected to a spontaneously formed committee called Ouest-Expansion which was launched in April 1927 and aimed to cover the whole area of the country west of a line from Dieppe, through Paris, Orléans, Limoges, Agen and Tarbes. It received the adhesion of a number of regions including Bordeaux and Lower Normandy and from chambers

[81] REBSO, novembre-décembre 1927, 601.

[82] 'Réunion constitutive de l'Office d'Énergie électrique (OEE) du 4 avril 1932,' REBSO, no. 30, juillet 1932, 63–7.

[83] 'Réunion de l'OEE du13 juin 1932,' REBSO, no. 35, décembre 1932, 124.

[84] 'Procès-verbal de la réunion de l'OEE de la VIIIe région économique du 23 janvier 1933,' REBSO, no. 40, mai 1933, 47.

[85] 'Réunion de l'OEE 20 novembre 1933,' Ibid, janvier 1934, 125.

[86] 'Réunion de l'OEE du 26 janvier 1936,' REBSO, no. 61, 15 février 1936, 376.

of commerce on the coasts, and also from private companies. It claimed to cover a large number of interests including commerce, industry and agriculture, shipping and ports, the importation of coal and other vital raw materials, the extractive industries, transport and tourism. It was connected to le Redressement Français headed by Ernest Mercier. Its president was a chief engineer from Ponts-et-Chaussées. The interests of importers who used the coastal ports were particularly important. They were concerned about any barriers to their trade such as tariffs.[87]

Economic expansion was also the concern of the *Revue Économique de l'Ouest* set up in 1920. This described itself as a "regional publication covering industrial, commercial and agricultural expansion" based in Rouen. It aimed to develop the resources of Normandy and Maine, as well as Brittany, for the good of France. In the thirties it extended its coverage to the Vendée and Charente. The editor commented that there was no similar publication in the North West, although there were similar publications in Flanders and the East. It claimed to have gathered a high quality team of writers. The journal discussed the development potential of different industries in the region.[88] The Revue published two articles on regionalism as a doctrine, arguing that business men working together to develop their region did not need the state to pass difficult administrative reforms. They were adopting a pragmatic approach to defending and enhancing a region's interests. The modern industrial economy, particularly the growth of transport networks, had made the confines of a department a block to reform and development.[89]

A third publication with a similar theme was called *Normandie Économique, organe bi-mensuel des IIIe et IVe regions économiques.* It was sponsored by these regions in a similar way to *Union Économique de l'Est*, the journal of the Lorraine region. It advertised itself as a brand-new journal to defend the interests of Normandy in all their variety. It claimed to represent chambers of commerce, chambers of agriculture, industrial unions, leagues of commerce, maritime associations, *syndicats d'initiative* for tourism and private companies. The first issue contained an article on regionalism as a phenomenon of expansion by Lucien Romier, an editor of

[87] *L'Ouest Économique*, bimensuelle, première année, no. 1, 1927, I-III; 1ère année no. 10 30 novembre 1927 2.

[88] *Revue Économique de l'Ouest*, 1e année no. 1, 15 novembre 1920.

[89] M. Masson, 'Le Régionalisme', REO, 1 août 1923, 1–2; M. Masson, 'le Régionalisme et la Réforme administrative,' REO, 1 mars 1927, 53–55.

Figaro and Parisian journalist specializing in economic affairs. He claimed that economic regionalism was successful while administrative regionalism was being left behind. Economic regionalism strengthened national solidarity rather than weakening it. Economic regionalists really wanted to develop the local economy. They understood the benefits for the nation of regional economic specialization.[90] In June 1927 *Normandie Économique* highlighted the dinner of the committee of Ouest-Expansion, which it said was not just a mouthpiece for coal importing interests. France needed good ports in the West for national security reasons to import food in time of war. The regions had an important role to play in mobilizing the country's economy behind a war effort. The government had recognized this when it asked economic regions to prepare economic mobilization plans.[91]

The future of the ports was clearly of concern to this maritime region. For example, the president of the chamber of commerce in Cherbourg put forward the case for a statute of autonomy for smaller ports like his own. Larger ports like Le Havre and Bordeaux were already autonomous. This would mean Cherbourg could manage itself independently, although it would need financing from the government, local authorities and chambers of commerce.[92] The economic region of Lower Normandy supported the proposal to grant autonomy to the port of Cherbourg.[93] Auguste Pawlowski, the editor of the *Revue Économique de l'Ouest*, set out the case for a much more comprehensive plan to re-equip and develop the ports of the region.[94] *Normandie Économique* took a similar position on the need to develop the ports, particularly Rouen.[95] The Normandy region also needed to modernize the waterways around ports, particularly the Seine between Rouen and Le Havre. Lucien Romier had written about this in *Explication de Notre Temps* (Paris, 1925). Now another book had been published on *La Seine, artère vitale de l'économie nationale*.[96] In 1928 a project commenced to examine the feasibility of a canal from Rouen to the coast, but this was entrusted to an inter-departmental commission rather

[90] L. Romier, 'Le régionalisme, phénomène d'expansion,' *Normandie Économique*, 1e année no. 1, 30 janvier 1927, 1–2.

[91] *Normandie Économique,* 1e année, no. 8, 8–15 juin 1927, VII, col.1.

[92] 'L'Autonomie de la port de Cherbourg,' rapport de M C-Th. Quoniam, Président de la chambre de commerce, *Revue Économique de l'Ouest (REO)*, 1 septembre 1927, 38–41.

[93] REO, 1 octobre 1927, 45.

[94] 'Pour une politique des ports normands et bretons,' REO, 1 janvier 1929, 9–10.

[95] *Normandie Économique*, 1e années, nos 3 et 4, 1 mars 1927, 3; 15 mars 1927, 1, col.1.

[96] *L'Ouest Économique*, première année, no. 4, 30 août 1927, 1.

than the economic region. This was sometimes the case with such projects as inter-departmental commissions could draw on a wider range of participants from elected members of *conseils-généraux* and also government engineers.[97] In 1920 the regional committee of Lower Normandy discussed a project regarding a canal from the Loire to the Channel. An inter-departmental group met at Angers at which chambers of commerce but also *conseils-généraux* were represented.[98]

Naturally regional actors wanted to see improvements to railways, particularly where they linked to ports. Existing links from Dieppe and Le Havre to the west of France, the Centre and the Midi were weak. Everything had to go via Paris.[99] Neither did they want to see Normandy miss out on the development of new air services. The chamber of commerce in Rouen and the region wanted Rouen airport to have good provincial connections and to England. They wanted to avoid all air services to other parts of France going through Paris like the railways.[100]

There is very limited evidence that the economic regions of Normandy were more than lobbying and publicity organizations. However, all these initiatives discussed in the press and regional bodies were helping to establish the concept of "l'aménagement du territoire," pioneered by Philippe Lamour in the inter-war years and developed into programmes of improvement under the new planning regime after 1945.[101] Regional discussion also concentrated on deficiencies in the distribution of electricity. There was a need for a better regional network in Normandy connected to thermal power stations fired by coal. There was also the opportunity to develop tidal power.[102] Pawlowski urged an electrification strategy for the whole region which took in thermal, hydro and wave power.[103] Some departments like La Manche presented a considerable challenge to engineers trying to design a cost effective network. Clearly reaching every remote

[97] *Revue Économique de l'Ouest*, 1 novembre 1928, 25.

[98] 'Séance du comité régional 23 décembre 1920,' *IVe région économique, groupement de Basse Normandie (Caen)*, bulletin, octobre-décembre 1920, 11.

[99] M. R. Groult, 'Sarthe, Office des Transports de l'Ouest,' *Revue Économique de l'Ouest*, 1 août 1928, 51.

[100] 'Coup d'oeil sur les quelques récents travaux de la chambre de commerce de Rouen,' REO, 31 août 1926, 13. *Normandie Économique*, 1e année, no. 4, 15 mars 1927, 1, col.1.

[101] J-R. Pitte, *Philippe Lamour, 1903–1992, Père de l'aménagement du territoire en France* (Paris, 2002).

[102] REO, janvier 1929, 7–8.

[103] A. Pawlowski, 'L'Électrification de la Normandie et de Bretagne,' REO, 1 octobre 1927, 9–11; 1 novembre 1927 9–11; 1 décembre 1927, 9–11.

rural area would be expensive. However, in La Manche there were signs of progress with inter-connections being made between different power stations. The *conseil-général* was driving electrification forward.[104] Yves Le Trocquer, technocrat, polytechnicien, engineer in the Ponts-et-Chaussées, former Minister for Public Works and senator for the Côtes-du Nord, urged the need to build more power stations close to coal supplies because of high transport costs, with a good distribution network for the resulting electricity. Moreover, everything had to be done to increase usage of electric power and thus reduce prices—electrification of the railways, construction of rural networks and more domestic use.[105] As elsewhere, Norman electric consumers started to band together to protect their interests against the suppliers.[106]

Le Trocquer in the Senate represented Brittany and was involved in pressing the case for economic development there too. An article on regional development in the West referred to the activities of a Consortium Breton whose aim was to make better use of the riches of the Finistère. Le Trocquer was involved as a contributor to the organization's publication.[107] The *Revue Économique de L'Ouest*, which was equally concerned with Brittany as with Normandy, believed Brittany had to open up to the rest of France and not just be concerned with its own affairs. It would benefit from business brought in by improved rail connections to the east and not just to Paris, from better roads and from improved air services. Events like the fair in Rennes would help.[108] If we read the proceedings of the sixth region based in Rennes, we find the same motions for better canals, roads and railways as we found in Normandy and elsewhere.[109] What was also fundamental to the development of Brittany was agriculture and tourism. It is not surprising that by the 1930s we find the regional

[104] A. Pawlowski, 'L'Électrification de la Manche,' REO, 1 septembre 1927, 43–44; 'Les progrès de l'électrification rurale dans la Manche,' REO, 1 janvier 1929, 49.

[105] Yves Le Trocquer, 'La Politique de L'Électrification dans L'Ouest,' REO, 1 octobre 1929, 49.

[106] REO, 1 février 1928, 16–17.

[107] Jean Leluc, 'Le régionalisme se développe dans l'ouest,' REO, 1 juillet 1927, 55–56.

[108] H. Quilgars, 'Ille-et-Vilaine, vers une orientation économique,' REO, 1 octobre 1927, 75, 77.

[109] 'Séance 10 octobre 1930,' *VIe region économique, groupement régional économique de Rennes*, extrait du registre des déliberations du groupement, 12–15; 20–22; 'Séance 20 mars 1931', 7–12; 'Séance 12 octobre 1934,' 3–8; 'Séance 10 juillet 1936,' 31–6. 'Compte rendu de la réunion du comité régional tenue à Rennes le 8 janvier 1937,' *Bulletin Trimestriel de la VIe région économique (Rennes)*, 1937, no. 1, 1e année, 3–6.

agricultural organizations conferring regularly with the Breton region. We shall return to these two important parts of the economy in the next chapter.

If we look outside the regions we have covered so far to the rest of France, we find the same themes covered in regional deliberations. Again a lot of lobbying went on; publicity but no executive action. Regions lobbied for new canals and improved railway services almost everywhere.[110] New technical institutes sprung up in many places with regional support.[111] Some *Offices régionaux d'Énergie électrique* were particularly active—in Marseille, Lille, Limoges, Montpellier.[112] We have seen that some leading chambers of commerce like Bordeaux got involved in the management of autonomous ports. The autonomy regime which derived from a law of 1920 also applied to Strasbourg, Le Havre and Marseille. Ports needed investment in new plant and machinery. In some cases, as at Le Havre, the port had to bring in outside concessionaires to help, in this case, with building an oil terminal.[113]

## Bibiliography

Anglade, J. (1928). *Les Troubadors de Toulouse.*

Bouneau, C. (1990). Chemins de Fer et Développement régional en France 1852-1937: la contribution de la Compagnie du Midi. *Histoire, économie et société*, Année, 9-1, 95–112.

Bouneau, C. (1985). *La contribution de l'électricité à la génèse de l'aménagement du territoire en France, pendant la première moitié du xxe siècle.* In F. Caron & C. Bouneau (Eds.), *L'UPEPO, 1922–1946 : génèse et logiques de l'interconnexion, Bulletin d'histoire de l'électricité.*

Bouneau, C. (2008). *Entre David et Goliath : la dynamique des réseaux régionaux: réseaux ferroviaires, réseaux électriques et régionalisation économique en France du milieu du XIXe siècle au milieu du XXe siècle.*

Bouneau, C. (1997). *Modernisation et Territoire, L'Électrification du Grand Sud-Ouest de la fin du XIXe siècle à 1946.*

Brun, P. (1928). *Les Régions Économiques* (Thèse de doctorat, Sciences Politiques et Économiques, Montpellier).

[110] Prevet, 126–7, 133–141.

[111] Prevet, 88–92; Duplantier, 241–2.

[112] P.Brun, 73–4; Prevet, 115–6.

[113] Duplantier, 159; P. Brun, 75–7; dirn. A. Corvisier, *Histoire du Havre et de l'Estuaire de la Seine* (Toulouse, 1983), 230–3; Prevet, 130–1.

*Bulletin de la Chambre de Commerce de Toulouse*, 1923, 1925, 1927, 1928, 1929, 1931, 1932, 1934.

Bulletin Trimestriel de la VIe région économique *(Rennes)*, (1937).

Corvisier, A. (dirn.). (1983). *Histoire du Havre et de l'Estuaire de la Seine.*

De Gélis, M. F.. (1921). La Vraie Langue d'Oc, l'ancienne et la nouvelle langue d'oc,' *Mémoires de l'Académie des sciences, inscriptions et belles-lettres de Toulouse*, 1 janvier 1921 (pp. 115–140).

Druelle-Korn. (2014). La Modernisation inachevée de l'aménagement du territoire, le cas de la VIIe région, (Limousin, Poitou, Charentes). In A. Aglan, M. Margairaz, et P. Verheyde (Eds.), *De la croissance à la crise (1925–1935) Le moment tannery; Une tentative avortée de modernisation conservatrice et libérale à l'heure de la mondialisation*, 155–172.

Duplantier, J. (1929). *Le Régionalisme économique et spécialement la région économique de Bordeaux et du Sud-Ouest.* Thèse de doctorat, Faculté de Droit de Bordeaux).

Dutil, L. (1929). *La Haute-Garonne et sa région*, t.1.

*Eck J.F., Une expérience de modernisation économique: la première région économique in Aglan A., Margairaz M., Verheyde P., (eds) De la Croissance à la crise (1925–1935): Le moment Tannery*, une tentative avortée de modernisation conservatrice et libérale à l'heure de la mondialisation (2014), pp. 139–154.

Gachon, P. (1921). *Languedoc.*

Giandou, A. (1999). *La Compagnie Nationale du Rhône 1933–1998; histoire d'un partenaire régional de l'état.*

*IVe région économique, groupement de Basse Normandie (Caen)*, bulletin, 1920.

L'Express du Midi, 1924.

*L'Oeuvre Méridionale*, 1918, 1919, 1922, 1936.

L'Ouest Économique, 1927;

*La Dépêche de Toulouse*, 1913, 1915, 1924, 1925.

*Le Cri de Toulouse*, 14 décembre 1913, 1927, 1929.

Le Cri du Midi, 1929.

Le Midi Républicain, 1930.

Le Soleil de Toulouse, 1925.

Normandie Économique, 1927.

Pasquier, R. (2004). *La Capacité Politique des Régions: Une comparaison France, Espagne.*

Pitte, J.-R. (2002). *Philippe Lamour, 1903–1992, Père de l'aménagement du territoire en France.*

Prevet, F. (1929). *Le Régionalisme économique, conception et réalisation.* Thèse de doctorat, Faculté de Droit de Paris.

Région Économique de Bordeaux et du Sud-Ouest, REBSO 1924, 1926, 1927, 1928, 1929, 1930, 1931, 1932, 1933, 1934, 1935, 1936.

*Région Économique de Toulouse et des Pyrénées* (Bulletin officiel du Groupement des Chambres de Commerce), *abbreviation RETP*, 1920, 1927, 1928, 1929, 1930, 1931, 1932. 1933, 1934, 1935, 1936.

*Revue Économique de l'Ouest*, 1920, 1923, 1926, 1927, 1928, 1929.

*Sud-Ouest Économique*, 1923, 1926, 1927, 1928, 1929, 1933.

Veitl, P. (2013). *L'Invention d'une région : les Alpes françaises.*

*VIe region économique, groupement régional économique de Rennes*, 1930, 1931, 1934, 1936, 1937.

CHAPTER 8

# Agriculture and Tourism

Agriculture and tourism had regional organizations separate from the chambers of commerce representing commerce and industry and also from their regional groupings which constituted the economic regions. Individual chambers and the regions discussed agricultural issues less frequently than commerce and industry. The Nancy chamber did have a commission on agriculture in the 1920s.[1] Some regions took more interest in tourism. In this chapter we will explore the growth of these agricultural and tourism organizations, the issues they covered and how these were also important to the economic regions.

## Agricultural Organizations

Before 1918 there were broadly two important types of agricultural organization. Firstly, there were the *sociétés d'agriculture*, independently formed societies to promote agricultural best practice in growing crops and animal husbandry. They also discussed other issues affecting farming like electrification. They were conservative organizations frequently dominated by local *notables*, landowners and local clergy. The *sociétés d'agriculture* usually covered one department and had federated into the Société des Agriculteurs de France. The *comice*s agricoles, which were also

[1] *Bulletin Chambre de Commerce Nancy*, 25e année, no. 101, janvier, février, mars 1927, séance du 8 février 1927, 45–47.



T. Cudbird, *The Origins of Economic Regions in France, 1918-1940*,
https://doi.org/10.1007/978-3-032-04422-8_8

independent of the state, had a similar purpose. There were also *offices départementales* set up with state money to research into better practice. Following the law passed on 6 January 1919, an *Office régional agricole du Massif Central* was created as well as departmental offices. They focused on research on the improvement of crop types including vines and fruit, which were important in the Limagne around Clermont; the spreading of best practice; the use of fertilizers and the control of pests.[2] Then there were *Syndicats agricoles*, again independent of the state and federated into a national organization. These started off as cooperatives to give the smaller farmers the chance to buy and sell at better prices like large farmers, although specialist selling cooperatives also developed. After the war the *syndicats agricoles* gradually moved from being solely cooperatives to agitating on behalf of farmers on a whole range of issues. More departmental and regional federations were formed. The federation for the Puy-de-Dôme (1921) and the wider Fédération Centre-Sud in the Massif Central are good examples. These syndicates had their own journals. For example, *The Revue du Syndicat départemental agricole du Puy-de-Dôme* represented the views of a *syndicat* which had over 10,000 members in 1920, having grown from 7000 at the end of the war. The review published 12–15,000 copies every month, and in 1922, it converted into a bi-monthly publication called *La Terre d'Auvergne*. Other militant organizations of peasant defence developed alongside political parties like the Parti Agraire. The detail of all these organizations, of which I have only given a very brief sketch, need not detain us here. However, to understand the full scope of economic regionalism in inter-war France, we need to focus on their developing relationship with the economic regions and the particular concerns they brought to discussions in the latter.[3]

After the war a law of 1921 brought into being *chambres d'agriculture*, officially elected bodies chosen for each department. They were chosen partly by the general population and partly by the *syndicats*. After a delay they started meeting in 1927, and they added another layer of consultation for central government. Some of them federated into regional chambers such as the *Chambre d'Agriculture de l'Est* covering the Ardennes, Aube, Marne, Haute-Marne, Meurthe-et-Moselle, Meuse, Moselle,

[2] *Région du Centre*, no. 4 (novembre–décembre 1921), 2.

[3] For a fuller discussion of the growth of agricultural organisations in France see P. Barral, *les agrariens francais de Meline a Pisani* (Paris, 1968), pp. 110–216.

Bas-Rhin, Haut-Rhin and Vosges.[4] A similar regional federation existed in Toulouse and also Bordeaux.[5] The *chambre d'agriculture du Puy-de-Dôme* discussed the idea of regional chambers for certain issues at a meeting on 17 December 1927. This was permissible under the legislation setting up the chambers.[6] The *chambres d'agriculture* operated on similar lines to chambers of commerce. They examined a whole range of issues affecting farmers and made their views known to government in formal resolutions.

These agricultural organizations, many of which had a regional base, adopted positions on a number of key issues which seem to have been common throughout France. One defining issue for the *syndicats* was agricultural prices. After the war, prices for foodstuffs, particularly grain, fluctuated. During the war farmers benefited from high prices, but after the war agricultural prices came under pressure from imports, particularly from the Americas. The collapse of the franc in the mid-twenties raised inflation including for agricultural products. Prices collapsed during the recession of the thirties. *Le Bon Grain*, representing the views of agriculturalists in Lorraine, noted a flood of cheap grain and meat imports in 1931.[7] The *syndicats* agitated constantly for protection through tariffs. They complained bitterly about the attacks of townsfolk who thought the farmers were exploiting them by raising prices. They felt that the contribution of agriculture to the national economy was not appreciated. G. Benes summed this feeling up in an article in the *Journal d'Agriculture du Sud-Ouest* in 1928. The public wanted cheap food as if the farmers should not make a profit.[8] The journals of the agricultural organizations are full of calls for more peasants to join *syndicats* or, if they were members, to turn up to meetings. Solidarity, according to the leaders, was the only way to

[4] *Le Bon Grain*, organe de l'union Lorraine des syndicats Agricoles, 15 août 1930, 136–139. *La Terre Lorraine*, 29 mai 1927, 209–212.

[5] 'Réunion de la chambre d'agriculture de la Haute-Garonne 25 août 1927,' *Bulletin de la Société départementale d'agriculture et du syndicat des agriculteurs des Hautes-Pyrénées*, Septembre 1927 413.

[6] Chambre d'agriculture du Puy-de-Dôme, 2e session ordinaire de 1927, procès verbal du 17 décembre 1927, création d'une chambre régionale, *Terre d'Auvergne*, 7ème année, no. 140, 8 janvier 1928, 2.

[7] *Le Bon Grain*, 15 novembre 1931, 257; 'Réunion de la chambre d'agriculture de l'Est,' 21 novembre 1931, *Le Bon Grain*, 1 janvier 1932, 3–5.

[8] *Journal d'Agriculture du Sud-Ouest*, janvier 1928, 131.

improve farming conditions. Marc Blatin wrote in *Terre d'Auvergne* on 26 October 1930:

> Peasants, unite to defend the soil which is threatened!

Joseph Faure, a farmer from the Corrèze, senator, creator of the *chambres d'agriculture*, and defender of the agricultural interest, wrote an article with the same message the year before.[9]

Many agriculturalists argued for improvements in agricultural techniques which would improve returns. These were discussed in the various organizations. However, there was also a widespread perception in these bodies that peasants with small farms were very conservative in their agricultural practice and resistant to new methods. Lagardelle in the South-West agreed with this view.

Rural depopulation had been a concern in many agricultural communities before the war.[10] This was certainly the case in Lorraine and even more so in a predominantly agricultural area like the Auvergne. Support for encouraging a return to the land continued in the Auvergne during the war years as evidenced by the article in *Le Moniteur du Puy-de-Dôme* under the signature of H. Gomot, senator for the Puy-de-Dôme. Gomot noted the opportunity to persuade school-children who were helping on farms during the war to remain in agricultural work.[11] The prominent agriculturalist Michel Augé-Laribé highlighted the effect of the huge loss of labour as a result of the war. He quoted estimates that 673,000 agricultural labourers had been killed or disappeared during the war and 500,000 were so badly wounded that they could not work again.[12] A remedy was suggested by the natalist movement which started during the war and wanted government measures to encourage couples to have more children. This was particularly active in Lorraine, for example, in the Nancy chamber of commerce.

The lack of labour on farms continued to be a constant theme. All the agricultural bodies were concerned with the depopulation of the countryside and the drift to the towns. This, they believed, was made worse by low

[9] Joseph Faure, Les agriculteurs auraient-ils enfin voix au chapitre, *Terre d'Auvergne*, 8ème année, no. 195, 28 juillet 1929, 1.

[10] Barral, *Agrariens français*, 180–202.

[11] Le Moniteur du Puy-de-Dôme (15 juin 1918), 3 col a.

[12] M. A-Laribé, *Le Paysan français après la Guerre* (Paris, 1923), 43–47.

prices and poor financial returns.[13] A writer in the October 1920 issue of the *Revue du Syndicat départemental agricole du Puy-de-Dôme* pointed to the decline in population in his village from 800 before the war to 600 in 1920, including 30 killed during the war. Like many others he believed positive measures were needed to keep people on the land, such as financial help for the renovation of old villages and more instruction on agriculture in schools.[14] Charles Guyot, from Lorraine, wrote about the industrialisation of agriculture and the decline of the rural population. We examined his views in the chapter on Lorraine.[15] During the war the Clermont-Ferrand chamber of commerce had supported the Nancy chamber to press for faster consolidation of agricultural holdings in order to give a much needed boost to agricultural production after the war.[16] This was particularly significant as the division of land into small parcels was common in fertile areas like the Limagne near Clermont-Ferrand.

Victor Boret, Minister of Agriculture during the war and later a senator, conducted a campaign to stem the rural exodus. He wanted agriculture to be better appreciated by urban citizens and the state and to have more state support.[17] Jules Méline in *Le Retour à la terre et la surproduction industrielle* (1905) had argued that a permanent crisis of overproduction in industry would drive workers back to the land, if the right measures were put in place to make rural life more attractive and agriculture more profitable.[18] Méline had long been a supporter of agriculture and was author of the pre-war Méline tariff on imports. He published his post-war support for a programme of encouraging people to return to the land in *Le Salut par la terre et le programme économique de l'avenir* (Paris, 1919). A national *Ligue pour le retour à la terre* was formed under the patronage of Méline and Boret as well as Émile Loubet, a former president of the Republic. The government issued a decree on 17 October 1922 asking for a *comité de retour à la terre* to be set up in each department by the prefect. They were to undertake publicity and to assist candidate farmers to find

[13] "Nos campagnes se vident, '*Le Bon Grain*, 15 octobre 1930, 24ème année, 169.

[14] *Revue du Syndicat départemental agricole du Puy-de-Dôme*, 33e année, no. 10 (octobre 1920), 280–1.

[15] C. Guyot, 'À propos d'un livre récent, le passé et l'avenir de la Lorraine, agriculture et industrie', *Extrait des Mémoires de l'Académie Stanislas 1918–1919* (Nancy, 1919), 27–46. Guyot was Secrétaire perpétuel de l'Académie Stanislas.

[16] *Travaux Clermont-Ferrand*, 1918, (séance 12 novembre 1918), 58–61.

[17] V. Boret, Pour et par la Terre (Paris, 1921), 133–155.

[18] J. Méline, *The Return to the Land* (London, 1906), 90.

jobs, properties and training.[19] The committee wrote to schools asking them to use their influence on young people to persuade them to remain on the land.[20]

*Le Bon Grain* which represented the views of the Lorraine agricultural syndicates posted two editorials in 1927, which took a very nostalgic look at the issue of peasants leaving the land.[21] A thorough article the following year highlighted various factors in migration from farms. Industry was competing for labour. Many men had met town dwellers in the army and thought that life in the town was easier. Farm machinery was expensive and some small farms were short of capital. There was a shortage of housing for young married farmers. The article suggested that better education in rural schools could combat this trend. Foreign workers could also help make up for labour shortages.[22] A publication of the Office Régional Agricole de l'Est in 1925 noted a similar trend of rural depopulation in the neighbouring Vosges.[23] Pierre Caziot was an agricultural engineer who later became Minister of Agriculture under Vichy. Writing in *La Terre Lorraine*, the organ of the agricultural syndicates in the Moselle department, he said there was depopulation in some areas in the East and in many other rural areas of France. He believed a crisis for the peasantry was also one for the whole of nation.[24] Two more articles entitled 'L'Abandon de Nos Campagnes' by the president of the Comices de Metz et de Boulay appeared in the journal in 1927.[25] Jacques Le Roy Ladurie, the secretary-general of the Union nationale des Syndicats Agricoles, returned to this theme when addressing a Journée Rurale in Thionville on 19 December 1936. He talked about 500,000 peasants who had left their farms between 1931 and 1935, many of whom would be unemployed.[26]

Lucien Gachon, the friend of Henri Pourrat and advocate of the virtues of a rural society in the Auvergne, hoped that difficulties in industry in

[19] *Bulletin de la Société départementale d'Agriculture et du Syndicat des Agriculteurs des Hautes-Pyrénées*, janvier 1923, 372.

[20] Ibid, juillet 1924, 542–44.

[21] 'Aimer la Terre,' *Le Bon Grain* 15 avril 1927, 21e année, 9; 'Réflexions d'un Terrien qui médite,' Ibid, 15 novembre 1927, 121–22.

[22] *Le Bon Grain*, 1 novembre 1928, 313–314.

[23] J. Perette, G. Adam, *L'Agriculture dans les Vosges en 1925* (Nancy, 1925), 2.

[24] P. Caziot, 'la Vérité sur la Richesse agricole, conclusion: la crise agraire' La Terre Lorraine, 15 août 1925, 6–8.

[25] *La Terre Lorraine*, 11 septembre 1927 452; 18 septembre 1927, 468.

[26] *La Terre Lorraine*, 27 décembre 1936, 835.

1927 would encourage some people back to the land and said they should be welcomed.[27] A little later a humorous piece appeared in *Terre d'Auvergne*, a dialogue between two peasants which suggested that conditions in the countryside would improve and in a few years they too would have electric light and cinemas and other entertainments which were now attracting young people to the towns.[28] However, another writer in the same journal thought that, once a peasant had left the land, he was unlikely to be attracted back. This remained true even in rural areas where conditions for growing crops or raising cattle were favourable.[29] On 15 December 1932 at the meeting of the *chambre d'agriculture* of the Puy-de-Dôme, it was noted that it was the young who were leaving and the farmers who remained were mostly over 40 years old. Of 110,000 farms in the Puy-de-Dôme, 80,000 had less than 10 hectares. They seemed unlikely to survive.[30]

This concern about the effects of rural depopulation was linked to a fear among conservative and Catholic circles on the right of politics that French society was changing for the worse. The declining importance of agriculture in the national economy and the move of population to the towns would lead to moral decay. This was articulated by a number of writers such as Henri Pourrat, both an ardent Catholic and close to the Action Française. His lament for a disappearing peasant world led him eventually to sympathize with the Vichy regime and its wish to preserve a traditional rural society. The same might be said of Caziot.

The agricultural bodies asked for measures to retain young people on the land and one of the most popular was to train teachers to instruct young people in the schools more effectively about agriculture and the benefits of staying rooted on the land. Another was electrification which would make life more comfortable and reduce back-breaking labour. A third was improved transport which would make farms less isolated. Technical education, electrification and transport were of equal interest to

[27] See also Terre d'Auvergne, 6eme année, no. 113, 2 janvier 1927, 2.

[28] 'G. Gardet, président du syndicat agricole de Champeix, La Désertion des Campagnes, dialogue entre Cadet et Bregillon,' Terre d'Auvergne, 6eme année, no. 123, 26 juin 1927, 3.

[29] Frantz Redon, L'exode rural et l'agriculture, *Terre d'Auvergne*, 8eme année, no. 239, 9 novembre 1930, 2; Jacques Bainville, Dépopulation et répopulation rurales, ibid., 9eme année, 4 janvier 1931, 247, 1–2. Extrait de la Revue des Agriculteurs de France.

[30] Ibid, 11e année, no. 324, 26 février 1933, procès-verbal d'une réunion de la fédération des syndicats 15 décembre 1932, aperçu général, 1.

the economic regions. Farmers and industry wanted better transport, for example, and access to cheap electric power with no minimum charges.

Improvement in transport, whether by road or rail, was a universal concern for agricultural communities. Louis Michel, senator for Meurthe-et-Moselle 1920–1936, drew attention to the need for better rural roads at a regional meeting of agricultural associations in the East in 1927.[31] The Puy-de-Dôme *syndicats* did so in 1931.[32] Rail transport was equally a concern in Lorraine four years later.[33] At the Annual meeting of the federation of *syndicats* for the Puy-de-Dôme on 28 March 1926, freight rates on the railways were a great concern.[34] Nine years later the *chambre d'agriculture* for the Moselle was demanding lower freight rates for fruit and vegetables.[35]

This was even truer for the issue of electrification of rural areas. Calvet, an engineer in the Génie Rural, put his finger on some of the key issues in articles for the *Journal d'Agriculture du Sud-Ouest* in 1928. The journal was the organ for various agricultural organizations in the area. Rural electrification would be expensive so there needed to be a fair sharing of costs among the local authorities. At the same time farmers had a responsibility to make better use of the new electrical machines available. There was a need for flexible tariffs. We have already seen this idea discussed in the Office Régional d'Énergie Électrique du Sud-Ouest in the previous chapter.[36] In Lorraine, Senator Michel referred to the issue of electrification in his remarks on transport cited above.[37] *Le Bon Grain* subsequently printed an article about how farmers could be persuaded to use more electricity.[38] In 1927 in the Puy-de-Dôme the newly formed *chambre d'agriculture* gave the issue due weight when it set up various commissions to progress its most important business.[39] Its organ *Terre d'Auvergne* published

[31] *Le Bon Grain*, 1 juillet 1927, 51.

[32] Fédération des syndicats et associations agricoles du Puy-de-Dôme, assemblée générale, chemins ruraux, *Terre d'Auvergne*, 9ème année, no. 263, 14 juin 1931, 1.

[33] *Le Bon Grain*, 15 avril 1931, 95–6.

[34] *Terre d'Auvergne*, 18 avril 1926, 2.

[35] 'Réunion de la Chambre d'Agriculture de la Moselle mai 1936, '*La Terre Lorraine*, 15 novembre 1936, 738.

[36] E. Calvet, 'Le problème de l'électrification des campagnes,' *Journal d'Agriculture du Sud-Ouest*, janvier 1928, 208.

[37] *Le Bon Grain*, 1 juillet 1927, 51.

[38] *Le Bon Grain*, 1 novembre 1928, 316–7.

[39] Chambre d'agriculture du Puy-de-Dôme, réunion du bureau du 9 juillet 1927, *Terre d'Auvergne*, 6ème année, no. 127, 4 septembre 1927, 2.

numerous articles on electrical machinery, for example, in 1929–30, also arguing for more flexible tariffs.[40] Using such machines, the journal argued, was not a leap in the dark. Moreover, it was easy to meet the minimum charge requirements. The Compagnie Hydro-Électrique d'Auvergne had revised its charges favourably.[41] However, later the chambre d'agriculture du Puy-de-Dôme was still arguing for special concessions on charges for using small motors and lighting.[42] The journal evidently felt this was an issue to which continuous education was the key, hence more articles on the facts about electricity in 1931.[43] Hence also the request from the *syndicats* to the Compagnie in 1933 to help with the education effort with advice on machines and installation.[44]

The need for agricultural education was also a constant discourse in the regional agricultural bodies. Leygue, Professor of Agriculture, made the case for better training for those who taught agriculture in schools. Their role was vital in persuading their pupils to stay on the land. He thought it was vital to train young women teachers in agriculture as well as men. After three years' teacher training at the regional école normale, a fourth postgraduate year was offered at the Institut Agricole de Toulouse. Women entered this course for the first time in 1929 and performed well. However, the writer felt that the teaching of *normaliens* needed to be even further oriented towards agriculture.[45] In Lorraine there was a similar discourse. At a general assembly of the Union Lorraine des Syndicats Agricoles, Joly presented a report on agricultural education. This described young men learning in winter through correspondence courses by the fireside. It also referred to young girls leaning to be good farm wives and mothers. This comes across as very paternalistic in tone.[46] However, the union renewed its commitment to agricultural education and correspondence courses the

[40] 'Utilisation de la force motrice dans nos campagnes, Terre *d'Auvergne*, 8ème année, no. 202, 1 novembre 1929, 1; Chronique de l'électrification rurale, ibid., 8ème année, nos. 229, 230, 233, 234, 29 juin, 13 juillet, 31 août, 14 septembre 1930, page 1, then page 2 in each case.

[41] *Terre d'Auvergne*, 13 juillet 1930, 1.

[42] Chambre d'agriculture du Puy-de-Dôme Ibid, 11ème année, no. 33?, 26 février 1933, 4.

[43] Caron, Notions d'électricité, *Terre d'Auvergne*, 9ème année, nos. 274–6, 15, 22, 29 novembre 193, page 2 in each case.

[44] Fédération du Puy-de-Dôme XIIIe assemblée générale, procès-verbal, cours agricoles par correspondance-divers,Ibid, 11ème année, no. 33?, 31 mai 1933, 2.

[45] J. Leygue, Les institutrices rurales et l'éducation agricole, *Journal d'Agriculture du Sud-Ouest*, 11 avril 1932, 77, 80, 83.

[46] *Le Bon Grain*, 1, 15 février 1927, 164–5.

following year.[47] Post-school agriculture courses had been facilitated by the national government in a law in 1918.[48] The *chambre d'agriculture* for Meurthe-et-Moselle was also committed to agricultural education. It also saw the importance of better training of teachers for rural schools so that agriculture had greater prominence in the curriculum. At the moment schools taught academic subjects suitable for the sons of lawyers but not for the sons of farmers.[49] Agriculture was becoming more technical and therefore more effort had to be put into agricultural education.[50] Hottenger in an article on agriculture in Union Économique de L'Est in 1932 recognized the contribution made by agricultural syndicates to spreading knowledge of modern methods.[51]

This emphasis on agricultural education was definitely shared in the Auvergne region. A piece on its importance appeared in *Terre d'Auvergne*, for example, in 1927. Young people had to be convinced that agriculture was not just about back-breaking routine. It was a noble profession demanding intellectual skills as well.[52] It was a preoccupation of the agricultural syndicates in the Auvergne and also of the *chambre d'agriculture* of the Puy-de-Dôme. It was listed as a responsibility of one of its commissions at a meeting in July 1927.[53] In 1930 H. Cote, the president of the *chambre d'agriculture* in the Puy-de-Dôme, presented a report on agricultural education. He said improvements had been made but further steps were needed to make sure enough suitably trained teachers reached the schools. Some of them must come from rural areas. Training must emphasize practical skills. There must be greater use of agricultural specialists in the training process. Post-school courses must be developed further including correspondence courses.[54] This emphasis on practical training

[47] *Le Bon Grain*, 15 octobre 1928, 305–6.

[48] Barral, Agrariens français, 211.

[49] *Le Bon Grain*, 15 décembre 1928, 340–1

[50] *Le Bon Grain*, 1 octobre 1931, 221–2.

[51] G. Hottenger, 'Si nous parlions un peu d'agriculture?' Union Économique de L'Est, 15 juin 1932, 149.

[52] P. Roux, L'Enseignement agricole, *Terre d'Auvergne*, 6ème année, no. 124, 10 juillet 1927, 1.

[53] Chambre d'agriculture du Puy-de-Dôme, réunion du bureau du 9 juillet 1927,*Terre d'Auvergne*, 6ème année, no. 127, 4 septembre 1927, 2.

[54] 'Assemblée générale de la fédération des syndicats et associations agricoles du Puy-de-Dôme,' *Terre d'Auvergne*, 18 avril 1926, 5e année, no. 98, 1–2; 'La réorganisation de l'enseignement agricole et post-scolaire, rapport de H.Cote, président de la chambre d'agriculture du Puy-de-Dôme, Ibid, 19 janvier 1930, 8ème année, no. 213, 1–2, Ibid, 26

for teachers and students was ratified at a meeting of the *chambre d'agriculture* on 2 June 1930.[55] In 1932 the *chambre d'agriculture* of the Puy-de-Dôme declared itself in favour of subsidizing a school of horticulture which the *maire* of Clermont-Ferrand proposed to create in order to provide a three-year training course.[56]

Gradually, in some regions, the *chambres d'agriculture* were absorbed into discussions within the Offices des Transports and the Offices Régionaux d'Énergie électrique, which had been set up by the regions to liaise with transport and energy companies. We have already seen in the previous chapter that this started to happen in the Toulouse region in 1929. The *chambre d'agriculture* for the Puy-de-Dôme noted in 1929 the nomination of a representative to sit on the Office des Transports du Centre-Ouest.[57] On 14th April in the same year the chamber of commerce of Clermont-Ferrand took the initiative in organizing a congress for the *chambre d'agriculture* and departmental chambers of commerce. Clémentel was present as president of the *conseil-général*. They agreed that there were many common issues to discuss and further meetings were planned.[58] At its first meeting in 1931, the *chambre d'agriculture* of the Puy-de-Dôme received a report on meetings of the Offices des Transports in Guéret, Lyon and Avignon. The railways were in deficit and the government proposed to put up passenger fares but not charges on freight which would affect farmers. The chamber felt the proceedings of the Offices were of great interest and called for better liaison in future with both the Offices des Transports and the chambers of commerce.[59] At a meeting of the *chambre d'agriculture* on 16 décembre 1932, it was noted that they

janvier 1930, no. 214, 1–2; XIIe Assemblée générale de la fédération des syndicats et associations agricoles du Puy-de-Dôme, instruction professionnelle, Ibid, 10ème année, 297, 29 mai 1932, 1; 31 mai 1933.

[55] Ibid, 8ème année, no. 230, 15 août 1930, 1.

[56] Création d'une école d'horticulture à Clermont-Ferrand, Ibid, 10e année, no. 260, 6 mars 1932, 2.

[57] *Terre d'Auvergne*, 8ème année, no. 179, 3 février 1929, 1, col. 1.

[58] Congrès de la chambre d'agriculture et des chambres de commerce du Puy-de-Dôme, *Terre d'Auvergne*, 8ème année, no. 189, 5 mai 1929, 3.

[59] Chambre d'agriculture du Puy-de-Dôme, procès-verbal de la première session ordinaire de 1931, commission des offices de transports, *Terre d'Auvergne, 9ème année, no. 266,* 26 juillet 1931, 3.

had been consulted on the joining together of railway networks as the chambers of commerce had been.[60]

This willingness of *chambres d'agriculture* and chambers of commerce to work together was seen in other regions too. For example, the economic region in the East backed closer cooperation with the new *chambres d'agriculture* at a meeting in March 1927.[61] It repeated this commitment in 1929 in response to a question from the Ministry of Commerce.[62]

In summary we can see how a set of local and regional agricultural organizations grew up in parallel to the chambers of commerce and the economic regions. They did so largely independent of government, except in the case of the *chambres d'agriculture* which required legislation. We can also see how the spontaneous growth of this multitude of agricultural organizations supported the economic regions in their work. They increased the pressure brought to bear by the regions for improvements in regional transport, distribution of electricity and technical education. This cooperation between the economic regions and the agricultural organizations was supported by Clémentel. In agriculture as in industry we see an example of spontaneous economic regionalism. The agricultural bodies were powerful lobbyists and their influence and action effected change in agricultural education, through *remembrement*, and by participation in local syndicates to carry out rural electrification.

## Tourism

Tourism developed very rapidly in the early twentieth century, despite the interruption of the war. Exploring regional cultural and historical sites, enjoying the diverse beauty of the countryside and tasting regional food and wine became a popular pastime for middle-class town dwellers. They now had access to the countryside in motor cars as well as by bus and train. Some went for winter and summer sports. Others sought a cure in one of the many spas, particularly in areas like the Massif Central and the Pyrenees.

Like agriculture, the tourist industry set about forming its own local and regional organizations in the early twentieth century to promote the

[60] Chambre d'agriculture du Puy-de-Dôme 16 décembre 1932, office des transports, projet de fusion des reseaux de chemin de fer, Ibid, 11ème année, no. 325, 5 mars 1933, 2.

[61] Région économique de l'Est, assemblée générale du 9 mars 1927, *Union Économique de l'Est (UEE)*, 11e année, no. 7, 1 avril 1927, 80.

[62] Région économique de l'Est, assemblée annuelle du comité économique régional, UEE, 13e année, no. 7, 1 avril 1929, 83–84.

attractions of each area, provide useful information to tourists, lobby for better transport and seek support from government and local authorities. Creating these organizations was entirely spontaneous and they were independent of government. They were activist in the sense that they not only lobbied others but also found resources and committed them to specific improvement programmes. They also had to cooperate with the economic regions and chambers of commerce on matters of common interest. They can certainly be regarded as effective expressions of economic regionalism.

These organizations grew from the bottom up. First came the opening of local offices known as the *syndicats d'initiative* to help tourists. One of the first was in Clermont-Ferrand in 1898, followed by the Cantal in 1900. The Velay followed in 1901, Vosges et Nancy in 1903 and Vichy in 1906.[63] These were founded on local initiative. A good example of local initiative is the role played by Henri Gutton, a Nancy municipal councillor and architect who was the first director of the *syndicat* in Nancy. He saw the opportunity to open up the Vosges to tourism by improving transport.[64] *Syndicats d'initiative* gradually got involved in a number of activities—creating publicity, publishing guides and lists of hotels, and providing information on transport.[65] It was soon realized, however, that the *syndicats* would be more effective if they banded together into regions on a number of issues like lobbying railway companies or commissioning publicity. Moreover, it was the different aspects of regional cultures which attracted tourists in the first place, for example, regional gastronomy or folklore. Certainly it was not the department which was the attraction. It was the region which pulled people in. Stephen Harp has explained how Michelin re-packaged the cultural features of each region, principally its gastronomy but also sites of historical interest, for the prosperous middle classes to encourage them to explore France, using their cars and Michelin tyres. In so doing Michelin re-defined what it meant to be French, to enjoy the country's richness and diversity. The green guides and the red

[63] B. Larique, 'L'Économie du tourisme en France des années 1890 à la veille de la seconde guerre mondiale, organisation et développement d'un secteur socio-économique' (Thèse de doctorat d'histoire, Univ. Bordeaux III—Michel de Montaigne, U.F.R. d'histoire, 2006), 128.

[64] J. Manfredini, *Les Syndicats d'initiative: naissance de l'identité touristique de la France* (Tours, 2017), 71.

[65] Ibid, 124.

guides to hotels and restaurants revived the *petites patries* as a tourist experience and as quintessentially French.[66]

So, beginning before the First World War, the *syndicats* started getting together. Congresses of *syndicats* were held before the war including one in Clermont-Ferrand in 1905 and Nancy in 1908.[67] Then they federated permanently into larger units, for a department but soon for a region or even, where it was useful, a grouping of regions.[68] The Vosges federation was created before the war and included Meurthe-et-Moselle, the Moselle (after the war), Bas-Rhin and Haut-Rhin but not the Meuse. By 1914 there were six federations of SIs in France—Sud-Centre, Sud-Ouest, Provence, Côte d'Azur, Bourgogne and Vosges.[69]At the end of the war a federation was created for the Massif Central which covered the Allier, Puy-de-Dôme, Haute-Loire and Cantal.[70] The federations for the Pyrenees similarly started with wartime meetings in Cauterets in 1916 and Toulouse in May 1918.[71]

Soon after the war there were 20 regional federations covering the whole of France, all of them active in promoting tourism. There were also some supra-regional confederations like the Confederation of the South-East which took in the regional federations for the Alps, the Valley of the Rhône, Provence and the Côte d'Azur.[72] There was also a special federation for the Cévennes.[73] The federations created a national union after the war known as UFSI, Union Française de Syndicats d'Initiative. This could interface more effectively with important agencies in Paris, not only government departments but also the quango Office National du Tourisme, which provided some government funds, and the powerful Touring Club de France (TCF), which had a regional presence as well. The meetings of the national union discussed similar issues to the regional federations—road and rail improvements, navigation, databases of hotels and sites, guide books, telephone and postal services, route signs, tourist events,

[66] S. Harp, Marketing Michelin: advertising and cultural identity in twentieth-century France (Johns Hopkins, 2001), 226, 235–45, 256–67.

[67] Larique, 'L'Économie du tourisme', 201–2.

[68] Larique, 'L'Économie du tourisme', 129, 234–5.

[69] P. Mieille, 'Tourisme et Décentralisation,' *Pyrénées et Océan*, 1 octobre 1919, 1–2.

[70] Larique, 'L'Économie du tourisme', 421.

[71] Assemblée Générale de la Fédération des Syndicats d'Initiative - Pyrénées, Bordeaux 5–6 avril 1919, *Pyrénées et Océan*, 15 juillet 1919, 7.

[72] *Bulletin de l'Union des Fédérations des Syndicats d'Initiative*, 1 janvier 1922, 6–7.

[73] Ibid, 1 janvier 1921, 18.

publicity. It wanted to see a plan to upgrade hotels in each region. It encouraged subsidies to the network of federations. In 1921 it noted that the railway company PLM gave 5000 francs to each federation within its network. The total public subsidy to the federations at this time was 150,000 francs a year, channelled through the Office National du Tourisme and the TCF.[74] UFSI also articulated views about how the federations should interface with the economic regions. Chambers of commerce could join a federation like the Fédération des Pyrénées-Languedoc-Roussillon as associates and contribute toward publicity. Representatives from the federations could likewise sit in on chambers of commerce. However, it was suggested they should make their views on transport matters known there, rather than joining the Offices des Transports as full members which might involve a heavy subscription.[75]

We will now look in more detail at how these regions operated and how they interfaced with government both nationally and locally, and also with the economic regions. We will study three regions in some detail—the Auvergne, the Vosges and the Pyrenees, but also draw some references from other regions.

## The Auvergne

The difficulty of operating during the war brought home to the region how essential to the future this sector could become. In March 1915 the chamber of commerce in Clermont-Ferrand noted the shortage of personnel in the hotel industry caused by conscription, but approved of the efforts made by the large thermal establishments to keep open. It expressed the hope that these establishments would have adequate supplies of coal and other materials and sufficient transport services.[76] The chamber repeated this request in the case of Mont-Dore in 1917. Supplying coal, flour and sugar caused particular problems.[77] In the same year an article appeared in *Le Moniteur du Puy-de-Dôme* entitled *L'Auvergne, pays de tourisme, doit s'organiser pour l'après-guerre*. It appealed to all the various interests in the region to get together to effect changes.[78] In 1918 a

[74] *Bulletin de l'Union des Fédérations des Syndicats d'Initiative*, septembre-novembre 1919 104, 105, 110, 115, 122, 139, 151–4, 156, 163. 1 janvier 1921, 3–4.

[75] Ibid, 1 janvier 1922, 13, 16–17

[76] *Travaux Clermont-Ferrand*, 1915, (séance 31 mars 1915), 18–21.

[77] *Travaux Clermont-Ferrand*, 1917, (séance 25 mai 1917), 48–9.

[78] *Le Moniteur du Puy-de-Dôme* (27 mars 1917), 3 col d.

*Fédération régionale de Tourisme de l'Auvergne et du plateau central* was set up after a large meeting in Clermont-Ferrand. It grouped together all the local *syndicats d'initiative* of the region including the most important for the Auvergne and Clermont-Ferrand and also the *Fédération thermale de l'Auvergne* and other organizations. Its main focus would be on hotels, transport and publicity. It sought to exploit economies of scale in producing brochures. It also wanted to focus on coordinating local bus operations. Such federations were linked to the Office National du Tourisme in Paris. However, delegates to the Clermont meeting were assured that:

> The Office Nationale du Tourisme is a state organization. It is however the enemy of centralization. Those at its head are regionalists.[79]

What we can observe in the Auvergne, and elsewhere, is the spontaneous growth of activities to promote tourism in the regions themselves. The initiatives were truly local and regional. Effective organizations were created, and they identified the key issues. What is particularly significant is that local organizations federated on a regional basis. Other regional bodies, such as departmental *conseils-généraux* and the economic regions, provided support. Such promotion of tourism linked practical economic regionalism to the cultural movement which celebrated each region's character.

The driving force behind the Massif Central federation was a Dr. Cany. He practised in the mountain resort of La Bourboule. Generally, assemblies of the *syndicats d'initiative* in the region took place once a year but committee meetings every three months. At the committee meeting on 20 November 1921, Dr. Cany acted as secretary-general, and Mathiot, the secretary-general of the economic region, was present along with representatives of 22 *syndicats*. The federation channelled 19,000 francs of subsidies from central government and *conseils-généraux* and other sources, passing on 11,000 francs to local *syndicats* in 1921 and retaining the rest for its own expenses. Guénot, the secretary-general of the Franche-Comté and Jura federation, came to talk about the benefits of union to local *syndicats*. For example, federations found it easier to get support from public authorities like *conseils-généraux*. Mathiot regarded tourism as very

[79] *Le Moniteur du Puy-de-Dôme* (24 juin 1918), 3 col b; (26 juin 1918), 2 col f; (27 juin 1918), 2 col b–d; quotation (27 mai 1918), col d. *L'Avenir du Puy-de-Dôme* (25 mai 1918), 3 col c.

important to the economy of the Auvergne. He offered the federation space every month in the journal *Région du Centre* in the section headed *Région touristique*.[80] By the beginning of 1922 the federation was operating out of offices in the main Place Jaude in Clermont-Ferrand.[81] Fairly soon it had 40 members.

The federation tried to work closely with other organizations with an interest in tourism, soliciting financial help where appropriate. For example, there was clearly a common interest with the new *Fédération thermale d'Auvergne* (stations of La Bourboule, Royat, Le Mont-Dore, Chatel-Guyon and Saint-Nectaire), which became the genesis of a national federation for this tourist sector. A French association was set up in January 1922 at the Mont-Dore resort with representatives from other French thermal resorts present.[82] Dr. Cany wrote about the importance of thermalism throughout the centre of France in the *Région du Centre*.[83] The federation of *syndicats d'initiative* clearly had to cooperate with the railway companies on services and also on investments in tourist infrastructure. Likewise, it approached the *conseils-généraux* for further financial support.[84] The Office National du Tourisme was also a financial partner.[85]

The federation identified a major block to the development of tourism in the shortage of reasonably priced hotels, particularly in the mountain areas. At one stage they contemplated opening their own mountain hotels in conjunction with the railway companies, the Office National du Tourisme, chambers of commerce or the Touring Club de France, the latter bodies providing interest guarantees on loans.[86] They calculated that 2000 more rooms were needed. Eighty per cent of sites of interest had no hotel nearby. The matter was urgent for the reputation of the whole industry.

By the beginning of 1923 the federation had realized that they urgently needed a bank which would make loans to small- and medium-sized hotels

[80] *Région du Centre*, no. 6 (février 1922), 17–18.

[81] Ibid, 15.

[82] Dr. Moncorgé, président de la fédération thermale d'Auvergne, 'Fédération thermale française 26 janvier 1922', *L'Auvergne thermale,* bulletin médical officiel des cinq stations de la fédération thermale d'Auvergne, février 1922, quatrième année, no. 23, 1.

[83] *Région du Centre*, no. 6 (février 1922), 7–13; no. 35 (juin 1924), 203–208.

[84] *Région du Centre*, no. 14 (octobre 1922), 25–7.

[85] *Région du Centre*, no. 26 (octobre 1923), 15–19.

[86] *Région du Centre*, no. 13 (septembre 1922), 21; no. 14 (octobre 1922), 25–7, no. 17 (janvier 1923), 17–19.

on a long-term basis, to improve existing rooms and provide new ones. In 1923 the Crédit National Hôtelier was born as a *banque populaire* based in Paris.[87] It enjoyed access to public funds but private companies and individuals could subscribe for shares. Although the bank was based in Paris, it operated through a series of regional committees consisting of representatives of *syndicats d'initiative*, federations, hotel groups and chambers of commerce. They examined plans submitted for consideration and sent a report to the bank.[88] The first regional committee meeting in the Auvergne took place in May 1924. Cany was present. The *Banque populaire* of the Auvergne region provided a banking organization on the ground for the *Crédit Hôtelier* and generated publicity. There was also a national consultative committee. André Michelin was on the board of directors of the central bank in Paris. Casenave, the president of the *Syndicat des Hôteliers* in Royat and an administrator of the *Banque populaire* in Clermont, urged local businessmen to show their love for their *petite patrie* by supporting the bank, thus demonstrating:

> that we are above all good citizens, excellent Auvergants who love their small fatherland, resolved to do the impossible to make it more beautiful, more prosperous and therefore more hospitable.[89]

The region also took steps to provide suitable education for hotel employees and hotel management. The École Pratique Hôtelière was moved from Vichy to Clermont-Ferrand and a specialist training course for females from 13 years onwards was also started there. Both gave a certificate of study after three years. A higher level qualification in hotel management was offered by the École Supérieure de Commerce. Charles Mathiot, the regional secretary, felt there was a need to improve the intellectual level of managers.[90]

The federation also sought to address the hotels' issue by providing practical guides of accommodation available, in which local hotels committed to a fixed price for the season, in return for a listing. The guides also covered sites of interest and related material on the region. In 1922 the federation published in Clermont 5000 copies of *Le Massif Central,*

[87] *Région du Centre*, no. 29 (janvier 1924), 11.

[88] *Région du Centre*, no. 32 (avril 1924), 177; no. 33 (mai 1924), 169.

[89] *Région du Centre*, no. 34 (juin 1924), 227; no. 40 (décembre 1924), 403–9, quote 410.

[90] C. Mathiot, 'L'Enseignement Hôtelier dans la XVIIe région économique,' *Région du Centre*, juin 1925, 203–205.

*l'Auvergne, Bourbonnais, Vélay, guide pratique de renseignements de tourisme.*[91] In 1924 they had to increase the print run of this practical guide to 10,000.[92] As well as publishing information about places of interest in the Auvergne, they also helped tourists find sites by better signposting and also to enjoy them once there with information boards. In so doing they worked alongside national organizations like the Touring Club de France.[93]

The federation and the Clermont chamber also lobbied railway companies for improvements to the rail services and the local authorities for road improvements. For example, in October 1923 the federation was asking for service improvements from Clermont to Paris and the chamber of commerce supported their request, at the same time supporting Vichy's demand for improvements to the roads. Charles Mathiot, the regional secretary, wrote in support of improvement to the latter.[94] The chamber of commerce complained again about railway services at the beginning of 1924.[95] At their annual general assembly, the federation returned to agitate yet again about railway services and improvements to the roads for their clients.[96] This was a constant refrain throughout these post-war years.

## Pyrenees

From 1919 there came into existence a well-established structure of tourist federations for the whole mountain chain. The two main federations were the Fédération de Pyrénées-Gascogne-Guyenne and the Fédération de Pyrénées-Languedoc-Roussillon. To keep the Pyrenees together as a tourist region, *syndicats* were allowed to federate to both organizations. There were specialist federations for sports and for hoteliers.[97] There was also a Confédération pyrénénne climatique, thermale et touristique. Intermediate between the *syndicats* in individual towns and the regional federations were federations for departments. For example, there was a

[91] *Région du Centre*, no. 9 (mai 1922), 15; no. 11 (juillet 1922), 23; no. 14 (octobre 1922), 25–7.

[92] 'Assemblée générale de la fédération Saint-Flour 6–7 septembre 1924', *Région du Centre*, no. 38 (octobre 1924), 335–9.

[93] Ibid.

[94] *Travaux Clermont-Ferrand*, 1923 (séance 30 octobre 1923), 81–2. C. Mathiot, 'L'Angoissante Question des Routes,' *Région du Centre*, octobre 1925, 323–5.

[95] *Travaux Clermont-Ferrand*, 1924 (séance 8 janvier 1924), 19–24.

[96] *Région du Centre*, no. 38 (octobre 1924), 335–9.

[97] *Région de Toulouse et des Pyrénées*, avril 1921, 41.

federation for the Haute-Garonne and a Union Thermale et Touristique de l'Ariège founded in October 1919. This grew rapidly after the war from two to twelve members. It encompassed a hotels federation and specialist societies for fishing and hunting. The local chamber of commerce was affiliated. It received a subsidy from the *conseil-général* who sent three representatives to federation meetings.[98] Within this departmental federation the *syndicats d'initiative* looked after routes, published maps and guides and maintained an information office. The departmental federation coordinated relationships with the departmental administration, dealt with transport services, contacted hotels with particular problems, protected historic sites and monuments, and undertook more general publicity.[99] The larger regional federations tackled major publicity for the region as a whole, the Pyrenees, and also used their muscle with the railway companies.[100]

We owe some of our knowledge of this remarkable burst of activity to organize tourism from the pages of *Pyrénées et Océan*. This was a specialist journal founded after the war to maintain a regional focus on the development of tourism. It fought against a narrow parochial approach. It emphasized how much there was to do after the war to re-establish a full railway schedule and also return hotels to civilian use and repair them.[101] This work was vital because tourism was an important contributor to national recovery.[102] The agenda for the joint Pyrenean federation meetings in April 1920 gives some idea of the enormous task they faced. They had to gain the willing cooperation of a host of other organizations local, regional and national, from local councils and railway companies to the Office National du Tourisme, a source of funds. Secondly, they had a huge publicity programme to undertake, which meant gathering much data on local attractions and photos. Re-organizing transport to cope with an influx of tourists was a big job. Lastly they had to encourage the development of hotels, and for this finance was needed.[103] This could be provided eventually by the establishment of the Crédit Hôtelier and its network of

[98] *La Région de Toulouse et des Pyrénées*, novembre 1921, 224–5.

[99] *La Région de Toulouse et des Pyrénées*, novembre 1921, 224–5.

[100] 'Organisation du Tourisme aux Pyrénées, '*La Région de Toulouse et des Pyrénées*, avril 1921, 40–41.

[101] P. Mieille, 'Tourisme et Décentralisation,' *Pyrénées et Océan*, 1 octobre 1919, 1–2.15 juillet 1919, 1–3.

[102] *La Dépêche de Toulouse*, 11 avril 1920, 3.

[103] 'Assemblée Générale des Fédérations Pyrénéennes Toulouse 10–11 avril 1920,' *Pyrénées et Océan*, 1 avril 1920, 1–3.

regional offices.[104] At a further meeting of the western of the two federations in December 1920 focus shifted to opening relations with the 8th economic region, particularly to put more pressure on railway companies. The doctors wanted to set up a separate association for thermal resorts offering cures, modelled on the Fédération Thermale d'Auvergne. They welcomed delegates from other regions, like Dr. Cany from the Auvergne, and sent representatives to other regions to see what they could learn. They also cemented relationships with the tourism committee in the Chamber of Deputies and worked hard on getting coverage in the press. They were beginning to show that they were politically astute in cultivating relationships with people who could help their cause.[105] As regards rail routes the federation started to look further afield in its aim to attract tourism. It wanted to see better rail links to Nice and also across the Pyrenees to Spain.[106]

The thermal industry extended its cooperation further at its congress in Pau four years later. The confederation for this industry wanted to extend its reach to the east. They now covered 37 establishments across the Pyrenees and had laid down minimum tariffs in an effort to maintain standards. They also took steps to publish an annual directory on the various cures offered and laid down hygiene standards.[107] The meeting at the same time of the Fédération de Pyrénées-Gascogne-Guyenne took the proposal for joint publicity a step further with discussion of a 60,000 francs budget for such activity. Joint promotional activity also included visits to tourist regions before congresses so that delegates could see facilities on the ground. Discussion of transport increasingly moved on to local bus services, particularly those run in conjunction with railway companies. For example, the Languedoc federation asked for a Route des Cévennes bus service to the Gorges du Tarn and Carcassonne to be operated by the

[104] Raymond Bertin, sécretaire-général de l'Union Thermale et Touristique de l'Ariège, *Pyrénées et Océan, 1 octobre 1924, 4–5.*

[105] 'Congrès de Tourisme de Pau, Fédération de Tourisme Pyrénées-Guyenne-Gascogne, 4–5 décembre 1920,' *Pyrénées et Océan*, janvier-mars 1921, 20–23.

[106] P. Mieille, 'Autour du Congrès de Tourisme de Toulouse, 13 novembre 1921,' *Pyrénées et Océan*, 1 novembre 1921, 2–3.

[107] 'Congrès de la Confédération Pyrénénne Climatique, Touristique et Thermale, 14 novembre 1925,' *Pyrénées et Océan*, 1 décembre 1925, 13.

PLM railway.[108] Air services also started to appear in the federations' discussions in the mid-twenties.[109]

Lastly at this time the hotel industry was turning its attention to training and the founding of hotel schools. The interest in technical education in the economic regions was reflected in the tourist industry's agenda. The general assembly of the *Congrès Hôtelier*, a national organization, met in Biarritz and its deliberations attracted attention locally. It wanted to see apprentices working in hotels and also schools offering more general training in hotel management.[110]

## Vosges

We find the same preoccupations in the deliberations of the Vosges federation. The departmental archives only contain the full records of one meeting in 1931, although there is evidence of similar meetings in 1921, 1924 and 1932. From this it is apparent that they were prosecuting their programmes both before and after this date. The Vosges federation encompassed the departments of the Bas and Haut-Rhin, Meurthe-et-Moselle, the Moselle, and the Vosges itself. Its extraordinary general meeting on 27 September 1931 included representation from the *mairie* of Épinal, the railways in Alsace-Lorraine, the Club Vosgien, plus various businessmen and hotel owners. The summary of activities included study tours organized with the railway companies, an increased budget for joint publicity and developing an inventory of natural and historic sites. The federation was building up a collection of photos of the region to respond rapidly to newspaper requests. They had prepared a publicity programme for the Paris Colonial Exhibition in 1931, had received a US delegation and organized other study tours for overseas travel agents including from the UK. The Chemins de Fer d'Alsace-Lorraine et de L'Est were continuing to pay generous subsidies. The president of the tourist federation had also written to the prefect asking if the *conseil-général* could continue their previous subsidy. The federation continued to publish guides to

[108] 'Fédération des syndicats d'initiative Pyrénées-Gascogne, 15 novembre 1925, Toulouse,' 'Assemblée Générale de la Fédération Pyrénées-Languedoc-Roussillon,' *Pyrénées et Océan*, 1 décembre 1925, 14–15.

[109] 'Hubert Lagardelle, La Confédération pyrénéenne touristique, climatique et thermale à Toulouse, Fédération des Syndicats d'Initiative Pyrénées-Gascogne 12–13 novembre 1927,' *Sud-Ouest Économique*, 8ème année, nos. 167–8, 15–31 décembre 1927, 1454–6.

[110] *Pyrénées et Océan*, 1 février 1925, 7–10.

accommodation including popular village bed and breakfast accommodation. They also published guides to the main sites of the region, including to the *stations hydrominérales*.[111] A *Credit National Hôtelier* visit was scheduled for June 1932 to persuade localities to improve tourist provision, particularly local hotels.

The resolutions passed demanded yet further improvements in train and bus services, particularly those ancillary to the trains, and in roads. The federation's members also wanted more reasonable tariffs.[112]

## Conclusion

The creation of regional tourist federations covered the whole of France and their concerns were similar-transport improvement, publicity, hotel refurbishment and the construction of new hotels, publication of guides to hotels and sites. They also wanted to link up with other interested parties, including the chambers of commerce and the economic groupings, to press their case. These universal concerns were reflected in the bulletin of the national union, which contained summaries of the proceedings of most regions. In 1922 several regions were actively pursuing joint publicity for example.[113] The Limousin and the Alps (Grenoble) were actively pursuing the construction of hotels and worked with the Crédit National Hôtelier.[114] The pages of the economic journals in Normandy and Brittany show that tourism was appreciated as important to their regional economies. In the 1930s there was a renewed commitment of funds to its promotion from the economic regions and individual chambers of

[111] ADV JPL 957 1 Vosges guides.

[112] ADV (Archives Départemental Vosges), 8 M 128.

[113] *Bulletin de l'Union des Fédérations des Syndicats d'Initiative*, 1 janvier 1922, 21.

[114] F. Prevet, *Le Régionalisme économique, conception et réalisation* (Thèse de doctorat, Faculté de Droit de Paris, 1929), 177. C. Druelle-Korn, 'La Modernisation inachevée de l'aménagement du territoire, le cas de la VIIe région, (Limousin, Poitou, Charentes), in A. Aglan, M. Margairaz, et P. Verheyde (eds), *De la croissance à la crise (1925–1935) Le moment Tannery; Une tentative avortée de modernisation conservatrice et libérale à l'heure de la mondialisation* (Paris, 2014), 165.

commerce.[115] Duplantier in his doctoral thesis of 1929 picked out these developments as perfect examples of spontaneous economic regionalism.[116]

In this chapter we have seen how local and regional organizations covering agriculture and tourism flourished during the inter-war years. They were powerful lobbying organizations, bringing their economic needs to the attention of local authorities and government ministers. They also used what powers they had to effect improvements. They worked with the economic regions in a cooperative manner on matters of common interest such as transport. While lacking the focus that only a centrally directed regional planning system could give, they carried out some important changes in their regions.

## Bibliography

A-Laribé M. (1923). *Le Paysan français après la Guerre.*

ADV (Archives Départemental Vosges), 8M 128.

ADV JPL 957 1 Vosges guides.

Barral, P. (1968). *Les agrariens francais de Méline à Pisani.*

Boret, V. (1921). *Pour et par la Terre.*

*Bulletin Chambre de Commerce Nancy*, 1927.

Bulletin de l'Assemblée Régionale Professionnelle (Toulouse), 1924.

*Bulletin de l'Union des Fédérations des Syndicats d'Initiative*, 1919, 1921, 1922.

*Bulletin de la Société départementale d'agriculture et du syndicat des agriculteurs des Hautes-Pyrénées, 1923, 1924,* 1927.

Druelle-Korn, C. (2014). 'La Modernisation inachevée de l'aménagement du territoire, le cas de la VIIe région, (Limousin, Poitou, Charentes). In A. Aglan, M. Margairaz, & P. Verheyde (Eds.), *De la croissance à la crise (1925–1935) Le moment Tannery; Une tentative avortée de modernisation conservatrice et libérale à l'heure de la mondialisation.*

Duplantier, J. (1929). *Le Régionalisme économique et spécialement la région économique de Bordeaux et du Sud-Ouest.* Thèse de doctorat, Faculté de Droit de Bordeaux.

[115] *Revue Économique de L'Ouest* Rouen, 25 octobre 1922, 15–17, 25 novembre 1922, 15–19; 1 novembre 1923 3–6; 1 avril 1929, 29–31. IVe région économique de Basse Normandie (Caen) mars-juillet 1930, 17–18; 25 novembre 1937, 43–48. VIe region économique, groupement régional économique de Rennes, séance 12 janvier 1934, 18; séance 6 juillet 1934, 9–10; séance 11 janvier 1935, 6.

[116] J. Duplantier, *Le Régionalisme économique et spécialement la région économique de Bordeaux et du Sud-Ouest* (Thèse de doctorat, Faculté de Droit de Bordeaux, 1929), 238–240.

Guyot, C. (1919). *À propos d'un livre récent, le passé et l'avenir de la Lorraine, agriculture et industrie*. Extrait des Mémoires de l'Académie Stanislas 1918–1919 (pp. 127–46).

Harp, S. (2001). *Marketing Michelin: Advertising and cultural identity in twentieth-century France*.

IVe région économique de Basse Normandie (Caen) 1930, 1937.

*Journal d'Agriculture du Sud-Ouest*, 1928, 1932.

*L'Auvergne thermale*, 1922.

*L'Avenir du Puy-de-Dôme* 1918.

La Dépêche de Toulouse, 1920.

*La Terre Lorraine*, 1925, 1927, 1936.

Larique, B. (2006). *L'Économie du tourisme en France des années 1890 à la veille de la seconde guerre mondiale, organisation et développement d'un secteur socio-économique*. Thèse de doctorat d'histoire, Univ. Bordeaux III—Michel de Montaigne, U.F.R. d'histoire.

*Le Bon Grain* 1927, 1928, 1930, 1931, 1932.

*Le Moniteur du Puy-de-Dôme* 1917, 1918.

Manfredini J., Les Syndicats d'initiative: Naissance de l'identité touristique de la France (2017).

Méline, J. (1906). *The return to the land*.

Perette, J., & Adam, G. (1925). *L'Agriculture dans les Vosges en 1925*.

Prevet, F. (1929). *Le Régionalisme économique, conception et réalisation*. Thèse de doctorat, Faculté de Droit de Paris.

*Pyrénées et Océan*, 1919, 1920, 1921 1924, 1925.

*Région de Toulouse et des Pyrénées*, 1921.

*Région du Centre*, 1921, 1922, 1923, 1924, 1925.

*Revue du Syndicat départemental agricole du Puy-de-Dôme*, 1920.

*Revue Économique de L'Ouest* 1922, 1923, 1929.

*Terre d'Auvergne*, 1926, 1927, 1928, 1929, 1930, 1931, 1932, 1933.

*Travaux de la Chambre de Commerce de Clermont-Ferrand*, 1915, 1917, 1918, 1923, 1924.

*Union Économique de L'Est*, 1927, 1929, 1932.

Vie region économique, groupement regional économique de Rennes, 1934, 1935.

CHAPTER 9

# The Legacy of the Inter-War Economic Regions After 1940

To assess fully how far the economic regions of 1918–1940 laid the foundations for today's regions, we need to examine developments after 1940 and particularly since the advent of the Fifth Republic. It is not enough to say that there were further attempts to map France's regions after 1945. We need to understand the thinking behind the various developments of regionalism after 1945 to see if there are any common threads with Clémentel's original vision. Decentralization and deconcentration of the state machine, as well as regionalism, were debated more intensively in the post-war period than ever before. There were many different proposals for reform implemented but sometimes the changes were not clear cut. Some would argue that the Jacobinism of the older centralized administration is still alive and well in the twenty-first century despite the dramatic changes implemented by the Socialists in 1982.

The first consideration is what continuities there were between the Third Republic and the Vichy regime. How far was Vichy truly regionalist? The Vichy government introduced regional prefects in 1941 to ensure better administrative coordination and set up the Délégation générale à l'Équipement national (DGEN). Twenty regions were defined in 1942. The expression "l'aménagement du territoire" first appeared in a government document under Vichy, in a report on industrial decentralization for the DGEN. The Vichy emphasis on a traditional society based on agriculture attracted some regionalists. So did the more corporatist approach to



T. Cudbird, *The Origins of Economic Regions in France, 1918–1940*,
https://doi.org/10.1007/978-3-032-04422-8_9

organizing business. Lagardelle, who worked for the Toulouse region after the First World War and espoused some corporatist ideas then, served as Minister of Labour in the Laval government. Caziot, who made his name in the inter-war years as a commentator on agriculture supporting the peasantry, became Minister of Agriculture under Vichy.

Another example of regionalist collaboration is the writer Lucien Romier. He worked unofficially on a plan to recreate the old provinces of the *Ancien Régime* and was the architect of Vichy's regional policy. He wanted if possible to avoid further annexations by the Germans as happened in Alsace. He hoped his reform would anchor the remaining provinces more firmly in France. He had been a prominent political journalist in the inter-war period. At one time he worked closely with *Redressement Français*. He became very critical of the Third Republic's inability to reform its governance. He was close politically and personally to Petain but later fell out with the occupiers, dying in January 1944 just before he could be arrested.[1]

Vichy's support for the peasantry as well as its alliance with the Catholic church earned the approval of Henri Pourrat, the Auvergnat writer who set his face against modernity. Even the Auvergne economic journal *Région du Centre* supported Petain in 1940.[2] Jean Charles-Brun, the secretary–general of the FRF made no political statements during the occupation, but was privately pleased about the regionalist developments. He accepted some symbolic honours.

Yet was Vichy truly regionalist? Barral argues that in fact the *état français* reinforced the power of regional prefects to keep control of is territory. Encouraging words about regional cultures were simply window dressing. Some people in the regime could see dangers in regionalism and Laval was not interested. The supremacy of the state had to be maintained.[3] Notwithstanding that Vichy's devotion to regional reform was

[1] J-P. Cointet, *Les Hommes de Vichy, l'illusion du pouvoir* (Paris, 2017), Lucien Romier 115–120.

[2] P. Cornu et M. Ozouf, 'la rencontre de trois mondes. L'agrarisme de Lucien Gachon,' in dir. N. Ginsburger, M-C Robic, J-L Tissier, *Géographes Français en Seconde Guerre Mondiale* (Sorbonne, 2021), 129–145.

[3] P. Barral, 'Idéal et pratique du régionalisme dans le regime de Vichy,' *Revue française de science politique*, 1974–10, Vol. 24 (5), 911–939.

skin deep, regionalism as a movement was tainted by its fascist associations after 1945. It did not really recover until the 1950s.[4]

If there was continuity in thinking about the role of regions across the Vichy divide, it came from individuals who survived to continue the debate. We have already noted the views on regionalism of a number of intellectuals from the thirties who were concerned to revive the French economy more widely and believed in organized state planning. One example is Hubert Lagardelle who worked on the journal *Plans*.[5] There were a number of other members of this influential modernizing elite sympathetic to regionalism including Raymond Aron, who supported federalist decentralization in the pages of *Ordre Nouveau* in 1933. Thierry Maulnier, the New Right journalist of the thirties, and Claudius-Petit, who later worked in the Ministry of Reconstruction and Urbanism, were also sympathetic to regionalism. Some of the men who worked for the Vichy DGEN later worked on the first Plan.[6] Clearly there is a continuity of thinking here with the post-war planning regime. Roland Pasquier has written that the connection between the inter-war period, Vichy and the post-war is clear on planning issues.[7] It is interesting that J-F Gravier, whose book *Paris et le desert français* kick started the implementation of *aménagement du territoire*, was quite close to Vichy's views at the beginning of his career. The early edition of his book contained some traces of anti-democratic sentiment, was anti-urban, and favourable to regionalism, elements which were later suppressed.[8]

Before we consider the evolution of regional policy in the years after 1945, we need to note the profound shift in the role of central government in the economy. In the nineteenth century it was not considered appropriate for governments to get involved in the day-to-day workings of firms and other enterprises. Its job was to set a regulatory framework in the general interest and allow them to make their own decisions. This

[4] J. Burnham, *Politicians, Bureaucrats and Leadership in Organisations. Lessons from Regional Planning in France*, (Palgrave, 2009), 29.

[5] J-L Loubet des Bayle, *Les non-conformistes des années 30: une tentative de renouvellement de la pensée politique française*, (Paris, 1969) 94–5.

[6] R. Pasquier, *Le Pouvoir régional, Mobilisations, décentralisation et gouvernance en France*, (Paris, 2012), 127–132.

[7] R. Pasquier, *Le Pouvoir régional*, (Paris, 2012), 131.

[8] N. Ginsburger, 'Pour la révolution nationale, J-F Gravier un parcours engagé,'in dir. N. Ginsburger, M-C Robic, J-L Tissier, *Géographes Français en Seconde Guerre Mondiale* (Sorbonne, 2021), 195–200.

attitude started to change during the First World War as the government had to ensure the economy functioned in a way which would support the war effort. Clémentel had hoped that some government involvement could continue after the peace to help make sure French industry was competitive again. However, he was defeated. There were some tentative government incursions in industry in the inter-war years, for example, in creating *sociétés d'économie mixte* to finance new power stations on the Rhône. However, such moves were the exception rather than the rule.

After 1945 the situation could not have been more different. France faced an even greater task of recovery than after the First World War. The Commissariat Général du Plan was set up to plan economic expansion under the government's leadership. One of the deficiencies in France's economic performance was the very uneven pattern of development in different regions of the country. Apart from being the centre of government administration, the Paris region was also attracting a disproportionate share of the country's enterprises. Other areas across France were much less fortunate. This was the focus of Gravier's book, *Paris et le desert français*. Out of a wide ranging debate within government, the policy of *aménagement du territoire* was adopted. The seeds of this can be seen in the work of people like Philippe Lamour in the thirties and in certain practical initiatives taken by the economic regions at that time. However, it was only after 1945 and especially during the fifties that it became a recognized national government priority. Investments were needed in industry and infrastructure to spread development more evenly across France. Gradually the national plan incorporated a regional element, so that it looked at regions as well as industrial sectors. Eventually planning contracts were instituted between the successive regional bodies and the state to carry out the national plan's proposals.[9] It is important to understand that debates about regional institutions were framed within an acceptance that the government had a role in regional economic development. But how should it carry this out?

It is worth stating at this point that Clémentel would have wished to create regional institutions with a wider membership than chambers of commerce. He was forced to adopt a more limited reform because of opposition in the Chamber of Deputies from those suspicious of government interference in the economy. He was in favour in principle of

[9] J. de Lanversin, L'aménagement du territoire et la régionalisation (Paris, 1970), 61, 125–6.

decentralization of government decision making. He would have liked to create regional councils but gave up the idea after opposition expressed by the general administration commission of the Chamber of Deputies on 5 December 1917.[10] We will see how the idea of regional councils created many years of debate after 1945.

By and large *aménagement du territoire* was driven until 1982 by central government. In itself it was not a policy for decentralization or regionalization of government. It was more a case of administrative deconcentration. Regions were areas for study to create the right mix of central policies, what Hayward has called *le régionalisme fonctionnel.* At the same time various attempts were made to enlist some people with expertise in each region to advise on the content of plans. Generally, they only had an advisory role. This created tensions between government and the regions.[11] Brittany is a prominent example. The *Comité d'étude et de liaison des intérêts bretons* (CELIB) was founded in 1950 to promote Brittany's economic interests. It was the pioneer of a number of regional expansion committees composed of local business interests, deputies, regional councillors, chambers of commerce and representatives of the professions and universities. Something similar had existed in the west of France before 1940, for example, *Ouest- Expansion* (see chapter seven). They studied problems and agitated for solutions. They persuaded Jean Monnet and the planners to include regional proposals in their overall national plan. However, after De Gaulle's party, the UNR, decisively won the 1962 elections, they could not gain more traction on policy. The government pursued a bureaucratic regionalism, creating the Délégation à L'Aménagement du Territoire in 1964 as a ministerial advisory group. This was followed in 1964 by the CODER, *commissions de développement économique régional*, which were advisory consultative committees in each region with a similar membership. To reinforce the government policy, regional prefects were also created in 1964. Resistance to a wider role for these committees came not only from government centralists like Michel Debré, but also from leaders in the *conseils-généraux* in the departments, the *notables* who feared a loss of influence. Some of these *notables,* under the *cumul des mandats* system prevailing at that time, could also hold

[10] Journal officiel de la République Française, Débats parlementaires, chambre des députés, 18 octobre 1918, 2739 in dir. M-C Kessler et G. Rousseau, *Étienne Clémentel, politique et action publique sous la Troisième République*, (Bruxelles, 2018), 336.

[11] Edward Welch, Making Space in Post-War France, (Cambridge, 2023).

office as say *maire* of an important commune, as well as being a deputy in the National Assembly. The *notables* would continue to protect their control over the levers of power. The prefectoral corps was also opposed to the regional committees.[12]

The one exception to this progress of bureaucratic regionalism was the regional policy pursued by the government of Pierre Mendès-France 1954–55. His book *République Moderne* contained a chapter on Vie Régionale. Under his government there were 21 regions, not so different from those set up by Clémentel. Mendès-France wanted the elected local representatives and the leaders of the professions, universities and industry to take an active role in the regional councils in order to construct a regional plan which had their commitment. He wanted the councils to coordinate the action of all the regional economic organizations like the regional development companies and the *sociétés d'économie mixte*. He wanted the councils not only to submit proposals for the plan but also to carry them out.[13]

De Gaulle put forward a regional reform after the events of 1968. It seems he wanted to encourage wider participation of local citizens in regional affairs. This reform of 1969 included regional councils consisting of deputies, elected departmental and municipal councillors, and socio-professional figures nominated by organizations representing agriculture, companies and public sector organizations, liberal professions, families, teachers and universities and social and cultural organizations. His proposal was combined with a reform of the Senate and was lost in the referendum, after which he resigned as president. Since 1969 the Senate has taken a conservative position on further measures of decentralization. The Senate has contained a disproportionate number of mayors of small

[12] J. Hayward, 'Functional Regionalism,' *Pouvoirs* 1981, no. 19, 105, 107, 109–10. 'From Functional Regionalism to Functional Representation in France: the Battle of Brittany,' *Political Studies* XVII, no. 1, 1969, 49–75. Michel Michel Masson, L'*Aménagement régional en France, du territoire aux territoires* (Paris, 1994), 40–1. Pasquier, *Pouvoir Régional*, 151. J. Burnham, *Politicians, Bureaucrats*, 38, 41, 171–96. Y. Mény, *Centralisation et Décentralisation dans le débat politique français 1945–1969* (Paris, 1974), 182, 219–20, 240, 250–1, 319–27. J. Perrilliat, 'La Révolution de la Ve République dans la représentation, objet et modalités,' in dir. L. Hamon, la Région de De Gaulle à nos jours (Paris, 1992), 5. 'Décentraliser vraiment,' *Projet*, mai-juin 1984, 185–6; numéro special 1984, 573–583 for the role of the *notables*. 'Décentralisation,' Les Cahiers français, janvier-février 1982, 15.

[13] P. Mendès-France, *République Moderne* (Paris, 1962), 199–212. Burnham, *Politicians, Bureaucrats*, 174. Mény, *Centralisation et Décentralisation*, 207–9.

communes and members of *conseils-généraux*. They have advocated inter-communal cooperation by *conseils-généraux* rather than regions.[14]

De Gaulle's successor Georges Pompidou did not share his enthusiasm for regional reform. His measures in 1972 kept regional activity firmly under bureaucratic control. The regions became simple agglomerations of departments.[15] Apart from regional councils consisting of deputies and local councillors, Pompidou continued with economic and social councils for each region, which consisted of qualified people selected by the prime minister. So there was some participation in planning but funds for investment were very limited.[16] His successor Valéry Giscard D'Estaing, a former *inspecteur des finances*, did not think France could afford four levels of government by adding regions to municipal councils, departments and the central government.[17]

Jean-Jacques Servan-Schreiber (JJSS) summed up this period of centralist regionalism with a blistering critique of regional planning, which was in sympathy with developing Socialist ideas. JJSS was the founder of *L'Express*, president of a now centre-right Radical party and supporter of Giscard D'Estaing in the 1974 presidential election. His *Le Pouvoir Régional* was a strong polemic against the centralized state and the prefects. He said that most decisions on local matters were really taken in Paris, despite decentralizing proposals in the past. He quoted opinion poll evidence that there was still an attachment in the regions to the cultural identity of the old provinces. He wanted to see elected regional assemblies with an executive taking over from the prefect, who just became an administrator of regional services. He believed regions should invest in transport infrastructure, and other regional development projects, and should also run schools and hospitals. All this was prescient of the radical reform of 1982.[18]

Much was achieved in this period of bureaucratic regionalism in the period 1945–1979. New infrastructure was built in the regions,

[14] Pasquier, *Pouvoir regional*, 176–7.

[15] C.Grémion, 'Decentralization in France, a historical perspective,' in G. Ross et al., *The Mitterrand Experiment: Continuity and Change in Modern France* (Oxford, 1987), 237. Mény, *Centralisation et Décentralisation*, 323.

[16] M. Philipponneau, *La grande affaire, décentralisation et régionalisation* (Paris, 1981), 68–73.

[17] Hayward, 'Functional Regionalism,' 111–113. B. Ducamin, 'Forces vives et élus locaux,' in dir. L. Hamon, *La Région de De Gaulle à nos jours* (Paris, 1992), 62.

[18] J-J Servan-Schreiber, *Le Pouvoir Régional* (Paris, 1971), 57–64, 81–86, 91–7, 195–200.

particularly for transport. The Canal de Provence is but one prominent example.[19] The emphasis on *métropoles d'equilibre* as the focus for regional development echoed the role of the *grandes villes* foreseen by Vidal de la Blache many years before.[20] Naturally the pace of development slackened after the end of the *trente glorieuses* and the oil crisis.

Meanwhile a debate on decentralization and regionalism had started on the left in the sixties. There were several factors driving this debate which eventually led to a radical change of policy and the reforms enacted under Mitterrand in 1982. The theorists in the Socialist Party, and a bit later in the PCF (Parti Communiste Français), perceived a social and economic crisis in many regions of France.[21] The post-war years saw the consolidation of industrial firms into very large often foreign conglomerates. These could dominate smaller traditional industries in the regions. Some of the latter went to the wall. When economic conditions were adverse, for example, after the oil price hike of 1973, larger firms would lay off workers and close factories. Often there was no alternative employment. Most of these firms were controlled by Paris and were seen as alien to the regions where their plants were located. In addition, small peasant farmers were leaving the land and their holdings were being rationalized into larger units. Some Marxists saw this as a struggle between the bourgeoisie who controlled the levers of economic and social power and the working class of the regions. This ruling class, it was also believed, had no interest in encouraging the survival of authentic local cultures. The regions were being exploited by outside interests just like colonies. Wealth was being extracted with almost nothing offered in return. To put this right power in the regions needed to be passed back to the people through elected regional assemblies with real power and budgets. This would be a process of decolonization.[22]

This analysis was most eloquently expressed by the writer Robert Lafont and by Michel Rocard, the leader of the small PSU (Parti Socialiste Unifié). He later played a prominent role in the Socialist governments of the eighties. The debate was fostered by a Socialist discussion meeting in Grenoble in 1967 and further by the events of 1968. Workers in 1968 were taking

[19] J. de Lanversin, *L'aménagement du territoire et la régionalisation*, 76–7, 105–9.

[20] Pasquier, *Pouvoir Régional*, 149.

[21] For a discussion of the evolution of the PCF on this issue see Y. Mény, *Centralisation et Décentralisation*, 92, 105–110.

[22] Ibid, p. 382–4.

over factories and running them for themselves. Regional leaders should do the same. The word *autogestion*, or self-management, entered the political vocabulary of the French left.[23] In *Décoloniser la France* Lafont framed the regionalist struggle as part of the anti-imperialist movement. Workers had to take control of the movement for greater regional freedom or it would be betrayed. Part of his programme was to combat cultural alienation in regions like Brittany and Occitania. He also said the struggle to improve the lot of the peasantry was key and urged action against the large estates. He wanted to see the creation of more cooperatives under popular control. He suggested that riches under the ground should become collective regional property. In the countryside he was against second homes and wanted to tax them.[24]

Another influential militant was Michel Philipponneau, Professor of Geography at Rennes and a local Breton politician who had championed CELIB and worked for both Defferre, who guided the 1982 regional reform through the National Assembly, and Mitterrand. He too talked about colonial exploitation and looked to a leftist victory to change the position of the regions. He hated the *régionalisme fonctionnel* run by bourgeois énarques (graduates of the École Nationale d'Administration). Although half the members of a CODER were from local organizations, the regional prefect controlled the agendas and the outcomes. The CODER could only offer an opinion on the regional development plan, not on other regional economic issues. The answer was popular control of the regions and state directed investment in the regions. To combat capitalist concentration, state controlled enterprises were needed. It was a scandal that all Breton milk was processed by firms outside the region.[25]

By the time of Mitterrand's second run for the presidency in 1974, he had adopted the pro-decentralization position and supported the delegation of powers to the regions. The common programmes of government adopted with the PCF included a decentralization policy.[26] This was a

[23] H. Dubedout, 'une nouvelle citoyenneté,' in Décentralisation, *Nouvelle Revue Socialiste*, septembre-octobre 1981, 27–30. Dubedout was Deputy Mayor of Grenoble.

[24] R. Lafont, *Décoloniser la France, les régions face à l'Europe* (Paris, 1971), 287, 290–1, 295–99, 303.

[25] M. Philipponneau, *La Gauche et les Régions* (Paris, 1967), 9–10, 102–3, 106–108, 148–9, 151, 154–6, 169.

[26] D.S. Bell, *François Mitterrand a political biography* (Cambridge, 2005), 67. *Programme commun de gouvernement du PCF et du Parti Socialiste* (Paris, 1972), 158–9. Programme commun de gouvernement, propositions socialistes pour l'actualisation (Paris, 1978), 66–7,

surprising turn of events given the left's traditional suspicion of regionalism as being a tool of the right to preserve a traditional patriarchal social structure. It had also been seen as a threat to the unity of the Republic. In the thirties the focus of the Socialists was to gain control of the centralized state and to use its powers to affect change. However, Léon Blum had said in 1939 that he had no objection in principle to regional institutions.[27] The ideological shift was considerable but ideology was not enough. The Socialists also saw a strong decentralizing and regionalist position as a route back to power. In the 1970s, with the stasis in government regional policy, the Socialists and their allies started to win seats in local bodies—municipal councils, conseils-généraux of departments, even advisory regional bodies—on their new platform. Regionalism was becoming popular. The Socialists wanted to disrupt the power of the *notables* on departmental councils with new regions which might garner support from the rising middle classes who were not part of traditional elites.[28] Some Socialist mayors, like Pierre Mauroy in the Nord or Defferre in Marseille, started to employ people on regional projects. The Socialists had taken over a number of towns and used their position to champion social reform.[29] In Provence, Defferre financed useful regional organizations like the Association régionale de Tourisme.[30] Socialists also had an influential voice on many of the consultative region councils. In *Nouvel Horizon* written in 1965, Defferre had urged the left to have the political will to move government nearer the people. The state, he said, would have to learn to convince, instead of ordering and controlling.[31] The three key concepts of greater local democracy, cultural identity and good public administration appealed to the party and also to its voters after 20 years of right wing power.[32]

102–3. F. Mitterrand, *Oeuvres II* (Paris, 2016), un socialisme du possible (1971) 67–8; le contrat socialiste (1969), 666–7. M. Rocard, 'La région, une idée neuve pour la gauche,' *Pouvoirs*, 1981, vol. 19, 131–138.

[27] M. Philipponneau, *Décentralisation et régionalisation*, 41.

[28] J.W. Friend, *Seven years in France, François Mitterrand and the Unintended Revolution 1981–1988* (Boulder, 1989), 141.J.de Lanversin, *L'Aménagement du territoire et la régionalisation* (Paris, 1970), 136.

[29] M. Philipponneau, *Décentralisation et régionalisation*, pp. 73–77, 87–8.

[30] P. Sadran, 'Les socialistes et la région,' *Pouvoirs*, 1981, vol. 19, 139–147.

[31] G. Defferre, *Nouvel Horizon* (Paris, 1965), 130–2.

[32] Pasquier, *Pouvoir Régional*, 170–2. Y. Mény, *Centralisation et Décentralisation*, 132–151, 475–502. Ed. J. Loughlin and S. Mazey, *The End of the Unitary State, ten years of Regionalisation 1982–1992* (London, 1995), introduction 1–8.

The reform introduced by Gaston Defferre to the National Assembly in 1982 affected municipal councils and departments as much as regions. Regions were to be given elected assemblies and a president who would take over the executive responsibility of the regional prefect. The *tutelle*, or legal oversight by the prefect of every decision a local body made, would be abolished. Twenty-two regions were created, three more than in Clémentel's day. Defferre, the boss of Marseille, was in a hurry. He wanted to run his fief in Marseille without being answerable to the local prefect.[33] No doubt he feared an adverse reaction in the National Assembly where many such reforms had eventually been defeated before. He was given total responsibility for the whole decentralization programme and introduced bills enshrining the general principles very quickly so there could be no backsliding. Clémentel did not enjoy the support of a substantial majority that Defferre enjoyed in 1982.

The regions were set up with their own budgets and staff. Their main agreed focus was on economic development. They had the power to make grants to attract firms and also to invest in regional development companies. They negotiated national plan contracts with the state for certain projects.[34] They had responsibility for transport infrastructure. They maintained university buildings and lycées. They were responsible for a programme of ongoing professional training which would improve the technical skills of the population. All these things were seen as vital to improving each region's competitiveness, as they had been after 1918. The spread of responsibilities of Clémentel's regions and those of 1982 is not dissimilar. In addition, they now have responsibility for the environment, running regional parks, for example, and also for cultural activities.[35] Elections to the new regional assemblies were delayed but eventually held in 1986. Was the battle for democratic control of regional affairs won for all time in 1982?

There is some evidence that the victory for decentralization proposals in 1982 cannot be seen as final. Regional budgets are relatively small. There is still an ongoing discussion about the split of responsibilities between municipalities, departments and regions. Sometimes the central

[33] C.Grémion, 'Decentralization in France, a historical perspective,' in G. Ross et al., The Mitterrand Experiment: Continuity and Change in Modern France (Oxford, 1987), 241–7.

[34] Ibid, 220–232.

[35] P. Bernard, 'la région aujourd'hui, pour quoi faire?' in dir. L. Hamon, *La région de de Gaulle à nos jours,* (Paris, 1992), 165, 167, 175. Pasquier, *Pouvoir Régional*, 194–5.

state becomes involved in a conflict with a region over how the state's guiding rules, for example, on finance, should be applied.[36] Sometimes there are disputes over the implementation of regional planning contracts, where the state holds the whip hand. There are overlaps in responsibility for aids to industry. Sometimes responsibilities have been transferred, but this has not been given concrete legal form. All three types of authorities—municipal, departmental and regional—make such grants.[37] The regional element of these is not so large. Europe has also presented a challenge to the French regions because some other European regions have wider powers than those in France. Rausch, the president of the Lorraine region, managed to conclude an agreement for investment with Luxembourg and the Saar, two similar regions on his borders.[38] Prime Minister Raffarin in his reform of 2003–4 gave ground to the departments, transferring responsibility for roads and university buildings to them. After this reform it was evident that the Senate was in control of any further changes and that it would normally support the departments. However, Raffarin changed the electoral system for the regions, in a way which created majorities and greater stability. The Balladur report of 2009 put its accent on bodies bringing together large communes rather than on regions. In France large cities are getting together to drive regional development, for example, in Nord-Pas-de-Calais, the Île-de-France and Rhône-Alpes.[39]

Regional leaders are becoming significant national figures, as well as very much bosses in their local areas. Regions are now an established part of the government structure and have achieved much of benefit. However, the change to the lives of ordinary people is not as dramatic as Rocard or Lafont might have imagined. On the whole, however, the public are supportive of their new regions, although uncertain as to whether their powers should be expanded. There has been a national conversation for over a hundred years about decentralization and regional identity, starting in the nineteenth century and still going on today. Decentralization and the creation of functioning regions has been a slowly evolving process. No doubt

[36] Dirn. S. Barone, *Les Politiques régionales en France* (Paris, 2011), 31.

[37] 'La décentralisation en marche,' *Cahiers français*, 220, mars-avril 1985, 42.

[38] Friend, *Seven Years*, 145.

[39] Pasquier, *Pouvoir Régional*, 179–182, 191–3, 195–197, 210–213, 289, 309–313. J-C Douence, 'Evolution of the 1982 regional reforms, an overview,' in Ed. J. Loughlin and S. Mazey, *The End of the Unitary State*, 10–22. J-M Rausch, 'Un président de région s'explique,' in *Réalités regionales*, Projet 185–6, 1984, 576–7, 581–3.

it has not finished yet. The Clémentel regions of 1918–1940 are very much part of that story. There was no clean break in 1940.[40] This brief sketch has shown the continuity of thinking on regional development and regional representative institutions between 1918 and 1982. The regional assemblies adopted by the Socialists in 1982 were nothing new even if the rationale and environment were. They were first proposed before 1914 by the FRF.

## Bibliography


'Décentralisation,' Les Cahiers français, janvier-février 1982.

'Décentraliser vraiment,' *Projet*, mai-juin 1984, 185; numéro special 1984, 573–583.

Barone, S. (dirn.) (2011). *Les Politiques régionales en France.*

Barral, P. (1974). Idéal et pratique du régionalisme dans le regime de Vichy. *Revue française de science politique, 24*(5), 911–939.

Bell, D. S. (2005). *François Mitterrand a political biography.*

Bernard, P. (1992). La région aujourd'hui, pour quoi faire? In dir. L. Hamon, *La région de de Gaulle à nos jours.*

Burnham, J. (2009). *Politicians, Bureaucrats and Leadership in Organisations. Lessons from Regional Planning in France.* Palgrave.

Cointet, J.-P. (2017). *Les Hommes de Vichy, l'illusion du pouvoir.* Lucien Romier (pp. 115–120).

Cornu, P., & Ozouf, M. (2021). la rencontre de trois mondes. L'agrarisme de Lucien Gachon. In N. Ginsburger, M-C Robic, J-L Tissier (Eds.), *Géographes Français en Seconde Guerre Mondiale* (Sorbonne, 2021) (pp. 129–145).

Defferre, G. (1965). *Nouvel Horizon.*

Douence, J.-C. Evolution of the 1982 regional reforms, an overview. In J. Loughlin & S. Mazey (Eds.), *The end of the Unitary State* (pp. 10–22).

Dubedout, H. (1981). Une nouvelle citoyenneté. In Décentralisation. *Nouvelle Revue Socialiste*, septembre-octobre 1981, 27–30.

Ducamin, B. (1992). Forces vives et élus locaux. In dir. L. Hamon, *La Région de De Gaulle à nos jours.*

Friend, J. W. (1989). *Seven years in France, François Mitterrand and the unintended revolution 1981–1988.*

Ginsburger, N. (2021). Pour la révolution nationale, J-F Gravier un parcours engagé. In N. Ginsburger, M-C Robic, J-L Tissier (Eds.), *Géographes Français en Seconde Guerre Mondiale* (pp. 195–200).


[40] Pasquier, *Pouvoir Régional*, 166, 225, 319–20, 325, 339–40.

Grémion, C. (1987). Decentralization in France, a historical perspective. In G. Ross et al, (Eds.), *The Mitterrand experiment: Continuity and change in modern France* (pp. 220–247).
Hayward, J. (1981). Functional regionalism. *Pouvoirs, 19*, 105–110.
Hayward, J. (1969). From functional regionalism to functional representation in France: The Battle of Brittany. *Political Studies, XVII*(1), 49–75.
Journal officiel de la République Française. (2018). Débats parlementaires, chambre des députés, 18 octobre 1918, 2739 in dir. M-C Kessler et G. Rousseau, *Étienne Clémentel, politique et action publique sous la Troisième République*, 336.
'La décentralisation en marche,' *Cahiers français*, 220, mars-avril 1985.
Lafont, R. (1971). *Décoloniser la France, les régions face à l'Europe.*
Lanversin, J. de (1970). *L'aménagement du territoire et la régionalisation.*
Loubet des Bayle, J.-L. (1969). *Les non-conformistes des années 30: une tentative de renouvellement de la pensée politique française.*
Loughlin, J., & Mazey, S. (Eds.). (1995). *The end of the unitary state, ten years of regionalisation 1982–1992.*
Mendès-France, P. (1962). *République Moderne.*
Mény, Y. (1974). *Centralisation et Décentralisation dans le débat politique français 1945–1969.*
Michel Masson, M. (1994). L'*Aménagement régional en France, du territoire aux territoires.*
Mitterrand, F. (1969). *Oeuvres II* (Paris, 2016), un socialisme du possible (1971); le contrat socialiste.
MUCEM, Fonds FRF 6 AP 8 for the agendas of FRF Congresses in the nineteen twenties.
Pasquier, R. (2004). *La Capacité Politique des Régions: une comparaison France, Espagne.*
Pasquier, R. (2012). *Le Pouvoir régional, Mobilisations, décentralisation et gouvernance en France.*
Perrilliat, J. (1992). La Révolution de la Ve République dans la représentation, objet et modalités. In dir. L. Hamon, *la Région de De Gaulle à nos jours.*
Philipponneau, M. (1967). *La Gauche et les Régions.*
Philipponneau, M. (1981). *La grande affaire, décentralisation et régionalisation.*
Programme commun de gouvernement *du PCF et du Parti Socialiste* (1972).
Programme commun *de gouvernement, propositions socialistes pour l'actualisation* (1978).
Rausch, J.-M. (1984). Un président de région s'explique. In Réalités regionales. *Projet, 185*, 576–583.
Rocard, M. (1981). La région, une idée neuve pour la gauche. *Pouvoirs, 19*, 131–138.
Sadran, P. (1981). Les socialistes et la région. *Pouvoirs, 19*, 139–147.
Servan-Schreiber, J.-J. (1971). *Le Pouvoir Régional.*

CHAPTER 10

# Conclusions

## Achievements of the Economic Regions

The regionalist reformers after 1945 did not start with a blank piece of paper. Regions were established as a unit of government before 1940. The economic regions and other bodies pre-1940 had set the agenda for *l'aménagement du territoire*, a concept of regional development which became important after 1945. Before 1940 regional leaders acting as lobbyists and publicists drew attention to the development needs of their regions. The encouragement of hydro-electricity in the Alps is a good example. In the pre-1940 period there were some pointers towards what would be achieved later, for example, in the initiation of power generation on the Dordogne and the Rhine, in the canalization of the Moselle, the exploitation of the Rhône, or the setting up of technical colleges. The pre-1940 economic regions gained improvements by exercising pressure on transport companies and electricity producers through the *Offices des Transports* and the *Offices régionaux d'Énergie électrique,* as well as protecting the interests of consumers. Spontaneously formed regional bodies took effective action to promote tourism. Agricultural syndicates cooperated with the economic regions on matters of common interest like transport and electrification. Chambers of commerce managed autonomous ports and started to get involved in the management of airports, for example, in Toulouse and Bordeaux.





T. Cudbird, *The Origins of Economic Regions in France, 1918–1940*,
https://doi.org/10.1007/978-3-032-04422-8_10

Prevet in his inter-war doctoral thesis on the economic regions tried to isolate factors which accounted for some being more successful than others. He referred to some having a powerful centre or a major port such as Nancy, Clermont-Ferrand, Bordeaux and Nantes. Others, he said, had a geographical unity such as Limoges and Toulouse, although I have suggested the latter is open to dispute. An area like Lille benefited from having some powerful industries, but, as Eck has argued, there was not much regional solidarity in the Nord. Some regions, Prevet said, had no homogeneity. Examples are the regions centred on Besançon, on Rennes which had little industry, or those centred on Bourges and Grenoble which had few chambers of commerce, although Veitl argues the latter achieved much.[1]

Regions with active elites in influential regional centres and a good university certainly seemed to be more effective. Fundamental to the effectiveness of an economic region was a strong sense of identity, as in Lorraine and the Auvergne. In Lorraine the development of local and regional cooperatives to undertake the massive task of reconstruction after the Great War demonstrates what a sense of regional solidarity could achieve.

The achievements of a region also rested on the quality of leadership. In particular, Lorraine, the Auvergne and the Rhône benefited from powerful leaders: the tightly knit group of ironmasters in Lorraine, the continued influence of Clémentel himself in the Puy-de-Dôme, and leaders such as Léon Perrier and Herriot in the Rhône. Romain Pasquier has identified the 'capacité politique' of regions as a crucial factor in their success. As we have seen political capacity involves institutional resources, strategic vision, leadership, coalition building and administrative know how to carry out a regional programme. It also involves the capacity to construct and project a territorial identity, which helps legitimize the region's role. He is homing in on the same political leadership skills which I have identified in Lorraine and the Auvergne.[2]

Despite this record of achievement, some historians have considered that Clémentel's regions were a failure. We find this view, for example, in Thiébaut Flory's book on regionalism.[3] J R. Pitte in his book on Philippe

[1] F. Prevet, *Le Régionalisme économique, conception et réalisation* (Thèse de doctorat, Faculté de Droit de Paris, 1929), 187. P. Veitl, *L'Invention d'une région: les Alpes françaises* (Grenoble, 2013).

[2] R. Pasquier, *La Capacité Politique des Régions: une comparaison France, Espagne* (Rennes, 2004), 26–9, 206–7.

[3] T. Flory, *Le Mouvement Régionaliste Français* (Paris, 1966), 94–6.

Lamour said that Clémentel's regions had no juridical basis and were therefore a failure. Pitte says Lamour, the father of regional development, saw the reform of 1918 as a missed opportunity.[4] The new regions did not gain the full legal powers of a public authority. *Les Échos*, the financial newspaper, wrote in 1926 that the groupings of chambers of commerce were more theoretical, inactive and powerless.[5] They were simply groupings of chambers of commerce, who legally could only commit themselves independently. Clémentel knew that a more comprehensive measure would not be accepted by the Chamber of Deputies.

A negative view of the economic regions post-1918 needs challenging. Contemporary critics and later historians have focussed too narrowly on what the economic regions did directly as opposed to their wider influence. This book sets out to provide a more balanced assessment. Regional elites came together, without the direction of the French state, to solve the problems posed by the First World War for their economies and societies. While regionalism was frustrated in the corridors of the Chamber of Deputies, it was alive and well in the provinces in the post-First World War period. The political scientist R. K. Gooch developed the concept of spontaneous regionalism, as a bottom up form of regional development and cooperation which emerged independently of central government initiatives. Gooch contrasted this with state imposed regionalism, such as the top-down creation of economic regions by Étienne Clémentel. Such regional cooperation arose from shared economic, social, cultural or geographic interests of local communities. The initiative came from local institutions like chambers of commerce and was focussed on practical needs like transportation or education. Such spontaneous regionalism emerged gradually. Although the framework for regional action was provided by Clémentel, the initiatives some regions took had many of the features of Gooch's 'spontaneous regionalism.' Hubert Lagardelle in the Toulouse region supported the growth of economic regionalism from the grass roots and tried to encourage it with his regional association of professionals.[6]

[4] J.R. Pitte, *Philippe Lamour, père de l'aménagement du territoire en France 1903–1992* (Paris, 2002), 24 (fn. p. 297), 32.

[5] 'L'activité de la région économique de Basse Normandie,' *REO*, no. 45, 31 août 1926, 45.

[6] R.K. Gooch, *Regionalism in France* (New York, 1931), 104–124.

## Regionalism and Economic Liberalism

Describing Clémentel's regions as failures also ignores the prevailing economic philosophy which taught that private enterprise should be left to its own devices and that proposals for government intervention in the economy should be viewed with grave suspicion. This was the classical economic liberalism of the late nineteenth century. During the First World War, Clémentel saw the need for government to get more involved, for example, in controlling the use of precious raw materials. The state also ran railways, levied an income tax, provided more welfare payments and planned manpower to keep vital production going.[7] But his plans to continue with a planned economy after the war were rejected. Government might set the guidelines, but it was reluctant to invest, for example, in power projects. State firms had a reputation among business leaders for waste. In addition, public finances were very constrained for most of the inter-war period, and there were very limited funds available. Some *sociétés d'économie mixte* with state participation were set up after the First World War, where, for example, a vital defence interest was involved or there was an opportunity to exploit German patents ceded to France in the Treaty of Versailles (e.g., the Office de L'Azote for making ammonia products in Toulouse). The Compagnie Nationale du Rhône was also such a company, set up to exploit the river's resources. Another example was the Compagnie Française des Pétroles. Government-backed loans were also made to some railway companies to keep the railway network afloat.[8] There were also some tentative moves towards more government involvement. Under the second Cartel des Gauches government, a National Economic Council was set up in 1925 which brought together the government, industrialists and labour to manage economic policy more effectively.

Under Président du Conseil Tardieu in 1930, proposals were put forward for a renewal of national infrastructure through some centrally funded projects. Gradually economic liberalism gave way to government management of the economy as the Great Depression took hold. Some firms like Compagnie Générale d'Électricité (CGE) were rescued from bankruptcy. The Popular Front, while not reluctant in principle to intervene in industry, was constrained by lack of finance, fear of capital flight and the more moderate stance of the Radical party. Blum wanted to soften

[7] Gaffney, *France and Modernization*, 18.
[8] Kuisel, R. F., *Capitalism and the State,* 66–69.

the impact of the capitalist system on workers, but he was not in favour of state planning and a fully socialized economy. The Banque de France was regulated but not nationalized, although some armaments manufacturers were brought under state control. The SNCF was created in 1937 out of the privately owned railway companies. The government did improve labour rights, introduce a 40-hour week and paid holidays, recognize trade unions and institute collective bargaining. The successor governments to the Popular Front continued with the hybrid system of a guided economy.[9] More industries were nationalized after World War Two.

So the economic regions set up by Clémentel received limited encouragement from the government for economic interventions. Moreover, they had to operate in an economic climate which was unfavourable. The dispute over reparations with Germany was followed by the crisis of the franc. High interest rates constrained investment after the war. The currency collapse necessitated a stabilization plan under Président du Conseil Poincaré and it was only in the late twenties that conditions improved for a few years before the onset of the Great Depression. Crucial investment and modernization of industry was deferred for much of the inter-war period.[10]

## Regionalism and Modernization

I argued in the introduction that the inter-war period marked a fundamental shift in the orientation of regionalism, from nostalgia for a traditional society based on agriculture to a commitment to modernization of regional economies and an interest in regional cultures for their own intrinsic interest. This modernization was facilitated by an institutional framework for regional elites to exercise leadership.

In the period both before and after the Second World War, there was a debate about the exact meaning of the term 'modernization.' Back in 1918 Clémentel and his advisers had blamed an atomized industrial structure, individualistic habits, and a pinched outlook for France's poor commercial and industrial performance. The process of industrial rationalization moved forward slowly in the inter-war period. Kuisel has suggested that in the 1920s economic modernization tended to be associated with what was going on inside a factory. It was concerned with product standardization

[9] Kuisel, R. F., *Capitalism and the State*, 90–92, 96, 114–127.

[10] A. Broder, *Histoire économique de la France 1914–1997* (Paris, 1998), 31–78.

and the rational organization of work; what was known as Taylorism.[11] There are many references to this in regional economic journals, for example, in Lorraine. However, those who worked in the economic regions would have pointed to developing electric power and the large scale industries which depended on it, improving road, rail and air transport or creating technical training institutes, as examples of modernization to which they were making a contribution.

Kuisel argues that a broader vision of the modernization process only fully arrived post-1945. Apostles of modernization after 1945 like Fourastié argued that historically France had suffered from certain deficiencies which held it back—a prevalence of small firms and entrepreneurial conservatism; a lack of competition; a dominant state sector; a state which was very reluctant to get involved in private enterprise; a protectionist mentality. The post-1945 modernizers also drew attention to political and societal factors such as an inefficient bureaucracy, a conservative bourgeoisie and compartmentalized classes involved in ideological conflict, a stagnant provincial society which was more concerned to defend acquired benefits than take risks, and lastly weak parties leading to weak government and immobilism.[12] Kuisel has brought to our attention the modernization process which came to fruition after 1945 with the advent of a planned economy and the creation of nationalized enterprises.[13] Planners looked for faster capital formation and rising standards of living, a reduction of the agricultural work force and mechanization, a growth of international trade and less dependence on the USA.[14] They espoused a 'Fordist' vision of mass production and consumption. Reading some writers on economic affairs post-1945, you might be forgiven for thinking pre-1940 France lived in the Dark Ages.[15] I argue that this was very far from the case.

[11] Kuisel, R. F., *Capitalism and the State in Modern France: Renovation and Economic Management in the Twentieth Century* (Cambridge: CUP, 1981), 45, 84–5.

[12] Ibid.

[13] Ibid, 59–127, 187–271, 305.

[14] R. F. Kuisel, 'Post-War economic growth,' in (ed.) G. Ross et al., *The Mitterrand Experiment: Continuity and Change in Modern France* (Oxford, 1987), 23–32.

[15] For the debate on modernization see also (ed.) J. Gaffney, *France and modernization* (Aldershot, 1988) P. Cerny, 'Modernization and the Fifth Republic,' 9–10, 18; C. Pessis, S. Topcu, C. Bonneuil, *Une autre histoire des Trente Glorieuses: modernisation, contestations et pollutions dans la France d'après-guerre* (Paris, 2013), 6–9.

## Evolution of Regional Cultures

Interest in France's regional cultures continued to flourish in the inter-war period. Regional cultures were studied by academics and also in museums and regional societies. Charles Sadoul in Lorraine built up the collection of Lorrraine cultural artefacts in the Musée Lorrain in Nancy and there were lively discussions of Lorraine's culture in the journal *Le Pays Lorrain*. The year 1937 saw the foundation of the Musée des Arts et Traditions Populaires in Paris. After the war the *Fédération régionaliste française* (FRF) turned its attention more to folklore and the promotion of the cultures of different regions. This was apparent from the discussions at its national congress in 1926.[16]

The character of regionalism changed gradually and this evolution contained several conflicting elements. After the First World War some in the regions looked back to the past and the pre-war world which had been lost for inspiration. They sought to reinforce the pre-war rural society and the cultural identity which accompanied it. Except for a few exceptions like the regionalist novelist Jean Giono, they were often associated with a political conservatism which emphasized the structures and traditions of the past and was encouraged by the Catholic church. Many of those who advocated a return to the land talked about encouraging mechanization but also about the moral virtues of a society close to the soil. When the post-First World War generation sought regional symbols to reinforce the *devoir de mémoire* in war memorials, they tended to look to figures from the past, peasants dressed in traditional costume or Vercingétorix, the Gallic leader of the Arvernes against Caesar. In the Auvergne we find a combination of attachment to the mainly peasant cultures of the past and social conservatism exemplified by Henri Pourrat and his circle. Similar features can be found in some circles in Lorraine.

However, there was never a clear division between those looking to the past and those preoccupied with the future. For example, many local cooperatives reconstructing villages in the north and east of France wanted to use traditional building styles rooted in the past but at the same time provide modern sanitation and other contemporary features. Even a figure like Vercingétorix was reconstructed as a modern republican hero fighting

[16] O.Grenouilleau, Nos *petites patries, identités régionales et état central en France, des origines à nos jours (Paris, 2019)*, 190. MUCEM, Fonds FRF 6 AP 8 for the agendas of FRF Congresses in the nineteen twenties.

for freedom. While there was a growing interest in folklore, this was not necessarily backward looking. The interest in folklore, which was manifest at the Paris Exhibition of 1937, was not the sole preserve of social conservatives. It fuelled a wider interest in the culture and history of France's regions which was manifest in the regional guides published by Michelin and the growth of tourism and therefore directly connects to the economic focus of this book.[17] However, we have seen that during the Vichy period, nostalgia for a more traditional way of life still had many supporters.

Post 1918 particularism in the Moselle gained strength from inept interference in the special status of the Catholic church there from the Cartel des Gauches led by Herriot. In the twenties and thirties, separatism in Alsace and Brittany was still a threat, particularly in the case of Alsace after the rise of Hitler to power. Alsace was removed from French control after 1940, but Vichy avoided any other annexations. It made a concession to Breton feelings by setting up a Breton consultative committee in October 1942, which included representatives from key Breton pressure groups like the Union Régionaliste. Its competence was purely advisory and limited to cultural issues. Vichy refused to consider a request for a provincial assembly with financial and legislative powers in 1943. Breton Nationalists derided the consultative committee but only a small minority broke away to collaborate actively with the German occupying forces. Collaborationists were dealt with very harshly at the Liberation.[18]

After 1945 the desire to celebrate these regional cultures became less of a political issue. In the 1960s and 1970s, Socialists mobilized an interest in regional cultures behind their programme of decolonization and regional reforms. However, the main impetus behind this progamme was a desire to right economic injustice outside Paris rather than to protect dying regional cultures. As a result of these reforms, today the regions promote these cultures, but they are not political controversial except perhaps in Corsica. There is no space here to tell the story of how the study of regional cultures evolved in the twentieth century. Grenouilleau's book cited above is a good introduction. However, as we have seen, a regional sense of identity has underpinned the operation of economic regions and continues to do so today. Opinion polls have shown that the voters are still attached to the identity of their region, but they want the French state to

[17] T. Cudbird, *The Impact of the Great War on French Regionalism 1900–1924* (Oxford DPhil, 2020), 178–9.

[18] R. Gildea, *The Past in French History*, (Yale, 1994), 205.

be the guarantor of national solidarity.[19] Today there is indeed discontent in deprived areas of France which has expressed itself in more extreme political movements of right and left. This has little to do, however, with regionalism in the sense it is used in this book.

## Regionalism and the Evolution of the French State

At the start of this book we identified two key influences on Clémentel's reform—a regionalist inspiration and also a desire to engage intermediary bodies between the central state and the private citizen in the modernization of the country. We have seen that the changing character of regionalism is a key theme, but this is not to neglect the change in the organization of the French state in the twentieth century, a change analysed by Rosanvallon. Rosanvallon has drawn our attention to the evolving resistance in the nineteenth century to the philosophy of the general interest, a resistance which manifested itself in the construction of various intermediary bodies between the central government and the private citizen. However, in his book *The Demands of Liberty,* Rosanvallon says nothing about regionalism and its effect on governmental structures in the twentieth century. Nor does he cover the parallel movement supporting the decentralization of government.[20] My analysis extends Rosanvallon's analysis into a study of regionalism and complements it.[21] At the same time it recognizes that regionalism as a phenomenon was a force free of the state originating from elsewhere in society with many different features. It clashed with the state in some forms, for example, in the work of Charles Maurras or later separatists, and found an accommodation with the state in the creation of economic regions.

Before 1918 the strand of regionalism which wanted to preserve regional cultures and a past way of life tended to be dominant. From 1918 regionalism was gradually re-oriented to harnessing the energies of the regions to modernize regional economies. Clémentel's reform anchored regionalism in the modernization camp rather than within a backward-looking nostalgia.

[19] Pasquier, *Pouvoir régional*, 340.

[20] P. Rosanvallon, *The Demands of Liberty, Civil Society in France since the Revolution* (Harvard, 2007) was originally published as *Le Modèle politique français: la société civile contre le jacobinisme de 1789 à nos jours* (Paris, 2004).

[21] See also Cudbird, T. 'The Clémentel Moment: the reform of 1918 and the beginnings of regional economic planning in France,' *French History*, volume 37 number 2, June 2023, 126–141.

## Bibliography

Broder, A. (1998). *Histoire économique de la France 1914–1997.*

Cudbird, T. (2020). *The impact of the Great War on French Regionalism 1900–1924* (Oxford DPhil).

Cudbird, T. (2023). The Clémentel Moment: The reform of 1918 and the beginnings of regional economic planning in France. *French History, 37*(2), 126–141.

Flory, T. (1966). *Le Mouvement Régionaliste Français.*

Gaffney, J. (Ed.). (2013). *France and modernization* (Aldershot, 1988) –P. Cerny, Modernization and the Fifth Republic. C. Pessis, S. Topcu, C. Bonneuil, *Une autre histoire des Trente Glorieuses: modernisation, contestations et pollutions dans la France d'après-guerre.*

Gildea, R. (1996). *The Past in French History.*

Gooch, R. K. (1931). *Regionalism in France.*

Grenouilleau, O. (2019). *Nos Petites Patries, identités régionales et état central en France, des origines à nos jours.*

Kuisel, R. F. (1987). Post-War economic growth. In G. Ross et al. (Eds.), *The Mitterrand experiment: Continuity and change in modern France* (23–32).

Kuisel, R. F. (1981). *Capitalism and the state in modern France: Renovation and economic management in the twentieth century.*

MUCEM, Fonds FRF 6 AP 8.

Pasquier, R. (2004). *La Capacité Politique des Régions: une comparaison France, Espagne.*

Pasquier, R. (2012). *Le Pouvoir régional, Mobilisations, décentralisation et gouvernance en France.*

Pitte, J. R. (2002). *Philippe Lamour, père de l'aménagement du territoire en France 1903–1992.*

Prevet, F. (1929). *Le Régionalisme économique, conception et réalisation.* Thèse de doctorat, Faculté de Droit de Paris.

Revue Économique de l'Ouest, 1926.

Rosanvallon, P. (2004). *The Demands of Liberty, Civil Society in France since the Revolution* (Harvard, 2007) was originally published as *Le Modèle politique français: la société civile contre le jacobinisme de 1789 à nos jours.*

Veitl, P. (2013). *L'Invention d'une région : les Alpes françaises.*

# Bibliography

## Manuscripts and Archives

### Abbreviations

Blois, Archives de Saint Gobain, Fonds Camille Cavallier, "SGA"
Clermont-Ferrand, Archives Départementales du Puy-de-Dôme, "AD P-de-D".
Clermont-Ferrand, Bibliothèque du Patrimoine, "Patrimoine".
Épinal Archives Départementales Vosges "ADV".
Marseille, MUCEM, "MUCEM".
Marseille, MUCEM, Fonds Charles-Brun, "MUCEM, Charles-Brun".
Nancy, Archives Départementales de Meurthe-et-Moselle, "AD M-et-M".
Paris, Archives Nationales, Pierrefitte, "AN".
Paris, Bibliothèque Nationale de France, "BNF".
**Nancy, Archives Départementales, Meurthe-et-Moselle**

### Archives privés 1 J

AD M-et-M, 1 J 30: 'Rapports Caserne Molitor 12/1914 – 9/1915 and 9/15 – 12/1916'.

AD M-et-M, 1 J 268: 'C. Muller et A. Richy, Journal tenu à Baslieux, Meurthe-et-Moselle, village occupé par les Allemands en 1914–1918'.


T. Cudbird, *The Origins of Economic Regions in France, 1918-1940*,
https://doi.org/10.1007/978-3-032-04422-8

AD M-et-M, 1 J 270: 'M. Laurent, Tonnerre des Hommes, récit autobiographique d'un soldat de la Grande Guerre'.

AD M-et-M, 1 J 1045/9: 'Paroisse de Nomény'.

AD M-et-M, 1J 1045/10: 'J. Godot, Journal de guerre, Loisy, 31 juillet–14 septembre 1914'.

AD M-et-M, 1J 1055: 'Emprunts de la défense nationale 1915–1917; emprunts nationaux 1920'; 'Journée du Poilu 1915; "Semon du blé" 1916; divers 1915–1920'.

AD M-et-M, 1 J 1183: 'Journal d'un habitant de Pagny'.

AD M-et-M, 1 J 1206: 'Journal de marches et d'opérations du Général Léon Durand—défense de la Grand Couronné de Nancy août-septembre 1914'.

AD M-et-M, 1J 1275: F. Sagot, '*Journal d'un témoin de la guerre à Pont-à-Mousson et au Bois-Le-Prêtre 7 août 1914–janvier 1915*'.

AD M-et-M, 1J 1276: 'Affiches-oeuvres de guerre'.

AD M-et-M, 1 J 1288: 'Journaux de tranchées et divers'.

AD M-et-M, 1J 1305: '1914. Pages de guerre écrites au jour le jour', (Édité Imprimerie Lorraine Rigot et Cie, 51–53 Rue St.-Georges Nancy; Chants du soldat, Imprimerie Lorraine.

AD M-et-M, 1 J 1334: 'Journal d'un évacué de Toul'.

AD M-et-M, 1J 1572: J. Hoffmann, 'Souvenirs de la première guerre mondiale 1914–1915 à Mailly-sur-Seille'.

AD M-et-M, 1 J 1575: 'Agenda de poche de Maurice Schmidt; son carnet de route'.

AD M-et-M, 1J 1600: P. Suisse, 'Récit des premières semaines de la guerre dans Le Lunévillois, à Moncel-lès-Lunéville, août–septembre 1914'.

AD M-et-M, 1J 1601: 'Carnet Auguste Marcilly: récits des évènements survenus à Nancy et sur l'ensemble du front entre le 28 juillet 1914 et le 14 janvier 1915'.

AD M-et-M, 1J 1602: L. René, 'Journal de guerre d'un village lorrain par l'instituteur, Halloville'.

AD M-et-M, 1J 1630: 'J-M. Itant, Mon grand-père Auguste Bertrand durant la guerre de 1914–1918'.

AD M-et-M, 2 P 123: 'Versement et échange d'or'.

AD M-et-M, 2 P 147: 'Emprunts nationaux'.

AD M-et-M, 8 R 213: 'Rapatriement des réfugiés'.

AD M-et-M, 8 R 216: 'Allocations aux familles de réfugiés'.

AD M-et-M, 8 R 217: 'Secours aux réfugiés'.

AD M-et-M, F/7/12936-7: 'Rapports du Préfet au Ministre de l'Intérieur'.

## Clermont-Ferrand, Archives Départementales du Puy-de-Dôme

AD P-de-D, La Grande Collecte: 'Correspondance Léger Debost, Adolphe Féneyrols, correspondence et carnets Eugène Martin'.
AD P-de-D, M 4582: 'Journées 1915, dossier préfet, la Journée Française 23, 24 mai 1915'.
AD P-de-D, M 4585: 'Fêtes de Vercingétorix'.
AD P-de-D, M 4628: 'Dossier préfet — *Leurs Crimes*'.
AD P-de-D, T 1462: 'Autorisation de manuels scolaires 1911–1921'.
AD P-de-D, T 1504: 'Conférences pédagogiques'.
AD P-de-D, T 3214: 'Cours à l'Université de Clermont-Ferrand'.
**AD P-de-D, Fonds Clémentel-archives privés AJ**
AD P-de-D, 5 J 27: 'Notamment: discours devant les élèves de l'École centrale en mars 1919; discours prononcé aux obsèques de Rodin; discours pour les inaugurations de foires (foire aux échantillons de Lyon, foire de Paris); discours devant des chambres de commerce'.
AD P-de-D, 5 J 28: 'Brouillons et notes, extraits du Journal officiel. Notamment: audition de Clémentel par la commission d'Organisation économique en 1918, dépositions devant la commission des Douanes, discours devant la commission des Entraves au commerce'.
AD P-de-D, 5 J 56: 'Études, notes et rapports, lettres de parlementaires, d'industriels sur la réorganisation économique. Notamment: dossiers sur les prohibitions d'importations, sur les surtaxes "ad valorem", sur la politique commerciale de la France, les produits viticoles, le change, les idées ouvrières'.
AD P-de-D, 5 J 58: 'Coupures de presse, revues, brouillons de discours de Clémentel. Notamment: discours d'inauguration des Régions Est et Auvergne, préface par Clémentel à l'ouvrage "Les Régions économiques" de Henri Hauser'.
AD P-de-D, 5 J 105: 'Lettres reçues'.
AD P-de-D, 5 J 109: 'Recueil de coupures de presse, 1916–1920'.

## Archives Départementales des Vosges

ADV JPL 957 1 Vosges guides.
ADV (Archives Départemental Vosges), 8M 128.

## Paris, Archives Nationales, Pierrefitte, AN

### AN 355 AP Archives privés Louis Madelin.

AN 355 AP 1: 'Correspondance reçue incl. Barrès'.
AN 355 AP 3: 'Correspondance reçue incl. Gaxotte'.
AN 355 AP 5: 'Correspondance reçue incl. Louis Marin'.
AN 355 AP 6: 'Lettres reçues incl. Pourrat, Poincaré, Nolhac, Méline'.
AN 355 AP 7; 'Correspondance avec C. Sadoul'.
AN 355 AP 16: Personal Journal 1909–1934.

### AN 317 AP Archives privés Louis Marin

AN 317 AP 48: 'Réformes administratives et économiques 1922–1924'.
AN 317 AP 119 and 122: 'Réparation des dommages de guerre et reconstruction 1915–1921'.
AN 317 AP 183: 'Dossiers hommes politiques lorrains 1915–1952'.
AN 317 AP 190: 'Lorraine'.
AN 317 AP 201: 'Agriculture'.

### AN 424 AP Archives privés Paul Boncour

AN 424 AP 34: 'Correspondance'.
AN 424 AP 35: 'Articles politiques 1919–1923'.

### AN F 12 Ministère du Commerce

AN F 12 8000: 'Coupures de journaux sur des questions économiques 1916–1917: régionalisme (division de la France en régions économiques) 1917'.
AN F 12 8001: 'Dossier 3 conseils consultatifs économiques régionaux'.
AN F 12 8037: 'Ministère du Commerce réorganisation'.

## Service historique de la Défense, Vincennes

16 N 1418 Contrôle Postale; 'Analyse de la correspondence militaire, 6e armée, 1916–1917'.

## Marseille, MUCEM

### MUCEM, Fonds Charles-Brun 2 AP

2 AP 2: 'Box 2 Correspondance domaine privé Courrier I 1892–1946, dossier 1911–1918'.
2 AP 3: 'Courrier II'.
2 AP 4: 'Courrier III et cartes'.
2 AP 10: 'Collaborations diverses — Collège des Sciences sociales; Institut des Hautes Études Internationales'.
2 AP 13: 'Oeuvres manuscrites III, genèse et écriture de "Une Formule, le Régionalisme"'.
2 AP 18: 'Cahiers de coupures de presse'.
2 AP 19: 'Cahiers de coupures de presse'.
2 AP 20: 'Cahiers de coupures de presse'.
2 AP 21: 'Coupures de presse'.
2 AP 22: 'Coupures de presse'.
2 AP 26: 'Coupures de presse et journaux; régionalisme et régions; généralités 1899–1945'.
2 AP 28: 'Coupures de presse et journaux: organisation administrative et réformes 1907–1946; Régions économiques 1916–1944'.
2 AP 29: 'Coupures de presse et journaux FRF 1900–1946'.
2 AP 30: 'Coupures de presse et journaux'.
2 AP 31: 'Coupures de presse et journaux 1898–1946'.
2 AP 32: 'Coupures de presse et journaux'.
2 AP 34: 'Coupures de presse dans les livres de sa bibliothèque'.
2 AP 35: 'Coupures de presse 1913–1937'.
2 AP 36: 'Coupures de presse 1918–1921'.
2 AP 37: 'Coupures de presse 1922–1926'.
2 AP 38: 'Coupures de presse 1927–1929'.
MS 74-66 B 250: 'Charles-Brun, Conférence sur le Régionalisme'.

### MUCEM Fonds FRF (Fédération régionaliste française) 6 AP

6 AP 1: 'Organisation interne'.
6 AP 2: 'Administration, Finances, membres'.
6 AP 4: 'Documentation organismes divers'.
6 AP 8: 'Congrès de la FRF 1901–1929'.

6 AP 17: 'Projets de réorganisation régionale de la France; projets officiels 1915–1952'.

6 AP 18: 'Projets de réorganisation régionale de la France; projets annexes, voeux de la FRF, des régions; discours et articles 1918–1921'.

6 AP 21: 'Papiers divers, hommages à Charles-Brun'.

6 AP 22: 'Papiers divers presse 1901–1936'.

## Paris, Bibliothèque Nationale de France, BNF

BNF, Fonds Z-Barrès, Z BARRES-18478, Desaymard, J., *Artiste Auvergnat Emmanuel Chabrier* (Revue d'Auvergne, Clermont-Ferrand, 1908).

## Clermont-Ferrand, Bibliothèque du Patrimoine

### MSS Henri Pourrat

MSS Henri Pourrat HP 38: 'Causerie d'Henri Pourrat sur l'Auvergne en son hiver 1939–1940, lue le 17 mars 1940 à l'Assemblée Générale de l'Auvergne de Lyon.La Geste Paysanne L'Entr'aide, Henri Pourrat'.

MSS Henri Pourrat HP 120 2–4: 'MSS divers Pourrat'.

MSS Henri Pourrat HP 125 1–7: 'Prières'.

MSS Henri Pourrat HP 128 1: 'Les Baumes aux Prairies, pages sur J-F Angéli'.

MSS Henri Pourrat HP 130: 'Nous qui sommes Auvergnats' copy.

MSS Henri Pourrat HP 137: 'Comptes rendus des ouvrages d'Henri Pourrat, coupures de presse, documents, manuscrits'.

MSS Henri Pourrat HP 163: 'Joseph Desaymard, Du temps qu'on se battait'.

MSS Henri Pourrat HP 215 42: 'La Pensée magique de Jean Giono'.

MSS Henri Pourrat HP 237: 'Notes de lecture, Henri Pourrat mss livres'.

MSS Henri Pourrat HP 247: 'Épreuve des Montagnards'.

MSS Henri Pourrat, cote A 33098, fo 1: 'Douze chansons pour les Poilus d'Auvergne par H. P. [Henri Pourrat], sur des airs populaires notés par Émile Ossedat'.

Patrimoine Overnia web site: 'Documents d'Henri Pourrat, HPC Correspondance avec la Famille Armilhon HPC 197, HPC 200, HPC 260, HPC329, HPC 335. HPP 221 — La Vie 4e année no. 8 (Septembre 1915).

MSS Henri Pourrat HPG 25, Correspondants d'Henri Pourrat, (Société des Amis, inventaire de Suzanne Montagne, Avril 2007): 'Lettres de Maurice Barrès, Étienne Clémentel, Claude Dravaine, Gandilhon Gens-d'Armes, L. Pastourel, D. Halevy, J. Paulhan'.

MSS Fonds Guillaumin hors catalog: 'Lettres de Guillaumin à Pourrat et réponses de Pourrat'; 801098 lever arch Guillaumin.

## MSS Desdevises du Dézert

Georges Desdevises du Dézert (1854–1942).

Dossiers documentaires sur les savants, les écrivains et les artistes de l'Auvergne contemporaine: 'MS 1740 Gandilhon, 1658 Clémentel, 1608 Boyer, 1538 Angeli, 1453 Poètes d'Auvergne, 1720 Louis Farges, 1671 Courchinoux, 1561 Bardoux'.

Carton DESD 19, Correspondance Desdevises–Pourrat: Letters from G. Desdevises to H. Pourrat 1911 to 1942.

MS 1453: 'Les Poètes contemporains de l'Auvergne [Manuscrit]: dossiers contenant textes et documents divers / réunis par Georges Desdevises du Dézert'.

MSS 1454,1455: 'Savants, artistes et lettres d'Auvergne [Manuscrit] / notices et correspondances réunies par Georges Desdevises du Dézert'.

## MSS Joseph Desaymard

MSS Joseph Desaymard JD12: 'Brouillons et manuscrits 1910–1914'.

MSS Joseph Desaymard JD21: 'Doubles disponibles de pièces etc. Joseph Desaymard'.

MSS Joseph Desaymard JD 24: 'Brouillons et manuscrits'.

MSS Joseph Desaymard JD 25: 'Brouillons et manuscrits 1937–1943'.

MSS Joseph Desaymard JD 38: 'Journal Joseph Desaymard, extraits de lectures, remarques personnelles, projets d'écrits, notes rédigées depuis 1896, classés et mises au net en novembre 1942'.

MSS Joseph Desaymard JD 39: 'Histoires et faits divers Desaymard'.

MSS Joseph Desaymard JD 47–50: 'Correspondance René Albert Fleury'.

## MSS Lucien Gachon

MSS Lucien Gachon LG 28: including 'L'Expérience rurale dans l'oeuvre d'Henri Pourrat, allocution prononcée à la salle des fêtes de Chamalières à l'occasion de la remise du prix Goncourt à Henri Pourrat par Pierre Caziot, Ministre de l'Agriculture, 8.II.1942'.

## Blois, Archives de Saint Gobain, Fonds Camille Cavallier

SGA 6754: 'Divers 1891–1918, dossier Congrès Natalité, Nancy'.
SGA 7225: 'Divers 1912 –1926, dossier Arts et Métiers'.
SGA 7229: 'Divers 1920–1926, dossier Assistance aux réfugiés, évacués (1920)'.
SGA 7234: 'Divers 1899–1926, dossier bourse des Valeurs'.
SGA 7289: 'Divers 1908–1926, papiers divers: dossiers École professionnelle de l'Est et L'Est républicain'.
SGA 7247: 'Chambre de Commerce de Nancy 1918–1926'.
SGA 7248: 'Chambre de Commerce de Nancy 1917–1924'.
SGA 7249: 'Chambre de Commerce de Nancy 1903–1925'.
SGA 7305: '1922–1925, dossier Camille Cavallier et la Grande Famille Lorraine 1925'.
SGA 7310: 'Divers 1856–1926, Habitations bon marché 1922-23'.
SGA 7313: 'Divers1915–1926, dossier Institut métallurgique et minier de Nancy 1920–1926'.
SGA 7319: 'Divers 1915–1926, dossier correspondance avec Albert Lebrun'.
SGA 7328: 'Maisons du conseil d'administration: note (1919–1925); dossier Michelin à Clermont-Ferrand: correspondence (1923–1925)'.
SGA 7331: '1915–1926, dossier natalité (1918–1922)'.
SGA 7341: 'Dossier politique 1918–1926'.
SGA 7342: 'Divers 1908–1926, dossier Pupilles de la Chambre de Commerce de Nancy (1918–1926)'.
SGA 7359: 'Divers 1914–1926, dossier régions économiques (1919–1926); dossier Le Rhône et Le Rhin (1920–1923)'.
SGA 7360–1: 'Occupation de la Ruhr 1921–1925'.
SGA 7383: 'Divers 1919–1926, dossier Testament industriel: note (1924–1926)'.
SGA 7385: '1917–1926, dossier L'Union économique de l'Est'.
SGA 7393: '1919–1926, dossier Visite du Président de la République Raymond Poincaré à Pont-à-Mousson le dimanche 23 novembre 1919; dossier voies navigables: note (1919–1920)'.
SGA 7398: 'dossier Association nationale d'Expansion économique 1917–1919; dossier commission de la Natalité'.
SGA 7420: '1904–1909, Chambre de Commerce de Nancy: pupilles et natalité, congrès de la natalité, bourse des valeurs à Nancy, Messieurs Vilgrain et Fayelle (ou Fayolle), région économique de l'Est et divers (1918–1919)'.
SGA 7447: '1914–1920 dossier Régions économiques (projet de division de la France en régions économiques): documentation, correspondance (1917–1920)'.

SGA 7448: 'Divers 1916–1922, dossier Société d'Assistance aux Réfugiés, Évacués, Sinistrés de Meurthe-et-Moselle: compte rendu de réunions, divers (1918–1920)'.
SGA no catalogue number: 'C. Cavallier, *La France Victorieuse* (Nancy, 7 septembre 1923)'.
SGA no catalogue number: 'C. Cavallier, Notes d'Un Sourd Sisyphe, 44 vols'.
*SGA* no catalogue number: 'Sagesse du Chef, Lettres et Notes inédites de Camille Cavallier' (Paris, 1937).
SGA DOC PAM 21.24, Série A fasc. 31 A: 'Fête de la Reconstitution aux Usines de Pont-à-Mousson 18 juillet 1920'.
SGA DOC PAM 21.47, série C fasc. 15 C: 'La Métallurgie: la situation des grandes industries françaises au début de 1922'.
SGA DOC PAM 21.49, Serie C fasc. 17 C: 'Crise de l'Habitation 16 janvier 1923'.
SGA, DOC PAM 21.50: 'Notes Économiques d'un métallurgiste, 20 Septembre 1923'.
SGA DOC PAM 21.51: 'C. Cavallier, La France de Demain, Paix et Prospérité par le Travail, la Natalité, l'Hygiène, août 1923'.
SGA DOC PAM 21.52: 'La Crise Économique: Transports par Chemins de Fer, 1 février 1924'.
SGA DOC PAM 21.65: 'Office des transports, séance du 24 février 1922'.
SGA DOC 22.11: 'C. Cavallier, Après Guerre; La Métallurgie Française, 19 avril 1917'.
SGA DOC PAM 22.12: 'Vers La Démocratie nouvelle, pages choisies (Union Économique de l'Est, 1917)'.
SGA DOC PAM 22.13: 'C. Cavallier, L'Avenir de la France, Réformes Nécessaires, Avant Propos de Maurice Herbette'.
SGA DOC.PAM 22.14: 'Documents précieux - Camille Cavallier'.
SGA, DOC PAM 22.21: 'La Sarre par un Franco-Sarrois, June 1923'.

## Printed Primary Sources

### Posters

Poulbot, F., *Journée du Puy-de-Dôme, paquetage du soldat, 23 janvier 1916,* 'Avec ça, il ne serait pas enrhumé, papa,' BNF, IFN-9013081.
Willette, A. L., *Journée du Puy-de-Dôme, Vercingétorix soldat au front, paquetage du soldat, 23 janvier 1916,* Imprimeur Devambez (Paris, 1916), Clermont-Ferrand, Patrimoine, web site Overnia, GR 12017.

## Newspapers

*Auvergnat de Paris*, 1919–1920.
*Avenir du Puy-de-Dôme* (Clermont-Ferrand), octobre 1903, 1914–1918.
*Cri de Toulouse* 1913, 1927, 1929.
*Cri du Midi*, 1929, 1932, 1934.
*Croix de Meurthe-et-Moselle* (Nancy), 1914.
*Dépêche de Toulouse* 1913, 1915, 1920, 1924, 1925.
*Écho de Lorraine* (Nancy), 1914.
*Éclair de l'Est* (Nancy), 1914, 1915.
*Électeur Lorrain* (Nancy), 1914.
*Est républicain* (Nancy), 1914–1924.
*Étoile de l'Est* (Nancy), 1914.
*Express du Midi*, 1924.
*Impartial de l'Est* (Nancy), 1914.
*Journal de la Meurthe* (Nancy), 1914.
*Le Temps* (Paris), 1918.
*Midi Républicain (Toulouse)*, 1930.
*Moniteur du Puy-de-Dôme* (Clermont-Ferrand), octobre 1903, 1914–1918.
*Phare de la Loire* (Nantes), 1914.
*Union républicaine des Vosges* (Épinal), 1915.

## Periodicals

*Action Française,* 1918–1919.
*Action Régionaliste*, 1906, 1920, 1926, 1927, 1939.
*Alauza d'Auvernha*, Organe de la Maintenance d'Auvergne et des Sociétés Auvergnates à Paris 1928–1936.
Auvergne Littéraire, Artistique et Félibréenne, 1924.
*Auvergne thermale,* 1922–1923.
*Bon Grain*, organe de l'union Lorraine des syndicats Agricoles, 1919–1921, 1927, 1928, 1930, 1931, 1932.
*Bulletin de l'Assemblée régionale professionnelle (Toulouse),* 1923, 1924, 1926.
*Bulletin de l'Office Régional Agricole du Massif Central, 1919–1920.*
*Bulletin de l'Union des Fédérations des Syndicats d'Initiative*, 1919, 1921, 1922.
*Bulletin de la Chambre de Commerce de Nancy*, vol. 7, 1909; vols. 12–22, 1914–1924, 1927, 1934, 1936.
*Bulletin de la Chambre de Commerce de Toulouse*, 1920–1931.
*Bulletin de la société départementale d'agriculture et du syndicat des agriculteurs des Hautes-Pyrénées* 1923–1931.
*Bulletin de la Société Industrielle de l'Est*, (Nancy, 1914–1924).

*Bulletin historique et scientifique de l'Auvergne*, Académie des sciences, belles-lettres et arts de Clermont-Ferrand, 1896, 1902–03, 1910, 1911.
*Bulletin l'Office Agricole Régional du Massif Central*, 1925 (Clermont-Ferrand, 1926).
*Bulletin mensuel du Redressement français*, 1927 2eme année, 1930, 1931.
*Bulletin Trimestriel de la VIe région économique* (Rennes) 1931, 1934, 1935, 1936, 1937.
*Commerce*, bulletin mensuel, L'Association du Commerce et de l'Industrie du Puy-de-Dôme, des Syndicats Patronaux et de la Fédération des Groupes Commerciaux et Industriels de la région du Centre.
*État moderne*, 1930.
IVe *région économique, groupement de Basse Normandie (Caen)*, bulletin 1920, 1928, 1930, 1937.
*Journal d'Agriculture du Sud-Ouest* 1928, 1932.
*Journal d'Agriculture Pratique, de Viticulture et d'Économie Rurale pour le Midi de la France* 1921–1927.
*Journal officiel de la République française*, débats parlementaires, Assemblée Nationale 1915–1921, 1924, 1938.
*Le Journal*, 1918.
*Les Cahiers français* 'Décentralisation,' *Les Cahiers français*, janvier-février 1982.
*Lorrain de Paris*, 1927.
*Musette*, 1908.
*Normandie Économique*, 1e année no. 1, 1927.
*Notre Temps* 1928–1933.
*Nouveaux Cahiers*, 1937–1940.
*Nouvelle Revue Socialiste*, Dubedout H., 'Une nouvelle citoyenneté,' in Décentralisation, *Nouvelle Revue Socialiste*, septembre-octobre 1981, pp. 27–30.
*Oeuvre Méridionale*, 1918, 1919, 1922, 1936.
*Ordre Nouveau* 1933, 1934.
*Ouest Économique*, 1927.
*Pays Lorrain*, 1907, 1908, 1909, 1913, 1919–1925, 1931.
*Petit Parisien*, 1918.
*Plans*, 1931.
*Populaire de Nantes*, 1914.
*Projet*, 'Décentraliser vraiment,' *Projet*, mai-juin 1984, 185–6; numéro spécial, 1984, 573–583 for the role of the notables.
*Pyrénées et Océan*, 1919, 1920, 1921, 1924, 1925.
*Reconstruction Lorraine*, 1917–1919.
*Réforme Sociale*, 1916–1919.
*Région du Centre*, 1921–1927.

*Région économique de Bordeaux et du Sud-Ouest Bulletin Officiel*, abbreviation REBSO, 1924–1936.
*Région Économique de Toulouse et des Pyrénées* (Bulletin officiel du Groupement des Chambres de Commerce), *abbreviation RETP*, 1921–1938.
*Revue d'Auvergne, 1892–1914.*
*Revue de la Haute-Auvergne, 1900–1914.*
*Revue du Syndicat Départemental Agricole du Puy-de-Dôme,* 1920–1922.
*Revue Économique de L'Ouest*, abbreviation REO, 1920, 1922, 1923, 1926, 1927, 1928, 1929.
*Revue hebdomadaire,* 1915, 1918–1919.
*Revue Industrielle de l'Est*, 1917–1918.
*Soleil de Toulouse* 1925.
*Sud-Ouest Économique,* 1923–1933.
*Terre d'Auvergne*, 1920–1933.
*Terre Lorraine*, 1925, 1927, 1936.
*Travaux de la Chambre de Commerce de Clermont-Ferrand*, 1915, 1917, 1918, 1923, 1924.
*Union Économique de l'Est,* 1917–1924, 1926–1936.
*Veillée d'Auvergne,* 1909–1914.
Vie region économique, groupement regional économique de Rennes, 1934; 1934; 1935.

## Other Primary Sources

'Le décentralisation en marche,' *Cahiers français*, 220, mars-avril 1985 (Paris, 1916).
*35e Congrès du Parti Républicain Radical et Radical-Socialiste 26–30 Octobre 1938, Marseille.* (Paris, the Executive Committee, 1938).
A-Laribé, M. (1923). *Le Paysan français après la Guerre.*
Achalme, L. (2013). *Le Maître du pain.*
Aimond, C. (1957). *Essai sur le caractère et le génie Lorrains.*
Aimond, C., *La Guerre de 1914–1918 dans la Meuse: Argonne-Les Éparges-Saint-Mihiel-.*
Ajalbert, J., *Auvergne* (1932).
Ajalbert, J., *En Auvergne* (1893).
Ajalbert, J., *Les Livres du Pays* (Clermont-Ferrand, L'Auvergne Littéraire, 1926).
Alphaud, G., *La France pendant la Guerre 1914–1917* (1918).
*Aménagement Hydro-électrique de la 2ème section du bassin de la Dordogne: Notice Technique et Financière* (1924)
Angeli, J. *La Métairie de Jean L'Olagne, suivi de poèmes divers et d'équinoxes,* préface d'Henri Pourrat (Saint Félicien-en-Vivarais, 1925).

Anglade J., *Les Troubadors de Toulouse* (Toulouse, 1928).

Appert, B., *Le Régionalisme administratif*; préface de M. Charles-Brun (Paris, 1939).

Ardouin-Dumazet, V-E., *Voyage en France: Auvergne, Vol. II Haute-Auvergne: Cantal* (Paris, 1927).

*Association amicale des anciens Élèves de l'École Nationale supérieure des Industries chimiques (Institut chimique)* (Nancy, 1920).

Auburtin, J. M., & Blanchard, H. (1917). *La Cité de demain dans les régions dévastées.*

Augé-Laribé, M. (1925). *L'Agriculture pendant la guerre.*

Badel, E., & Courtin-Schmidt, L. (1914). *Gerbéviller la martyre, des ruines à la gloire.*

Bardoux, J. (1936). *La France de Demain, son gouvernement, ses assemblées, sa justice; textes du comité technique pour la réforme de l'état.*

Barrès, M. (1909). *Colette Baudoche.*

Barrès, M. (1917) *L'Âme française et la guerre: les voyages de Lorraine et d'Artois.*

Barrès, M. (1913). *La Colline inspirée.*

Barrès, M. (1919). *L'Appel au Rhin, la minute sacrée.*

Barrès, M. (1919). *La Lorraine dévastée.*

Barrès, M. (1922). *La Politique rhénane: discours parlementaires.*

Barrès, M. (1899). *La Terre et les morts: sur quelles réalités fonder la conscience française.*

Barrès, M. (1921). *Le Génie du Rhin: les bastions de l'Est.*

Barrès, M. (1897). *Les Déracinés.*

Bellard, A. (1929). *De Nancy à Nancy* via *Morhange et Vitrimont, feuilles de route et remembrances d'un combattant d'active de la Division de Fer.*

Bellessort, A., Pourrat, H., Olive, P., Leriche, R., Charles-Brun, J., & Bertin, P. (1941). *La Revolution Nationale Constructive, un bilan et un programme.*

Berlet, C. (1913). *Les Provinces au XVIII siècle et leur division en départements: essai sur la formation de l'unité française.*

Berlet, C. (1916). *Réméréville: un village lorrain pendant les mois d'août et septembre 1914.*

Bertrand, L. (1917). *Le Sens de l'Ennemi.*

Besson, P. (1914). *Le Pâtre du Cantal.*

Van Bever, A. (1909) *Les Poètes du terroir du xve siècle au xxe siècle.*

Bigey, J., & Minarie, T. (1999). *Étain Août 1914-Novembre 1918.*

Blanchard, R. (1922). La Houille blanche dans le Massif Central français. *Revue de géographie alpine, 10*(3), 353–396.

Bloch, C., Lafitte, L., Letaconnoux, J., Levainville, M., Maurette, F., Rousiers, P. de, Schwob, M., Vaillaux, C., & Vidal de la Blache, P. (1913). *Les Divisions régionales de la France; leçons faites à l'École des Hautes Études Sociales.*

Blum, L. (1954). *Oeuvres*, vol. III.i.

Bonnefoy, G. (1903). *Canal Latéral de l'Allier.*
Bouchot, L. (1919). *Vingt-Cinq Leçons sur l'histoire de la Lorraine et du Barrois.*
Boule, M., & Farges, L. (1898). *Le Cantal, Guide.*
Boule, M., Glangeaud, P., Rouchon, G., & Vernière, A. (1901). *Le Puy-de-Dôme et Vichy, guide du touriste, du naturaliste et de l'archéologue.*
Bourderon, R., et al. (1981). *Le PCF: étapes et problèmes 1920–1972.*
Bourgeois, L. (1896). *Solidarité.*
Branchet, L., & Plantadis, J. (1904). *Chansons populaires du Limousin.*
Bréhier, L. (1912). *L'Auvergne.*
Brocard, L. (1913). Le Développement économique de la Lorraine Française. *Séance de la Société d'Économie Sociale* (727–745).
Brun, P. (1928). *Les Régions économiques.* Thèse pour le doctorat, Université de Montpellier, Faculté de Droit.
Brunhes, J. (1910). *La Géographie humaine: essai de classification positive, principes et exemples.*
Brunhes, J., & Vallaux, C. (1921). *La Géographie de l'histoire: géographie de la paix et de la guerre sur terre et sur mer.*
Buffet, J. (1917). *Du Régionalisme au nationalisme financier.*
Busset, M. (1919). *En Avion: vols et combats.*
Busset, M. (1924). *Le Vieux Pays d'Auvergne: recueil des costumes, des types et des coutumes de Haute et Basse-Auvergne, notés et dessinés en l'an 1923.*
Cadilhac, P.-E.. (1921). *Les Projets de régionalisme administrative.* Thèse pour doctorat, Faculté de Droit de Paris.
Cathala, E. (2008). *L'Auvergne.* Facsimile de l'édition de Paris, fin du 19e siècle.
Cathala, E. (2008). *L'Histoire de l'Auvergne racontée aux jeunes Auvergnats.*
Cellérier, H. (1916). *La Politique fédéraliste.*
Centenaire de la Chambre de Commerce de Clermont-Ferrand 1826–1926: discours de MM. Jouve, Maupoil, Clémentel et Fighiera (1927).
Chadefaux, R. (1924). *La Région économique de Clermont-Ferrand.* Thèse pour le doctorat, Faculté de Droit de Paris, Aurillac.
Charles-Brun, J. (1913). *La Division de la France en régions*, rapport présenté au xviie Congrès national de la Propriété bâtie les 5, 6, 7, mai.
Charles-Brun, J. (1911). *Le Régionalisme.*
Chaton, E. (1922). *Historique du 2e bataillon de chasseurs à pied 1914–1918.*
Chevalier, P. (1935). *Bar-Le-Duc pendant la guerre.*
Clémentel, E. (1905). Organisons la Démocratie. In J. Paul-Boncour & C. Maurras (Eds.), *Un Débat nouveau sur la République et la décentralisation*, opinions de E. Buré, G. Clemenceau, E.Clémentel, J. Dessaint, E., & Fournière, J. Reinach, L. Xavier de Ricard, P. Strauss, Le "Temps", A. Varenne (1905). (pp. 148–161).

Clémentel, E. (1914). *Un Drame économique, les délimitations, le passé, l'avenir.*
Colin, L. (1915). *Les Barbares à la Trouée des Vosges,* récits et témoins avec préface de Maurice Barrès.
Collé, A. (1925). *La Bataille de la Mortagne, la Chipotte. L'Occupation: Ménil et ses environs; liste des héros.*
*Communications de la Chambre de Commerce de Metz, 1922–1924.*
*Compte-Rendu des travaux de la chambre de commerce de Clermont-Ferrand 1914–1920, 1923–24* (1915–1921 and 1924–25).
*Congrès national de la natalité 1919, premier congrès de la natalité tenu à Nancy du 25 au 28 septembre 1919, compte-rendu part I* (1919).
Conseil-Régional de la Lorraine, (1998) *14–18 côté civils: témoignages d'habitants du canton de Fresnes.*
Dalet, C. (Ed.). (2013). *Correspondance croisée Henri Pourrat–Joseph Desaymard 1913 à 1918: la Grande Guerre.*
Dalet, C. (Ed.). (2007–8). *H. Pourrat–B. Zimmer, Correspondance 1923–1942.*
Dalet, C. (Ed.). (1983). *H. Pourrat–C. Silvestre, Correspondance 8 mai 1920 au 4 août 1925.*
Dalet, C. (Ed.). (1996). *H. Pourrat–L. Gachon, Correspondance 13 janvier 1940 au 18 septembre 1942.*
Dalet, C. (Ed). (1994). *H. Pourrat–L. Gachon, Correspondance 21 janvier 1934 au 15 décembre 1939.*
Dalet, C. (Ed). (1997). *H. Pourrat–L. Gachon, Correspondance 23 septembre 1942 au 29 décembre 1946.*
Dalet, C. (Ed.). (1991). *H. Pourrat–L. Gachon, Correspondance 31 janvier 1921–25 décembre 1927.*
Dalet, C. (Ed.). (2010). *Henri Pourrat: Actes du cinquantenaire de la mort de l'écrivain; conférences prononcées à l'Université catholique de Lyon et à Paris au Collège de France.*
Defferre, G. (1965). *Nouvel Horizon.*
Delille, L. (2002). *À La Veillée d'Auvergne, contes, légendes et menteries: les histoires extraordinaires de mon grand-père.*
Delmas, J. (1931). *Mes Hommes au feu avec la Division de Fer; à Morhange, sur l'Yser, en Artois 1914–1915.*
Delzangles, F. (1933). *Biographies et morceaux choisis d'écrivains d'Auvergne.*
Delzangles, F. (1910). *Folklore Cantalien, chants populaires d'Auvergne.*
Demangeon, A. (1933). *Paris, la ville et sa banlieue.*
Desaymard, J. (1908). *Artiste Auvergnat Emmanuel Chabrier.*
Desaymard, J. (1935). *L'Art et Les Artistes en Auvergne.*
Desdevises du Dézert, G. (1916). *Pour la Maison de Rééducation des Aveugles de la Guerre à Montferrand.*
Diez, J. (1925). *Le Régionalisme Économique, Organisation de la Région Économique de l'Est (Nancy).* Thèse pour le doctorat, Sciences Politiques et Économiques.

Doniol, H. (1900). *La Basse-Auvergne.*

Driant, E. C. (1903). alias Capitaine Danrit, *La Guerre fatale: France–Angleterre* (3 vols).

Dubest, Dr. (1896). La Dépopulation des Campagnes et la Défense nationale', *Bulletin historique et scientifique de l'Auvergne* (Académie des sciences, belles-lettres et arts de Clermont-Ferrand, mai 1896) (133–161).

Duplantier, J. (1929). *Le Régionalisme Économique et spécialement la Région Économique de Bordeaux et du Sud-Ouest* (Thèse de doctorat, Faculté de Droit, Bordeaux).

Dutil, L. (1929). *La Haute-Garonne et sa région*, t.1.

Élardin, J. (1963). Souvenirs et Impressions: Senones et sa contrée sous la botte allemande 1914–1918. *Bulletin de la Société Philomatique Vosgienne,* 89e année, vol LXVII.

Estourbeillon, R. de L'. (1918). *Le Régionalisme et la France de demain.*

Exposition internationale (1937, Paris), Exposition internationale des arts et des techniques dans la vie moderne. Tome I (2e édition), Liste des exposants.

*Exposition Internationale (1937). Arts and Crafts in Modern Life. Official Guide* (English Edition).

Farges, L. (1928). *La Haute-Auvergne: une description, une histoire, un voyage de tourisme et d'art.*

Favareille, R. (1919). *Réforme administrative par l'autonomie et la responsabilité des fonctions (self-administration).*

Ferry, A. (2005). *Les Carnets secrets d'Abel Ferry 1914–1918, suivis de lettres et notes de guerre.* A. Loez and N. Offenstadt (Eds.).

Fèvre, J., & Hauser, H. (1909). *Régions et pays de France.*

Fiel, P. (1935). La Reconstruction des régions dévastées en Lorraine. *Le Pays lorrain,* 27e année, nouvelle série quatrième volume, 6.

Fombaron, J.-C., & Prouillet, Y. (Eds.). *Senones, une ville vosgienne sous l'occupation allemande, journal de guerre de l'abbé André Villemin* (Société Philomatique Vosgienne, Raon-l'Étape).

Foncin, P. (1898). *Questions du temps présent: les pays de France, projet de fédéralisme administratif.*

Franck, J. (1921). *La Région économique de Basse Normandie.* Thèse de doctorat.

Gaber, S. (1998). *Mémoire de la Grande Guerre en Lorraine.*

Gachon, L. (1948). *L'Auvergne et Le Velay.*

Gachon, P. (1921). *Languedoc.*

Gachon, L. (1925). *Maria*, préface d'Henri Pourrat.

Gaultier, L. (1917). *Exposition de la Cité Reconstituée (Salle du Jeu de Paume and Terrasse des Tuileries (25 mai–15 août 1916), Association Générale des Hygiénistes et Techniciens Municipaux, Rapport Général.*

Gaxotte, P. (1975). *Les Autres et moi.*

Gaxotte, P. (1968). *Mon Village et moi.*

Ginisty, S. G. (1917). Mgr., Évêque de Verdun, *Verdun.*

Ginisty, S. G. (1918). Mgr., Évêque de Verdun, *Jeanne d'Arc et la France de la Grande Guerre: panégyrique de la bienheureuse Jeanne d'Arc prononcé dans la Cathédrale d'Orléans le dimanche 12 mai 1918 pour le 489e anniversaire de la délivrance de la ville.*

Gobin, L. (1896). *Essai sur la géographie de l'Auvergne.*

Gourbeyre, A. (1900). *La Petite Propriété rurale dans le Puy-de-Dôme.* Thèse de doctorat, Faculté de Droit.

Gravier, J.-F. (1947). *Paris et le désert français.*

Gréau, E. (1908). *Le Fer en Lorraine.*

Gréau, E. (1908). Société industrielle de l'Est, *La Métallurgie en Lorraine.*

Guillaumin, E. (1904). *Vie d'un Simple.*

Guyot, C. (1919). À propos d'un livre récent, Le Passé et L'Avenir de la Lorraine, Agriculture et Industrie. *Extrait des Mémoires de l'Académie Stanislas 1918–1919.*

Guyot, C. (1921). Un Problème urbain, logements insalubres et habitations à bon marché. *Mémoires de l'Académie Stanislas,* CLXXIe année, 6e série, t. xviii 1920–1921 (1–4).

Hadjadj, D. (Ed). (2015). H. Pourrat–A. Vialatte, *Correspondance tome 7, Les Temps Noirs II janvier 1943–décembre 1946.*

Hadjadj, D., Milkovitch-Rioux, C., & Schaffner, A. (Eds.) (2001, 2003). *Correspondance Alexandre Vialatte–Henri Pourrat Tome I Lettres de Collège 1916–1921, Tome 2 Lettres de Rhénanie février 1922–avril 1924.*

Halévy, D. (1935). *Visites aux Paysans du Centre 1907–1934.*

Hannotin, E. (1998). *Le Canton de Spincourt pendant la Guerre 14/18.*

Hauser, H. (1924). *Le Problème du Régionalisme.*

Hauser, H. (1918). *Les Régions économiques*; préface de M. Clémentel.

Hennessy, J. (1916). *Régions de France 1911–1916.*

Hennessy, J. (s.d.). *Réorganisation administrative de la France.*

Hérouville, M. (1923). d', *Les Conditions de la réforme administrative.*

Hinzelin, E. (1913). *Coeurs d'Alsace et de Lorraine.*

Hinzelin, E. (1918). *Français de la Moselle, des Vosges et du Rhin.*

Hinzelin, E. (1915). *La Lorraine Martyre.*

Hottenger, G.-A. (1923). *Introduction à l'histoire économique de la Lorraine au xixe siècle.*

Hottenger, G.-A. (1927). *L'Ancienne Industrie du fer en Lorraine.* Société industrielle de l'Est.

Hottenger, G.-A. (1913). *La Cité moderne et ses fonctions, conférence faite à l'hôtel de ville de Nancy, le 6 mai 1913, à l'occasion de l'exposition de la "Cité Moderne".*

Hottenger, G.-A. (1925). *Le Mouvement économique en Lorraine: 1920–1924.*

Hottenger, G.-A. (1911). *Le Pays de Briey.*

*Inauguration du monument Bichat: 23 avril 1911* (1911).

*Inauguration solennelle du musée historique lorrain 28 juillet 1912* (Palais Ducal, Grande Rue (Ville-Vieille) Nancy, 1912).

Israel, A. (1934). *La Réforme de l'État devant les partis.*

Jean-Desthieux, F. (1919). *Produire: d'une organisation économique du pays.*

Jean-Desthieux, F. (1918). *L'Évolution régionaliste: du Félibrige au Fédéralisme.*

Jean, J.-P. (1929). *Livre d'Or du Souvenir français.*

Jean, J.-P. (1922). *Lorraine et Alsace.*

Joanne, P. (1904). *Itinéraire Général de la France: Auvergne et Centre.*

Joucla, E., & Cortat, R. (1929). *Lectures d'Auvergne.*

Jouve, A. (1910). *Création d'un canal latéral à l'Allier.* Chambres de Commerce de Clermont-Ferrand, Riom et Issoire.

Jouvenel, B. de. (1928). *L'Économie dirigée.*

Jouvenel, H. de (présidence). (1924). *Réformes politiques de la France*, conférences faites à l'École des Hautes Études Sociales par MM. Louis Loucheur, Georges Leygues, A. de Monzie, Paul Raynaud, H. Lemery, Henry de Jouvenel.

Krug, A. (1920). *L'Industrialisation de l'agriculture.* Nancy, Union économique de l'Est.

Krug, A. (1916). *La natalité française.* Nancy, supplement to the Bulletin de la Société industrielle de l'Est.

Krug, A. (1918). *Pour La Repopulation.*

*La Société industrielle de l'Est pendant la guerre 1914–1918* (1919)

Labbé, E. (1938). *Exposition Internationale des Arts et Techniques dans la vie moderne 1937.* Rapport Général, Tome 1. Ministère du Commerce et de l'Industrie.

Laffitte, L. (1912). L'Évolution économique de la Lorraine. *Annales de Géographie*, t.21(20), 393–417.

Laffitte, L. (1912). *Rapport général sur l'exposition internationale de l'Est de la France, Nancy, 1909.*

Lafont, R. (1971). *Décoloniser la France, les régions face à l'Europe.*

Lagardelle, H. (1929). *Sud-Ouest, une région française.*

Landouzy, le Professeur (1906), *Le Mont-Dore, station hydrominérale et station d'altitude.*

Laufenburger, H. (1924). *L'Industrie sidérurgique de la Lorraine désannexée et la France.*

Lebrun, A. (1920). *La Politique du fer au cours de la guerre, la question de Briey, conférence faite à la Société industrielle de l'Est, le 18 juin 1920.*

Lemaigre, M. *Haute-Auvergne, département du Cantal, monographie* (Aurillac, sd but post WW1).

Léoutre, J. (2005). *Chronique cordiale d'un Mussipontain des XIXe et XXe siècles 1887–1980.*

*Les Instituteurs meusiens, témoins de l'occupation allemande 1914–1918* (Meuse Archives Départementales, 1999).

Lyautey, H. (1923). *Hommage d'un Lorrain à un Lorrain.*
Lyautey, H. (1926). *La Réunion de la Lorraine à la France.*
Macaigne, A. (1917). *Notre France d'après-guerre: comment réorganiser la France, comment développer ses forces productives, solutions pratiques.*
Madelin, L. (1907). *Croquis Lorrains.*
Madelin, L. (1919). *Heures merveilleuses d'Alsace et de Lorraine.*
Maire, P. (2014). *Lunéville pendant la Grande Guerre 1914–1918.*
Mansuy, E. (Ed.). (2001). *Carnet de guerre de Georges Curien territorial vosgien.*
Marcoline, C. (Ed.). *Un Auvergnat dans la paix et dans la guerre, chroniques auvergnates autour des journaux de la guerre 14/18 de Jean et Jacques Lacoste* (s.d.).
Marin, L. (1944). *Contes traditionnels en Lorraine. Institutions de transfert des valeurs morales et spirituelles.*
Marin, L. (1966). *Regards sur la Lorraine: réflexions sur des notions fondamentales, particularités du caractère lorrain.*
Marin, M. L. (1973). *Louis Marin 1871–1960 homme d'état, philosophe et savant par lui-même et ses contemporains.*
Martin-Froment, C. (2010). *L'Écrivain de Lubine, journal de guerre d'une femme dans les Vosges occupées 1914–1918.* P. Nivet, J-C. Fombaron, Y. Pouillet (Eds.).
Martin, J. (1927). *La Représentation politique des intérêts économiques. Une solution: les conseils économiques régionaux.* Thèse de doctorat, Université de Lille.
Masfrand, J. (1896). *Le Cantal, guide du touriste, du botaniste et du géologue.*
Masson, P.-M. (1917). *Lettres de guerre août 1914–avril 1916.*
Mathé, R. (Ed.). (1969). *Cent dix-neuf lettres d'Émile Guillaumin dont 73 inédités 1894–1951; autour du mouvement littéraire bourbonnais.*
Mathiot, C. (1926). *La Mobilisation Économique.*
Maurras, C. (1919). *l'Idée de la décentralisation* (1st ed. 1898, 2nd ed.). Action Française.
Mazel, H. (1917). *La Nouvelle Cité de France, réorganisation nationale d'après-guerre.*
Imbart de la Tour. (1916). Réforme administrative après la guerre: organisation des cadres territoriaux et de l'action locale. *Séances et travaux de l'Académie des sciences morales et politiques.*
Megglé, A. *Atlas, guide économique et touristique des régions de France et d'Algérie; vol 1 Auvergne et Bourbonnais; vol 2 Région de l'Est et Lorraine* (1922 and 1923).
Méline, J. (1919). *Le Salut par la terre et le programme économique de l'avenir.*
Méline, J. (1906). *The Return to the Land.*
*Mémoires de l'Académie des sciences, inscriptions et belles-lettres de Toulouse,* 1921.
*Mémoires de l'Académie Stanislas 1918–1919,* Nancy (1919).
*Mémoires et procès-verbaux, Société agricole et scientifique de la Haute-Loire* (Le Puy-en-Velay), 1907–1909.

Mendès-France, P. (1962). *République Moderne* (199–212).

Mény, J. (Ed.). (2009). *Jean Giono-Henri Pourrat Correspondance 1929–1940.* Hors-série de la revue Giono 2009; Association des Amis de Jean Giono; Société des Amis d'Henri Pourrat.

Mer, G. (1934). *la Réforme de l'État en action.*

Mercier, R. (1917). *Journal d'un bourgeois de Nancy, Nancy Sauvée.*

Mercier, R. (1914). *La Guerre de 1914: la vie en Lorraine août 1914.*

Ministère du Commerce et de L'Industrie, Direction des affaires commerciales et industrielles, *Organisation des régions économiques* (5 avril 1919).

Ministère du Commerce, de l'Industrie, des Postes et des Télégraphes, *Projet de division de la France en régions économiques* (1917).

Mirman, L., Simon, G., & Keller, G. (1917). *Their Crimes.*

Mitterrand, F., Oeuvres II (2016), un socialisme du possible (1971) 67–8; le contrat socialiste (1969).

Moselly, E. (1990). *Le Rouet d'ivoire: enfances lorraines 1907,* P. Goudot (Ed.).

Nolhac, P. de (1888). *Pages Auvergnates.*

Nouel, J. (1978). Carnets de route d'un officier lorrain, le capitaine Édouard de Warren, dans les combats en Lorraine de l'automne 1914. *Le Pays lorrain,* 59e année (4), 179–194.

Pange, J. de, *Journal vol. 1 1927–1930* (4 vols, 1964–1975).

Pange, J. de (1921). *La France et les Pays rhénans.*

Pange, J. de (1922). *Les Libertés rhénanes: pays rhénanes, Sarre, Alsace.*

Pange, J. de (1951). *Les Meules de Dieu.*

Pange, J. de. (1927). *Les Soirées de Saverne.*

Parisot, R. (1924). *Histoire de Lorraine, vol iii 1789–1919.*

Parisot, R. (1909). *La Lorraine Région Française.*

Paul-Cavallier, M., & Fayolle, B. (1936). *Trente Ans d'Action Économique 1905–1935, la Chambre de Commerce de Nancy.*

Paulhan, J. (1930). *Le Guerrier appliqué.*

Pézard, A. (2001). *Nous autres à Vauquois.*

Philipponneau, M. (1967). *La Gauche et les Régions.*

Philipponneau, M. (1981). *La grande affaire, décentralisation et régionalisation.*

Pineau, L. Le Foklore de l'Auvergne. In A. Van Bever (Ed.), *Auvergne et Limousin: Histoire, Tableaux Pittoresques, Poésies, Chansons Populaires, Contes et Légendes* (s.d.).

Poincaré, R. (1906). *Idées Contemporaines.*

Pourrat, C. (Ed.). (2000). *Amitiés suisses d'Henri Pourrat; correspondence avec Ramuz 1922–1946 et autres.*

Pourrat, H. (1913). Nous qui sommes Auvergnats. *Revue d'Auvergne,* 73–92, 160–187.

Pourrat, H. (1928). *Ceux d'Auvergne, Types et Coutumes.*

Pourrat, H. (1959). *Histoire des Gens dans les Montagnes du Centre.*

Pourrat, H., & L'Olagne, J. (1927). *La Colline Ronde, films auvergnats.*
Pourrat, H. (1942). *Le Chef Français.*
Pourrat, H. (1940). *Le Paysan Français.*
Pourrat, H. (1923). *Les Jardins Sauvages, la Vie et Oeuvre de Jean-François Angeli, Soldat au 140e de Ligne tué à l'ennemi le 11 juin 1915.*
Pourrat, H. (repr. 2016). *Les Montagnards, chronique paysanne de la Grande Guerre.*
Pourrat, H. (1921). *Liberté.*
Pourrat, H. (1936). *Toucher Terre: bois d'Angeli.*
Pourrat, H. (1941). *L'Homme à La Bêche, Histoire du Paysan.*
Pourrat, H. (1941). *Vent de Mars.*
Préaud, R., & Fiel, P. (1922). *Les Coopératives de reconstruction du département de Meurthe-et-Moselle.*
Prevet, F. (1929). *Le Régionalisme économique, conception et réalisation*; préface de M. Étienne Clémentel. Thèse de doctorat, Faculté de Droit.
Probus alias, (Jules Corréard). (1916). *La Plus Grande France; la tâche prochaine.*
*Programme commun de gouvernement du PCF et du Parti Socialiste* (1972).
Programme commun de gouvernement, propositions socialistes pour l'actualisation (1978).
Proudhon, P. J. (1959). *Du Principe fédératif et oeuvres diverses sur les problèmes politiques européens*, précedé d'études sur le fédéralisme par G. Scelle, L-L. Puech et T. Ruyssem.
Puy-de-Dôme Conseil-Général. (2014). *Des Armes aux larmes 1914–1918, l'engagement patriotique du Puy-de-Dôme.*
Rausch, J.-M. (1984). Un président de région s'explique in *Réalités regionales*, Projet 185-6, 576-7, 581-3.
Renan, E. (1882). *Qu'est-ce Qu'Une Nation? conférence faite en Sorbonne le 11 mars 1882.*
Reynaud, B. L. (1911). L'esprit agricole et le retour à la terre. *Bulletin historique, scientifique, littéraire, artistique et agricole de la Société scientifique et agricole de Puy-en-Velay et la Haute-Loire*, fasc.*3*, 195–213.
*Rhin Français, Projets d'aménagement du fleuve, force motrice, navigation* (Union Économique de l'Est, Nancy, 1920).
Rocard, M. (1981). La région, une idée neuve pour la gauche. *Pouvoirs, 19*, 131–138.
Rochemaure, Duc de La Salle de. (1909). *Régionalisme Auvergnat, conférence donnée à la Faculté des Lettres de l'Académie de Clermont-Ferrand, le 23 janvier 1909.*
Romier, L. (1925). *Explication de Notre temps.*
Sadoul, C. (1920). *L'Art Rustique en France 1. La Lorraine*, Ph. de Las Cases (Ed.).
Sadoul, C. (1926). *Le Mobilier lorrain (Ensembles et détails).*
Sanson, A. (1922). Les Coutumes chrétiennes en Haute-Auvergne. *Revue de la Haute-Auvergne, xxiv*, 4e fasc., 357–371.

Servan-Schreiber, J.-J. (1971). *Le Pouvoir Régional.*
Solet, B. (Ed.). (1981). *Quinze Histoires d'Auvergne.*
Tardieu A. (1934). *La Réforme de l'État.*
Taussac, F. (1934). *Contribution à l'étude de l'agriculture dans la Haute-Garonne.*
Teilhard de Chardin, P. (1961). *Genèse d'une pensée: lettres 1914–1919.*
Tiravy, L. (1922). Instituteur à Siran (Cantal), *Instituteur et Paysans.*
Tollab, F.-X. (1931). *Jusqu'à l'infini.*
Tuffet, L. (1895). *Le Problème social.*
Turinaz, C.-F. (1900). *Discours patriotiques.*
*Université de Clermont-Ferrand* (1900).
*Université de Clermont-Ferrand et le pays d'Auvergne* (1919).
Université de Nancy (1923). *Vingt-Cinq Années d'une Université Nouvelle 1897–1922.*
Vaillat, L. (1917). *La Maison des pays de France: les provinces dévastées.*
Van Gennep, A. (1942) *Le Folklore de L'Auvergne et du Velay.*
Van Gennep, A. (1924). *Le Folklore, croyances et coutumes populaires françaises.*
*Verdun; Livre d'or du clergé du diocèse de Verdun* (1922).
Veysset, G. (1982). *En Amitié avec Henri Pourrat.*
Vidal de la Blache, P. (1910). Régions de France. *Revue de Paris*, 821–849.
Vidal de la Blache, P. (1917). La Rénovation de la vie régionale. *Foi et Vie*, 103–110.
Vidal de la Blache, P. (1917). *La France de l'Est.*
Vidal de la Blache, P. (1911). Sur la relativité des divisions régionales. *Athéna, 11*, 1–8.
Vidal de la Blache, P., & Camena d'Almeida, P. (1897). *La France: cours de géographie à l'usage de l'enseignement secondaire.*
Vidal de la Blache, P. (1903). *Tableau géographique de la France.*
Viriot, A. (1916), *Les cités martyres de Lorraine, les Allemands à Nomény Août 1914*, préface Louis Marin.
Vital-Merle. (1923). *Petit Recueil de notes sur l'Histoire de l'Auvergne à l'usage des écoles primaires élémentaires.*
Vogt, A.-P. (1920). *Nancy pendant la guerre 1914–1918 d'après les documents officiels.*
*XVIIe* Région Économique, Groupement régional de Clermont-Ferrand, *Compte-rendu des travaux du comité régional et du comité consultatif régional économique, séances des 29 avril 1918, 17 juin et 19 août 1919* (s.d.)
XVIIe Région Économique, Groupement régional des Chambres de Commerce. *Aménagement hydro-électrique de la 2ème section du bassin de la Dordogne, demande de concession présentée par la Région économique du Centre* (1922).

Zingerlé, M.-F. (2003). *Toujours fidèle à la France: journal de guerre 1914–1918 d'une paysanne Lorraine.*

## Electronic Primary Sources

Rollet, L. *Liste des membres des conseils de la Société industrielle de l'Est (1883–1920).* Laboratoire d'Histoire des Sciences et de Philosophie, Archives Henri Poincaré, Histoire des Institutions scientifiques et éducatives de Nancy (HISE), Université de Lorraine, http://hise-nancy.ahp-numerique.fr/items/show/13.

## Secondary Sources

### Books and Articles

Aglan, A., Margairaz, M., & Verheyde, P. (Eds.). (2014). *De la croissance à la crise (1925–1935): Le moment Tannery, une tentative avortée de modernisation conservatrice et libérale à l'heure de la mondialisation.*

Amalvi, C. (1988). *De L'Art et de la manière d'accommoder les héros de l'histoire de France.*

Amossy, R., & Herschberg-Pierrot, A. (1997). *Stéréotypes et clichés: langue, discours, société.*

Anderson, B. (2016). *Imagined Communities: Reflections on the Origin and Spread of Nationalism.*

Annales du centre régional de documentation pédagogique de Clermont-Ferrand. (1987). *Henri Pourrat, sa vie, son oeuvre, ses illustrateurs.*

Antenucci, M.-L. (2004). *Parcours d'Italie en Moselle: histoire des immigrations italiennes 1870–1940.*

Appert, B. (1938). *Le Régionalisme administratif.*

Asselain, J.-C. (1995). *Histoire économique du XXe siècle, la montée de l'état 1914–1939.*

Audoin-Rouzeau, S., Becker, A., & Temerson, C. (2002). *1914–1918: Understanding the Great War.*

Audoin-Rouzeau, S. (1992). *Men at War 1914–1918: National Sentiment and Trench Journalism in France during the First World War.*

Barone, S. (dirn.) (2011). *Les Politiques régionales en France.*

Barral, P. (1974–10). Idéal et pratique du régionalisme dans le régime de Vichy,' *Revue française de science politique, 24*(5), 911–939.

Barral, P. (1966). L'Opinion Lorraine devant Jaurès. *Actes du colloque Jaurès et la Nation organisé par la Faculté des Lettres de Toulouse et la Société d'Études Jaurèsiennes (23–24 mai 1964)*, 157–173.

Barral, P., Charpentier, F.-T., & Bonnefont, J.-C. (1978). La Capitale de la Lorraine mutilée 1870–1918. In R. Taveneaux (Ed.), *Histoire de Nancy* (pp. 375–430).

Barral, P. (1989). *L'Esprit Lorrain, cet accent singulier du patriotisme français.*

Barral, P. (1968). *Les Agrariens français de Méline à Pisani.*

Baudin, F. (1992, 1993, 1997). *Histoire économique et sociale de la Lorraine, ii L'Essor 1870–1914* (3 vols).

Bazoche, M. (2008). *Département ou Région? Les réformes territoriales de Fénélon à Jacques Attali.*

Beaupré, N. (2014). La Grande Guerre littéraire au prisme des régions. *Siècles*, nos 39–40. http://journals.openedition.org/siecles/2714

Beaupré, N. (2006). *Écrire en guerre, écrire la guerre: France, Allemagne 1914–1920.*

Becker, J.-J. (1987). L'Opinion publique française en 1917. *Historiens et Géographes* (315), 1497–1507.

Becker, A. (1994). L'Étranger au temps de la guerre de 1870–71. In J.-P. Jessenne (Ed.), *L'Image de l'autre dans l'Europe du Nord-Ouest à travers l'histoire* (Actes du colloque Villeneuve d'Ascq, 123–132).

Becker, A. (1994). *La Guerre et la foi, de la mort à la mémoire 1914–1930.*

Becker, A. (1988). *Les Monuments aux morts, patrimoine et mémoire de la Grande Guerre.*

Becker, J.-J. (1995). La France de l'Est (Lorraine-Alsace) 1917 de Paul Vidal de la Blache. *Vingtième Siècle revue d'histoire*, no. 48, 175–176.

Becker, J.-J. (1986). Les Classes populaires françaises et la guerre de 1914. *Bulletin du Centre d'histoire de la France contemporaine* 7, 67–91.

Becker, J.-J. (1985). Sentiment national et doubles fidélités: l'exemple de la guerre de 1914. *Mélanges Robert Mandrou, Histoire sociale, sensibilités collectives et mentalités*, 449–456.

Becker, J.-J. (1985). *The Great War and French People.*

Becker, J.-J. (1997). *1917 en Europe: l'année impossible.*

Becker, J.-J., Audoin-Rouzeau, S., & Duroselle, J.-B. (Eds.). Les Sociétés européennes et la guerre de 1914–1918. *Colloque 8–11 décembre 1988 Université Paris-X Nanterre, Centre d'Histoire de la France Contemporaine.*

Becker, J.-J., & Krumreich, G. (2008). *La Grande Guerre, une histoire franco-allemande.*

Becker, J-J., & Kriegel, A. (1964). *1914, la guerre et le mouvement ouvrier français.*

Bell, D. S. (2005). *François Mitterrand a political biography.*

Bellon, C. (1903). Étienne Clémentel et l'organisation administrative de la France. Rapport parlementaire sur le budget du Ministère de l'Intérieur. *Parlement[s], revue d'histoire politique, 20* (2013/2), 127–131.

Berdoulay, V. (1995). *La Formation de l'école française de géographie 1870–1914.*

Berstein, S. (1980-2). *Histoire du Parti Radical, vol.I La recherche de l'âge d'or 1919-1926; vol. II Crise du radicalisme 1926–1939.*

Berstein, S. (2006). *Léon Blum.*

Bertho-Lavenir, C. (1988). La Géographie symbolique des provinces: De la monarchie de juillet à l'entre-deux-guerres. *Ethnologie française*, nouvelle série t. *18*(3), Régionalismes, 276–282.

Birck, F. (2006). La Société industrielle de l'Est et la diffusion de l'information scientifique et technique, de la fin du XIXe siècle à la veille de la Première Guerre mondiale. In S. Benoit, G. Emptoz, & D. Woronoff (Eds.), *Encourager l'innovation en France et en Europe* (173–198).

Birck, F., & Grelon, A. (Eds.). (2006). *Un Siècle de formation des ingénieurs électriciens, ancrage local et dynamique européenne, l'exemple de Nancy.*

Birck, F., & Grelon, A. (Eds.). (2007). *Des Ingénieurs pour la Lorraine XIXe–XXe siècles.*

Birck, F. (2013). *L'École des Mines (ENSMN) 1919–2012; entre université, grand corps d'État et industrie.*

Blanchet, P. (2000). Les Cultures régionales et l'extrême droite en France: entre manipulations et inconscience. *Les Temps Modernes*, 55e année no. 608, 100–116.

Bled, J. P., Faucher, E., & Tavenaux, R. (Eds.). (1988). *Les Habsbourg et la Lorraine.*

Bodis, J.-P.. (1991). *Cent Ans de Rugby à Toulouse.*

Bontemps, D. (1982). L'Anniversaire de la bataille de Mars-la-Tour (avant 1914). *La Revue lorraine populaire,* 8e année (47), 224–227.

Boswell, L. (2000). From Liberation to Purge Trials in the "Mythic Provinces": Recasting French Identities in Alsace and Lorraine 1918–1920. *French Historical Studies, 23*(1), 129–162.

Bouillon, J., & Petzold, M. (1999). *Mémoire figée, mémoire vivante: les monuments aux morts.*

Boulanger, P. (2001). *La France devant la conscription: géographie historique d'une institution républicaine 1914–1922.*

Bouloc, F., Cazals, R., & Loez, A. (Eds.). (2011). *Identités Troublées 1914–1918: les appartenances sociales et nationles à l'épreuve de la guerre.*

Bouneau, C. (1985). La contribution de l'électricité à la génèse de l'aménagement du territoire en France, pendant la première moitié du xxe siècle. In F. Caron, & C. Bouneau (Eds.), *L'UPEPO, 1922–1946: génèse et logiques de l'interconnexion, Bulletin d'histoire de l'électricité* (6, pp. 75–102).

Bouneau, C. (1990). Chemins de Fer et Développement régional en France 1852-1937: la contribution de la Compagnie du Midi. *Histoire, économie et société*, Année, 9-1, 95–112.

Bouneau, C. (2008). *Entre David et Goliath: la dynamique des réseaux régionaux: réseaux ferroviaires, réseaux électriques et régionalisation économique en France du milieu du XIXe siècles au milieu du XXe siècle.*

Bouneau, C. (2000). *Hubert Lagardelle, un bourgeois révolutionnaire et son époque 1874–1958.*

Bouneau, C. (1997). *Modernisation et Territoire, L'Électrification du Grand Sud-Ouest de la fin du XIXe siècle à 1946.*

Bouneau, C. (2002). La Contribution de l'électrification à la genèse de l'aménagement du territoire en France durant la première moitié du XXe siècle. In P. Caro, O. Dard, & J.-C. Daumas (Eds.), *La Politique d'aménagement du territoire: racines, logiques et résultats* (31–52).

Bour, R. (1989). *Histoire de la Banque Populaire de Lorraine.*

Bourlet, M., Lagadec, Y., & Le Gall, E. (Eds.). (2013). *Petites Patries dans la Grande Guerre.*

Broder, A. (1998) *Histoire économique de la France 1914–1997.*

Brubaker, R. (1992). *Citizenship and Nationhood in France and Germany.*

Brun, G. (1985). *Techniciens et Technocratie en France 1918–1945.*

Brun, M. (1939). *Départements et régions* (pref. J. Charles-Brun).

Brustein, W. (1988). *The Social Origins of Political Regionalism: France, 1849–1981.*

Bullock, N., & Verpoest, L. (Eds.). (2011). *Living with History 1914–1964: Rebuilding Europe after the First and Second World Wars.*

Burnham, J. (2009). *Politicians, Bureaucrats and Leadership in Organisations. Lessons from Regional Planning in France.*

Bury, J. P. T. (1964). *France 1914–1940: A History.*

Candar, G., & Duclert, V. (2014). *Jean Jaurès.*

Canini, G. (1988). *Combattre à Verdun. Vie et souffrance quotidiennes du soldat 1916–1917.*

Canini, G. (1984). La Lorraine dans la guerre de 14/18.

Caro, P., Dard, O., & Daumas, J-C. (Eds.) (2002), *La Politique d'aménagement du territoire: racines, logiques et résultats.*

Caron, F. (Ed.). (2005). *Les Grandes Compagnies de chemin de fer en France 1823–1937, archives économiques du Crédit Lyonnais.*

Caron, F. (1997–2016) *Histoire des Chemins de Fer en France* (3 vols).

Carrol, A. (2011). Regional Republicans: The Alsatian Socialists and the Politics of Primary Schooling in Alsace, 1918–1939. *French Historical Studies, 34*(2), 299–325.

Cazals, R. (Ed.). (2013). *500 témoins de la Grande Guerre.*

Cazals, R., & Loez, A. (2012). *14–18, vivre et mourir dans les tranchées.*

Cazals, R., Picard, E., & Rolland, D. (Eds.). (2005). *La Grande Guerre: pratiques et expériences.*

Chaline, N.-J.. (2014). *Émile Guillaumin paysan-écrivain bourbonnais, soldat de la Grande Guerre.*

Chanet, J.-F. (1996). *L'École républicaine et les petites patries.*

Chanet, J.-F. (1988). Maîtres d'école et régionalisme en France sous la Troisième République. *Ethnologie française*, nouvelle série t.18(3), Régionalismes, 244–256.

Chanet, J.-F. (2000). *Les Félibres cantaliens: aux sources du régionalisme auvergnat 1879–1914.*

Charbonnier, P. (1999). *Histoire de l'Auvergne des origines à nos jours; Haute et Basse-Auvergne, Bourbonnais et Velay.*

Chassaigne, P., & Largeaud, J.-M. (Eds.). (2004). *Villes en guerre.*

Chatriot, A. 'Les corps intermédiaires en République: un problème ou une solution pour l'État (France xix-xx siècles),' *Histoire, Économie, Société,* 2016,1, 35e année, 36-44.

Chatriot, A. 'Un débat politique incertain: le corporatisme dans la France des années 1930,' *Les Études Sociales*, 2013/1, no. 157-8, 231-44.

Chaunu, P. (1982). *La France: histoire de la sensibilité des Français à la France.*

Checinski, J. (1999). *Les Poilus de Mulhouse à la crête des Vosges.*

Chiron, Y. (2000). *La Vie de Barrès.*

Clarke, J. (2011). *France in the Age of Organization: Factory, Home and Nation from the 1920s to Vichy.*

Claval, P., & Juillard, E. (1967). Région et régionalisation dans la géographie française et dans d'autres sciences sociales, bibliographie analytique. *Cahiers de l'Institut d'Études politiques de l'Université de Strasbourg III.*

Claval, P., Nardy, J.-P. (1968). Pour le Cinquantenaire de la mort de Paul Vidal de la Blache: Études d'histoire de la géographie. *Cahiers de géographie de Besançon*, no. 16, *Annales littéraires de l'Université de Besançon, 93.*

Cleary, M. C. (1918). *Peasants, politicians and producers, the organisation of agriculture in France since 1918.*

Clemendot, P. (1973). Population de Nancy (1815–1938). *Annales de démographie historique*, hommage à Marcel Reinhard sur la population française au xviiie et au xixe siècles, 119–134. https://doi.org/10.3406/adh.1973.1135

Clément, F. (2000). Monuments aux morts du canton d'Aigueperse. *Sparsae*, no 46, spécial 1914–1918 Association Culturelle Aigueperse et ses environs, semestre ii, 25–50.

Clout, H. D. (1997). War and recovery in the countryside of north-eastern France: The example of Meurthe-et-Moselle. *Journal of Historical Geography, 23*(2), 164–186.

Clout, H. D. (1996). *After the ruins: Restoring the countryside of Northern France after the Great War.*

Clout, H. D. (Ed.). (1977). *Themes in the Historical Geography of France.*

Clout, H. D. (1975). Structural Change in French Farming: the case of the Puy-de-Dôme. *Tijdschrift voor economische en sociale geografie, 66*(4), 234–245.

Clout, H. D. (2005). The great reconstruction of towns and cities in France 1918–35. *Planning Perspectives, 20*(1), 1–33. https://doi.org/10.1080/0266543042000300519

Clout, H. D. (1993). The Revival of Rural Lorraine after the Great War. *Geografiska Annaler, series B, Human Geography, 75*(2), 73–91.

Cobb, R. (1983). *French and Germans; Germans and French: A personal interpretation of France under two occupations, 1914–1918, 1940–1944.*

Cochet, A. (1982). Les Paysans sur le front en 1916. *Bulletin du centre d'histoire de la France contemporaine, Paris-X Nanterre, 3*, 37–48.

Cochet, A. (1986). *L'Opinion et le moral des soldats en 1916 d'après les archives du contrôle postal.*

Cohen, A. P. (Ed.). (1982). *Belonging, Identity and Social Organisation in British Rural Cultures.*

Cointet, J.-P. (2017). *Les Hommes de Vichy, l'illusion du pouvoir.*

Cornu, P.. (2014). Auvergne dans la Grande Guerre. *Les Montagnards* d'Henri Pourrat et la rhétorique de la dette. *Siècles* [En ligne], 39–40. http://journals.openedition.org/siecles/2799

Corvisier, A. (dirn.). (1983). *Histoire du Havre et de l'Estuaire de la Seine.*

Coudert, C. (2015). *Le Cantal et la Grande Guerre 1918–1939: mémoire et représentations du premier conflit mondial dans une société rurale.* Société des Lettres, Sciences et Arts "La Haute-Auvergne", Aurillac.

Courmont, J. (2010). *L'Odeur de l'ennemi, l'imaginaire olfactif en 1914–1918.*

Cudbird, T. (2023). The Clémentel Moment: the reform of 1918 and the beginnings of regional economic planning in France. *French History, 37*(2), 126–141.

Cudbird, T. (2020). *The Impact of the Great War on French Regionalism 1900–1924* (Oxford D Phil thesis).

Dalbin, S. (2007). Visions croisées franco-allemandes de la Première Guerre Mondiale: étude de deux quotidiens, la Metzer Zeitung et l'Est Républicain.

Dalet, C., & Guittard, J.-M. (Eds.). (1990). Centenaire de la naissance d'Henri Pourrat 1887–1987. *Cahiers Henri Pourrat, no. 7 conférences et articles.*

Den Boer, P., & Pomerans, A. (2014). *History as a Profession, the Study of History in France 1818–1914.*

Descouturelle, F., Ponton, B., Roth, F., & Sicard-Lenattier, H. (Eds.). (2008). *Nancy 1909: centenaire de l'Exposition internationale de l'Est de la France: triomphe de l'industrie, de la science et de l'Art Nouveau.*

Doucet, H. (2004). *Art nouveau et régionalisme: Emile André (1871–1933), architecte et artiste.*

Druckman, D. (1994). Nationalism, Patriotism, and Group Loyalty: A Social Psychological Perspective. *Mershon International Studies Review, 38*(1), 43–68.

Druelle-Korn, C. (Ed.). (2011). *Les Corps intermédiaires entre l'état et le marché.*

Druelle-Korn, C. (2012). De la pensée à l'action économique: Étienne Clémentel (1864–1936) un ministre visionnaire. *Histoire@Politique, Politique, culture, société, 16*, 40–54.

Druelle-Korn, C. (2014). La modernisation inachevée de l'aménagement du territoire, le cas de la VII[e] Région (Limousin, Poitou, Charentes). In A. Aglan, M. Margairaz, & P. Verheyde (Eds.), *De la croissance à la crise (1925–1935): Le moment Tannery, une tentative avortée de modernisation conservatrice et libérale à l'heure de la mondialisation* (155–172).

Dubasque, F. (2007). Jean Hennessy 1874–1944: itinéraire militant d'un politique entre milieux reformateurs et réseaux d'influence. *Parlements, revue d'histoire politique, 7*(1), 21–33.

Dubasque, F. (2008). *Jean Hennessy 1874–1944, argent et réseaux au service d'une nouvelle république.*

Duplaix, P (1932). *L'économie rurale en Auvergne depuis 1914*: thèse pour le doctorat en droit, Montpellier.

Duroselle, J.-B. (1988). *Clemenceau.*

Duroselle, J.-B. (2002). *La Grande Guerre des Français 1914–1918.*

Duroux, R. (2018). *Les Auvergnats de Castille. Rennaissance et mort d'une migration au XIXe siècle.* Clermont-Ferrand, Faculté des Lettres et Sciences-humaines, Université de Blaise-Pascal.

Eck, J. F. 'Une expérience de modernisation économique: la première région économique. In A. Aglan et al. *De la Croissance à la crise (1925–1935)* (139–154).

Ehrard, A.. (1980). *Vercingétorix contre Gergovie?* Nos ancêtres les Gaulois. Clermont-Ferrand June 1980. https://hal-clermont-univ.archives-ouvertes.fr/hal-01410214

El Gammal, J. (Ed.). (2006). *Dictionnaire des parlementaires lorrains de la Troisième République.*

El Gammal, J. (Ed.). (2014). *Régions, courants, transferts: histoire et politique.*

El Gammal, J. (2010). 'Être "National" dans l'Est durant l'entre-deux-guerres', *Annales de l'Est,* dossier patrie et nation xviiie–xxe siècles, No. 1, pp. 61–71.

Eriksen, T. H. (1993). Formal and informal nationalism. *Ethnic and Racial Studies, 16*(1), 1–25.

Eriksen, T. H. (2004). Place, Kinship and the case for non-ethnic nations. *Nations and Nationalism, 10*(1–2), 49–62.

Eriksen, T. H. (2010). *Ethnicity and Nationalism: Anthropological Perspectives.*

Eriksen, T. H. (1995). *Small places, large issues: An introduction to social and cultural anthropology.*

Faure, C. (1988). *Littérature et Société, la Mystique Vichyssoise "Du Retour à la Terre" selon l'oeuvre d'Henri Pourrat.* Hors-série 11 des Chroniques Historiques d'Ambert et de son arrondissement, Édition Régionale du Livradois-Forez, Revue Archéologique.

Férier, G. (1987). 'Les Conséquences démographiques de la Grande Guerre en Auvergne *Guerres mondiales et conflits contemporains, 145*, 81–94.

Ferro, M., Brown, M., Cazals, R., & Mueller, O. (2005). *Frères de tranchées.*

Ferry, B. (2014). *L'Art patriotique face à l'annexion.*

Flory, T. (1966). *Le Mouvement Régionaliste Français.*

Fontana, J. (1997). 'Le Prêtre dans les tranchées 1914–1918,' *Guerres mondiales et conflits contemporains, 187*, 25–37.

Foucault, M. (1994). *Power: essential works of Foucault 1954–1984 vol 3.*

Friend, J. W. (1989). *Seven years in France, François Mitterrand and the Unintended Revolution 1981–1988.*

Gaber, S. (1994). *La Lorraine fortifiée.*

Gaffney, J. (Ed.). (1988). *France and modernization.*

Galloro, P.-D., & Boubeker, A. (2013). *Histoires et mémoires des immigrations en Lorraine.*

Gardes, R. (1987). *Henri Pourrat, sa vie, son œuvre, ses illustrations.*

Gerson, S. (2003). *The Pride of Place: local memories and political culture in 19th Century France.*

Gervereau, L. (1991). *La Propagande par l'affiche.*

Giandou, A. (1999). *Compagnie Nationale du Rhône 1933–1998, histoire d'un partenaire régional de l'état.*

Gildea, R. (2009). Eternal France: Crisis and National Self-Perception in France 1870–1945. In S. Carvalho & F. Gemenne (Eds.), *Nations and their Histories.*

Gildea, R. (2008). *Children of the Revolution: The French 1799–1914.*

Gildea, R. (1994). *The Past in French History.*

Gilles, B. (2013). *Lectures de poilus: livres et journaux dans les tranchées.*

Gilles, B., & Weinrich, A. (2014). *Une Guerre des images: 1914–1918, France–Allemagne.*

Gilles, H., Guironnet, J.-P., & Parent, A. (2014). 'Géographie économique des morts de 14–18,' *Revue économique, 65*(3), 519–532. https://doi.org/10.3917/reco.653.0519

Ginsburger, N., Robic, M.-C., & Tissier, J.-L. (dirn.). (2021). *Géographes Français en Seconde Guerre Mondiale.*

Girardet, R. (1953). *La Société militaire dans la France contemporaine 1815–1939.*

Girardet, R. (1966). *Le Nationalisme Français 1871–1914.*

Godfrey, J. F. (1987). *Capitalism at War: Industrial Policy and bureaucracy in France 1914–1918.*

Gooch, R. K. (1931). *Regionalism in France.*

Grandhomme, J.-N. (Ed.). (2008). *Boches ou Tricolores: les Alsaciens-Lorrains dans la Grande Guerre.*

Gras, C., Livet, G. (eds) (1977), *Régions et régionalisme en France du XVIIIe siècle à nos jours* (based on colloque in Strasbourg 1974).

Gregori, S., & Pellegrinetti, J.-P. (Eds.). (2017). *Minorités, identités régionales et nationales en guerre 1914–1918.*

Grémion, C. (1987). Decentralization in France, a historical perspective. In G. Ross et al., *The Mitterrand Experiment: Continuity and Change in Modern France.*

Grenouilleau, O. (2019). *Nos Petites Patries, identités régionales et État central en France, des origines à nos jours.*

Grivel, G. (1984). 'Les Idées politiques de René Mercier,' *Annales de l'Est*, 5e série, 35e année no. 2, 123–138.

Grohmann, C. (2008). From Lothringen to Lorraine: Expulsion and Voluntary Repatriation. In C. Fischer & A. Sharp (Eds.), *After the Versailles Treaty; Enforcement, Compliance, Contested Identities* (153–169).

Grossmann, R. (2004). Deux Académiciens de Metz face à l'Europe: Maurice Barrès et Jean de Pange. *Académie Nationale de Metz*, 187–217.

Guéno, J.-P., & Laplume, Y. (2003). *Paroles de Poilus: lettres de la Grande Guerre.*

Gueslin, A. (1992). *L'État, l'économie et la société française xixe–xxe siècles.*

Guiral, P. (1994). *Clemenceau et son temps.*

Hamon, L. (dirn.) (1992). La Région de De Gaulle à nos jours.

Hanna, M. (1996). *Mobilisation of the Intellect: French Scholars and Writers during the Great War.*

Hanna, M. (2006). *Your Death would be Mine.*

Haraucourt, E. (1932). *Étienne Clémentel.*

Harel, V. (Ed.). (1998). *Les Affiches de la Grande Guerre.*

Harp, S. L. (1998). *Learning to be Loyal. Primary Schooling as Nation Building in Alsace and Lorraine 1850–1940.* North Illinois University.

Harp, S. L. (2001). Marketing Michelin: advertising and cultural identity in twentieth-century France.

Harris, R. (1993). Child of the Barbarian. *Past and Present, 141*, 170–206.

Hayward J. (1969). 'Functional Regionalism,' *Pouvoirs* 1981, no. 19, 105–10; 'From Functional Regionalism to Functional Representation in France: the Battle of Brittany. *Political Studies* XVII, no. 1, 49–75.

Hazareesingh, S. (2015). *How the French Think.*

Hirtz, C. (1973). *L'Est Républicain; naissance et développement d'un grand quotidien régional 1889–1914.*

Hobsbawn, E., & Ranger, T. (Eds.). (1983). *The Invention of Tradition.*

Hopkin, D. (2000). 'Identity in a Divided Province: The Folklorists of Lorraine, 1860–1960,' *French Historical Studies, 23*(4), 639–682.

Horne, J. (1994). L'Étranger, la guerre et l'image de "L'Autre" 1914–1918. In J.-P. Jessenne (Ed.), *L'Image de l'autre dans l'Europe du Nord-Ouest à travers l'histoire; actes du colloque à Villeneuve d'Ascq 24–26 novembre 1994* (133–144).

Horne, J., & Kramer, A. (1994). 'German "Atrocities" and Franco-German Opinion, 1914: The evidence of German Soldiers' Diaries,' *The Journal of Modern History, 66*(1), 1–33.

Horne, J., & Kramer, A. (2001). *German Atrocities 1914, A History of Denial.*

Irvine, W. D. (1979). *French conservatism in crisis: The Republican Federation of France in the 1930s.*

Israel, A. (1934). *La Réforme de l'État devant les partis.*

Jeanenney, J.-N. (2019). *François de Wendel en République: l'argent et le pouvoir: 1914–1940.*

Jeanneney, J.-N (2000). *Une Idée fausse est un fait vrai: les stéréotypes nationaux en Europe.*

Jeismann, M. (1997). *La Patrie de l'ennemi: la notion d'ennemi national et la représentation de la nation en Allemagne et en France de 1792 à 1918.* Paris CNRS.

Joly, L. (2015). *Naissance de l'Action Française.*

Kalaora, B. (1992). 'Georges Hottenger ou les débuts de la sociologie urbaine (1868–1934),' *Communications*, no. 54, Les Débuts des sciences de l'homme (77–87). https://doi.org/10.3406/comm.1992.1814.; https://www.persee.fr/doc/comm_0588-8018_1992_num_54_1_1814

Keen, S. (1988). *Faces of the Enemy: Reflections of the hostile imagination.*

Kemp, T. (1972). *The French Economy 1913–1939: The History of a Decline.*

Kessler, M.-C., Rousseau, G. (Eds.). (2018). *Étienne Clémentel: politique et action publique sous la Troisième République.*

Kidd, W. (1999). *Les Monuments aux morts mosellans.*

King, S. M. (1933). *Maurice Barrès: la pensée allemande et le problème du Rhin.*

Kriegel, A. (1964). *Aux Origines du communisme français 1914–1920, contribution à l'histoire du movement ouvrier français* (2 vols).

Kuisel, R. F. (1981). *Capitalism and the State in Modern France: Renovation and Economic Management in the Twentieth Century.*

Kuisel, R. F. (1987). Post-War economic growth. In G. Ross et al. (Eds.), *The Mitterrand Experiment: Continuity and Change in Modern France*, 23–32.

Laborie-Barrière, L. (2014). Été *1914: Nancy et la Lorraine dans la guerre*; exposition Musée Lorrain.

Labrude, P., Legras, B., Mezzarobba, L., & Richard, C. (2016). *La Faculté de médecine et l'école de pharmacie de Nancy dans la Grande Guerre.*

Ladmiral, J.-R., & Lipiansky, E.-M. (2015). *La Communication interculturelle.*

Ladurie, E. Le Roy. (2001). *Histoire de la France des régions: la périphérie française des origines à nos jours.*

Langman, L. (2006). The Social Psychology of Nationalism: To die for the Sake of Strangers. In G. Delanty & K. Kumar (Eds.), *The Sage Handbook of Nations and Nationalism* (66–83).

Lanversin J. de. (1970). *L'aménagement du territoire et la régionalisation.*

Larcan, A., Schwindt, F. (Eds.). (2010). *Les Bastions de l'Est de Boulanger à De Gaulle.*

Lauras, A., & Pourrat, C.(1996). *Les Travaux et les Jours d'Henri Pourrat.*

Lawrence, P., Baycroft, T., & Grohmann, C. (2001). '"Degrees of Foreignness" and the construction of identity in French Border Regions during the Interwar period,' *Contemporary European History, 10*(1), 51–71.

Le Bras, H., & Todd, E. (1981). *L'Invention de la France.*

Le Naour, J.-Y. (2006). *Le Corbeau: histoire vraie d'une rumeur.*

Lebovics, H. (1988). 'Le conservatisme en anthropologie et la fin de le Troisième République,' *Gradhiva, Revue d'Histoire et d'Archives de l'Anthropologie, 4*, 3–17.

Lebovics, H. (1992). *True France, the Wars over Cultural Identity 1900–1945.*

Legendre, J.-P. (Ed.). (2010). *Lorraine.*

Lemercier, C. (2003). *Un si discret pouvoir: aux origines de la Chambre de Commerce de Paris, 1803–1853.*

Lenormand, P. (Ed.). (2008). *La Chambre de Commerce et d'Industrie de Paris 1803–2003, II études thématiques.*

Lévy-Leboyer, M., & Morsel, H. (Eds.). (1994). *Histoire générale de L'Électricité en France, T.II 1919–1946 L'Interconnexion et le Marché.*

Logette, A. (1964). *Histoire de la Faculté de Droit de Nancy 1768–1864–1914.*

Loubet des Bayle, J.-L. (1969). *Les non-conformistes des années 30: une tentative de renouvellement de la pensée politique française.*

Loughlin, J., & Mazey, S. (Eds.). (1995). *The End of the Unitary State, ten years of Regionalisation 1982–1992.*

Luzzatto, S. (1996). *L'Impôt du sang: la gauche française à l'épreuve de la guerre mondiale 1900–1945.*

Lyons, M. (2008). *Reading Culture and Writing Practices in Nineteenth Century France.*

MacDonald, W. (1922). *Reconstruction in France.*

Manfredini, J. (2017). *Les Syndicats d'initiative: naissance de l'identité touristique de la France.*

Manry, A. G. (1974). Un Siècle somnolent. In A.-G. Manry (Ed.), *Histoire de l'Auvergne.*

Marin, S.-A., & Soutou, G.-H. (Eds.). (2006). *Henri Hauser 1866–1946 humaniste-historien-républicain.*

Mariot, N. (1913). *Tous unis dans la tranchée: les intellectuels rencontrent le peuple 1914–1918.*

Martin, D. (ed). (2002). *L'Identité de l'Auvergne, mythe ou réalité historique, essai sur une histoire de l'Auvergne des origines à nos jours.* Université de Blaise-Pascal.

Martin, P. (Ed.). (2006). Sion colline d'histoire. *Annales de l'Est*, no. 2.

Martin, P., & Roth, F. (Eds.). (2003). *Mémoire et lieux de mémoire en Lorraine.*

Masson, M. M. (1994). L'*Aménagement régional en France, du territoire aux territoires*.

Mathé, R. (1966). *Émile Guillaumin, homme de la terre et l'homme de lettres*.

Mazières, J. (1965). *Arsène Vermenouze 1850–1910 et la Haute-Auvergne de son temps*.

Mény Y. (1974). *Centralisation et Décentralisation dans le débat politique français 1945–1969*.

Mercier, G. (1994). *Lyautey Prince Lorrain*.

Meyer, J. (1991). *La Vie quotidienne des soldats pendant la Grande Guerre*.

Meynier, A. (1969). *Histoire de la pensée géographique en France*.

Millington, C. (2020). *Searching for a French Mussolini during the 1920s, A History of Fascism in France: From the First World War to the National Front*. https://doi.org/10.5040/9781350006577.0007

Miossec, J.-M. (2008). *Géohistoire de la régionalisation en France, l'horizon régional*.

Mitchell, A. (2006). *A stranger in Paris: Germany's role in republican France, 1870–1940*.

Mitchell, A. (1991). *The divided path: The German influence on social reform in France after 1870*. University of North Carolina.

Mitchell, A. (1979). *The German influence in France after 1870: the formation of the French Republic*. University of North Carolina.

Mitchell, A. (1984). *Victors and vanquished: The German influence on army and church in France after 1870*. University of North Carolina.

Moine, J. (1989). *Les barons du fer; les maîtres de forges en Lorraine*.

Monnet, F. (1993). *Refaire La République, André Tardieu, une dérive réactionnaire 1876–1945*.

Mosse, G. L. (1990). *Fallen soldiers: reshaping the memory of the World Wars*.

Moulin-Bourret, A. (1997). *Guerre et Industrie Clermont-Ferrand 1912–1922: la Victoire du pneu*. Faculté des Lettres et Sciences Humaines de l'Université Blaise Pascal (Clermont II), Centre d'Histoire des Entreprises et des Communautés.

Moussié, E., Manière, Y., & Déat, J. (1997). *Histoire du Rugby Auvergnat*.

Musée Francisque Mandet, Riom. (2003). *Entre chien et loup. La veillée, naissance d'un mythe? Les veillées en Auvergne en milieu rural et urbain, du XIXe siècle à nos jours*.

Nguyen, V. (1991). *Aux Origines de l'Action Française: intelligence et politique à l'aube du xxe siècle*.

Nicot, J. (Ed.). (1998). *Les Poilus ont la parole: dans les tranchées, lettres du front 1917–1918*.

Nora, P. (ed), *Les Lieux de mémoire* (3 vols, 1984–1992).

Nord, P. G. (2010). *France's New Deal, From the Thirties to the Postwar Era*.

Northrup, T.A., The Dynamic of Identity in Personal and Social Conflict. In L. Kriesberg, Oakes, P.J., Haslam, S.A., Turner, J.C., Stereotyping and Social Reality (Oxford,1994).
Ory, P., & Sirinelli, J-F. (1992). *Les Intellectuels en France, de l'affaire Dreyfus à nos jours.*
Oualid, W., & Gide, C. (1931). *Le Bilan de la guerre pour la France.*
Ozkirimli, U. (2010). *Theories of nationalism: A critical introduction.*
Ozouf, M. (1984). *L'École de France.*
Paillard, R. (1986). *Affiches 14–18.*
Paillard, Y. (1991). 'Domination coloniale et récupération des traditions autochtones: le cas de Madagascar de 1896 à 1914,' *Revue d'histoire moderne et contemporaine*, tome *38*(1), 73–104.
Pasquier, R. (2004). *La Capacité Politique des Régions: une comparaison France, Espagne.*
Pasquier, R. (2012). *Le Pouvoir régional, Mobilisations, décentralisation et gouvernance en France.*
Paxton R. O.. Vichy France, old guard and new order, 1940-44
Peer, S. (1999). 'Les provinces à Paris: le Centre régional à l'Exposition internationale de 1937,' *Le Mouvement social*, No. 186, 45–68.
Peer, S. (1998). *France on display, peasants, provincials and Folklore in the 1937 Paris World's Fair.*
Pessis, C, Topcu, S., & Bonneuil, C. (2013). *Une autre histoire des Trente Glorieuses: modernisation, contestations et pollutions dans la France d'après-guerre.*
Pitte, J. R. (2002). *Philippe Lamour, père de l'aménagement du territoire en France 1903–1992.*
Planhol, X. de (1994). *A historical geography of France.*
Pouget, G. (1998). *Le Cantal dans la Grande Guerre.*
Pourcher, Y. (1995). *Les Jours de guerre: la vie des Français au jour le jour entre 1914 et 1918.*
Pourrat, A. (1994). *L'Auvergne au temps d'Henri Pourrat.*
Price, R. (1987). *A Social History of Nineteenth Century France.*
Prochasson, C. (1993). *Les Intellectuels, le socialisme et la guerre: 1900–1938.*
Prochasson, C., & Rasmussen, A. (1996). *Au Nom de la patrie: Les Intellectuels et la Première Guerre Mondiale 1910–1919.*
Prost, A. (1992). *In the wake of war: 'les anciens combattants' and French society.*
Prost, A. (2002) *Republican Identities in War and Peace: Representations of France in the 19th and 20th Centuries.*
Pupier, P. (1999). *Henri Pourrat et la Grande Question.*
Purseigle, P., & Macleod, J. (eds) (2004). *Uncovered Fields: perspectives in First World War studies.*
Purseigle, P. (2013). *Mobilisation, Sacrifice et Citoyenneté, Angleterre-France 1900–1918.*

Puymège, G. de (1993). *Chauvin, le soldat-laboureur: contribution à l'étude des nationalismes.*

Raison-Jourde, F. (1976). *La Colonie Auvergnate de Paris au XIXe siècle.*

Raphael, F. (Ed.). (1993). Image de soi, image de l'autre: la France et l'Allemagne en miroir. *Colloque à la Maison des Sciences de l'Homme de Strasbourg*, 4–5 mai.

Reshef, O. (1984). *Guerre, mythes et caricature: au berceau d'une mentalité française.*

Rieber, R. W. (Ed.). (1991). *The psychology of war and peace: the image of the enemy.*

Rive, P., Becker, A., Pelletier, O., Renoux, D., & Thomas, C. (1991). Secrétariat d'État aux Anciens Combattants et Victimes de Guerre, Mission permanente aux commémoration et à l'information historique. *Monuments de mémoire: les monuments aux morts de la Première Guerre Mondiale.*

Rivière, G.-H. (1947). *Un Musée-laboratoire; le musée des arts et traditions populaires.*

Robert, J.-L. (1995). *Les Ouvriers, la patrie et la Révolution, Paris 1914–1919.*

Rollet, L., & Choffel-Mailfert, M.-J. (Eds.). (2007). *Aux Origines d'un pôle scientifique; faculté des sciences et écoles d'ingénieurs à Nancy, du Second Empire aux années 1960.*

Rondeau, D., Baudin, F. (1979). *Chagrin lorrain: la vie ouvrière en Lorraine 1870–1914.*

Roper, M. (2009). *The Secret Battle; Emotional Survival in the Great War.*

Rosanvallon, P. (2007). *The Demands of Liberty: civil society in France since the Revolution* (A. Goldhammer, Trans.).

Rosenthal, L. (2014). *Villes et villages français après la Grande Guerre: aménagement, restauration, embellissement, extension.*

Rossiter, A. (1986). Experiments with Corporatist Politics in Republican France 1916–1939.

Roth, F. (Ed.) (2006). Lorraine et Alsace, mille ans d'histoire. *Annales de L'Est*, no. special.

Roth, F. (2010). *Alsace-Lorraine, Histoire d'un pays perdu de 1870 à nos jours.*

Roth, F. (1992). *Encyclopédie illustrée de la Lorraine: L'Époque contemporaine, de la Révolution à la Grande Guerre.*

Roth, F. (2012). *Histoire politique de la Lorraine, de 1900 à nos jours.*

Roth, F. (2011). *La Lorraine annexée: étude sur la présidence de Lorraine dans l'Empire allemand, 1870–1918.*

Roth, F. (1986). *La Vie Politique en Lorraine au XXe siècle.*

Roth, F. (1983). *Le Temps des Journaux; presse et cultures nationales en Lorraine mosellane 1860–1940.*

Roth, F. (2002). *Lorraine, France, Allemagne: un parcours d'historien.*

Roth, F. (2000). *Raymond Poincaré, un homme d'état républicain.*

Roth, F. (2008). *Robert Schumann, du Lorrain des frontières au père de l'Europe.*

Rousseau, F. (1999). *La Guerre censurée: une histoire des combattants européens de 14–18.*

Rousseau, G. (1989). 'Impressions dans la tourmente: le journal d'Étienne Clémentel dans l'été 1914,' *Guerres mondiales et conflits contemporains, 156*, 89–103.

Rousseau, G. (1998). *Étienne Clémentel 1864–1936.* Conseil Général du Puy-de-Dôme, Archives Départementales, Clermont-Ferrand.

Rousseau, G. (1991). *Le Temps du Gouyat: l'enracinement socialiste dans le Puy-de-Dôme 1870–1914.* Université Blaise Pascal Clermont-Ferrand.

Sadran, P. (1981). 'Les socialistes et la région,' *Pouvoirs, 19*, 139–147.

Samuel, R., & Thompson, P. (1990). *The myths we live by.*

Sandole, D. J. D., Byrne, S., Sandole-Staroste, I., & Senehi, J. (Eds.). (2011). *Handbook of conflict analysis and resolution.*

Sauvy, A. (1984). *Histoire économique entre les deux guerres* (Vol. 2).

Schmauch, J. (2013). 'Novembre 1918. L'administration française s'établit en Alsace-Lorraine,' *Revue d'Alsace* [En ligne], no. 139. http://alsace.revues.org/1951.https://doi.org/10.4000/alsace.1951.

Schmauch, J. (2017). 'Réintégrer les départements annexés: le gouvernement et les services d'Alsace- Lorraine, 1914–1919,' *Revue d'Alsace* [En ligne], no. 143. http://alsace.revues.org/2609. https://doi.org/10.4000/alsace.2609

Schmidt, V. A. (1990). *Democratizing France: the political and administrative history of decentralization.*

Schmidt, M. (1985). *Chansons de la revanche et de la Grande Guerre.*

Service Éducatif des Archives Départementales des Vosges, Centre Départemental de Documentation Pédagogique des Vosges. *La Vie des civils dans les Vosges pendant la Guerre 14–18.*

Service pédagogique du service régional de l'Inventaire d'Auvergne. (2015). *Les monuments aux morts en Auvergne.*

Sherman, D. J. (1999). *The Construction of Memory in Interwar France.*

Sicard-Lenattier, H. (2002). *Les Alsaciens Lorrains à Nancy 1870–1914, une ardente histoire.*

Slater, C. (1981). *Defeatists and their enemies: political invective in France, 1914–1918.*

Smith, A. (1986). *Ethnic Origins of Nations.*

Smith, A. (1999). *Myths and memories of nations.*

Smith, A. (1991). *National identity.*

Smith, A. (2008). *The Cultural Foundations of Nations: hierarchy, covenant and republic.*

Smith, L. V., Audoin-Rouzeau, S., & Becker, A. (2003). *France and the Great War 1914–1918.*

Smith, P. (1996). 'À La Recherche d'une identité nationale en Alsace (1870–1918),' *Vingtième Siècle, revue d'histoire, 50*, 23–35.

Sternhell, Z. (1972). *Maurice Barrès et le nationalisme français.*

Stevenson, D. (1982). *French War Aims against Germany, 1914–1919.*

Northrup, T. A., & Thompson, S. J. (Eds.). (1989). *Intractable conflicts and their transformation* (55–82).

Taillefer, M. (2002). Nouvelle Histoire de Toulouse

Tandonnet, M. (2019). *André Tardieu l'incompromis.*

Thiesse, A.-M. (1992). 'L'invention du régionalisme à la Belle Époque,' *Le Mouvement social*, no. 160, Paris–Province 1900, 11–32.

Thiesse, A.-M. (2002). La République des régionalistes. In V. Duclert (Ed.), *Dictionnaire critique de la République* (433–438).

Thiesse, A.-M. (1991). *Écrire la France; le movement littéraire régionaliste de langue française entre la belle époque et la libération.*

Thiesse, A.-M. (1997). *Ils apprenaient la France: L'exaltation des régions dans le discours patriotique.*

Thiesse, A.-M. (1999). *La Création des identités nationales, Europe xviii–xx siècles.*

Thull, J.-F. (2008). *Jean de Pange, un Lorrain en quête d'Europe.*

Tilmans, K., Vree, F. van, & Winter, J. M. (2010). *Performing the Past: memory, history and identity in modern Europe.*

Tombs, R. (Ed.). (1991). *Nationhood and Nationalism in France, from Boulangism to the Great War, 1889–1918.*

Tombs, R. (1996). *France 1814–1914.*

Tonkin, E., McDonald, M., & Chapman, M. (Eds.). (1989). *History and ethnicity.*

Tronquart, G. (1980). *La Lorraine de Barrès: mythe ou réalité?.*

Turetti, L. (2008). *Quand la France pleurait l'Alsace-Lorraine 1870–1914: les provinces perdues aux sources du patriotisme républicain.*

Varley, K. (2008). Under the Shadow of Defeat, the war of 1870–1 in French Memory.

Veitl, P. (2013). L'Invention d'une région: les Alpes françaises.

Viallaneix, P., & Ehrard, J. (1982). Nos ancêtres les Gaulois; *Actes du colloque international de Clermont-Ferrand 1982.* Faculté des Lettres et Sciences humaines de l'Université de Clermont-Ferrand II, nouvelle série fascicule 13, Clermont-Ferrand.

Vigato, J.-C. (1994). *L'Architecture régionaliste: France 1890–1950.*

Vuorinen, M. (Ed.). (2012). *Enemy Images in War Propaganda.*

Wahl, A. (1974). *L'Option et l'émigration des Alsaciens-Lorrains, 1871–1872.*

Wahl, A., & Richez, J.-C. (1993). *L'Alsace entre France et Allemagne 1850–1950.*

Weber, E. (1962). *Action Française: royalism and reaction in twentieth century France.*

Weber, E. (1976). *Peasants into Frenchmen: the modernisation of rural France 1870–1914.*

Weber, E. (1980). *The Nationalist Revival in France, 1905–1914.*

Welch, E. (2023). *Making Space in Post-War France.*

Whalen, P., & Young, P. (2014). *Place and locality in modern France.*

Whyte, W. H., & Zimmer, O. (2011). *Nationalism and the reshaping of urban communities in Europe 1848–1914.*

Winter, J. (1995). *Sites of memory, sites of mourning, the great war in European cultural history.*

Winter, J. (2014). The Editorial Committee of the International Research Centre of the Historial de la Grande Guerre (Eds.), *The Cambridge History of the First World War* (3 vols).

Wright, J. (2003). *The regionalist movement in France 1890–1914: Jean Charles-Brun and french political thought.*

Wright, J., & Jones, H. S. (Eds.). (2012). *Pluralism and the Idea of the Republic in France.*

## Unpublished Theses

Chalchat, G. (1986). *Les Monuments aux Morts des deux Guerres mondiales dans le Département du Puy-de-Dôme.* Thèse de Troisième Cycle, Histoire de L'Art, Clermont-Ferrand Université II, octobre–novembre.

Druelle-Korn, C. (2004). *Un Laboratoire réformateur, le Département du Commerce en France.* Thèse de doctorat, Institut d'Études Politiques.

Druelle, C. (1993). *Le Ministère du Commerce et de l'Industrie pendant la Première Guerre Mondiale: Étienne Clémentel ou la volonté de moderniser la France.* Mémoire pour le Diplôme d'Études Approfondies, Institut d'Études Politiques.

Grivel, G. (1997). Le Parti Républicain dans les Vosges de 1870 à 1914. Thèse de doctorat, Nancy II.

Grohmann, C. (1999). *The problems of integrating annexed Lorraine into France 1918–1925.* PhD, University of Stirling.

Kent, C. H. (1972). *Camille Cavallier and Pont-à-Mousson: An Industrialist of the Third Republic.* DPhil Thesis, University of Oxford.

Lang, G. (1979). *L'Opinion publique dans le Puy-de-Dôme pendant la première guerre mondiale.* Mémoire de maîtrise, Université de Clermont-Ferrand.

Larique, B. (2006). *L'Économie du Tourisme en France des années 1890 à la veille de la seconde guerre mondiale, organisation et développement d'un secteur socio-économique.* Thèse de doctorat d'Histoire, Univ. Bordeaux III–Michel de Montaigne U.F.R. d'histoire.

Thouvenel, C. (1967). *Étude sur la Chambre de Commerce de Nancy d'après les procès-verbaux des séances de 1871 à 1914.* Thèse D.E.S., Université de Nancy.

## Websites

M. François, 'La France savante', (Notice on comité des travaux historiques et scientifiques web site https://cths.fr/an/prosopographie.php, 15.12.2008).

www.monumentsmorts.univ-lille.fr, results of search for 'Vercingétorix'.

# Index[1]



[1] Note: Page numbers followed by 'n' refer to notes.



T. Cudbird, *The Origins of Economic Regions in France, 1918-1940*, https://doi.org/10.1007/978-3-032-04422-8

FSC
www.fsc.org
MIX
Papier | Fördert
gute Waldnutzung
FSC® C083411

Kolibri 360 GmbH
Ferdinand-Jühlke-Straße 7
99095 Erfurt, Deutschland
produktsicherheit@kolibri360.de